W9-DBU-826

By EMIL LUDWIG

WILHELM HOHENZOLLERN

BISMARCK: THE TRILOGY OF A FIGHTER

CONSISTING OF THREE PLAYS—

1. KING AND PEOPLE (1862-1864)
2. UNION (1870)
3. DISMISSAL (1890)

NAPOLEON

BISMARCK: THE STORY OF A FIGHTER

GOETHE

JOHANN WOLFGANG VON GOETHE

In Closing Years

GOETHE

The History of a Man

1749~1832

By

EMIL LUDWIG

Author of
"Napoleon," "Wilhelm Hohenzollern," etc.

Translated from the German
by
ETHEL COLBURN MAYNE

Illustrated

G. P. PUTNAM'S SONS
New York — London
The Knickerbocker Press
1928

First Edition, with portrait in photogravure

G. P. Putnam's Sons

Made in the United States of America

INTRODUCTION

Dear Mr. Shaw,

When I ask you to accept the English edition of this book, I have three motives for so doing. In the first place you are—I beg your pardon—an Englishman after all, and the most eminent among the authors of that land. Moreover, there was a swifter and deeper understanding of Goethe among English authors than among those of any other nation. He himself was led by this English comprehension into some bitter reflections on the incomprehension of his own people—sentiments which are not, perhaps, entirely unknown to yourself. Carlyle, who was underrated simply because he was of British birth, was properly speaking the first to perceive the significance and dimensions of the drama which, for the first time in centuries, was once more being unfolded in the breast of a mortal; at the time of the Master's death he anticipated what the course of a hundred years has revealed to posterity at large.

A second link between this book and yourself lies in its purpose of reconstructing the genuine man, who really lived, from the æsthetic divinity. In a succession of splendid plays you have convinced our age of the fruitfulness of such a reconsideration, commended and attempted by Goethe a hundred years ago. It is because the Germans had so long been inured to the idea of a young Apollo and an old Zeus that he was always kept at an Olympian distance which precluded any direct influence upon his nation. And so this century has gone by as though he had never existed. Our present generation has been the first to love him for the sake of that inward conflict, to depict his temptations and inconsistencies as the motive-forces of his endeavour. In the following pages this new conception of him is embodied. Here you will be a spectator of the sixty-yeared battle which his Genius fought with his Dæmon, and from which he finally wrested a kind of tragic victory. If Goethe's incessant effort is made plain in this way, he may well become a more potent influence than he ever could be through an apotheosis of his experience or an analysis of his work—more potent, indeed, than *Faust* itself.

That Goethe's was neither a happy nor an harmonious nature, but one in the highest degree enigmatic—that he was neither a Don Juan nor a sycophant of princes—that as observer and sage he was no less great than as poet—is known to you, though not to the mass of men. Hence I can offer you no more than these various confirmations of your own insight. To that end this book will display in a slowly-moving panorama the landscapes of his soul; wherefore I have, in mercy towards any foreign readers, abridged the German edition by half. Thus he will be lifted above the sphere of national and moral prejudices—just as you have shown the world some historical figures who have not thereby been diminished, but only made more humanly comprehensible. Goethe himself wished to be no otherwise seen; for he inveighed against all delineations "which weigh merits and demerits with feigned impartiality, and thus are far worse than death in their obscuring of a personality, which can only be made to live through the unification of such contradictory traits of character."

To conclude—I see between the veteran Goethe and the veteran Shaw some similarities which both will kindly permit me to enumerate. In London I see a man who, during the War, held himself aloof from the strife of the nations, who in particular was the first to distinguish Potsdam from Weimar, the obsolete from the immortal Germany, and who repeatedly acknowledged his debt to German civilisation. Not otherwise, to the dismay of his nation, did Goethe hold himself during the war with France, and in his intercourse with foreign civilisations. When at the conclusion of the War I wrote this book, the thought of some few Europeans acted as a stimulus.

And further, I see two fearless spirits who have always prized the idea above æsthetics, and the truth above the idea; two great realists in life, because both were idealists in thought, were innovators and critics; two masters of ethics, two preceptors. It is true that in this respect Shaw more strongly resembles the old Voltaire. But I hope that the following delineation may make it clearer that Goethe as a political and social observer, as a biologist and a teacher, not only surveyed his century but transcended it.

You will see with admiration how, for that strenuous nature, work was never the aim of life, but only one of the means whereby to keep one's-self alive. Hence in this book his slow spontaneous evolution is shown as the reward of his active patience; and to this end portraits, conversations, and letters are assuredly no less important than works.

That Goethe wrote, besides, the most magnificent poems which the German language has produced, and that even in his advanced old age he could not shake off the habit, you will very cordially forgive in view of his great merits as a prosaist. You have, dear Mr. Shaw, a profound understanding of German music. Accept me now as your Guide to Goethe; he was a brother of our great musicians.

Yours,
EMIL LUDWIG.

CONTENTS

PART I

GENIUS AND DÆMON

PART II

THE EARTH-SPIRIT

PART III

TRAGIC VICTORY

ILLUSTRATIONS

GOETHE

THE HISTORY OF A MAN

PART I

GENIUS AND DÆMON

"All your ideals shall not prevent me from being genuine, and good and bad—like Nature."

CHAPTER I

ROCOCO

"These ravings and rhapsodies will give you some idea of the young fellow."

IN a fancy-shop at Leipzig stands a sixteen-year-old student, choosing among powder-puffs and hair-ribbons; and as he turns them over, he glances at a graceful gilt-framed mirror, and does not soon look away. Two dark eyes look back at him, complacently if critically: the nose is a little too prominent, seeming to bear the full weight of the lofty brow; a mouth lifted charmingly at the corners smiles mockingly and sceptically, and if he turns slightly to the left he can see his powdered side-curls. He pulls at his lace cravat, polishes one of his buttons with his glove, then, turning again to the counter, sets his left hand on his hip, plays with his dagger as if it were an epigram, and looks very well pleased with himself.

When this young gentleman, on leaving the shop, encounters a fellow-student and begins to talk, the charming mouth emits phrases of precocious wisdom, the outcome more of vanity than conviction, and full of a confident omniscience alert to bring everything—God, universe and art—down to a level whereon nothing need be venerated. Through the old streets they wander; and as they go, the admiring or wanton glance of every girl they greet is a mark for their disillusioned ribaldry, as are also the faces, figures and teaching-capacities of all their professors, to say nothing of the German State and King Frederick. Young cynicism, early resigned to a malicious outlook, must have its gibe at any price; the young lips curl as though beneath the laces pulsed an elderly heart. Insatiable without ardour, sensual without the least illusion, our witty student trifles with his own desires; and if he puts them into verse, the rhymes are as stiffly corsetted as the bosom of the girl to whom they are addressed.

> As for our Goethe! [writes a school-friend]. He is the same conceited coxcomb as ever. . . . If you were to see him you'd either fly into a rage or burst with laughter. . . . For all his self-assurance, he's nothing but a fop, and no matter how handsome his clothes are, there's a kind of absurdity about them which makes him the talk of the school. . . . Everywhere he goes, he makes himself more laughed at than liked. . . . The way he goes on is simply unbearable.

Had he not lately—on his sixteenth birthday—poured out the wisdom of a lifetime in his friend's album?

Dieses ist das Bild der Welt,
Die man für die beste hält:—
Fast wie eine Mördergrube,
Fast wie eines Burschen Stube,
Fast so wie ein Opernhaus,
Fast wie ein Magisterschmaus,
Fast wie Köpfe von Poeten,
Fast wie schöne Raritäten,
Fast wie abgehatztes Geld,
Sieht sie aus, die beste Welt![1]

With a forbearing smile he enters the lecture-room. Are his stockings properly pulled up? What is the Professor talking about to-day? Supreme Courts, Presidents, and Assessors. Interminable—and it's all printed in the compendium! Well, the book has a white margin—the best thing about it, and one can sketch the gentleman of this tedious speech. The clock strikes, he stretches himself, free to get off to a lecture on Physics

[1] "Here I would the world portray,
'Best of all,' as people say:—
Something like a robbers' den
Or the 'digs' of first-year men;
Something like an opera-house
Or a stuffy dons' carouse;
Something like a poet's hair
Or a bibelot rich and rare;
Something like your cash 'gone west'—
That's the world you call the best."

—perhaps that will be more interesting. Monads—quaint little beggars! And he writes to his sister:

We scientists look upon you girls as so many monads. Really, since I've learnt that a sunbeam consists of some thousands of atoms, I feel ashamed of ever having bothered my head about a girl who most likely had no idea that there are little animals which could dance a minuet upon the point of a needle.

He is always owing some old friend a letter. And when he does write:

I am in two minds! Shall I stay here with you, or go to the theatre? I declare I'll throw dice for it. No, I can't, for I have no dice. I'm off—goodbye. Wait a moment, though—I'll stay where I am. And to-morrow I shan't be able to get away, for I must go to College, and then pay visits and sup out in the evening. . . . Imagine a little bird on a leafy green branch in full ecstasy, and you have me—society, concerts, plays, parties, suppers, picnics, when this weather permits of them. Oh, it's mighty fine, and costs a mighty fine lot of money!

But before very long the Leipzig families drop him; and we see why when he writes:

Another reason why they can't stand me in the great world is this—I have a little more taste and knowledge of what is beautiful than our smart folk, and often I could not help showing them, *coram populo*, how despicable their opinions were.

No—he was not cut out for a society-favourite, though he was making foolish sacrifices to that end.

Nor was it the Leipzig atmosphere which first developed this vein in him. The earliest letter which contains an illusion to Goethe—a letter from a nobleman, to whose influence the young student (incidentally offering a false reference) had presumptuously and vainly appealed for election to a certain club—commends him "more as an amusing chatterbox than a person to be taken seriously"; and in his old age Goethe himself speaks of his early self-conceit, when he imagined that all eyes were fixed on him.

In his letters to his sister at home, who was only a year younger and every bit as accomplished, the tone is contemptuously playful or pedantically dogmatic:

To-day is your birthday, and I ought to be lyrical in my wishes for you, but I haven't time, or room either. . . . Write your letters on alternate pages, and then I'll answer and criticise them on the blank ones. Further, I want you to become a perfect dancer, to learn the card-games most in vogue, and thoroughly master the art of dress . . . . These latter demands will strike you as very singular, coming from so stern a moralist as I am, especially as I'm hopelessly bad at all three myself.

And no sooner has he sealed the letter than the stern moralist hurries off to his mistress, with whose "art of dress" he is very intimately concerned. Thus does he fritter away his time—will nothing induce this young dilettante to take a grip on himself?

One fancy he does take more seriously, because it really takes a grip on *him*. This is Art, both the painter's and the writer's. Sometimes he goes of a morning to the Academy, there to resume his boyish studies. There he is simpler, more single-minded; there he has no inclination to gibe or dogmatise—he wants only to learn. And why? Because a natural aptitude makes the work easy to him—for he enjoys nothing which does not, so to speak, drop into his mouth; and also because the man who instructs him had charmed him at first sight. So it will be with him all his life long—with him and the world about him; scarcely anyone who does not at once charm him will later, when he is powerful, have any chance at all of his favour.

This, too, was adumbrated in the boy: "I was generally either too vivacious or too silent, and appeared forward or sullen, according as people attracted or repelled me. . . . I was often accused in a friendly way, but often derisively too, of putting on a certain amount of airs."

And now this painter and professor of painting, the gentle dignified Oeser, with his delicate feminine features, captivated the volatile young gentleman, because he encouraged him without either over-praising or over-criticising. He alone divined beneath the youth's flippant attitude an underlying vein of energy; and far too wise to hector him, he let him drift, he gave

GOETHE AT THE AGE OF SIXTEEN

him scarcely anything but his own example, unurged, unspoken of; he suffered him to play at etching with an engraver, and ere long to try his hand at woodcuts too.

Was it not this silent, subtle Oeser who had shown Winckelmann the way? Italy was the supreme influence; and when Oeser showed his pupils that the Southern antique was the model for the North, the youthful Goethe produced his earliest Greek outline studies—but abandoned them ere long, as if he felt: "It is too soon." Indeed he even avoided the Classic Gallery at Dresden, for just then his genius forbade him a direct approach to those divinities who were later on to regain life through him. It was written that the decisive experiences of his long life should be fruitful only after wide circumlocutions.

Susceptible to personality as he was, Goethe was now on the point of contact with Winckelmann. The master was coming home, and the Leipzig students were preparing a grand reception for him, when there came the news of his assassination at Trieste. This was the first side-tracking of Italy, and Goethe was then eighteen; there were to be three more such delays, and not for twenty years was that door to be opened to him.

His life grew as a tree grows; and standing at the end before that eighty-yeared stem, one feels that nourishment and refreshment, wind and weather, obeyed some organic law in nearly always coming to him at the right moment.

Wieland was still the lode-star. Every novice stood spellbound before those gossamer verses; and Goethe, from boyhood remarkably facile, imitated him like the rest—disporting himself pliantly and buoyantly on the surface of graceful rhyming, so much so that his very earliest lyrics have been set to music. He had a dangerously quick ear for measures, and used much variety of rhythm in his rhymed letters; while as a boy he had been apt at reproducing the style and speech of women and actors. In these days he would write one friend an English poem and another a French one, would translate Italian madrigals for this correspondent and copy a graceful myth for that, all the while deriding these exercises, warning his sister, to whom he would send them, against such parroting, ironising his own little artistries:

Von kalten Weisen rings umgeben,
Sing' ich, was heisse Liebe sei;

Ich sing' vom süssen Saft der Reben,
Und Wasser trink' ich oft dabei.[1]

Was he, then, self-critical and scornful of his own attempts? Not always; and woe to anyone else who might take that tone! If his Professor found fault with a poem, Goethe would resent it for six months; when he dedicated one to his grandfather for New Year's Day, he demanded a meticulous report of its effect upon the audience. He spent months over his pastoral, he was indefatigable in rewriting *Die Laune des Verliebten.* But when a friend compared that piece with a renowned contemporary model, Goethe was much offended and wanted to burn every scene that could be said to resemble those in the other play.

In truth, these were no more than porcelain toys—these lyrics and plays, baked in the most modish ovens and polished till they shone again and were fit to be put in the glass case which would protect them from a breath of wind. Children of the brain, they treat of things gone by; artificial creations without any real background, they generally end with an epigram; even when he addresses a mistress, she must figure as Chloe or Ziblis. Whether he depicted art as a lure for the prudish, or sang the triumph of virtue, in these Leipzig songs Nature always appears as a smooth green lawn, the maiden ventures to its utmost limits, then she flies, then pleads and vows and (according to the mood of her piquant poet) is led by her shepherd either into the temple of Venus or round and round its precincts. For Venus lives in a well-pruned garden, and the very waters of the brook are seen by this son of the Muses as no more than a symbol of sweet inconstancy:

Und buhlerisch drückt sie die sehnende Brust,
Dann trägt sie ihr Leichtsinn im Strome darnieder,
Schon naht sich die zweite und streichelt mich wieder,
Da fühl' ich die Freuden der wechselnden Lust.[2]

[1] "Circled around by frigid sages,
Of Love's impetuous warmth I sing;
Juice of the vine my Muse engages,
While I gulp water from the spring."

[2] "She wantonly presses her passion-stirred breast,
Then down in the water the hussy has vanished;
But here comes the next—at her touch grief is banished,
And mine are the pleasures of change that is best."

What has Nature to with that? Sometimes he does betake his poetic self to the woods "on the hunt for similes," but mostly he stays indoors or strolls to a beer-cellar. Even riding is abandoned; and afterwards he called the Leipzig years a sedentary, slinking existence, and said that

my very restricted means, the indifference of my companions, the reserve shown by my tutor, the total lack of any cultivated society, and the extremely uninteresting country that surrounded me, obliged me to look into myself for everything I needed.

What did he find there?

Were there seething emotions, biding their time for attack, hidden behind his over-intellectualised spirit? What sign can we detect of the dæmonic force that soon was to set this perilous life aflame? If at twenty-two he was to shape the earliest tumultuous image of the vastness in his soul, it would seem miraculous, had there been nothing to foreshadow such an issue.

Three odes and a dozen letters to a friend: these reveal in a flash the dæmonic, gifted youth whose demeanour, tastes, and intellectual activities served but to disguise him. For while in these years he was "merely groping among the things of Art and Nature," in some remoter region of the spirit there had broken a mysterious storm, a tempest undefined, which spent itself in a supreme appeal to a vocation, and was confided to no song, no play, but only to his one close friend.

At first, amid this new strange tumult, he took refuge in the planning of great works, long acts of which he toiled at—only to burn them. These were all torsos; he felt that it was too soon for anything of the sort:

But I wish people would leave me alone! If I have genius I shall be a poet, whether they correct my stuff or not. If I haven't, their criticisms can do me no good. My *Belshazzar* is finished, but I can say no more for that than for any of the other mammoths which I, an impotent dwarf, have attacked.

A little later: "So there's my life—scarcely a friend or a girl in it, and I'm half despairing. A very little more, and I shall be entirely so."

But in fact he *had* a friend, and a girl.

Who was the friend to whom these strange gloomy letters, and these odes, went streaming? Was the touchy sensitive trying to find an admirer—the dogmatic novice a disciple—the high-spirited youth an aristocratic patron? He who received them was a poverty-stricken man of nearly thirty, private tutor to a nobleman's son; a haggard man with a long nose and sharp features, decently but quaintly attired, true to the buckled shoes, the hat, the little rapier, as an old Frenchman might have been. He was a man whose greatest delight it was to investigate absurdities with the utmost gravity, to follow up some crazy proposition to the bitter end. An intellectual grotesque, in short, but not in the least malign or brutal; a mournful cynic, a ribald philosopher, a singularly touching donkey. This is Behrisch, who demolished every author alive but took Goethe's poems seriously and (among meticulous comments upon lettering and ink, paper and binding) set about making a fair copy of the finished pieces, despite the author's one condition—that nothing should be printed.

Such was the eccentric with whom he would spend whole nights in Auerbach's cellar, caricaturing, spinning verses, "as if we were in an invested fortress . . . whence two misanthropic philosophers shoot down the Leipzigers with pellets of derision." But when it became known that young Goethe had exalted a confectioner at the expense of a Professor, Behrisch was dismissed from his tutorship on account of having such a friend.

Was it really the same hand which wrote the odes to that friend, and some of the other verses? To-day that hand writes this:

Ich sah, wie Doris bei Damoeten stand,
Er nahm sie zärtlich bei der Hand;
Lang sahen sie einander an
Und sahn sich um, ob nicht die Eltern wachen,
Und da sie niemand sahn, geschwind—
Genug, sie machten's, wie wir's machen! [1]

[1] "I saw fair Doris with Damœtas stand,
He took her gently by the hand,
They looked in one another's eyes,
Then looked around—did parents watch this wooing?—
And seeing no one nigh, quick, quick—
Enough, they did as we are doing!"

And to-morrow, when his friend is leaving the city, it writes this:

Sei gefühllos!
Ein leichtbewegtes Herz
Ist ein elend Gut
Auf der wankenden Erde.
Behrisch, des Frühlings Lacheln
Erheitre deine Stirne nie;
Nie trübt sie dann mit Verdruss
Des Winters stürmischen Ernst . . .
Du gehst, ich bleibe.
Aber schon drehen
Des letzten Jahres Flügelspeichen
Sich um die rauchende Achse.
Ich zahle die Schläge
Des donnernden Rads,
Segne den letzten—
Da springen die Riegel,
Frei bin ich wie du.[1]

What is left of all the lyric rapture—where have the charm of rhyme, the magic of half-confessed joys disappeared to? Here is a heart oppressed with the sadness of autumn, throbbing with the bitter sense of being left behind, yet no less with a chaotic impulse towards liberty, symbolised in the anarchic rhythms. Some obscure strife of the spirit forbids the victim to resign

[1] "Banish feeling!
A too-responsive heart
Is not worth its keep
On this ramshackle cosmos.
Behrisch, may April's laughter
Illume thy brow no day that dawns,
For never then shall it cloud
'Mid winter's tumult and gloom . . .
You go, I linger.
Ah, but already
Last year's winged spokes are revolving
Swift round the blistering axle;
I count its pulsations,
That thundering wheel's,
Blessing the last ones—
The staples are giving,
I'm free as you're free."

himself too soon—*his* harbour gleams afar. In letters, often resembling a diary, the absent friend was now besieged with laments and objurgations; the long-stemmed ardour of a hitherto unawakened heart broke out for the first time—for Goethe was in love.

He had "ranted" before then, when he was robbed (in tragi-comic circumstances) of his first fancy, a Frankfort Gretchen; but that was a boy's defiant fury. It had been like wounding a sleeper for the relation was an idealistic one, to be classed among youth's morning-dreams. But in Leipzig there were pitfalls, and the lover's feet were sore beset. What did she look like, this being for whom he contended? Was she a passionate experienced woman of thirty, formed to attract the sensual worldling in him—an artist, an Egeria for the budding poet—or a dazzling coquette, amusing herself with a raw boy?

She was Käthchen Schönkopf, a vintner's daughter, twenty years old, "well-grown, but not very tall, with a round, pleasant, though not remarkably pretty face, a frank winning gentle manner, very ingenuous and not in the least coquettish; and she is gracefully intelligent though by no means highly educated." Other women of Goethe's adolescence were to resemble her; at no time, indeed, was he apt to be attracted by beauty or intellect; it was always a sweet nature which charmed him most. The law of polarity ordained that his prodigious temperament should seek a soothing influence.

But she was an innkeeper's daughter, and at first the Councillor's son was torn between pride and inclination. Away from her, he dressed more extravagantly than ever and made love to his girl-acquaintances, so as to avert curiosity from the wine-shop. He was still the prey of social conventions, his bringing-up prevailed against Nature; it was but slowly that he threw off such prepossessions.

Soon, however, he did grow more urgent, for every sensual impulse he possessed was stirred by the girl's vitality, and eagerly demanded the semi-surrender by which at that period maidens were wont to allow themselves to play with danger. Some rococo verses, dedicated to her under her other name of Annette, are unmistakably coloured by the delights of satisfying hours which were not hours of dream.

He was her suitor, and her servant. For though his soul was but gradually to flower into a reverence which should extirpate its early cynicism, it was instinctively subservient with women; and hence he was always the one to suffer most from the complexities of love.

Goethe was never the handsome seducer, never proud of his conquests, never a Don Juan; he was always the suppliant, always the giver of thanks—and much oftener a rejected than an accepted suitor! It is only when we regard him as utterly self-surrendering, and recognise how unquenchable was the will-to-love which ultimately subdued itself to the facts of existence, that we shall clearly understand the legend of his passions, the cosmogony of his work, the history of his soul.

But behind the blissful lover's gratitude there hovered even then, at seventeen, such doubts as Faust might have cherished. Half-submissive, half-morbid was his attitude; and the irony he had toyed with became a quivering experience:

Das reinste Glück, das wir empfunden,
Die Wollust mancher reichen Stunden
Floh wie die Zeit mit dem Genuss.
Was hilft es mir, das ich geniesse?
Wie Träume fliehn die warmsten Küsse,
Und alle Freude wie ein Kuss! [1]

Here for the first time appears the tragic problem of his life. At every period he was to ask himself anew, and at eighty-two inexorably to reiterate in the words of his centenarian Faust: "What gain is mine, though mine were blisses?" Goethe's recoil from the immediate, the momentary, which nevertheless he ceaselessly pursued, began at eighteen.

And yet again it was too soon! He knew it, and he and his were to pay a heavy price for that consciousness. His tempestuous spirit could not yet strike the balance between insight and experience, and so there came trouble for all concerned.

[1] "The purest joy that e'er was given,
Hours that were rich in gifts from heaven,
Like time and happiness are fled.
What gain is mine, though mine were blisses?
Vanished like dreams the warmest kisses,
And as a kiss my rapture dead."

His genius guided him better in the sphere of art, in that it made him abandon his "mammoths." But in actual life he was unable to distinguish between time-worn generalities and a personal distrust of this Käthchen. He was a poet, born with a soul whose gift and penalty it was to universalise every experience; and his difficulty was to reconcile his insight with the course of daily life. Moreover, he was now left entirely to himself, for his friend was far away; and he was neurotic and sensitive, an exacting lover.

With his own hands he destroyed the tranquillity of this earliest attachment. He refused his troubled senses their instinctive confidence in the girl he loved; it was not long before she threw him over—and so, for the first time, he unconsciously set himself free for his destined task.

For it had been his definite intention to marry Käthchen. Her mother was a Frankfurt woman, her father too favoured his suit; and he, sensuously steeping himself in the beloved's atmosphere—hearth and home, taproom and billiard-room—and temperamentally attracted by its orderliness and security, dreamed of himself as her husband. But then, after he had been more than a year in love with her, he began to torment her; restless as he was, he could not suffer his heart to rest where it listed.

His letters to the absent friend reveal such a degree and variety of passionate emotions as were only once again to colour Goethe's life; ferocity and scepticism, sensual and spiritual chaos, moralities and cynicisms—Faust and Mephistopheles, in a word. In these letters, written at eighteen, the mighty forces warring in his heart are first made manifest. The duality of that spirit is laid bare in these upheavals of the restless senses.

One more night like last night, Behrisch, and for all my sins I shall never have to go to hell! . . . A jealous lover, who had drunk quite as much champagne as was good for him, so as to enkindle his imagination to the utmost! At first I couldn't sleep, tossed about my bed, jumped up and raved; and then I tired myself out and did get off. But idiotic dreams arrived before long. . . . They woke me up, and I consigned everything to the devil. Afterwards I had an hour of peace, and pleasant dreams—of her looking like herself, waving her hand from the doorway, giving me a fleeting kiss; and then all of a sudden—she had thrust me into a sack. . . . I philosophised in my sack, and bayed out a dozen or so of allegories in the Shakespearean manner, when he went in for rhyming. . . . Then suddenly it struck me that I should never see you again, and that gave me a sort of feverish paroxysm, for I was light-headed, you see. I flung my bedclothes to the winds, gnawed a handkerchief or two, and then slept till eight o'clock amid the ruins of my palatial couch.

Erotic struggles with Käthchen were probably the origin of this state of mind, and of its later aggravation.

A few days later he suddenly explodes again:

Well, Behrisch, this is one of my bad moments! You are away, and my paper is but a chilly substitute for your arms. O God, God! If I could only be my own man again. Behrisch, may love be damned! Oh, if you could see me, see this raving wretch who knows not at what he raves, you would be sorry for me. Friend, friend, why have I only *one?*

Then, in a sort of diary-letter extending over four days and more than eight pages, he gives a frenzied description of the fever into which her coldness has driven him:

Well—but oh, Behrisch, don't expect me to tell you in cold blood! My God! This evening I sent down a message. . . . My servant . . . came back to say that she was at the theatre with her mother. I had just had a shivering fit, and this news set my blood on fire. At the theatre! When she knows that her lover is ill! Good God. . . . Could she possibly be at the theatre, with *him?* That thought shattered me. I *had* to know. I dressed myself, and tore like a lunatic to the Comedy.

And now listen! Behind her seat was Herr Ryden, in a very tender attitude. Ha! Picture me. In the gallery—seeing that through my opera-glasses. Curse them! Oh, Behrisch, I thought my brain would burst with fury. . . . Sometimes he would lean forward . . . then sit back, then bend over her chair again and say something. I had to gnash my teeth and watch it. Tears came into my eyes, but they were tears of eye-strain, for I haven't been able to cry this whole evening. . . . All of a sudden the fever took full possession of me, and I thought I should die that very instant. . . . Do you know of a more unhappy mortal, with such abilities, such views, such advantages, than I am? . . . Another new pen. A few moments' rest. . . . But I love her. I believe I would take poison from her hand. . . . What am I to do to-morrow? . . . If I once lay eyes on her, I know I shall think, "God forgive you as I forgive you, and grant you as many years as you have robbed from my life. . . ." Ha! All our delights are in ourselves. We are our own devils, we drive ourselves out of our Edens.

By next evening all was well—her innocence established. Reconciliation-scene. Nevertheless he finishes his letter, but

would tear it up if I *could* feel any shame at your seeing me as I really am. This violent desire, and this equally violent detestation, these ravings and rhapsodies, will give you some idea of the young fellow. . . . Yesterday the world was made a hell by the very thing that makes it a heaven to-day. . . . The remembrance of sufferings survived is bliss. And such a compensation! My all of happiness in my arms!

This is the earliest Goethe. Passion, which mostly tends to obscure a character, in him was illuminative of every trait. Sensuous and contemplative, hot-headed and shrewd, dæmonic and naïve, self-reliant and subservient: it was a chaos of emotions, all of equal intensity, clamouring, undisciplined, unguided.

In this last Leipzig winter it would seem that after two years of courtship he had the girl completely in his power. The confidences to his friend are less outspoken, rarer too; the lovers seem to meet more regularly, his nerves are in better order, he toys with the drama, sketches, visits a few families—and then in March he makes this remarkable avowal to his friend:

Listen, Behrisch. I never can or will desert the girl, and yet I must and will get away from here—but she shall *not* be unhappy. If she goes on being as sweet to me as she is now! She ought to be happy. And yet I have grown so cruel that I drive her to despair. . . . If she could get hold of the right man, if she could be happy without me, how delighted I should be! I know my duty towards her; my hand and fortune are hers by right; she ought to have all that I can give her. A curse on the man who thinks of himself rather than of the girl whom he has made miserable! She shall never know the pain of seeing me in another's arms until I have felt that pain for her.

This is a new tone—the unmistakable tone of the young man possessive, who has had his pleasure and cooled off, who has a vague sense of indebtedness, but decks his resolution to be free with moral platitudes.

A few weeks later the tone is a free man's. They have parted, and he loves her better than ever, for

passion grows stronger when it is calmer, and so it is with mine. Oh, Behrisch, I have begun to live! If I could only tell you all—but I can't; it would be too much for me. Enough that we have parted, and are happy. It was a business; but now I sit like Hercules when he had finished all his labours, looking at the glorious reward. It was a dreadful time, until we understood one another. . . . We began with love, and we end with friendship. But not for me! I love her still—how dearly, O God, how dearly! O that you were here to comfort me and love me!

This letter, full as it is of reservations, evasions, and untruthfulness of every kind—though the writer was more taken in than the recipient—reveals an increasing violence and instability of temperament. He hovers like a feckless phantom about the love that is supposed to be over and yet not over; pretends he will be satisfied with a problematic future outcome, is very sorry for himself and not particularly sorry for her—impossible to say whether it is the heart or the senses which prevails. Thus it never occurs to him that the girl, who is older than he and is without social standing or fortune, has much more at stake and so must look after herself—no, he is shocked beyond measure when, her liberty regained, she does what he professes to desire for her, and becomes engaged to another man.

And now again Goethe's heart was as a seething volcano of passion and jealousy.

My passion grew stronger [so he wrote afterwards in his Reminiscences], but it was too late, I had really lost her; and I reproached myself so bitterly for my mistake, and wrought such havoc in my physical constitution, merely to scout the moral law, that it contributed greatly to the bodily ills which wasted the best years of my life. . . . I put such a strain on the organism with which I was blessed that every separate element in it was bound to conspire in violent rebellion, if the whole were to escape destruction.

Was he alluding to erotic excesses? Unquestionably his life in that last Leipzig year was licentious. Even if this were not the natural consequence of his general temperamental trend, a few words to his friend would drive us to the same conclusion: "I'm going downhill faster every day. Three months will see the end of me, Behrisch. Good-night—I hope I shall know nothing about it." This short epilogue brings the curtain down sensationally; for here ends the correspondence with his friend.

His collapse came sooner than the apocalyptic hint at suicide had arranged for. Two months after this letter—in July—he woke one night to find himself bathed in blood. It was a hemorrhage. He retained sufficient consciousness to awake the man in the next room to his; then was confined to bed for weeks, and for six months was in a state so critical as only once again he was to experience, and that a generation later. He calls the attack consumption first, then quinsy, then dysentery. We can arrive at no certain conclusion. The one thing that signifies is that this illness, important as it was for his spiritual development, was the result of an abandoned way of life, to which he was driven by a spiritual conflict. It was a concatenation of psychic causes and effects.

Nervously, when he was convalescent, did he revisit the tavern. He met the beloved with outward composure, but was alert for indications of her intercourse with the new possessor. True, he had handed her over; and this admirer, older and quieter, would know better how to treat her. But the sight of him was too much for the invalid; he fled, with no farewell, from the girl who had long ceased to be his.

This was Goethe's first flight from a woman whom he loved. It would be repeated, and now proved an instinct which gradually became an experience, teaching him how far he could trust his heart, and what he must spare it, in the catastrophes which convulsed his early years. Here we see the beginning of Goethe's spiritual hygiene, whereby he found salvation in each successive development.

It was a depressing household to which the invalid son came home after three years' absence. An embittered father, whose own long-shattered hopes of rank and influence were now centred on his children, and who had lost four of them in swift succession, to see but two grow up. On his only son he had fastened all his ambition, and three years ago had sent a gifted youth, the product of his anxious personal training, out into the world of men.

Was that father a born misanthrope? His essential traits were pride and energy; his suffering was the outcome of disappointed ambition. His aim was now to obtain rank for his son. Goethe's father—son of a ladies' tailor—had, thirty years before, lost all hope of the eagerly-desired position on the Council of his native town, because of the absurd pretensions he had put forward, and now had lived for a generation, unemployed, upon an inherited income. He had been the heir of his own far-seeing father's hardly-earned fortune; and that he might extend his knowledge of the world and obtain a wider outlook, had been permitted, at so early a period as the beginning of the century, to take his education in the shape of prolonged tours both southward and northward.

And in precisely the same spirit he had given his son an extraordinarily complete education—such learning and such training as would fit him to be either a great dilettante or a universal genius. Three living, and three dead, languages had the boy acquired from his father and his father's chosen tutors; he could play the piano and the 'cello, could sketch and paint, was acquainted with the history of the world and of the arts. He knew something about exploration and cartography, he could ride and fence and dance, had come into personal contact with municipal and governmental affairs, with painters and diamond-cutters at their work, with the stage both before and behind the footlights—nay, his father was actually the first to induce him to make verses.

. . . But now that hard-featured face clouds over, as the father stands near the staircase in the broad vestibule, and sees the object of all his anxiety transformed into a pale-faced, languid, dissipated-looking student, devoid of all energy, all vitality.

Not, indeed, that there is much harmony to be disturbed by this home-coming; his aspect merely serves to increase the discord in a joyless household. She who stands beside the grim old master, that mother of just thirty-eight, has always looked forward to her son's return as a relief from the dullness of her home-life. For Goethe was the child of an unhappy marriage. The father who could be so kind to his son showed little kindness to his vivacious wife. Stinginess and distrust made a gloomy atmosphere round the unoccupied, embittered husband; with increasing age there came indications of pathological disturbance, the outcome of his inward unrest.

When in the past the mature, reclusive bachelor had courted the magistrate's daughter, who was only half his age, he could not but have been tempted by the much-desired connection with the Town Council; and his father-in-law, Textor, heir of an old-established legal family, was equally of course attracted by the fortune of the tailor's son. When the event proved that the ambitious elder Goethe was not to get what he wanted out of his purchased title of Councillor, his coldness to the young wife grew more marked than ever, for her innate gaiety of disposition had from the first been uncongenial to him. Soon he fell out with his father-in-law as well, and it ended in his accusing him of having betrayed the city to the French. The conduct of such debates between Goethe's father and grandfather is depicted by a constant witness of them, in these casual words: "Textor threw a knife at him, whereupon Goethe whipped out his dagger."

Even in his old age, Goethe could not bring himself to reveal more than the most superficial aspect of all this to the world at large—yet the revelation is far-reaching enough when he describes his father as a stern man who,

> because his nature was essentially of the tenderest, assumed, and kept up with amazing consistency, an adamantine severity of manner. . . . On the other hand, my mother, still little more than a young girl, could hardly be said to mature in any sense until her two eldest children were old enough to be companions to her. . . . She was full of vitality, eager to enjoy the passing moment. The atmosphere created in a family by such incompatibility grows more and more trying as years go on; my father went his way relentlessly and uninterruptedly; my mother and her children could not sacrifice their every feeling, claim, and aspiration.

Goethe, who in extreme old age wrote some good-humoured rhymes about his inheritance of both parents' qualities, derived all his passion, scepticism, and ambition from his father, but from his mother the correctives of these three elements—blitheness, *joie de vivre*, and even, in a sense, imagination. The chiaroscuro of his temperament, so strangely commingled as to be the source of all his joys and pains, originated in this heritage from parents so disparate as his; but genius is never of mortal provenance—"the mind is always autochthonous." So he summed up in his old age.

If, however, we measure the formative influence of such experiences as his father alone subjected him to, we shall find that the credit for his development in this period must be given to the paternal side; and that for the next seven years the elder Goethe's genuine interest in his son's career did much to heighten his influence by its untiring helpfulness. The mother, with her charm and spontaneity, was like an elder sister to him, and to her he drew much closer than to the father. But he learnt nothing from her; she added in no way to his experience. Neither in Goethe's own narratives nor in those of his friends is any deep influence attributed to his mother during the formative years, which henceforth were mostly spent at home. If the mother did take the son's side against the father, it was only in matters of the passing hour; she was never his confidante, his refuge, or his solace. Even in his Reminiscences, so constantly eloquent of gratitude to his unloved father, he characterises his mother only once, calling her "a good woman, never without some mental interest," who found her dearest solace in her religion.

. . . Now, on his home-coming, she stood in the hall and welcomed her son as a deliverer from strife and ennui. Still more ardently, because her heart was heavier, had his sister set all her hopes on him; she had borne much in the last three years. Her father had wreaked his pedagogic enthusiasm, her brother his self-conceit, on her; but the mother, with her craving for amusement, was entirely alien to the girl's nature. Perhaps she was already mentally affected.

This brother and sister strongly resembled one another in the elements of their characters, but were totally dissimilar in the combination of those elements—and this it was which decided their respective destinies. When Goethe, in later life, called his sister an inextricable mixture of strength and weakness, he might have said the same thing of himself without thereby revealing the essential. Those moods of depression which at all times, but especially in his adolescence, were wont to attack him, he could always overcome by the virile cheerful elements in his nature, and this up to the ninth decade of his life. In Cornelia there was nothing to redress them, and Goethe went so far as to call her a creature devoid of faith, love, and hope. It is written in both their faces: the same forces which convulsed her inharmonious nature were, by a colossal lifelong effort, fused into unity in him. Though the physical likeness between them was so marked that they were sometimes taken for twins, the traits which in the brother were attractive, even beautiful at times, were in her repellently masculine; moreover she stooped and had an unhealthy complexion. Goethe was rescued from the perils of his nature by the grace of his senses, which inspired him with devotion for men and deeds; his sister's morbid lack of sensuality was fatal to her happiness in love, and marriage, and daily life.

Never were the two more alike than in this moment when the suffering youth of nineteen was greeted by the disillusioned girl of a year younger, who had no admirers such as her girl-friends had, and "showed terrible harshness towards my father." To such a stormy atmosphere, which the mother's native kindliness was but seldom able to dispel, the shipwrecked adventurer returned. There was a violent scene at the very moment of his arrival. "I suppose I looked worse than I knew."

Then they settled down as best they could. The three younger members of the household breathed again, though cautiously, and left the old man to his grumbles. The student had to tell the women all about Leipzig; he collected his Leipzig verses, published them anonymously, though he utterly scorned them, and began on a one-act play, first entitled *Lustspiel in Leipzig*, and then *Die Mitschuldigen*.

It is a remarkably gloomy sort of comedy, closely allied to a tragedy. A cynical, dæmonic man of feeling is depicted from the ludicrous point of view, and the misanthropic attitude adopted by him is evidently that of the author, for he is undeniably the most interesting figure in the piece. For neither here nor in his later plays is Goethe's character to be deduced from the hero only; his dual nature shed the same light on the hero's antagonist—whence the entire absence of the "villain" from Goethe's works.

His illness was not quite over. It was hanging about him still and now attacked his throat, so that with bandaged head he would sit in his dressing-gown on the sofa in his attic-room, under the eaves of the old house. He would usually be reading. What musty old folio had he got hold of? Paracelsus? How came the scoffer to hit upon the old alchemist's work?

Suffering as he was in heart and limb the youth had seemed a good subject for the Moravian teaching; and when Fräulein von Klettenberg, an aristocratic old maid, his mother's confidante in the many sorrows of her marriage, drew the sceptic into her circle in the hope of converting him, he went obediently like a good son, and listened quietly for a while, concealing his amusement. For in his view he was now "on very good terms with my God. Indeed I considered that, after my many and various experiences, he really owed me some amends, and I was impudent enough to think that I had something to forgive him."

So it was in vain that the gentle cheerful lady, whose soul had more purity than depth, cast her net for this disciple of Voltaire. But Goethe was attracted by the transparency of her nature; and so he lent an ear when her doctor and friend, in their transcendental conversations, pointed him to certain occult writings, to the practice of alchemy, and hinted that he had found such useful in his medical work. At nineteen, one had read so much—why not a mystical book into the bargain? And without perceiving its significance, the reflective patient took his first step—more out of curiosity than for his soul's sake—towards an approach to that mystic world, having closed the other door, the Bible of his childhood, with a gesture saying "I know too much about this."

There he would sit, reading the old mystics; even Swedenborg's name had ceased to be a mere legend for him. So close had his tireless genius drawn him to the source of things. But since the scholar in him was still obdurate, he was sore beset. In December he had a serious relapse, so alarming that he was convinced by his sufferings that he must be on the point of death, and that no power could save him. And then, when it was touch-and-go, his distracted parents begged the mystical doctor to use his magic panacea. His refusal increased their anguish; at last he did rush home one night, and returned with a little phial of crystallised salts, which he administered to the patient. There was an immediate improvement; the illness took a favourable turn; convalescence soon followed. "I need not say how greatly this enhanced my confidence in our doctor."

The great crisis, which had begun five months before in Leipzig, was at its height. To-day we call this sort of thing "suggestion," which after all is only a word. The important point is that Goethe's psychical life took a turn precisely synchronising with the physical one.

For when after weeks of misery he rose from his bed of fever, something had awakened in him which gave his unsettled nature the first clear note of stability. We might call it belief, which does not mean the faith of his childhood; rather it was but readiness for belief. That this should have originated in the means which he believed to have cured his physical body could not prevent his searching intellect from following. The thing that matters is that he found a support.

Such a psychic evolution, regarded not as a miracle but merely as the result of much that had gone before, is not likely to achieve wonders over-night, as one might say. In the mind as in the body we perceive a general alleviation, a gradually growing sense of clearer air. The incident as a whole—physical crisis and psychical deliverance—is the significant fact. This illness (so he wrote in his old age) "made me a different man. For I had attained a wonderful lightness of heart. . . . I was happy, conscious of my spiritual emancipation, though threatened by a period of tedious physical suffering."

Tied by the leg, he sat there at his table, sketching the room, his furniture, his visitors and everyone the visitors gossiped about. And while the convalescent's spontaneity and other charming characteristics struggled with his former arrogance, he felt an increasing reverence for those magic forces which had drawn him back into the light. But at the same time his curiosity was aroused—it kept a parallel course with belief throughout the life of Goethe; and he made himself a little blast-furnace and a sand-bath, and tried, by some eccentric method of his own invention, to produce medicinal salts—in a word, was definitely busying himself with the craft. In this way the quasi-adept got a general idea of it; it was by this circuitous path that he reached the confines of pure physics. Bodily torment, originating in that of the spirit, led the nineteen-yeared Goethe to the alchemy he made use of in *Faust*, and to that scientific chemistry which he was not to pursue seriously until decades had gone by.

His thirst for universal knowledge was now renewed, and on a higher level. During his long convalescence he made a drastic clearance among his books, and banished Manilius and Voltaire, Propertius and Quintilian from the shelves in his room. Well-prepared by education, and by the progressive though undisciplined Leipzig period, this great dilettante was ready for a much wider flight.

And now the darkness which had so perpetually enshrouded his prehensile brain began very slowly to lift. The clouds dispersed, and he could write:

> Oh, my dear lady, light is truth, and though the sun is not itself the truth, yet from the sun streams light. It is night which is the unreality. And what is beauty? It is neither the light nor the night. A twilight, born of truth and untruth, a something intermediate. In beauty's realm there is a parting of the ways, so deceptive, so sinuous, that a Hercules among philosophers might lose the track. . . . Once I begin on this sort of speculation I don't know where I am; and yet I like it better than any other.

Now he rises and sinks upon the quivering waves of light that come and go, now strives to shake off his insensibility, now pantingly, desperately, grasps at every ray! The utterances of his scepticism are more restrained, more tentative; and he continues this letter to Oeser's daughter in a totally new strain, wherein we hear the modulations of a panic-stricken soul:

> He who takes the strait path should follow it in silence absolute. Humility and circumspection are the indispensable accompaniments of our steps thereon, and we shall have our reward in the end. I owe it to your dear father that my soul was ever touched to such an issue. Time will bless my labours, and grant them to accomplish what has been begun.

Can this be the same Goethe—are these the words of a boy scarce twenty? Has he who began by being omniscient turned diffident all of a sudden? Nay, rather call this the earliest perception of himself. For the flickering insight of his confidences to his Leipzig friend is now a still flame burning upward from the deeper stillness within. One of Goethe's fundamental beliefs was that we should feel ourselves to be organisms, accepting our seasons as they pass, silently bearing all they bring us, even as the tree does. His self-consciousness was now, without a tinge of vanity, transmuting itself into consciousness of his vocation; and the loftier his flight was to be, the longer he must take to prepare himself for it. At this time he spoke of himself, quite frankly, as a poet in the germ, and said with equal candour that no very young man could expect to be a master.

In those years he wrote scarcely anything—the surest indication that he was meditating new modes of expression. He burnt the plays and verses he had begun on, burnt his letters too, and while "verses refused to flow" he was exploring the field of criticism. So that now we have our first tangible evidence for the way in which critical insight and plastic powers, cool perceptions and glowing emotions, worked on equal terms in the depths of his spirit; for before his poetry was inspired by the pantheistic impulse, he had recognised that impulse as indispensable. Such self-recognition vehemently turns against its own endeavours. That was why he burnt most of the Leipzig lyrics, and abandoned that phase once for all.

Käthchen alone survived for him; and while Leipzig became a thing of the past, the bitter-sweet after-taste of that first passion remained with him for years. After a few letters which hovered between friendliness and love-making, with a tendency to exaggerate the portentousness of the past, he heard of her formal bethrothal to his successor in her favour; and instead of exchanging his tender avowals for the phrases of ceremony, all the painfully repressed passion broke out afresh. His sensual male imagination was stirred to picture the beloved in another's arms, and a malign compulsion kept his eyes perpetually fixed upon that vision.

Soon memory distorted the truth, and he persuaded himself that she had refused him; three years later, even, he told his friends so; and—long after his next love-affair—his grief for Käthchen was so poignant that no one thought he could possibly fall in love, so obsessed did he seem by the Leipzig episode. And forty years later, he reiterated this falsification of a biographical fact, and that with full conviction: Käthchen had thrown *him* over!

He felt now that her betrothal had shattered his last secret hope. Bridal songs he could not send her—those he had attempted were all either too intimate or too cold; and when shortly before his twentieth birthday he was seized by bitter resentment for his wasted years, it is as though he were seeking to atone for the pain he had given her when in the Hamletian manner, but with a challenge underlying the self-reproach, he laments:

> Three years ago I would have sworn that things should be very different. . . . There was a time when I never could have my fill of talk with you, and now all the wits that I possess are insufficient to cover a page of letter-paper. . . . If you could write me a line . . . to say that you are happy in every possible way, I should be glad. . . . O, if I could call back these last two and a half years! Käthchen, dear Käthchen, I swear to you that I should show more wisdom!

Thus did his lovelorn heart, which for more than two years of his adolescence turned to no other woman, find sustenance in its dreams of the past.

A year and a half after their amicable separation, he suddenly begged her not to write to him again.

> A sad request, my dearest, my one and only love, whom I cannot call my friend. . . . I would rather not see your handwriting again, just as I would rather not hear your voice; it is bad enough to have my dreams so taken up with you.

But no less suddenly he pulled himself together, and concluded as with a wakening prescience of great things to come: "You are always a dear girl, and you will be a dear woman too. And I—I shall always be Goethe. You know what that means. When I say my name, I say all that I am."

CHAPTER II

PROMETHEUS

"When you stand boldly erect in the chariot, and four fresh horses are tugging frantically at the reins, and you control their energies . . . till all sixteen hoofs are taking you at a measured pace to where you want to go—that's mastery!"

"ENLARGE the place of thy tent, and let them stretch forth the curtains of thy habitation. . . . For thou shalt break forth on the right hand and on the left." On his first day in Strasburg, in the small room near the Fish-market, Goethe opened the little prayer-book, his mother's gift, at random, seeking a sign; and when he saw that the Book was Isaiah and the passage that quoted above, he was strangely moved. Was the new-old book to prove a "lively blessing" after all, and could that heart of his, purged of its thirst for knowledge, recapture the one and only radiance, in his childhood so familiar and so bright? His endangered life and all his disappointments did, in the beginning, lead him to a resumption of the childish faith which he had hastily abandoned, rather from perplexity than from conviction. True, what Fräulein von Klettenberg had instilled at home seemed no less problematical than the worthy doctor's alchemy. But behind it all, behind it, there must be something—and that sense was urgent in appeal.

And while, that evening, he installed himself, arranging clothes and ink-bottle and pens (for everything must be in good order); while he compared the pleasant new quarters with his Leipzig workshop, he suddenly remembered the man in the next room there, who had nursed him so kindly. Was he still prayerful, that purblind theologian? It was the night of Good Friday. What about writing him a religious letter? Money would be more welcome, for he was badly off. And he sent some, and wrote:

When I remember what an intolerable creature I was last summer, I am filled with amazement that anyone could put up with me. . . . If things are as they were—if you are still in twilight while others enjoy the light of day, you don't lose much. It is twilight everywhere in this world, a little more or a little less; some comfort in that. . . . I am changed, much changed, and I thank my Saviour for it; that I am not now what I threatened to become is another cause for thankfulness. Luther says: "I fear myself more for my good works than for my sins." And when one is young, one is nothing—nothing.

The old effusiveness, the old ardours here in this strange Good Friday outpouring from the believer dubious of his belief, the sceptic dubious of his scepticism! If in the first weeks at Strasburg he sometimes consorted with religious people, he soon found them tiresome, narrow-minded. Vacillating between the allurements of a haven of rest, and a yearning for the splendours of the perilous ocean, Goethe cruised for a while along the coast.

He was still looking sallow and haggard; still clinging to the God of his childhood, "whom we call Lord, until we can call him Our Lord." But within new sap was rising, and it broke forth into Spring.

At that time Strasburg was a French town, its inhabitants were called *sujets allemands du Roi de France.* Society aped Paris more eagerly even than in Leipzig, which was the reason why the shrewd father had chosen these two universities, for once the boy had got his doctor's degree he was to go to Paris and behold the sun. Only among the French could he learn to be a man of the world; then he would come home to dazzle his native town. What a pity he wasn't a born patrician! But this was at any rate the best chance of his touching the fringe of society; he would have to make good therein himself. Would he bring it off this time?

He was unchangingly eccentric, more inclined to be reclusive than to look up successful people. With youthful contrariness he now disdained the ladders which it had cost him so much to climb, he passionately abjured the tastes which had once absorbed him, and accused civilisation as a whole of having led him astray. This young æsthete seemed to abominate everything that was French, though in fact he was only disgusted with his own recent behaviour.

And besides, he had been hit on the raw. French, which as a child he had mastered, he now spoke badly, for he had too often imitated servants and sentries, actors and parsons; and so the Strasburghers laughed at his *patois*, as the Leipzigers had of yore at his Frankfurt accent. Proud and offended, he resolved to abjure French; he would make it his business to speak his mother-tongue and show them how forcible and expressive it was. The German Goethe had to tread French soil before a trace of German instinct woke in him; but still stronger incentives were needed to arouse him from mere passive emotion to productive ardour.

He never led the student's life. The academic forms and ceremonies bored not only the young dandy, but the eccentric, in him. Some violent prejudices, however, began to give way; for now, at twenty, he no longer declined to play cards, but learnt whist and piquet. Though he was more sociable than in Leipzig, he was very tenacious of his liberty; and this alternation between sociability and reclusiveness, which went on until he was quite an old man, was—like all the paradoxes in his conduct—no more than reflex action. During his adolescence Goethe went from the scholarly to the amusing, and slowly retraced his steps in his old age.

In Strasburg, where his too-sophisticated young heart was longing to beat high once more, he strove against his misanthropic tendencies—and not until he was nearly sixty was he ever again so amiable a creature as in those three college-terms. Returning health, a new faith, his surroundings and sympathies, forbade him any intellectual affectations; he was gradually arriving at a spontaneity which gave play to the best part of his nature, and was ere long to inspire his genius. But for Goethe's responsive temperament a human relation was indispensable, if he were to disentangle himself from his conflicts.

Before any such relation could bear fruit, Nature demanded a whole summer-season for the ripening of her disciple. In those early Strasburg months fresh energies were developing at every point; and when he felt himself unequal to their urgency, he took to a régime. He sought to render himself immune from noises, morbid sensations, giddiness, and adopted violent measures to that end. He would stand close to the drummer at a tattoo; he

SILHOUETTE OF GOETHE AT THE AGE OF TWENTY-ONE

right teacher and in a swift flash of insight had now grasped eagerly at what this stranger might have to offer him. And so in these weeks, whose results were incalculable for Goethe and for German culture, the unexpected happened—Herder, born for domination, with every day surrendered himself more completely, though much against his will; while Goethe, born for self-surrender, took all he wanted and gave the lonely invalid little more than the pleasure of his company in return.

For Herder's nature never wanted to yield, to know repose. His first impulse was towards knowledge; his second towards display. It was the effort which primarily attracted him; ambition came next. There he sat in the half-light with one eye bandaged; his features sharp, his forehead high, his nose somewhat blunt, his mouth perhaps too sensual for such a thinker . . . there sat Herder, pedagogue and preacher, tutor of princes and discoverer of new connecting-links in folk-lore; twenty-six years old, renowned, a subject of controversy, in the darkened room, waiting to see if the lachrymal gland would open. His genius was in his brain; his eye was diseased. He who sat before him, his visitor, had just begun to escape from over-exercise of the brain to exercise of the eye—a young student, not dazzling, of middle height, well-built, nicely dressed, his hair carefully curled, with a head whose beauty might have been spoilt by a large nose, if a nobly-curved mouth and a high clear brow had not made it attractive. But the dominating features of that head were two dark eyes that could light up with ardour, could sparkle, muse, enkindle, probe. For eight decades these, and only these, betrayed the stirrings in a mighty spirit, and all the more when they sought to conceal them.

And where was the point of contact between these two—Herder and Goethe, sitting in front of one another? True, they had mockery in common; and if we figure its degrees as steps of a staircase, there they could meet, Herder going up and Goethe coming down. But it was only the elder of the pair who expressed himself in ribaldry; the younger was withheld from it by two other feelings. Reverence and gratitude made Goethe the inquiring disciple. Herder's critical comments were eagerly snapped up by Goethe; what the one scattered freely about him in his conflict with himself and the surrounding world, the other was earnest to make the most of. What, then, did Goethe give Herder?

He gave him the ideal listener. For Herder's spell for others was his talk. Goethe, during the next few years, developed great narrative power; Herder talked. He preached, guided, convinced. Meanwhile, what of the young man before him? "You're all for the eye!" said Herder more than once to him, and in those cavilling words he summed up the difference in their natures. Was it his to perceive the genius in this student? Even two years later, when his personality and his work made the prognosis easier, only two persons really grasped what the youth was; and at this time Herder merely wrote to his betrothed:

Goethe is really a good fellow, only somewhat light and superficial (*spatzenmässig*), for which I everlastingly rebuke him. . . . He is a good noble-hearted boy, full of feeling—too full indeed; and, as is proper and best for us in this charming existence of ours, the half of it will resolve itself into the rosy dreams of dawn.

Herder undoubtedly saw Goethe at his most unsophisticated, as did none other in those years; for he saw the enraptured disciple. But the outward frivolity, the nonchalance of such an adolescence, which his own struggles made still more obnoxious to him, awakened his distrust; in his view this young man had neither suffered nor struggled enough—nor had he learnt enough, for at twenty Herder had had his doctor's degree.

Hence his sarcastic temper made him the more insistent to take back with one hand what he gave with the other. Yesterday, for instance, Herder would have written a lampoon on Goethe's name; to-day he would rally him about a flirtation; to-morrow rebuke him for having been so overwhelmed by *The Vicar of Wakefield*, which Herder was reading aloud to him. Directly he felt that he had got hold of the boy, he wanted to master him completely. And yet Goethe, nervous, proud, and defiant as he was, would not let go; every day he clung closer to this vexatious sort of a teacher, feeling spellbound as by a Mephisto—whom Herder resembled in some respects, without being a Mephisto at all.

Goethe was not only learning a new æsthetic—but also its

moral foundations. Herder had already decided on his own life-work—he was to preach intuition, and exalt it above observation; thus, in obedience to a biogenetic law, glorifying his personal temperament. Creative intuition was what he loved and preached to the world; he had just written a history of the mind, based upon that hitherto unheard-of thesis. In this unprinted piece upon the origin of language he put before his disciple not only the historical side—he showed the nursling of the rococo that the art of poetry is a universal gift, a folk-gift, not the private property of educated people. In proof of this he led him to the fountain-heads of poetry, urging him to regard Homer and the Bible as a succession of pictures, as the rhapsodies of shepherds, warriors, and hunters; he introduced him to Ossian and made him translate from him—but at the end of it all, he showed him perfection in the work of Shakespeare.

All this was fruitful for the disciple because it did not really astonish him, only confirmed what he had already surmised. True, no one else in Germany could have given the twenty-yeared Goethe so far-reaching, so weighty and largely-conceived an exposition. But educative influence has the same effect upon genius as dramatic treatment has upon an audience—the more powerful it is the less it surprises, the better it has been prepared for. In these weeks Herder confirmed, deepened, accelerated the perceptions germinating in Goethe, who secretly related every pronouncement on genius to himself and his future works. Herder was all for emancipation from the Parisian-Attic tyranny, for the primitive force of natural language, for folk-legends—these were to furnish the forms and materials for a revival of the drama.

From the sick-room Herder exercised this kind of spell upon Goethe; even his handwriting had such "magic power" that Goethe never destroyed a single note, nor even an envelope of his. And yet he never loved him. At first he admired him, then avoided him, then again sought him out; but in the following decades there was only one really intimate passage between them. As long as Goethe lived, he learnt something from every type of individual, not only from humanity in general; but this was the last of his definite instructors.

When Herder, at this time, wrote a satirical poem in which he compared Goethe to a woodpecker, Goethe politely retorted that a woodpecker was far from being a common bird. He seems to have grown more and more reserved. Goethe, who as a lad had been filled with a desire to surrender himself to others' influence, was now more reticent; and was nearly always, throughout his life, misunderstood by other men. With this man he was quick to conceal his real self. It amazingly came about that the sarcastic teacher, renowned and misanthropic, read to the disciple his treasure, the scarce-finished manuscript, while this latter, listening and saying nothing, kept from the teacher his own recently-begun drafts of *Götz* and *Faust,* which he owed indirectly to Herder.

While Goethe was learning, his heart was in pain; while Herder was teaching, his eye was. The lachrymal gland would not open; he left the clinic and the town, an angry man. He felt that all his weeks there had been wasted. His disciple, issuing from the darkened room into the light of everyday, was conscious of a sense of relief. He had laid his veneration at Herder's feet, and yet felt that he had but received what he already possessed. For under the snow-mantle of fashion Goethe had it all in him, soon to break through as does the earth from its glittering veil.

But as yet his mind was in a state of chaos. A poet through and through, a research-student not at all, what charmed him in Herder's poetically-inspired investigations was to see how thought and intuition imposed their own manner of expression.

This first Strasburg experience, which was not only Goethe's own but soon to be that of a generation—this awakening to the primitive, the natural, in style—began with a negation. The first return to the primitive is apt to be the outcome of a revolt against the artificial; and as in Goethe's life everything was of slow growth, so with this apparently most violent of revolutions. For years it had been silently preparing, and did not even now spring to light so abruptly as his friends and imitators boasted.

This epoch, then, begins with an emphatic No. Nature instead of convention; spontaneous diction instead of Alexandrines—the landscape which gave one birth, in which one moves at large: such were the urgencies, emotional rather than intellectual, which made this young German wish to prove himself a German. Not till then did Goethe find the Strasburg Minster impressive; hitherto it had baffled his classifying eye.

But since these recognitions are always the outcome of vital emotions, Goethe's first written confession of faith was dithyrambic in form. In his pamphlet, *Von deutscher Baukunst* (*On German Architecture*)—a collection, made a few years later, of notes taken in Strasburg—the inspiring influence is Erwin von Steinbach, that master to whose name he constantly appeals.

Admirable man! before I again put out to sea in my cobbled skiff, more probably to perish than to reach the desired haven, behold how in this grove where the names of those I cherish encircle me with vernal beauty, I now carve out thine own upon a beech as slender and as strong as one of thy tall towers; and from its four crests suspend this kerchief filled with offerings—with flowers, buds, and leaves.

Did the art-experts call this Minster Gothic? They ought to

thank God that they can tell the world: "This is German architecture, *our* architecture, for the Italians can boast of none like it, still less the French. . . ." The more rapturous the sense of those proportions which alone are beautiful and rooted in eternity, whose grandest harmonies, whose deepest secrets, man may do no more than feel, in whose celestial rhythms alone the God-like genius circles like the stars of heaven . . . the more fortunate, the more glorious is the artist, and the more reverently do we bow our heads in prayer to God's Anointed!

That might be Goethe on Shakespeare. Very much like this are his flamboyant stammerings before the poet of whom in Leipzig he had thought no more than of many others. This adolescent, roving where he listed, found in Shakespeare alone (not even in Homer) and only now was finding such an inspiring source of energy

as one born blind might be conscious of, if a wonder-working hand should cause him, in a single moment, to see like other men. . . . I rushed out into the open air, and felt as though for the first time that I had hands and feet.

A poet, feeling the lightning of a poet strike across the centuries! Is it surprising that Goethe's worship, in a speech on Shakespeare's birthday, was mingled with a proud sense of affinity? The boy's heart, kindling, tumultuous, fearless, holds equal speech with the high gods in this discourse.

This life, gentlemen, is far too short for our souls. . . . For let our course be ever so long and ever so fortunate, at the end we must fall out . . . and be as nothing. As nothing! I! I who am everything to myself, who know everything through myself! Such is the cry of all who are self-aware, and take this life in giant strides. . . . Shakespeare, my friend, wert thou still with us, I could live nowhere but with thee. How gladly would I play the subordinate part of Pylades, if thou wert the Orestes!

In such a rhapsody from genius to genius did his soul first soar above the clouds, for every day seemed more confidently to assure him of what lived within and would in time be manifested. In the group of young people who now began to draw together, diffidence was a thing unknown; every one of them claimed the laurel for his mere enthusiasm. But none put forth such unbounded pretensions to genius as did Goethe, who had as yet done nothing. At the conclusion of *Deutsche Baukunst* he invokes himself thus, in a sort of cosmic rapture:

All hail, thou boy endowed at birth with a keen eye for the relations of things, with a prehensile grasp of form! When the day shall come for wakening to the joy of life, to the sense of exultation in man's works, his apprehensions and his hopes . . . oh, lift him in thine arms, thou heavenly fairness, mediatrix between gods and men, and may he bring down to this earth the happiness of those Olympians, a Prometheus more triumphant than he of old!

This comes from the depths—it is at once humility and pride. Here is the high-mettled heart of budding genius, and here, no less, the yearning of the earth-born; here are desire and impulse for which no achievement, no rapture, can be too exalted, but here too is the prescience of pain and disappointment, sustained by a manly hopefulness towards the Olympian Powers, though patiently seeking sustenance on earth below. Here we have Prometheus.

But though the artist thus anticipated his future, there were to be long days in which he dragged the burden of his earlier experiences, striving to make these, too, productive. The fruit of these Promethean ecstasies is not perceptible for two years to come. The mirage of his childhood's teaching gently dissolved before the eyes of twenty-one; and though when his sophisticated scepticism was shattered, he had striven to regain that faith, if not to any certain end, all vestiges of orthodoxy now vanished in the light of an ardently accepted Pantheistic impulse.

Pan was reborn in him; Pantheism had transformed his faith.

> Wie herrlich leuchtet,
> Mir die Natur!
> Wie glänzt die Sonne,
> Wie lacht die Flur!
> Es dringen Blüten
> Aus jedem Zweig,
> Und tausend Stimmen
> Aus dem Gesträuch,
> Und Freud und Wonne
> Aus jeder Brust.
> O Erd', O Sonne,
> O Glück, O Lust! [1]

Goethe's faith had opened its eyes. Virile, paternal, was the Immanence to which now, and even as a white-haired man, he confidingly submitted his spirit.

He was then translating Ossian. Everything that was rhapsodic in him had to find its outlet; and when intoxicated by words, he wanted to intoxicate others by them. If in Leipzig Goethe had always been alone with his eccentric friend, it was very different now—a circle of young people had "put their shirts" on his originality; and since the really gifted are known to invent their own uniforms, one of these fervents regarded the revolution in Goethe's attire as emblematic of his development.

[1] "How bright, how glorious,
The world I see!
The sun how radiant,
How glad the lea!
The buds are thrusting
On branches tall,
And myriad voices
From thickets call,
And joy and rapture
From every breast—
O earth, O sunlight,
O bliss, O zest!"

When the consciousness of his genius awoke in him, he took to going about in a slouched hat with his hair out of curl; he wore the same suit every day, and very remarkable it was. He would wander about the woods, fields, hills, and valleys just as the fancy took him. His look, his gait, his speech, his very walking-stick were those of an extraordinary personality.

One of his Professors records that

Herr Goethe behaved himself here in a way which caused him to be regarded as a meretricious pretender to scholarship, a frantic opponent of all religious teaching. . . . It was the well-nigh universal opinion that he had a slate loose in the upper storey.

This may be true, but it is of no importance. His panache of "frenzy" was important to his circle, not to him. The effect he could make at that time on an unprejudiced observer is best conveyed by Jung-Stilling, who at his first dinner with the group "was particularly struck by one man, who had large, bright eyes, a magnificent brow, and a beautiful figure. He came in with such an air!"

But the friend whom he singled out from all others was no contemporary, but a man of fifty, another bachelor and another pernickety eccentric in buckled shoes, breeches, and three-cornered hat. To this clever oddity of a Salzmann, who founded the first German Club, all his letters were now written, as of yore to Behrisch. What in those earlier days had been spurious ardour was now the authentic outpouring of a youth's fervent heart.

He accepted his friends and their atmosphere; and yet there was a warning voice within—the voice of that unconquerable perplexity of mind which made him seem older than his years, and questioned whether he and those around him were not mistaken in establishing this mutual admiration society. He wrote to one of them who was living at a distance:

I don't get any good at all out of the much too favourable view you've all chosen to take of me. . . . We love our friends as we love our sweethearts . . . so keen on having the best there is. . . . We find that we've deceived ourselves—but we won't admit it, and flatter ourselves that on the contrary the other person deceived us.

How mature—and how wise, as well, never to have sent this letter! We have only the draft of it. Goethe was always sociable, but always reserved; devotion, with dæmons lurking in the background.

Only to women did he wholly surrender himself, and so he always gave them more than they gave him. The love-affair which marks these months was neither *Sturm* nor *Drang*, though this period has been so characterised. It was idyllic. This experience of the heart is an oddly tranquil interlude between the shocks of the same year, and seems to have scarcely any connection with them. Nothing that we know of it implies the kind of passion which he had felt in Leipzig, and which was ere long to make havoc in his heart no less than thrice. Three women were epoch-making in Goethe's adolescence; Friederike was not. She was the mildly-radiant star of the moment; in his work of this year one immortal poem scintillates. The ending of that love was productive for him; but even Weislingen and Clavigo (in whose weaknesses he masked and unmasked his own) are of no importance in Goethe's life-work.

Goethe did not frequent the parsonage at Sesenheim in quite so literary a spirit as he afterwards represented. He was always something of the condescending visitor with these worthy folk—the intellectual attempting a return to nature in art, in scenery, and consequently in love. But there were at any rate some literary results of his nine months' attraction. Anyhow, he captivated the blonde maiden at first sight, on a ride through the mountain-region, and captivated her once for all. Her rustic style of dress—so German!—was refreshing to the young man from town; moreover, she too was his type: "Slender and light, she walked as if she had no weight at all to carry; and her dainty little head looked almost too delicate for the big blond plaits. She gazed very frankly out of her mirthful blue eyes."

His quest of the primitive, soon to set him collecting folk-songs from the old wives of Alsace, made him rejoice in Friederike's incapacity for the drawing-room ballad, though she could warble the most delicious old country-ditties in the open air. She was cheerful, even-tempered, tranquil; and so had everything that Goethe then and always wanted from women, because he had himself so uncertain a hold on it.

It took only a few days to attract him in the way that women often did by her whole environment, her parents, her brothers and sisters, the farmyard, trees and animals. There was always a trace of *amour goût* in Goethe's infatuations, though *amour passion* might be the original magnet.

I have been spending some days in the country with most agreeable people [he wrote to one of his other hostesses on the day after his return]. The companionship of the charming daughter of the house, the lovely neighbourhood, and the exquisite weather stirred in my heart every slumbering sense, every memory, of the things I love best.

In the tranquil warmth, the sympathetic thrill which gently touched his nerves on this first evening after their first encounter, we perceive the idyllic amorist in the youth who nevertheless was now, as a poet and thinker, vehemently, boldly casting his earlier skin. He thankfully lingered in the girl's little world, precisely because an infinite world was beginning to reveal itself to him; Nature-worship and Love were seeking mutual completion. The girl was one of those who look particularly well out-of-doors; he had a picturesque vision of her on a path high above his head. "I was immensely happy with Friederike. I was talkative, gay, witty, impudent, yet all this was modified by emotion, respect and attachment."

Is this the insensate, gloomy Goethe, who had so recently driven a girl to despair? Here we have a tame sort of affection, out of which his essential nature plucked no fruit. He wrote her some verses. Only sixteen poems of this Strasburg year-and-a-half survive, and probably but few are lost to us. Half of these were for the girl, but he retained no more than two in the subsequent collection of his verse. One of these is world-renowned.

It was not till after his meeting with Herder that this *Willkommen und Abschied* (*Welcome and Farewell*) was written. This is Goethe's earliest "Goethean" poem—the harbinger of a new lyric, a new German, a new literature. For while the odes to Behrisch were visionary and stiff-jointed, here the vision has subdued the material to its plastic purpose. With these verses, which were the first to depict Goethe's passional life, begins the long succession of mystifications by which, to the detriment of his work, he shielded the women concerned, throughout the whole course of his life.

> Ich ging, du standst und sahst zur Erden,
> Und sahst mir nach mit nassen Blick. . . .[1]

It ends thus; and even if we did not also possess a sheet of paper on which the text of this poem is headed *Den . . . Abend*, and the story is completely revealed, the whole would sufficiently vouch for a ride to a night of love and the parting in the morning. But Goethe began his precautions, and the poem was thus printed in a newspaper:

> Du gingst, ich stund und sah zur Erden,[2]

—which ruins the entire conclusion; and not for twenty years did he set it right again in the more callous mood of a "collected edition."

During these summer months Goethe almost lived at Sesenheim. The idyll lasted too long, grew faded, lamentable.

> Things are not very bright with me [he wrote in May to Salzmann]. The little girl is still out of spirits and health, and that makes everything go wrong. To say nothing of the *conscia mens*, but unfortunately not *recti*, that I carry about with me. . . . If you would send me a two-pound box of confectionery, there would be sweeter lips, at any rate, than the faces we have been seeing lately. . . . I danced with the elder girl last Whitmonday, from after dinner to twelve o'clock at night. . . . I gave myself up to it body and bones. And yet if I could say I was happy, it would be far better than that sort of thing.

A few days later:

> The world is so beautiful! So beautiful! For a man who could enjoy it! . . . It is difficult to punctuate it as one should. Girls never use commas or full-stops, and it is no wonder if I am turning into a species of girl.

[1] "I went, and you stood looking downward,
Then looked at me with tearful eyes. . . ."

[2] "You went, and I stood looking downward."

At the end of June:

It is high time for me to come back, and I want to, and mean to; but what good is "meaning to" against the faces that surround me! My heart is in a strange state. . . . The most delightful neighbourhood, people who love me, a circle of friends! "Have not the dreams of your childhood all come true?" I often ask myself, when my eyes are feasting on this blissful horizon. "Isn't this the magic garden you longed for?" It is, it is! I feel it, dear friend, and feel too that one isn't an atom happier when one gets what one wanted. The counterpoise! The counterpoise that fate always weighs in with our blisses! Dear friend, it takes a lot of courage not to lose heart in this world.

So there we have Goethe at Sesenheim. We can read between the lines—the girl's condition and the mute looks of a family, which plead when they would do well to be angry; the boredom, impatience, and remorse of the young man who is longing to get away from the sweet maiden: it is Faust and Mephistopheles. What could he do? He fled the place.

This is Goethe's second flight, but only stupidity could call it cowardice. Every time that gentle and strong nature, that heart of devotion, forced by the law of evolution to inflict pain upon others, was driven to confess his inner conflicts, he avoided scenes and explanations, and withdrew into himself to save himself. A strange mixture of fear and courage.

When he was about to ride off, leaving his beloved in her deplorable situation, he leant down from the saddle to shake hands with her again. "The tears stood in her eyes, and I felt anything but comfortable." But he bade her the real farewell in a letter. She answered it with one "which rent my heart," for it was written "at a moment which well nigh cost her her life."

Is it necessary to point out what drove the seducer to this conscience-stricken flight? He could do no other—that is all. In Leipzig such a vehement passion enchained the idling student that he felt himself cheated of lifelong happiness. In Strasburg it was not from dreams of happiness that he fled; by that time his passion was concentrated on the strenuous future. In Leipzig he fled from a passion; in Strasburg from an idyll. On the day before his departure he drew a picture of himself which is very different from the cool confessions of his old age.

Last night I was sentimental, but early this morning I was in such a pother about my arrangements that I leaped out of bed. Oh, my head is as disordered as my room. . . . Nor is my soul precisely cheerful; I am far too wide-awake not to feel that I may be grasping at shadows. And yet—to-morrow at seven o'clock the horse shall be saddled, and then adieu!

One seems to see his agitation, the fevered sparkle in his eyes. How utterly he ignores the girl, whose fate was afterwards to haunt him as a symbol! "Send it to the good Friederike, with or without a note, as you like." So he wrote a few weeks later to his friend, enclosing a sketch. Eight months after their parting, he was telling his intimates in Darmstadt that he *had* been in love once before—but it was only of Käthchen that he spoke.

Once more the law of love, as creative spirits know it, was affirmed. The girl he could not win turned the adolescent Goethe into a poet; her whom he won too easily he soon forgot.

While Goethe, by his flight, broke through the obstacles set up by his heart, he was simultaneously in flight from the prescribed course of study; for though officially speaking he finished it, his sensuous temperament—involved, moreover, as it was in the general upheaval—was alien to theoretical jurisprudence, in Strasburg as elsewhere.

Thus his graduation at the end of the term was merely a form demanded of him by his father; and in his Dissertation on canon-law, which set forth that the lawmaker is entitled to ordain the form of worship, the only interesting passage is the tolerant afterthought that there should be no question of what anyone present might be thinking, feeling, or imagining. This specimen of logic was returned to him by the Dean, with a cold word of praise, for private printing; and one of his Professors was only partly wrong when he wrote that Goethe's insanity was plainly shown by this Dissertation—for apart from his attacks on the Christian religion, if any one of the Doctors had approved it he would have been obliged to resign his office.

Ultimately, Goethe discussed some uncontroversial question of the sort which provided after-dinner mirth; and by so doing displayed for the first time that submission of genius to recognised authority which afterwards distinguished him, and was unlike so many of his colleagues. It was because he then and there perceived that the external forms of revolt are not of any real importance.

For Goethe always, even in this year, kept apart from the indiscriminate revolutionaries, the mere hotheads, among his fellow-students. His "storm and stress" was never concerned with politics or law; the anarchism of his period was alien to him. As a critic his quarrel was with spurious forms of literature; as a poet he used the symbols of all time to frame man's wrathful challenge to the gods.

If it be said that these are but forms, was it not for the formulation of existence, of thought, that his soul strenuously sought? It was indicative not only of the well-bred young gentleman, but of the poet, when soon after this he was disgusted by Basedow's bad tobacco and soggy sponges. And beside these manifestations we must set the reiterated comments from friends and strangers: "The kind fellow; the kind-hearted boy; his kindness."

About this time Goethe began to think with his eyes. Already he had surprised a Strasburg connoisseur by the just remark that the Minster tower was not really finished, for there ought to be four slender spires to contrast with the four squat arches.

> But that was always to be the way with me. It was only after a long process of observation and reflection that I could form any real conception of things; and perhaps this would not have been so fruitful in its effect upon me if I had gained it from others.

That henceforth Goethe's eyes were to be the principal factor in his artistic evolution was one of the reasons why he was attracted to the classic, as opposed to the German, world.

He was still in a state of chaotic unrest when he left Strasburg; but his internal development had little in common with his external life. A like contrast between his inner self and his production will now and again recur. Though Goethe himself enjoins us to regard his work as one prolonged confession, but its successive phases rather as a means of living-down his experiences, this should be taken as a mere summary. The creative spirit would at one time keep step with that which determined his daily life, and at another be far in advance, occasionally expressing itself in images which the more actual side of him had either left behind, or had still to attain. To foresee and prophetically embody, in moments of insight, the phases of his own experience was Goethe's appointed destiny; but nothing was further from his native impulse than any idea of consciously making his life a work of art.

In these early days he displayed all the accepted marks of genius. On his first home-coming after three years' absence he had been a pale, broken-down invalid. Now he arrived in good health, it is true, but in so nervous a condition that he owned to not being mentally at his best. Nor did he come alone; the astonished parents beheld at his side a boy-harpist, to whom he had taken a fancy in Mainz the day before, and for whom he now proposed to find employment during the Fair.

So there he was, back in Frankfurt, the gifted son of an Imperial Councillor, caged again, and now as it seemed for good and all; for when on his twenty-second birthday he applied for a post as advocate, his idea was to become a useful citizen of the Free—but unemancipated, narrow—Town, which he never really liked. In fact that stormy nature was never in any sense outwardly revolutionary. In the new journal for which he then wrote, his social confession of faith soon appeared:

> When we find a place in the world where we can settle down among our possessions, with a field to grow food in and a roof to cover us, have we not found a Fatherland? . . . And do not thousands live happily under such limitations? Why then strive after an emotion which we neither feel nor want to feel? . . . The Roman sense of patriotism! God preserve us from that, as from an ogre! We should find no chair to sit on, no bed to sleep in, in that country of the mind.

It might be an old man speaking, and it is a boy of twenty-three.

Inwardly, however, that boyish mind was restlessly vacillating, under obscure urgencies, between its desire for tranquillity and its determination towards the vortex. Domesticated in the comfortable confines of his father's house, by no means desirous to confront the world at large, yet with a soul so agitated that it could not know rest in such an atmosphere, he devoted himself to imaginative work. What made the little attic-room that he inhabited now as in his boyhood a pleasant place for him?

Hier meine Welt, mein All!
Hier fühl' ich mich,
Hier alle meine Wünsche,
In körperlichen Gestalten.
Mein Geist so tausendfach
Geteilt und ganz in meinen teuren Kindern.[1]

Prometheus, shaping his inward visions, longing for them to take life! There Goethe sits, foreseeing the figures of which as yet not one is more than adumbrated, but which will in time grow definite before his inward eye. . . .

If only I had not so many forebodings, or more often only vague hauntings, if I could really hope, if beauty and greatness were more vital elements of thine emotion, then thou mightst do, speak, write something good, something beautiful, without knowing it!

Aspiring thus towards greatness, he sought his subjects among great men. He wanted a hero, and tried Cæsar, Socrates, Prometheus first; then Götz and Mahomet, who succeed one another as examples of his hero-worship; and for the guiding conception he shaped this phrase from his own intimate foreknowledge: "All that genius, through the character and the mind, can do for humanity . . . and what it gains and loses thereby."

With such prescience, such prophetic knowledge of his own destiny, he roved among the great figures of legend and history, conceiving himself, experimenting on himself, in the characters of prophet and demi-god, while room and town and period hemmed him in. Only a few fragments of his *Cæsar* survive. For Socrates, whom he shortly attempted, he took Herder as model; he himself was to be Alcibiades!

But again it was all fragmentary. His soul was too deeply stirred to find its outlet in a well-made drama; the flame of his intellect consumed all the formulas. But the more these dramatic torsos are imbedded, as it were, in the block from which they

[1] "Here is my world, my all!
Here I am I,
Here every wish is with me,
Incarnate, visibly present.
My myriad-minded self
Dispersed and whole in these my well-loved children."

spring, the more they seem to issue from the depths of his inarticulate emotion. Only in a work like *Götz*, where a consecutive artistic purpose has made of a similar kind of sketch a finished stage-play, are we in some degree unconscious of the inward stress.

And *Götz* itself was begun by accident, so to speak. When Goethe was reading Berlichingen's Life, he invented some scenes for Cornelia out of his own head, and was finally tempted to write them down. So he began one morning, without any sort of a plan, wrote a few scenes, and read them to Cornelia in the evening. Her praise was tempered by doubts of his perseverance; this piqued him, and he pushed on. But of this period he confesses that he would never have cherished such schemes and fancies if he had had a sweetheart, though in the same breath he describes work as an "unexpected" passion.

At the end of six weeks he called the piles of manuscript that lay before him "a sketch," and decided on a drastic overhauling. But none the less he perceived that this was like all his writings in being "a milestone, whence one starts on a long walk, knowing one will have to rest for hours at a time."

Here we have the earliest exposition of Goethe's method—a perpetual sense of probation, together with as perpetual a sense of responsibility for giving every attempt as high a finish as it would take; so that ultimately sixty volumes of rewritten pieces survive, and fragments in even greater numbers.

This first *Götz* he revised at the end of six months—distilling, clarifying, recasting, transposing, till a new piece lay before him, to be in its turn regarded as practice, and subsequently rejected for yet another re-modelling.

Götz was written three times, the third rendering after a generation had gone by; and *Götz* did more to make Goethe famous in his lifetime than any one of his later dramas. Is it therefore in the canon of masterpieces? What experience shaped it—since experience remains the open sesame for all Goethe's works? Was impulsive pity for the oppressed, as in the drama as a whole—was active Christianity, as in the knight—a characteristic of Goethe's youth? Where—since all the documents have been searched and meticulously analysed—where, in earlier sketches or later works, do we find any indication of such a characteristic? In which letters, which poems, of this period? Renowned for things which are not the essential marks either of Goethe's nature or his poetry, this brilliantly-coloured picture occupies a place apart in the gallery of his works—not as an achievement never again reached, but rather as a lesson learnt and swiftly left behind.

The personages shaped in his own image are, and were bound to be, the antagonists of Götz. Goethe's vacillating spirit lives again in Weislingen, his ardour in Franz, his radiance in Adelheid. And these are by far the best realised figures in the drama. Weislingen, with his good heart but his weak will, is definitely Goethe—so well-comprehended, partly by experience, partly by prescience, that he was continually to crop up again in subsequent works, first of all as Clavigo.

But whence came his vision of that heroic, amoral Adelheid? Here is a new feature in his poetry; for with that commingling of male and female elements without which genius cannot be, Goethe is no less present in his feminine than in his masculine figures—often indeed more so; and sometimes he needed two women for the subtlest refinements in presentation of the duality within himself. Hence there is more of him in Adelheid than in Götz, and afterwards he expressed this by saying that, while he was at work, he fell so much in love with Adelheid that she cut out Götz.

He was Adelheid's prototype, and Franz's too. His fierce sense of power, his lust for experience, burn in the woman; in the boy blazes his own young dream of love, hovering between sensuality and devotion.

> A thousand years are but half a night! [cries Franz in Adelheid's arms—the Franz of the first *Götz*]. How I hate the day. . . . O that on thy breast I were one of the immortal gods, who lived self-centred in their passionate, brooding ardour, and in a single moment engendered myriad teeming worlds, and felt the raptures of those myriad worlds in one swift instant touch themselves. . . . I would slay my father, if he disputed this place with me!

Fantasies of the dæmonic youth who for years had scarce known actualities of this kind!

When Goethe diffidently sent the play to Herder, the latter criticised it sharply, and accused the author of having been utterly ruined by Shakespeare. It took Goethe only a few months to know all about himself and his work. But to save this play, he had to do it violence. When shortly afterwards he wrote the second *Götz*, the most powerful passages—Franz in Adelheid's arms, the murder of Adelheid, Sickingen's love-affair, the symbolical opening to the fifth act—were cut out; a great deal was toned down in the interest of economy of material and pointed dialogue—the story, in short, was thoroughly pulled together.

But Goethe did all this reluctantly, in defiance of his passion for divagations. He felt that spontaneous inspiration was being sacrificed to stagecraft, and wrote of his second *Götz* to a friend:

> . . . und bring, da hast du meinen Dank,
> Mich vor die Weiblein ohn' Gestank,
> Musst all die garstigen Wörter lindern . . .[1]

He was twenty-three when he wrote the first *Götz*. In the year which he then spent at home he was sometimes sociable, sometimes reclusive, but the "storm and stress" was far more vehement in the latter mood. At first there were difficulties; his moods were unaccountable, he was fond of taking long walks at dead of night, and moreover his people looked upon poetical activities as a protest against the civic sphere. The mother had to smooth things down—no easy task; the father was from the first a good deal disappointed, perceiving that though the advocate's robe was worn—and worn becomingly, successfully, and with dignity—by his son, it was regarded as being nothing to be proud of. The elder did what he could; and indeed even more lavish hands than his might have hesitated to bestow the surprising amount of $700 for nine months of life at Frankfurt.

The first literary triumph altered the family atmosphere. The proud embittered man wanted fame and success for his son, though it were only through writing verses! And so, with all his eccentric overbearing zeal, he sought to further the youth's worldly interests. But now a friend stepped forward, more sophisticated than the father, experienced both in things of the mind and of business, and willing to be a buffer in the assault of genius on the public; and he succeeded in keeping the elder Goethe

[1] ". . . and bring me to the fair ones' feet—
For this I'll thank you—smelling sweet,
Not one coarse word may you leave unsoftened . . ."

within the bounds of moderation. This is Merck, to whom Goethe afterwards ascribed the greatest influence.

Again an oddity, again older, again long-limbed and haggard, with a pointed nose and grey-blue eyes which glanced about him watchfully, giving his aspect something of the tigerish. Just thirty, and if not precisely a man of the world at any rate a man who knew something about it, resolute, free-handed, with much literary perception and critical instinct, something of the publisher-type, though companionable only for those

whom he did not intimidate by his irrepressible sarcasm. . . . By nature a gallant, noble-hearted, reliable man, he had become embittered with the world, and gave his spleen such free vent that he could never resist the temptation of purposely playing the fool, not to say the knave.

Merck was a dilettante in verse and prose, he had even published; and whenever one scheme turned out badly, he would instantly meditate fresh undertakings which were not only to enrich but amuse him. He was prone to infatuations for the sentimental ladies whose circle was dominated by the Herder influence; would be tender as long as might be, but was at the mercy of his malignity, when he would suddenly write impertinent spiteful verses of which Goethe says that he could not possibly reproduce them. And yet Merck detested himself for these ebullitions, and told his friend that he envied him his "harmless choice of subjects."

A silhouette seems to dawn on us. This is Mephistopheles. Faust always seeks Mephisto—and especially when he is not only Faust.

Merck, on practical things intent, advised Goethe to get something ready for the press. Goethe, hitherto discouraged by Behrisch's serio-comic adjurations against all publication, and then by Herder's criticism, now—in the businesslike Frankfurt atmosphere—allowed himself to be persuaded, printed a few fugitive pieces at his own expense, gave some copies away, and at the same time put several on sale in a book shop, as a better means of "getting rid of them."

To take money for verses had not long since been regarded as simony. But when Goethe published for the first time, he yielded to his bourgeois blood and made up his mind that talent, illect, and industry ought to be paid for by the world. In thourse of his sixty years of authorship he was to become the moschly-remunerated of German authors, and this long before anf the few "booms" made by his books.

Merck's practical good sense influenced Goethe to e recasting of *Götz*. Merck paid for the printing, Goethe · the paper. Then the two friends launched the novice's dram

It made a great sensation. The edition was soon sol ut, a second appeared; and though the author was much congra ated, he was much embarrassed too by the huge bill for paper ue to irregular payment for the copies sold.

Götz was the only play of Goethe's which made a gre success on the stage—and yet, even with this most easily-mprehended of his dramas, the effect was partly due to misundetanding. Young people thought that turbulence was there grified, their elders quarrelled with such commendation of "mht is right," many believed the author to be a *savant* and wishe there had been erudite notes.

He himself soon came to regard the work with indifrence. He left the second edition unaltered, on the ground that tis was his trial-essay and must remain as it was. "If I ever aga write a German drama, which I very much doubt, I want tl truly critical spirits to perceive how much I have improved."

So clearly did he grasp the experimental nature of th play; and at the same time showed how he could stand back fom his work, while claiming from his readers the same unusual orm of contemplation, even at this early stage. The inviolabe conviction that his was to be a long and patiently-accepted evolution was persistent in him from the days of his youthful self-absorption to those in which the veteran sank slowly to his rest in th bosom of mother-earth. In these years, especially, when his companions were rhapsodising over his emergence, Goethe's self-restraint was so remarkable as really to seem imposed by a highe hand.

Meanwhile the drama has shown you that the aims I cherish are dearer to me than ever, and I hope they may gradually inspire me to some purpose. I see more to be done every day, and my way grows clearer. . . . There may be many a day of schooling still to put thrh. For I tell you once for all: one *cannot* overleap one's adcence.

nfined to a côterie of adoring young *literati*, who were lavish of praise which they hoped would be mutual, he felt at this timhat he was in danger of taking things too easily, of accepting barren adulation which might well be destructive of selfdiscine; and while he shunned all clubs and associations, it was for rder's voice that his ear was stretched.

had scarcely abandoned this captious friend before instinct drohim to institute a correspondence which might forge the linkresh. His attitude hovered between pride and veneration —wnever Goethe turned towards Herder, his heart quivered. It w a secret rivalry, a mute measuring of himself with one whoas to be overborne:

Im making myself write to you in the first rush of my feeling. I *wot* be stiff-necked! Your withering letter is worth three years of ar experience I can get here. . . . My whole ego is convulsed, man,s you may suppose, and I'm still in such a fever that I can hardl put pen to paper. Apollo Belvedere, why dost thou show us thy nedness but that we may be ashamed of our own. . . . Herder, Herd go on being what you are to me! If I am born to be your satell, I accept my fate, and gladly, loyally. A moon that loves its eth! But—make no mistake about this—I would rather be Mercy, the last, the least of the Seven that revolve with you round the Sc Sun, than the first of the Five that belong to Saturn! Adieu, dear mn; I will not let you go. I hold fast to you. Jacob wrestled with te angel of the Lord. And though it cripple me, so will I!

Never before or afterwards did Goethe write thus to a man, and oly to one woman—and this after Herder's contemptuous attack! There was fever in his blood; he clutched at the man as in walking dream, and yet his pride revolted tremulously at thisbending of the neck. We can catch the arrogant intonationas this storm-tossed youth, set on his own proud course, flings own the gauntlet:

I amelectrified by those words of Pindar's: ἐπικρατεῖν δύνασθαι! When you stad boldly erect in the chariot, and four fresh horses are tugging frantically at the reins, and you control their energies, whipping the fiery ones in, the unruly ones down, urging and guiding, with a turn of the wrist, a flick of the lash, pulling them up and then giving them their heads, till all sixteen hoofs are taking you at a measured pace to where you want to go—that's mastery!

Goethe had sent the first *Götz* to Herder, frankly confessing that the best powers of his mind had been expended on it, but adding that Herder's judgment would open his eyes to its real value. After reading it, Herder wrote to his betrothed: "You have hours of enchantment before you. There is an uncommon degree of authentically German power, depth, and sincerity in the piece, though now and again it is merely an intellectual exercise." But all he vouchsafed to the author was some satirical verses. What was the explanation? About this time he said to his betrothed: "I love Goethe as my own soul; only—shall I, *ought* I to let him see it?"

It was the rivalry of master and disciple; and the disciple's soul is laid bare when in the *Cæsar* fragment he makes an elder man say of the young hero: "It's an atrocious thing to have a boy growing up beside one in whose every limb one can see that he's going to overtop one by a head!" It was thus that he heard Herder's soul speak to him of Goethe; and Herder's uneasiness would have been comprehensible indeed if Goethe had read the enraptured letters about *Götz* which came from Herder's betrothed.

This girl, Caroline Flachsland, whom Goethe often met in their *al fresco* gatherings during these months, was never tired of saying what a kind pleasant boy he was, what a thoroughly good-hearted companion of their walks, not a bit erudite, and very fond of playing with children.

Schlosser—afterwards his brother-in-law—saw more clearly, and thought Goethe was to be honoured for his efforts "to purge his soul, without emasculating himself." In those seven words almost the whole history of that soul is forecasted.

He took up several sociable pursuits; he rode, fenced, and—not omitting the literary touch which was then so fashionable—he began a new art with his twenty-third year. For it was with Klopstock's verses on his lips that he leaped out of bed one frosty morning, and hurried to the ice that he might learn skating without spectators. He got on so fast that this soon became a mental resource, for he felt that the swinging motion vaguely inspired him, so that his thoughts as it were ripened of themselves.

But it was when walking that he got nearest to himself. He would disappear without a word; the pleasant friendly companion would withdraw himself, that the stirrings in a soul which was preparing for so mighty a stretch of the pinions should not suffer enervating dispersal. These solitary rovings through forests, up mountainsides, often at night, often in rain, were Goethe's most characteristic manifestations of storm and stress. One day he braved a threatening tempest; and when it caught him, he sang passionately to himself:

Wen du nicht verlässest, Genius,
Nicht der Regen, nicht der Sturm,
Haucht ihm Schauer übers Herz.
Wen du nicht verlässest, Genius,
Wird dem Regengewölk,
Wird dem Schlossensturm
Entgegensingen,
Wie die Lerche—
Du da droben. . . [1]

And in long sweeping dithyrambs he invokes in this ode, which is akin to those written to Behrisch, the Muses and the tutelary spirits (*Charitinnen*), and feels near, ever nearer, to Nature.

But suddenly the god-like poet, lustily singing, pulls up the chariot with a jerk and thus concludes:

Glühte?
Armes Herz?
Dort auf dem Hügel,
Himmlische Macht!
Nur so viel Glut:

[1] "He with whom thou bidest, Genius,
Not in rain and not in storm,
Ever knows dismay of heart.
He with whom thou bidest, Genius,
Shall to threatening cloud,
Shall to pelting hail,
Bid sweet defiance,
Like the skylark—
There, above me!"

Dort meine Hütte,
Dorthin zu waten! [1]

There it is again—the young Goethe turning aside from ecstasy, leaving the storm for the calm, a tranquil observer hand-in-hand with a restless rover; no unity as yet between the contrasting traits. And in his one successful attempt, at this time, to portray these paradoxes of the spirit, he used the dramatic form, dividing (in *The Wanderer*) his emotions between the pilgrim and the woman. In this piece, how exquisite is the passage where, on the mountain-crag, his wanderer meets the woman with her nursling at her breast, coming from the antique temple where she dwells, and takes the sleeping boy in his arms—but when she invites him to linger in this freedom, this vast, narrow sphere, he passes resolutely onward, saying to himself:

Leb wohl!
O leite meinen Gang, Natur! . . .
Und kehr' ich dann
Am Abend heim
Zur Hütte,
Vergoldet vom letzten Sonnenstrahl,
Lass mich empfangen solch ein Weib,
Den Knaben auf dem Arm! [2]

[1] "Soul-stirred?
Ah, poor heart,
There on the hill-top,
Touching high Heaven!
One pulse, no more:
Low lies my dwelling,
Thither we stumble!"

[2] "Farewell!
O lead me, Nature, guide my steps!
And coming home
To some roof-tree
At evening,
All golden with dying sunset-rays,
May she await me—such a wife,
Our boy upon her arm!"

CHAPTER III

EROS

"Mir gaben die Götter
Auf Erden Elysium—
Ach, warum nur Elysium!"[1]

". . . Sie nähert sich mir,
Himmlische Lippe!
Und ich wanke, nahe mich,
Blicke, seufze, wanke—
Seligkeit, Seligkeit!
Eines Kusses Gefühl!"[2]

A FAINT sigh runs through the elect little group of ladies under the beech-trees; and Urania, to whom the young Goethe dedicated these verses, may have blushed. It is a small gathering which awaits the spring under the fresh green foliage of the mountain-path. Each of the ladies bears a good German name, most indeed an aristocratic one; but all have assumed romantic pseudonyms, and the one called Psyche is Herder's betrothed. A wave of mystic fervour, a transcendental atmosphere of æsthetic maidenhood (for though none of the girls is in her first youth, there are no married women among them), a virginal world where latent ardours may be smouldering, but where decorum rules the scene—all this has its very special effect

[1] "The gods did accord me
On earth an elysium—
Ah, why elysium only!"

[2] ". . . Close, closer they come,
Lips like an angel's!
And I tremble, nearing them,
Gaze and sigh and tremble—
Ecstasy, ecstasy!
Oh, the sense of a kiss!"

upon the wanderer, whenever he visits his soul-mates at Darmstadt. The storm and stress is modulated into a minor key: "Morgennebel, Lila, hüllen deinen Turm um."[1]

This wondrous little coterie reads and recites amid the moss-grown boulders, the high-souled girls uncertain whether to be rapturous or analytical; and as Herder is far away and Merck—though in true Mephistophelean fashion particularly captivated by these ladies—is not a real poet, the ardent sisterhood bestows its suffrages on Goethe. His adolescent heart stirs in this chaste company, to which he is drawn neither by his own internal flame nor their fresh beauty, but simply by a common zest for culture and the aspirations of youth. It is an Atlantis of the mind, a plane of contemplative ardours, a tranquil return to Nature, somewhat feminine in feeling; and in this period of vehement self-absorption he is soothed by such intercourse with sympathetic women.

At this time Goethe was, like many of his contemporaries, extremely impressionable. His feeling for religion, too, was hovering between paganism and Christianity. He harked back more than once. He consented to attend the Synod of the Moravian Brotherhood; but his interest quickly cooled. The strenuous young man could not resign his will and "await the blessing," for he was too profoundly penetrated by a sense of Nature's potent influence upon the human spirit. This spring-time was to make her votary something more than the enthusiast of landscape, the plastic recipient of impressions. He became the Goethe who could love her—and hence, the solitary. Those around him could not read the riddle of his heart.

> I've had many another blow [he wrote at this time]; but I came here with whole-hearted ardour, and it's like the torments of hell to be received in a spirit so unlike my own. . . . People say that the curse of Cain is upon me. What brother have *I* slain! And so I say to myself that people are fools. . . . To be so utterly alone!

Such was his mood. "Love me—*you!*" His letters would end thus.

More remote from his fellow-men than his expanding soul

[1] "Mists of morning, Lila, shroud thy turret-window."

desired, yet perforce reserved with the crowd whose pioneers were in touch with him; not specially desirous of cultivating the Muse, but still less so of living a practical life; contemplative, expectant, hovering between two worlds as it were—at the end of May Goethe passed some time in a smiling region, where the thrusting shoulders of the hills were like the side-scenes of a theatre, and the valley was always hazy, and the crests of the impenetrable forest tempered the sunlight. Here he would lie in the tall grass by the leaping brook, where

I observed a great many different kinds of grasses . . . . When I listen to that susurrant little world which has its being amid the green blades . . . and feel it grow dearer to my heart, and feel the presence of the Almighty who made us after His own image, and the breath of the All-loving who lifts us and sustains us in infinity of rapture . . . then I think longingly: "Oh, if you could but utter it, if you could but breathe on to the paper all that in yourself has such abundant pulsing life, so that it should be the very mirror of your soul!"

Or else he would sit in the open air and drink the wine of the country, reading Tibullus and seeing a girl by the brook, who looked round for someone to help her lift the brimming vessel to her head. And he went and helped her, smilingly; or played with some children on the hillside and sketched them, and then the young mother arrived and told him how her husband had gone on a journey and hadn't written for a long time; and he gave the children a kreutzer and passed on, at peace and happy.

Was this retreat a watering-place? Or a mountain village? It lay outside the gates of a town; and Wetzlar, dirty and confined, was nevertheless illustrious because in its heart there stood a large building which was the Court of Appeal of the Holy Roman Empire, whither the German Princes and Cities sent ambassadors. There young jurists acquired the final polish, so tradition said; but in truth the teaching was far too vague and diffuse. Goethe put down his name on the list—hardly more—at his father's desire. With those whom he liked he would foregather at the inn, where they instituted a parody of the Round Table and baptised him, the youngest, as "Götz the Honest Man."

The Embassy folk did not dine at this table; and as Goethe did not go to the Court of Appeal, it was some time before he made the acquaintance of the serious-minded, intelligent Secretary from Bremen. This gentleman had merely heard that a young doctor from Frankfurt had arrived in the place—eccentric, a writer, a philosopher. A *bel-esprit?* Sceptically he repeated the unknown name: "Goethe?" And then, after two or three weeks had gone by and people could meet in the open air, he beheld the new arrival.

He saw a pale, thin young person lying on the grass, with a long face, rather a big beaky nose, dark hair and eyes; he was leaning on one soft and not very beautiful hand, and arguing vehemently with some other young fellows. A few minutes' listening revealed that these were philosophers in dispute—one was Epicurean, another Stoical, a third neither one thing nor the other. When the introductions were made, Kestner, who was just thirty and a man of the world, looked searchingly at Goethe as he shook hands.

Near by stood Kestner's colleague from Brunswick, still graver-looking than he, a man of few words, punctiliously attired in the English fashion—blue frock-coat, buff waistcoat, boots with brown tops. His name was Jerusalem. Goethe and he seldom met; all Goethe knew of him was what everyone said—that he was passionately in love with the wife of a friend. The young diplomat and philosopher who bore so pregnant a name was prejudiced against this Goethe who was holding forth so vehemently; and when he got home he wrote to a friend: "Goethe was at Leipzig in our time, and was an ass. Now he's a writer on the *Frankfurter Zeitung* into the bargain." The youth in the grass was soon to make these two diplomatic personages immortal, but one was never to suspect it and the other to know it only too well. There was nothing to forewarn them that a woman and a genius were to make such a marvellous link between the three.

A week later they were all at a party, and so was a girl who danced a great deal with the young doctor from Frankfurt. The slender blooming creature, in her simple summer frock, moved like a sylph, if less yieldingly than Friederike, less ardently than Käthchen; a girl of the middle-class, accustomed to society and quick-witted.

> No faultless beauty [so Kestner, to whom she had been engaged since she was sixteen, describes her], but a pretty girl. Her greatest external attraction for me is her sweet engaging expression. She has plenty of sense besides, and a pleasure-loving disposition. She is amusing and can say witty things. Not forgetting her heart, which is of the first order—noble, affectionate, kind and generous.

And so, too, after forty years had gone by, she was to be described by the poet with whom she danced that evening.

Lotte Buff was his type, once more. The women of his adolescence were all slender and airy, all light-hearted—the sedative influences which his dæmonic nature required.

That summer night saw the poet over head and ears in love; and he was not slow to display the qualities which were sure to attract her to him. Had he not almost everything which Kestner lacked—passion, ingenuousness, and the charm of novelty besides? On the other hand, Kestner had much that was lacking in Goethe—knowledge of the world, cool judgment, impeccability, and such tact that he contrived to bring his betrothed, himself, and his new friend unscathed out of the three months' romance which was then beginning. For nothing speaks better for Kestner than the fact that he could become Goethe's friend, despite jealousy, envy—the whole impossible situation. Soon he came to know him so well that he could deliver the following verdict:

> He has a great deal of talent, is a real genius and a man of character; he possesses an extraordinarily lively imagination, which is the reason why he usually expresses himself in images and symbols. He often declares that he cannot help using figurative language, that he never can express himself literally, but that when he is older he hopes to be able to utter the idea as it really is. He is extremely impressionable, but often shows great self-control. He has fine ideals, is quite unprejudiced, and does as he likes without caring whether other people like it or not, or whether it's the fashion, or generally accepted in society. He hates constraint of any kind. He loves children and will play with them for hours. He's bizarre, and there's something about his manner which might easily make him disliked. . . . He has a very great reverence for women. His principles are unsettled as yet, and he's beginning to long for some definite system of belief. . . . It is only to a few that he will talk about certain vital matters—he avoids upsetting other people's peace of mind. . . . He hates scepticism; it

GOETHE AT THE AGE OF TWENTY-THREE

is the truth that he's after. . . . He doesn't go to church, not even to the Lord's Supper, nor does he often pray. . . . Sometimes he takes these things lightly, sometimes quite the reverse. . . . He believes in a future life, and a better one. . . . In short, he is a very remarkable fellow.

Kestner's understanding of Goethe—for this letter is the best contemporary portrait of his adolescence—was equalled by that which he displayed in the affair now brewing. He acted cleverly all along. Kestner's was the active part, Goethe's the passive.

In Lotte's home there were her father and several brothers and sisters—children to be played with and older ones before whom caution had to be observed; and Lotte's hands were full, for she was at once housewife, mother, and betrothed. The poet's eye, accustomed to observe domestic details and always attracted by an idyllic picture, was rested and cheered; and moreover this was good material. The restrictions of that respectable household, effective in warding off many of the risks attendant on actual romance, were no less so in lending a charm to the written narrative.

Passion was soon at its height, and the sentimentality of the time would lead us to anticipate such a climax as the following: conflict between love and duty in the hero's heart, victory of his friendship with the fiancé, self-sacrifice and withdrawal, then the final conflict between mortal ennui and love of life. Little consonant with Goethe's nature, it is true; yet the atmosphere surrounding the young people would seem to answer for it.

But no, Goethe, yielding to his passion and more and more intimately drawn in spirit to the girl, neither transgressed against friendship nor wallowed in self-sacrifice. Like any other young man he wanted a wife. As always, he was thinking less of passion and romance than of home and marriage. But the girl—restrained by respectability and prudence, faithful to her four-years' engagement, too prosaic and much too timid to yield to the vehement wooing of this stormy genius and let the whisper of the senses urge her heart to a choice which would endanger her own happiness, her father's peace of mind, and the credit of the family name—the girl drew back, keeping him at a distance with kindly tact and remaining her own sensible, cheerful self. So little overwhelmed was she that the alternative never really presented itself at all; and she had only to think quietly, weighing habit and common-sense against the new prospect, to decide, as her equable nature bade her, in Kestner's favour.

Goethe soon made preparations for flight from this situation, but he did not carry them out. Kestner, of course, admired Lotte all the more for the way she kept the other man in check.

> His peace of mind [so he was soon writing to a friend about Goethe] was much disturbed; there were several extraordinary scenes, which made me think all the more of Lottchen, and of him too as a friend. Usually I felt very sorry for him and was much perturbed in spirit. . . . He began to see that he must pull himself together, for his own sake.

The cardinal point is this. Our lover never entirely lost his head; or rather he found it again in the moment when Lotte, called upon by him after eight weeks of courtship to decide the question once for all, chose—at the cost of one sleepless night—not him, but Kestner. Genius, battering at the door of a maiden's heart, had to learn that a mere human being was already in possession. And genius drew the sleep-walker away from the inhospitable threshold. The heart which could contain the flood of inexpressible emotions, old as time, that surged within it—was that heart likely to break for a Lotte? Nothing we know of this incident points even indirectly to the girl's refusal having sapped her young lover's prodigious vitality.

Disdained by the woman he loved, and rejected for a lesser man, his dæmonic nature asserted itself. He accepted the position and took the strongest line—to go, and go at once, no matter what it cost him. Had not Merck invited him to join a party on the Rhine? That would be a good pretext.

Goethe went, and made no scene at all; he did not even say goodbye.

And then the swift revulsion! From the moment he left her neighbourhood, from the very night on which he packed his trunk, his soul was possessed by a sense of fatality. Once an incident was closed, Goethe's heart was prone to feel in all its manifold anguish the inexorable determinism of all experience, the stern law of nature which decreed his course. The environment and the girl's sweet gaiety, the intimate daily intercourse, the joy of loving service had until that evening blinded him to the possibility of a final renunciation. But now, when he had left her, when kindly chance could do no more for him, the elemental forces in his heart broke bounds. In the farewell notes which he left for the two lovers we hear the first mutterings of the tempest in his soul:

He is gone, Kestner; when you get this note, he will be gone. . . . I had felt composed, but your conversation was too much for me. . . . If I had stayed one instant longer, I could not have controlled myself. Now I am alone, and to-morrow I depart. Oh, my poor head!

And early next morning:

Packed up, Lotte, and the dawn is breaking; in another quarter of an hour, I shall be gone. . . . You know all, you know how happy I have been throughout these days. And I am going to the dearest and best of people, but why away from you? So it is, and this is my destiny. . . . Adieu, a thousand times adieu. Goethe.

This is Goethe's third flight from a girl, and again it is only when his love is coming to an end that he regards it as fatality. That is the way with dæmonic natures. If he had won and possessed the girl he would have been intoxicated for a little while; renunciation and flight let loose the mysterious powers within him.

His passion grew with absence, and he indulged in raptures of renunciation. Goethe's love for Lotte Buff—an idyll of two summer months with a third month of rivalry and rejection—was now to increase throughout the course of twenty months. For thenceforth the ruler of his spirit was not so much Lotte as Eros; and never was he more the prey of Eros than just now—like Romeo, who loved because he *had* loved.

A week after his flight Goethe was sitting in a charming villa on the Rhine, where people of many interests lived in luxury with a hostess who was responsive, intelligent, full of sensibility and in the early forties. This was Sophie Laroche, at one time the beloved of Wieland, and now becoming known as an authoress. She had a daughter too. The sixteen-yeared Maximiliane was not so tall as Lotte Buff, but hers was the same kind of open countenance and clear complexion, and she too had the darkest of dark eyes.

It was the rhythmic quality in Goethe's nature which at regular and recurrent intervals attracted him towards definite groups of women. He spent five days in this house. Fifty years afterwards he had not lost sight of the mother, daughter, and granddaughter.

But no sooner had he returned to Frankfurt than he immersed himself afresh in Lotte's world, and began to bombard her with letters, full of yearning and relinquishment, half adoring and half teasing, charming and challenging, much tinged (at that safe distance) with sensuality, charged with memories of all he had resigned—and always, always pleading for her love, her remembrance, as though he had no dearer wish than to be unforgettable for the heart which had rejected him.

So Lotte didn't dream of me. I am offended at that, and insist on her dreaming of me to-night, and not telling you anything about it, either. . . . Here I can only go on as best I may, and I don't want to see Lotte again until I can tell her in *confidence* that I've fallen in love. . . . It would be better if I didn't write to you, and left my imagination in peace—yet there hangs the silhouette, and that's the worst of all. . . . It's very much the same rose-coloured ribbon, only paler, I think, than the one she wore out driving that day.

Eight weeks of this was as much as he could stand, and he went to Wetzlar, ostensibly on business. There he stayed a few days in a state of ecstatic friendship; when he was going he regretted not having made his formal goodbyes:

I came short of a kiss which she could not have denied me. I very nearly went over there this morning. . . . Indeed, Kestner, it was time I took myself off. Last night, on the sofa, my thoughts were concerned with hanging, and very hangworthy they were.

His passion and his enjoyment of his own pangs were both increasing. And if now, when he could have kissed his friend under the eyes of his friend, there was audible—so many weeks after the decision and the earlier parting—a sigh over the futility of existence, it was no more than a momentary mood of dejection.

For Goethe, so long as he drove the chariot of his life, was conscious of the mastery within him; and the nearer, the dizzier the abyss that yawned beneath—the abyss upon whose edge almost the entire eighty-yeared course was run—the more firmly did he grip the reins, rejecting the thought that the goal might be unsatisfactory and loyally fulfilling the day's demand. In this spirit he now became an advocate at Frankfurt, and so remained during the three succeeding years of the last and longest stay he was obliged to make at home.

He had twenty-eight cases, most of them for Frankfurt Jews; not a remarkable number. Although Goethe was not an excellent speaker (and never a persuasive one), no fighter either, and although he was entirely devoid of worldly ambition or desire for a popular success, thus lacking all the stimulations which go to make great advocates, his feeling for actualities might have kept him in this sphere, if the formulas, conventions, and hair-splitting, the whole pedantic procedure of the calling, had not scared him off.

His début was quite in the manner of a fierce poetic diatribe, and the Court snubbed him on the spot! Goethe was practical enough to keep for his poetic workshop that dispassionate attitude towards both parties which distinguishes the dramatist from the advocate, and to aim at cumulative effect in his first case for the defence. He was representing a son whose father refused to grant him undisturbed possession of a porcelain-factory. Goethe's ten-paged brief, in answer to the indictment, began with such extravagant periods as the following:

> If blustering self-sufficiency can affect the decision of a learned judge, and the most malignant of invectives prevail against a well-established verity . . . in such circumstances as these, how could I, how should I, be expected to add fuel to the fire which is to consume me? When jurisprudence, that mysterious veiled goddess, after long grievous travail has brought forth—what do we see? A couple of ridiculous mice that creep from the pages of some compendium of definitions and proclaim themselves her children. Run away, little mice!

While this speech was in progress the lawyers, sitting among their arid briefs, shook their heads and smiled forbearingly; and the opposing counsel, in his reply, observed that all the clever fooling they had just been listening to proceeded from a man whom even in their school-days he had perceived to be an arrogant type of person.

But Goethe, never a revolutionary in the narrow sphere of established custom, changed his tactics after this first effort; and thenceforth it was only very rarely that his briefs had to suffer the irruption of epigram. We can follow the process of getting into line in his successive cases—the phrasemonger gradually becomes an advocate. The father must have had some influence here. He was an accomplished lawyer; and though as an Imperial Councillor unable to practise, he was often helpful as a confidential intermediary, and he now frequently lent a controlling hand.

But directly the son became known as an author, the old gentleman resolutely altered his course. It was Goethe's father who cleared the way for his son's imaginative life. When he wanted to travel, he could hand over his work to his father—and to his brother-in-law as well, for at this time Cornelia married Schlosser, who was a lawyer.

Soon after their engagement, Goethe turned jealous. He was used to this confidante, he liked to tell her about his schemes for work, his letters, and even his answers to them; and the conservative side of him was vexed by any intrusion from without. A sort of hypochondria of the spirit set in; he complained of being deserted, and although the sister had never been anything more than an echo, or possibly a timorous ally against the father, he wanted to find her always there when he came home and needed a confidante.

This year brought one of those nervous crises which at fairly regular intervals—usually every seven years—would run their course with Goethe. Eros, languishing for a distant heart, sought a substitute in sentimental friendship. A distant female relative became his mother-confessor—one Johanna Fahlmer, not young, a single woman but safe. For her nephew, the poet Fritz Jacobi, Goethe cherished a prejudice; he refused to make any approaches to him and his brother, would not even contribute to their new magazine. But a sudden fancy took him, after all, to pay Jacobi a visit on a trip up the Rhine; and he found him an idealistic, delightful-looking man. From the first moment he was conscious of the closest kind of affinity, and the ice was melted by words of flame. It was as if two ardent spirits had rushed into one another's arms—but there was a definitely literary atmosphere about it all, with recitations by moonlight, soon to be followed by incoherent letters which might have been those of lovers.

Götz had made his name famous; in North Germany and Vienna it was tried on the stage, and though it had no run, this measure of success was useful in selling the book. Goethe looked upon it all as a lark. He wanted the suffrage of the few, while the applause of the many-headed was heaped on him. "I wish Lotte cared a little about my play. I have all sorts of laurels, and flowers too—even Italian flowers—and I try my wreaths on by turns and grin at myself in the glass."

He himself was a reviewer at this time. The *Frankfurter Gelehrten Anzeigen*, organ of the literary revolt, had accepted contributions from Goethe before *Götz* appeared, and it was there that he began his critical career. But always as a poet condescending to criticism—or, as Herder said, an arrogant young cock of the walk with very formidable spurs. In these writings his mocking spirit coruscates through the critical comments, a malign sort of wit after Mephisto's heart. The chaotic youth had scarce one attribute of the true critic.

One day there came strange tidings from Kestner. Jerusalem had killed himself,—that singular visionary, philosopher, and lover of literature, who was also something of an artist and a collector of lonely landscape-scenes. He was the son of rich parents and was cultured, independent. He had a love-affair with a friend's wife, it was true. . . .

Unfortunate man [wrote Goethe], the poor, poor fellow! Once, when I was coming back from a walk and he met me in the moonlight, I said to myself immediately: "He is in love." Lotte must remember how I used to laugh about it. Loneliness played the mischief with his heart, God help him, and—I've known him by sight for seven years; we never saw much of each other, but when I was leaving Wetzlar I borrowed a book from him. I shall keep it, and remember him as long as I live.

A vague sense of shortcoming—the unfortunate man—a sad ending—poor fellow—and a dash. . . . That represented all Goethe felt on hearing of Jerusalem's suicide, yet he himself was living in a rising tide of passion, seven weeks after his parting from Lotte.

It was because he divined how different his nature was from Jerusalem's. This latter had once written an essay to prove that complete surrender to passion was despicable; but when it did get hold of him he made the greatest of all surrenders—self-murder. Goethe, who had never moralised on the subject, who defended every manifestation of passion, and who moreover was emancipated from all semi-religious scruples, yet had a safety-valve in his dæmonic temperament; and in his spirit such instinctive, life-giving humility before destiny and Nature that to his tempestuous soul the thought of death by his own hand could never seriously present itself. At that time he had been wont to lay a valuable dagger from his collection of weapons on his bed-table every night;

and before I put out the light I used to try if I could bring myself to plunge the sharp point a couple of inches in my breast. But as I never could, I finally laughed myself out of the attempt, got rid of all such mumpish affectations, and made up my mind to live.

But what manner of life did he then adopt? Where was the fire, the craving to learn, to shape a course, which had been so intense the year before? He now stood remote from the world around him; Eros possessed his fervid, lonely heart; his walks were almost all he had to cling to. The winter season in Frankfurt was in full swing; he was young, brilliant, famous, good-looking; he could go into society, he did help to dress a girl for a ball, but would not join in the carnival.

You complain of loneliness [he wrote]. Alas! That is the fate of the noblest spirits, to sigh in vain for a reflection of themselves. . . . Ye sacred Muses, pour the *aurum potabile* . . . from your chalices for me, for indeed I languish! What a price we pay for sinking wells in the desert and building a house there. . . . One strand snapped! And all your seven-ply ropes are of no avail.

"Perfectly aimless and planless"—such were Goethe's manifold activities at this time; a life, an art, directed to no central point. He knew he was drifting all the time between sceptical waiting and curious expectancy, wholly passive: "Since I am playing no part in the world as yet, I devote my best hours to shaping forth my phantasies, and my greatest delight is when somebody I respect and love will take an interest in them."

Phantasies—sometimes they took form under his pencil. White and black on grey paper, profiles of his friends; but as they never satisfied him he would take to verse once more.

Let us look at one of these drawings. It represents three people—his sister and her friends in a group, in everyday attire, the treatment academic. We turn the paper and read:

> Wer half mir gegen der Titanen Ubermut?
> Wer rettete vom Tode mich,
> Von Sklaverei?
> Hast du nicht alles selbst vollendet,
> Heilig glühend Herz. . . .[1]

With its tame drawing and its fiery verses this sheet is an epigram on the poet's plastic ambitions, which were then beginning, and were to prove well-nigh a tragedy for many years. For Goethe had no plastic talent; and when he took to the pencil it can scarcely be said to have been from a genuine plastic impulse, though it was to take him thirty years to realise this. That one great mistake about himself casts light upon a hundred other impulses; and thus the barren effort was fruitful for posterity's understanding of the man.

"My heart is beating high to-day. This afternoon I am to use the paintbrush for the first time. With what lowliness, reverence, and hope I can't express—my fate hangs on that moment." In such a high-flown mood did Goethe begin a new

[1] "Against the Titans' overweening pride of rule,
Who helped me, rescued me from death,
From slavery?
Hast thou not done it all unaided,
Heart of sacred fire?"

art, for which nevertheless he had been preparing throughout years of sketching, etching, and silhouette-drawing. And yet as a poet he had never once trembled before the blank sheet which awaited his hand, nor taken the beginning of any such task with a like solemnity. Why then for painting? Was it a case of the impotent coveting the master's throne? Was his hand not a painter's at all?

Not so. His line was firm, he caught good likenesses (especially in profile), his tones were transparent—he *had* learnt something, and his best drawings are no worse than the trivial lyric dramas he was presently to write. But the impulse of his soul was not to be denied. To give form and verisimilitude to things of the imagination was the at first unconscious aim of his writings; and because he had an eye which could discern the particular in the universal, Goethe ranks as the pioneer of imaginative realism. His vision was as a dove sent forth by his genius to survey the universe and bring back tidings of the terra firma rising above the tumultuous flood of dreams, which would afford a base for the constructive mind. Never was it his aim merely to find words for what he saw; his insight had already revealed that to him; but such was his reverent love for the thing seen that he could not but express it in phrases of clairvoyant tenderness.

Since in plastic art he was no more than the amateur whose aim it was precisely to reproduce the object, his efforts in that sort are futile soulless imitations, often devoid of any sensibility whatever; and nothing better proves the subordinacy of this aim than the fact that when on his rambles a landscape tempted him to sketch it, he was wont to scribble notes on the margin, pointing out his inadequacies in form and colour. "How we long to find expression for what we feel! . . . Blessed be the good impulse which told me to sketch my room for you, just as it stands before me, instead of writing any more about it!" As a painter Goethe aimed only at veracity, while the poet's eye was "in fine frenzy rolling."

This chiaroscuro of the spirit held him from any surrender to absolute beauty. Though plaster-casts of classic heads, bought from itinerant Italians at the Fair, lit up his attic-room, he was possessed by that love for the fantastic and untamed which is a trait of solitary natures, and in him found an outlet in screaming farce. A visitor describes at this time "his grave, sad look, in which nevertheless there was a gleam of mockery and satire. He is very eloquent, and full of extremely witty notions. He turns everything into a sort of drama." He loved to talk in images, and here again the duality of his experience is made manifest; for his impassioned searching vision, all-embracing as it was, supplied him with images at every turn, while the poet's eye beheld each particular as symbolic of the universal—and at the end of eighty years it was to be no different with him.

Sometimes, waking in the night, he would find verses running in his head; and then he would rush to his desk and write, obeying his inspiration, without a pause and straggling anyhow across the paper, so as to preserve the somnambulistic mood. Mostly he wrote in the very early morning, often after having had a dream. "Anything with real stuff in it would set me off."

One day he read in Wieland's magazine that Wieland had critically defended his own *Alcestis* against that of Euripides. This wakened the spirit of derision; he sat down with a bottle of Burgundy beside him and on that afternoon wrote—in such haste that he used initials to designate the characters in the play —*Götter, Helden und Wieland*. Did he hate Wieland? Not at all. He kept a sharp ear for the verdict of that pope of literature. In attacking Wieland now, he was once more attacking his own outgrown rococo-phase; and with a characteristic flash of self-illumination he instantly asked himself in a letter: "Do I hate Wieland or love him? It's all one, really—I take an interest in him."

Soon chance was to put him to the proof. Pride and good-manners, the self-consciousness and the detachment of a budding poet, veneration, audacity—all were involved. For Goethe's friend Lenz, out of either malice or impudence, printed this farcical piece on his own responsibility, thus turning a private lark into a literary scandal; and it was Wieland who, with a man of the world's shrewd chivalry, laid his young opponent in the dust. For he chose this moment to write an eulogy on *Götz*—a somewhat feline amenity, it is true. The post brought it to Goethe—the latest number of Wieland's magazine; and a friend who was present testifies emphatically to the mutterings she could hear while Goethe read.

Well, Wieland, you're a decent fellow! A thorough good chap! What? Is this what he's after? . . . Wasn't I always kindly-disposed to him? I always did say he was a good fellow, a kind fellow. . . . I wrote that damnable muck when I was drunk. . . . There—that's what always annoys me about Wieland . . . that tone he takes. . . . I don't mean to say that I was right and Wieland wrong, for one takes different views according to one's age and period. . . . Perhaps when I'm Wieland's age, or even sooner, I shall think precisely as he does. . . . "In time." Oh, of course—just the way my father talks. . . . Awfully decent! Well, Wieland, our feud is over—I'm done with attacking you!

All this, while he was reading the critique on *Götz*. Then he turned to Wieland's retort to the comic piece. He flushed up; his friend could see that he was agitated; he exclaimed: "He couldn't have been cleverer! . . . Wieland gains enormously with the public, and I lose. I've prostituted myself!"

But he wrote another satire at this time—less genial and less gay, but deeper and more personal: *Satyros*. Here he was mocking at another man, but also at himself and the phase he had recently outgrown. The duality of Goethe's nature always made him quick to watch himself upon the stage, as might one behind the scenes who had been taking part in the performance. In this deified satyr he was ridiculing not only Herder whom he venerated, but also *Sturm und Drang*, and Rousseau, and the Return to Nature.

But behold, ere the mocking author quite realised it, Herder's potent spirit had possessed him, breaking through the limitations of farce! And this quite against Goethe's will. He had just been making Satyros, the apostle of Nature, ridicule the flowing vesture worn by Hermes, when the ironic side of him suddenly turned upside down, revealing the sentimental—and Herder's ideas about the instinctive method flashed through the Goat-foot's diatribe.

Goethe was more careful with this piece; he allowed only a few friends to read it, and it was not for forty years, when all the prototypes were dead, that he suffered it to see the light. When he was writing it, he was on fire—not against, but *with* Herder; and likewise "with" himself, who was toying with the Return to Nature and yet recoiling from it.

For here was the extraordinary thing—Goethe's duel perception was parodying himself as he then was. The farce of *Satyros* dates from the same summer-months which saw the birth of *Prometheus*.

In no work of his adolescence are the dæmon and the genius, who disputed Goethe's soul for eighty years, so completely fused in a single figure as in this Prometheus, at once rebel and artist. His very first words are defiant of the gods: "Tell them I will not! Once for all, I will not!" And his last are no less bold a challenge: "To heed thee never, as myself not heeds thee!"

Yet this rebel is likewise a constructive spirit. Nowhere can we more plainly perceive the distinction between Goethe's "Storm and Stress" and that of his comrades. The latter revel in the chaotic; for Goethe it is a primitive state to be escaped from as soon as possible.

For while Goethe, all defiance and indignation, surveying the round earth, feels like his Prometheus, the defiant shaping spirit who to Destiny alone is subject . . . suddenly the artist in him, ever haunted by his veneration for the higher powers, bends the knee before his genius, and he makes Prometheus answer Minerva:

> Durch dich, o meine Göttin,
> Leben, frei sich fühlen,
> Leben! Ihre Freude wird dein Dank sein![1]

All these poems seem play to him; he regards them as practice, not as finished work; he scarcely has a word to say about them. . . . Disporting himself thus in challenge and mockery, the toys of his passion-tossed spirit, Goethe sought to pacify that Eros whose sad eyes were ever present to imagination. When Lotte was preparing for her wedding and Kestner was transferred to a post in Hanover, Goethe's neuroticism reached its climax; and just as, four years earlier, he had brooded with all the sensual ardour of a lover upon Käthchen's nuptials, so now his erotic excitement rose to fever-point after the wedding-day. His letters during these weeks are unparalleled throughout the whole course of his adolescence.

[1] "Through thee, O thou my goddess,
Thus to live, enfranchised,
Live! Thy guerdon shall be in their rapture!"

He refused to go to the wedding; personally he wished to be as far away as possible, though in spirit nearer than ever before.

Why would they not let him buy the wedding-ring? he demanded. "And her silhouette . . . shall be cast out of my room on her wedding-day, never to hang there again until I hear she is in childbed."

Later he was perpetually imagining his rival's blisses, and wrote of them with classical outspokenness, a week after the wedding:

. . . So good-night, Mr. and Mrs. Kestner. I would have ended my letter there if I had anything better to expect in bed than my dear brother Sleep. Just look at that bed of mine—it's as sterile as the desert-sands. How I could leave Lotte I have never yet been able to understand . . . and tell me, was it heroic or what? I'm proud and not proud of myself. It cost me little, and yet I can't imagine how I could do it. . . . But one thing I know, and that is that our Lord God must be a very cold-blooded fellow to let *you* have Lotte.

Evidently his nerves were all of a twitter during those honeymoon-days, seven months after the parting. This letter is, unlike all others, written in a shaky hand, untidy and straggling. After some days:

But I do think it unkind to pull a face at me and lie down beside your wife. . . . And to call me an envious fellow! . . . O Kestner, when did I ever grudge you Lotte in the human sense—for if I didn't grudge her to you in the sacred sense, I should have to be an angel without lungs or liver. . . . My poor existence is petrifying into barren rock.

In these weeks—not in the year before, when he was wooing her, and still less in that to come, when he depicted her—Goethe's heart was convulsed by the anguish of a young lover compelled by the beloved herself to relinquish all hope, and in imagination perpetually seeing her in the arms of another man.

In the summer he dreamt of her sometimes, and wrote: "And so I dream, and dawdle through life, conducting beastly law-suits, writing dramas and novels and such-like." Towards autumn he sent her a loose gown. She would want one shortly, he supposed.

But while the stormy sea was gradually growing calm above the passion drowned, a new ship with gaily-coloured flags was appearing on the horizon; and perhaps the abandoned lover unconsciously let the earlier infatuation sink the sooner below the surface because he felt the new one drawing near. That Maximiliane Laroche who had charmed him at the time of his flight from Wetzlar, now arrived in the nick of time at Frankfurt, as a fascinating young woman and moreover a wife "misunderstood." At this period Goethe had broken away from the asceticism which he had long preserved in memory of Lotte; he had written some erotic poems to a certain Christel, of whom we know nothing, and this makes a healthy interlude among the letters of that year.

He was ready, in short; and it is no wonder that the pretty, warm-blooded creature, just become the wife of a rich elderly merchant (and a stepmother into the bargain), and brought from the high-souled atmosphere of the charming villa on the Rhine to a gloomy ancestral house in Frankfurt, should have in a fortnight renewed her full intimacy with Goethe. By that time he was talking of the "joy of his life"; but now he did not mean the woman herself, but his feeling for her, and the difference is profoundly significant. At first the husband, Herr Brentano—who was supposed to have no cause for jealousy—seemed to him a worthy man, a strong character, the motive-power of his great business.

Mephisto knew better.

> *Goethe est déjà l'ami de la maison* [wrote Merck to his wife]. *Il accompagne le clavecin de Madame avec la basse. M.B., quoique assez jaloux pour un italien, l'aime. . . . G. a la petite Mme. B. à consoler sur l'odeur de l'huile, du fromage, et des manières de son mari.*

This passion of Goethe's was brief and violent. He returned her letters and she must have burnt his, for all that remains is an unfinished copy of a single sheet, where he sentimentalises about one of her dark curls:

> When I am in the mood I have the hair to gaze at, and reflect that it represents my possession in all the other curls which are not actually in my power. For to which of the many with whom we consort has she given anything so intimate! . . . A spade will push through the

earth and bring to light what had been consigned to darkness, and the earth does not resent it. I suppose that symbolises all the happiness I can wish you. And if you had it, I should be as happy as you.

In a few weeks all was over. Mme. Laroche made no concealment of her grief about her daughter's marriage. Goethe was malicious about the sharp nose of the husband—roughly awakened from his brief dream of love. The Brentanos had arrived at New Year; by February Brentano had forbidden Goethe the house.

Even in the summer, when the mother, who was on a visit in Frankfurt, begged him to come and see her, he answered in a gloomy strain:

If you knew what I went through before I ceased to go to the house you would not want to lure me back, dear Mamma. In those frightful weeks I suffered enough for all my future; now I am calm, and let me remain so!

Is not this little lady the third from whom Goethe had to tear himself in the full tide of passion? And was it not always for the woman's sake—for her peace of mind or security—that he left her? That was Goethe's appointed rôle with the women of his adolescence—unlimited surrender, and in the midst of his surrender, flight, to protect the woman.

But himself as well. For behind these women—whom he never wanted to possess for the moment only, but always wholly and for life—stood the stern form of his genius, driving away the dæmon with invisible hands lest blisses should enervate that temperament. Never in his life is this more evident than in those agitated winter weeks. For then, on fire once more and once more driven from the loved one's house—then, once more a fugitive, once more established in his attic-room at home . . . the memory of his last parting leaped to life, and he thought how different it was, since then he had been driven out by the beloved woman's own free choice.

How different—and yet there might be some resemblance between his mood of to-day and that of the unhappy man, the young diplomat and philosopher from Brunswick, who had likewise been forbidden his mistress's house by her husband. Had he not blown out his brains that very night! . . . "Ah, *now* I understand you, Jerusalem—*now* I can show how you felt! Show—yes! There are the white sheets of paper, whose fellows have received the raptures and the agonies of my soul year after year!"

And Goethe sits down, and without a plan, without a preliminary draft, writes *Werthers Leiden.* The whole work, begun as by a sleep-walker, shut away from all his friends, was finished in a month; but no sooner had he written the first of Werther's letters than the constructive impulse took a hand, so that in full tide of work he could write to one friend: "I never had any idea of making a coherent whole of this subject," and soon afterwards to another: "The sufferings of this precious youth . . . and now I have put my own feelings into his story, and it makes a marvellous whole."

That *Werther* survives to this day, although the spirit of the age was accountable for its immediate success, is due to the wealth of circumstantial detail, the spontaneity and freshness which inspire it; and this was enhanced by a master-stroke of Goethe's. It is almost certain that he got Merck to give him back his letters from Wetzlar, with the intention of making use of them; and this is the more probable because in those days letters were composed as literary exercises, which explains the vogue then beginning for novels written in that form.

So strong is the similarity between Goethe's and Werther's letters, even in dates and punctuation, that in the first part of the book we can read Goethe's soul through the medium of Werther's —although the work was written a year and a half after the parting and Jerusalem's death, when the passion had long been got over—nay, in the midst of a new one, so that it is but a semi-relapse, as it were.

Goethe to Kestner:

The morning is so splendid and I feel so happy that I can't stick in the town, and intend going to Garbenheim. Lotte said yesterday that she would like to take a longer walk than usual to-day. . . . Not that I expect you both out here—but wish! *That,* with my whole heart; and I shall hope . . . just enough to make up for the uncertainty. So I shall spend my day in uncertainty, hoping and hoping.

Werther to Wilhelm:

I shall see her today—so I say every morning and look as gladly at the glorious sunshine as it looks at me. I shall see her! And that's the one wish I have all day. That prospect swallows up every other.

Goethe must even have looked up Kestner's letter about Jerusalem's death, for he used whole sentences from it word for word. Apparently he re-read all Kestner's letters while he was at work on *Werther*. And then he felt impelled to write to him and Lotte more fully, more intimately, than of late. The consciousness of having concealed his new love and his flight, together with a secret fear that this book might impair their friendship, made him insist ambiguously, but with ever-increasing emphasis, upon his affection. Suddenly a piece of news relieved the situation—Lotte had given birth to a son, immediately after Goethe had brought *Werther* into the world.

And now every instinct that is part of Eros sprang to life in Goethe. He was lover, friend, and sponsor; and it was a touch of the paternal too which caused him to make the impossible suggestion: "I wish Lotte . . . might have said, 'His name is to be Wolfgang' . . . and I want him to have that name, because it is mine. . . . Tell me at once what you decide upon." . . . At the same time the day for the novel's publication was approaching, and the author was feeling nervous about it.

"I shall very shortly be sending you a friend who resembles me a good deal, and I hope you will like him. His name is Werther, and he is and was—well, let him tell you himself!"

Meanwhile, rejuvenated, revivified, he plunged into manifold activities, till at last—it was then more than two years after his departure from Wetzlar—he was able to dispatch the book.

And this copy is as precious to me as if it were the only one in the world. It shall be yours, Lotte; I have kissed it a hundred times, I have locked it up so that no one else should touch it. O Lotte! [But after all he forgot to enclose this note in the book.] I live in such a racket! The Fair is at its noisiest, my friends are with me, and past and future are strangely mingled. What will be the end of me? Go on loving the live man, and respect the dead one.

How remote he was at heart, already!

But then fell a blow. Kestner felt injured—and justly, in so far as he stood for Albert; but his resentment was for Lotte as well. His limitations were now made evident. The sensation created by the book was certainly trying enough for an official; we cannot blame him. And what was to be Goethe's attitude? The earliest scintillations of prodigious fame were flashing through his father's house, his own little attic-room. Would he not retort: "You don't understand—these are all questions of art"?

No—he pleaded, expounded, coaxed.

You have cut the ground under my feet—what can I say in excuse? I can only hold out this hope of requital . . . that Fate may grant me to have done what will ultimately draw us closer than ever before. . . . But even then I must be your debtor, and your children's, for the bad moments that my—call it what you like—has caused you.

When Kestner, before long, changed his tone, Goethe's pen could not keep pace with his emotion.

Thank you, thank you! . . . Oh, if I could fall on your neck, could fling myself at Lotte's feet. . . . O ye of little faith! If you could feel the thousandth part of what *Werther* is to a thousand hearts, you would not reckon with the cost you now deplore. . . . Give Lotte my hand—warm with affection, and say to her, "To know that your name is uttered in reverence by thousands of adoring lips—is not that an equivalent for any uneasiness?" . . . If you're both good, and don't carp at me, I'll send you some of the letters, effusions, suspirations about *Werther*. . . . Farewell, Lotte, and Kestner too—go on loving me—and *don't* carp at me——!

Tender, pleading—yes; but half-withdrawn from these two, already borne from Eros to Eros on the mighty wing-beats of his dæmon.

CHAPTER IV

DÆMONIC

"Accursèd destiny, that will never suffer me to be in equilibrium!"

"Mir ist das liebe Wertherische Blut
Immer zu einem Probierhengst gut,
Den lass ich mit meinem Weib spazieren,
Vor ihren Augen sich abbranliren,
Und hintendrein komm' ich bei Nacht. . . ."[1]

AND if one could quote further, readers would be strengthened in the conviction that here is a cynical pot-bellied jester invading Werther's high-flown sphere, and tearing down the veils of illusion. Nothing surprising in a worthy citizen's writing this doggerel as the protest of all healthy-minded folk against Werther's tear-dimmed universe. But the verses are by Goethe, introduced—immediately after the publication of *Werther*—into the crazy orchestration of *Hanswursts Hochzeit*, which he thought well to eliminate from the list of his works, but which we need as a document.

For here, more strikingly than anywhere else, we are shown the immense reaction in Goethe's dual nature after the writing of *Werther*.

It was the fate of this passionate young man to love five women in his adolescence, four of whom he either failed to win or lost too soon to others. In this period of sheer eroticism he surrendered himself so completely to the luxuries of relinquishment and the spell of imagination that all his vital forces, repressed for more than a whole year, were bound to break out in

[1] "That dear old strain of Werther in my blood
I always can trot out when in the mood;
It sometimes takes my wife out driving
And goes to pieces, myself conniving,
And I slink home at night somehow. . . ."

full force directly such passivity had sown its wild oats in *Werther*.

Goethe's genius, whose task it had hitherto been to combat his dæmon, in that one instance gave it free rein. His prodigious temperament blazed out uncontrollably, and his genius had to follow those flames whither they would.

It was reaction, too, from the sensation caused by the work. At twenty-five, astounded and alarmed, he was confronted by such success as he never again either achieved or desired. In sceptical moments he clearly perceived that it was not so much his self-revelation as the coincidence with a national sensation—the mysterious suicide of a German diplomatist—which had caused the multitudinous success.

For fifty years Goethe was for most Europeans the author of *Werther*. Since the novel responded to a contemporary phase which Goethe himself quickly outgrew, it did as much harm to its readers as it had done good to him. Every young man was wearing a blue frock-coat and a buff waistcoat, many tears were shed, there were some suicides. Though in Leipzig the book was prohibited and a fine of ten dollars imposed on sales, there were sixteen editions in Germany and more in France and England; it penetrated to China, was dramatised, imitated—and parodied.

In his attitude towards these parodies, Goethe was something like a wandering minstrel who should willingly suffer his adventures to be derided, but not his songs. When Nicolai in his *Freuden des jungen Werthers* depicted an abortive attempt at suicide with a pistol full of hen's blood and Werther's subsequent wedding with Lotte, Goethe was at first delighted with the charming vignettes. He cut them out, and that evening went tranquilly on with his new lyric drama. But he could not get the parody out of his head; in three poems and many letters he gave utterance to his wrath, and finally travestied the travesty in a dramatic scena.

Nor was it only the uproar itself which spoilt his triumph. It showed him too plainly the spuriousness of contemporary fame. He had flung his book into the world on an impulse of reaction from a strain which had shaken him to the remotest depths of his being; and the world, with its tactless, shrewd curiosity, was chiefly intent on discovering how much of the story was actual fact.

On that point he was so susceptible that one of his friends, writing about Lotte Kestner's view of Goethe's delineation of herself, warned his correspondent not to tell Goethe, lest he should fall upon him tooth and nail.

Goethe, whose own experience coloured all his works, was always afterwards desirous to obliterate any trace of this, and suffer no one to detect the links between his life and his publications. When to that was added the further necessity of concealing any incoherence caused by frequent re-writing, he took great pride in accomplishing the feat.

No one earlier perceived, or at any time better expressed, this peculiar correlation between the work and the experience of Goethe than did Merck, who wrote him these pregnant words: "Your irresistible tendency is to give poetic form to the actual, while others seek to give actuality to the so-called poetic." Even after fifty years the veteran was freshly struck by his worldly old friend's profound comment, made so long ago. And now, with *Werther*, he had to bear the consequences of this tendency, as imposed by the world at large.

Nevertheless, despite the offensive curiosity, despite the uncomprehending nature of the applause, the youth who scorned the outward show was having his first glimpse of what real glory might mean for his soul; and though he reiterated, to himself and his friends, his view of the earlier writings as not worth considering, he did feel that the present uproar was a confirmation of loftier hopes, in that his melodious name was ringing through all the nations. For the first time he beheld himself as *called*—the unattainable dream was visibly nearer. The stream of homage, pouring in from unknown readers, moved him to the core; and he, who in utter tranquillity of spirit had laid aside his pen in March, now in the autumn, when the book appeared, wrote in a kind of ecstasy: "If my life were at stake, I would not suppress *Werther!*"

He gained greatly in self-confidence that year. When an anonymous farce appeared, which both copied and made fun of him, Goethe published in a newspaper a manifesto "for those who love me and trust my word"; and to this public declaration he added the lordly remark: "For the rest, I was very glad to have an opportunity of quietly obtaining a better knowledge of various people, by their behaviour towards myself. Goethe."

He even caused a play to be offered to a Berlin bookseller, without revealing more than the title. Renowned older poets, whom he had not before known, he now met as on equal terms. He asked a friend to say to Lessing that he had always felt sure of him, and was seldom deceived in people.

And as to the most illustrious of all: "Why should I not write to Klopstock? . . . Why not address myself to the live man, when I would make a pilgrimage to his grave?" When the master did visit the young author, they talked of little but some new type of skate which Klopstock recommended. Even to Saltzmann he now first used the phrase which as an old man he was often to repeat: "Maintain your kind interest in me and mine." These words sound very arrogant from the lips of twenty-five, suddenly become unapproachable!

Praise of his universality reached him in a very exaggerated form, as a consequence of this renown. It was not to be really his until a lifetime of hard work had gone by. Women were foremost in this; and his native town was so full of gossip about him that Merck declared he could have made a book out of the secrets entrusted to him on the subject of Goethe. He received many begging-letters, adventurers borrowed money from him, and his funds began to run low.

A fateful year for Goethe had begun—his twenty-sixth.

How far he could be divined from his outward appearance we learn from the greatest physiognomist of the period. Lavater writes in this fervent strain:

> Intelligence is here, with sensibility to kindle it; and sensibility, with intelligence to illumine it. Observe . . . the form of the energetic brow; observe the eye, so swiftly penetrating, searching, enamoured, narrowing so gradually, not very deepset, clear, quick, mobile . . . and the nose, in itself enough to proclaim the poet, with that lyrical transition to the full-lipped . . . mouth. With its virile chin, its well-opened, vigorous ear—who could question the genius in this head?

There was one peculiarity in that head, which henceforth becomes noticeable in the full-face portraits and busts of Goethe.

The right side of the forehead was a little contracted, so that the right eye was deeper-set than the left, and smaller too. How self-conscious he was about this disparity, which he called a "pinch from old Nick," we know from some remarks of his later years. But in his youth, at any rate, the physical irregularity may be regarded in a less material light.

For never was Goethe's dæmonic nature, perpetually rent by its own contradictions, more vehemently displayed than in this twenty-sixth year, when his genius assumed control in the battle of life.

His existence was one long self-contradiction. He was sensual and transcendental, amoral and Spinozaistic, all egotism and all self-surrender, now delighting in companionship, now imperious in his demand for solitude; to-day religiously, to-morrow cynically, inclined; misanthropic, philanthropic, arrogant and kindly, patient and impatient, sentimental and pornographic, absorbed in form or intent on act, untamed and pedantic, a far-reaching thinker but an instinctive doer, coldly objective yet essentially and passionately erratic, entirely masculine yet very feminine—a dual being, if ever there was one; and so unlimited in scope that circumstance would have its way with him whose avid thirst for all experience, intent though it was on form and measure, found satisfaction in one faith alone, and that the faith he now shaped into verse:

> Nenn's Glück! Herz! Liebe! Gott!
> Ich habe keinen Namen
> Dafür. Gefühl ist alles.[1]

The few who knew anything of him confirm this view, in their letters of the period: "You would idolise Doctor Goethe. He is the most terrible and the most lovable of men" (Lavater). "He is pure energy, sensibility, imagination. But he acts, on the other hand, without knowing why or wherefore, as though borne on a current" (Lavater). "How often did I see him, in the course of one quarter-of-an-hour, all tenderness and all fury!" (Stolberg). "Goethe is too much for me. You are right—he is

[1] "Call it Joy! Heart! Love! God!
For me there is no naming
Of this. We can but feel it."

GOETHE AT THE AGE OF TWENTY-FIVE

womanish; but if he doesn't go to pieces in the next few years, we shall probably become better friends" (Schlosser).

"'Give all for love,' says Goethe; and everyone who sees him knows how by his charm he conceals the energy of his mind, and the gravity of his solitary hours" (Zimmermann). "Goethe is a man possessed, who is hardly ever able to act voluntarily. . . . It is utterly absurd to require him to think and act as others do. . . . I don't mean to suggest by this that there is no possibility of a change to better, lovelier things; but he can only expand like a flower, ripen like a seed" (Jacobi).

Such was the radiance of the rising star. Let us analyse that iridescence.

At this time, when Goethe conceived his greatest works and made his most vital decisions, his duality was never more arresting. His whole being, ardently seizing, critically examining, the content of the passing moment, and productive in every breath it drew, was at the mercy of its manifold antitheses; but though tempestuous passions stirred the surface, a harmonising energy was at work in the "dark backward and abysm" of that unfathomable soul. It was to take him forty years to sail into God's sunlight, on a tranquil surface with a halcyon breeze around his head. For the present we can but hear the ever-conflicting voices.

Here is the amoral Goethe: "And so the word of men is to me the word of God, whether parsons or whores . . . have promulgated it. I embrace my brother-man with my inmost soul. Moses! Prophet! Evangelist! Apostle, whether Spinoza or Machiavelli! But I take leave to say to every one of them: 'Dear friend, we're all alike!'"

In *Clavigo* he puts into Carlos' mouth the doctrine of genius exempt from the moral law; but none the less there is evident, in the original draft of *Faust* (which he wrote in the last two Frankfurt years), some conflict of conscience. May a genius forsake a maiden in her need?

His unconquerable faith in his genius kept him ever intent, as though for comparison, on personality. The teaching of Spinoza could only have attracted him by the law of contraries—as a nobly-conceived system, nothing more.

Thus concentrated on personality, he was all for deeds.

Lavater's impeachment of a provincial governor set him aflame; he insisted on being told all about it, without any false modesty, "so that I may fully appreciate your action. . . . A deed like that is worth a hundred books; and if such days could come again, I would compose my quarrel with the world."

He was alert for movement, activity: "I am not weary; so long as I live on earth, I intend to conquer at least my own little foot of territory afresh every day." Much of this found an outlet in satires, critical writings, duels of the mind; but at other times he would scorn that kind of thing as second-rate, and exclaim: "Why do we judge by works? . . . Are they our real fruits—these soilings of paper, whether written or printed?"

It was a propensity for kindly deeds which drew this amoralist to children, friends, and strangers. He would send books to Lotte's brothers, so that they should not buy newspapers; a falling-out with her little sister worried him for a long time; to another child he sent a new Frankfurt penny, for a musician he tried to obtain publication and performance, defrayed the expense of Klinger's entire course of study, twice pressed his assistance on him, and finally supported him for an indefinite period.

But this was not pure philanthropy. Scorn and mockery were more native to him, and hence his desire for friendship and intimacy was always at war with his nervous craving for solitude. This explains his behaviour to acquaintances, which was at once charming and repellent; and the constant marked alternations between gaiety and dejection.

He instituted poetic gatherings of a few fervents in his attic-room—they would read aloud, open their hearts to one another, cultivate enthusiasms. On a trip up the Rhine, immediately after *Werther*, he was positively boisterous, calling himself "the worldling"; and when guests were invited, he could not sit still, but would go dancing round the table.

But there was no radiance in this gaiety—it was dæmonic. "When one's in company," he confessed at this time, "one takes the key out of one's heart and puts it in one's pocket. Those who leave it in its place are simpletons. . . . I should have lots to say if you didn't let everyone see my letters. . . . I can't bear a man, to whom I wouldn't tell the tenth part of them by word of mouth, to see my letters." When the Freemasons approached him, he drew back "from love of independence"; and after a stay in Zurich, Goethe was reproached with having made no friends, because he had been too haughty and self-opinionated.

To the crowd he was alien. Humanity in the lump he pronounced intolerable; and in the tumult of the Fair he recalled Ariosto's phrase about the mob: "They should have been killed at birth."

Nevertheless his dual spirit could comprehend the two spheres.

> The magnet attracts filings from the dust and chaff; and at bottom it is much the same with the aristocrat. He uses his active beneficence as a magnet, ferreting out from the mob the few kindred souls he can attract. But can you blame the mob if it revolts against the ferreting and the beneficences which disturb and unsettle such elements as are not susceptible to the special influence?

That defines, twenty years beforehand, Goethe's attitude towards the Revolution. He liked the idea of the people and studied it in individuals, but by the mob as a phenomenon he was alternately repelled and bored.

And now, at twenty-five, Goethe was becoming aware of an encircling desert-region where his soul could find no pasture; and in this period of ardently creative adolescence he was driven to a woman-friend:

> For hours I have been lying self-absorbed, turning over and over in my mind the question whether I possess the fortitude which will enable me to bear what inexorable destiny may design for me and mine—whether I shall ever find within me the rock on which to build a stronghold, whither in the ultimate resort I can betake myself with all I cling to.

Such were the nocturnal agitations of his being, though its activities were manifold, and friends and foes and fame came in full measure. In that midnight hour, writing to his woman-friend, the youth who was renowned, courted, wealthy, with good prospects, chose the symbol of the Wandering Jew to represent himself.

He wanted everything and all things, wanted to feel and exist to the uttermost; yet none the less, though time was hurrying on, he was possessed by that inviolable consciousness of a vocation which would only very slowly ripen to fulfilment. "The amazing fellow," he wrote of a colleague, "actually thinks that he need only trust to luck—the Lord God will do the rest."

And then again his spirit would soar high, and he would see life as a post-chaise speeding up hill and down dale, and from that image frame his vision of Circumstance. Time sat upon the driver's box, but though he might invoke his "Postilion Chronos," the four horses were not now the Pindaric simile for passions held in check—it was the conflict known to Faust which alone absorbed him.

The pendulum of his senses oscillated in like manner between *Werther* and *Hanswursts Hochzeit*—say, between Petrarch and Aretino! Thus, in the first *Faust*, Gretchen's song "*Meine Ruh ist hin*" is made more burning by the use of a single word, for there it runs: "*Mein Schoss! Gott! drängt sich nach ihm hin!*"[1] And in her cell she says, in that version: "*Wie sonst ein ganzer Himmel mit deiner Umarmung gewaltig über mich eindrang! Wie du küsstest, als wolltest du mich in wollüstigem Tod ersticken!*"[2]

This enigmatic duality was usually confined to his private moods of excitement; it was but very seldom perceptible to outward view. Once when he was sitting with some friends in Mainz, he said very gloomily, after a gossip about some literary enmities: "And now I'm good friends with everyone . . . and I don't quite like it. It is a condition of my nature that just as I must have something which I can regard as a lifelong ideal of the admirable, so I must have something as an ideal object of indignation. I know they're all the most worthy folk; but precisely *because* they are—I want to know what sort of harm I can do them."

Even from the look of his letters, their punctuation and handwriting, we can divine the pursuing Furies; and when he sent his manuscripts to the press, the printers had to interpret mere

[1] "O God! My womb that throbs for him!"

[2] "How all heaven would rush upon me when I lay in your embrace! How you would kiss, as though you fain would stifle me in that voluptuous death!"

hieroglyphics and even correct the spelling. And his papers were in utter confusion; a visitor tells us that he would fetch them from every corner of the room. But on the other hand, he could be so meticulous that in sending a sketch to his woman-friend he begged her "by all that is holy to take the greatest possible care of it, for slovenly as I am in other respects, the slightest crease in a thing like this infuriates me."

Trivial as they are, such symptoms are suggestive of the vast convulsions in that antithetical nature. The two souls, of which Faust was to speak in later days, symbolise but in part the inner conflict. Goethe never put all his duality into any single figure; not one of Goethe's characters stands for Goethe. He always split up his own personality, dividing it between two antagonists, or even two women; and that is perhaps the cardinal reason why a poet whose sensibility was chiefly of the lyrical and epical order should have turned to the dramatic form, and never entirely abandoned it. That was also the reason why in this youthful period, when the conflict was at its keenest, he found the dramatic dialogue so congenial, and would make a miniature play out of the most trifling of parodies. So, too, he almost entirely abstained from writing poems. In this most agitated of all phases two lyric dramas, besides *Clavigo* and *Stella*, were completed, and long passages of the *Urfaust* "fired off."

But the completion of these short works, while *Faust* (like *Prometheus*, *Mahomet*, and *Cæsar*) remained a fragment, is not to be regarded either as caprice or self-discipline.

Claudine von Villa Bella was composed, with sure dramatic instinct, by the same hand which, after writing four lines, would reject a scene for *Faust*. And the very man who would finish his operettas down to the indications for the orchestra, and was perpetually ordering additional fair copies, kept the first draft of *Faust* a dead secret; and when he wanted to go on with it twenty-five years later, could find nothing but a yellowed, dog-eared, long-relegated bundle of sheets, which had quite the effect of one of Faust's old books.

Clavigo and Carlos are the first unmistakable examples of his dual portraiture. Indeed, Carlos the man of the world came easier to the youthful Goethe's hand than did Clavigo the poet. It is as though he had some prescience that the spiritual side of him, in its perpetual self-contradiction, was shortly to take on a worldly disguise.

But it was in *Faust* that Goethe's duality was first fully revealed. True, in the original draft he was only approaching the dæmonic dialectic which was so peculiarly his own, and in that sense the fragment has more the effect of a monologue than has the later work. But otherwise the *Urfaust*, because the fable is less overlaid with intellectualities (and also because it is shorter) seems more dramatic than the later First Part. He was then well-nigh solely absorbed in the tragedy of Gretchen.

Is this girl Friederike? Since Goethe in all his works, and particularly those of his youth, was skilled in and enamoured of the portrayal of familiar figures, our question naturally is—why are none of Friederike's personal attributes presented here? A love-affair which to Goethe was only an idyll, not a passion, is here so universalised that (as in *Werther*) the issue is almost the reverse of the actual truth. But in *Faust*, is not everything universalised—were not Merck and Herder mere suggestions for Mephisto? In *Faust* we are given, not a Faust-like Goethe withstanding the caustic Merck, not a constructive, striving spirit who with untroubled upward gaze can meet the feline fascination in those tigerish eyes; but a man who felt the deep affinity which drew him to such natures, and in mirroring them shed light upon that consciousness.

Both figures, Faust and Mephisto, are dæmonic through and through; but it is only by adding them together that they can stand for an exhaustive symbol of the dæmonical in Goethe's self. Their dialogues are the stormy dialogues in his own heart. Neither of the two is pure goodness or pure malignity. Mephisto, in the original draft, is not by any means the Devil; he is merely the cleverer, the more far-sighted, of the two—a stronger Carlos.

Which is Goethe's part in these dialogues—which is his portrait? On both sides.

To another problem of his duality Goethe gave expression in the opening monologue of *Faust*. His fluctuation between the contemplative and the active life informs the long introductory passage in the original draft. First he exclaims: "*Bin ich ein Gott? Mir wird so licht!*" Then: "*Du, Geist der Erde, bist mir näher!*" Repulsed, he loses heart and cries: "*Ich, Ebenbild der Gottheit! Und nicht einmal du!*"[1] At this moment Wagner enters; the question is left unsolved. It was to torment him all his days, and never be more than half-answered.

And yet it was this self-confession of a nature rent in twain which lit the path to one way of escape. When in the character of Faust, the disillusioned Goethe, surveying symbols of the macrocosm, exclaims: "*Welch Schauspiel! Aber ach! ein Schauspiel nur!*" ("Vast drama! But alas, no more—no more!"), it is but a metaphor, after all; for he goes on to ask:

> Wo fass' ich dich, unendliche Natur?
> Euch Bruste wo? Ihr Quellen alles Lebens![2]

Nature—the focussing-point of his faith, the solitary polar-star, unerring guide for this chaotically storm-tossed youth! If there had been left some glimmers of his early faith to light some segments of the universe, those church-candles were now put out. Two of his friends were clergymen; but one said to him: "You are no Christian"; and to the other, to Herder, he wrote himself in these unseemly words: "If only the whole teaching of Christ were not such bilge that I, as a human being, a poor limited creature of desires and needs, am infuriated by it!"

In this darkness and perplexity Goethe found nothing he could cling to, except Nature—but now not so much as an idyllic luminary as "the incoherent stammering expression of our submission to an overpowering sense of the Infinite."

The same idea, rhapsodically conceived in the form of a hymn, all yearning and yet harmonious in the loftiest sense of the word, it was his to grasp for a brief while just then:

> Wie in Morgenglanze
> Du rings mich anglühst,
> Frühling, Geliebter!
> Mit tausendfacher Liebeswonne

[1] "Am I a God? I see so clear!"
"Earth-Spirit, thou art nearer to me!"
"I, image of the Godhead! And not even thou!"

[2] "Thou Infinite, O Nature, where art thou?
Ye mother-breasts, ye sources, where abide ye?"

Sich an mein Herz drängt
Deiner ewigen Wärme
Heilig Gefühl,
Unendliche Schöne! . . .
Das ich dich fassen möcht
In diesen Arm!' [1]

In this twenty-sixth year, when the passionate lightnings flashed fiercest, Goethe was no more than the servant, not yet the master of his life. That agitated lonely soul was always desirous of comprehension, friendship, love. His first impulse was towards writers, and he found and kept a few of these as friends. Never again did Goethe mix so freely in literary society as at this time; and just as the world and he were periodically attracted to and repelled by one another, so it was with the literary groups.

As regards those who were influenced by him and copied him, it is easy to understand Goethe's isolation, even when there was an instinctive sense of fellowship. Klinger venerated and envied him; Lenz hated and loved him. Klinger's perceptiveness is sufficiently established by one monumental phrase which he, at twenty-one, wrote of the Goethe of twenty-four, then scarce to be divined for what he was: "A marvellous fellow . . . the things he has in him! Posterity will learn with amazement that there ever could be such a man!"

With Jacobi Goethe did not get on too well; and the lightnings played dangerously between him and Herder. The ardour of his first impression was indelible in Goethe's feeling; but the further he advanced—he who had the world before him!—the more captious was the attitude of Herder, aware that his best days were behind him. Their original relation had been so high-flown—was it now to take a more everyday aspect? Two years of estrange-

[1] "Like the morning-radiance
Around me thy sheen,
Spring, my belovéd!
A thousand thrills of loving rapture,
Heartfelt, thou bringest—
Children they of thine ardour,
Deathless, divine,
Thou infinite fairness! . . .
Oh, in these longing arms
To clasp thee once!"

ment went by, without meetings or letters; then Herder—married, well-placed, an important personage—got over his soreness and was the first to re-open correspondence. Five years had passed since the meetings in the sickroom at Strasburg. Quickly and warmly, yet with a curious aloofness in his cordiality, almost like that of a stranger, Goethe answered: "I had just been recalling vividly the ups-and-downs of our intercourse—and behold, you walk in and stretch out your hand! Here's mine; and let us begin a new life together."

Yet aloof he was; and when he offered his hand it was really no more than a gesture. But even Herder understood Goethe better with his heart than with his head—sufficiently remarkable in a man who all his life had fought against his heart!

Goethe's nerves were tried to the uttermost by one of his new friends, for truly we can only wonder at his patience during the prolonged intercourse of this year with Lavater. This is the first example—of which there were few, and those much later—of Goethe's being attracted to another man by the mere fact of his proficiency. Since as a poet he could not be taught anything, it could only be some science thoroughly understood which cast the spell. But to attach him really closely, mere knowledge did not suffice; there had to be something purely personal, a something by which one temperament could affect another, before he succumbed. And certainly physiognomy, which Lavater had just brought to Germany like a new discovery, for the moment almost as his patented invention—that something between an art and a science demanded as much intuition as observation, as much of the poet's fervent apprehension of psychic elements as of the scientist's objective scrutiny of material ones. The two men could meet on this quasi-scientific ground, Goethe learning and in learning producing, under his teacher's forcible influence.

There are pages in Lavater's great work on physiognomy where one can study both authors, side by side, in their tempers and handwritings. In the text, Goethe's hurried, slanting, violent characters reveal his swift prehensile mind; Lavater's dainty upright script encircles this fiery core with its sage comments.

"You're all for the eye!" So Herder had said to Goethe in Strasburg, and said it with all the captious arrogance of an intellectual whose own eyes were in danger. But now, with physiognomy the matter in hand, who should reign with more of a right divine than he who was all for the eye? Knowledge of human nature and observation here went hand-in-hand to make Goethe the first of physiognomists; and while he subdued his intuitive powers of perception to the scientific method, he was entering quite unconsciously upon another line of activity as the man with eyes to see—and that line he pursued to the end of his life.

For while Lavater raved or depreciated, Goethe always looked for, and found, the law. Instead of seeking, in the traits of an historical head, these things which would confirm his prepossession, Goethe was able to say at once to whom an unnamed head could alone belong. This was intuition; and it is as though one heard him improvising at ease over a glass of wine, when we read this of a bust conjectured to be Homer's:

This man is not an observer, or a hearer, or a questioner, or a combatant, or a doer. In this head the focus of all the senses is the upper portion of the flattened, slightly hollowed forehead—which is the seat of memory. There everything is retained as a *picture;* and the muscles are strained upward, as though their function were to carry those vivid images down to the eloquent cheek—that of expressive genius. These brows were never knit in speculation over the relation of things; there was no attempt to comprehend them apart from their tangible forms. All experience, in that head, is gladly reconciled—at peace with itself in all its manifestations. This is Homer!

This warmly personal sense of personality, this ardent, piercing insight into human nature, tender and ironic, compassionate and mocking—but never malignant—and as a consequence quite without sentimentality, this highly temperamental perceptiveness led him (and that in his most neurotic period) to study the soul in its physical aspect. That was why he was so particularly interested in the skulls of animals, whose habits and natures are so infinitely various. Moreover, they afforded him indications, *points d'appui*, even justifications, for the impressionism of his method.

Because Lavater was for a while his instructor in these matters, he forgave him many things throughout many years.

Lavater's quietism soon got on his nerves. At the very first

Goethe had written in four plain words: "I am no Christian." On this, Lavater declared him to be an atheist who would at once, and inevitably, seek to make *him* one too.

Lavater's letters were of many pages, on large paper, interspersed with scraps of verse, frequent dashes (a habit which infected Goethe for a short time), headings, divisions, exclamation-marks—all in miniature script, all feeble, uncritical. Lavater's ambition was to force the confidence of Goethe and all other men, not really out of tactlessness, but solely from his thirst for anything psychical which might give depth and significance to physical things.

Goethe answered this bombardment at ever longer intervals, much more briefly, much more reticently, but always fraternally—often warning Lavater, on the subject of their collaboration, that he must not print or engrave everything, must not let everything be seen.

It was with peculiar sensations that friends and students of human nature looked about them in Goethe's house at Frankfurt, while strangers were full of excited curiosity. This was the frame which to-day would reveal him to, the next day would conceal him from, the world at large; and in that frame the young illustrious son was king, sometimes a delightful, sometimes a tyrannical one; inviting his friends to his father's table, and sometimes to stay—so that "Frau Aja"—as the two Counts Stolberg nicknamed his mother—had frequently to fetch from the cellar a bottle of her oldest and best.

Now at last the vital instincts of this unchangeably young-hearted woman were satisfied by her son. His renown entitled her to idolise him without reserve, and forget all the discontents of her joyless marriage. The father's love, based as it was on ambition, was certainly more actively serviceable than hers; but the son, though his intercourse with the blithe mother was more cordial than that with the cross-grained father, found in neither a confidant for the spiritual agitations of this storm-tossed period. Neither in his letters to her (which in his absence would surely have testified to it), nor in his journal-letters to friends, nor in the accounts given by visitors to the house, do we find any hint of that complete mutual comprehension which creates unreserved confidence.

The house was his haven of refuge. It was a pity that his sister should just then have left it. For her it was well—better, indeed; since her inharmonious temperament had, to her, made it insufferable. Would she draw clearer breath in the little town in Baden whither a good appointment had called her difficult-natured husband?

Once more we are led to compare her ravaged countenance with Goethe's strenuous one. Cornelia's rounded forehead, to which the then fashionable mode of hairdressing was horribly unbecoming, is far from attractive. The erotic instincts of this pathologically sexless girl were still further repressed by the intellectual intercourse with her brother; and he himself in his old age depicted their relation in these remarkable words: "Frank, pleasant, though often rather bold."

A wife of twenty-three, she now went forth with Schlosser, a man of thirty-four, the son of an Imperial Councillor of Frankfurt. Goethe called him his own antipode. His was a gloomy, sensual nature, oppressive to the girl. The destiny of this second fusion of Goethe-blood both illumines and obscures—and that as much retrospectively as prospectively—the physical conditions in which the battle of Goethe's life was fought.

And now another passion was to be the first real revelation of its intensity. For none of Goethe's love-affairs was without its effect upon his inward development; were it otherwise, they might —for him and for our presentment of him—have afforded a mere background to our encounter with a mighty intellect, a re-born nation, a new philosophy. It is because Eros represents the most powerful element and the motive-force for his highest flights in character and work—it is because Eros could so possess him and therefore so inspire him—that we can interpret Goethe best through these experiences.

A year so spiritually disturbed was bound to have its external conflicts also. Since, at eighteen, he had lost his Käthchen at Leipzig, Goethe had but seldom been actually and obviously in love—perhaps only during the few weeks of his affair with the youthful Mme. Brentano. Now, seven years after the Leipzig parting, he was ripe and ready for a different and more brilliant recipient of his surging temperament. The world was open to him now; the glamour of his young renown enhanced the dreams of a tirelessly energetic spirit, and loveliness—such loveliness as he had never before had to do with, for none of Goethe's women had been lovely—to-day smiled on him, all allurement, captivating and capturable, and well worth keeping when once caught. From its golden frame it called imperiously until, obeying it, he sought to climb those heights of freedom and escape from his dæmonic haunts.

Something infinitely blithe he tried to grasp at in his love for Lili. "Magic": such was the attribute he ascribed to the slim fair girl. The word incessantly recurs in all the verses and letters which for the next nine months were inspired by her; and when he said she was as lovely as an angel, and declared, after half-a-century had gone by, that in reality she was the only woman he had ever loved, each statement needs the other for full confirmation.

This year saw him for the first, and last, time a young society-man—of Frankfurt society—in the full sense of the word. On the ice, at the Carnival, at balls, he mixed with the young patricians and Englishmen of the town as an equal among equals—though his companions no more reckoned him as a member of the Upper Ten than he did them as the friends of his heart. For it was more the brilliant oddity of whom the papers were writing than the son of the retired Imperial Councillor who was invited, and it was more curiosity than social ambition which attracted *him*. Thus he could be forgiven even the unceremonious way in which he invaded the fashionably-furnished drawing-room of a Frankfurt banker. There was an evening-party, and a friend had persuaded him to "come along."

It was quite late in the evening. . . . There was a big party; in the middle of the room stood a piano, at which the only daughter of the house was just sitting down to play. She played with great facility and charm. I was standing at the end of the piano, so that I had a good view of her figure and attitudes; there was something childlike about her, and her movements in playing were graceful and easy. When the Sonata was finished she came towards where I stood. She said a few words of welcome but we could not talk, for a quartette was just beginning. . . . I noticed that she looked at me closely, and that I was, quite literally, "on show."

This was Lili Schönemann; and that the scene was not invented for *Dichtung und Wahrheit,* we can tell by the preliminary drafts. It was a *coup de foudre.* In those first minutes he stared at her until, with a naïve sensuality which was almost Olympian, his eyes were holding hers; and if it was her tall blonde blue-eyed brilliancy which first attracted him, there was that in her whole personality—the way her hair was dressed, her gowns, her fans, her riding-horse, her carriage, the Park and the balcony, the whole arsenal of fashionable allurements—which gripped his imagination; and from which, in the early days at any rate, he would not have wished to separate her.

This was the real thing! For what he always wanted from women—something lasting, binding, a community of interests, a haven, house and home, conjugal life—he thought to see awaiting him here. She was free, rich, a fellow-townswoman; his constant craving for a home where he might shelter from his inward unrest seemed to have found its earthly goal. Enchanted by the lovely seventeen-yeared girl, he wanted to make her his own; he was dazzled by the glitter and glow of her setting; the inward conflicts, he obscurely felt, might be resolved by paternity . . . in short, everything combined to carry away a young man (in the full swing, moreover, of the carnival-season) and draw him into these opulent civic circles, there to assert himself as Lili's lord and loyal servitor.

Let us look at his account-book:

Flowers, drawing-paper, horse, a little golden heart, eight boxes of tin soldiers, countermanding horse, 100 Dutch quill-pens, wig-maker; flowers, dagger-ornaments, boot-buckles, cleaning leather gloves, brass labels, an ounce of Italian chalks, tongues for silver buckles, half a pound of shot, half a pound of powder, hair-ribbon; flowers, a white Venetian mask, a pair of white gloves, thirty-two copper-plate illustrations of Klopstock, a pound of bonbons, tailor's bill, flowers . . .

Such were the requisites of Goethe's one society love-affair, which filled him with delight and drove him distracted, and which he never forgot. But for all that, he did not really ape the other young exquisites. This bourgeois luxury and elegance soon repelled him, for he felt from the first the difference between the real and the mock Upper Ten.

Here, among the rich citizens of his native town—whose stereotyped witticisms upon his own personality he was conscious of and despised—he often purposely played the part of "Nature's gentleman."

This spirit of opposition issued in an ambiguity of conduct which went hand-in-hand with his secret uncertainty. He, who was wont to embrace the whole environment of the loved woman and make it a part of his passion, took up the sanctioned attitude of the brilliant middle-class young man, and vehemently defied the world to which he belonged—yet all the while was fully conscious that it was precisely this setting which made Lili so entrancing! But it was not until he had spent six months of such torment that his distrust of these circles became a feeling which demanded action.

It was a strangely profound distrust, which overshadowed his love in the very moment of complete surrender to her charm. We can hear its undertones even in the three songs, light as her own footsteps, which were inspired by her. A new love, a new life—yes; but he was at heart an alien in that life, and cried in a sort of terror:

> Muss in ihrem Zauberkreise,
> Leben nun auf ihre Weise—
> Die Verändrung, ach wie gross!
> Liebe! Liebe! lass mich los![1]

Can this be the same heart which always hitherto had called to Love, had needed it and grasped at it, and never let it go until, so strangely, it was reft from him?

He gives us a kind of answer in the second song, when he poses as the poor obscure dreamer, who has never seen the world at all. But the passionate duets between Stella and Fernando are the

[1] "From her magic breaking never,
Living as she lives for ever—
Oh, too great the change for me!
Bid me go, Love! Set me free!"

first real revelation of how the poet, throwing aside his many masks, could long for Lili, ignoring all the glitter which had dazzled him but yesterday and was to-day despised; for in a quarter-of-an-hour of dream his genius showed him greater splendours than the Schönemann family and their Offenbach friends could ever find in all their parks and villas.

He knew himself very well. The dual part which he now felt compelled to play, he could regard with an eye as coldly clairvoyant as the heart within was hot. And he expressed his feeling, though not to the lovely girl, to whom he showed only so much of his enigmatic nature as she was capable of understanding. At this time he loved, in a totally different fashion—as of the moth for the star—a woman of the aristocracy whom he knew only through her letters to her brothers.

To this young Augusta, Countess Stolberg—wholly unknown to him, on whose sympathy he relied from her letters—Goethe wrote, in the perplexity of his heart, the most intimate letters of his youth; and the more remote she was from him on her North German estate, the more vehemently and unreservedly did he pour out upon her his dialogues with himself—as though, thus separated, he felt safe from all the disillusions of actuality. It is as if with trembling hands he were building himself a distant stronghold, whither he could flee in all dejections of the heart, and which indeed might come to be the only hope he possessed.

If you can imagine a Goethe, who in a frogged coat and otherwise quite consistently arrayed from head to foot for conquest, with the meaningless glitter of girandoles and chandeliers about him, surrounded by crowds of people and kept chained to the card-table by a pair of lovely eyes—a Goethe hunted from concert to ball by the alternating demands of social amusement, and making love to a dainty blonde with all the fervour of a fribble—you have the Goethe of this very Shrove-Tuesday, who lately blurted out to you some deep confused emotions, who has no right to address you, who often sets himself to forget you, because in your presence he feels himself to be quite insupportable.

But there is another Goethe, in a rough grey overcoat, with a brown silk muffler and strong boots, who can scent the spring in the soft February breezes, to whom the dear wide world he loves will soon be reopening, who tries—for ever living an internal life of effort and achievement—as best he can to express the guileless emotions of youth in little poems, the stronger savours of life in dramas many and various, and to portray his friends and his environment and his familiar surroundings on grey paper with a morsel of chalk . . . because he seems to climb a step higher on the ladder when at work, because he is not clutching prematurely at his ideal, but seeking to develop his emotions half in fiercest earnest, half in play, until they can be used as trusty instruments. . . . That is the Goethe . . . whose greatest happiness it is to live with the best men of his time.

God knows, I am a luckless young man—on the 28th we danced till Shrove-Tuesday was a thing of the past . . . and then—much gaiety and affection surrounding me—in the morning, getting home, I felt I must write to you. . . . What am I to say to you, since I can't tell you quite all about my present state of mind. . . . Go on being kind to me—I wish I could hold your hand, could rest under your gaze. Great God, what a thing is the heart of man! Good-night. I thought I should feel better when I had written. But it's no good; my brain is overwrought.

To-day was wonderful. I have sketched a little, and written a scene [of *Stella*]. Oh, if I didn't write plays in these days, I should perish. Soon I shall send you one.—This is another period of joy and woe for me, so that I don't know whether I'm on the solid earth or in heaven itself. . . . Thanks for the description of yourself and your life—how truly I had divined it beforehand! Hold me in your heart. . . . Now good-night, and no fever-dreams! But whenever you are ill, tell me—I want to share everything with you—oh, promise you won't forsake me in the time of trouble, which may come, when I shall flee from you and all whom I love! Pursue me then, I implore you—pursue me with your letters and save me from myself!

Such frantic cries had never issued from that breast since he had loved seven years ago and confided in Behrisch; nor was he ever again to find such tones. The chaotic emotions which had been so painfully repressed seemed now to be breaking forth once more, and far more perilously—for those seven years had been devoted to the building of a dam, and there had even been moments when he could think himself secure against them.

Goethe became engaged to Lili—and all the details of his future domesticity began to obsess his imagination in the very moment when his being was so riven with contradictions that it could but bend before the storm. The only result was sheer terror lest his wishes should reach fulfilment. The first external opposition came from his father, who made himself extremely disagreeable, saying that his house was quite fit for a daughter-in-law, but not for a "fine lady" like this, and he would have to build a new storey. And the respective parents, when brought together, could not get on at all, the tragic reason being that the Schönemanns were Reformed-Church people, and the Goethes Lutherans!

Between parents and friends, all disapproving in their different spheres, the future bridegroom led distracted days as a lawyer, a cavalier, a courted celebrity, obedient to Lili's wishes when she wanted him to be "sensible"—for in reality she was a cold beauty, and when she took it into her head to coquet with other men, this man with his prodigious capacity for feeling must indeed have known the stings of jealousy as he looked on at the wiles of her superficial upbringing.

He eased his heart in poetry, and if *Stella* loses something by having been written in the full tide of a passion—instead of, like *Werther*, after it was over—the piece is but the more ardently conceived for that, and is justly described as "a drama for lovers." Simultaneously, under Lili's spell, he finished and altered the lyric play called *Erwin und Elmire*. In this he again puts Lili on her defence; and although in both works he affects discretion, he makes us witnesses of a probably authentic scene:

> If he had not been so . . . reverential [says Stella], I should not have loved him so much, and he would not have been unhappy. . . . Oh, when he brought me the two peaches which he had watched over so carefully, borne by a tree he had propagated himself—its first-fruits! He brought them to me and my heart beat fast, for I knew all he thought of his gift, and I knew what it *was*. And yet I was frivolous enough—no, not frivolous, but malicious . . . I presented them to some other people who were there. I saw him wince and turn pale—I had trodden his heart underfoot.

A sample of Lili's provocations, coquetries—a summary of her heart-breaking devilry!

But between the scenes and the misunderstandings—what hours of blithe happiness, what abandonment in her arms!

> Lovely as an angel, and I had not seen her for four days! . . . Yesterday we were out riding. You should have seen the angel in her riding-dress on horseback! . . . I am full of wonderful things, new things; in three hours I hope to see Lili.

Round Lili hovered alternately, incessantly, hope and despair. On the same day that he cried to his other friend "Save me from myself!" he told Herder that he hoped everything would soon go well, and the twin threads of his destiny be united. "For the rest, many circumstances are rather paralysing, but they don't destroy my fine youthful spirits." Immediately before this: "Daily I strive and labour to be more courageous, and thank God I *have* been able to get fresh horses to go on with." Or to a stranger, in the middle of a first ceremonious letter: "I live, as I always do, in an immoderate turmoil of pleasure and pain."

When he was writing that sentence, in the beginning of May, the immoderate pain was at its worst; and it was Spring, and the two Counts Stolberg were announced—they wanted him to travel with them. What the lovers' intimate relations were at that period is not known to us, nor is it of great importance. She may have been all his, on rare occasions; for from the nature of their intercourse and Lili's temperament, it could only have been a brief, snatched episode. His later biographical notes, very extensive about Lili, contain these words: "Episode with Lili. Prelude. Seduction. Offenbach."

There seems then to have been a semi-rupture.

> I am in the same boat with you, dear brother [he writes to Herder]. I am sending my balls against the wall and playing at battledore and shuttlecock with the women. A short while ago I fancied I was approaching the haven of domestic felicity and a firm footing in the authentic world of pain and bliss, but I have been distressfully swept out again upon the weltering sea.

Goethe's fourth flight from a woman, again without a farewell, though this time not without "some indications." No sooner is he gone than he feels himself emancipated! He calls himself the bear out of the cage, the escaping cat; he no longer feels the slender golden chain with which he had desired to be bound, and "everything is better than I thought it would be. Perhaps it's because I love that I find everything sweet and kind."

In this mood, definitely as a man in love, he entered his sister's house for the first time.

At once the happy turn of mind was overshadowed. Had marriage proved a fatality to his sister? His keen eyes instantly divined what Schlosser wrote himself to an intimate: "She sickens at my love." He saw his brother-in-law at work in the forenoon as a high official, then at gardening and turnery after the midday meal, then off to the office again, then for an hour at Greek, and in the evenings with his wife. He heard Cornelia complain about her housekeeping, which she disliked, saw her ailing, never going out. And when, as of old, he made his confession to her and set forth the case for and against Lili, he felt the whole disaster of this marriage in the quiver of her voice as she implored him never to marry Lili—never to marry anyone! He half agreed; but she wanted a promise, and that he refused.

When a year later Cornelia gave birth to a child, she would not keep it with her, but gave it into the care of strangers because it was "noisy." Her mind became diseased; a cure was tried, with short-lived success, followed by collapse. Her brother wrote to her but seldom.

Goethe left her house at this time with body and soul oppressed and anxious. Her misery weighed upon his spirits; he went to Switzerland, but in less than a fortnight he complained that his journey had failed to do what he had hoped for him.

The farther he got from Lili, the more vehemently he longed for the familiar charm of her presence. He learnt and enjoyed a good deal, for all that; he interested himself in people and things; and on this summer-tour with his friends among the lakes and peaks of Northern Switzerland, we hear of "festivities that lasted till midnight," or else of "rude health and projects." Only his heart refused to beat in tune with the rest; at bottom, Goethe was always alone in the company of others.

To Lili herself he did not write; and it was only once, when gazing at a splendid view, that his verse remembered her:

Wenn ich, liebe Lili, dich nicht liebte,
Welche Wonne gäb mir dieser Blick!
Und doch, wenn ich, Lili, dich nicht liebte,
Wär, was wär mein Glück?[1]

At a convent he took a little coronet out of the casket and held it aloft—how well it would become Lili, if he could lead her to the mirror! Never again did such a fancy occur to Goethe, not with any princess. Lili alone among his women was to him the princess; at her side he thought he could have worn the other crown . . . but all this was condemned to exist in imagination only. At Frankfurt her smiles would have made him forget the invisible diadem. Ought he to have eloped with her? When he was over eighty he described this period of his life, and still declared emphatically that she would have gone with him to America. But Goethe was never an adventurer, any more than he was a Don Juan. And that he was to prove once more, in these very weeks.

For at last he had climbed St. Gothard with a friend; and there he sat in the Pass and sketched (with more feeling than skill) himself and his friend, the hills and the valley, at first so precipitously, and then so smilingly, opening to the South.

To the South—to Italy. He saw it at his feet—that Italy to which even his old father wanted him to go. And when the saintly host of the hospice came riding up the path, having only a few days back bent the knee amid the rose-flushed marbles of Milan Cathedral, and when his companion urged him to do likewise, and behold the flowering islands in the long blue lake—he, Goethe, sat irresolute upon the Gothard Pass, his look turned southward, powerless to decide, though he suffered his companion to make ready for the road. But he remained on his rocky promontory—alone. Germany, dear and familiar, was at his back; and yet his every thought must have drawn him whence the Prior had come.

But, pondering the project, he felt round his neck the chain

[1] "If I, dearest Lili, did not love you,
What a joy this landscape were for me!
Yet if I, O Lili, did not love you,
Whence my ecstasy?"

of Lili's gift—a golden heart; and quickly he stood up, took leave of the Prior, and turned northward without a word.

No sooner was he back in Frankfurt, no sooner had he rapturously held her in his arms again—she smiling at him as a somewhat crazy sort of *fiancé*—than he regretted his pitiful return, than perplexity, doubt, desire for solitude, invaded his two-sided being, and far more violently than before!

A fortnight after the return, to friend Merck:

> I am . . . stranded, and should like to box my own ears because I didn't go to the devil when I was well on the way there. I am ready for print again, on the first opportunity; only I should like to know if you would stand by me in the matter of funds. . . . Anyhow you might . . . make my father see that early next year he must let me go to Italy—that means I must be off again by the end of this year.

Like a hunted creature he strayed among the various bourgeois families, who kept him closely to Lili's side, for still (or again) they were supposed to be engaged. He felt like a bear chained at her feet by silken bonds; but the numerous relatives and friends were continually with them, and Lili's park, where he had a sense of being in a trap, exasperated him.

His whole being longed for Lili's blithe light nature; his whole being drove him away from her. Outside the town, where Lili's relatives, after the manner of rich bourgeois, had metamorphosed the country into another sort of town, Goethe's heart went through a long series of convulsions, amid the luxurious setting of the fashionable rococo. But now he had become a stranger in a world left behind. To Countess Stolberg he turned for confession—from his *fiancée's* writing-table, she unaware of the other woman's existence; and the outpourings were scrawled anyhow, left lying for days, then dashed at again, and finished in a sudden spasm.

> . . . That's the only way, when I write at such odd moments. . . . At a desk of inlaid cane, bright and frivolous—that's where these letters . . . are written, these tears are shed, these torments endured. What an anomaly! O that I could say all! Here in the room of the girl who is making me wretched, not by her fault, who has the soul of an angel, whose bright days I am troubling—*I!* . . .

Accursed destiny, that will never suffer me to be in equilibrium! Either clutching at some point and holding on to it like grim death, or drifting to the four winds of heaven. . . . On the table here are a handkerchief, a basket covered with a scarf; and over there the dear girl's riding-boots are hanging. (N.B.: we are to ride out to-day.) Here lies a gown, there hangs a watch, there are ever so many band-boxes for caps and hats. . . . I hear her voice—I may stay; she will want to dress in here. . . . I have described all this to you, so as to drive away my spectres by the things I can see. . . . The man who cannot rest.

With autumn came the climax. The Fair brought a troop of business-friends to her father's house, all of whom Lili welcomed as old acquaintances. Each had some claim on her; her eccentric *fiancé* was taken seriously by none of them. His way with them was half comic, half sentimental:

Here is some cheese, dear lady, and may it soon disappear to the pantry! The stuff is like myself: as long as it doesn't see the sun, and *I* don't see Lili, we are sturdy, gallant chaps. . . . Yesterday an evil spirit led me to Lili in an hour when she could so very well do without me that my heart felt as if it were being mangled, and I hastily made off.

A note to a woman-friend:

I've just come from Offenbach! I can't give you any sort of an idea of that household. My heart is still like a stocking turned inside out. Please, please, find something at the Fair for Lili. Some trifle, a trinket, the newest, smartest! You alone know how to find it—and give her my love with it. But this is between ourselves, a sacred secret—not a word to her Mamma. And let me know what it costs!

Meanwhile, his utter longing was for that high tranquillity which he imagined to dwell in the young Countess Stolberg's heart. To her went his dreams, he called his hours with her his blessed ones.

Unfortunately the distance she keeps me at only tightens the bond which enthralls me. . . . Can it be anything but excessive arrogance which insists that I must know the girl through and through, and so knowing love her? Perhaps I don't know her in the very least? And being different from me, may she not therefore be better than I?

However, the moment I saw the sun I hopped out of bed and ran up and down the room, and my heart pulsed so warmly and I felt so gay, and had a sort of assurance that I should be saved and make something of myself after all. . . . It is *here* and *now* that we need happiness. . . .

18th September: Is my heart at last to feel in its full intensity of joy and pain such happiness as is permitted to humanity, and not be for ever . . . driven from the heights of heaven to the depths of hell? . . . I saw Lili to-day after dinner. . . . Couldn't get in a word with her—and so said nothing to anyone! I wish I could get away from it all. . . . And yet I tremble to think of a time when she might be indifferent, and I hopeless. . . . Seven o'clock in the morning! Off somewhere! Gussy! I am drifting, and grip the helm only to prevent myself from being stranded. But I *am* stranded, I can't leave this girl—early this morning my heart was all for her. . . . I am a wretched, distracted, good-for-nothing fellow. I ponder this of nights. Just out of the theatre, and now I must dress for the ball. . . . If I feel like that again—feel that in the midst of all this nothingness so many husks are peeling from off my heart, so many convulsive tensions yielding in my silly little composition—if I feel that I can look more cheerfully at the world and make my human relations more assured, more steadfast, more broad-minded, and yet know that in my inmost soul I am for ever dedicated to that sacred thing called Love which gradually drives out, by its own pure influence, the alien elements within, so that at last the whole is pure as virgin gold . . . I will just let things go on as they are, deceiving myself maybe—and thank my God. Good-night.

In all that long life there is no other document which thus unreservedly sets forth the dialogue in Goethe's heart; and so this letter, regarded as the reflection of his inward conflict, is as valuable to posterity as are *Werther* and *Tasso*. For while *Stella*, a finished drama, suffers from its immediacy, this letter, of vague moods all compact, is more than a passage from the man's history—it shows how a dæmonic heart can quiver at its contact with the world. And yet that world, that girl who drove him crazy, were no more than the flint at which the element takes fire. Again, as seven years ago, his senses were ablaze from intimacy with one of those *demi-vierges* of the rococo-age; but now the syncopations of the battle were fiercer in their alternation between melody and droning bass, between ecstasies and energies, between pleasures and predestination.

In those very weeks of fooling about the pretty girl, he wrote "much" at *Faust*—translated the Song of Solomon in the very hours which were holding Eros at bay!

During the days referred to in that letter the crisis reached its climax; it may have been the night of that ball which decided Goethe's more obvious fate. Henceforward the tone is harder, there is a more manly note of defiance, emotion deepens, time is preparing changes—and like a herald from the great world which lies beyond the renunciation of Lili's kisses, a Prince steps forth for Goethe.

Dined, rather worried, dressed, the Prince of Meiningen introduced to me, went as far as the town-gate, then to the theatre. Said half-a-dozen words to Lili. And now here. [*21st:*] I took it into my head to be smart to-day, and am expecting a new coat from the tailor—which I have had embroidered in Lyons, grey with a blue border—with more impatience than the acquaintance of a man of intellect, who has this very hour announced himself as arriving. . . . My wig-maker spent an hour curling my hair and as soon as he was gone, I tore it all down and sent for another whom I sometimes employ. [*23rd:*] There has been mad work. I haven't had a moment for writing. Yesterday nothing but Dukes.

Dukes? And some interest in tailors and barbers, which no former note had hinted at, and which was only half ironical in this one. Mad work? And the way he relegates the Prince of Meiningen to a place between a worry and a walk, casually divided by a comma! Was something fresh looming up? And he was conscious of it—and suddenly came to a pause of fifteen days in the passionate confessions which had been wont to cover weeks. Then he continued, on the same sheet: "*October 8th:*—A long pause till now. I in a queer state between coldness and fervour. Soon there will be a still longer pause. I am expecting the Duke of Weimar." Exactly like a Prince. Exactly as in a novel.

It was nearly a year since the sudden apparition of a stranger in the half-light of Goethe's room, announcing himself as Knebel, from the Ducal Court at Weimar; and a few days later Knebel escorted Goethe to his sovereign's hotel. A boy of eighteen, Carl August had just come to the Ducal throne—and when at the door of the hotel-room the poet bowed deeply to the Prince and then raised his head again, two pairs of eyes encountered, but with their owners' traditional rôles exchanged—for the Prince's were curious, the poet's searching; the former asked questions, the latter perceived at a glance.

Captain von Knebel, of the Ducal suite, quickly made friends with Goethe; but Goethe's letters to him, for all their cordial intimacy, were full of uncertainties. The air of courts was unfamiliar to him, but he was not in the least the dreamy poet (a part which he brilliantly assumed in a few words of gratefully-surprised acknowledgment). His eye had instantly fastened on the flowers which might possibly bloom for him in those unknown gardens.

This was the first time Goethe had thought an indirect relation with the great world worth a spontaneous effort—it was indeed the first time he had ever resumed correspondence with a man, after a few weeks of silence, in such a strain as this: "I do most earnestly beg you for a word. . . . Am I kindly remembered among you all?" And for the third time: "Do you still care for me? Write me a lot about yourselves. And about the dear Duke. Give him my fond remembrance." There had been small sign of such sudden affection when the two had met in the Frankfurt hotel, or later in Mainz. Goethe was simply feeling: "In case . . ."

He had met Carl August again at the Margrave's and received a cordial invitation to Weimar. On this his first appearance at a Court, he had made a good impression on the Margrave of Baden; "Quite tolerable for a novice. Besides, one was in some sort challenged to be natural and yet striking." He soon fathomed the young Sovereign, choosing from his works for Carl August the lyric drama *Claudine*, which would just suit his taste—light, somewhat conventional, romantic, with bandits in it.

Goethe had mixed with the aristocracy, though never with princes; but a close and lifelong relation, or a marriage, was in those times denied to a scion of the middle-classes, a tailor's grandson.

Now, at the climax of his inward crisis, in spirit continually at flight from Lili, he met the Duke again, and the invitation to Weimar was pressingly repeated; now it was well-nigh a "call" with which he had to deal.

To Goethe's ear it sounded as a clarion note through the fog. Everything had urged him to yet another flight—the fifth of his youth. The engagement had grown more and more stormy, his love more and more tormented. That long letter to Augusta was nothing but a cry for deliverance; a flight to North or South was, if not exactly arranged, continually pondered as a means of salvation . . . when suddenly there fell a word from a Prince, a friendly steadfast word; the smiles of a young Princess summoned him to a Court which his imagination saw with widely-opened doors and lit by Wieland's genius. Moreover, it would lend him prestige with Lili's parents, while with his own it supplied a long-desired pretext for leaving Frankfurt. Was he really expected to grow grey in the narrow old town, to remain an advocate to the last, shut up in the old gabled house—and all this only for Lili's sake? All this, that her blonde, blue-eyed loveliness, her slimness and freshness, might be his to the end of time?

> A pleasant afternoon, which is unusual—and with great folk, which is more unusual still. I could make love to two Princesses, both in one room. . . . For a fortnight now I've been positively wrapt up in studying the great world.

But right on top of this comes the self-assertion:

> If I can get to Weimar I certainly will, but not . . . for love of anyone whatever, for I have a crow to pick with the whole world. . . . My heart is sick because of this. It's autumn weather there too, neither warm nor cold.

The Ducal pair departed, but a travelling-carriage and an escort were soon to come for Goethe. He packed up, said goodbye to everyone, dressed for the road—the carriage failed to arrive. His father made fun of the Court-equipage; trying (as he had done before) to influence his son against the scheme, he offered to send him to Italy, and pointed out how much more useful this would be to his art than a journey in a carriage—which had not come—to a small, unimportant capital.

Well, should he yield? It was all uncomfortable enough; his kind friends were grinning, and he never went out till evening, muffled in his cloak like a stranger in his native town. Lili, to whom again he could say nothing decisive, for they had fallen out with one another, he never visited at all. But one night, slinking past her home, he heard her singing one of his songs, he saw her slender silhouette upon the blind, and it haunted him all the way back. He sat down at his desk, wrote the opening scene of *Egmont,* read it aloud to his father, went out again, came home again—it was as though he were his own ghost.

Yet there was something in him of confidence, of manly acceptance of the moment, of faith that all would be well somehow. For as the carriage still failed to arrive and as to travel privately to Weimar would be unsuitable, and all the while his father was urging and Italy beckoning, Goethe found a middle course. He travelled southward, whence the carriage must come—to Heidelberg first, where at any rate one could talk about Lili with Lili's friends; and, halting for a while on the mountain-road, he looked things in the face. It was goodbye to Lili—goodbye for the second time. . . .

> . . . And you! How shall I name you, whom I bear in my heart as a flower of spring! Fair-Flower should be your name. . . . What may be the actual political, moral, epical, or dramatical purpose of all this? The only answer to that, gentlemen, is . . . that there is no purpose at all. One thing is certain—it's glorious weather, stars and a crescent-moon are shining. . . . And I throw my cap over the windmill!

This is a new note. It would seem that Dæmon had given place to Tyche! And, "in case," one leaves word at the post-office in Heidelberg that if a carriage *should* come . . . It comes. A polite Court-marshal, with many apologies, carries off the guest. The guest writes a half-obliterated scrawl in pencil to a friend:

> These nights . . . when one soars into Our Father's vast and glorious firmament—the infinite ocean of the sky. Oh, my brother! I am tossed upon a sea of emotions—there are words for them, but

they are past my telling. . . . That lamentable "dust to dust," Fritz! And the fretting of the worm—I swear to you by the heart in my breast that it's nothing but old wives' tales, but childish prattle, like *Werther* and all that stuff—I call to witness the soul I have within me!

And, sitting beside the polite Court-marshal, Goethe drives to Weimar.

CHAPTER V

ACTIVITY

"The joy of life darkens my spirit."

MY life is like a sledge, slipping along to the sound of tinkling bells. God only knows what I'm meant for, to be put through such schools as I have been. This one gives existence a new turn, and it will be all right. . . . I am quite like one of the family, and the Duke grows dearer to me, and our friendship closer, every day. . . . I hope you may soon hear that I know how to take the stage on the *Theatro mundi*, and cut a decent figure in all its tragi-comic farces.

On a loose rein, jocund, nimble, and assured, Goethe rode into the new arena; and whatever the above words, written during the first two months, may have signified, it was not so terrible as outsiders believed. The new Duke of Weimar had made a housemate of that outrageous young Goethe (so they said and wrote in Germany), and they threw plates out of the castle-windows, and had holes cut in the ice that they might bathe at New Year; they kept boys for their pleasures and shared the same mistress, and the poor young Duchess spent her days in tears. The bourgeois found a good pretext for his dual distrust of sovereigns and geniuses; and when Goethe's old friends came to see him, Germany was soon provided with the desired catchword of "Weimar and its new *mode à la bohêmien*."

In reality this kind of thing lasted barely three months. They tired themselves out with shooting and hunting, noisy riding-parties, drinking and burlesque theatricals, and a few peasant-girls may have been hugged by Prince and Poet. This eighteen-yeared ruler, volcanic of temperament and married to a shy girl, felt strongly attracted to the poet of twenty-six, two of whose books he had devoured, wherein tenderness was veiled in strength and strength in tenderness. The personality he actually had to deal with, it was beyond his age or his capacity to divine. Goethe's splendid German, his spirited aspect, his natural virility, together with a certain romance surrounding his name (which he did not seek for), so captivated the Duke that he set himself to defy the training and tradition from which he had so recently emerged. An instinct of rebellion drew him to the townsman's son, and he may have hoped in secret for a clash with the old-fashioned elements in the Court he had inherited.

That did not occur. Court, nobility, and society took off their hats to the parvenu, and saw to it that the door was shut before they confided the least disapproval of this genius's ways to one another. Was he not the young ruler's favourite? But how long would *that* last, even if reasons of State should not separate Prince and Poet? Anyhow, he was charming. Why did people say that the author of *Götz* was a "nature's gentleman," who looked indulgently on every kind of barbarianism? He was easy-going enough, but knew how to behave in this novel sphere. The majority of courtiers soon agreed that—*salva nobilitate*, of course—they could get on with him all right, for he would never presume to emulate them. And the ladies too were soon confiding to one another that this savage whose extravagances in the Thüringian Forests they were never weary of relating in the speech of boudoirs, was after all an acquisition to Weimar—always gallant, always witty, only seldom eccentric, and then not impossibly so.

At last they had an elegant *maître de plaisir*. There were balls and masquerades innumerable; everyone adopted the Wertherian mode of dress, and if anybody was too poor to afford it, the Duke provided the costume as though it were a uniform. There was a new theme for court-gossip. And who else could, like this young author, add an appendix out of his own head to the *Muses' Almanac*, as it circulated round the tea-tables, and make fun of absent and present in verses of every kind?

In a corner would sit the principal Minister in the country, and think:

May he always be able to amuse as he does now—for the Duke is fully occupied and doesn't any longer pester me with his youthful absurdities. This poet certainly doesn't trouble himself with affairs; if he ever *was* a lawyer, he seems to have forgotten all about it.

Wieland, for some years now the intellectual leader at Court and in the town—he who really was menaced, since his had hitherto been the prevailing influence with the youthful ruler—Wieland was enchanted. With his infinitely subtle critical perception, he had long divined from his distance that the man who was coming to Weimar was the greater poet. In the next number of his *Merkur* he printed an ode on Goethe.

For the present, then, Wieland with his powerful name had "legitimised" Goethe in Weimar—and his years counted too. At forty-two, he was the senior in this youthful circle. The Master of the Horse, von Stein, was forty, his wife thirty-three; Knebel was thirty-two, the Dowager Duchess thirty-six; the Duke and Duchess were both under twenty. Goethe stood between; he was eight years older than the Duke, and seven years younger than the wife of Stein.

But his spirit was the oldest by far, and his intellect had a wider grasp of experience than his twenty-six years seemed to warrant. Did no one at this juvenile Court perceive that the young favourite could discriminate shrewdly between people and things at Weimar—or at any rate that his vision and purpose far transcended anything that the place could offer? Was the feather-brained Goethe really so feather-brained, after all?

All of a sudden the whole thing, which to a bourgeois should have meant such glory, got on his nerves. He turned his back upon Duke and Court; and the man who had appeared in the town at the beginning of November, had by Christmas-time fled, with a few others, to the hills. He wrote to the Duke—a high-spirited, confused sort of letter, telling about his having seen the portrait of a former Duke of Weimar. "There is something stiff, shrinking about it—it represents a man who never really reflects, but rather obeys his first impressions . . . yet there's a distinct touch of the tyrant. . . ." And he added these lines:

> Gehab dich wohl bei den hundert Lichtern
> Die dich umglänzen,
> Und all die Gesichtern,

SILHOUETTE OF GOETHE AT THE AGE OF THIRTY

Die dich umschwänzen
Und umkredenzen.
Findst doch nur wahre Freud und Ruh
Bei Seelen grad und treu wie du.[1]

Thus subtly, so as not to startle the Duke (who would pore upon the livelier passages of the letter, with a longing to be there too)—thus subtly did the mentor from the mountains convey his prescient warning to the young ruler, between tales of pranks and laughter. And looking at the morning-star in the wintry sky (which he proposed to adopt as his blazon), he was tormented by one question: "It's confoundedly present both to my head and heart that I don't know whether I shall stay or go."

In the course of ten weeks he seems to have made up his mind, but only to one person did Goethe confide the reason for his wish to stay.

I am so mixed-up now with all the Court and political affairs [he wrote to his worldly old friend Merck], that I scarcely see how I can ever get away. My position is advantageous enough, and the Duchies of Weimar and Eisenach are certainly good places for discovering what sort of a part one is likely to bring off in the great world. So I'm in no hurry; and liberty and a sufficiency of means will be the cardinal conditions for any new orientation, though I am more capable now than I ever was before of judging how utterly despicable is all this temporal splendour.

The Duke spared no pains to keep him. He gave him a summer villa outside the town, wrote to his parents, summoned (against the advice of most of the Weimar clergymen) the free-thinking Herder to the chief place in his church, because Goethe wished it. Four months after Goethe's arrival, in the beginning of March, we find this: "I have now tried Court life. I shall do the same with the Government, and so on." Again his most

[1] "Thou farest well; and around thee gleaming
Are lights and faces,
And friendly seeming
And courtly graces.
Yet happiness, peace shalt find alone
With hearts as true as is thine own."

intimate words went to Mephisto. Were they the most intimate? What was Faust thinking of the scheme?

Faust knew well enough what he was giving up, nor was he in the least intoxicated by his position. He accepted it in the spirit of one who proposed to treat it in the grand manner. He knew all about the Duke, and intended to serve him affectionately, but was not blind to the dangers in so unequal a relation. Those, however, he was ready to risk. To train a petty ruler to some greatness, to shed upon a petty realm the illumination of a vaster sense of human destiny, to do by means of intellect what hitherto had been done only through exalted birth or from interested motives—these were contributory motives, half-hidden even from himself.

When Goethe made up his mind to stay, his conscious motives were to find a wider field for his energies, to open a far-flung sphere of influence, to fight the fight against men with that unwearied valour which had hitherto been his against invisible spectres of imagination. His dæmon, so inspired, urged him onward as it were in a consuming flame of energy. In the very whirl of the introductory excitements—

> when I have to screw myself up afresh every day, when there are a thousand big things and little things to be put through, and I am struggling, brain and heart, with love and hatred, rascality and despotic power—

in the very week of that salutary turmoil, Goethe, on one of his long walks, wrote down these words:

> Der du von dem Himmel bist,
> Alles Leid und Schmerzen stillest. . . .
> Ach, ich bin des Treibens müde.
> Was soll all die Qual und Lust?
> Süsser Friede,
> Komm, ach komm in meine Brust![1]

[1] "Thou that dost from Heaven fall,
Every pain and sorrow stilling. . . .
I am weary now of ferments.
What shall pangs and thrills betide?
Sweetly soothing,
Come, O Peace, with me to bide!"[1]

There was only one man in Weimar who could understand what was secretly brewing.

> But oh [wrote Wieland after three months to Lavater], how much more could and would that glorious intellect achieve, if he had not let himself go under in this chaos of ours! I was not thirty-eight when I suffered myself to be drawn to this Court, to this dangerous . . . and (looked at in the broad light of day) this eternally impossible experiment. I was led away by the spell of imagination, and the still more irresistible spell of the seductive idea that I might accomplish some great and enduring good. Goethe is only just twenty-six. How should he, conscious as he is of such powers, have withstood a still greater temptation? . . . His existence here reminds me of a game of faro. The Duke keeps the bank, and Goethe bets against him. Goethe stakes 1, 2, 3, 4 and often eight or more days upon a card, and frequently loses; but as he plays high, he only needs one good win . . . to recoup himself. . . .
>
> But having entered on this new career, he won't rest until he has reached the goal, and is as great a Minister as he was an author.

Wieland's powerful insight thus predicted Goethe's course and way of escape. No one else grasped the position with like mastery.

Weimar took a more commonplace view. When the Duke decided to appoint Goethe to his Privy Council—that is to say, to the centre of his Government—two parties immediately sprang up. The minority consisted of courtiers who sided with the favourite and Modernists who sided with Goethe; the majority of the Traditionalists and the Die-Hard nobility, who resented the advent of a middle-class amateur. At their head stood the Prime Minister, von Fritsch, who on account of his loyal services during the Regency could not be allowed to go; and so even Anna Amalia, the Dowager-Duchess (who in other ways encouraged her son's choice of Goethe) had to thank her stars that Carl August (desirous above all things to rule alone) was for the moment content with offering him the most subordinate place in his Council of Six—namely, that of a Privy-Councillor of Legation with a salary of 1,200 thalers.

For all that, Fritsch was on the war-path. Was he not ten years older than this poet, coming in as it were like a thief in the night? Had he not long been of the Council, and its chief for the last four years?

And he risked all. Suppose he *was* dismissed. . . . He pointed out that

> he could not any longer sit on a Council of which the said Dr. Goethe was henceforth to be a member, since he could not hope to be of any further service to His Highness, and should feel it dishonouring to himself; hence he resigned the position he had held and laid it at His Highness's feet . . . feeling himself superseded.

The Duke stood up stoutly for his friend.

> The world takes a prejudiced view of these matters, but I . . . am not ambitious of glory; my only desire is to justify myself before God and my own conscience. . . . Goethe is an upright man, with an unusually kind and sympathetic nature.

Fritsch exacted further proofs of confidence, but finally stayed where he was—and Goethe was his colleague in office for the next ten years.

The poet took the great step resolutely and wholeheartedly. Those outlets which he had hitherto kept open to himself—lingering, hesitating, for three months on the threshold—he now shut with a bang, excluding the young man from Frankfurt, the literary leader, the lover of a girl, the friend of many friends, and even the son and brother.

He wrote often to his father and mother, but few of his letters remain. They were always affectionate but remote, always full of commissions and business-matters, reticent, uncommunicative. The most heartfelt was that on his sister's death:

> I can feel nothing but the natural human grief, and I rely on Nature, who never suffers us long to endure extreme sorrow and sense of bereavement. . . . With my sister something so radical . . . has been uprooted that the upper branches . . . can but wither and die.

And he added for his mother that Bible-text of fire and ice: "I am too accustomed now to the idea: 'These are my mother and my brethren.'"

This was, and continued to be, Goethe's relation to his people, once he had left them. In the some thousand letters of these ten years, there are scarcely ten references to his mother. When the Dowager-Duchess wanted to ask her to Weimar, Goethe prevented it.

So recently as February he had sent two messages to Lili. By April it was: "Nothing more of Lili; that is over and done with." Soon afterwards his servant one evening brought him a letter. He was half-asleep. "I read in a sort of stupor—that Lili is married! Then I turned round and went to sleep. How I blessed Fate's dealings! Everything at the right moment, that's it!"

When he wanted to set up house, he sent a message through Johanna Fahlmer to his mother.

> My father owes me a trousseau and a dowry, and mother must manage this in her own way, but she mustn't be childish about it, when I am brother and everything else to a Prince. The Duke has conferred on me a hundred ducats. *Given* them to me, if you like.

Then, taking leave of his youth, he found a fine symbol for the farewell, and set it in verse before the die was cast for good and all. In his *Seefahrt* he depicts his friends sitting at the quay on his departure, rejoicing in the idea of the treasure-trove he will bring home when he comes back; but when contrary winds endanger the seafarer, they cry in instant anguish from the shore:

Ach, der Sturm! Verschlagen weg vom Glücke!
Soll der Gute so zu Grunde gehen?
Ach, er sollte, ach, er könnte?—Götter!
Doch er stehet männlich an dem Steuer:
Mit dem Schiffe spielen Wind und Wellen,
Wind und Wellen nicht mit seinem Herzen.
Herrschend blickt er auf die grimme Tiefe
Und vertrauet, scheiternd oder landend,
Seinen Göttern.[1]

[1] "See the storm! Oh, driven back from fortune!
Shall our dear one thus be baffled, ruined?
Shall he—oh, it may be . . . Gods above us!
Nay, he stands intrepid—see, he steers her!

Imperious? This was not a time for deeds, but merely for getting busy. It was not the world, not power, which were opening their massive portals to that giant intellect; for even if one is to regard the Duchies of Weimar and Eisenach as samples of the great world, it was surely indispensable to be master in them! But Goethe was entering the Council of State in a petty realm as the youngest and least of Ministers, without any special office beyond that of backing up the Duke against his strait-laced old officials. He was at first wholly, and afterwards in great measure, excluded from foreign affairs. He was not sufficiently master of the chessboard to be entrusted with those.

Only the things he could tangibly grasp fascinated that humane intelligence. He hoped to influence home-affairs, to improve and deepen the outlook. To achieve the greatest of tasks in the most restricted of spheres, to identify himself more fully with people and territory, was inevitably a stronger attraction for a temperament like his than to take his place at the green table with the so-called great ones of the earth. Goethe was neither desirous of, nor born to, domination; in this place he had still to learn his first lessons both in command and obedience. He took up office in that spirit, wishful to develop himself, to stimulate himself, not reckoning much with his potential usefulness to the Duke of Weimar and Eisenach. And so it was only fair that he should sacrifice something.

But in the first four years (which we shall here summarise) his genius took care that he should, generally speaking, fasten only on the matters which were useful to himself, though in everything he had to do with he proved valuable to others. The mines at Ilmenau had lain unworked for forty years; to open them up again was an old ambition of the dynasty. Goethe undertook to do this. He accepted, and thenceforth carried on, an Office of Works which he was the first to entrust with the reconstruction of the Ilmenau mines. Three years later he was appointed to select, maintain, and arm the recruits, and superintend the

---

Sport, ye winds and waters, with the vessel,
With his heart ye sport not, winds and waters.
On the angry deep he looks imperious;
In his gods, for shipwreck or for haven,
Trusting fearless. . . ."

making of roads throughout the region—so that at thirty he was a lesser Minister of War and of Public Works.

In the countless documents of that first decade there is scarcely a single instance of Goethe's view having needed supplementing. He owed this insight to the far-reaching dilettantism which had ruled him from his boyhood. Had not his ten years of research, which were now being dovetailed into ten years of activity, been full of unremitting efforts to attain to an unsystematic, as it were accidental, mastery of art and science?

The village of Apolda was in flames—the wooden villages of that time often went on fire. The *Herr Geheimrat* galloped to the place and

was roasted and boiled all day long. . . . And so were many of my plans, ideas, and the arrangement of my time. That's how life will always go on, and others will come after us and have the same experience. . . . My ideas about fire-brigades found fresh confirmation. Especially in places like this, where they take their chance in that as in everything else. The Duke will believe me at last. My eyes are smarting from the blaze and the smoke, and the soles of my feet are sore. It's all becoming as much a matter-of-course as the fire in one's grate. But I cling to my ideas, and wrestle with the unknown angel—aye, even to the dislocation of my loins. No one has any idea of what I'm doing, and the foes I have to contend with, before I can accomplish the least little thing. I implore ye not to mock me, watchful deities, as I strive and contend and labour. But after all ye may smile, so long as ye stand by me.

A wooden village is gutted. Usually, in such an event, Ministers demand a report, an investigation into who was to blame, relative statistics of the sufferers and the amount of compensation required, and then disbursement. Goethe, being a poet, helped to put out the fire; and while the flames were singeing him, he was considering how best to organise the fire-brigade, for he was a Minister too. But meanwhile from the smoke and blaze emerged the symbol. That very angel with whom at twenty he had reverentially wrestled in the shape of Herder's captious spirit, "though it should lame me for life," now appeared to him as, at thirty, he fought the stupid world around him, and he meant to wrestle with this one too—"aye, even to the dislocation of my loins." But over the whole scene there hovered the beneficent gods, and they might smile at the champion if it so pleased them.

For this contemplative intellect, desirous to work and learn, had now to turn combative—a state it had never known. In a few months he was exclaiming inwardly: "*Aequam memento!*" And though he increasingly felt that here he had done something fine and well worth doing, it was but a few more years ere he was penetrated by the sense of having distilled from it all it could give towards his development. Imperceptibly a course of study had been transformed into a duty; as imperceptibly, that duty came to stand for a symbol.

When three years afterwards he was made Minister of War, he thus recorded the event: "Impending fresh disgusts, as a member of the War Commission." And soon:

> Nothing but that business today. I steeped myself in it, and am now pregnant with ideas and certain I can stick it out. Pressure of business is very good for the soul; when it's got rid of, one's spirit has freer play and enjoys life. No one is more wretched than a prosperous man with nothing to do; the fairest of gifts is dust and ashes to him. Strenuous work, this setting earthly machines going and keeping them going! Text-books and histories are alike absurdities to the busy man. But there is no more arrogant prayer than that for wisdom, since the gods have once for all refused it to mortal men. They do hand out some common-sense.

A few weeks later:

> I stand well with the War Commission, because I keep imagination out of the business, never by any chance suggest anything, and only want to know what there is to know and get things going. And it's the same with road-making.

These notes are vividly representative of the atmosphere in which Goethe's soul could best breathe, when head and hand were making ready for new activities. One clearly perceives how science, sense of duty, and symbolism traced his path for him. During these years of endeavour to strike a balance between his conflicting faculties, he used each task as a stimulus for the next.

Fatigue evoked fresh energies, he made up his mind to be one-sided, and the consciousness of leaving a minor office a cleaner place than he had found it became to him a symbol of our earthly limitations. Hence it is less important for posterity to consider what he did than the typical way he did it; and since our portrait, as a whole, is designed as a picture of what a man can make of himself, we shall not here dwell upon the details of the administration he belonged to, but on the manner of his personal administration.

Recruiting-work soon leads to politics; and so his little world of uniforms and discipline served him as a bridge to the great art of statesmanship, which is so individual. Goethe never saw "Old Fritz." He had been respectfully silent when the King who dabbled in poetry made a senile attack on *Götz*, but the War-Minister and Poet did not spare that King when he sought to grab his recruits! When the militarist Duke showed a desire to grant his ideal, the soldier-king, recruiting-facilities in his Duchy, Goethe warned him in a long report of the political consequences in Vienna, which his knowledge of human nature enabled him to foresee.

These practical concerns inspired him with the idea of a Confederation of the Princes, which might be useful to Central Germany, situated as she was between two hostile Great Powers. It was not an abstract historical view which led him to this idea of an alliance, but the direct pressure of events. Otherwise the whole trend of his spiritual development, as we shall here follow it, kept him aloof from diplomatic experiments.

Nevertheless, Goethe's letters to Fritsch were even then masterpieces of diplomacy. He would give the home-keeping President most courtly snubs, in the course of his own shooting-trips—cool and friendly, kindly and respectful, as from a subordinate who was none the less the better man, a Divisional Commander but the Duke's friend, a Councillor of Legation—but Goethe.

He practised this art with ever-increasing subtlety. Even before he became an official personage, he had sometimes touched up the Duke's drafts with his own hand, smoothing down too plain-spoken passages. The style of Goethe's own letters is evidence of how, as he mixed with the great world, he learnt the art of being all things to all men; for just as he would always find a few robust adjectives for the Duke, or for Merck some cynical *aperçu,* so for his mother he would affect the simple bourgeois outlook which to her seemed natural in him, though it did not seem so to himself.

Yet there was no dissimulation in all this—and least of all at Court, where in the early days his "tone" was epoch-making. "You need only be what you are—that's the policy for this place," he wrote ironically to Herder. But though the chosen attitude of Weimar society—their spontaneous affectation, so to speak—made his initiation easier for him, the Court soon got used to him and he to the Court; and by the time the first strain was over, he was an adept in the privileges of aristocracy—indeed he was sometimes held to be over-punctilious.

When after something like a year he became a recognised official rather than a recognised appanage of the Duke, he was obliged to frequent three ducal Saxon Courts instead of only one. That is to say, he frequented the Duke's, the Duchess's, and the Dowager-Duchess's.

But these three reigning heads were all equally attracted by the stranger; and that this lasted for decades is the more remarkable because all three were periodically at odds with one another. True, he made it his principle never to let anything he heard in confidence go any further at Court. Goethe's dual nature, consciously disciplined to these social ends, made life easier for him; for he could give Anna Amalia the benefit of his satirical moods, his prehensile intelligence, and his musical proclivities; for the young Duchess he kept the melancholy and reserve of his spirit, "communing only in looks and monosyllables"; while for the Duke he lavished all the ardours which were the cause of his election. It was all genuine; but the balance kept was his art and his secret—a secret more profound than the Weimar courtiers could at all have dreamed.

With regard to the Court his feeling was of this kind:

After dinner I played up to the Prince-Boy. Chasing each other in the garden. Ball at night. Was incapable of any sense of Nature. . . . To Tiefurt, where every soul I saw annoyed me. So I made my way home. Couldn't enjoy anything. . . . I pitied these courtiers—

I wonder the majority don't turn into toads or basilisks. . . . Four or five Dukes of Saxony in one room are not the best of company. Except the Duke himself, not one has the breath of life in him; the others are like wooden dolls turned out by the dozen, and most of them not even coloured.

What manner of man was it for whom a poet endured all this—who could know him and not know him, and was to bear with him here for fifty years. What manner of man was the Duke?

Carl August was shorter, more thickset than Goethe, who was of good middle-height and slenderly built; his eye was dark like Goethe's, but not so keen as it was fierce; his mouth, in complete contrast to Goethe's nobly-curving lips, was somewhat crooked. What held them to one another, what made the elder a model for the younger and the younger a sort of reflection of himself for the elder, was the dæmonic element in Carl August's nature. The stormy enigmatic strain in the Duke might have made him seem a younger brother of Goethe's, if he had had genius instead of only having many gifts. But he lacked the corrective supplied by a creative nature; and as the idea of self-discipline was uncongenial to him, he remained essentially inharmonious. It was only time, not reflection nor riper judgment, which gradually calmed him down, and made him appear better-balanced. He was often a victim to self-reproach—a sensation wholly unknown to Goethe; and while Goethe's emotional capacity was unlimited because his heart was impassioned to the core, the Duke was unbridled because he was dissatisfied with himself. *Dæmonia activa—passiva.*

Goethe's dæmon urged him to activity, Carl August's to perpetual movement. Goethe recognised the privilege of princely birth, Carl August that of royal intellect—each with the secret reservation that that which he himself possessed was after all the higher of the two. The Duke was drawn to the poet by personality, the poet to the Duke by the opportunity of playing the latter-day Voltaire and installing Rousseau's ideas into a real live Prince. But if the Duke was also influenced by the desire to deck his Court with the poet's renown, this latter was wholly devoid of courtly ambition. We must remember that at that time even the most liberal-minded of Princes would quite naturally speak of his Ministers as "servants," and of Goethe as a man on the "possession" of whom he was to be congratulated.

Carl August, who felt that Goethe's nature and his own were akin, perceived that in him he had found an older friend and mentor; and as he exaggerated their points of resemblance while taking their relation as a whole somewhat superficially, he was merely preparing for himself a moderate sort of disappointment. The poet, who saw in the Duke's impetuosity a reflection of his own without the corrective of genius, saw him in the light of a friend so much younger as to be easily influenced, and was quite ready to defer to his authority if by so doing he could find scope for his own energies. But as his connection with the Prince involved him in a vital decision, he would be proportionately disappointed if the Prince should fail him.

Thus an easygoing ruler was making an experiment with a poet who took his fancy, and was at first but little concerned for his State, in whose interest he did not immediately utilise the newcomer. Goethe was making his experiment with a Prince and that Prince's realm, but was soon absorbed in the realm to the neglect of the Prince. Both began their connection in a spirit of adventure. For both it proved fateful.

From the first day Goethe tried to influence him, more in the way of training than of culture. As he himself could never learn anything from books, he did not offer his friend books, but a living model; he thought it more important to form his heart than his intellect, for the heart was more accessible and more nearly akin to his own. Certainly the young man was sagacious, nimble-witted, quick to understand, with fewer prejudices than most Princes; but he was vain as well. His intellect played scarcely any part in his friendship with Goethe. In the first ten years we hear nothing of the Duke's studies; even Goethe's works made little real impression on him. Like all Germans, Carl August had raved about *Götz*, which appealed by its power to his own crudity. The great works which were to come left him entirely uncomprehending.

In his efforts to develop him as a Prince, Goethe did not lose sight of the mere man. He described the dæmonic young ruler retrospectively in later years:

Noch ist, bei tiefer Neigung für das Wahre,
Ihm Irrtum eine Leidenschaft.
Der Vorwitz lockt ihm in die Weite,
Kein Fels ist ihm zu schroff, kein Steg zu schmal;
Der Unfall lauert an der Seite,
Und stürzt ihn in den Arm der Qual.
Dann treibt die schmerzlich überspannte Regung
Gewaltsam ihn bald da, bald dort, hinaus,
Und von unmutiger Bewegung,
Ruht er unmutig wieder aus.
Und düster wild an heitren Tagen,
Unbändig ohne froh zu sein,
Schlaft er, an Seel' und Leib verwunden und zerschlagen,
Auf einen harten Lager ein.[1]

Shooting and boar-hunting and camping at night in the open, high jinks with country-girls of easy virtue, were the favourite excesses of the young Prince; for the desire of his heart—campaigning—was as yet refused to him. Goethe, who was neither a sportsman nor a libertine, joined in these amusements only at first. Sometimes, in the tumultuous initiatory summer, he was obliged to take part in them three times a week. But in a few months his contribution to the shooting-trips took the form of sketching the various incidents and places.

At first he tried to accomplish many things by gentle lectures. Sometimes he spoke out:

I want to give you another talking-to about that! For on my way here I was thinking about your very excessive impetuosity on such

[1] "And yet this love of truth in him is mingled
With error, ardently pursued.
His active mind thus onward urges—
No height too tall for him, no path too steep;
The giddy precipice then emerges,
And panic terrors on him leap.
So, in a mood of woebegone distraction,
To find escape he rushes here and there;
Soon in as reasonless reaction
Will sink to earth as in despair.
His mirth will change to savage sorrow;
Unruly he, and yet not glad;
On some hard couch he sleeps, oblivious of the morrow,
Heart-sick, and wounded sore, and sad."

occasions [he was referring to a conflagration], which always exposes you to the risk of doing something which, if not mistaken, is at any rate unnecessary, and a useless expenditure of your own energy and that of your officials.

After the early weeks of wild excitement the Duke seemed to calm down a little, and Goethe could adopt more courtly methods. If the young monarch had been too eloquent at the Council-table, Goethe would take an opportunity, after dinner, of letting fall some remarks on moderation of speech, on giving one's self away, on heated orations. If he found him reactionary, he would give an allegorical turn to his own ideas on politics and jurisdiction. His constant aim was to be a lively example of how a man could be adventurous without being eccentric, and to warn the Prince against taking eccentricity as the mark of an adventurous nature.

The Court stood amazed. They saw their monarch acting upon suddenly-acquired convictions; "and when he is really all out for them, making such a to-do about it that people get exasperated." At such moments Goethe's hopes for the Prince rose high; these were his brightest days, for in upholding the youth he felt that he was proving his own worth as a man, and that was the first and the abiding aim of his genius.

Goethe taught his Prince to despise the forms of authority, while reverencing the spirit. In a letter written in collaboration with him, he derided "the Council's sublime session" under the Duke's very nose. But shortly afterwards Goethe wrote this *Königliche Gebet* (*Royal Prayer*), which might have been dedicated to his Prince's temper:

Ha, ich bin Herr der Welt! Mich lieben
Die Edlen, die mir dienen.
Ha, ich bin Herr der Welt! Ich liebe
Die Edlen, denen ich gebiete!
O gib mir, Gott im Himmel! dass ich mich
Der Höh' und Liebe nicht überhebe. [1]

[1] "Lord of the world am I! They love me,
My nobles, they that serve me,
Lord of the world am I! I love them,
My nobles, sworn to my allegiance.
O grant me, God in Heaven! ne'er to set
On rank and love an unbefitting value."

Moreover, at this time he became a mediator between the Duchess and the Duke. His duality enabled him to win the confidence of both the disunited couple. When he could not prevail with words, he had recourse to poetry. In the curious lyric drama, *Lila,* he designed to cheer the Duchess's melancholy by figuring it forth, to cure fantasy by fantasy; and when in a later farce he made the ladies of the Court comment upon the gallantries of the Fairy-Prince, he could venture on it simply because he was the favourite of both parties.

In this restless medium Goethe's nature craved a place of repose—he found it in his garden. Beyond the City gate, near the Castle but removed from its bustle, stands an old-fashioned little house, with only four rooms:

> Übermütig sieht's nicht aus,
> Hohes Dach und niedres Haus.[1]

But a large garden surrounds it, and the neighbouring park is extensive. For nearly seven years this was Goethe's abode, and it was a place where his spiritual growth could proceed amid all the outward activities; the soil of his garden did that for him. There he planted his affections deep; thence his happiness flowered high. Had he not, pent in the narrow streets of towns, for years craved such a plot of ground? And now he devoted a good part of his time to the garden, for this too he had to learn to tend—it was as new a thing to him as affairs were. Whole days of the early bustling period were spent in the mere preliminaries of installation, in tending, planning, enlarging; and then his diary says: "These most exquisite days continue."

If, in his solitude, he woke early after a night spent between dancing, talking, and riding, he would feel as if enwrapped in an atmosphere of celestial peace, and was never weary of saying what a delightful sensation it was. For Goethe never worked at night, in any period of his life; and in his old age requested that the lamp as a symbol of industry might be omitted from the first of the memorials to him, for he had never written except in the mornings, "when I skimmed the cream off the day and used the rest of the time for cheese-making."

[1] "Nothing here for pride or show,
Roof is high and house is low."

In that garden he steeled his frame, bathing in the brook by the hedge on November evenings and December mornings, and on snowy January days, "so as to freshen up my deplorably stagnant wits." And he gave up drinking coffee and took less wine, that he might get the very most out of himself. He speaks of his thinness at that period, and his servant declared that he could easily carry him. Moreover, he ceased to wear a wig—that badge of the rococo.

He was inclined to utilitarianism at that time; and so he kept bees, grafted young fruit-trees, wrote "love-letters with fingers greasy from grafting-wax," and told how he had gone exterminating caterpillars too late in the day, "and so I always failed to see them. A poet and an amateur are bad managers, both."

But now and again there are hints at more inward things. "I am planting trees now, like the children of Israel setting up pillars of witness." In this third year Wieland could already say that planting and sketching were Goethe's favourite occupations. A mind so speculative that "in the evenings my whole being seems to be concentrated between my eye-sockets" needed sedatives like these.

This garden-life was not in the least sentimentalised, and so he could take an interest in his little house as well. But he never wanted more space; it was on interior order that he concentrated. "To live within limits, to want one thing, or a very few things, very much and love them very dearly, cling to them, survey them from every angle, become one with them—that is what makes the poet, the artist, the human being." And while the illimitable spirit strove to concentrate on some definite aim, while the giant intellect confined itself to narrow activities, he found that garden and house inevitably kept his mind fixed on their economy—and this too was a new thing for him. Till then he had never had much, and only seldom enough, money; he had repeatedly borrowed, and as a young man had in fact lived like one who knew there was a heritage behind him. Now, with money and house of his own, he began to keep accounts with very much greater care, and continued to do so for fifty years. "Ever-increasing pleasure in housekeeping, saving, making both ends meet. Delightful tranquillity in my home-life. A certain sense of restriction, resulting in a sense of real liberation."

The man whom in these years he most heartily admired was Batty, a farmer recommended by Merck, whom he now employed as land-agent. The practical, straightforward procedure of this man struck the poet, in this his first real contact with the soil, as a pattern of efficiency; for Batty

> doesn't indulge in vague dreams, as we used to do about creative art. When he has to get something done, he sees at a glance what is necessary to his purpose. Agriculture is a very fine thing, because you get such an unmistakable answer as to whether you're making a fool of yourself or hitting the mark.

In these first four years he acquired a thorough elementary knowledge of husbandry as practised in the Weimar region. It was even with a view to making economies in favour of the land that he undertook the War-Commission; thenceforward he was set on reforming Weimar's finances.

As a youth he had been alternately Bohemian and pedantic in his dealings with documents and money; now he trained himself to exactitude and sought by such methods to clear away the confusion in his mind. "Since in my position it is so easy to obtain money" (he wrote to a *protégé*), "I must be all the stricter in my household management." And he asked for an account of what his correspondent had received, for there was an entry missing in his account-book. Once, when away, he wrote to Weimar ordering twelve plain frames for the Academy, as he was bringing back some drawings, and they were to use the glass they already had. If this were large, the frames might be made to suit it.

Even in his literary schemes he did not forget economies. From Merck, who was writing a novel, he demanded the full dramatic rights, for he himself proposed to dramatise the book. When, during his visits to the German Courts, he made an ironic list of Court-types, he begged the recipient of his letter to keep it a secret, lest someone should plagiarise the idea.

The documents to which he entrusted these weighty trifles soon waxed into a series of 1,700 letters and notes, kept in a woman's casket, and covering ten years. Goethe was more devoted to this woman than to any who preceded or followed her; he gave her all himself. She was as a reservoir in which he could concentrate the flood of imagination and thought which was Goethe, and find all clarified when he was ready to direct it elsewhere. The superhuman attempt to unify his antithetic nature in the course of three short years is as it were symbolised in this woman; and what he and posterity had and have to thank her for is the nobility of the measures she adopted with him. It was not her fault that the experiment was premature, and that it was not until long after the tremendous tension which his soul underwent in this battle for chastity had been relaxed, that liberty and harmony could ensue. Her merit is that, nevertheless, she represented as it were a shore whose tranquil harbours can withstand the fierce tempestuous sea.

She loved the idea of Goethe, not Goethe himself. He loved the idea of her, not the woman herself. In that resides all which was fine, all which was fruitful, in their relation. They could not hold communion like celestial spirits; they divined each other visually, through the senses, in their daily contact, knowing one another too late, and yet (as it proved) too soon; they were constrained to live for these ten years apart yet not apart, two temperaments which differed widely in their conception of surrender to feeling, pent in a narrow circle, a restricted space, with prejudice and intrigue around them—and from *that* sprang all the bitterness and distrust they mutually suffered from. Their romance is no tale of bliss that ended in tragedy, but a long, unequal story with a hundred moments of exaltation and a thousand hours of torment.

Charlotte von Stein was small, graceful, slender, at no time beautiful but always attractive with the tranquil oval of her countenance; and when Goethe first met her she was, at thirty-three, more sensitive, more delicate, more transcendental and oftener ailing than she became in later years—not a woman in her bloom, at her zenith; but a resigned and melancholy being. Her voice is said to have been soft and low; she was a type of suffering virtue, of gentle seriousness, a mistress of court-etiquette, but (so they said of her) with a frankness which was all her own. A friend writes of her that no one would have imagined, from her exquisite dancing, that quiet moonlit hours and midnight musings were as the peace of God to her heart.

Finely-curved, rather thin lips, dark hair and great Italian eyes, she had in common with Goethe; but while his eyes gleamed or pierced, hers seemed to swim in flame which never wholly kindled, never wholly went out. Not sensual as Goethe was, nor sexless as his sister was, the best pictures of her give the impression of a disillusioned rather than of a cold-natured woman.

She was well provided-for by her marriage with the good-naturedly unaffected, unintellectual, robust-minded Master of Horse, von Stein, who was of a type completely alien to her; and when Goethe left school at sixteen, she was twenty-three and the mother of a son. But in the course of the next eight years she had seven children, and her health had seriously suffered.

In December Goethe was still lamenting Lili in verse. In January he wrote his first letter to Frau von Stein; and even this earliest one reveals the half-unconscious, but at bottom very definite, prevision of a breaking-point which haunted his love for her. His earliest written word to her is concerned with a falling-out. She had given him a seal, he had passed it on to his sister, and Frau von Stein was offended. Goethe wrote: "That is the reason, then! . . . What I give to my sister is mine, in more than one sense mine! But that is the reason—*I* shall never seal with it. And I should not be worthy of it, if I had not felt that."

However, not more than a couple of notes had passed between them before he was calling her his balm in Gilead. His feeling, in the first few months, hovered between love-sickness and an attempt at Platonic friendship, between *Du* and *Sie;* he did not write tempestuously, but restlessly, pleadingly; and yet these early love-letters reveal something of disappointment in her.

> It vexed me to find no word that came from *thee*. . . . Dear lady, let me love you. If I ever find anyone I can love better, I will . . . leave you in peace. . . . Perhaps it's all imagination—no matter. For the present, it is so with me; and if it changes, that will soon be evident. . . . And yet it troubles me that I love thee so much, and just *thee!*

But then his troubled spirit lectured itself into a celestial frame of mind towards the adored one.

O you the one woman who has breathed a love into my heart that makes me happy! . . . The one woman I can love without suffering torments—and yet I live in a state of terror half the time. . . . What a sister I have in you. Think of me, and press your hand to your lips. . . . Good-night. Once more I could see nothing but your eyes throughout the whole masquerade.

Written at midnight, after he had known her two months: a conflict between desire and renunciation, a massacre of longings, with doubts of his own constancy.

But the letters immediately following are panting, distracted.

O peerless among women! . . . who would wish me to be happy if I could love anything better than you! How happy I should have to be, in that case! Or how unhappy! . . . Fritz [her three-years-old boy] has been with us. I gave him a great many kisses. . . . Good-night, angel, I think of you asleep at this moment. . . . You who are so saintly I cannot make into a saint, and can do nothing but torment myself because I would so much rather not torment myself.

Out of these fragments—all from one voice, for we have none of her answers—we can reconstruct the erotic conflicts of the pair, in which the older, calmer woman imposed upon the younger, stormier man a friendship of the soul. Once more this poet—sought after, renowned, full of fire and charm, a childlike suppliant, a fierce desirous lover—had to recognise that he stood before a half-closed door, the door of her whom he loved.

What prevented this worshipped woman from now becoming Goethe's mistress? Did she think the enigmatic poet unworthy of such surrender?

The greater a man's grasp, it seems to me [so she confided to a doctor], the more he is perplexed and repelled by the totality of things, the more easily he misses the way to tranquillity. We know that the fallen angels were more intelligent than the others. . . . What will be the end of me, with him? For when he is here, he never leaves my side. I call him my saint now.

Did she love her husband? He was as a stranger to her. Did she dread Weimar's opinion? They had been gossipping from

Goethe's earliest visits; and Weimar society was almost more accustomed to marriages *à trois* than to normal ones.

Did she, or did she not, perceive that by the refusal of herself she made her friend as restless as by her caustic or gentle comments, her broad outlook upon men and things, she soothed his inward conflict? An ideal of chastity haunted her soul—to that she sacrificed her lover's equilibrium.

After three months of this he put his secret longing into verse. Only that once did he tell himself and the woman, in poetry, of the mysterious bond between their souls, though there were many little love-songs throughout the following ten years.

Sag, was will das Schicksal uns bereiten?
Sag, wie band es uns so rein genau?
Ach, du warst in abgelebten Zeiten
Meine Schwester oder meine Frau.
Kanntest jeden Zug in meinem Wesen,
Spähtest, wie die reinste Nerve klingt,
Konntest mich mit einem Blicke lesen,
Den so schwer ein sterblich Aug durchdringt.
Tropftest Mässigung dem heissen Blute,
Richtetest den wilden irren Lauf,
Und in deinen Engelsarmen ruhte
Die zerstörte Brust sich wieder auf.[1]

Such was Goethe's avowal of the tragic intimacy felt by both to be a part of that relation which denied them the sorcery of the unexpected, the immunities of a fool's paradise. But in their closeness he perceived a call to something higher, more inspiring; and forcibly restraining the earthlier elements in his nature, he entered thenceforth upon a losing battle.

[1] "Tell me, what is Destiny preparing?
Tell me why we two have drawn so near?
Æons since, were you a sister, sharing
Kin with me, or else a wife most dear?
Everything I am, my every feature,
You divined, my every nerve could thrill,
Read me at a glance—no other creature
Knows me as you know, nor ever will.
You could calm my fevered blood, could guide me
Better than my erring will has led;
In your angel-arms I ran to hide me,
Care from out my troubled bosom fled."

She was for renunciation, for a vaguely spiritualised friendship; he was and remained the young ardent man, intent on possession. His only course was to make renunciation a form of sensuous pleasure; and (as when Lotte had married) he steeped himself in that inverted joy. "If only you were thinking of me, as I am of you! . . . No, I don't wish that! I intend to feast upon the melancholy of my well-known destiny—not to be loved, when I love."

But on the back of his letter she wrote these lines:

Ob's unrecht ist, was ich empfinde—
Und ob ich büssen muss die mir so liebe Sünde,
Will mein Gewissen mir nicht sagen.
Vernicht es, Himmel, du, wenn mich's je könnt anklagen.[1]

Such was her saintly eroticism, fleeing from its own passion.

And yet she was fully conscious of her submissive friend's desires, for ever at her side, for ever stirred afresh—and that for years! It was precisely this—this wholly uncharacteristic vacillation between spiritual longings and sensual desire, this division (so utterly alien to Goethe) between the beast and the God in man—which to Frau von Stein appeared as a stage on the road to purity of soul! And Goethe followed that path for years, his feet entangled in his lady's Web of Maya.

But though she racked his senses by these ecstasies of earthly renunciation, she did by her ripe wisdom in some other things allay the tempest in his soul. When two years had gone by, he was one evening, after he had left her side, moved to such thoughts as this: "I wonder if I really do love you, or whether to be near you is no more than being near a mirror so crystal-clear that it is delightful to look at one's self therein." And he gives neither himself nor her any conclusive answer to the question, which indeed may be said to answer itself.

Nowhere more plainly than in *Iphigenie* can we perceive the soothing influence which her soul could exercise on his. He wrote it in his fourth year at Weimar.

[1] "Can it be wrong, this deep emotion—
Shall I repent of this my sinful dear devotion?
Conscience all answer doth refuse me.
Oh then, destroy it, Heaven, if ever it accuse me."

In this play he delineated the most untroubled moments of their friendship; and he afterwards said that the passage where Orestes finds himself again in his sister's presence was the turning-point of the drama. But in Thoas walking in darkness, Goethe likewise appealed to his friend's beneficent lucidity of spirit; and we are listening to his dialogues with Charlotte when we read the opening scene of the first *Iphigenie:*

Iphigenie: [Die Götter] reden nur durch unser Herz zu uns.
Thoas: Hab ich kein Recht, sie auch zu hören?
Iphigenie: Es überbraust der Sturm der Leidenschaft die zarte Stimme.
Thoas: Die Priesterin vernimmt sie wohl allein?
Iphigenie: Der König sollte sie vor allem andren merken. . . . Ich trage nun die Schuld von dem Vertraun zu dir.
Thoas: Ich bin ein Mensch, und besser ist's, wir enden.[1]

Never was Goethe's capacity for suffering more manifest than in his relation to this generous but extortionate woman. He was devoted to her without possessing her; she wanted to possess his heart, without being devoted to him. He suffered in silence; she vehemently bewailed herself. Then he would write to her tenderly.

At other times pride would have its way, when she had attempted to banish him from her presence.

I don't wish to see you. Your presence would make me sad. If I am not to live near you, your love is of as little good to me as that of any of those absent friends in whom I am so rich. Proximity in our moment of need is what matters—it resolves our doubts, soothes our distresses, fortifies us in every way. . . . I am, alas, so dependent on your love that, often as I try to break loose, it gives me such pain that I would rather let it be.

Thus he wrote eight years before the end—foreshadowed in this outburst.

[1] "*Iphigenie:* [The gods] speak to us only through our hearts.
Thoas: Have I no claim to hear them too?
Iphigenie: The storm of passion drowns that gentle voice.
Thoas: And the priestess hears it only?
Iphigenie: The King should need it more than any other. . . . I am now bearing the penalty for my trust in thee.
Thoas: I am a man, and it is better we should say no more."

She often suddenly betrayed her heterogeneous nature by keeping apart from him socially. It had scarcely been decided that he was to remain at Weimar (a decision to which she must have contributed), when she departed for a cure of some weeks and left the unfortunate man to himself at the very moment when she ought to have stood by him. The Duke, and many other gentlemen of the Court, visited her in Kochberg; Goethe alone was left to fume in Weimar, forbidden all access to her. His reproach is a foreshadowing of Tasso's:

> Oh, you can torment a man as Fate does; he dare not complain or cry out, it goes too deep. . . . Of me you shall hear nothing more. . . . If you could but imagine how I felt, when the Duke took leave of me, and Einsiedel dressed for the journey in my uniform!

The innumerable things he sent her from his garden she would dispense to her household as though they had been bought in the market-place, and he constantly had to remind her that they were love-tokens and meant for her alone. When he asked her to return a little poem for copying, she wrote on the back of the sheet: "I don't like returning anything that I have from you." As all her letters to Goethe were demanded back and destroyed, by herself, some value attaches to so rare a piece of evidence. The little sentence expresses, prettily enough, the jealous sense of possession by which she grappled her ethereal affection to the earth she thought so slightly of. With all her tranquil wisdom, all her dignity—Charlotte had but little sweetness of disposition.

Now as always Goethe included the woman's environment in his love for herself. This attachment, with its accepted mystic decrees, was even extended to her house and children. Food and its preparation, gifts of and requests for things to eat, play a large part in his letters to his friend.

The desire for offspring was stronger in his heart than ever before. The "little monkeys" make their appearance in a hundred letters, getting presents—and instruction. He would let little Fritz play and pick flowers and fruit in his garden all day long, would toss pancakes for him, and invite him in to look for Easter-eggs.

Amid his innumerable studies, duties, activities and speculations, Goethe laid all the tenderness of his nature, fresh as in his adolescence, at the beloved woman's feet.

> I've spent this whole week in tending the flowers for your bouquet to-morrow. . . . If I ever return to earth after death, I mean to implore the gods to let me love but once; and if you were not an enemy of this world I would ask for *you* as that dear companion.

And even when four years had gone by he hid himself in the bushes near the street, just to see her drive by to the town. "That you should think of me or write to me, I do not ask. . . . I take everything as a favour."

Her favours consisted in being always ready for him when *he* was ready to be reverential, to instruct her, to spend himself for her. He dictated to her, sketched and read with her, taught her English and physics—he was always the giver. Her tranquil spirit poured oil upon the troubled waters of his dual nature. It never stimulated his intellect. Nowhere do we read of her judgment having influenced him in art or literary work; and if at first she could so judge for him in social matters, he soon surpassed her in that field.

But Charlotte von Stein did stimulate Goethe's imagination in a deeper sense than any of the women who came before her. To them he owed idyllic figures only. Two of the masterpieces of his dramatic creation were drawn from her—or more precisely, from his idea of her. These excepted, all he wrote for her in those first four years was that one elegy and some few short pieces which are not in his collected works. The first half of Goethe's life was filled with passions and is almost empty of love-poems—a very few for Friederike and Lili are all that we have, as against the hundred love-songs of the second half. And this too is symbolic.

But even his urgent impulse to confess himself to his friend was singularly intermittent. When he withdrew for weeks to the Wartburg—there to hearken, remote from men and business, for the strenuous inward voice—he (who once had written her diaries in his absences) now for nearly a month, and for long after his return as well, wrote never a word to her.

In the spring and at the end of the third year such absences became frequent; and by this time it was unmistakable that though he thought her more charming than ever, she seemed less of an affinity. And at the end of these weeks, though he saw her every day, he did not tell her of his resolve to go to Switzerland. She did not know of it until a few days before he left, and even then he did not tell her why he was going.

Charlotte von Stein, who figures as the sun in Goethe's sketch-books, was in her mild grave radiance much more like the moon. The beauty of Corona Schröter was to break upon Goethe like the rising sun. When soon after the beginning of his friendship with Frau von Stein, he called, with an introduction from the Duke (who had himself wooed her in the past), upon this artist in Leipzig, he wrote to Carl August:

> May I be preserved, soul and body, from that angel of a Schröter woman, of whom God forbid that I should say a word of any kind. . . . For the last twenty-four hours I have scarcely been in my right senses—which means that I am in my senses a good deal too much. . . . I'll leave the actual details till I come back, as in them there are pp. . . .

These were their erotic hieroglyphics.

In the autumn he brought her to Weimar. Before that he wrote a great many letters to one of her most devoted friends: "Console the angel! If I could only spend an hour with her . . . Never mind the handkerchiefs! And buy only the dress." With this he sent twenty louis d'or, and commended the middleman. Only a few of these letters (whose numbers are known) have been preserved, and none of those which he enclosed for herself; but the few we have give a picture of a headlong love-affair in which a poet finds himself reflected in an artist, and the courtier lavishes presents on the singer. To the intermediary: "Send me my bill when the Fair opens. . . . I have no fears for the Schröter, her destiny is bound up with my own."

From the first day she appeared in Weimar, there to be the crowning attraction of her lover's theatre, Corona ranked as the most beautiful woman in the town. Tall, slender and yet Junoesque, with her refined simplicity and her favourite Grecian attire, she was soon the Muse of all the masquerades. Her head (she was only twenty-five), with its tawny colouring and long curling hair, was like that of an archaically sculptured young lioness; the wonderful hand, of which the mere plaster-cast can enchant us to this day, could play upon the zither, flute and pianoforte. Her voice, pure, soft and slightly veiled, had the thrill of an inspired priestess's, yet its pathos was never wearying. She was as yet much too timid, too sensitive, to appear upon the public stage; quite unworldly, and not in the least of the actress-type, she had no ambition for a Court-existence. She soon took her place in the little circle which was ruled by Goethe's influence, but rarely consented to join in the festivities to which she was eagerly invited. A lucid intelligence, wide culture, the mastery of three languages, skill in drawing and composition, raised her far above the level of the theatrical world; and she was never ill, she was able for anything.

How should this beautiful gifted being, the like of whom Goethe had never beheld till now, have failed to take the poet by storm? And when the figures of his imagination were actually incarnated by her, how irresistible must have been this Muse with her morning freshness! Had she not everything that the eight-years-older Charlotte lacked, and a great deal too of what Charlotte could offer? Never again was Goethe to meet a woman who, like Corona, summed up all that beauty and art had meant to him; to her alone could he have chanted those dedicatory lines:

> Es gönnten ihr die Musen jede Gunst,
> Und die Natur erschuf in ihr die Kunst.[1]

As unhesitatingly as he had courted her in Leipzig, he now appropriated the lovely creature. Frau von Stein, who would not allow him to visit her at her country-seat, had left him languishing in Weimar for two months. When she returned to the town in early November, Corona had just arrived and was beginning to rehearse *Die Mitschuldigen*, with its author in one of the parts. There are no letters from Goethe; but his diary, though by way of

[1] "The Muses showered favours on her head,
And Art in her by Nature's self was bred."

keeping the secret, gives it away by indications clear as daylight: "November 16. Rehearsal. Corona at night! . . ." A suspensive punctuation which does not reappear for decades. "17th . . . Love-making. Rehearsal! . . . Corona." And yet he writes to Charlotte of her remoteness: "Ah, these eight weeks have played havoc with me, and I am still the completely sensual man."

The most remarkable symptom is that instead of exulting in his natural attraction towards a beautiful and gifted woman, Goethe—he who prostrated himself before the laws of Nature—felt remorseful and confessed his remorse to the other woman, from whom nevertheless he concealed his *bonne fortune!* His friend had jealously forbidden him to yield to the seductions of other women, while refusing to yield to him herself; she stayed away from the performances because Corona was acting with Goethe, and for that reason actually refused to witness the first night of *Iphigenie!* Was she really the poet's Muse? Their relation was falsified in a way which was utterly unlike him. For Goethe was immensely reticent, but he never lied.

The swift passion was soon to be complicated by the Duke's rivalry with Goethe.

Possibly Goethe, remorseful and unhappy between these two strangely-constituted women, was inclined to welcome the rival as one who would serve as an occasional substitute for himself, especially as his increasing melancholy may have made him feel unequal to Corona's brilliant personality. Only one word relating to the situation between these three young people has been preserved to us. In February Goethe's diary says: "In the evening I caught Corona and the Duke at L." Such scanty indications also throw some light upon the difficult days he must have had with his idolised friend; and it is vain to seek expression for all that is unexpressed in the situation.

Corona's share in the character of Iphigenia can only be divined. When Goethe wrote this work in his fourth year at Weimar—though its theme must surely belong to the first—he was wholly under the more intimate spell of Frau von Stein. All that is spiritual in Iphigenia is certainly drawn from her, as he knew her in their best days; the dramatic presentment and the outward semblance reflect Corona's influence.

In the six weeks of mere manual labour at this play, the division of Goethe's energies is made manifest.

> I've brooded all day long on *Iphigenie,* until my head is spinning. . . . It will be very difficult to get it finished at all, so interrupted as I am, with only one foot in the stirrup of my hippogryph's saddle. I've sent for musicians to soothe my spirit and free the phantoms of my brain.

A week later:

> My spirit is gradually escaping, through those lovely sounds, from the red tape of documents and protocols. A quartette is going on in the green room next door, and I am sitting and gently summoning the distant phantoms to my side.

Then again four days of "attendance at the Council and the War-Commission, of recruiting and street-surveying work."

From Apolda sounded lamentations about fuss and everlasting calls upon his time. "No chance for the play here; it's damnable. The King of Tauris ought to be holding forth, as if there were no starving stocking-weavers in Apolda." There are lengthy notes about the weavers of the town, and how the overseers cheated them in the weighing-out of goods. "March 9 . . . Alone in the evening. Pulled the three acts together."

Goethe's rendering of Orestes was a rendering of himself, at one remove as it were; that was why he was so good in the part of that dæmonic personage. These years, this very point of time, saw him set foot upon a path which was to be his way of escape from his innate duality—but this was only the first step.

In *Iphigenie* Goethe chose a tragic way of soaring above the chaos within; a year earlier, when he was in a state no less susceptible, he had administered a kick to himself by means of a farce. In the *Triumph der Empfindsamkeit* (*The Triumph of Sensibility*) the dolorous Prince, who travels about with a mechanical imitation of Nature and adores a doll, is made to ask: "Are my pistols loaded?" "As usual," is the answer, "but . . . for God's sake don't shoot yourself!" And hidden within his doll, among straw and shavings, they find copies of *La Nouvelle Héloïse* and *Werthers Leiden!*

But immediately after this the same Prince breaks out into the splendid lines, beginning:

> Dich ehr' ich, heiliges Licht,
> Reiner, hoher Gefühle Freund![1]

This amazing farce is a testimony to the confusion of styles arising from Goethe's duality; and as it was written in his third Weimar year, it is plain proof that the author of *Iphigenie*, when he let himself go, could still express the contrasted sides of his nature as uproariously as he could tragically.

Drawing served him as a sedative. It was one way of compelling his soul to tranquillity; and it was no less precious to him as a means of perpetuating the memory of such hours of quietude.

But then, once more, his critical spirit would be vexed by his own inadequacy, and he complained that he would never be an artist. This too was quite a Faustean situation; and in these particular years it made him now melancholy, now happy, and then furious with himself again. A hundred letters testify to this; and thus, while he was striving towards unity, the problem of his state assailed him as it were from every side.

His worldly activities inevitably made the spiritual struggle still more complicated. To wear himself out in the daily round of work, which had once been represented by the exaltations of literary production, now became his definite purpose—he regarded it as his destiny, and it *was* his danger. Writing took a secondary place; he looked upon his genius as a beautiful, irrelevant gift.

In those first four years he wrote only seven or eight longer poems; for the rest, we have but a quantity of brief quasi-axiomatic verses—exhortations to himself and his friends.

Again and again we ask ourselves: "Why all this? Why all the road-making and recruiting, wire-pulling and spiritual discipline at Court? Why did he learn to command and obey, to

[1] "I praise thee, holiest light,
Of pure, exalted emotions friend!"

wear himself out in actualities for which another would have served as well, and let his incomparable poetic powers lie fallow?" And from the hills he loved we seem to hear these Faust-like lines to Destiny resound:

> Mein Carl und ich vergessen hier,
> Wie seltsam uns ein tiefes Schicksal leitet,
> Und ach, ich fühl's, im Stillen werden wir
> Zu neuen Szenen vorbereitet.
> Du hast uns lieb, du gabst uns das Gefühl:
> Dass ohne dich wir nur vergebens sinnen,
> Durch Ungeduld und glaubensleer Gewühl
> Voreilig dir niemals was abgewinnen.
> Du hast für uns das rechte Mass getroffen,
> In reine Dumpfheit uns gehüllt,
> Das wir, von Lebenskraft erfüllt,
> In holden Gegenwart der lieben Zukunft hoffen.[1]

And still more audible was the inward voice to himself, when he praised the country at a later period: "Where you continue to lead a tintinnabulating sort of existence between enjoyment and its contrary."

In his fourth year there, he felt on an official trip,

like someone coming out of a town where he has long drunk the water from a well in the market-place, to which all the streams of the neighbourhood were conducted. And then he arrives, after walking and walking, at the source of one of those streams; and is never tired of gazing at the ceaseless ripple of the water and delights in every weed and pebble.

[1] "Here do my Carl and I forget
Our sense of thee, O stern Predestination;
And yet methinks the stage is set
E'en now for some supreme initiation.
Thou lik'st us well—hast taught us both to feel
That thou art lord, and we but prematurely
Strain to the goal, nor ever know it surely.
And thou hast known the measure best befitting—
Kept us in passive trust enwrapped,
Aware of energies untapped,
Our future hopes to present bliss submitting."

In all these reflections about his work there is never a word of its value or helpfulness, little either of its management or efficiency—he is scantly concerned with anything but what stimulates or absorbs his moral sense. Everywhere we can discern that flight from his illimitable self to a restricted, definite sphere of activity, that humble faith in a slow process of evolution, that proud aloofness from the turmoils of the world, which when all was said but came and went before his poet's eye as do the changes of scene in a theatre.

This symbolic way of looking at his work gave rise to a more concentrated mood; he became more self-confident than he had been for years, and his tone was more virile:

Schaff, das Tagwerk meiner Hände,
Hohes Glück, dass ich's vollende!
Lass, o lass mich nicht ermatten!
Nein, es sind nicht leere Träume:
Jetzt nur Stangen, diese Bäume
Geben einst noch Frucht und Schatten.[1]

He saw more clearly, and avoided, the suicidal results of his former irresolute way of life, and strove for concentration and reposefulness.

This dread of spiritual disintegration stood like a stern incorruptible sentinel in the background of Goethe's worldly life; and—fifty years before he made his dying Faust perceive the phantom form of Care—he implored it, if it must disturb his equilibrium at moments, at least to enlighten him:

Kehre nicht in diesem Kreise
Neu und immer neu zurück!
Lass, o lass mir meine Weise,
Gönn, o gönne mir mein Glück!
Soll ich fliehen? Soll ich's fassen?
Nun, gezweifelt ist genug.

[1] "Yield, O thou my daily striving,
Best of all the joys of living,
This—to see his consummation!
Empty dreams? Nay, never, never!
Naked boughs, but not for ever:
Fruit and foliage—by creation!"

Willst du mich nicht glücklich lassen,
Sorge, nun, so mach mich klug.[1]

But he remained the victim of his duality. When he was thirty, Wieland could still describe him as a man who was nearly always in a state of exasperation, though he (Wieland) had happened to hit on a good-tempered day.

So, in creating his Orestes, he had not overcome him; and when Goethe was twenty-seven Lavater was to hear this striking declaration: "All your ideals shall not prevent me from being genuine, and good and bad—like Nature!"

At that time he would still write inflammatory farces, the attacks on the Court being merely toned-down a little. All the dualism of his youth flames forth in his words, at thirty, to the actor Iffland:

> Take my advice and do your damnedest, never anything less, whether in the lowest farce or the loftiest tragedy! The fellow who is fit for anything worth speaking of is contemptible if he's content with mediocrity. Ugh! [and he got into a highly excited state]. Excelsior, Excelsior—or you'll stick in the mud!

It is clear that no one could really influence this man. It was not Frau von Stein who formed that spirit—at most she was the harder diamond which could often grind down Goethe's angles. Like Herder before her, she was symbolic of an epoch on whose threshold he had entered before he met her.

But since he did not meet her at so propitious a moment, since he never was (generally speaking) so intent on self-development and so able to go the right way about it, as in the ten years of his first Ministerial work, the influence of this woman was more transient than Herder's. For the chaos in his soul was still far

[1] "Nay, thou shalt not haunt me ever,
Coming back and back to me!
Let me live—I willed thee never,
Grant me rest at last from thee!
Shall I fly? Or boldly grasp it?
He who questions thus replies.
Joy—if never I may clasp it,
Troubled spirit, make me wise!"

too immanent for any attainment of that celestial harmony, her ideal of which he reverenced and strove to realise in himself.

His nerves were rent in the attempt: "Feverish depression. . . . Strain, depression and religiosity. . . . Fever at night. . . . Strange swift melancholy alternations of feeling": such were the repeated entries in his diary. Or else he would be "very sad without knowing why. . . . I sent for the woman clarinet-player. . . . It was all so splendid, but my heart was like a log." Bad weather put him out of temper; he began to be his own weather-prophet.

And yet the passage of those years, in which for the first time he could feel as one transferred from a boat upon the high seas to a steady-going vessel, was richer than any earlier period in happy prospects and sensations. Ἀγαθὴ τύχη was his favourite motto for a while: a happy dispensation, blissful hours—so familiar to his thought was the well-nigh untranslatable phrase that in his diary he used the Greek abbreviation.

This epoch, from twenty-six to thirty, held fewer disappointments for Goethe than any that went before. "Strivings of the heart . . . Vague ardencies . . . For I am so happy . . . I must accept good fortune as my mistress—and recognise that that is why she is always urging me on, as one whom she loves." And once, all of a sudden, quite irrelevantly, he sums up this period in a note of four lines to Frau von Stein. The words are Rembrandtesque in their chiaroscuro: "The joy of life darkens my spirit."

Everything he enjoyed was to Goethe a gift from the gods; he always knew that they might bereave him of it. At first he still felt as though wandering reluctantly. "Suppose I had to leave this land, with my staff in my hand," he asked himself, and burst into tears—yet felt in himself "the force even to bear that. The force—that means the passivity." To brace himself for suffering—in thoughtful moments that seemed to him the aim of all his discipline; unlike Prometheus, who in truth was never the only symbol of this nature, always aiming at self-control.

Wonderful—how henceforth Goethe sought to reconcile his faith in an appointed destiny with the most strenuous form of endeavour, striving in its flexible vigour against immovable force. It was as though he sought to wrest a favourable intention from the Olympian decree, though it were but by the faintest of indications. For the next fifty years this was to him the dearest of all his spiritual processes; and as his dæmon clung to the idea of destiny, but his genius to that of relentless self-mastery, the drama now beginning seemed sometimes to be paving the way to the equilibrium which would reconcile all dualities. His self-discipline in holding the balance true between desires and energies becomes more and more evident from this time forward.

Signs of superstition multiply; certain days of the year are looked upon as propitious or ominous; esoteric speculations lead him to secrecy, as also his greater worldly wisdom and growing distrust for men. He seeks oracular answers in the brightening or obscuring of the constellations, believes in omens, and at the end of this epoch he listens to the sound of a waterfall and cries:

> Seele des Menschen, wie gleichst du dem Wasser,
> Schicksal des Menschen, wie gleichst du dem Wind![1]

During these years of his most pronounced phase of worldliness, Goethe always resorted to seclusion from social life when he wanted to commune with himself. His garden, his friend, his drawing were only the daily sedatives. Though he frequented society to fortify himself and measure himself with others, he was conscious of some uneasiness at the rarity of his solitary hours, and could write half-ironically, half-sadly: "Then for a wonder I stayed at home, alone. Sat down in my chimney-corner and read." At another time: "I have . . . nothing in common with these people, nor they with me; some actually imagine they are fond of me, but they aren't in the least." Or else: "My destiny is completely hidden from my fellow-creatures —they can hear and see nothing of it."

At the end of two years he withdrew quite alone to the Wartburg, leaving the Duke and his companions "to their boar-hunting" below in Eisenach. Even Knebel's arrival worried him. For weeks he abode there in solitude, completely idle. A stranger who forced his way in compared his taciturnity to

[1] "Spirit of man, thou art like to the water,
Fortune of man, thou art like to the wind!"

that of an Englishman, "who should stand before one, glum and cold, as if in a fit of spleen."

At this time he wrote to a friend that he was "dead to the world," though people were amusing themselves with fables about him, as of yore with the *Werther* fables.

And he was twenty-eight, world-renowned, a Minister, the friend of a Prince, of remarkable women, of distinguished men!

The deeper his absorption in worldly affairs, the more he avoided the intrigues connected with them.

Formerly my soul was like a city with low walls, which had a mountain-fortress at its back. I guarded the fortress, and left the town defenceless both in peace and war; but in these days I am beginning to make that stronger too. . . . Alas! the iron bands around my heart grow more and more constrictive, till at last it will be completely impenetrable. . . . The higher the sphere of society the more contemptible is its comedy; and I will take my oath that no clowning at a country-fair is as revolting as the attitude of the classes, from the highest to the lowest, towards each other. I worship the high gods, and yet I feel it is in me to bid them eternal defiance if they should ever choose to behave towards us mortals as do their human prototypes.

What with his official life, his reclusiveness, his friend, and the Duke, there was little room for other friends. Many of them were already out of sight, as it were. "Remember me to Lotte," he wrote to Kestner, "and if I occasionally put on the official manner, the rest of me is very much the same old Goethe. . . . Apropos—is Lotte still as cheeky as ever?" Four years after *Werther!*

Lenz and Klinger, the friends of his youth, soon followed Goethe to Weimar, not by his request. He did not wish to be reminded of what he had been—and still less to remind the Weimar folk. Both men quickly left the place.

Even Merck got it hot, when it was a question of Goethe's dexterous establishment of his position at Weimar. He was prevented from writing about the Court and social conditions at Weimar. But Merck was undoubtedly the one who knew most about Goethe's real opinions, because he alone could understand the active side of Goethe's life.

In two decades, Goethe made only one friend in that new

world of Court and society. This was Major von Knebel; and their intimacy was of slow growth. Besides Wieland—with whom his relation was a cordial, but not a very intimate one—there was Herder once again; when he came to Weimar at Goethe's request, Goethe superintended the furnishing of a house for him. No sooner had Herder arrived than his capricious temper brought him into collision with the Court and society in general; and so the younger man involuntarily became a sort of protector to the elder. But Herder got over these difficulties; and at that time laid the foundation for his second masterpiece. He and his wife (who soon, it is true, developed some jealousy of Goethe's other friends), together with Knebel, Wieland and Frau von Stein, were in those years the sole members of Goethe's "little public," to whom he would read scenes or chapters from the works he was engaged upon.

As to Lavater, Goethe's liking kept equal pace with his exasperation. Already Lavater's intolerance was greatly endangering their friendship, for he was increasingly persistent in urging his pagan friend to adopt the path to salvation which *he* believed in.

Despite all this, Goethe loved Lavater's active benevolence, called him the most humane of human beings; and when at last he set forth to meet him, begged him beforehand—but in friendly words—not to talk about religion.

For at the end of this epoch he again went on a journey, and again to Switzerland. But it was no flight this time. With his thirtieth year Goethe's vitality was growing in force, and he felt its inspiration. On his twenty-ninth birthday we have this: "A queer sensation, this entering on one's thirtieth year. And many points of view are changed." Goethe, who combined the passive patience of a plant with the analytic spirit of a botanist, was unerring in his perception of the periodical ebb and flow of his vitality. This knowledge he gradually developed into a source of strength.

Just then he must have felt something like a farewell to youth; and he also believed the Duke's development to be proceeding more rapidly.

After innumerable talks between the two in the course of these four years, upon every topic under the sun, from the complexities of the heart to the finances of Weimar, we now find indications of a crisis. Some of Goethe's notes point to his having adopted a new plan, trying the influence of change of scene upon the Duke, which signified new duties for himself—though he too felt desirous of a temporary escape from the limitations of Weimar.

In the early days of August he began a serious review of the decade which had just expired; he sorted and burnt his papers, and with remarkable brevity summed up his youth in this modest outline-sketch:

A quiet retrospect on my life, on the perplexity, restlessness, curiosity of my adolescence, drifting in every direction, intent on finding something satisfactory. The peculiar pleasure I took in the mysterious, in the dimly-divined relations of things. My inadequate grasp of all scientific matters, and the way I would then let them drop; the sort of modest complacency which ran through everything I wrote in those days. My narrow-minded gyrations in matters human and divine. The barrenness of my activity, and even of my practical ideas and writings; the time thrown away in vague sensations and nebulous passions, which were of so very little service to me; and that is my life half-over, and there is no turning back. Nay, rather I am like a man who has saved himself from drowning, and whom the beneficent sun is drying and warming. The time I have spent in the turmoil of the great world, since October '75, I dare not as yet envisage as a whole. . . . May the idea of purity, which embraces the very food I eat, become ever clearer to my spirit!

Yet at the same time he told his people at home to expect him and the Duke on a visit; and from his letter there plainly emerges the remoteness and reserve of his chosen isolation—in the part of Goethe—from his parents. The letter is cool, and begins without personal invocation:

My wish to see you once again has hitherto been only restrained by circumstances. But now an opportunity seems to offer. . . . I want to find you [his mother] in the best of spirits, and wish you such a Good-Day as never before. I have everything that a man could wish for—a life in which I daily exert myself and daily develop; and this time I come to you in good health, untroubled by a passion or a perplexity, free from vague restlessness, like one beloved of the gods who has reached the meridian of his life and hopes that past sufferings will work to his future good, and has moreover steeled his heart against all sufferings that may be to come.

There was a purpose in this. The man who, conscious of standing on the watershed of youth, on the heights of his material and spiritual existence, had but now held the most humble-minded dialogue with his soul, a dialogue which might have been that of a vanquished creature . . . that very man strides like a conqueror into the house and land of his fathers, where once he had known himself to be completely misunderstood. Not a word of the son's own joy at coming home—nothing but formality, pride, biography. And yet that son loved his parents in his own way. But here is the first monumental sign of that double life which for so long could obscure the picture of Goethe's old age for contemporaries and posterity.

In his next letter he gave orders about their quarters in his father's house—all in the imperative tone of an Imperial Court-Marshal.

However, on the birthday itself he felt "frolicsome and free." Then: "I got my nomination as Privy-Councillor. The turmoil of terrestrial affairs, and also all sorts of similar private feelings, take possession of me. It is better not to write down these inward agitations."

By this comment, which has no parallel in Goethe's diaries, we perceive that he could be reserved with himself, or at any rate with his pen.

The impending trip turned into a sort of review of his youth. A good-humoured, yet rather derisive, glance was cast upon Frankfurt. At Strasburg he left the rest of the party and took his way to Sesenheim.

The second daughter of the house had loved me in days gone by, better than I deserved. . . . I had been obliged to leave her at a moment when my departure well-nigh cost her her life; and her reference to the delicacy which had never since left her was tactfully slight. But she was extremely cordial and friendly to me from the first moment of my arrival, when I startled her by suddenly appearing on the threshold.

Only eight years since he had ridden away! The soul can travel far.

Immediately after this, Strasburg and Lili:

> And I found the lovely minx playing with a doll-like creature of seven weeks old, and her mother with them. There too . . . I asked after everybody and looked into every corner. And I found, to my delight, that the dear girl is very happily married.

Soon he was standing on the glaciers which were the aim of the trip; and his spirit was untroubled as the light on the snowy mountain-side, and cold as the ice-forms around him, "unperturbed by circumscribing passion." At heart he was sad in that saddening landscape—he saw in its colourlessness the reflection of himself. "One dimly guesses at the origin and life of these strange shapes," he wrote of a ravine. "However and whenever such things come to be, these masses have fused into large, simple forms, according to the weight and similarity of their parts." And we perceive how self-contemplation amid the mountains can take Nature in its stride.

In this exalted mood he was sometimes annoyed by the Duke's boisterous conception of "playing up," and when once they were rolling stones down a glacier and the Duke was inclined to overdo it, "I told him that would do, and we could not get any more fun out of it."

On their way back they visited some of the South German Courts; and Goethe, who knew only the unusually cultured Weimar one, was filled with contempt for heirs-apparent and princelings, turned the cold shoulder to everyone, and was bored to extinction. "They are badly organised, and consist chiefly of noodles and rascals. . . . My endeavour now is to find out what these so-called men of the world are really made of"; and he drew up a satirical list of such typical courtiers, which he once tried to dramatise—it wound up with the description of a lackey "who has more to say than most of them."

Such was the confidence he now felt in himself, such was the pilgrim's incorruptible outlook on Nature and humanity. Only once was the self-conscious young man exposed to temptation. In Lausanne he paid a visit to the Marchesa Branconi.

This was Goethe's first encounter with a renowned society beauty. Few European women and scarce one German—for the Marchesa was German—of those with whom Goethe came into contact seem to have been of so rare a quality as this flawless creature, who as the one-time mistress of a Duke was no less notorious in her day than Lady Hamilton in hers.

But he, in her presence, asked himself "whether she really *is* so beautiful. A mind—a way of life—a frankness . . . one positively doesn't know where one is"; but he was unaffectedly relieved to find that he was not going to assume the damnable position of one of her adorers, "and melt like butter in the sun all the year round, *par devoir*."

That was all the impression made by a fascinating woman upon the thirty-yeared Goethe, who never possessed any beauty but Corona. Yet perhaps not all. On his departure, he was struck by what he was abandoning of his own free will, and said to one of her cavaliers: "What could not that woman make of a man!" It was Goethe's destiny always to chase the moment, yet hesitate to grasp it. Was she not more dazzling in every way than Charlotte at home? Had she not made advances to him? And yet there was that dread of losing himself, which lies at the heart of all the renunciations in an artist's life.

So that when he finally stood on the Gothard Pass, he was cooled-down in more than one sense. For the second time he gazed southward from the Pass, but

> even now Italy does not draw me to her. This trip is not going to be of any service to the Duke, I can see; there is no sense in staying away any longer; I shall see *you* again—all this turns my eyes for the second time from the Land of Promise (which I hope I shall behold before I die) and draws my spirit homeward to my own humble roof, where I shall be happier than ever to see you by my hearth and give you a good dinner.

Extremely sensible and even Philistine are these remarks—and for the jealous friend to whom he writes not one word of intimate longing, merely *Ihr* and *Euch!* At the same time he wrote to Knebel, grimly saying that casting one's skin was always a hellish business; and if he were to turn savage again, Knebel could not say he had not been warned by this letter.

A new note of all-embracing self-restraint had become audible; passion of every kind was to be strenuously kept at bay, his youth seemed to have flickered out. When Lavater sent him a disciple, Goethe wrote these memorable words:

> He is indeed akin to me, and trusts me. But alas, I am conscious of my thirty years and worldly-mindedness. Far as I have travelled from this state of germination, of burgeoning, I know it when I see it, and rejoice; in spirit I am with it, but my heart is far away. My soul is filled with vast conceptions of which this boy cannot so much as dream; a new realm opens to my energies; and so I cannot turn back for a moment, as it were, into the dewy vale where the sweet turtle-doves coo to their morning-mates.

CHAPTER VI

DUTY

"The daily work which is laid upon me, and which daily becomes at once easier and harder, demands my waking and dreaming consciousness."

THERE were three gods to whose images Goethe, in his thirty-first year, offered praise and prayer. Tyche, the "happy dispensation," occupied the central place; at her right stood Terminus, the setter of boundaries, the moderate-minded counsellor; but on the left was Genius with the torch, striding steadfastly onward, urgent and eager. Such was the strange Ex Voto which, after the return from Switzerland, Goethe erected in the shady park at Weimar—more as a monitory than a reminiscent symbol.

Goethe entered upon his fourth decade in a mood of buoyant seriousness. He was clearer about himself, less imaginative—a thorough man of the world. He observed with amusement that his adversaries at Court were full of congratulations upon the trip with the Duke, for Weimar found the home-coming ruler quieter and more sober-minded.

Tyche was the central star in Goethe's firmament. He was intent on complete submission to the happy fate which had drawn him from afar to this sphere of activity; he meant to hearken to the voice of worldly wisdom; and his genius, though it stood on the left side, the side of the heart, was to be near him only in the capacity of a mute, beloved presence. The dæmon seems to have vanished. We are in contemplation of the most highly organised of attempts—initiated by a man who demanded from his nature the very utmost of which it was capable—to attain, by means of forced labour, the clearer atmosphere in which he could draw as full a breath as mortals may, the atmosphere for which his native turbulence had craved through fifteen years. He hoped that he was entering on an epoch—and could not know that it was to last but a year.

His first sensation was of a refreshing satisfaction in his exertions.

> The greatest gift I have to thank the gods for is the swiftness and variety of my ideas. This enables me to divide a good day into a million parts and make of it a lesser eternity. . . . No one who doesn't deny himself in every possible way is fit or able to rule. . . . *Nemo coronatur nisi qui certaverit ante.* So I take the rough with the smooth. . . . I succeed in everything I put my hand to.

Nowhere in the whole course of Goethe's confessions do we retrieve so cheerful a tune, underscored though it be with some unrest, as in this thirty-first year. It is a well-made—one might say a well-invented—melody, which has not yet the staying-power to develop; and so it occasionally breaks off while its tones are still in possession of our ears.

For all of a sudden, from one day to another—or indeed within the compass of a single day—this happy mood would change; and Tyche, who had smiled on him a moment ago, would turn her Janus-head and like one of the Dark Sisters gaze wide-eyed and sombre into Goethe's own dark eyes. Then in a flash would rise that isolating sheet of glass which he must always have beside him as a shield against the world. "If only men were not so poor in spirit, and those who are rich so helpless!"

And the man engaged in social activities felt an ever-growing contempt for the men he laboured for. "In our youth we are confident that we can build palaces for our fellow-creatures, and when it comes to the point we find it is as much as we can do to get their dung-hills out of the way."

Even in this year of chosen submission to the actualities of the present, Goethe found a refuge in his confident sense of a future.

> New mysteries are being revealed to me. Some day I shall have a good time. I am drilling myself to be ready for the biggest possibilities. . . . What I intend for myself and others is hidden from every eye. The best thing I have is the unbroken silence which I

preserve with the world at large; in that I live and grow, and what I gain thereby not fire nor sword can deprive me of.

He used his intellect like a violin; and the more stringently he manipulated the bow, the more closely he kept his eye upon the strings he touched. And as in more tranquil periods he studied the laws of his being, taking the lull in the tempest, with its resulting depths and shallows, as an opportunity for diagnosis of the storm that should next blow up, so he was particularly attentive to his bodily health when he was feeling particularly well. In this year of accentuated self-control there are very many notes about the laws of his constitution.

For some time now he had taken to dictating; because he found that the manual labour of writing got on his nerves and made him lose the thread; and though he would make a rough draft beforehand, his verse, prose, and letters thenceforth assumed something of an oral tone, so much so that in his old age he once made a list of odd mistakes occasioned by his amanuensis having heard him wrong. This year he resolved to do more dictation than ever, because all his best ideas and images occurred to him when he was walking up and down.

He was at all times so dependent on light and warmth that he said his nature was like a flower which closes when the sun sets. He was intent on studying the cyclic alternation of good and bad days to which he was subject; he was conscious that conception, execution, arrangement—to say nothing of enthusiasms and impulses—kept a regular rhythm, no less than cheerfulness and depression, strain, elasticity and lassitude, composure and excitement; and "as I live by a strict regimen, the pace is even; and now I must work out the time and measure of my own rotation."

Still more astonishing is the dispassionate lucidity of a note made, immediately after the above, in days of volcanic energy:

This was my day for conceptions. Dullish at first, and I clung to business-matters; but soon things got livelier. . . . Walked to Tiefurt. A good idea for *Tasso*. . . . In the evening a few moments of lassitude. I must look into this. Why was it?

Next day:

The lethargy of sleep was soon banished by fresh air and water. My soul was longing for rest, even at that hour, and I should have liked to make a bolt. Pulled myself together, and dictated some of the Swiss trip. . . . No wine these last three days. I must be careful about that English beer. If I could knock off wine altogether I should be very glad.

Again Goethe was watching over the Duke as in the earlier phase; again he was ascribing all his absurd ideas to his youth; and he only smiled when Carl August, imitating him, introduced short hair at Court. He helped him with his diet-sheet, and through an awkward affair about a miscarried love-letter. His hopes for ruler and friend were renewed; some ideas of the Duke's were noted down by Goethe as worth having. He was still counting on Carl August for the self-control he had resolved on for himself.

The more he concealed his inward self from others, the more skilful he became in the management of them. He cut down his social engagements; and though he consented to join the Freemasons on the somewhat arrogant ground that he was desirous of good-fellowship, every detail of his private and public life proves that this was but a pretext concealing deeper motives. When he visited the neighbouring Court he complained that he never felt at ease nor could be open-hearted with people, unless he had lived with them for some time. But at his own Court he was tenacious of his standing, though he began to feel more and more of an alien there. When the Duke's brother met him on a walk, Goethe thought him discourteous not to have offered him hospitality. As Court-poet he did only what he was obliged to do, rather automatically—the pageants he arranged for the winter-festivities were put together bit by bit, so that when the parts were assigned he could note: "All departments fixed up."

He used ministerial changes and chances as material for his art, studying the life of a Duke of Weimar so as to dramatise it later on; and seems to have touched bottom in the paradox of this existence when he wrote these extraordinary words:

My writing is subordinated to this life—nevertheless I do permit myself, like the great King who devoted some hours daily to the flute, a frequent exercise of the talent which is peculiar to me. I have a mass of writing . . . but I need concentration and a sense of ennui before I can do anything with it.

At such moments this chosen Art of Life reduces itself *ad absurdum;* and he who had constructed it for himself realised that in a flash of insight. "Yet I feel," he writes in the middle of an outburst about his satisfaction with his work, "like a bird caught in a snare. I feel that I have wings and cannot use them." Another time he had been actually praising Marcus Antoninus for not allowing himself to be absorbed in authorship—yet how did he continue?

I am, so far as in me lies, withdrawing the water from these fountains and cascades, and turning it on to the mills and irrigations; but before I can look round some evil genius turns the tap and it all runs away in a splutter. And when I think that I'm sitting on my hack and riding to the station I am in duty bound for, all of a sudden the mare under me will turn into a glorious creature with uncontrollable desires and wings, and run right away with me.

In this thirty-first year Goethe wrote nothing to speak of, beyond a burlesque on critics and literature.

This week I have something to do to it; if I can work it in between Saturday and Sunday it may be all right . . . and as I have it well in my head, twelve hours, inclusive of eating and drinking, ought to see me through. . . . I want to snare my birds. . . . After all, it brings people together, amuses the Duke (who is to play a big part) and gets him away from Tiefurt.

And so he dictated it on Sundays, just like an overworked official to whom authorship is a recreation.

Must not his unquiet nature have brooded on death in the midst of such organised drudgery? At the close of this year we have the first tangible evidence of Goethe's presentiments. If from his youth he had been familiar with death and always haunted by the thought of it, he now gave practical shape to these ideas. In good health and a tranquil frame of mind, he made the draft of a will; and in a curiously agitated letter struck out this arresting metaphor for his endeavour as a whole:

The daily work which is laid upon me, and which daily becomes at once easier and harder, demands my waking and dreaming consciousness. This duty grows dearer to me every day, and my aspiration is to equal the greatest men in that sphere, and in no wider one. This ardent desire to build my existence, on the basis assigned me, into a pyramid which shall cleave the upper air, outweighs all others; and I can scarcely ever for a moment forget it. I dare not delay, I am far from being a young man now, and Fate may perhaps break me in the midst of my endeavour, and the Babylonian tower survive as an unfinished stump. At any rate men shall be able to say it was a gallant attempt.

And about the same time, a few days after his thirty-first birthday, Goethe wrote on the wooden wall of a belvedere in the Thuringian forest:

> Warte nur, balde
> Ruhest du auch.[1]

Was Eros doing nothing, amid this labyrinth of toil, to turn the poet's thoughts aside from death?

When he returned from Switzerland, he visited Frau von Stein and Corona by turns; but in a week the latter's moods became a source of torment to him, and depressed him greatly. Two months later, it appears, he broke off the relation with her.

The songs he afterwards sang in her praise for contemporaries and posterity, may possibly have consoled the artist in her, but not the mistress. For he who always gave thanks for love, would as invariably seek an occasion to pay tribute when he could love no longer; and immediately after their parting Goethe apotheosized Corona in an ode. Her heart can have taken no pleasure in it. It may have been six months after the rupture that he wrote her the only letter of his to her which we possess:

How often I have taken up my pen to explain myself to you! How often that explanation has hovered on my lips. . . . I cannot excuse myself without touching upon strings which may not again be sounded between us. Would to God that you would make peace without explanation, and forgive me. . . . I feel no anger against

[1] "Wait but a little—
Thou too shalt rest."

GOETHE AT THE AGE OF THIRTY-TWO

you now—don't repulse me and spoil the hours I can still spend with you. . . . If you demand more, I am ready to tell you all. Adieu! If only our relation, so long uncertain, could be clear and steadfast again! G. Thanks for the cakes and the song, and I am sending in return a gay little bird.

The weight upon his spirits lies in these lines, which no one would attribute to a man of thirty. They come from the man with the furrowed brow and darkly-musing countenance whom we behold in the five busts of him by Klauer; and that man indeed has little in common with the flame of erotic life which was probably the atmosphere of this beautiful woman. The short postscript alone breathes the blither, simpler air of her artist's life; and for that Goethe was not fit until a decade later.

And when in the summer the Marchesa Branconi arrived for a few days—and assuredly she came to see Goethe—he was more like a sculptor enraptured by her beauty than a poet; and we get a good idea of her coquetry when we hear him make this intimate confession:

I behaved to her as I would to a Saint or a Princess. And if that was only my illusion, I would not have wished to sully such an image by the delights of a passing desire. But God defend us from a serious tie, for she would drag my soul out of my body with it.

Never was there greater evidence for Goethe's effort, at this time, to escape from the sensual spell of women that he might breathe a presumably clearer air in a more ethereal atmosphere.

In the melancholy Court-lady our disabused worldling had the idol he really wanted during this year of strenuous self-control. His letters are tenderer, calmer, more fraternal in tone. The more he immersed himself in work, the farther he stood from poetry, the closer did Charlotte von Stein draw to him, for only in worldly things was she ever his counsellor. The rare quality of her spirit, early ripened by sorrow, made her an ideal figure for Goethe; but as the Minister's companion this older woman, with her twenty years' experience of Court, could be no more than a friend, a sister.

And that was what she preferred. Instead of playing the Egeria and urging the poet back to his natural sphere, she sedulously bound him to the world. The end of their relation will demonstrate what she meant for him at this period.

He was lighter-handed in making up their quarrels. He sent her a tiny broom to brush away the things she did not like in him; and when she became jealous about his writing verses to her youthful cousins, he promised never to do it again. Though he confided all his interests to her, he felt none of the earlier need to unburden himself in poetry.

Yet we have a witness to how much, in this very year, he withheld from his friend. Never again was Goethe's diary, which had been wont to resemble a mere calendar of the passing months, so heavily scored with self-confessions. But his numerous letters to Charlotte, written in the most critical moments of development, are devoid of any real revelations of his deeper self. He was sternly teaching himself to be reticent about almost everything.

With this new, this thirty-second year, began a new era for Goethe's soul. It was to last for six years. At its beginning his love, for all its fondness, was preparing a change.

Throughout the five years he had lived in Weimar Goethe had loved his friend; but with the new turn in his life, which was always moving around hers, she was obliged to adopt a new form of devotion to the man who for five years had been the centre, the very sum and substance, of her days.

The crisis was brought on by Goethe, in an impassioned appeal. It was the first outbreak of all the darkling energies which had been so long kept under; Eros was merely the messenger on whom was laid the task of proclaiming the new dispensation. He wrote, suddenly, from his house to hers, rent by some erotic conflict of which we know nothing.

What you ended by saying to-day has hurt me very much; and if the Duke had not been with me as I climbed the hill, I should have wept out my pain. . . . But it has had the result of turning me, with all my thronging ideas, into a child again—utterly perplexed, quite in the dark about myself, though I can judge for others as by some all-consuming flame of fire. . . . If this must be so, I shall have to avoid you at the moments when I need you most. It terrifies me to have to destroy my best hours with you, for before I could be so complaisant I should have to rend every individual hair from my head. And then to be so blind, so callous! Have pity on me!

She read this, and her heart stood still. In a flash the Platonic soul-mate saw her five-years' work threatened. Goethe's conquest of the senses, chastening of the spirit, had been purely artificial; and now the Greek pagan in him was defying her asceticism.

He tried at first to conform to her wishes and hold himself in: "Only I implore you to tell yourself daily that everything which may displease you in me comes from a source of which I am not master." They were reconciled; but the erotic spark had flashed out afresh, and was no longer to be extinguished. In his diary that symbol of the sun becomes more and more frequent . . . then suddenly the book breaks off, is mute for eight months, and not until August is it resumed with the words: "This half-year has been a very significant one for me."

A physical crisis, at this time, testifies to the spiritual one; he says he is "mostly ailing," but helping on the cause of social life.

During these weeks his wooing became more urgent than ever before. He had no sooner left her neighbourhood and gone to the Countess Werther's castle (she was the Duke's mistress) than he drew a grand composite picture of their five-years' conflict—but not as one who tenderly pleaded with her. No, as a proud antagonist; and he implied conditions in his chosen metaphor!

I have been comparing my heart to a robbers' stronghold, of which you have now taken possession. The rabble has been driven forth, and now it's your business to guard it! We can keep our possessions only by taking a jealous pride in them. . . . You hold it now, and gained it neither by force nor craft; in a case of voluntary surrender people are bound to be extremely magnanimous, and reward the confidence shown them!

Guardianship and jealousy; obligations and rewards—quite new turns. And simultaneously he reinforced his attack by singing the praises of another woman, prettier and younger, in whose hourly company he was living. This gave him a weapon against his friend. Why otherwise should he have made such a point of admitting his weakness for the lovely lady to her?

> She seems to give everyone just what he wants . . . to live her life in other people's. The reason why the tune she plays is so lovely is that she doesn't touch every note, but only the special one desired. . . . What genius does in all the arts, she does in the art of life. . . . I have still three days with nothing to do but look at her; in that time I propose to master many more of her attributes.

And so on for pages, affecting to be merely the psychologist intent on analysing a new phenomenon, but most artfully choosing every phrase so as to show his friend where *she* falls short. After years of groundless jealousy she felt, reading this, that real danger threatened her. And next day, he continued:

> She loves the Duke more nobly than he loves her, and in that mirror I have beheld myself, and seen that you too love me more nobly than most of us can love at all. But I don't give up, I feel I am challenged to the combat, and I beg the Graces to show every possible favour to my passion, and go on showing it. . . .

But then, the next instant, he is all self-surrender, he flings his prudence to the winds in one comprehensive gesture, and falls at her feet with this supreme appeal:

> My soul has grown into yours; I may say what I will—you *know* that I am inseparable from you, and that neither heights nor depths can part us . . . and my novitiate has surely been long enough for me to know what I am talking about. Adieu. I can't write *Sie* any more, just as I could not say *Du* for ages.

After his return he sent her a few more tender little notes, which by their use of *Sie* betray the tension of these early days at home.

Suddenly, with the last weeks of March, a new note is struck—that of one who has conquered after long wooing, almost the note of youth:

> Your love is as the morning and evening star to me. . . . I cannot

tell you and scarcely dare comprehend myself, the overwhelming effect of your love in my inmost being. It is a state which, old as I am, I have never known before. . . . Adieu, my New One! . . . I kissed your soul in little Fritz. . . . My five-years' love passes before my vision in all its beautiful pageant of ennobling emotions. Oh, if I could only tell you all I owe you! . . . Farewell, and be sure that you make me very happy. . . .

And so on and so on for ten days, full of such phrases and images as he had not known for five years.

. . . "My last throw." So the mature woman, scenting the crisis as she surveyed her friend's most recent letters, may have said to herself. The crowning proof of her art would be to keep him now, and keep him for evermore. She did not dare venture on a separation and a marriage in Weimar; besides, it would make difficulties for him, in his position, if he were involved. The value of the gift she had so long refused had been, she judged, enhanced by the refusal. Moreover, she was in her thirty-ninth year; and Goethe was thirty-one. It was the end of her youth—though she was looking younger, as a medallion of her shows: fuller cheeks, a rounder chin, even the ascetic lips more sensuously curved.

And yet Charlotte von Stein lost her friend, just when she believed she had won him wholly. A justice deeper-lying than she knew, a justice immanent in the decrees of Eros, bade her atone in the end for the too long-drawn-out refusal. Now she could make him happy but for a little while, and could never intoxicate him; and she, who had woven so strange a spell by her remoteness, must now as time went on lose all by her surrender.

It was too late, after so many fruitless appeals, to establish the illusion of perfect communion with the most clear-sighted of men—and yet it was too soon to have solved an enigma of the heart which might have continued to enthral him by its ambiguity.

Thus the period of passionate love-letters was a brief one—it lasted barely five weeks. He was once more haunted by the superstition of throwing a ring into the sea, for he "added up his happiness to an incalculable amount." By May the tone was quieter. "If you will permit me to tell you, at sunset, that I love and revere you as much as ever." Then he went this length: "The Werther lady wrote me a most charming little note in returning *Wilhelm Meister*. The Schröter comes at noon. I am and remain the favourite of women, and as such too you must love me."

Never before had Goethe so described himself—nor was it at all often true of him, in that sense.

The playful tone of the possessor sounds in a postscript: "'You know who is my little love,' as the old song has it." There is something painful about these ostensibly light words, as used in a letter to a saddened older woman by a man whose soul was struggling towards a difficult development. The phrase is the *cliché* of boy-and-girl lovers; and behind it one seems to catch a glimpse of some profound renunciation.

For Renunciation was the first word Goethe had to inscribe on the portal of a new epoch; and though it was to be written again, and very strangely, in his declining years, it was now—between his thirty-first and thirty-seventh—no sad tenebrous giving-up as in the *Werther* period, but a manly, steadfast, yet not uncheerful relinquishment of freedom to work and write. In a grand crescendo we read of overwork and disappointments, till those inhibiting forces slowly awakened the impulse towards escape. This spectacle too proceeds with all the deliberation peculiar to his leisurely mode of development, especially as, when it begins, he had just undertaken new burdens. Not till he had fought a six-yeared combat was Goethe to break away.

The exterior difficulties were the limitations of official life, which he had to regulate, and the recusancy of the Duke, whom he had to guide; together with the opposition of the stupid world around him to a genius who, after all, had invaded their sphere by a side-door—and was not born to rule therein.

At the end of his thirty-first year he revealed to his mother, in a long retrospective letter, the resignation which underlay all other moods. He gave her a Pisgah-sight of the broad realm he governed, yet even in that gesture there was the first hint of a farewell to it:

And yet now, could I possibly wish for a position more fortunate in every respect for the sort of person I am than one which has something of the illimitable about it? . . . so that nothing but the weightiest considerations . . . could induce me to forsake my post; and it would show little sense of responsibility even towards myself if I . . . were to leave it for reasons of personal inconvenience, and destroy the fruit of my labours. Nevertheless, believe me when I say that a great part of the good-humour with which I can carry my load and toil from day to day, flows from the thought that all these sacrifices are free-will offerings, and that I have only to order my post-horses to retrieve with you the necessary and pleasant things of life, and absolute peace and quietness. For without that prospect, when I have to attend to the demands of others in hours of depression as though I were a serf and a day-labourer, I should feel a much greater bitterness.

Yet at this very time, when routine had sunk from the tranquil glow of a symbol into the smoulder of dull obligation, he concentrated all his capacities for action and undertook a double burden by becoming President of the Ducal Chamber, and "buckling on my armour in real earnest."

It was not exultantly, however, that the envied poet took possession of a relegated courtier's desk. Goethe, as even his opponents testify, had got up no intrigue against the President. What attraction could there have been for him in becoming Administrator of the Ducal Estates and the finances of the realm—or, as we should say, Chancellor of the Exchequer at Weimar?

Again he relied on his knowledge of the country and the people, whom he had thoroughly studied; again he underestimated the unwieldiness and complexity of the antique feudal machinery which was the motive-power for the whole. The President was confronted by four Governments, besides three provinces with three or four estates of the realm, all of which were at variance about laws, conventions, class-distinctions and, being accustomed to an unequal division of burdens, were determined to stick to it. Goethe now designed to challenge his colleagues in the administration, together with the assessors who stood between them and the people; he cherished far-reaching schemes for the relief of agriculture, for in his years of official travelling he had thoroughly investigated the inadequate system which prevailed.

But very soon his hand was stayed. After two short years of it, he gave up the attempt to fight single-handed (and moreover not as head of the State) against the obstinate coalition of the Tories. A victor in the grand manner he saw that he could never be. At thirty, Goethe had known why the peasant was impoverished; at thirty-two, he had perceived that to partition the great estates and increase the number of lease-holders would be one way towards amelioration of conditions; at thirty-four, he wrote from the *Landtag* saying he was resigned, no longer involved in a foolish hopeless struggle—

> although I miss many agreeable sensations associated with earlier days. . . . But alas! out of nothing can come nothing. I know very well what ought to be done, in place of all the endless shilly-shallying and all the propositions and resolutions! Meanwhile, one waters one's garden, since one can procure no rain for the country at large.

This is the period of his social embitterment; these were the experiences which were later, with their consequences of misanthropy and resignation, to make him a reactionary.

> Our damnable system of consuming the very marrow of the country destroys any prospect of a green and pleasant land. . . . I go on patching up the beggar's cloak which is gradually slipping from my shoulders. . . . Our moral and political world is undermined by subterranean passages, cellars, and cess-pools . . . to whose intercommunications and those of the creatures who inhabit them not a soul gives a thought. But to one who has some personal acquaintance with these things, it will be a good deal more comprehensible when the earthquake does arrive . . . and strange voices become audible in these clefts of the earth.

Written by Goethe in Thuringia, eight years before the great Revolution broke out in Paris.

How Goethe watered his garden, how he managed the "Household," is shown in his reports. Take three letters to the Duke, for instance. He was superintending the reconstructed mines at Ilmenau, he was establishing manufactories, visiting wool-factories, carting about samples and catalogues, trying a new method of selling timber, ordering well-water to be analysed for minerals, buying a laboratory, having a castle renovated, an old hospital demolished, the arch of a bridge widened, demanding twenty louis-d'ors from a Prince for mining-shares unpaid-for, getting money out of the Jesuits for a courtier, establishing a marble-mill in a brick-factory, reckoning the profit, in a favourable season, of the Ducal corn after deducting all the demands of the Court, the servants, and the military.

He hastened to Jena, which was overwhelmed by avalanche and flood; and—as before in the Apolda fire—immersed himself in ice and water, grasping and controlling the situation. His most edifying hours were those in which he rode round his district with Batty, his farmer-friend; for Batty had no theories, but his practical common-sense exactly chimed in with those which Goethe held by. "In the smallest village, or on a desert island, I could not exist unless I were just as busy as I am here."

Thus manifold were the claims and representations which, amid his exertions, Goethe did manage to bring forward despite the age, the environment, and the fatiguing work of documentation. But though he exacted the utmost from himself and nothing from the world around him, there was one factor whose energy and good-conduct were indispensable, yet whom he could not bend to his will. Because he could not, Goethe's own energy and zest diminished. That factor was the Duke.

When five years earlier they had gone hand-in-hand, a Prince and a Prince's friend and mentor, everything had depended on their sympathy with one another. But the first lustrum had scarcely come to an end before Goethe had had to ask himself, "Have I been able to influence the Prince's mind in any way?"

Carl August would stand for Goethe's one complete failure if he had not been a half-finished product before the latter undertook him, hoping to finish him in his own way. The rare prospect of being able to do this in the grand manner, and yet as a thoroughly humane achievement, had tempted him to touch material from which his shaping hand could at any moment be removed. Now, after these five years, he had the proof that affinity of temperament is no sure foundation for friendship or enduring influence.

For while Goethe went more deeply, and ever more earnestly,

into matters human and divine, investigating society and solitude, Nature and her sources, to say nothing of Art—the Duke evaded friend and duty, family-life, every educative influence, and kept up an establishment of eighty persons in the snow-clad hills for the sake of boar-hunting, thus maintaining a few impoverished aristocrats who gave him no thanks for it, and irritating the farmers whose land was trampled down. "And all this with the best intentions, to give pleasure to himself and others. God knows if he will ever learn that fireworks at noon have no effect at all." The shoots and driving-parties, the breakneck exploits and love-affairs of the Duke, oppressed the little realm with ever-growing expenditure.

Goethe wrote of these shoots:

> If at the end of it all we were the richer by a single province, I should commend it; but as it only amounts to a few broken ribs, slaughtered horses and an empty purse, I will have nothing to say to it.

With good abilities and worthy intentions, Carl August, despite faithful servants and costly tutors, wasted his time from sheer boredom, merely wearing himself out; and though he saw the right, desired the good and even insisted on it, he could never stick to anything, was for ever craving new sensations, sick of his own puerility; and with all his fine ambitions, was at bottom stubborn and intractable.

The poet had taken until now to see all this; for it was only now, when he was stricter than ever with himself, that he kept a sharper eye on the Duke and began to acknowledge that he was disappointed in him.

Never had the intimacy between Prince and Poet which had been so oddly, so idealistically, conceived, stood in greater danger, never had Goethe's position with Carl August been more precarious than in these four or five years when he undertook the Ministry of Finance—which, in the system of State prevailing at Weimar, included that of steward to his reckless and extravagant ruler and friend. True, the Duke was obliged to promise his friend some retrenchment at Court and in his private life, before Goethe would accept such a responsibility. For ere now he had felt a good deal of anxiety, not to say anger, in connection with the Duke; there had been many heart-to-heart talks about economy—all fruitless.

The Duke has an essentially narrow outlook, and when he takes a bold step it is usually the result of momentary excitement; he is not logical enough to carry out a far-reaching scheme which as a whole would be an equally daring experiment. He is not really a statesman.

The "daring experiment" alluded to, and propounded in long reports by Goethe, was for a reformation in the financial system. The Duke would have none of it; and it is almost as though he hoped to atone to his friend by official compliments for what he was too weak to grant his Minister. On Goethe's thirty-second birthday the Duke ordered a pageant in his honour, and arranged for the Emperor Joseph to ennoble him.

These things left Goethe cold. When, as Privy-Councillor, he had reached the highest rung in the German citizen's ladder, the middle-class man in him had known a momentary tremor, and he had confided to his diary that he would rather not say exactly how he felt. Now, when at thirty-two he was raised to that social altitude which had so often proved a source of disillusion to him, he declared himself to be "so strangely constituted" that he felt nothing whatever when he looked at his patent of nobility; and for years afterwards he signed even official letters and reports as he had always done. But in his coat-of-arms the worldling did set that morning-star which the poet had long ago fancied.

His letters to the Duke now became colder and colder. When Carl August broke his promise and demanded fresh expenditure, Goethe wrote laconically to the Treasurer:

By this arrangement, you will have nothing more in hand this quarter. At the beginning of April you may include all that month's revenues. But afterwards, in May, I wish them to be held over until the end of the month. Have the goodness, dear Sir, to make your arrangements in this sense; for I must either get things straight by Midsummer, or resign.

That these lines would be submitted to his master by the frightened Treasurer Goethe well knew, and it was what he desired. The indulgent mentor had turned, in the course of seven years, into a stern trustee who seemed resolute to keep at any rate the Duke's money-affairs in order—if the young man was bent on squandering his energies.

Only once in these years did his hopes for his friend revive. That once, Goethe really believed the Duke to be on the right path, and confided to his intimates that he foresaw better days both for his friend and his friend's family.

In this mood of renewed confidence he summed up the history and outcome of their companionship in a great Ode; and while affecting merely to look back upon the days when both of them were younger and wilder he ruthlessly holds up the mirror to the Duke as he now was.

Ilmenau, composed in the Thuringian forest for the Duke's birthday, is anything but the amused retrospect of a poet conjuring up youthful follies from the harbour now safely gained by him and his friend. The writer imagines himself stealing in a dream past the hut of the sleeping Duke; and when he interrogates his own phantom form, the embittered Minister is answered by the Goethe of twenty-six in these foreboding words:

Ich brachte reines Feuer vom Altar—
Was ich entzündet, ist nicht reine Flamme. . . .
Nun sitz' ich hier, zugleich erhoben und gedrückt,
Unschuldig und gestraft, und schuldig und beglückt.
Doch rede sacht! Denn unter diesem Dach
Ruht all mein Wohl und all mein Ungemach:
Ein edles Herz, vom Wege der Natur
Durch enges Schicksal abgeleitet,
Das ahnungsvoll nun auf der rechten Spur
Bald mit sich selbst und bald mit Zauberschatten streitet. . . .
Kein liebevolles Wort kann seinen Geist enthüllen,
Und kein Gesang die hohen Wogen stillen.[1]

[1] ". . . I brought pure fire from off the altar high—
What I have kindled is no flame from heaven. . . .
Now I sit here, at once exalted and depressed,
Am guiltless yet chastised, am guilty yet am blessed.
But softly said! For under this roof-tree
Lies all my weal, and all that troubles me—
A noble heart, from paths that Nature chose
By narrow Fate diverted wholly,

No word of gratitude for many gifts—for Goethe in his retrospect regards himself solely as the benefactor of his immature and dissipated friend.

And at the end, when there should have come a ceremonial tribute to the royal personage, he confines himself to a grave wish for tardy improvement, a paternal word of admonition:

So mög', o Fürst, der Winkel deines Landes
Ein Vorbild deiner Tage sein!
Du kennest lang die Pflichten deines Standes,
Und schränkest nach und nach die freie Seele ein.
Der kann sich manchen Wunsch gewähren,
Der kalt sich selbst und seinem Willen lebt;
Allein wer Andre wohl zu leiten strebt,
Muss fähig sein, viel zu entbehren.[1]

Had poet ever before handed his Prince so stern a festal ode? Must not Carl August—himself at the end of his twenties, surrounded by many secret enemies of Goethe, and now deserted by his boon-companion in sports and other weaknesses—have inwardly regretted that he had ever made so much of him, that he had given this poet control of his cash-box? What had become of the complaisant literary personage who had been eager to surpass all others in proficiency and inventiveness? Was it not tacitly understood that his being here was a whim? And moreover, he was even losing his looks. Those eyes that used to be so brilliant were now sunken, those lips of yore so rich in song were now as close as wax. An eccentric, almost a hermit, seeking the society of no woman but that of the elderly "Mistress of the Horse," self-shackled by his official duties—and if ever he

---

That now, more prescient, grasps the good it knows,
Assailed by its own self and wizard-forms unholy. . . .
That spirit still is deaf to loving exhortation,
No siren-song can calm the billows' wild elation."

[1] "The angle of thy realm, O Prince, discloses
The pattern set thy every day!
Thou long hast known the duties rank imposes,
And slowly framed thy wilful soul its debt to pay.
He who lives self-absorbed, unheeding,
May at his pleasure wreak his callous will;
But he who takes command is subject still—
He must renounce, who aims at leading."

did relax a little, doing nothing but study stones or plants or engravings!

And moreover, Goethe was not even his Prime Minister. They had duties in common, but their pleasures and foibles were poles apart. The Duke was but scantly interested in Goethe's writings; Goethe hated the Duke's wild-boars. He had given up talking about the injury to the farmers; now he spoke only of the effect upon the public, who could not be expected to understand this passion of their monarch's.

Towards the end of this period they came into open conflict. Other Princes were urgent that Weimar should join the Princes' Alliance, under Prussia, against Austria; and the Duke, burning for warlike exploits, at last saw a chance of achieving them. He rushed into the Alliance, disregarded its clauses, acquiesced in the military demands of the Allies, and by his incautious behaviour awakened suspicion at Vienna—all this against the advice of Goethe, who was trying to gain their point by subtler tactics, and believed he could obtain his end from the old King Frederick.

But the Duke was dreaming of battle. Jingoism became fashionable at Weimar, and

> is like a subcutaneous itch in our Duke, while it wears me out as a bad dream might. . . . Well, we must leave them in their fools' paradise, and hope that the prudent measures of the greater powers will keep the lesser ones quiet, and prevent them from acting at the expense of others, which is what they would like. On this article I have no pity, no sympathy, nor any hope or patience either.

Goethe as a statesman—in this instance to be judged by history—saw right, and the Duke wrong. During these negotiations Carl August was again sternly lectured by his friend: "However your affair turns out, behave with moderation and—if there's no help for it—extricate yourself without quarrelling with those whom you have involved and compromised." This is not even fraternal in tone. It is much more like a gruff father.

Goethe fled to Jena, where his friend Knebel was, took refuge in Nature-study, tried to get rid of some of his Council-work, even considered resigning it. How entirely in his secret heart he had given up the fight, we can guess from these cynical words:

The Duke is happy with his (new) pack. I don't grudge it him. He is getting rid of his courtiers and getting keen on his dogs—it's always the same, no end of racket just to kill a hare. And I have to make nearly as much fuss to keep one alive.

As money was scarce, the Court-dinners were given up, people dined in the ordinary rooms, and Goethe complained of the close quarters; but said there would be worse to bear than that.

Three lyric dramas and a few masques were the semi-official productions of the Court-poet; and when after reading these things one suddenly catches a glimpse of Goethe's bust, one is inclined to admire the self-abnegating person who could condescend to such trifling almost as much as, in the scenes of *Tasso* (written at the same time), one admires the authentic poet!

> So zwingt das Leben uns zu scheinen, ja
> Zu sein wie jene, die wir kühn und stolz
> Verachten könnten. Deutlich seh' ich nun
> Die ganze Kunst des höfischen Gewebes![1]

It was thus that Goethe, in the very years when he suffered his greatest disappointment in the world of action, learnt his lesson to the end, and became the complete man of the world—at Court, with his fellow-men, and in affairs.

Before his first big contract with a publisher, which he signed at the end of this period, he let it be known through a third person that he would not accept any lower price than his—for that time—very high demand of £300; and he asked the same price for unprinted and printed works, since these latter would be re-written and be "as good as new." He ordered a thousand copies of the announcement of his edition to be sent to him at Carlsbad, that he might distribute them himself. He accepted money from Merck to redeem some capital that was not paying enough interest.

He now made a system of saving time. He rarely read a book through. When the visits of passing strangers disturbed

[1] "Thus life constrains us to appear—nay more—
To be like those whom yet our haughty hearts
Could scorn how coldly! Plain I see it now,
The great machine that turns us into courtiers!"

him, he would bring out some bones after a quarter-of-an-hour, "which bores them so that they take their leave."

The stage on which his life was set now altered—and this too was symbolic. When the poet had been made a Privy Councillor, he stayed in his garden; as "von Goethe," President of the Chamber, he took a large house in the town. Again it was not pride, but humility, but sorrow, that he felt at this change of residence. He knew quite well that he was giving up something irretrievable; and though it seemed like advancement, it was abnegation once more. This was no mere removal, but a final step.

The suburban abode had always had something of the romantic, the accidental about it, from which it would be easy to break away; the Minister possessed in it a refuge, close by the river, under the trees and stars. When he moved to the mansion in the *Frauenplan*, he was really casting anchor for the first time in his eight years' sojourn, never again to set sail. He lived exactly half a century in that house. In that house he died.

But when the time came for this quasi-farewell, he felt it as deeply as he had those of his younger days. His emotion overswept all the systematic self-restraint and common-sense.

Every rose said to me, "and you are going to give *us* up?" At that moment I felt that I could not do without that abode of peace. . . . I wandered round my deserted house as Melusina did round hers, to which she was never to return; and thought of the past that I did not understand, and the future that I did not know. How much I have lost. . . .

In a long life Goethe found few partings from his fellow-creatures so hard to bear as that from the trees which he had planted himself.

To him, at thirty-three, his big house was not merely "the proper thing," but an instrument of culture as well. Had not the boy collected knowledge and proficiencies, ideas and objects? Now a man was collecting. Slowly, in the various rooms of his house, he accumulated engravings and drawings, pictures and books, silhouettes and busts, and above all stones, bones, and plants.

As the self-taught inquirer, Goethe still (as in the strenuous days of yore) directed all his mental energies towards scientific knowledge. When he was studying the situation of one of the great estates which were to be partitioned, the economic purpose would at once suggest the geological conditions, and wonderfully dramatic he found it to have a visible presentment of the origin and formation of the earth, and at the same time that of the sustenance which it could afford to humanity.

Never in Goethe's varied life and activity did he lose sight of the great concatenation of past and present which links every action and achievement as in willing obedience to some master-mechanism. His apparently strange destiny seemed the most inevitable of sequences to a nature which believed in fate's decrees.

The practical out-of-door life at Ilmenau led him spontaneously to the study of geology. "The mountains and ravines promise me much entertainment. It is true they don't now strike me as so picturesque and poetic—but it is merely a different sort of painting and poetry that they suggest to me, when I go climbing among them." This is a turning-point; and, as it might seem, an alteration in him. But behold!—on an official mission, when he was clambering up a dangerous slope, he stood on the shoulders of the young man who was with him so as to break off an interesting fragment compounded of primeval rock and red granite with a blue-black tone on the surface. When the other spoke of risks in their upward climb, Goethe cried: "No matter—let's get on! We both have great things to do before we break our necks!"

He was President of an aristocratic Chamber, a poet of European reputation, a cold and misanthropic official—and from those lips broke those words, as he craned from the shoulders of a guide to touch the primeval rock! We might be still in Strasburg.

Mountaineer and mineralogist, rhapsodist and epic poet were combined, when with the fragment in his hand he examined the granite and began with this confession:

I do not fear the reproach of capriciousness because I turn from the contemplation and description of the human heart, of the most mobile and unaccountable portion of creation, to the observation of . . . the most steadfast, the most infrangible, product of Nature. To me, who have suffered and still suffer from the alternations of my fellow-creatures' opinions, it may surely be granted to enjoy the sublime repose afforded by proximity, in solitude and silence, to the great heart of Nature, which speaks to our hearts so gently.

Visual conception was everything to him. Raphael without his arms would have been more productive than Goethe without his eyes. "As I never can learn anything from books, and had got through the miles and miles of pages represented by our neighbourhood, I now began to study and utilise the experiences of other men."

At this time Goethe turned from plastic art to science. True, he studied bronze-casting with Klauer, and had an occasional "attack of sketching-fever"; but during these middle thirties he quite abandoned serious work, for he saw that he could not "take pot-shots" in that sphere. In plastic art this man who could construct so patiently, who was content so slowly to investigate, and learn, and live, felt conscious that his genius stood aloof, and would impede his progress as a painter all too effectively.

But he retraced his steps as of old—and from scientific research looked back to art, both as teacher and pupil. The rapidly acquired knowledge of anatomy which marked the Jena sojourn he immediately imparted to the Weimar School of Art, in the form of lectures for masters and students, treating osteology as a commentary on human biology. In lecturing he learnt the art of public-speaking, and found in his demonstrations "that the logical processes of Nature are a solace for the illogical actions of humanity."

Rarely and briefly—never for more than a week—was Goethe able to steal away to Jena, there to study osteology.

All of a sudden, like a bolt from the blue, Herder received this note:

Jena. March 27. At night. I have found—neither gold nor silver, but something that unspeakably delights me—the human *Os intermaxillare!* I was comparing human and animal skulls with

Loder, hit upon the right track, and behold—Eureka—! Only, I beg of you, not a word—for this must be a great secret for the present. You ought to be very much delighted too, for it is like the keystone of anthropology—and it's there, no mistake! But *how?*

In his thirty-fifth year, then, Goethe discovered the intermaxillary bone in the human upper cheek-bone, hitherto known only in animals, but which some were hopeful, some sceptical, about finding—the characteristic which distinguished the ape from the human being.

How did Goethe come to discover what had escaped the adepts? Because, as a dilettante, he examined the skull with an open mind, because his eye was unprejudiced—he was not looking only for what system and instructor had pointed him to. That eye was thinking while it gazed; and during its years of a roving apprenticeship to natural phenomena, it had perceived relations, transitions, gradations. And how, once more? Because there was a soul behind that eye which divined, from the gradual development of its own powers, from the slow difficult unwinding, coil on coil, of the mighty cable, that Nature obeyed a kindred law. Self-conscious yet humble-minded (as he had developed since his youth), his genius felt the cosmic laws immanent in itself. The same psychic emotion which could bend that head, so haughtily confronting men, in reverence before the gods—the same sense of a sure and certain brotherhood to all plants or animals of the primeval mother-soil . . . that emotion and that sense alone could enable Goethe so to scrutinise a human skull as to cast new light upon the problem in so spontaneous a fashion.

It is only when subject to such a spirit—a spirit which in the moment of apprehension can crystallise its passion into abstract observation—that the eye discovers hitherto unknown correspondencies. When he discovered that bone, Goethe gave us no less precious a document for his inmost self than was *Tasso* or *Faust.*

But in a then unprinted draft, of which he allowed only a few savants to see a copy—confident of their scepticism!—he carefully kept silence about his ultimate conclusion

that we cannot discern the distinction between human beings and animals in any isolated detail. On the contrary, man [so he wrote privately at this time] is very closely akin to the brute-creation. It is the harmony of the whole which makes every individual creature what it is, and man is as much man by the form and nature of his cheek-bone as by the form and nature of the smallest joint in his little toe. And thus we have the further proof that every creature is only a tone, a modification, in a mighty harmony which must be studied in all its length and breadth—else every individual part will be no more than a dead letter.

All this, which he declared to be the quintessence of the little article, and which in truth was its source, he—man of the world and hierarch of the mysteries—withheld from those who, as he knew beforehand, would be incredulous.

The animosity of legitimate scientists against the intruder quickly justified his precautions. Goethe's first step in Nature-study aroused that opposition which not until a century had gone by was to be changed into admiration of his far-sighted conclusions.

He was to immerse himself still more profoundly in problems of this nature during the next decade, but was never to synthesise his vision as a whole. His reverence was such that he feared to propound an all-embracing summary.

But he had given one to a young Swiss. In some expansive hour he must have said—less *to* him than *before* him—what he felt in the presence of Nature; and it may have been the higher meaning of that young life to have embodied Goethe's dithyrambs on Nature in a memorable achievement—that great ode to Nature, which begins: "Natur, wir sind von dir umgeben und umschlungen." [1] Let the reader find that poem, and read it slowly aloud, more than once!

When this Hymn to Nature appeared in the privately-printed journal of the Tiefurt Association, Knebel guessed Goethe to be the anonymous author. Goethe denied it, but would not reveal the secret—admitting, however, that he had often talked of these things with the author, and that he admired the grace and melodiousness of the composition, which he would have found it difficult to achieve in that form.

This hymn gives us an idea of Goethe's character which far

[1] "Nature! we are by thee encircled and included."

surpasses its rendering of his feeling for Nature. He can only be understood in his entirety, as he understood Nature. We perceive how he manifested himself in his most trifling works, although it is only in the sum of his production that we apprehend him as a whole. It needs little skill, but a good deal of perception, to substitute Goethe's name for that of Nature in many of the rhythms of this Hymn—thus gaining some insight into a soul which was untiring in its quest for enlightenment, and which, amid all its contradictions, was subject to a coherent law. And indeed one might say that though Goethe conceived of himself in terms of the microcosm, he could transmute that conception—by some miracle of treatment—into the image of a man who should be a prototype of Nature.

The rhythms of this Hymn, breaking upon the now impregnable coast, might be the ultimate billows of that tempestuous, impassioned adolescence. The lyric impulse was quiescent; in the well-nigh seven years of this period Goethe (if we exclude his two-lined aphorisms) wrote barely ninety poems; and the few which stand out are the appanages of lyric dramas and novels. The impetus of passion seldom stirred him.

A life which was in some sort epical, as his was in these years, is propitious to the epic form. But if Wilhelm Meister's countenance often gazes through the sedulously-barred windows of Goethe's existence, his presence did not mean any liberation from immediate tension (the origin of all his earlier poetic works) nor even any critical remarks on the present age and environment; rather, the novel was a pretext for critical retrospection. It is true that the foundations had been laid in the earliest Weimar years; but only the beginning was written, and despite all the parallels which are so easily to be found for this period, the book remains more of a retrospect than a survey of surrounding conditions. In treatment it resembles the novel rather than the autobiography; and even in his old age Goethe spoke feelingly of the terrible loneliness in which the work originated.

Undoubtedly it would be easy to point out from what living models some of the characters were drawn. But the most vivid figures—the Harper, Mignon, Philina—were the work of insight, not of actual experience; and in general there are far fewer transcripts from life than in the earlier *Werther* or the contemporary *Tasso*. Wilhelm, above all in the original draft—it was entitled *Wilhelm Meisters Theatralische Sendung*—resembles the author more in his social dilemma than in the structure of his soul; and despite all his medley of projects and undertakings, seems gayer, happier-natured than Goethe was. Round Wilhelm, Goethe wove the web of any fancies which refreshed his own imagination in these years—the novel is a gleam of romance in the restricted, joyless life of that period. It lies like a little convent-garden, crowded with bright pagan blossoms, between the stony strenuous paths of concentration, experiment, and toil.

This duality of artist and worldling, alternating with each other, characterises the first shape of the book; and we should find it hard to say on which side the author took his stand, for he himself was uncertain of Wilhelm's predilection.

There is some bitterness in the words which the overburdened man assigns to his hero:

> How the man of the world longs, in his distracted life, to preserve the sensibility which the artist must never let go if he designs to produce a consummate work of art. . . . Believe me, my friend, it is with talents as with virtue—if we do not practise them for their own sake, it is better to have nothing to do with them.

Egmont, too, which Goethe then provisionally finished, is biographically ambiguous, if only because of his long hesitation over it. Drafted at twenty-six, the play was at thirty-three temporarily, and at thirty-eight finally, laid aside—and besides, the plan of an historic drama precludes such reflections on a long course of authorship as were later to enliven the more imaginative *Faust*.

Precisely because in Egmont he was delineating a different type which he sometimes longed to resemble, the imagined figure was more objectively perceived than his own could ever have been. The dæmonic youth beheld in Egmont the happy-natured and gifted creature that he must often have wished to be. Egmont's lighter-hearted, more transparent nature seemed enviable to him at a time when Lili's cynical innocence, her featherweight character, dancing as it were on small buoyant feet, her skilful manipulation of the problems which distracted *him*, had transported Goethe with delight. From Lili's fluttering youth he borrowed a few of the elements for Egmont's suppleness; and if now and then some of the poet's perplexities were discernible in his hero, they were, so to speak, smuggled in.

That is another reason why *Egmont* is less of a help than a hindrance towards a knowledge of Goethe's soul—indeed, it may even be said to show a distorted image of it, for it is easier to understand Egmont than Goethe.

Elpenor, likewise a product of these years, is more intimately conceived; but here the external rather than the internal conflicts are illustrated. This piece, too, was interrupted by documents and duties. So was a *Roman über das Weltall* (*A Cosmic Story*), which remained a mere sketch. In this, certain pathological-ethical phases were to have been symbolised by planets and earth-tremors. And fortunately *Die Geheimnisse* too was cut short—an epic poem in stanzas, with a distant affinity to the cosmic novel.

Of these *Geheimnisse* a stanza was to be written every day, and the author resolved to give himself a double dose until he had made up his "arrears." "I dragged a stanza out of myself yesterday, somehow or other." Nowhere is our sense of the busy President so overpowering as when we traverse the desert of this poem, where there are but few oases to remind us of the author.

> Welcher Unsterblichen
> Soll der höchste Preis sein?
> Mit niemand streit' ich,
> Aber ich geb' ihn
> Der ewig beweglichen . . .
> Der Phantasie.[1]

The dark eye which once, either flashing or penetrating, had sought to wrest from fleeting life its utmost secrets and im-

[1] "Say, which Immortal one
Merits highest praises?
With none I quarrel,
But I would give them
To her, the capricious . . .
Protean Fancy!"

prison them in anarchic rhythms or steadier rhyming-measures, now gazed with saddened yearning towards a country more congenial to genius, freedom—in a word, to a happier man. The poet's attitude to the world was undergoing a significant change.

Now, when he had traversed one of that world's paths from end to end, when his monarch had disappointed his hopes, when he was conscious that without supreme authority he could not alone achieve the right—*now* the old sense of a vocation possessed his mind. At thirty-two, when a chapter in a novel satisfied him, he told himself quite naïvely, as though it were a new discovery: "In reality, I am a born writer!"

In bitter-sweet words he at this time imparted to his friend Knebel the essential reasons for, and results of, his dual mode of life.

The Duke lives only for hunting and shooting. . . . The Duchess has settled down, she leads her Court-life—I seldom see either of them. And so I have begun to live for myself again, and know what I am made of. The illusion that those germs of nobility possessed by both my friends could be ripened in this soil, and that celestial gems could be included in this Prince's earthly crown, has quite abandoned me; and I feel happier than I have felt since I was a young man. When I lived at home I never allowed myself to confuse intellectual vision with juristic routine, and I now make a similar distinction between the Councillor and my other self, who is by no means essential to a Councillor's success. Only I do secretly keep faith with myself in the inmost conception of all my plans and intuitions and undertakings, and in this way establish a hidden relation between my social, political, moral and poetical existences—fasten them together with a knot that no one perceives.

The secret conflict between dæmon and genius took this form in the years we are now considering; and the masterpiece of this period inevitably touched upon that conflict. So long ago as his thirty-first year—when he was constraining himself to a life of action remote from all poetry—he had, a year after *Iphigenie,* conceived the idea for *Tasso;* but in obedience to his chosen attitude, had never put a finger to the work. At the beginning of this new period he returned to it, wrote an act in the autumn, began the second at the time of his friend's final surrender, and finished it shortly before his thirty-second birth-

GOETHE AT THE AGE OF THIRTY-EIGHT

day. Then he broke off, and not for six years was the work resumed, remodelled, and finished.

When in later years a Frenchman remarked that *Tasso* was an elevated *Werther*, the comment pleased Goethe; and indeed this work is a document for the Goethe of thirty-two who conceived and began it, rather than for the older man who concluded it.

The play is wholly concerned with the Goethe of that phase—who was then erecting his image of Terminus, who now, in his Antonio's cautious moderation, ironises the enthusiastically toiling poet, and who all through is subject to his Prince's caprice. And if he did exaggerate his susceptibility in *Tasso*, it was not its intensity, but its duration, which he exaggerated.

Five years before he broke through its meshes, Goethe had recognised the net of entangling self-deceptions—noble though they were—in *Tasso;* and so once more in his character of poet, Goethe saw his life before he enacted it.

But we must not extend the analogy too far. The play contains no compliments to Weimar or the Duke; and all his intimate confessions of that period would lead us to expect this. It was not the Court of Weimar to which the poet gratefully referred in his picture of Ferrara—but the Court of Weimar as the poet would have had it. The Duke of Ferrara displays no single trait of kinship with Carl August, for Alfonso is zealous and moderate-minded, mature and good-humoured.

The two women are more certainly drawn from life; and as in the Sanvitale we can recognise the Countess Werther, though the slight sketch of her in Goethe's letters is all we have, so in the Princess he undoubtedly gives us an idealised portrait of his mistress. Charlotte's mature melancholy speaks here:

> Es gibt ein Glück, allein wir kennen's nicht:
> Wir kennen's wohl, und wissen's nicht zu schätzen.[1]

And here is her soulful yearning for her friend:

> Wie mehrte sich im Umgang das Verlangen
> Sich mehr zu kennen, mehr sich zu versteh'n!

[1] "There is a joy, but we may know it not:
Or else we know, and know not how to prize it."

Und täglich stimmte das Gemüt sich schöner
Zu immer reinern Harmonien auf. . . .
Ihn musst' ich lieben, weil mit ihm mein Leben
Zum Leben ward, wie ich es nie gekannt.[1]

But here too is Charlotte's determination to be alone in the possession of him; and when Eleonore says of Tasso "*Was ich besitze, mag ich gern bewahren,*"[2] they are almost literally the words of the one little note of hers which has come down to us. And here, again, is her poignant uncertainty, the tearful complaint of the woman who is growing old:

Wir sind vor keinem Männerherzen sicher,
Das noch so warm sich einmal uns ergab.
Die Schönheit ist vergänglich . . .
Wenn's Männer gäbe, die ein weiblich Herz
Zu schätzen wüssten, die erkennen möchten,
Welch einen holden Schatz von Treu und Liebe
Der Busen einer Frau bewahren kann. . . .[3]

And finally, in the second act of *Tasso*, Frau von Stein's elusive treatment of Goethe brings on the crisis—he reproduces the dangerous way in which his transcendental friend had allured him spiritually, only to repulse him physically. When Tasso ventures on a vehemently passionate declaration, the Princess does not interrupt him, considerately repressing his outburst, but encourages and incites him all the more.

Yet at the height of these allurements (which are clearly to be divined from Goethe's letters to his friend) she is dexterous enough to make use of her position as the cool-headed woman of the world, doubly protected by her rank; and the man whom she has been leading on so subtly is shown his place in these insufferably priggish words:

[1] "With intercourse the yearning still grew stronger,
Better to know, yet more to understand!
And daily was the spirit stirred to fairer
And ever purer harmonies of thought. . . .
Him I must love, for life with him beside me
Became such life as I had never known."

[2] "What I possess, I fain would keep for ever."

[3] "Of no man's heart can we be ever certain,
Though warmly once it beat upon our own.

Nicht weiter, Tasso! Viele Dinge sind's,
Die wir mit Heftigkeit ergreifen sollen:
Doch andre können nur mit Mässigung
Und durch Entbehren, unser eigen werden.
So sagt man, sei die Tugend, sei die Liebe,
Die ihr verwandt ist. Das bedenke wohl![1]

So speaking, she turns her back on him, and with a final half-promise that he may possibly win her by long devotion, leaves him alone with the flaming passion she has excited in him! Can we wonder that Tasso, in his wounded pride and his distraction, falls in with Antonio? Or wonder that Goethe should have written those clamorous, despairing letters?

Encouraged by allurements of this kind, the poet very guilelessly pursues the Princess with his love. The visible catastrophe with which the play concludes is the natural consequence of this early scene of spiritual temptation.

When Goethe wrote this last scene, he had long escaped from the experience which inspired it. Before the first was written, she had yielded to him; and a poet appeased turned the previous unrest into song.

For a blissful tranquillity was the fruit of his friend's surrender, so that the succeeding two years—from thirty-three to thirty-five—were the quiet zenith of their affection. These were the real love-years; and though tempestuous adoration seemed quickly to abate after the crisis, Goethe never ceased to woo and serve her, even after he had possessed her.

Exactly a year after they had once for all established their relation, he wrote:

All loveliness is fleeting. . . .
If men there were, by whom a woman's heart
Were truly prized, who could in some sort measure
The wondrous wealth of constant fond devotion
A woman's breast can hold for him she loves. . . ."

[1] "No farther, Tasso! Many things there are
That we may seize with avid, hasty fingers;
But others we may only make our own
By gentle steadfastness and resignation.
Such, we are told, is virtue, such affection
Sister to virtue. So bethink thee well!"

All my life I have had an ideal of how I should like to be loved, and have sought it vainly in illusive dreams. And now that the world grows brighter for me every day, I find it at last in you, and so that I can never lose it.

For some two years this spiritual surrender was continually interwoven with erotic suggestions. Here are some verses which he wrote his mistress at that time:

Einen wohlgeschnitzten vollen Becher
Hielt ich drückend in den beiden Händen.[1]

But Amor appears to the drinker, and promises a more beautiful cup with different nectar, and:

O wie freundlich hat er Wort gehalten,
Da er, Lida, dich mit sanfter Neigung
Mir, dem lange Sehnenden, geeignet!
Wenn ich deinen lieben Leib umfasse,
Und von deinen einzig treuen Lippen
Langbewahrter Liebe Balsam koste,
Selig sprech' ich dann zu meinem Geiste:
Nein, ein solch Gefäss hat ausser Armor
Nie ein Gott gebildet noch besessen. . . .[2]

Between these verses (which Goethe conveyed to Frau von Stein in the graceful anonymity of a manuscript Court-journal, but had told her of beforehand) and the great Ode about their union in a former existence, lie five years of an unhealthily indefinite relation, scarcely balanced by a tardy union. Towards the prototype of Iphigenia and Eleonore the playful flatteries of a youthful husband were out of tune. This can hardly have escaped the delicate susceptibilities of both lovers, and may serve to explain much of the ensuing friction.

The more intimate their relation, the more heedfully did Frau von Stein preserve decorum—at that time for her children's sake, but possibly with an eye to posterity also.

[1] "Finely wrought and brimming was the chalice
Held between my hands with clasping fingers."

[2] "Oh, he kept his promise, and how richly,
Lida, when he moved thy heart to love me—
Giving thee to one who long had languished!

But though she so sedulously covered her tracks in an intercourse which, natural as it was, her soul persistently regarded as derogatory, she did not shrink from sending her friend suggestive keepsakes—for what other interpretation can we put upon the gift which, when Goethe opened it, so amazed him that he begged her "not to make him love her more every day by the delicious things she did, for since the time of Deianira no more inflammatory garment had been given to a lover"? He had shut it away in his despatch-case, otherwise it "would have burnt me up." And this was not sent or acknowledged from a distance—they were both in Weimar.

Whatever appearances may have been, theirs was nothing less than a marriage—except that she remained the wife of von Stein, Master of the Horse. Everything that Goethe was interested in, he shared with her; there were long evenings when the other members of her household were at the theatre, and the pair would go on imaginary journeys with the aid of books and atlases—though occasionally they would play whist with her friends.

Frau von Stein gave a luncheon-party for the Duchess in Goethe's summer-villa; she received his guests at the town-house, as if to emphasise their purely fraternal relations by such public displays. But when she did not wish to give her name on her visits to him, she would come in by the back-door of the garden, or stop her carriage near the bridge. When he was away from home, he would send her the key of his writing-table. He lent her money for her mother; he ordered boots for herself and sent her a chemise. His letters grew more and more frequent.

He looked after her children as if he were their father, fetched doctor and nurse for her ailing son; but the youngest, Fritz, he took to live with him altogether when the boy grew older, so as to relieve his friend's frequently overburdened household of one anxiety. The clever little boy was like a keepsake from her

---

When I clasp thy dear, thy worshipped body
And from thy fond lips, the dedicated,
Drink the love for mine devoutly treasured,
Rapturous, I commune with my spirit,
Saying: Of the gods none else but Amor
Ever shaped or owned so rare a chalice!"

when she was away. Goethe would show him English engravings, teach him the new Latin script, instil his own ideas about the progress of culture; and once he sent him to Frau Goethe at Frankfurt, where he saw the first air-balloon. How "thoroughly parental" Goethe's feeling was for him is evidenced by his proposal to his friend Jacobi that the latter should bring up his daughter to be the wife of this adopted son.

These strongly-developed domestic instincts had been perceptible in Goethe, even as the student who liked to have everything in order, and so often included the entire household in his love for a girl. His first impulse was always towards marriage; it was only on second thoughts that he fought shy of it.

With their intimacy Charlotte's jealousy increased. If hitherto it had been no more than the wayward determination to keep him to herself, not unnatural in one whose intimates were so few and whose temperament was so melancholy, it now, with the ultimate surrender, became a point of honour that no other woman should be suffered to dispute him. Corona, whom he invited to Weimar when he was versifying *Iphigenie*, was obliged to leave at once; whenever he went to visit her he had to apologise to Charlotte, and assure her it meant nothing.

Her jealousy even included his men-friends, his acquaintances. "Knebel," writes Goethe, "has been such a kind good fellow that, if you will allow me, I will paint him one of those flower-pots." And after a festival performance on his birthday: "If possible, let me thoroughly enjoy the pleasure of all these people's good-will."

From the fourth year onward—the ninth of their love—Goethe's declarations diminish; not in number, it is true, but in variety, in convincingness. Sometimes he seems to get tired of his favourite turns of phrase, and this is nowhere more evident than in the letters written in French, which he sent her when in France on a political mission.

It was then that he found the just word for the whole situation; and vainly did he seek to soften down its penetrating insight by a tender corollary: "*Non, mon amour pour toi n'est plus une passion; c'est une maladie qui m'est plus chère que la santé la plus parfaite et dont je ne veux pas guérir.*"

Very gradually had this sense of "a malady" grown upon

Goethe, and it was to take him two further years before he could cut loose from this and all other distempers—and then, free at last, could frankly exclaim that he had shaken off a mortal disease. In these concluding years of their relation his desire for solitude grew stronger and stronger; and in the New Year of the last he puts it all into this strangely ambiguous phrase: "Be still my own, even though we are less together than of old, which is frequently almost more than I can stand." About this time Frau von Stein was entering on her forty-fifth year.

From the early Weimar period there were now, in reality, only two friends left—Knebel and Herder.

At this time, when Knebel left the Court and went to Jena, there to do research work and immerse himself in Hellenism—in short, to become something of an oddity—Goethe's heart went out to him still more, and he wrote him his most intimate imaginings.

Herder was a stiffer proposition, but with him too this period of research drew the bond closer. Herder was conscious that his mind rather than his heart attracted him anew towards Goethe. This great researcher and thinker was encouraged in his cosmic interests by seeing Goethe—the greatest man in his circle—investigating and thinking more enthusiastically even than of yore. Goethe (so Herder said at that time) was on the right track in physics; fortune favoured his efforts, head and heart always guided him aright, and at every step he took he proved himself a man. In the most insignificant matters, and even those he most abhorred, he steadily worked on as though it were the only thing that mattered, and the one he thought most special to himself. This is a very unexpected tribute—something new from Herder.

How distant seem the perils of his youth! "Do write to me again about yourself," he begs that Countess Stolberg to whom he had once opened his heart, "and—if you will—let us knit up the old threads."

From Lavater Goethe had resolutely withdrawn. Even his friend's self-knowledge had lost its suggestive power; he could see nothing but the advocate, in and out of season, of Christ, and was so sick of the subject of the worthy Jesus that anyhow I would rather hear about it from someone else. . . . I am losing sight of the Lavater . . . whom I know well and love; I can see only the sharp outlines of his flaming sword of speech, and for the moment I feel that I can't stand it.

But he was ready to acknowledge himself in the wrong to his quondam friend: "Breathe into me the balm of kindliness, and banish my sense of estrangement. Estrangement blows from the four corners of the world, and the spirit of love and friendship from only one." But it was too late.

In financial and private matters, but also in those of geology and osteology, Goethe turned more and more frequently to Merck, and got from him what he needed. But when the Duke thought of asking him to Weimar, Goethe advised against it, giving as his reason that it was better not to transplant old trees.

His mother was more than ever a mere idea to Goethe. After the death of his father, who became weak-minded before the end, her spirits revived; but the son's letters grew rarer and less affectionate. "Take good care of yourself and love me." Cold, haughty, distant.

And in this narrow circle was there anyone really to sympathise with and understand Goethe's works, his apparently halting literary development? He who was always the giver was given but little when he longed for encouragement and sympathy. Charlotte and Knebel were in these years as before his best audience. Wieland's critical ear was attentive, but his sage lips rarely gave judgment. The Duke could but seldom be induced to listen. Lavater, to whom nearly everything was sent in manuscript, would (amid the maze of his letters—between corrections, Christ, visits, and freemasonry) devote perhaps three lines to *Iphigenie*. About *Tasso* he wrote, two years after receiving it, exactly two lines.

As he had published hardly anything in these seven years, Goethe's fame was decreasing; he wore it, on occasions, as he might have worn an Order.

And so loneliness, still more pronounced than of old, was Goethe's fate in this period of apparently excessive worldly ambition. He did not always seek it. On his official missions he had begun to study the cosmos from a fresh angle, and systematically sought society, trying to get from everyone what at some time he might come to need. He was never in quest of gaiety or relaxation. To observe and record was his dual mission as author and man of the world; he deduced the larger sphere from the smaller.

And indeed the small portion of the world accessible to him was narrowing still more. It was now limited to a couple of Thuringian Duchies; even the Court of Brunswick seemed like a foreign country, while Berlin and Leipzig were so rarely visited as to represent distant centres of civilisation. Out of such limitations the mind makes its own universe.

He was not moved by international events. Even Voltaire's Reminiscences of Frederick the Great, which he read in manuscript, at the most amused him; Frederick himself he regarded as a mere historical personage. Goethe's friends considered that he ought to reply to Frederick's attacks on him; he did think of doing so, and a fragment has been lost. But he was too broad-minded to have persevered in the task.

Goethe stood yet more aloof from the lower classes than from such illustrious persons as these; though his rare contacts with them, now and in the early years at Weimar, left a profound impression. But those who look to find contemptuous allusions (such as he heaped upon Court and nobility) to the people in Goethe's writings of this decade will be disappointed. Of all that he did to help needy young men who, socially or intellectually speaking, came from the underworld, we have only an incomplete record.

That Goethe should take the Conservative side in German politics was a natural consequence of his general sense of order and civilisation; and he who as a youth, in the period of his heaven-defying Prometheus, wrote in favour of upholding the Constitution and against any change in it, was as a Minister constrained to do the same for public and still more for private reasons. For it was his very official activities themselves which led him to make a complete severance between a narrowly-bounded Duchy and the unbounded realm of intellect.

On the other hand, Goethe's social work was extremely democratic in tendency, much more so than that of any other German of his time. His treatment of the land-question preserved to the farmer what it wrested from the feudal nobleman—his general trend towards limitation urged him to that course. It was Goethe who led the way in partitioning the Crown Lands, so as to provide sustenance for the poor and the half-poor. The age, which was one of parliamentary and feudal transition, was propitious to his aims.

In that century an official rarely came into direct contact with the people; but on his journeys Goethe sought them out.

> How greatly again . . . my liking goes out to the so-called lower classes, who are perhaps the highest in God's sight! In them all the virtues are combined—austerity, contentment, straight-thinking, loyalty, pleasure in the least good-fortune, guilelessness, endurance—endurance unto the end. . . ."

When, in his last year of office, he sent for a bookbinder to bind part of a novel, and the man, while working, told him about his life and its conditions, the poet listened as he watched *Wilhelm Meister* being put together by those toilworn hands. "Every word he said was worth its weight in gold, and nothing but a dozen or so of Lavater's pleonasms could give you any idea of the reverence I felt for the man."

When writing orders to his servant-man, he would use no form of address. But once the villa was cleared of the Princes, master and man would collogue over the kitchen-fire. In the early days they sometimes had to share a room when travelling, and then Goethe would have long arguments with him as to whether a nation were happier in subjection or in liberty.

Goethe did not, as of yore, turn to Nature that he might find himself. He was less interested in himself, indeed, than in Nature as Nature, and that not as landscape but as record. Nothing was more irksome to him in the years of his abnormal self-discipline than the indoor life he would impose on himself for weeks at a time. There is barely a mention of swimming, riding, or skating; his giving-up his house and garden was in that sense symbolic. And when in his *Ilmenau*, he gazes at the hills, it is as though his lips, long spellbound, had at last been opened.

> O lass mich heut an deinen sachten Höhn
> Ein jugendlich, ein neues Eden sehn!

Ich hab' es wohl auch mit um euch verdienet:
Ich sorge still, indes ihr ruhig grünet.[1]

A victim of duty, he had forgotten how to roam. What a transformation—the vagrant turned into a man of action!

Sociabilities dwindled to nothing. Every week he gave a general invitation to tea at his new house, and even of that he would say, "My tea-party gives me the shivers." Otherwise he saw hardly anyone at home. Even music was rarely heard within his doors, though in the early years he had been a patient auditor of the Duchess's compositions, and would play on Wieland's spinet himself. And he had given up acting altogether.

By this time he had quite abandoned the idea of making Weimar a centre of German culture—in any respect, one might say. He was not in the right frame of mind, the Duke did not understand, the Court was too poor. He often fled to Jena, there to work in peace; and while at Weimar there were thirty rooms in his house, he had to arrange these visits to Jena so that he arrived on a Sunday, for his room was close to a concert-hall and he could only stay a week before the Sunday music drove him away.

For his genius always urged him, when tempted into the larger world, back into the cell of contemplation—which alone is the *cella dei*, even though it be next door to a concert-hall.

And it was now too that he invoked the spirit of Truth:

Ach, da ich irrte, hatt' ich viel Gespielen,
Da ich dich kenne, bin ich fast allein:
Ich muss mein Glück nur mit mir selbst geniessen,
Dein holdes Licht verdecken und verschliessen.[2]

In such isolation he had sudden flashes of insight, revealing all the antagonism between the world and any earnest effort—the discord which precluded the harmony he sought. Then bitterness

[1] "To-day, O let me on thy gentle heights,
New-born, behold an Eden of delights!
I too have earned it, patient care bestowing,
While green thy branches tranquilly were growing."

[2] "Ah, while I strayed, how many were my playmates!
Now I possess thee, solitude I seek:
Joy such as mine is not for others' knowing,
Shielded thy light, too fair for outward showing."

and dissatisfaction would overflood his spirit; and at the very moment when he undertook the Presidency of the Chamber, he was driven to confess to Charlotte: "I was intended to be a private person, and I cannot understand what made Destiny want to involve me with a Constitution and a Princely house."

Socially he became more and more of an eccentric in these years. When he was thirty-five, he arrived at a party in the Steins' house when dinner was nearly over, and was silent and terribly forbidding in manner. At Court, sitting beside a lady, he once began to talk audibly to himself, till she turned a freezing countenance upon him and asked, "What are you counting?"

As Goethe grew more dissatisfied, he grew more haggard too. Klauer's busts, as well as the letters of friends, testify to the profoundly introspective expression of his face, the furrowed brow which a visitor said denoted subtlety and guile rather than suavity. Knebel records that on a walk Goethe, who had appeared quite happy, suddenly begged him not to smoke because it made him feel so feverish. His friend was surprised at this nervous irritation; but Goethe's discomfort increased every moment, he had an attack of shivering, and became so ill that he had to take to his bed. Knebel, however, observed "how Goethe's nature enables him to hold out to the last moment without any sign of a change; and then in the twinkling of an eye he will utterly collapse for a mere nothing. This in all sorts of ways."

This remark, appended by Knebel to his general observation of Goethe, is valuable as a clue to the way Goethe's psychic cataclysms would assert themselves and come to a head.

At last, in his thirty-seventh year, one of these cataclysms arrived, brought on by the seven years of self-discipline and the feelings which had oppressed him for a decade. In this, too, he held on to the last moment, apparently unchanged, only to break out with a suddenness which was not really suddenness at all. An eruption like this would seem to signify complete annihilation of that spiritual tranquillity for which he had striven through so long a period. What was left of it? When at this point we seek to obtain an insight into Goethe's soul, does not our analysis of him at twenty-five seem to be scattered to the winds? What had he been striving for, through those twelve years of ceaseless effort?

For purity and harmony. Trusting, seeking, working, he had sought for these; and trusting, seeking, working, he had gained some steps. The confident faith which was in him could not be shattered in the decade of his probation; and if its growth was not upward, it took but the deeper root for that.

For a while Goethe tried to believe in an abstract good, without forms or ceremonies. From thirty to about thirty-three—and at no other time in his life—he taught himself an ideal of abstract morality; and though the rarefied atmosphere of *Iphigenie* is sufficiently disturbed by the tempest in the soul of Orestes, Goethe afterwards said that the work was "diabolically humanistic." How much more so were the few poems of that period, which are wholly intellectual! Cold and unreal, something like the fragmentary *Geheimnisse, Das Göttliche* raises its head among Goethe's verses; and because it is easier to understand than a thousand characteristic poems by which he contradicted these frigid verses, it has done more than any other lyric to obscure the general view of the poet.

Edel sei der Mensch,
Hilfreich und gut!
Denn das allein
Unterscheidet ihn
Von allen Wesen
Die wir kennen.[1]

No—that is merely the creed born of Frau von Stein's experience; and because it is not his own conviction, the form is hopelessly inelastic. The man who at the same period declared that he was "good and bad—like Nature," could not be reduced to that magniloquent formula.

He eagerly defended the cause of his beloved Nature against philosophy. He himself sought the divine in plants and stones;

[1] "Noble man should be,
Helpful and kind!
For this alone
Doth distinguish him
From every creature
Known to science."

for though Jacobi had been cursed by God with a love for metaphysics, God had

> on the contrary blessed me with a love for physics, so that the contemplation of his works always does me good. . . . If you say that we can do no more than believe in God, I say that we can see him.

But in conjuction with this radiant vision of externals, of terrestrial things, there persisted now as twelve years earlier that internal brooding gaze, which like the moon drew every cosmic image of eye and mind back to the vastness of the soul.

Thus his mysticism tended at first to increase rather than to diminish as a result of his scientific work. He perpetually invokes the name of Swedenborg; and the sense of another world became in this anti-Christian and anti-philosopher something amounting to a certainty, when he would grant it free scope. Goethe derided a new book on spiritism, calling it charlatanry; but:

> No one is more inclined than I am to believe in another world besides the visible one; and I have imagination and vitality enough to feel that even my own limited ego can embrace a Swedenborgian conception of the spirit-sphere.

The man who pored upon infusoria and fragments of bone under his microscope was averse from any rationalist explanation of the macrocosm, and even shunned astronomy, of whose tremendous clockwork he had only the dimmest sort of an inkling.

At this time he was constructing, from his belief in a Beyond, a corresponding belief in a metempsychosis; but this was very vague, and belonged to the poetic side of him. Henceforth he more frequently speaks of death as a friend, and there are casual sentences in his letters pointing to that which he was later to embody in mystic song. "What a good thing it is that mortals die, if only to shake off the stamp of mortality and come back refreshed as by a bath!"

More than ever did he feel himself the creature of destiny. When he was sorting his papers, he stood in amazement before his past existence, and "less than ever understood" what he was and what he was meant to be. And writing to Knebel, he suddenly wound up with: "Farewell, and pray for me!"

For the clash of the internal discords was more alarming than he had ever before felt it, in this period of inward striving toward harmony. What he attained was no spontaneous coalescence of his powers—it was only a way out from his chosen renunciation! He said at this time that he permitted himself no longings for any good that Destiny denied or had bereaved him of. He shut himself away from his fellows, refused to leave home because he wanted to avoid new ideas—and at the end of it all, this was the best thing Truth had to say to him:

> Wieviel bist du von Andern unterschieden?
> Erkenne dich, leb mit der Welt in Frieden![1]

Does this represent the catchword of a premature harmony, the fruit of those many years of sacrifice and effort? No—the elemental battle was still raging unappeased in that turbulent spirit.

In addition to *Egmont,* where in the scene with the Prince of Orange the balance sways between worldly wisdom and freedom, *Tasso* gives us a vivid exposition of his dual personality. The work belongs to this decade, and has its analogue in the original draft of *Faust.* Amid all the speeches which betray the essential difference between Tasso and Antonio, there is one which summarises them all, and gives a clear idea of the superhuman drama which was still going on in Goethe's soul. All our sympathy goes to the poet who makes one half of himself say of the other: "He possesses, I might say, everything that I lack."

And is either of them proved right in the end? Exactly as in the first *Faust,* the poet's soul is so artfully divided between the two scales that the balance never swings true until the propitious moment arrives—the moment which Goethe himself so rarely seized.

It was not only the worldling and the poet who contended in Goethe's soul, but the old dæmons also—now exorcised by

[1] "Whereby art thou distinguished from thy brothers?
Know thyself, then, and live at peace with others!"

courtly ritual, though ten years before they had gnashed their teeth at one another in the curt cynical rhymes of the first *Faust*. Neither obtained the smallest advantage; and the insoluble psychic problem would have been no less insoluble in actual life if the antagonists had not realised that they were obliged to live together. It is the authentic Goethe who at the conclusion of the first draft of *Tasso* draws his dagger upon the other Goethe, and cries to his inseparable antagonist:

> Zieh oder folge, wenn ich nicht auf ewig,
> Wie ich dich hasse, dich verachten soll![1]

Throughout all these years Knebel was the one who understood him best, as these words are enough to show:

> I am well aware that he is not always agreeable company; there are traits to dislike in him. . . . But taken as a whole the man is as good as can be. . . . I insist that he sees aright, that his outlook is clear and fine. He is bound to be misunderstood, and he seems to find that state his native atmosphere. He is most attracted by the beauty which shows as from under a mask. He himself is an extraordinary mixture—or a being compounded of hero and histrion, but the former prevails. . . . He sees that things which one had imagined to be settled now will not be so for years, and other things he as it were wrests from the distant future. . . . His wings are at present pinioned by inexorable fate.

The mighty eagle, self-condemned to captivity, seemed now all suddenly to spread, to lift, those broad Fate-pinioned wings—suddenly, that is, for those around him, even those who knew him best; but not suddenly for posterity, envisaging the documents of this last year.

For now, in his thirty-seventh year, his pace—on every one of the various instruments he was playing—gained in velocity. The things that oppressed him oppressed him more, piled up as it were into a tower; and the things he enjoyed seemed more greatly to excite him. Aloofness, taciturnity, melancholy themselves reached such a height that he wished he could either rend

[1] "Draw or obey, if I am not for ever,
Even as I hate thee, to despise thee too!"

his bonds or go under once for all. Here are Goethe's enterprises in the last summer of his Ministerial life:—

An energetic campaign against a revolt of students in Jena. Spasmodic study of algebra. Observation of the passage of Mercury through the sun. Draft of six new parts of *Wilhelm Meister*. All his love-poems classed under general headings—for purposes of mystification—in a collected edition of his works. Re-modelling of *Werther*, in the course of which he came to the conclusion that the author would have done better to blow out his brains after he had finished writing it. Microscopic study of infusoria.

> The botanical kingdom has got possession of my brain once more—I can't lose sight of it for a moment. It forces itself on my attention, the whole thing—I don't have to *think* about it any more, it all comes to me naturally, and the tremendous business seems to be simplifying itself in my soul. . . . If I had time in this short life of ours, I should venture on a general investigation of Nature—of her entire kingdom.

Meanwhile, for months he had been planning out every detail of his flight.

Flight was the only resource by which Goethe's temperament, after it had held out to the last moment, could break free from all the cunningly-contrived encampments and intrenchments. Five years earlier he had once despairingly confessed to Charlotte that his evil genius depraved him when he was away; "it points out the most troublesome aspects of my present situation, and advises me to save myself by flight."

True, Goethe was not desirous only of leisure and quiet—he wanted a warm climate and some social life as well. In the summer before this, when he was thirty-five, he had for the first time spent a few weeks in a gay, animated, ever-changing society, and that as part of it—not as a celebrity passing through; and he said afterwards that he "owed a perfectly new existence" to Carlsbad. Now Italy was the one magnet for the wearied man. Twice he had gazed southward from the Gothard Pass, and twice turned away. It was the lode-star of his intellectual life; but to consummate that life he must see, must tread, that soil.

Yet he was still more irresistibly attracted by the freedom which—he felt beforehand—would be in the very air of the

South. Greece would have done as well, perhaps, for other reasons—he could have pursued his science there. But in his scheme of life, drawn up in the past year, he had written: "Trip to Italy decided on"; and now he was all regret that he did not speak and understand Italian as he did "that unhappy German." To visitors he said that it was a pity the Germans were not more temperamental. Take it for all in all, it was for the clearer southern atmosphere that Goethe inevitably yearned at the end of his thirties.

He intended to take the plunge from Carlsbad. No one was in the secret. His master and friend, his mistress and lover, the companions of this eventful decade, were only told that he would follow them to Carlsbad, and thence go on elsewhere.

So aloof was Goethe.

For in truth he was consciously putting an end to an epoch of his life, was fleeing from that mistress, from the office and duties of that Duchy, because he felt that he was at the breaking-point—only it was a more terrible, a more irreparable collapse than that of the afternoon when he had begged Knebel to stop smoking. In very truth he was determined to have liberty, poetry, warmth—rejuvenescence.

All was ready.

The President of the Chamber, Herr von Goethe, had applied to the Duke for leave of absence. When at the end of August he remained in Carlsbad after Carl August and Frau von Stein had left it, he put on speed and worked eagerly at getting the first volumes of his collected edition ready for the press. He read a good deal to his friends, and got very uneasy when his thirty-seventh birthday came and went, for it was to have been the day of days—the day of departure, the beginning of the new era. His last letters from Carlsbad grow more and more feverish and overcharged, like the chapters in a novel which lead to a new development of the story.

His mistress had of late been captious again, but they seem to have reconciled their differences. Nevertheless when she left he can only have given her a hint of his plans:

Then I shall live at large with you (which means, without you); and in blissful solitude, incognito, a nobody, shall draw near to the bosom of earth. . . . Hitherto I have endured many things in silence, and have had no dearer wish than that our relation might so re-establish itself that nothing on earth could endanger it. Otherwise I prefer not to live near you, and would rather remain in the solitude to which I am now departing.

That is the tone of a man who intends to retrieve his liberty at last. It is more resolute than ever before—this is an ultimatum. Where he is going and for how long he does not tell his mistress; at the end of September he will let her have his address.

His friends at Carlsbad were not to know that he was off next day. He grew more and more secretive, his excitement waxed daily, the last postscripts are exactly like those in *Werther:*

Eleven at night. At last, at last I am ready, and yet not ready, for really I had a week's more work here; but I intend to go, and even to you this is adieu once more. Farewell, sweetheart! I am thine. G.

Once more all the tenderness in his soul is brought into play, so as to console her for the days that are to come.

But he was imperturbable and resolute. He passed in review the past and the future of his actual position, as if to justify himself to himself. Then, the day before he was to depart under a name that none of them was to know, he could composedly write these arresting words to his master:

Forgive me for having spoken so vaguely of my plans and probable stay abroad, when we said goodbye. . . . You are happy; you are about to gratify your dearest ambition. Your domestic affairs are in order, and promise well; and I know you will now permit me to consider myself.

Generally speaking (he went on) he could now be dispensed with; he had arranged his private affairs so that even if he were to die there would be no trouble. He begged for an indefinite leave of absence, so that he might live at large for a while, restore the tone of his mind, and have leisure for the publication of his works.

All this and many attendant circumstances urge and compel me to lose myself in quarters of the world where I am entirely unknown. . . . Fare-you-well, it is my heartfelt desire; remember me kindly. . . .

May you be fortunate in all your undertakings, and rejoice in their happy issue.

After this cold formula comes a postscript:

His deputy on the War-Commission had hitherto dealt only with pressing matters; but now he was to look after everything. "Seeger has precise knowledge of all these matters, and Schmidt likes the work." This was his last word—conscientious in the most trifling details.

Then for the fifth time Goethe fled from a woman—but this time from a burdensome form of existence as well. Only his servant Philipp had his pseudonymous address. It was:—

"A. M. Jean Philippe Möller, Rome."

PART II
THE EARTH-SPIRIT

"First my errors made me objectionable to others, then my serious aims. So do what I would, I was alone."

CHAPTER VII

LIBERTY

"When you think of me, let it be as of a happy man."

IN the window of a large cool room stands a half-dressed young man, with slippers on his feet, for the floor is tiled and the Northerner in the South feels it rather chilly. True, it is spring-like out of doors, and girls look laughingly up to the window, whose one shutter he has only half-opened. Is he a foreigner? His eyes are large and dark enough for him to have opened them first here—here in Rome; but his nose. . . . Most likely he is only a poor German painter. One would think so from the way he stares—as if he would like one to sit for him. And while the girls speculate about the foreigner at the window, instead of flirting with him, he only stares the harder and seems to be taking stock of everything—their complexions and profiles, the way they walk and carry their arms, the colours of their aprons and the shapes of their caps; but is simultaneously observing a rearing horse in a wine-cart, together with the shape of the wine-barrels and the appearance of the driver. Nor does he fail to notice that the wind is blowing from the Porta del Popolo today, as it has not on the last few days, and he asks himself why.

As he thoughtfully turns back into the room, he casts a fondly-scrutinising glance on the little pots in which he has planted seeds and kernels, and on the tiny date-palm that he hopes to rear. For the hundredth time he deeply studies the position, length, and arrangement of the leaves—they puzzle him. Then he goes over to the opposite wall, to see how yesterday's sketch on the Via Appia looks this morning—is there any sense in going on with it? It is all right, but there's no stamp on the work. How is it that all Tischbein's sketches, across the room, have a stamp of their own? . . . To work!

And he sighs a little, and thinks he had better go back into his own small apartment, where *Egmont* awaits him. An hour every morning is devoted to *Egmont*, for it is better to get to work before his friends are up—otherwise they'll start an endless argument. The things Moritz says against Michael Angelo! Certainly, these fellows . . .

He halts on the threshold. So high that her conventionally-treated hair touches the dimly painted ceiling, there stands on a pedestal a plaster-mask of that Juno who is as inscrutable "as a song of Homer's." He gazes long and silently into her watchful eyes. Then he turns to her sleeping neighbour, Medusa, who seems to hover between death and voluptuous ecstasy. But oh, where is the colour of the marble?

When finally he sits down to the sallow pages of *Egmont* (covered ten years ago by his swift clear youthful handwriting), when he takes up the latest of them, written in the first Weimar years . . . all of a sudden he is in his attic-room at home, then in the green little study of his summer-villa in the Park at Weimar . . . and his whole existence, unguided, somnambulistic, and yet advancing with so sure a step, comes over him like a thing imagined, a passage from *Wilhelm Meister*. And he takes a firmer grip of these old pages which he is now to remodel and furnish with a new ending—the faithful mute companions of his path, the only things which prove that all he has been recalling is no dream.

Is this room really on the Corso at Rome? Is it the Roman sunlight which illumines the page before him? And when he goes out, will he only have to turn to the right and in a quarter-of-an-hour be gazing from the Capitol? Yet here he sits as of old, nailed to his chair, inventing, writing—because Göschen in Leipzig wants to set up his fourth volume, and Herder in Weimar will soon be wanting the copy for correction.

Weimar! How far away it seems, it and his mistress and his friend! After all, doesn't everyone think first of himself? Is not Charlotte more deeply possessed by pride and jealousy than by love and friendship? Is not the Duke much fonder of his war-game than of his friend's æsthetics? "I am cured of a mortal disease. . . . If I had not made up my mind to do what I am doing now, I should simply have gone to the dogs and become incapable of anything whatever." Liberty! Is it only liberty

GOETHE AT THE AGE OF FORTY

that he is enjoying in Rome? And is it really enjoyment—this feeling which possesses him?

Since his flight from Carlsbad on that September morning, Goethe had rushed to Rome, rather than merely travelled thither. Fifty-six days ago, and the mere getting there took sixteen. Still, half of Northern, and a good deal of Central, Italy had been seen. Some prescience had urged him irresistibly, some compulsion had driven him onward—as though the long dreamed-of goal might yet elude him. Here is Goethe on his first Transalpine day:

> I believe in God again! [he exclaimed in the Trentino]. I feel as though I had been born and brought up here, and had come back from a trip to Greenland, from whale-fishing. Everything smiles on me. . . . If this were read by someone who lives in the South, belongs to the South, he would think me very childish. Ah, what I am writing now, I have long known; all the time. . . . I was pining under a gloomy sky, and now I like to feel that this delight is one of those rare occasions for which one should be eternally grateful to beneficent Nature.

So does a long-banished exile feel, returning to his home. These are Goethe's first words in Italy—he seems to be returning to the land that he has never seen before. He stands incredulous as a prisoner released—and yet he had been twice in Switzerland—before the blue and white peaks of the Brenner Pass. Everything sad was disappearing in the North—the clouds and mists which happened that day to be drifting northward, were in his view carrying, as they had always carried, darkness and cold to his native land.

Travelling incognito was like being a boy again—it was delightful to eat pears and apples in the street, to talk to the people he met, to ask his way of every beggar. A carpet-bag and knapsack were all his luggage; he had a sleeved waistcoat and an overcoat against wind and weather. In Verona he adopted the dress of the middle-classes, acquired their ways of walking and behaving, and ended by wearing cotton stockings so as to climb a rung lower down the society-ladder. In the market at Vicenza he played with some children. And he enjoyed being without a servant and running about the town, after his years of a "sedentary, slinking" existence. In a week he found his spirits rising, "for being waited upon makes people old and incapable before their time"; and now he had to "keep an eye on the exchange, see about my drafts, pay bills, keep accounts, write to you, instead of only thinking, planning, brooding, giving orders, and dictating."

In the two years of his Italian sojourn, Goethe was never again so light-hearted as in these first two months. He was like a Prince who has evaded his Master of the Ceremonies, and is on the way to embrace a long dreamed-of foreign mistress instead of the royal cousin who has been assigned him as a bride. It was only the beginning of the tour which smacked of adventure; Goethe was late in enjoying the rôle of wandering scholar, with its feasts of grapes and figs under the blue of an Italian autumn, and the language and the common people.

But though he was roving, he was learning too. Why, he asked himself, were the dwellers near Lago di Garda less attractive to look at than those north of the Brenner Pass—and he came to the conclusion that it was their different way of eating polenta. "What does it cost to rent an archway in the arena?" he asked in Verona of the craftsmen who had their workshops there; and from Venice he wrote, quite in his old manner, that he wasn't wasting a single hour and would stay away no longer than was necessary. Here—only a month after his flight—he was very glad to provide himself again with a servant, and rejoiced in the assistance that a native of the country can render to a tourist. Now he could always go the shortest and cheapest way anywhere; and this, he said, was a great relief. Perhaps he was no longer young enough for the manner of life that a month ago he had so thoroughly enjoyed.

Very soon again he began, instead of calculating and paying (and the more gladly for the change), to think, plan, brood, and give orders. Even Venice got on his nerves, and after a fortnight he was glad to get away. With every degree of latitude the attraction of the great magnet increased. He scoured through Ferrara, from Bologna onwards he preferred merely to pass through the towns, he literally tore through Florence, stopping only three hours, the last two nights he slept in his clothes, left his inn before dawn, and: "To-morrow evening in Rome. After that I have nothing more to wish for, except to see you and my few belongings again, and find you in good health." But not until he reached the Porta del Popolo was

> Rome a certainty. The law and the prophets are fulfilled, and I shall be quit of my Roman hauntings for the rest of my days. . . . Only now am I beginning to live. . . . Now I *am* here I am tranquil and, it would seem, tranquillised for the remainder of my life.

This rapid travelling is like the impatience of a young man approaching the fulfilment of his heart's desire, sure of his conquest, and yet at the last moment—because doubt assails him—exaggerating his joyful expectancy. As if stunned, unable to enjoy or look at anything, Goethe at the end of this journey sank upon his bed, rid of the "Roman hauntings." Rome was a certainty now, and no one could ever take it from him. And exactly like one whose nerves were aching for the first step on Roman soil to be over, he said on his first day there, quite tamely and coolly, that he had seen St. Peter's and "the most important" ruins.

For here and now as everywhere and always Goethe knew the thing before he reached it. The image in his heart could only be confirmed by the actual scene or the literary presentment, but even in the deeper emotional life that soul could experience nothing which had not long been inwardly foreknown. Goethe could have dispensed with actions, landscapes, journeys, if he had trusted to his genius alone; but his dæmon perpetually impelled him to submerge himself in complications, actualities, the atmospheres of foreign lands—to prove on his own body the prescient powers of his mind. He whose internal vision could surpass the earthly actuality required the external vision also to content his insatiable, probing eye, and thus nourish his ideas by constant observation. He was unchangingly the supersensual yet sensual lover, even when Italy was the mistress he wooed.

In Italy he was to learn nothing that he had not known already, to enjoy little that he had not anticipated. One charm of travel (as indeed one charm of life), and to many the greatest, Goethe was deprived of—the element of surprise. What other tourists found exciting he found soothing, for what he was seeing only confirmed his prevision. But to be soothed was precisely what his restless nature wanted when it drove him to the land of art, of liberty, of Southern warmth—repose of spirit, the assurance of an intellectual gain. It was not because he had read a great deal about Italy that he felt at home there; he had read about her simply because he *was* at home there. And now the chain of causation was linked up.

Even in Venice he felt less inspired than relieved "that Venice is no longer a name to me, a name which had so often tormented me—*me*, who was ever the deadly foe of mere combinations of syllables!"

> For I never get any nearer through historical facts; the things I see were never at any time more than a hand's-breadth away from me, yet I was divided from them by an impenetrable wall. For really even now it is not as if I were merely seeing them, but as if I were seeing them again.

And it was just the same with the first days in Rome: "It is all as I thought it would be, and all new." His old ideas had, as he said, come alive; and in Naples he added: "On the whole, man is a creature who knows very early and acts very late!"

There was only one thing he did not know beforehand, and that was the issue. He had a suspicion of it, but even some months afterwards he was agitated by the dæmonic thought of all he had risked: "I have only one existence, and I have staked it all this time, and continue so to stake it."

He called upon nature, intellect, and fortune as good guides. Fortune did little for Goethe in Italy. His nature bore less fruit, but was so far tamed as to do him no harm; intellect alone bestowed on him inestimable treasures. But he owed more to the liberty which for two years he enjoyed there, after having been shackled for fifteen years first by his family and profession, then by friendship and society, finally by State and Court duties, often by women, and always by literary production. As a *savant* without rank or reputation, a German amateur of the fine arts, free from obligations and women, from social life and to some extent from production—free, above all, from the past . . . Goethe lived long in the great foreign city, intent on self-development before he should be forty.

For this was the purpose of his tour. Goethe lived in Italy to learn, not to enjoy, and so in the gay land his spirit took the same earnest fold as of yore. The painter Tischbein admirably rendered this frame of mind in a large painting where he depicted a wanderer meditating on the past among the ruins of a dead civilization. The only trait which does not fit Goethe is the romantic feeling in the composition—for that mind, at the end of its thirties, was for clear-sightedness at any price, for truth in art and Nature. Never was Goethe's eye keener, his vision shrewder, than in Italy; never was he less lyrically inclined than in the decade now beginning. Artistically speaking, he kept a tight hand on himself, living by rule and tranquilly, so that realities should not meet exaltation but should of themselves exalt the soul, for only in this way might errors be avoided.

My practice of seeing and studying all things as they are, my loyalty to the light of the eye, my complete shedding of all pretensions, make me happy here in a very quiet sort of way. . . . I was pretty sure I should learn something at Rome, but that I should have to go to school to such an extent, that there was all there is for me to learn, I had not imagined. . . . Already I have gained much, spiritually speaking . . . and feel ever so much freer. Daily I cast another skin, and hope to return as a normal person.

These confessions in his first months at Rome show the frame of mind which ruled his whole stay in Italy—for ever learning something, seldom shaping it into form, still more seldom amusing himself. For even in Naples, a metropolis of the rococo whose charms have tempted many a sober German to a gayer life, he remained unalterable:

Quite calm, as I usually do remain, and when things are beyond the beyonds I merely goggle at them. . . . Everyone (here) lives in a sort of intoxicated state of self-oblivion. And so do I; I scarcely recognize myself, I seem to myself an entirely different person. I am certainly learning to be a tourist on this tour; whether I am learning to live I can't say. The people who seem to understand that art are too different from me in every respect for me to lay any claim to possessing their talent.

So it was no sacrifice to his genius, but only to his temperament, when Goethe made use of this freedom to learn what he could. There could not at that time have been a more fruitful field for this than Rome afforded. Here he saw what he had known erroneously or only in part, realised what connections could be made, and only now did his co-ordinating sense succeed in constructing a scheme for the tour which had begun as an adventurous escapade. Now he declared that he should need a year and more before he could fully grasp the things which, though they did not take him by surprise, he felt that he must deeply study. Into the loose framework of the improvised route he now built columns and arches to make the tour a work of art—for himself, not for others. And at Rome he drew up a sort of educative programme so as gradually to master its marvels, and regarded his trip to Sicily as a means whereby to shape his experience into a whole, for to have ended the tour at Naples would have been to leave it an unfinished monument.

If in the methodical home-life Goethe's eye was his chief source of intellectual sustenance, how entirely it must have been master of the situation when he was travelling—an occasion when everyone tries to practise the art of seeing. "Here and now"—that was his motto in these years; sensuous impressions were what he was after, those which books and pictures could not afford him. He was testing his powers of observation, his clear-sightedness, his swiftness of apprehension;

and I want to see if my temper can get rid of its inveterate frowns and furrows. . . . I've been conversing with *things* all day long. . . . I want to open my eyes, gaze humbly, and await the image which my soul will make for me. . . . All roads are open to me, because I walk in a spirit of humility.

Nevertheless he could not but see according to the law of his vision—and Goethe always saw the object in its evolutionary aspect. Even here in Italy, where everything appealed to him to enjoy the "Here and Now," he sought instead to see how it came to be so. Rome, he said, he was considering as formerly he had considered Nature; and though, so doing, his delight in the object at rest, fully evolved, might be impaired or destroyed, he made for himself a profounder, more temperate delight in the thought of its struggle and development. Hills and pasture-land, arrangements of columns and shapes of vehicles—of all things that he saw he traced the genealogy.

If on entering the temple at Pæstum he was disappointed by the cumbrousness of the squat pillars, it only took him an hour to feel at home with them, once he recalled the age to which such architecture was germane. Instead of rhapsodising romantically in Venice, he saw that the city was as it was because of its origin and situation. The costume of the Northern Italians did not strike him as an eccentricity of fashion, but as a necessity for people who were not very clean, but were very fond of appearing in public. At Verona he could see the arena gradually growing, in the master-builder's conception and under his hands, into a place of which the aim was to contain a vast crowd of spectators; and from a mysterious never-opened gate on the Corso he deduced the frustrated purpose of an architect, planning new pleasure-grounds. Everywhere his travels were productive for Goethe, for he seemed to create anew whatever he saw. Even on the Apennines he conferred a new aspect, when he said that if they had not been so high they would have been more exposed to the action of the sea, and thus would have been more beautiful features of the landscape!

What Goethe's eye beheld in Italy was, above all, things rather than people—he had recently had to suffer so much more from people than from things!—and that was why, in his capacity of author, he brought home numerous images and still more numerous forms, but scarcely any material, and even fewer models for new characters. In these last years at Weimar he had been more of an author than a statesman, more of a scientist than an author, and the proportions did not alter on the Italian tour. His inner aversion from the affairs which had weighed so heavily upon him is plainly proved by his lack of interest in the government and politics of Italy. It was like the wilful blindness of a homesick artist.

Freedom of movement and anonymity strengthened his

democratic tendencies. He admired the Republic of Venice as a fitting monument, not to a ruling caste but to a people. Seeing the freer intercourse of the classes, here in the South, he realised more acutely the social mummeries of the little German sovereigns.

But in Rome he was not interested in the Papal State, either for its abnormality or its corruption; indeed he only once or twice had anything even derisive to say about it.

He was sometimes inclined to study the details of government, because in those the "Here and Now" suggested possible improvements to his practised eye. He devised a scheme for the sanitation of Venice, thought the painting of churches a mistake, praised a custom-house regulation for its stringency, however inconvenient travellers might find it, took note, for imitation at Weimar, of a method of paving the streets in Ferrara (this was the one point of comparison he made between Tasso's and Goethe's town!); and six lines of writing about Florence were followed by pages about agricultural methods, rotation of crops, the intervals between rows of wheat, and manuring in the Florentine region. Nevertheless, the paucity of these memoranda after a decade of practical routine is a striking testimony to the fact that he regarded all this in the light of a mere duty.

As a scientist, on the contrary, he worked with spontaneous enthusiasm at every stage of his tour. His love for truth prevailed over his love for beauty. Nature was to rescue him from his dæmon's complexities. Goethe's nature-study in Italy proves the growing power of the organic principle in his evolution. Here, where such art as he could find nowhere else awaited his attention, he spent half his time and energies on the study of Nature, which after all he could have done at home; and as if to clinch his attachment to the laws of evolution he now turned more and more decidedly from stones to plants. It was as though the North must always signify the petrified for him, while the South stood for germination and budding vitality.

On the third day of his tour he was still desirous to take a bit of quartz shot through with jasper along with him to Rome, for transport to Weimar later on; and up to the Brenner Pass he studied mineralogy. Then, crossing it, he was fascinated by the shapes of wind-blown clouds; and an entirely original theory of weather-conditions, which was later verified in principle, was suggested to him by the vague feeling that everything dark and oppressive was bound to drift northward. When later on he indulged in sporadic geological studies, it was merely because there was an opportunity of seeing, in activity on Vesuvius, the volcanic lava of his Thuringian observations.

But as soon as he reached the Lido he became absorbed in the sappy toughness of the shore-vegetation; he enjoyed seeing all this kind of thing become part of the world around him, instead of mere cabinet specimens. Goethe never went forth to discover; he saw, and so discovered. But here too he was guided by his insight into the laws of things. Everything he found outside he knew to be already in himself. Really (as he said in the beginning of his study of lava) he might have devoted the rest of his life to observation, there would have been so much for him to discern. From South Italy, where new plants and fishes made their appearance, he felt tempted to go to India,

> not to discover anything new, but to see what *has* been discovered in my own way. As I so often prophesied, I have found that everything here is more expanded, more evolved. Many things that I guessed at and looked for with the microscope at home, I can see here with the naked eye, an indubitable certainty.

Those words are symbolic of the whole tour.

"The botanical kingdom has got hold of me"; so he had written shortly before his flight. The law which he had unremittingly pursued he now found outside himself, without having actually looked for it. At Padua and Palermo, looking at the palm-trees, he was struck by the idea of a primitive plant. He felt that he was

> quite close to the mystery of procreation in plants; and that it is the simplest thing that could possibly be imagined. . . . This primitive plant of mine is going to be the most marvellous organism in the world, one that Nature herself might envy me. With this pattern and this clue to it, one will henceforth be able to invent new plants to all eternity, which cannot but be in the order of succession. . . . The same law will be applicable to all other living organisms.

Ten years afterwards he spoke of this discovery as the most glorious moment of his life; and again, twenty years later, long after the conclusion of his Morphology, he gave utterance to these glowing words: "To conceive, to sustain such an idea, to discern it in Nature, is a task which transports one into a region of tormented bliss." Then the study of Rome prevented him from working out his ideas; and so—entirely self-taught—he would gather plants from the gardens and fields, from wherever he went for a walk and wherever he came across them, "happy in that which is my Father's."

In Sicily he even gave up going to Syracuse, because he preferred to travel through the country-regions and see the corn which has given the island its nickname. He called Raphael's skull—very drolly, with a touch of scientific cynicism—a splendid structure of bones in which a beautiful soul could promenade at ease. When his friends in Naples tried to prevent his drinking a glass of water because there were insects floating in it, he quietly swallowed the liquid, saying that we ate crabs and eels, and that these little animals would do him no harm and might possibly nourish him.

This unromantic clear-sighted attitude is nowhere more evident than in his treatment of scenery. There are scarcely any long descriptions of Italian landscape in his letters and diaries. Here, where the German is wont to rhapsodise, Goethe kept his head. To the gardens and skies which in Thuringia had moved him to lyric yearning, he now—shaded by their trees and basking under their blue—devoted no long poem, and only a few descriptive verses in the dramas which were remodelled in Italy. But he was never tired of praising the climate—indeed it was the climate alone that he wanted to transplant, to "cut a piece out of, big enough for a strip round my house."

The scenery itself was coolly, not to say tamely, described; even the flame-belching Vesuvius was examined with a view to its inward rather than its outward aspect. Moonlight, which casts a veil over objects, is rarely mentioned. Even the sea did not surprise him, as a spectacle! From the tower of St. Mark's he saw it for the first time in his life, but described only the ships, hills, and lagoons. And standing on the Lido, he merely recorded: "So now I have seen this too with my own eyes, and followed its traces on the beautiful floor it leaves behind as it ebbs. I wished the children were with me, because of the shells!" He examined the seaweeds and sea-snails, and in this first contact with the sea he uttered, on seeing the crabs, these impressive words: "What an ineffably glorious thing is a live organism! How adapted to its environment—how real—how concrete!"

Here we have Goethe at thirty-eight—revering the Infinite in the little, but inclined to be suspicious of the vaster manifestation. This particular vastness of the ocean took some time to impress him, and in Naples he said that it was only when people had lived a long time by the sea that they could understand its being impossible to live without it. But when the sea revealed itself in storm, he studied the formations of the waves! Is it not as though, in his desire for proportion, he avoided all seductions even in Nature? Twenty years earlier Goethe would have seen in the ocean a symbol of his soul.

How useful his knowledge of the organic could be to him in art, he realised in Rome. On his arrival—so he recorded at the end of his tour—he had understood nothing about plastic art, had merely admired its reflection of Nature. Nevertheless here he found art confirming his ideas, He warned himself that he must always look at sculptures over and over again; in the first impression, "a mixture of truth and fallacy," he put no faith. He had delayed for a lifetime to acquire the technique of any craft; now, he said, he intended to do that, so that he might go on to something else.

> The great point is to get all these things, which have worked on my imagination for thirty years—and have thus taken too supreme a place in it—so arranged in the lower rooms of my house of life that they and I can breathe the same regular domestic atmosphere.

He used these words when standing before Palladio's buildings. He had tracked that classic spirit all over Northern Italy; his desire for purity of line, serenity, could be satisfied only by the Greeks. He studied very cursorily the Renaissance buildings of Florence and Perugia—the baroque remained wholly alien; its distorted pinnacles were no less irritating to him than the eccentricities of a Sicilian Prince, which nevertheless he took the trouble to catalogue rather pedantically. His derision of everything that he thought at all Gothic was utterly indiscriminating—so set was

Goethe's mind at this time on the linear, the serene, as opposed to the individual treatment. But in the multitude of buildings he did not ignore even those which were alien and disagreeable to him. Only once did he turn tail. In the Catacombs he experienced such discomfort that he instantly regained the light of day. He had often penetrated far into the bowels of the earth at the mines of Ilmenau, tapping with his hammer; in these Christian mortuaries his breath failed him, and Goethe escaped into the light.

Statues he at first found more impressive and striking than antique buildings. He could not help reconstructing the latter from their ruins, which only depressed him, since no romantic emotion stirred him to gloat upon things that have been demolished. The statues, when they were intact, revealed to him the secrets of their raw material. In Germany he had seen only plaster-casts, not any originals. Now, in Rome, he quickly learnt to distinguish the various Grecian epochs in statuary and gems, and would have gone so far as to buy a genuine piece. At first these works of art struck him chiefly as witnesses of the age they derived from—in a literary sense as it were; and in them he revered humanity in its pristine purity of vision. It was not until the final half-year, the most fruitful period of the tour, that they really came to life in his productive faculties. Aided by his anatomical knowledge, he learnt to draw the human head and body, began to model enthusiastically, and once again quoted those words of Jacob's: "I will not let thee go except thou bless me—though I should be crippled in the struggle!"

At twenty, on that cry, he had wrestled with Herder and his doctrine of the people as the source of poetry; at thirty, with the same prayer, he had sought to regulate and simplify the Weimar finances; now, at thirty-eight, he was struggling with his own shaping hand. For yet again Goethe was experimenting in drawing; and as it was in Rome this time, surrounded by art and artists, he put all his enthusiasm into the effort—and never tried again. For the first time he became so conscious of the affinity between plastic and literary art that he used the word artist in a dual sense, tried to attain realism in his modelling, divided his second Roman winter into five or six periods of plastic study, wished that, like a musician, he could set the harmonies he felt on the paper, believed he had discovered a principle, and finally did succeed in modelling a fairly good head of Hercules.

This study of modelling was useful to him as a writer. Impersonal though his drawings always were, the effort to attain line and colour showed him a new aspect of things, taught him to divine their essential features; and this entered into the manipulation of his sentences, verses, and images. One advantage of his tour, as he emphatically said when it was over, was that he had done with modelling henceforth, for he was "really born to be a writer."

In an amusing letter he said that he was fated always to forecast his own destiny in his writings, and this year they were telling him that he would fall in love with a Princess so as to write *Tasso*, and then sell himself to the devil so as to finish *Faust*. While he was revising *Egmont* in Rome, he read in the latest newspaper of just such disturbances at Brussels as he had described a decade ago; and if he transferred a few scenes of *Tasso* to the Florentine gardens, and gave the new *Iphigenie* a touch of the Southern atmosphere he was then breathing, these incidental moods in no way transgress against the deeper law of his prescient imagination. Goethe was like other poets in that he did not need to see the landscapes and costumes he wanted to present. In the Borghese Gardens he wrote the scene in the witches' kitchen, than which nothing could be more German in feeling; and under the orange-trees of Naples he merely remarked: "Mignon was quite right to long for them."

On one blue morning in spring, Goethe went to the public gardens of Palermo, "with the settled quiet resolution of going on with my poetic dream" (*Nausicaa*). "But before I knew, I was in the grip of another phantom which had been slinking about my path for some days." This meant that among the subtropical plants, he again began to search for the primitive plant of his faith. There *must* be a specimen! He compared, examined, got excited, but found nothing; and

> my good poetical intentions were done for, the garden of Alcinoë vanished into thin air, a cosmic garden had opened its gates. Why are we moderns so easily distracted, why are we fascinated by enterprises that are entirely beyond our grasp?

Though the scientist was heaping up treasure in Italy, and the connoisseur was mastering form, the writer was gaining but little; for even in the *Elegies* which he was to write on his return, Rome was rather the background than the theme. He brought home neither any considerable poems nor any important new conceptions. But for the completion of his fragments, which was his only literary work in those two years, he needed that intellectual liberty which he could find only in absence from Weimar. In that sense, Goethe needed liberty more than he needed Italy.

When he had decided to print his fragments, he had regarded himself—or so a confession from Rome would seem to say—as extinct. But now he went vigorously to work at finishing them; and, conscious that he had gained a new sense of style, he could compare himself with himself, and see his lights and shadows. It was with a peculiar sensation that one day he opened the parcel wherein the first four volumes of his collected edition "came to Rome with the results of half a lifetime."

He took great pains with *Iphigenie*, seeking to lay the yoke of verse upon the delicate conception without straining it. Sometimes, in his solitary journey home, he clung to it as if to a firm bond connecting him, among these foreign people, with the past.

With a strange mixture of distaste and affection Goethe reread this work; and if we compare his earnest absorption in *Iphigenie*, his years of devotion to her presentment, with the indifference he felt for the play within a year of his finishing it, we have yet another symbol of his love for the original model, and the destined issue of that love. Goethe could forget Lotte Buff in the end, could parody *Werther;* but from Frau von Stein and *Iphigenie*, less passionately experienced, he merely felt remote when his fervour had died out. A year after he had finished it, that work of Goethe's left him cold.

Even *Tasso* (to which he added more in the last six months at Rome than he did in the first twelve to *Iphigenie*) grew *in* Italy, not because of Italy. At Naples he was tempted to throw it into the fire, but felt himself pleasingly intimidated by the distant printer; and though he said he was amused and surprised by this sense of compulsion, it nevertheless throws a light on the completion of many of his works—for if he had obeyed the deeper law of his conceptions, the majority of Goethe's works might have remained unfinished, because in fact they were experiments. Indeed, there was only a certain number of his poems which he felt an inward compulsion to finish, and that was because they fell from his pen in the utmost perfection—something like Leonardo, who of his countless ideas and schemes completed only one, and that as it were by accident.

Again and again he was on the point of abandoning the troublesome *Tasso*, but the poet had put too much of himself into that other poet to be able to leave him in the lurch. He was now recasting the nebulous first act of the Weimar manuscript, seven years afterwards, and giving it rhythmic form. Crossing the sea, far from the world of men, he used the leisure and physical relaxation in the service of mental exertion; and when later on he took the manuscript with him on the homeward journey, it was probably because he felt a melancholy pleasure in its close connection with the land to which he was saying farewell.

His genius would not suffer him to continue *Faust* in Rome. Wistfully recalling his youth, he deluded himself into the idea that all he need do was to go on writing, and have the paper smoked—then nobody would know it had been composed at widely-separate intervals. But two scenes were enough for him. One of these, the Wood and Cavern scene, where Faust invokes the Sublime spirit, reveals a mood which later was to be constant with Goethe. How masterfully his strange genius could resist the attempt to subject it to classical forms is shown in the baroque scene of the Witches' Kitchen, which might have been written anywhere but under the tall spreading pine-trees of the Borghese Gardens. There is no trace of their umbrage, and still less of their form.

The later *Italienische Reise* remained a fragment, but has not the charm of the diary-form. The letters, on the other hand, are racy and spontaneous, though they too were designed for semi-publicity and somewhat written-up. For the first few weeks, up to his arrival in Rome, they were supplemented by a diary for Frau von Stein, of which Goethe then thought very highly indeed. All that was pedantic in him came out when, writing from an address she did not know, he adjured her (from whom he had concealed his plans, his destination, and was still concealing them when he wrote) to copy out the diary which would shortly reach her, on separate quarto sheets and read none of it aloud, so that he might have something to tell when he came back. In this way, he said, there would be a copy waiting for him on his return, which he would be able to "correct"!

He abandoned this diary in Rome, and confined himself to notes which he did not send home and which were not preserved. None the less to write and to depict was a necessity for him in travel as in life. It was only when he called himself to account that Goethe could comprehend himself at all; and to this highly personal impulse we owe the grand total of his work, which he called a prolonged self-revelation. When thirty years afterwards he collected his Italian notes, letters, and diaries for his volume, the material before him contrasted with his new outlook at every point; and yet he could not bring himself to rewrite what had been written in the style he had now shed. "These documents, dear things, are altogether too naïve; they would have had to be done all over again."

Since in the South Goethe was first of all the student, his manner of life was necessarily quiet, secluded, Southern only in the sense of environment. His incognito shows the degree of his reclusiveness. He was nearly forty, of European reputation, ennobled and a Minister, and he had—except for a few weeks at Carlsbad—never mixed with the great world, never set foot in Paris, London, or Vienna. He had disliked Berlin on a brief visit, had merely passed through Dresden, in Strasburg and Leipzig had known nothing of the higher social spheres; Frankfurt was a provincial town, Weimar a stupid little Residency. A free man for the first time in fifteen years, he could now, with the renown which was spreading wider every day, on his tardy overstepping of the German-speaking frontier have easily entered the most dazzling circles in the "Capital of the World." He could have travelled like Voltaire—have breathed the atmosphere of a great nation by exchanging ideas with the best minds it possessed, have intimately felt its history, and compared himself with its illustrious men.

Instead of this, he was upset even on the way there when a bookseller recognised him, and he denied that he was Goethe. His incognito was soon of course an open secret in Rome, and every German there wrote home the news. But as he chose to be known as the painter Möller, the fiction saved him from visits and publicity; and the one Prince whom he did visit, because he could give him useful introductions, he met first in a picture-gallery.

In Sicily he was forced to submit to some visiting. At the Palace in Palermo, a Knight of Malta asked about Central Germany (which he had visited ten years before) and finally about Weimar and a young man who there "*faisait la pluie et le beau temps*"—the author of *Werther*.

When he was told who his interlocutor was, the effect upon the Knight was to make him exclaim, with every manifestation of surprise: "There must have been a good many changes there." Goethe smiled: and reticent as ever about facts which concerned himself merely said "Oh yes. I've undergone a good deal of change between Weimar and Palermo." Soon after this, he happened on a market-place in the interior of the island where the citizens were sitting about in the antique fashion and they asked this German stranger and his companion to tell them about "the great King." Goethe sat down and recounted the exploits of Frederick the Great, saying nothing about his death lest the audience should be mortified. These anecdotes give us a flash-light on Goethe in Italy—he startled the Knight of Malta at the Palace by his alteration from a youth to a man; the nameless foreigner told the old Sicilian peasants about the deeds of the only German who, besides himself, is epoch-making for that period.

Between the two extremes lies nothing but a quiet life. Goethe was in good health throughout these two years and longer, and that really for the first time since Strasburg. He attributed it to the Southern climate and had reason to fear, from various indications, that he would relapse on his return to the North.

What I particularly like about him [Tischbein wrote home] is his simple manner of life. He asked me for a quite small room where he could sleep and work unhindered, and very simple food. There he sits now, and in the mornings works at his *Iphigenie* till nine o'clock; then he goes out and looks at the great works of art. . . . He doesn't let any of the big-wigs worry him, and will see no one but artists.

Economy was not the reason, was merely the mark, of this simplicity. In the first eighteen months he spent his official salary and the thousand thalers paid for the first four volumes of his works, apart from what his mere living cost him—that makes between six and seven thousand marks for a year in Italy, including all the expenses of travel, and the purchase of casts, pictures, and marbles. He was meticulous about details, told Frau von Stein that he was sending her seven pounds of the best coffee in Venice, which had cost one ducat, but that to this must be added the expense of transport; and he bought a marble replica on the Duchess's behalf, representing himself as the purchaser, which reduced the price by twenty ducats. He persuaded the Duke that certain volumes of the Vatican Museum Catalogue must be procured for Weimar. With the drawings which the painters Tischbein and Kniep did for him in South Italy he covered their expenses as his guests on the tour. For his return he intended to save the Easter quarter of his salary, and the advance payment for his fifth volume. Thus, though he lived comfortably, it was from hand to mouth.

Goethe—and it should never be forgotten when considering his most weighty decisions—had no capital of any kind until he was in his sixtieth year. He lived well, but always on his salary and his at first somewhat scanty remuneration from writing, which never brought him in any sums worth talking about until he was forty. That was why he was grasping with his publisher, Göschen—so much so that his Weimar friends actually called him petty, because on a slight difference of opinion arising he firmly stuck to his bond. He ordered his servant in Weimar not to let the manuscript of a new volume leave his hands for anything but cash down from the publisher—"the contract says so, and there must be no paltering with it." When the subscription for his works fell below what author and publisher had hoped, Goethe wrote in serious earnest that "people may think they are paying me a prodigious sum for a piece of work, when in reality all they are doing is to recoup me for the money I had to spend on collecting the material for it."

His studious temper often deprived him of opportunities for closer study of the Italian people. In Venice he would be coming home when the Venetian was going out; and when at last he thought of buying a mask the waste of money deterred him, and he preferred to purchase some lasting enjoyment in the shape of a volume of Vitruvius. That is Goethe at thirty-seven, in Venice—studying a Latin writer on the architecture of the Augustan age in the evenings at an inn, while outside Canaletto's pupils at the tables on the Piazza of St. Mark's, and Casanova's mistress in the boxes of the Commedia, were savouring the autumn glories of the rococo.

The Roman Carnival, of which he gives us a graphic but unenthusiastic picture, pleased him better after the event than it did at the time, when he said it "robbed him of a precious week," and thought it so dull that, once seen, no one could wish to see it again. And when he did look in at a masked ball, he fled in half-an-hour. The idleness and ostentation of Neapolitan life drove him away from the city—he liked it fairly well, but felt it was not for him; and when he met some men of the world he realised more clearly than before why he could never be one of them. When the Viceroy at Palermo invited him to the Court, he barely mentioned it in his letters. He avoided going into society at Rome because he knew he would be drawn into cliques, and obliged to praise certain artists and dilettanti. Why should he do in Rome what he tried to avoid at Weimar!

But in his small chosen circle he was sociable, and in fact was much less alone than in the recent years at home. His society consisted exclusively—and only in those two years of his life!—of artists and connoisseurs. And they were all Germans. His chosen position of complete personal independence, and his intercourse with none but total strangers, permitted him to do just as he pleased. He dreaded being drawn into society by the Italians in Rome, and wasting his time and energies on fashionable people; and as his scientific studies were a thing apart from the place, no one in Rome could have been of much use to him in that sense. Thus it came about that in Italy Goethe seldom spoke anything but German. Just then he would have found it dull to live alone. He was learning, and for that he needed the sort of assistance which could be dispensed with when it had done its work for him. Here, among more unconventional people and surroundings, he appreciated the value of mutual endeavour more deeply than ever before.

The travelling Goethe, then, needed companions both as master and pupil, but these could only be adepts, a select few.

Tischbein, with whom he made his longest stay, would by reason of his unconventionality and genuine knowledge have been the best possible company for him; and so he was for months. In his house, with his cheerful companionship, Goethe—the fugitive from his own stately abode in the sombre North—had his first rejuvenating draught of artistic domesticity, and was entirely contented until his host's unpunctuality began to irritate him. Finally he declared that Tischbein was a typical Bohemian—and Bohemians, for fifteen years, had ceased to suit Goethe's taste in friends. Ever since Weimar he had found them unendurable. In the end, too, he thought Tischbein less open hearted and unselfish than he had at first.

At times he would say that the best company he had in Rome was a melancholic, neurotic, gifted writer—the German, Moritz; and declare that Moritz had taught him anything he might have learnt there. Kaiser of Zurich, whom he persuaded to come to Rome, was his guide in musical matters. The German painters, Bury and Lips, completed this circle of artists,

> who are all kindly-disposed, all on the right path, and the proof of it is that they can put up with me. . . . For I am ruthless and impatient with everyone who dawdles and divagates, and yet wants to pass as a pioneer and an explorer. So I laugh and mock at them until they either alter their ways or give me the go-by. . . . Two of them—nay, three—already have to thank me for a new outlook and a new manner of life, and will be grateful to me as long as they live. On that count—my effect on others—I do feel that I have a healthy and inspiring nature. Only I can't walk in tight shoes, nor could I ever see through a stone wall.

Here he appears as a comrade with comrades, influencing them, living with them, a German artist in Rome as they were, working hard like them, like them unpretentious, their superior in only one thing—the power of a tremendous personality.

In one social quality he did surpass them—and that was a kindliness greater than we have hitherto had occasion to record. He wrote a long letter to Wieland—otherwise honoured with no correspondence—about a young art-expert whose acquaintance he had lately made, suggesting that he should do some work on Wieland's journal, for the young man was in need of money.

When the neurotic Moritz met with an accident, Goethe tended and cheered him, visited him daily for a considerable time, sat up at night with him, brought other fellow-countrymen to see him, arranging visits and vigils so that for six weeks the invalid was never without nursing and companionship.

But despite all this, he was as a rule so absent-minded and reticent, even in their company, that after a year he wrote home confessing that he could open his heart to no one in the place. It was not till later on that he met the only Roman acquaintance who was to influence him for his whole life—the Swiss Heinrich Meyer, a mediocre painter but a first-rate connoisseur, reserved, loyal-hearted, a typical Swiss. This man did more for Goethe's æsthetic enlightenment than anyone since Herder, but he taught him less in the way of ideas than of technique. His pupil took earnest note of every word he said, for what Goethe had learned in Germany was as the rind to the kernel, compared with Meyer's teaching. At only one house was Goethe a frequent visitor—Angelica Kauffmann's, a kind woman, a skilful painter, very much the fashion in Rome and very highly paid. She was married to an old, miserly Italian. But even on his intercourse with her he laid such restrictions that she had to root him out on Sundays to go to an exhibition, and dine with her afterwards.

This second Roman sojourn which was to have lasted one month and lasted eleven—because Goethe had by that time made up his mind to study and thoroughly master the artistic treasures of Rome—followed a strenuous course, as methodical as his life in Weimar.

In that summer he copied the heads in the lower part of the Day of Judgment in the Sistine Chapel. He and his friends would work there, because it was the coolest place in the August heat, and they tipped one of the custodians to let them encamp in the Chapel, bringing their food and drink. Once indeed the great pagan dozed in the midday heat upon the Papal Throne. Here, and later in the country, Goethe led a light-hearted youthful sort of existence, for they spent a few summer weeks on the Campagna in the house and garden of an English art-dealer. It was exactly like life at a watering-place, and there Goethe fell in love.

Not like a boy. For a year and more he had abjured women in Italy. To the Duke, who was fond of recounting his *bonnes fortunes* in his letters, Goethe explained his abstention by a dread of "French influences" among the models, of social encroachments among the middle-class ladies—in a word, of interference with his studies. Even Lady Hamilton's dancing, which at that time was regarded as the last word in erotic æstheticism, he curtly described as being very pretty and well-arranged, "and an original sort of lark."

But now, in this *villeggiatura* at Castel Gandolfo, he made the acquaintance of a beautiful Milanese who in appearance, character, and destiny was in many respects a specimen of the type which ruled the Goethean love-affair. Once more she was of the middle-class, and he met her unconventionally. Once more she was of clear brunette colouring, with a delicate skin, and "frank, engaging, not to say appealing, manners." She had blue eyes; and he met her in the company of a darker, more statuesque Roman lady, but in this instance too was more attracted by the suppler, gentler, airier type. Like an elderly man, almost paternally, he yielded to her wish that he should teach her English. His courtship began on the first day with the substantive in a sentence from the *Times*, and was soon extended to the relevant adjective—it was all in fun, but all in earnest too; and before long she appeared in his company at meal-time, when she was rather coldly received.

Then he heard she was engaged, and he was

> terrified. . . . I was old and experienced enough to pull up instantly, with whatever regret. "It would be a little too much," I exclaimed to myself, "if a Wertherish story were to crop up in Rome, and spoil the unforgettably delightful conditions you've been so successful in preserving."

Later, in Rome, she was deserted by her betrothed and fell desperately ill. Goethe often inquired for her; and finally he saw the convalescent in her carriage at the carnival, talked to her for a moment, receiving her thanks for his attentions—and went his way, feeling "tranquil and very happy."

This incident, as described in his old age, bears no resemblance to the mood of ever-increasing gaiety which characterised the concluding months in Rome—and particularly quarrels with a letter to the Duke in which, though rather pedantically, he recounts some love-affairs; as also with some verses to Cupid which are evidently the outcome of a prolonged love-affair, and in which the poet actually bemoans his wasted time. In these we have the studious Goethe, modelling, revising his literary work, who has somehow or other slipped into a flirtation and cries to the God of Love:

> Du hast mir mein Gerät verstellt und verschoben,
> Ich such' und bin wie blind und irre geworden.
> Du lärmst so ungeschickt; ich fürchte, das Seelchen
> Entflieht, um dir zu entfliehn, und räumet die Hütte.[1]

This is another astonishing instance of the way Goethe's writings persistently foretold his experiences—for in the spring of that year he had, in his *Nausicaa*, imagined such an attachment of a passing stranger for a woman of the region. Now he was enacting it, and again it is symbolic too of his prescient nature, that he had portrayed this love fifteen years earlier in the dialogue of the Wanderer with the Woman of the Temple.

If his flirtation with the Milanese girl was really the platonic relation he represented it to be, there must have been another love-affair. This is indicated not only in the verses referred to above, but far more explicitly in the Elegies which were soon to follow. "Faustina," whoever she may have been—and her name, rank, and place of abode are supposed to be known—was no phantasm, but Goethe's great adventure in Italy.

He had one of a different kind before he met her, in which the tourist-Goethe was called upon to prove his pluck and presence of mind. On his return from Messina he was in danger of being stranded on the rocks of Capri one summer-night. It was a sailing-boat; and when all was confusion on board, Goethe rose to the occasion and authoritatively bade them keep their heads, soothed the terrified passengers, and persuaded them to pray (which was one means of keeping them quiet), and reminded them of Christ walking on the waters.

[1] "Disabling, idling, thus to me thou comest—
Vainly I work, blind-eyed, distracted ever. . . .
Thou foolish, restless lad! My startled spirit
Takes flight from thee, but leaves thee in possession."

Such was the force of his personality, which in a long life had few opportunities of impressing itself upon the crowd. Sea-sick himself, speaking a foreign tongue, and in mortal danger, the poet yet contrived to act as priest, teacher, and practical man. Then, half-stunned, he sank upon his mattress, "yet with a certain sense of pleasure which seemed to derive from the Lake of Tiberias, for I could quite plainly see the picture from Merian's illustrated Bible hovering before my eyes." He fell asleep, and was wakened by the rope dragging along the deck. They were taking in sail, and a favouring wind lifted the vessel from the rocks.

Goethe's sensations in face of death are remarkable, even if he did touch them up a little in describing the scene later on. The fact remains that he seems to have based his action on the Bible. His earliest memories revived in that moment—he found himself seeing the picture with which he had just calmed down the terrified devout; and even if he did not himself pray as he bade others do, the thought of prayer was with him, recalling childish emotions, in that grave crisis; just as ten years later he was to make the equally sceptical Doctor Faust recall them on the night of Easter-Eve.

For Goethe's anti-Christian heart knew a still keener revulsion from the old teaching, when in the Italian churches he saw that the works of the great painters were injured by their fidelity to the legend. He could bear Titian's Assumption of the Virgin only because her earthward gaze was so tenderly compassionate of humanity; Raphael's Madonna della Sedia he called "our beautiful Goddess-Mother." Later, in Bologna, his tone was that of contemptuous dislike when he spoke of the stupid, detestable religious pictures that people went crazy about.

> It is as though when the sons of God engendered with the daughters of men, monsters were born. . . . These people are always concerned with the anatomy, or the execution, or the flaying—at any rate, with the sufferings of the principal figure, never with the artistic treatment. . . . Either miscreants or epileptics, criminals or fools.

The trend of Goethe's mind, intent on the true, the actual, which is to say on the classic, made him more clear-sighted than ever in this Catholic country. He said it was a mercy that the horses of St. Mark's had not been melted down into candelabra or crucifixes, that on the Greek tombs there was no man in armour waiting, in the attitude of prayer, for a joyful resurrection.

As a power and an organism he could admire the Roman Church. Before he left South Germany he had joyfully looked forward to steeping himself in the cosmopolitan atmosphere of Jesuit circles; but Venice was to teach him that one had to become a Catholic, like Winckelmann, if one wished to be admitted to any intimacy with that world. The irrational, when so sensuously portrayed, seemed to him an advantage of the Roman Church.

> What a beautiful invention is that of the Mother of God. . . . A thing which subdues the sense to its beauty, which has a certain intimacy of poetic charm that so delights one as to annihilate one's powers of reflection—it is the very pattern of a religious object.

So it was really with a prejudice in favour of the Faith that he went to St. Peter's and saw the Pope celebrate the Mass on Christmas and Corpus Christi—but inveterately he obeyed his nature and broke loose from these seductions. He could not do otherwise.

> It is a spectacle unique in its way, but I have grown too old a Diogenes to be impressed by it in any sense whatever. . . . All that fuss to bolster up a delusion seems to me simply silly, and the mummeries which impress children and sensuous-minded people are to me, when I regard the business as an artist and a poet, tedious and pettifogging.

Thus, with no intimate feeling for the country, the people, or the creed, friendless among comrades, unworldly in the capital of the world, methodical despite his liberty, Goethe during those two years never quite looked away from his native land. As long as his sojourn lasted, he kept up an affectionate correspondence with the friends from whom it had been his first delight to escape. His second was to be the reunion. Not for an hour did he seriously think of settling down in Italy; and his very first message to Herder, who got his most confidential letters throughout the two years, was to ask him to reconcile the Duke and Frau von Stein to his flight—he had not meant to hurt anyone by going.

But his mistress was irreconcilable. For two months, on his way to Rome, he had kept a diary for her—though she did not know where he was, and could make him no sign. His attitude was like a friend's—not a lover's. He wished Fritz was with him, but did not say the same about her. Their future was uncertain; and from Venice he wrote her these extraordinary words of half-reluctant appeal: "If when I come back you are good to me, you shall know all my secrets." But when he got nearer to Rome he did feel that he wanted her, had presentiments of disaster, and suddenly broke into a remorseful strain, like a lover in a novel:

> To have lived for ten years in your society, to be loved by you, and now to be here, in an alien world! I knew how it would be with me, and nothing but the utmost necessity could have made me resolve on this step. Let us have no other thought than to live our lives together to the end.

His presentiment was justified, and largely because Charlotte had none whatever, because even those ten years had left her unable to divine what he would feel when he was far away from her. Or *had* she any prescience of the great disintegration, which her lover had not yet confessed either to her or himself? If she had written despairingly, Goethe would have been moved; but she assumed the attitude of a fine lady—and her first thought was that since he could so "insult" her, she must take care that her love-letters did not endanger her reputation!

What her first letter to Rome must have been like we can see from Goethe's answer: "So this is all you have to say to a friend, a lover, who had been so long looking forward to a sweet letter from you. . . . I won't tell you how your little note has rent my heart." And then he implores her not to open the box containing her returned letters until she has news of his death. Next he accuses himself; and once more we have the ardent, lonely, pleading Goethe:

> You intend to keep silence? To take back the proofs of your love? You could not do this without great pain to yourself, and I am to

blame for it. But perhaps a letter from you is on the way, a letter which will uplift and console me—perhaps my diary has reached you. . . . I can only beg you most submissively, most imploringly, to make it easier for me when I return—not to banish me utterly. Be generous, forgive me my misdemeanours, and let me lift my head again. . . . Don't regard me as a separate person—nothing on earth could requite me for what I should lose in you, in what life at Weimar means to me. . . . I was engaged in mortal combat there, and no tongue could say what I had to suffer. This blow has brought me to myself.

But thenceforth her image gradually faded from his heart. It was not without reason that Goethe had always told Charlotte that he needed her presence. Quickly now did he pull himself together; his other letters show how thoroughly he had recovered the healthier mood of determination to make use of his liberty, press on, be no longer the victim of her caprices. Even to Charlotte herself he was soon writing more composedly, telling her that at Kochberg (her country-house) she must not finish any of her sketches, for he was coming back with a new technique, and in a year they would celebrate her birthday in better spirits—the tone of consolation, of one who would fain be helpful out of kindness, but would not retain the attitude of a lover. She, however, removed her son from his house! That grieved him, for he loved the boy—and he thought he had "arranged it all so very well," having installed Fritz in his own room and told the servant-man to sleep there too.

Gradually her letters grew more cordial, but now, in her anxiety, she made him promise to burn her answers at once. Goethe's letters were unchangingly kind, but grew rarer, and told her nothing of his arrangements. In the third half-year he wrote to her nine times; in the last (which was the period of his Roman love-affair) not once.

His relations with the Duke were simpler; there were no critical moments. Carl August had gone forth to battle, happy to be rid of Goethe's admonitions; and now, with him confronting the cannons and Goethe the Roman statues, their different paths were so thoroughly established that they could salute one another cordially from their distance. Goethe made a joke out of their "antipodean existences," and never failed to give amusing details of social events; he entertained the Duke with remarks about the Roman battle-fields, and sent him a fragment of a water-trough which the German troops had once used in the Alban Hills. Only once did he warn him against certain follies, for he had heard, with anxiety and vexation, of a fresh accident to the Duke.

For the rest, he kept carefully to the stipulation that his leave of absence should be renewed from month to month—saying he would return at a moment's notice, but otherwise would like a few months more to complete his education. He got his friends to send him private information of the general position of affairs at Weimar.

The Duke was only too glad to agree to every demand for fresh leave of absence. The longer the poet would stay away, the better it pleased the Duke, and the heartier were the poet's acknowledgments. The more they were apart, the more their friendship revived. A relation which recently had been muddled was cleared up, and seemed quite natural again—they were once more the artist and his Mæcenas.

All along Carl August wanted Goethe to do what was most useful and agreeable to himself, and Goethe put a new colour on this return to their original cordiality when he said that the crown of all his endeavour now would be to "embellish" the Prince's existence. But when the Dowager-Duchess wanted to come to Italy and have Goethe for her *cicerone*, the startled poet (in one of the longest letters he wrote to the Duke) pointed out how difficult it all would be . . . but of course he was quite ready—and the recipient must have smiled and said to himself that he would spoil all his friend's enjoyment if he laid this duty upon him.

In the delicate question—never really decided—of whether and how far Goethe should be relieved of his official position, both men displayed the tact of skilled diplomatists. Goethe held himself in readiness to return after his first spring-season in Italy, so as not to have been more than a year away. The Duke then cautiously proposed to appoint someone else Vice-President, and make Goethe "Director" of a sort of Committee of Cabinet-Control. Goethe was no less circumspect in following up the suggestion. On some formal pretext he put forward a request that the colleague in question should at once be appointed President, and he himself be simultaneously relieved of office in the usual way, with a cordial word or two added to the official formula:

As a matter of fact, I shall be of more service to you than I have often been of late, if you will only permit me to do what no one but myself *can* do, and entrust the rest to others. My position in public affairs has been the result of my personal position with you—now let a different one with you result, after all these years, from the public one I have hitherto held. . . . Give me back to myself and my country; give me *yourself* again, so that I may begin a new life with you!

I lay my entire destiny in your hands with perfect confidence. I have seen such a great, such a beautiful, part of the world, and the net result has been to show me that I can live only with you, and in your life. If I can do this, less burdened by details which are not in my line, I shall be able to give you and others pleasure by so living. . . . Farewell, and be sure that few men alive can feel more loyally towards you than I do, and that the best thing which can happen to me is to be always devoted to your service. Keep me in your heart! Goethe.

And in a postscript: "Do give the Steins and Herder a confidential hint, so that they may not be anxious and imagine all sorts of extraordinary things."

One of the cleverest letters that Goethe ever wrote! Certainly from no other can we make a clearer analysis of the combination of practical worldly wisdom and genuine gratitude, of loyalty and calculation, of freedom and sense of obligation, which marked his relation with the Duke. Tasso is in it, and Antonio too—Mephisto joins hands with Faust.

When he left Rome a year afterwards, he felt that the course of his development permitted him to speak more frankly. The colleague had in the meantime been appointed his successor; he himself was to hold an advisory position in the Cabinet. And now, homeward bound, he wrote to the Duke, saying that in his prolonged retirement he had found himself again—

but as what? As an artist! What else I may be good for, *you* shall decide, and shall use me to that end. . . . I shall willingly submit to your judgment. Accept me, then, as your guest; let me work out my destiny to the full, and savour the cup of existence, at your side—so shall my powers, like a mountain-source discovered, concentrated, purified, be yours to direct as you will."

Meanwhile, for Carl August it had been no easy task to uphold his friend's cause. Court-gossip and town-talk had been swelling high; there was a jealous grudge against the absent Minister; and Schiller, who then visited Weimar, had this to report of Goethe, almost as soon as he got there:

> While he is painting in Italy, the Toms, Dicks, and Harrys are sweating for him like beasts of burden. For doing nothing, he is squandering a salary of 1800 thalers in Italy, and they have to work double-tides for half the money.

Goethe never knew anything about this private letter; but when he was told that at Weimar they said he must be off his head, he resolved to answer this "good opinion" as Sophocles had done in writing Œdipus upon Colonos.

The opinion and the retort were reported and received by Philipp Seidel, who was now ceasing to be a mere servant and becoming a confidential right-hand man. He looked after money-matters, superintended the household, delivered messages, forwarded letters; but at the same time Goethe permitted him the frankest comments on the gossip of the servants, the town, and the general public, and wrote him confidential replies.

Meanwhile, however, the servant himself had ventured on authorship, and that on the subjects of the female sex and finance. Goethe advised him to go slowly with the latter and have his opinions on the former anonymously published, for in a moral question like that, anonymity left the writer in a better position to learn the truth by his effect upon public opinion. When Seidel, like a dutiful servant, went in for Nature-study too, Goethe praised his efforts, warned him against hasty conclusions, and so as to gain his full confidence, assumed the position of a colleague. "So your observations are very useful to me, if I am a little beyond you in deductions and combinations."

Though he had fled from home, he was always haunted by its spirit, and always welcomed the haunting. Not, indeed, that of the wholly forgotten Court (to whose ladies he sent the curtest kind of greetings) nor that of affairs either. It is a fresh proof, and an astonishing one, of Goethe's increasing alienation from his political activity, that he should so entirely have consigned it to oblivion. Very seldom did he answer, and that with mere complimentary phrases, his colleague's various inquiries; from the Duke he never requested any details; the progress of Ilmenau alone occasionally seemed to appeal to his imagination.

On the other hand, he wrote meticulous instructions from afar about the seeds and cuttings he sent home. Once, in Rome, Goethe had a dream about official affairs, and it is sure to have been a bad dream—for as long as he was uncertain of the Duke and his future liberty, he dreaded the moment when he should "have to resume the position of a Caryatid."

But his house, the little city, his friends above all, were missed during his travels; he knew well that he was too deeply attached to them for any thought of permanent absence. But it was only Weimar which so possessed his remembrance. In those two years he wrote his mother in all seven letters (of which she lost six), and one each to Merck, Schlosser, Jacobi and Kestner—curt and cool in every instance.

To the Herders' and Frau von Stein's children, though, he sent many a lively epistle, telling on the same page of the pomegranates on the trees and the electric fish, or of the Holy Father on his throne and a thousand dead pigs at the butcher's—all adapted to their age and outlook.

Herder got the most intimate letters of these years. His penetration, his unflinching outlook, just suited Goethe now—he hailed a friend in the man whose intellectual curiosity was so comprehensive. His verdict was impatiently awaited by Goethe in Rome—he frequently asked for Herder's impression of the completed *Egmont*. He had had a curious experience with *Iphigenie*. He had read it aloud three times in the early months at Rome, but it had always left the audience cold. They had expected something more like *Götz* and were disconcerted by this classic piece, of whose like they had so many examples. Now from Weimar too came scarcely-veiled expressions of disappointment; the earlier draft was preferred. That version, composed ten years before on an official tour, seemed to his friends more remarkable than the piece which had flowered under two blue skies.

And again Goethe felt himself alone. Slowly the premonition of his future as a poet dawned upon his consciousness—he would write no more for the nation, for his own period of time. Moreover, the disappointing subscription for his collected edition hit him hard both in the practical and the ideal sense. Had it been otherwise, he said, he could easily have put forth ten or twelve volumes instead of eight. This German poet, whom his fellow-countrymen have since been fain to crown upon the Capitol at Rome, caught so faint an echo of his fame when he published this first edition of his works that he had to importune his nearest and dearest for their opinions. "Do say something about my writings; it greatly encourages me to hear a reverberation from afar." It was all very well for the misanthropic traveller to say that henceforth he would write only such things as even people whose lives were full, and concerned with great matters, would really enjoy reading. He was over-emphatic in asserting his indifference to the general public, and declaring that he only wanted to please his friends. Judicious criticism was, as ever, what influenced him most, and in Herder he honoured the one man who could—and was permitted to—make comparisons. To him Goethe sent the finished *Iphigenie*, and actually gave him *carte blanche* about corrections!

He had scarcely reached Rome before he declared that all his ideas about shutting himself away from his friends were a fantastic delusion, which had vanished with his feverish symptoms. They were to send him a round-robin, and everyone whose name appeared in it should have a sketch in acknowledgment. In this there was perhaps a sense that after all he was the cynosure of their circle: "Just wait till I'm back!" Under the orange-trees of Italy this German pictured himself sitting by the winter-hearth among the beech-woods of Thuringia, telling his travel-tales; and when the miners sent him a poem for his birthday and hung up a wreath on the *Gartenhaus*, Goethe in Rome felt a sentimental longing for Ilmenau.

These moods became, in the second year of the sojourn, more the outcome of an idea than of an actual emotion, and recurred at longer intervals; while none the less he never dreamed of making his liberty a permanent possession or even of prolonging it for five years or so, instead of letting the question of his absence crop up every three months to worry himself and others. Observing all this, we cannot but feel dubious about the alteration in his character, and ask ourselves whether it was not a delusion when Goethe said that after three months he felt different to the very marrow of his bones. What was he like, in reality, when, turning round in the coach, he for the last time beheld the dome of St. Peter's vanish behind the Alban trees? Was he really a different man from the one who had stolen out of Carlsbad on that September morning?

He was a rejuvenated, a more freely-developed—above all, a happier—man; but in himself he was of the stuff which could be altered neither by travel nor women, activity nor knowledge. If we explore the soul of this man of thirty-nine, we find the old duality in a new shape—we might, indeed, anticipate himself, and describe him as his own Faust, his own Helen. He had sought repose from his ceaseless struggle in the classics, in the ever-elusive "Ideal Now" of the South, and was going home—not re-shaped, only with new ideals for the shaping. It is as though his genius had strayed into a by-path of style, only to leap once more upon his dæmon from that ambush.

For Goethe remained dæmonic, even in the sunny Southern atmosphere. When he fled with the boast that he was resolved to "stake his whole existence"—when he spoke of the mortal combat and the deadly disease—when he arrived in Rome, and it was for the non-classic masters that he instinctively contended—for Michael Angelo and against Raphael (whom he but coolly estimated)—still he was the dæmonic Goethe. When he came out of the Sistine Chapel, he could not give any attention to Raphael's Loggie, for "one's eye had been so expanded by those mighty forms that the brilliant trivialities of the arabesques gave it no pleasure."

Vesuvius allured him thrice, not only in the character of geologist. All his descriptions of Naples are coloured by the thought of that diabolic peak uplifted in the heart of a Paradise, by the incomprehensible paradox of that horror confronting that beauty. Men were as they were in Naples because they felt as though hemmed-in between God and Satan! At this time he commented on Herder's *Ideen* (of which the second part reached him in Rome) that assuredly humanity would be victorious in the end; "only I fear that simultaneously the world will turn into a vast hospital in which everyone will be the devoted nurse of everyone else." In this cynically-conceived phrase we have another proof of how the combat was always Goethe's interest—never the moral issue.

The most striking revelation of his dual nature occurs in that monologue in *Faust* (in the Wood and Cavern scene) which may be read as a separate lyric poem:

> Erhabner Geist, du gabst mir, gabst mir alles,
> Warum ich bat. Du hast mir nicht umsonst
> Dein Angesicht in Feuer zugewendet.
> Gabst mir die herrliche Natur zum Königreich,
> Kraft, sie zu fühlen, zu geniessen. Nicht
> Kaltstaunenden Besuch erlaubst du nur,
> Vergönnest mir, in ihre tiefe Brust
> Wie in den Busen eines Freunds zu schauen . . .
> Geheime tiefe Wunder öffnen sich,
> Und steigt vor meinem Blick der reine Mond
> Besänftigend herüber, schweben mir
> Von Felsenwänden, aus dem feuchten Busch
> Der Vorwelt silberne Gestalten auf
> Und lindern der Betrachtung strenge Lust.[1]

But then, at the very height of this flawless tranquillity of spirit—without transition Goethe continues the dialogue with himself:

> O dass dem Menschen nichts Vollkommnes wird,
> Empfind' ich nun. Du gabst zu dieser Wonne,
> Die mich den Göttern nah und näher bringt,
> Mir den Gefährten, den ich schon nicht mehr

[1] "Spirit supreme, who gav'st me, freely gav'st
All that I begged for! Not in vain didst thou
Turn from the flame thy countenance on me,
Giving for kingdom glorious Nature's realm,
With power to feel, to enjoy her. Not
One transient, shivering vision didst thou grant,
But sufferedst me to gaze in her deep heart
As in the bosom of a friend most dear. . . .
Mysterious hidden marvels open there,
And rises, as I look, the virgin moon
In gentle pure refulgence; from the rocks
There float, and from the bushes wet with dew,
The primal world's celestial silver forms
To breathe soft balms on stern reflection's joys."

Entbehren kann. . . .
Er facht in meiner Brust ein wildes Feuer
Nach jenem schönen Bild geschäftig an.
So tauml' ich von Begierde zu Genuss,
Und im Genuss verschmacht' ich nach Begierde.[1]

In this avowal, the last two lines of which are the profoundest formulation of Faust's problem, we get the first hint of Goethe's relinquishment of the hope for complete harmony. He had realised that the path taken under his mistress's guidance was the wrong one for him—otherwise he would not have fled her. It had been self-deception—all the sacrificial soulful chastity, the extirpation of fervency and complexity of emotion. But even while he was giving free play to his sensuous temperament, Goethe was oppressed in spirit, unchangingly resentful—grateful to his genius, but implacable to his dæmon. Never was the immutability of his enigmatic nature more evident than when, in presence of the Classic and the South—those two great examples of serenity and symmetry—he thus summed up their healing influence: "My being has now found the counterpoise which gives it the desirable inertia; I no longer fear the spectres which have so often had their way with me."

It was in this sense only, to this degree only, that Rome had a tranquillising effect on Goethe's nature. And in this sense we are to interpret his declaration, shortly before his return, that in Rome he had first found himself, been a happy and a reasonable being, made peace with himself. This was the halting-place he had reached, striving to moderate his heart's impulses, in the middle of his life. From classic serenity, Rennaissance actuality, he was still excluded; nowhere is there an image, or even an *aperçu*, which points that way. *Tasso*, which alone hails from that sphere, has nothing of these attributes; to the house where

[1] "Oh, that for man perfection may not be,
I feel this hour. Thou gavest this delight
That near and nearer draws me to the gods,
And with it him whom henceforth I no more
Can do without. . . .
He fans within my breast a fierce wild flame
For that sweet form, nor ever lets it die;
So am I tossed between desire and bliss,
And, having bliss, am with desire consumed."

Raphael lived Goethe paid the conventional compliment: "It is a sacred monument"; and everything unconventional and airy which charmed him in the Southerner, everything he thought enviable in the Italian's adaptability and contentedness, he declared to be utterly foreign to his own nature.

One spasmodic outburst is peculiarly expressive of Goethe's eternally unsatisfied desire to grasp the passing moment's happiness in all its actuality, to achieve a natural, spontaneous balance:

At all events I have been in contact with happy people, who are happy simply because they are all of a piece. Even the most insignificant of mortals, if he is *that*, can be happy and in his way complete. And that I will and must attain to also. I can do it—or at any rate I now know wherein it consists, and why it endures. I have gained a knowledge of myself, during this sojourn, which it is beyond me to define with any adequacy.

"I *can!*" he exclaims—but instantly abandons the resolve for the perception. If it had been true that he "could," he would not have gone home—or if he had, it would not have been Goethe, but another man who returned.

Watching him abroad, extending and fortifying his boundaries, then to return to the centre of his dominion, we speculate again on where that centre precisely was. The Italian sojourn gives but a negative answer—that it was not in activity as such, nor in excitement for excitement's sake. Statecraft and government as duties were finally relegated—not again would Goethe's centre be the world of affairs. But whether that centre lay in art or in scientific research, seemed long uncertain. Though he always insisted that in Rome he had found himself again as an artist, what he meant by that was a social, not a scientific, withdrawal. In Rome (he once wrote) his purpose was to gladden himself with the fine arts, to stamp their sacred forms on his spirit, but then, on his return, take up the study of chemistry and mechanics; "for the age of the beautiful is over; ours is one of emergency and implacable demands." Here is international prescience of coming evolutions.

True, during his second stay in Rome he was more the artist than the scientist; but even as an artist he seems more the scientist than the enthusiast of form. His love for truth was a stronger characteristic than his love for beauty; continually he spoke of classic art as true: "I have grown too old for everything, except the Truth. . . . There is nothing great but the True, and the least of that has greatness. . . . How glad I am that I have consecrated my life to the Truth."

Towards the end of the sojourn, he gave utterance to this unromantic remark, which at one time would have been thought unpoetic as well: "Lately I see only the object—not, as before, the accessories which do not really exist." Was the stress laid upon unvarnished truth a sign of departing youth? In Italy there are continual references to his being "too old" for this or that, to his earlier poetry being good because it was written with youthful ardour, to our taking far too much trouble merely to live, to his having at the most ten more working years before him, to his long life of toil demanding some relaxation now that it was nearing the end. On one sad evening shortly before he left Rome, he sat drawing a design for his tomb near the Pyramid of Cestius: "I will finish it when I can, in Indian ink, and then you are to have it." Nor could he have divined that the son of a woman whose acquaintance he was soon to make, would be buried under that Pyramid, forty years from that time, and that he would survive the death of that only son.

But for all the underlying seriousness of his mood, he *was* rejuvenated. A man (he wrote from Rome) must accept the good that comes to him as a beautiful accident, instead of worrying about good and evil in general. And in a happy hour he summed it all up for his friends in the words: "When you think of me, let it be as of a happy man."

Then, facing northward, dæmonic melancholy fell upon his spirit: "In every great sorrow there is the seed of madness—we must be careful not to brood on it and foster it." In Angelica Kauffmann's garden he planted a little pine-tree "as a memento," and afterwards he confessed that on his last days in Rome he had wept like a child.

But his farewell to the South did not weigh on him so heavily as his prescient dread of the reunions in the North, which nevertheless he longed for. A year before he went home he had written to his mistress, saying diffidently that he would like to mean something to those whom he should see when he came back. Later there are many faint hints and questions as to what he was to expect at home, and from Rome sounded brief, appealing adjurations: "Love me, want me, so that I may come back joyfully!"

Now in Milan the North wind blew upon his cheek; and as he, leaving statues and blue skies, once more approached the gloomier Northern peaks, he once more took it as a symbol—and there is a note of gentle melancholy in the words he wrote to his friend Knebel on the way home, saying that crystals "seemed interesting again" and a stone an object to be reckoned with. "Thus does human nature help itself out, when there is no help for things." And, possessed by foreboding, Goethe—who yesterday had written a gay letter—added this poignant sentence: "I am bringing back so much—if there is any chance of your caring about it."

Then he was told that the man he had been most confidently reckoning on had passed him on the way—Herder, bound for Rome. Goethe was startled as by an omen, spoke of the bitter pain the news had caused him, but from the German frontier looked back once more to the gayest weeks he had spent in the South:

If you go to Castel Gandolfo [he wrote from Lake Constance to Herder], ask to be shown a certain pine-tree. . . . I used to look out upon it, at the time when I wanted you most. . . . *Bon voyage*, and be well when you open this letter in the land where I was absolutely happy for the first time in my life.

CHAPTER VIII

LONELINESS

"I am not always in tune for great emotions, and without them I am negligible."

THE Belvedere. Tea with the Duchess in the little drawing-room. It is an evening at the beginning of August; all the windows are open.

Goethe stands at the table. On its inlaid surface he has spread out some Roman sketches, carefully mounted, many of them lightly framed, and now he unrolls a map of Rome and shows the Duchess, over whose chair he is bending, where he had lived. She finds the big map very puzzling.

Carl August, who has hurt his foot, sits in his invalid-chair; he looks ill. Another fall from his horse, when he had insisted on spurring the exhausted animal to camp after a whole day in the saddle. Only thirty-two, is he? When his well-drilled military figure is not in evidence, his head makes him look older than that. A Prince begins life early, especially when he comes to the throne at eighteen. He is smoking and gazing into vacancy. His mother yonder, on the contrary, looks younger than her age; she sits straight as a lathe upon the sofa. She is just fifty, but her bearing and her fine figure make her still attractive. Just now she has a little sketch before her and is showing it to Weiland who bends over her from behind, his sharp nose nearly touching her *décolletage*. With his long artistic hand he is pointing to a Watteauesque group which is prominent among the pine-trees of the picture.

On the left, with her back to the table, sits Caroline Herder. She does not seem to notice the prolonged silence of her neighbour, Knebel; her alert gaze is alert for her husband alone, and when it discovers him yonder in the window, absorbed in a volume of the Vatican statuary, she wonders whether it would annoy him if she went and joined him.

Opposite, with her beautiful but no longer youthful head supported on her slender left hand, Charlotte von Stein leans well back in her chair, very silent, replying but coldly and absently to the Duke's occasional remarks. By the open door to the terrace a Chamberlain is telling a Privy-Councillor a piquante story of Carl August's youth, but the other seldom smiles. He is only half-attending—like all these people, who are always absent-minded, though they may seem to be talking or listening. . . . "Would it really be worth while for a month or two?" thinks Herder—who has not yet started for Rome, after all. He turns over the pages of the Vatican Catalogue. "We can't all stay abroad for two years; only this upstart can do things of that sort. What wonderful things he has seen, and how wonderfully he has seen them! But who was his guide? My *Ideen* showed him how to see Rome—from my distance it was *I* who taught him the essential. People like us, with the centuries in our hearts, don't really need to travel. It takes one out of one's groove, though. . . . General-Superintendent, am I? But it's not good enough, not nearly good enough! Where are your youthful dreams, Johann Gottfried Herder? King of the realm of intellect, absolute monarch? And all you are is a Duke! This Goethe—well yes, he's the one man I could have borne to take my place, for one has hopes that he won't get a swelled head—and that's something, at any rate. . . ."

"How long the Duchess is listening to him!" thinks Caroline Herder. "It's time that Herder went to Rome—that trip of Goethe's has given him too great an advantage. If one could only be sure that Dalberg will cover the expenses! We ought to be 'raised' at last, Goethe will have to arrange it—it was he who brought us here, after all! Out of affection? I cannot get rid of the feeling that he never really does anything that isn't going to be useful to him. Perhaps he *is* the more gifted—but certainly not the more profound; and as to fame—our *Ideen* are talked of all over Germany, and who has a word to say about *Egmont!*"

"He doesn't care a button about all these things he's showing!" thinks Knebel. "How different it was on that Sunday evening,

GOETHE AT THE AGE OF FORTY-ONE

when we were coming down the road at Tiefurt, and he stopped and plucked a bit of myosotis and began to pull it to pieces, observing it and never saying a word. And he was so communicative about our stones, but now he won't say anything about his plants. O solitary spirit! You flee from me because you think I might understand you!"

"We might as well not exist!" thinks Anna Amalia, the Dowager-Duchess, remembering Goethe's enchantment with the Borghese Gardens, a picture of which she now has in her hand. "Certainly I should like to go South, too—but I shouldn't forget my own country so completely when I was there! Yesterday he was complaining about the rain and the cold, now that it's turned cool at last. Good heavens, one would have thought we were at the North Pole? What did he come back for, then? But all these middle-class people are the same. . . ."

"*Fine mouche!*" thinks Wieland, who is looking at the sketch without seeing it. "He knows how to look after himself. No sooner is he back, and sees that we have managed to survive his absence remarkably well, than he looks round for something to keep up the Italian mood—and takes a girl! She had to be Junoesque, of course, but *plus gentille*—we don't get used to Roman sumptuousness and write poems to Cupid for nothing. Young too, with brown curly hair; they even say she's a virgin—what does he want more? There will be a charming scene if the Mistress of the Horse catches him at it. . . ."

"He might be surrounded by glass walls!" thinks the Duchess, while she painfully follows Goethe's finger on the map of Rome. "One would have expected him to seem younger, when he looks so sunburnt and animated. But it's as if he wore a mask. I understand—yes, yes! He is not happy."

"The fellow's got a fresh lease of youth!" thinks Carl August, who has been talking to him this morning. "He understands at last that one isn't an old man at thirty or so, but must have some fun when one has to go through such a grind. This confounded foot of mine! My little girl will be unfaithful to me if I can't get about again before long! And there's the Review coming on. I'll give it till Sunday—then I'll be off, and devil take my foot! Goethe must come with me, as he used to. He can't put up an official excuse now, and I bet he's taken a liking to going about and will be glad to do it for nothing. *Parbleu*, I wish this tea-party was over. . . ."

". . . Never any more!" thinks Frau von Stein, and looks mournfully across at him out of her Italian eyes. "There he stands, prosing like Loder or some other wiseacre from Jena. He's getting stouter, more easy-going. How slender he once was! And his chin used to be so firm and clear-cut! Now it's almost a double-chin, and his lips are thicker—they say he's got fond of eating. That look about the mouth—it suggests kisses of a certain kind. . . . O Charlotte, why didn't you keep a firmer hand on yourself? Why—instead of making him unhappy all the time? He has tasted youth in the South—from creatures who could only fasten on his lips! No one will ever take hold of his soul as I did from the first day he saw me—no one will ever take hold of mine again. And now, in his desolation, he wants pleasure—and it's always to be found so easily. We're happier with lower ideals. Never any more—O genius that you are; and all that I gave you—done with! How is it I do not hate you?"

". . . Where am I?" thinks Goethe, showing his pictures and talking. "Are these the friends I was so glad to be coming back to? With whom I meant to share it all, in the long evenings? My public, my disciples, my teachers, my lord and lady? I feel their searching eyes upon me, and it's as uncomfortable as though my belt or my stockings were hanging down (I wonder if they are). And when I came back and felt their hands in mine—was it just an accident?—how cold they seemed! Only now do I realise what I have given up for them, and when I wonder why I gave it up, I have to keep a tight hand on myself or I should fly at them all this minute. Or perhaps it's really only the climate of this place? No, it can't be only the climate. That brown-haired child was born here too—and she's as alluring as any Roman girl!"

When Goethe re-entered the Weimar in which he had wasted more than ten years of his life, he felt, after a few days, that all his painful forebodings were confirmed. "Why have you come back?" asked the eyes of his friends. "Why have I come back?" his own heart retorted.

Two years ago, departing from the place, the chariot of his life had been drawn by those two rival steeds—his genius and his dæmon. They had borne him swiftly across the Alps, as though to retrieve the youthfulness which here was perishing, and only in the South could bloom again. But it was a mere remnant of it that he had retrieved. His days in Italy had been methodical and laborious; he had been overshadowed by the now wonted mood of deep seriousness, and any ripple of the gay Southern life which had reached him had been as it were a dance of wavelets on the shore beneath his watch-tower, which he was not yet too old to observe with indulgent amusement.

Nothing and no one urged him homeward—there was hardly a creature who called to him or needed him. The Duke had had enough of him, in a way; Goethe's place had been filled with his own consent; his mistress was, even at the time of his flight, little more than an idea for him, and during his years of absence her image had completely faded from his heart. The two Duchesses and Wieland had long been no more than friendly lookers-on at his struggle; Knebel, and still more Herder, were dear to him but were not irreplaceable, and their attraction was far from being powerful enough to allure him from the animated sphere of mutual endeavour and daily renewed stimulations. Weimar, its town, its Government-offices, its politics, its Court, were like vague mist on the horizon of a little State of which he had hardly known the name twelve years before, and to which nothing now attached him but reminiscences of what he had learnt and achieved there. As poet, as scientist, he was tied to no country: at thirty-eight, Goethe was free to remain in a land, and a condition of life, which he enjoyed. Why *had* he come back?

The answer might be—because in Weimar he had a certain standing, a house and possessions. On the surface it would be true. He had to make some money; his inheritance from his father was in the remote future; he could not have afforded the expensive Italian sojourn without his Ministerial salary, and the advance-payment for his collected edition. Whether he would earn much more by writing seemed doubtful. No longer young, not adventurous enough to risk all, though he had no one to keep but himself, he had been spoilt by his position and manner of life; and though in Rome he could live in one room and used only two small ones at Weimar, he was not prepared to do without the large handsome house in which he could collect his treasures and entertain his friends. Travelling incognito was all very well, but he had no intention of dropping his famous name altogether. This Weimar post was as a needful prop, enabling him to stand with a dignity akin to that which his gait had now assumed. Prudence, convenience, a touch of provincialism—these entirely Philistine motives might well have been the reasons impelling him to return to the place whither his genius had originally borne him.

And yet, in view of the second half of his life, we cannot be content with such an explanation. The impulses of genius may appear to be rational, but they will always prove in the end to have been the reverse. Goethe might have his reasons, but his destiny had not—it drove him on unconsciously. It was too late to settle down or even make a long stay in the clime and among the occupations and interests which he had so long desired. He came home because his spirit was not attuned to the dreamy measure of the Southern days, to the infinite suggestiveness of Rome, to the pleasant unconventionality of foreign life—but needed a narrow circle, fixed duties, and that Northern sky from which, to the end, he was to wish he could get away. Goethe left Italy of his own free will, of his own accord, because his antithetical nature needed the alternation of wish and fulfilment, because neither Faust nor Mephisto could long endure the "Here and Now." That alternation ruled his whole career.

He was hardly back before it began to take effect again. He had returned to the North, longing for the friendly use and wont of house and friends, and saying emphatically that the Southern people and their manner of life were to him as a beautiful, exotic picture. No sooner did he reach Weimar than the wish for what he had left behind deepened into a craving; and the more unlikely it seemed, after he had voluntarily made his choice, that he should ever see Rome again, the more he set his heart upon it. "Indifference to everything, since the loss of my Roman bliss"—so runs a note written some time afterwards.

If he had left that bliss with wet eyes, it was with eyes which dwelt too fondly on the past that he now gazed across the Alps. Now, as was his way, he celebrated the beloved place in verse;

and while he sighed over the low barometer and the want of colour, and accused the murky heavens of depressing him beyond belief, he sought escape by fancying himself in the South—exactly as he had lost all sense of the Roman pine-trees in the vapours of the Witches' Kitchen. Now, under the grey skies, he wrote thus:

> . . . Gedenk' ich der Zeiten,
> Da mich ein graulicher Tag hinten im Norden umfing,
> Trübe der Himmel und schwer auf meine Scheitel sich senkte,
> Farb-und gestaltlos die Welt um den Ermatteten lag,
> Und ich über mein Ich, des unbefriedigten Geistes
> Düstre Wege zu spähn, still in Betrachtung versank.
> Nun umleuchtet der Glanz des helleren Äthers die Stirne![1]

Can we wonder that in his friends the restless fluctuating temper which, though at home, seemed miles away from them, should have caused some estrangement? Much had happened to them while he had been in Italy, but Goethe could find no interest for it; their whole sphere seemed even narrower to him, coming back from the world outside, than it had while he was absent. Herder and the Dowager-Duchess were on the point of starting for the Rome whence he had come; the Duke was absorbed not only in military projects but in a new love-affair, and was for weeks confined to his sofa, restless on more than one count. Goethe had had a presentiment of how it would be; and had written to his friends a year ago, apparently for no reason whatever, that it was extraordinary how "there was a sort of eternal veil between even the best and most intelligent people."

Charlotte, whom disappointment, illness, and loneliness had aged—and the more because Goethe seemed to grow younger every day—was now in her forty-seventh year, and for more than six months had had no Italian letters from him. Whether the parting in Carlsbad had been an unconfessed eternal farewell,

[1] ". . . Those moments recalling,
Pent under skies of the North, here in the murk of the days,
Leaden, the lowering heaven pressed on my brain like a burden,
Colourless, formless, the world, wearily on it I looked.
And myself and my Ego, never satisfied spirits,
Sought us, how vainly, a path—silently fell into thought.
Now, in these crystalline skies, the glittering stars are as jewels!"

and the forgiveness in her letters to Rome but a half-forgiveness—certain it is that directly he came back, sunburnt and restless, both saw how far they had drifted apart. She might still send him little dainties, Fritz might return to his house as of old—these were mere gestures, concealing the emotions that neither wished to express. True, it was she alone who, privileged by the unlimited intimacy of the many years that had gone, spoke frankly to Goethe in the very first days of his return. And he, from old habit, resumed some of their old themes, sent her the manuscript of his poems before they were printed—but said to Herder's wife:

"Ah, with *Her* I can't do anything. She is out of spirits, and nothing seems to go right."

Herself he approached—not indeed as a lover, but with something of appeal as of a fellow-creature in distress. "I will gladly hear anything you have to say to me; I would only beg that you won't be too hard on me, so distracted—I won't say so torn in pieces—as I am. To you I may surely confess that I don't feel exactly as I appear. . . ."

He was franker with Herder's wife, whom he often visited after Herder had gone, interesting himself in her allowances and the children; and her view of him—subtle and kind as she was, but always unequal to understanding him—was given in her letters to her husband, so that through Goethe's mask we can guess at the state of his soul.

> Goethe has been saying some comical, I might even say bewildering, things about his domestic and general situation. . . . He has now reduced all happiness and well-being to a sense of proportion, and all unhappiness to that of disproportion. He says he is now perfectly satisfied with having a house, enough to eat and drink, and so on. Everything . . . depends upon a person's having a domestic nature. . . . On the whole I don't altogether approve of him. He is living now in a way that starves his heart. Charlotte Stein thinks he has become sensual, and she is not far wrong.

Once he paid Frau Herder a surprise-visit, and said: "I was well on the way to my garden, but I felt I must turn back—something drove me here, not love, but perhaps despair. I had just left the Duke." Equally laconic and obscure, gloomy and apprehensive, are the few words that surged from out the carefully-guarded depths of his soul into his letters:

> I am living very strangely, very self-controlled, waiting on time and the hour. . . . Everyone finds it convenient to keep away, and I feel very much like Epimenides when he woke up. . . . How utterly useless I am, on the whole.

On his birthday he danced till midnight—Goethe had to be thirty-nine before he could dance his birthday out in a mood of restless, bewildered apathy. And he was to be thirty years older before he could repeat the performance.

He remained in this "self-controlled" condition till the autumn, considering the possibilities presented by life. What he needed was a place for his collections, an income independent of his literary earnings, the proximity of a university, a circle which would be useful to him both as audience and disciples; and so he decided to stick it out to the end at Weimar, despite his retirement from office, despite estrangements—despite, perhaps because of, his isolation. Yes, to the end; since for a short span of time a man of his kind does not take such immense precautions as Goethe now took.

The first was clearing up the situation about his official posts. True, he was still a member of the Cabinet; but as his chair had always been empty for two years before he left for Italy, it was now removed, and Goethe was privileged, when he did wish to put in an appearance, to sit in the Duke's.

He was relieved of all responsibility; there were no more admonitions to the Duke, the Court, or the Government. Only rarely did the economically-inclined Treasury Minister flame forth, as for instance when he wrote to the Dowager-Duchess in Naples that her tour might involve her in many expenses: "Your Highness will pardon this expression of opinion, which though well-meant may seem to smack a little of an Ex-President of the Cabinet." In this spirit of self-mockery he played the part of an old intimate, and barely concealed behind his courtly blandishments the annoyance he felt at extravagant diversions. But in the same letter he begged the Dowager to patronise his friends, the German painters, in Rome!

He was gentler with the Duchess, whose resigned melancholy struck an answering chord. A certain strain of lovemaking, now and then tinging their expressions of platonic sympathy, can hardly be said to obtrude itself, but does occasionally strike one as one reads the documents. At this time he often read aloud to her, was very helpful to her after a miscarriage—and she gave him her husband's letters to read.

He continued to do some practical work for the Court, superintended the structural alterations in an old castle, tried to induce a foreign Minister, whose acquaintance he had made on his tour, to come to Weimar, interested himself for some old friends at Court, procured credit for a Chamberlain who was in debt, got a paid post for an old servant. Officially speaking, he was still Minister of Mines, but not for three months after his return did he inspect Ilmenau.

For the rest, he became Minister of Education in the little realm, which means that he undertook the direction and supervision of the University, the Institute, the Academy of Art, and the Theatre. And this was more than an office. In this, and this alone, what executive authority he had became an effective instrument of his plastic spirit. He clutched at the post because just then he felt some menace in the air—he would be the officially recognized intellectual leader in this Duchy at any rate, if he was no longer to be so for Germany.

For when Goethe returned, he found the literary atmosphere altered. If in the overburdened years before his departure for Italy he had scarcely noticed this, or perhaps refused to let himself notice it—now it asserted itself, he could not doubt that other gods were on the throne. While Goethe was in Rome, Schiller had come to Weimar. His plays were being acted over half Germany. When Goethe came back, nobody was talking or writing about his *Iphigenie*, which had just appeared, and even when *Tasso* followed hard upon it, the same silence reigned. Twenty years were to go by before the German stage saw his plays. All the world was raving about Don Carlos—even the Duke, whose cousin of Meiningen gave Schiller a title of honour.

But to Goethe—so he later described his feelings—Schiller's *Die Räuber* was detestable, because a powerful but immature talent has . . . abounded in the very ethical and theatrical paradoxes from which I have sought to get clear . . . pouring them out in a turgid, irresistible torrent. The applause which was lavished on that remarkable production was to me alarming. . . . I would have been quite glad to abandon the practice of authorship, had that been possible—for what chance was there of outbidding those works with their genuine talent and their outrageous form? You can imagine my state of mind!

At first he held his peace; and while he built himself a stronghold where he might write and analyse undisturbed, he took care to make it impregnable, a refuge and a *locus standi*, not easily to be invaded by anyone whatever. His position as Minister of Education—originally jumped-at so as to give some return for his salary—he now used as the corner-stone of that stronghold.

Resolute to abdicate the position of intellectual leader in this region neither for Schiller nor another, he lost no time. A criticism of *Egmont* had appeared, full of reverential fault-finding. Its author was Schiller, with whom for years Goethe refused to treat as an equal power; and its appearance coincided with his return from Italy, as if to welcome him home. Goethe spoke of it to the Duke with regal indifference, scarcely deigning to do more than make an all too prophetic allusion to Carl August as Schiller's new Mæcenas. Then he recommended the inconvenient poet, who was living in or near Weimar, as Professor of History—that is to say, he packed him off to Jena. Moreover, he removed the new elements from the Academy of Art, and introduced methods and teachers who would carry out his own severely classic ideas.

For the stronghold had now turned into an academy. Feeling himself less of the author, more and more of the scientist and æsthete, Goethe needed co-operation. He procured pass-men from the colleges who, for the sake of a living and a certain position, would give him the indispensable assistance. This intangible Goethe-Academy, which had its quarters in Goethe's house, was the grand annexe, so to speak, of his collective Roman studies, the ripe fruit of his dilettante adolescence, and was quickly supplied with professors. From Rome came Moritz, and stayed several weeks with Goethe. Then he was politely dismissed, handed over to his bewildered destiny—having unloaded all the æsthetics that his friend required. They were contained in a manifesto which was transferred to Goethe's Works, like that of an assistant-student to the archives of an Institute.

For Meyer, the art-historian and painter, Goethe contrived to procure two years' financial support in Rome for the completion of his studies, upon his promise that he would then come to Weimar.

The Duke was induced to grant these gratuities, salaries, and commissions by the slogan that a modern Florence was to spring up in his capital. In reality it was simply to give Goethe facilities for the work that was useful to him. For now, when he could see his way before him, with fewer calls upon his time and far-reaching purposes, he found himself unable to push forward on that level path unless certain material was prepared for his attention, as it is for a Minister's. His increasing absorption in scientific research henceforth made him dispose of his fellow creatures' destinies, claim certain people's brains as his exclusive property, and be highly indignant if any one he wanted was unable to come to him, or refused, or, once come, proposed to leave. Meyer's knowledge of art was as indispensable to him as a lexicon, and when his friend fell ill, Goethe wrote: "If he dies, I shall lose a treasure that I despair of finding again in a lifetime." But Meyer got well, and was for ten years his housemate, for forty his friend.

In Rome one final, systematic effort had proved to him that he was no painter. Thenceforth—and we can guess with what a heavy heart!—he gave up painting once for all, and persuaded his Roman friends to come North. He sent Meyer to Dresden to copy Titian; he lured Lips to Weimar by promises of commissions and journalism, and gave him enough money to travel in comfort; Bury too came later on. As Goethe was no longer responsible for the finances, he was ready to turn the Duke into a Mæcenas. In his passion for plastic art, indulged to the hilt at Rome, he tried to replace Rome at Weimar by pictures and statues; and as Goethe never in his life cared for possessions merely as such, and would certainly not have been a collector if there had been collections at Weimar, he satisfied his own ambition by enriching the Court, the town, and the Academy.

When he could not get at the Duke, he would approach the

two Duchesses for appointments and pensions for struggling artists. Or he would send a musical servant to the Berlin orchestra, or give an engraver lessons in lithography at Dresden. His house and his letters, which formerly were full of society-people, became, after the tour, alive with artistic figures; and when, at the end of the *Kunstlers Apotheose*, he causes his artist to implore the Muses to keep the needy student, it was really Goethe, pointing the Duke to Lips or Facius, and saying sternly:

> Und willst du diesen jungen Mann,
> Wie er's verdient, dereinst erheben,
> So bitt' ich, ihm bei seinem Leben,
> Solang' er selbst noch kaun und küssen kann,
> Das Nötige zur rechten Zeit zu geben![1]

One and a half millions—so, forty years later, he could reckon up—were given for great purposes, at his instigation, in that small sphere!

Goethe, who for the last few years had been almost invisible, now again went into society. "Forgive me; I am distraught today, and my head is spinning with the Carnival gaieties"—so he could now write to Friend Meyer in Rome. A year before, in Rome itself, he had fled after half-an-hour of the ridotto, and hoped never to see another! If nowadays he gave a big tea-party in his garden, he enjoyed it—it did not "give him the shivers" as before the tour. At Belvedere he served tea and sour milk, "so as to win the ladies' hearts, while the menkind are chained by the powerful Parcae to the card-tables."

Nevertheless he worked at full pressure. He invited a colleague for a discussion either in the evening at eleven, or next morning at six. He read aloud a great deal—the fragment of *Faust* three times running. In between he would make frequent visits to Jena; and there, though it is true that early in the mornings he would tramp through the snow with Fichte, Humboldt and

[1] "Wouldst thou, as merits this young man,
Ensure him future acclamations,
I pray thee, spare him all privations;
While yet he lives and comfortably can
Digest and kiss, fail not in thy donations!"

Meyer to the anatomy-lectures, the afternoons would be spent at tea-parties, the evenings at balls and concerts, and he was never tired of talking about Italy, for people best enjoyed hearing about that. "People" in general got more of his conversation than of old, and possibly more than his friends did. Knebel fell rather into the background, Goethe now found him too enigmatic; what he was looking for was simplicity, animation—youth, in a word. He hesitated to ask Knebel to accompany him on a trip, and remarked afterwards: "He is so kind that it is bad for one to be long with him—and I am so set in my own ways, by which I must live or be utterly wretched."

How kind he was to Caroline Herder, when her absent husband was offered a post at Göttingen, and she was full of hope and anxiety! He wrote again and again to his friend in Rome, and advised the wife to think well over all the pros and cons. He procured gratuities for father and children, and higher rank and greater liberty for Herder, so as to keep him at Weimar; was forever praising his new work to his wife—and yet, though nothing could have been more devoted than his counsel and his actions, though even Caroline perpetually assured her husband that he was their only friend . . . this was not Goethe's old, unmeasured devotion, either with Herder or any other friend.

A heartier tone, so to speak, was infused into his letters to everyone; they seem more friendly than before, and more superficial. Commonplace turns of phrase, a quantity of postscripts, testify to a carelessness which had not hitherto been his. They are more communications than letters; at any rate, they seldom have any literary charm. To his very good friends there is a frequent condescending "My dear fellow" or "Write to me now and then"; there are many requests to excuse his illegible writing, and if one compares one letter with another, one finds things twice recounted, or even metaphors and images used twice over on the same or the following day.

Were all these indications of a more pliable, sociable life, the symptoms of a nature more at ease? If so, we should expect to discover traces of a more genuine happy-heartedness. Or did they mean a flight from self-knowledge—the flight of an unhappy man who is trying to stupefy himself? Were that so, we should look for signs of a collapse, for reasons or at any rate causes at this particular time. No; rather this is a man whose conflict with the world has gradually so isolated him, whose inward life has finally become so withdrawn into itself, that there is no further danger for him in mixing with society; a man who after mighty efforts to attune his nature to the world at large has—not now defiantly, but astutely—abandoned all idea of that attunement. This is a man with a mask—and here is Goethe at forty-one, as Lips depicted him.

Middle-aged, but only in years; no longer young, but only if we go by dates. The features, that but four years ago were lean and nervous, are now becoming broad and massive; the nose, whose irregular lines spoke of a man at odds with himself, is now strikingly majestic—the lips beneath are folded tranquilly, making one think of noble treasure-laden ships at anchor. The chin is beginning to acquire a massy fullness; it can hardly be true that the brow has widened, but certainly the head is more set, is heavier and squarer—that head which not long ago had seemed to touch the clouds. But the eye, once inquiring, then impassioned, then fiery, then searching, now seems spellbound in impenetrable aloofness—from no other portrait does it gaze thus uncompromisingly, staring straight into your own and yet not seeing you. No mouth was ever more resolutely wordless, no eyes ever looked more inexpressively into vacancy, or—so looking—more profoundly into the man's own soul, than Goethe's do in this portrait. Yes—it is gone; that ardent youth, that inquiring, craving, dreaming, appealing youth. This is the first, the pathetically premature, attestation that Goethe is growing old.

Can we wonder that at last he, even he, resolved to possess, enjoy, retain what others had been granted sooner and in richer measure? He took a wife, he founded a family, he became the father of a son.

Here too his prophetic look had long been conscious of a new turn of fate. It seemed no more than the light touch of Tyche's flying wing, to his first apprehension. In a few months he knew it for fulfilment—in a few years, for destiny.

Ja, wir bekennen euch gern, es bleiben unser Gebete,
Unser täglicher Dienst Einer besonders geweiht. . . .
Diese Göttin, sie heisst Gelegenheit; lernet sie kennen! . . .
Gern ergibt sie sich nur dem raschen, tätigen Manne,

Dieser findet sie zahm, spielend und zärtlich und hold.
Einst erschien sie auch mir, ein bräunliches Mädchen, die Haare
Fielen ihr dunkel und reich über die Stirne herab,
Kurze Locken ringelten sich ums zierliche Hälschen,
Ungeflochtenes Haar krauste vom Scheitel sich auf.
Und ich verkannte sie nicht, ergriff die Eilende, lieblich
Gab sie Umarmung und Kuss bald mir gelehrig zurück.
O wie war ich beglückt! . . . [1]

Four weeks after his return, in July, Goethe one morning went for a walk in the Park. A girl, such as the above lines depict, approached him with a request that he would let her brother call on him—he was a writer, she said, penniless and unemployed. Christiane Vulpius was twenty-three, Goethe nearly thirty-nine, Frau von Stein forty-six. Youthful and fresh, the girl might have been Charlotte's daughter, though they were utterly unlike in character, temperament, and class. Or she may have resembled the Roman damsel whom Goethe had left a few months ago. The impression she made upon him that morning he has recorded twice to Johanna Schopenhauer in the beautiful phrase that "she was then like a young Dionysos."

Everything that was Southern in Charlotte—the melancholy night of her black eyes, the ivory pallor of her skin, the symmetry of her noble features—in this young creature was diametrically different. She was fresh as the dawn, impulsive, virginal yet budding into ardent womanhood, while in Charlotte a woman's instincts had been inhibited by her prolonged withdrawal from sexual life.

Goethe, who might almost have been her father, snatched at her as at a goblet filled with wine that would dispel his troubled

[1] "Aye, we acknowledge ye gladly, yet are our prayers and our service
Daily offered to One—she is the chosen of all. . . .
Goddess this of our hearts, Opportunity: learn ye to know her!
Him, the swiftly-deciding, swiftly-acting, she smiles on,
Him she meekly obeys, sportive and tender and kind.
Once to me she appeared, an olive-brown girl, and her tresses,
Dusky and rich, like a cloud covered her forehead and fell;
Tiny ringlets curled round her neck in delicate beauty,
Loose, unwoven, the hair sprang in thick waves from her head;
And I mistook her not then, I caught at her passing, and sweetly
Docile she clasped me and kissed, swift her response as my call—
O the joy that was mine! . . ."

restlessness, and did not too closely inquire into the provenance or vintage of the draught. It was a young, fervent, simple nature that he snatched at, rather than the actual Christiane Vulpius; it is as though her looks were at first more important to him than her personality, for he took possession of her more rapidly and more decisively than of any of the women in his earlier love-affairs.

For from the first moment it was his heart that ruled his desire. No one was ever less of a believer in the primitive dualism of the soul and the senses than was Goethe, whose "hygiene of the spirit" could never have misled him into giving only a part of himself to a woman. He, who in Venice had not been able to resist expounding Palladio to his servant-man, simply because they happened to be standing together before the masterpiece—he, who had tried to teach the boy at his side to observe the phenomena of Nature, because they so stirred himself—this man, so unreserved and self-surrendering with his intimates, who had never had a woman under his roof till now—was *he* the man to shut this first feminine housemate out of his heart, and like any vulgarian take his pleasure when he listed, consigning her at other times to the kitchen and the housework, and leading a separate existence with other men and women? That day would never come.

For the present he did not even exclude her from his work. True, she did not possess the freedom and breadth of Charlotte's culture, nor could she grasp the idea of plastic form. If Frau von Stein had never stimulated Goethe's brain, she knew very well how he had stimulated hers. Christiane's appreciation was more naïve, but when her friend explained optical experiments or botanical studies, she had mother-wit enough to get some idea of the things that Charlotte's intellect had fully grasped. Of the sciences to which Goethe was now entirely devoting himself, both women were completely ignorant; but it was in a very tender tone that he lyrically answered Christiane's questions about the *Metamorphosis of Plants*. That didactic poem, whose opening lines are enough to make it a love-poem, is like a rainbow spanning the distant horizons of the two lovers.

Between his seventeenth and twenty-fourth years Goethe had been thrice engaged, each time with a wish for children; and now again at forty he was thinking, if not of immediate marriage, at any rate of paternity. For the first time a second person was to be a permanent inmate of his house.

In Weimar, throughout the past ten years, he had taken no woman entirely to himself. With the Court-lady, as with the loveliest artist in the town, he had had intimate relations, but had never lived with either. Now, immediately after his second arrival, he identified himself with this girl, who was the penniless daughter of a deceased archivist, and had been obliged to work in an artificial flower factory. She was cheerful, simple, and domesticated, and though she was fond of dancing, there had never been a word of scandal about her. At first their meetings were only in his little *Gartenhaus*; when after scarce two years he established her and her mother in his town-house, he did not propose to marry her—what he wanted was a woman, a home, an abiding-place for his son. "I am married, except for the ceremony," he said, and referred to the anniversary as the date of his marriage.

Her bright exhilarating nature always reminded him of his native home. For fifty years this man vainly strove to love the Thuringian landscape, and longed not only for the Tiber but for the Main and the Rhine, when the absence of brooks and broad sheets of water weighed on his spirits. "Only love me" (so Goethe now read on his travels); "I think of you every minute of the day, and am planning to have the house looking ever so nice, so as to give you pleasure because you give me so much."

When had he ever before read such tenderly-imagined, timidly solicitous words? And soon he was to read that a little person had asked: "Did Father send me a kiss?"

His swift snatch at Christiane, the defiant attitude he took up, give us the impression of a man who, like him of fifteen years before, was fighting down his former prepossessions—and fighting too against the rank that now was his. Though this had first begun in Rome, it was not till now that it became apparent.

One day Goethe found his newly-written love-poems in a cupboard under the cast of Raphael's skull, where someone had put them away. He smiled, and took this too as a symbol—and indeed these poems are themselves the most definite symbol of the alteration he had undergone. Through the very first that he wrote for Christiane—*Der Besuch* (*The Visit*) and *Morgenklagen* (*Morning-Complaint*)—rings the cheerfully-assured tone of a man whose happiness lies more in being loved than in loving. Here is a lyric in which gossamer lightness is linked to passion, here is the playfulness of love at ease—it is not even rhymed, is just a whispered caress:

> O du loses leidigliebes Mädchen,
> Sag mir an; womit hab' ich's verschuldet—
> Dass du mich auf diese Folter spannest,
> Dass du dein gegeben Wort gebrochen? . . . [1]

Very likely he found her asleep, and sang that song to her; and when he sketched her, as he sang, in that position Goethe was for the first time, and unconsciously, illustrating one of his own poems.

A month or two—and even from that exhilarating contact he removed himself (as was his wont) to a little distance, there to take it in as a whole and at the same time see it in detail. When, with his devotion to the classic ideals, he found his beloved so easy-going, unexacting, and cheerfully selfless, he was reminded of the Roman girl who might have walked out of the pages of Horace; and soon her image became so fused with the more immediate relation that Rome, Faustina, and Christiane seemed one and the same thing.

He quite understood the process, and explained it to her by his classical predilections; and when in the third Elegy he distinguished between two kinds of love, one seems to detect some resentful reminiscence of Charlotte's feeling for him:

> Vielfach wirken die Pfeile des Amor: einige ritzen,
> Und vom schleichenden Gift kranket auf Jahre das Herz.
> Aber mächtig befiedert, mit frisch geschliffener Schärfe
> Dringen die andern ins Mark, zünden behende das Blut.
> In der heroischen Zeit, da Götter und Göttinnen liebten,
> Folgte Begierde dem Blick, folgte Genuss der Begier. . . . [2]

[1] "O you lazy love, you little rascal,
Tell me in what way I have defaulted,
Tell me why you rack me, tantalise me—
What are given words when they are broken?"

[2] "Amor's arrows are many and various—some of them rend us
And their poisons are slow, long will the heart be in pain;
Ah, but fleetly are feathered, skilfully pointed, some others,

Goethe, in the first four years with Frau von Stein, wrote her nearly four hundred notes, all of which we possess. There is not one page to Christiane, in a similar space of time. There was no sense in writing when they were both under the same roof, and his communications in the early years of travel are lost. Thus there are few direct testimonies to the strength of an attachment which no one who reads his verses could possibly dispute.

In the course of eighteen months Christiane became the mother of Goethe's first son. During the early weeks the least thing was enough to alarm the father. He was in Venice when something occurred to make him anxious, and he wrote to Herder about the woman who had now made him happy for two years: "Those whom I have left behind are very dear to me, and I freely confess that I passionately love the girl. How deep my attachment is I have only realised since I came away." So profound was the strength of his feeling, so entirely did he now feel her to be his destined mate, so heavily did loneliness weigh upon his spirits, that he was soon obsessed by the pessimistic fear of love's instability which filled that soul, so rarely happy as it was, with humble apprehension at the touch of good-fortune's flying wings. He was awaiting the Dowager-Duchess, whom he had come to Venice to bring home, and the days were slipping by, he was nervous, longing for the wife and child in the North. . . . He broke out into a cry which Hamlet might have uttered, quivering with a sense of former evil tricks of Fate, though to the world all might well have seemed glad fulfilment:

Oftmals hab' ich geirrt und habe mich wiedergefunden,
Aber glücklicher nie. Nun ist dies Mädchen mein Glück!
Ist auch dieses ein Irrtum, so schont mich, ihr klügeren Götter,
Und benehmt mir ihn erst drüben am kalten Gestad'.[1]

The full significance of these words (which we must accept in default of any other written confession) can be estimated only

---

These will go deep, and inflame the quick blood at a touch.
In the heroic old times, when the gods and the goddesses coupled,
A glance would engender desire—joys on desire followed hard."

[1] "Oftentimes I mistook, and often came to my senses,
Happier never I was. Happiness now is this girl.
Oh, if this too is mistake, spare me, ye gods that mistake not,
Suffer the dream to go on, till I wake on the lonely shore."

by those who have realised the passion for unvarnished truth to which, at this period, Goethe was resolute to sacrifice even his imagination. How little of love, of trust, had his forty years' quest instilled into the man who, nevertheless, would choose the sweet delusion rather than a rough awakening!

However, he was to be granted many years of happy domesticity. Eros soon made himself at home in the house; comfort and good order, entrusted to kind, capable hands, were at last to surround and soothe the restless spirit which had longed for them through twenty years. He was a man at ease, tranquil, self-assured and cheerfully resigned to the limitations that genius must ultimately accept in this world of ours.

The solitary found his happiness in the narrow home-circle. Now he was intent on founding his family, on increasing it—but in the succeeding years four children died almost as soon as born, exactly as it had been with his parents. Those were the first shadows to fall, as shadows had fallen in the past, on the well-being that Goethe had now begun to enjoy.

At last, four years after their union, we have an example of Goethe's letters to Christiane herself:

> There is no sense at all in going away from those one loves. . . . Dear angel, I am all your own. . . . Kiss the little man, of whom I often think. And of everything about you, down to the coal-rapes we planted. . . . If only you were with me! There are big broad beds everywhere, so you'd have nothing to complain of, as you often have at home. Ah, my darling! There is nothing better than being together. We'll say that very often, when we have one another again. . . . For I'm frequently jealous in fancy, and imagine that someone else might please you better, because so many men seem to me to be handsomer and more agreeable than myself. But *you* mustn't see that; you must think me the best of all, because I love you quite terribly, and no one pleases me but you. . . . While your heart wasn't mine, what good was anyone else to me? And now that it *is* mine, I want to keep it. And so I'm yours, you see. . . . We'll always stick together, for we'll never find anything better, after all. . . . If I ever write you anything you don't like, you must forgive me. Your love is so precious to me that I should be wretched if I lost it—so you must forgive me a little jealousy and anxiety. . . . Weren't the shawl and the frock pretty? I wish you lovely weather, so that you can often wear the frock.

That was how Goethe could write to this woman, in the fifth year of his attachment to her, and in the midst of the embarrassments and anxieties which are part of every adventure. In the whole series of his letters we find nothing like this simplicity, like this utter surrender to the normal relations between a man and a woman. It is his nearest approach to the typical lover.

And in fact it was a quiet, simple existence that Goethe led in the early years of this marriage which was not a sanctioned marriage. It was the form taken by a dæmonic personality for its tranquillisation, that genius might be set free to create.

His neglect of the marriage ceremony was the result of his choice. The domestic, not the social, aspect of marriage was what he wanted; neither the aristocratic nor the gifted woman would have been of any use in his house—each would have imposed those duties which for a decade he had avoided. It was no source of distress to Goethe that his young mistress was lacking in the education and social training suitable for his wife—indeed he needed her simply because of those lacks, and for a long time his view was justified. The large house, which he had inhabited since the years immediately before the Italian tour, was now superintended by a sedulous housewife; when he went away for a time he had it redecorated, and constantly impressed on her that she must have everything looking its best when he came back.

Money, far in excess of his salary, was now needed and earned. Directly he returned, he offered Wieland part of his Italian writings for the *Merkur* and these grew into a long series, running through fifteen monthly numbers. The form taken by Goethe's offer, which was almost exclusively concerned with the question of payment, shows that he made the proposal to that end alone. When Göschen, later, declined to publish the *Metamorphosis of Plants,* Goethe despondently made him a list of all the works he had ready, waiting for the propitious moment, and added this outspoken comment:

Since, as you say yourself, my things are not so popular as other people's which better please the public taste, I can only yield to circumstances; and I am sorry to say I foresee that I shall have to make a complete change in my arrangements for future works.

Dwelling in so limited a sphere, he continued to stand aloof from the dim figures of the past—from some, indeed, his estrangement grew more marked.

His mother, whom he had last seen when he was thirty, and who in the meantime had lost her husband and his father, he did not see again till he was forty-three—yet in the interval he had travelled as far as Sicily and Galicia. On his way to the Rhine, when he simply could not avoid it, he made up his mind to visit her at last.

When, shortly afterwards, Frankfurt was in danger of invasion, he offered his mother—whom for twenty years he had never invited, and whose suggested move to Weimar he had definitely prevented—shelter in his house; but she stayed where she was, for she was fearless. Then he urgently advised her to sell his father's house. She consented, and went to live in lodgings. All the furniture, so associated with the old man's life and work, was auctioned off—Goethe did not even add the good library, which had helped to educate him, to his own. So little family-feeling for the past did he evince—and for the future it was scarcely stronger. With no relative, old friend or companion did Goethe, who now stopped at Frankfurt three times running on his way elsewhere, keep up any intercourse; he even refused to visit his dying niece (whose letters grieved him), saying he did not wish to see his sister die "for the second time"—she whom in trouble, illness, and death he had for years neglected.

Could a man have shown more aversion from his own youth?

Nevertheless, his name inspired such confidence in his former home that very many people, during the French invasion, sent him their jewels, savings, and other treasures for safe-keeping at Weimar.

The only man to whom after years of very intermittent correspondence he did make a definite approach, was Fritz Jacobi, in whose house on the Rhine he spent several weeks; and this was not mere accident, for that friend lived in a luxurious country-mansion, where Goethe was glad to be a guest after the deprivations of camp-life. In this "most hospitable of all houses" the old scenes of friendship and confidence were now renewed, less buoyantly than twenty years ago, but more sagely, more humorously—for only in a spirit of high tolerance could Jacobi, now shedding his early enthusiasms in favour of theosophy, accommodate himself to the rational, bleak outlook of his guest. However, the personal beauty, the nobility, and the knowledge of the world possessed by his friend were enough to make up to Goethe for many other things.

Towards Lavater his aversion now developed into hatred. He did not answer his letters; in Mainz he was "not at home" to him; in Zurich, some years later, he avoided him by turning down an alley. In his *Gross-Cophta* he derided him along with Cagliostro, in whom Lavater believed; and this seems to be meant for Lavater: "What a knave! To interweave the Holy of Holies with his lies!"

Herder, on his return, remained intimate with Goethe. There was much to share with each other, and Herder even gave such vent to his affection as the jealousy and antagonism in his soul permitted. But can it be called friendship, when Goethe had to suppress nearly all of his deepest, most intimate emotions, those connected with his child and its mother? Before he left for Venice, he told Christiane that Herder was the person to whom she was to turn in any sudden emergency. But to Herder he did not dare to say this outright; it was not until the first stage of his journey, from Jena, that he wrote to his friend: "I told her in any such extremity to turn to you. Forgive me!" The clergyman, to show his freedom from prejudice, had to his wife defended Goethe's unsanctified union; but how entirely his partisanship was from the lips outward we can plainly see by comparing the active interest Goethe took in Herder's children and his attachment to his eldest boy, with that touchingly timid, almost shamefaced word on his departure: "Forgive me!" And yet a frank whole-hearted identification of himself with Goethe's private affairs would then have gained Herder an eternal, whole-hearted friendship. Knebel seems to have shown just this kind of chivalrous affection, and Goethe and he remained attached to the end.

Weimar, which winked at any *bonne fortune* of the Duke and his courtiers, turned against the eccentric favourite in whom for ten years it had vainly sought material for some scandal. He had been forgiven the "Mistress of the Horse," but the girl from the flower-factory was disgraceful. It is true that among his many enemies there was no one who could cast suspicion on her past life—but it was none the less an affront to society that so renowned a member of it should pick up a person of her class to establish in his stately abode. Herder advised him not to publish the Roman Elegies; Wieland called Goethe's son "the servant's brat"; more frequently than before Goethe was driven by the tattle of the town to Jena, whence he gave vent to ironies about Weimar: "My purgatory over there gets worse and worse . . . *Crescono le mie virtù, ma la mia virtù cala.*"

How deeply he felt certain slights in Weimar is to be read in the sixth Elegy:

> Also sprach die Geliebte, und nahm den Kleinen vom Stuhle,
> Drückt' ihm küssend ans Herz, Tränen entquollen dem Blick.
> Und wie sass ich beschämt, dass Reden feindlicher Menschen
> Dieses liebliches Bild mir zu beflecken vermöcht![1]

Along with all this went increasing jealousy and hostility, now that he no longer requited salary and house by the colossal toil of the Presidential office. "Goethe is a private person nowadays," said Weimar; and gossip about the big house was incessant.

The Duke alone held out. He defended Goethe's love, and stood godfather to his son August. He (whose Chamberlain's name was Venus) felt that Goethe's erotic rejuvenation cast its ægis backward over the years when Goethe had sought to bring him back to the Duchess. He felt that they were friends as of old, rejoiced in the tone of the new poems, saw much more of Goethe than of late, would ask him to come away with him. And again he took interest in Goethe's work, offering frank criticisms which were often just.

Goethe made wise use of his patron's mood, contrived to become indispensable once more, followed him to camp, and even, for the first time in eight years, adulated him in verse:

> Denn mir hat er gegeben, was Grosse selten gewähren:
> Neigung, Musse, Vertraun, Felder und Garten und Haus.

[1] "Thus my loved one replied—from his chair she lifted the baby,
Pressed him close to her heart, kissed him with tears in her eyes.
Oh, but I shamefaced sat, to think that malignant gossip
Could have sullied for me a picture so dear and so sweet!"

Niemand braucht' ich zu danken als ihm, und manches bedurft' ich
Der ich mich auf den Erwerb schlecht, als ein Dichter, verstand.
Hat mich Europa gelobt, was hat mir Europa gegeben?
Nichts! Ich habe, wie schwer! meine Gedichte bezahlt. . . .
Niemals frug ein Kaiser nach mir, es hat sich kein König
Um mich bekümmert, und Er war mir August und Mäcen.[1]

And just as formerly he had told him salutary truths in *Ilmenau*, so now he made no bones about letting the Duke see why still, when he had given up all hope of influencing him intellectually, he remained at his side.

In confidential letters he gave Carl August many intimate details—even telling him when his mistress was restored to normal life after the birth of a child. The tone is that of equality regained. When the Duke sent him to meet the Dowager-Duchess in Venice, Goethe wrote: "This free trip is great fun." He now ended his letters even to the Duke with that haughtily humble request of his: "Go on loving me." But he was sage enough to abjure entirely the Mentor's rôle which had been such a failure; there is not one written word of even political advice, though he was constantly asked for it by word of mouth. With finance he never interfered; and only once in several years did he use the tone of an *emeritus* Court-tutor: "Keep a particularly bright smile for the days when you are doing what of yore you were so keen on!"

On this basis of mutual tolerance he constructed, after his return, a new relation to his patron, which if not very productive had its own vitality, and bridged the former quasi-estrangement.

Not even the shadow of friendship was accorded him by his former mistress.

Charlotte's attitude towards Goethe's love-affair was that of a Court-lady. For quite a long time she knew nothing of what

[1] "For to me has he given what great ones but rarely have granted;
Affection, leisure, and trust; acres and garden and house.
No one but him must I thank, and great the beneficence needed,
Since, as a poet, but scant the reward I received for my work.
Europe—has Europe acclaimed me? Given me aught has this Europe?
Nothing! But heavy indeed the cost of my poems to me . . .
Never an Emperor summoned me, never a monarch
Thought of me—this my Augustus, Mæcenas, this man!"

half Weimar knew. Goethe made Christiane's acquaintance in July; the first Charlotte heard of it was in February, and as he was no longer her property in any sense of the word, she tried at first to avoid a breach. "But," wrote Caroline Herder, "she takes it very much amiss in him." She concealed her knowledge from Goethe; her first breakdown was like that of Hamlet's mother—the play was the thing. From a drama which portrayed a similar estrangement she came home in a state of collapse.

It has grieved me very much [wrote Goethe] to hear that that insipid, wretched play gave you such pain by reminding you of a sad reality. I shall expect you this evening. Let pain and joy be our bond of friendship, so that we may get some good out of the few years we have left.

But, for all that, both held back. Soon afterwards he wrote more resolutely, absolving her of all blame, though her reproaches hit him hard; "and if you are to suffer a great deal through me, it is only fair that I . . . should, through you"—exactly like the verses in *Tasso*. Better to close the account and keep out of one another's way than to dispute the items, since he could never be anything but in her debt. Strenuously did they try to save what might yet be saved. He told her about his optical secrets; in his letters he did seem urgent to bring matters to a head, but was unchangingly chivalrous and grateful. How uncertain his feeling about her was is evident from a letter which begins in this contrite but cautious strain:

Forgive me, my dear, if my last letter was a little confused. Everything will settle down and clear up—we must give ourselves and circumstances time. I am so nervous all round that I can hardly make up my mind to come to you.

Can Goethe have hoped for her return, in a situation so ambiguous? Certainly she hoped for his. There is no stronger proof of how whole-heartedly she was convinced of his love for her, in the recent years at Weimar, than the fact that she now resolved to give him his choice. Charlotte, in her transcendental phase, would not only have had to forgive her forty-yeared lover a mistress, but could scarcely have helped wishing that he would take one; but Charlotte as a woman scorned, blind to her forty-seven years, with a rival just half her age, felt that she had been betrayed; and, completely misapprehending Goethe's character, presented him with an alternative which was no alternative at all.

She did not do this until the beginning of May, and amazingly selected the moment in which she was about to visit Goethe's mother for the first time. It was as though the woman of the world, after the collapse of all her mystic dreams of elective affinities, were anxious to parade a more normal relationship so as to protect her fair fame. Goethe did not answer till July:

How very much I love you, how completely I recognise my duty to you and Fritz, I proved by my return from Italy. . . . Unfortunately, when I arrived, you were in a peculiar frame of mind. . . . I saw the Herders and the Duchess leave for Italy, and the place in the carriage which had been pressingly offered to me, remained empty. I stayed behind for my friend's sake, just as I had returned for her sake—and all I had to listen to was the obstinate reiteration that I might as well have stayed in Italy. . . . And all this before there was any idea of the relation which seems so greatly to offend you! And what sort of a relation is it? Who is deprived of anything because it exists? Who makes any claim to the feelings which are mine for that poor little thing? Who, to the time I spend with her? Ask Fritz, ask the Herders, ask anyone who is dear to me if I am less interested in their affairs . . . than before? Strange, indeed, if it is with *you* that I am to lose touch—you, the best and dearest of all my friends! How strongly I have felt that everything is as it has been between us, when you have been disposed to talk with me about the things that interest us!

But I will freely confess that I can no longer endure the way you have treated me of late. When I was most inclined to talk, you would silence me; when I was most sympathetic, you would accuse me of indifference. You wanted to regulate my behaviour to everyone; you found fault with everything I did and was. . . . What chance was there for confidence and frankness, when you had made up your mind to repulse me at every turn! . . . Unfortunately you have long scorned my advice about coffee, and have taken to a dietary which is most injurious to your health. . . . I won't give up the hope that you may again do me some justice. Farewell. Fritz is in fine fettle and often comes to see me.

A week later:

I have known no greater happiness than my confidence towards you, which once knew no bonds; now that I may no longer practise it, I am a different man, and must become more and more so. . . . What with this cold wet summer and the hard winter that is at hand, what with the Duke's frequent absences [as a Prussian General], and all the other circumstances which make things here so unsettled and confused that one scarcely knows a single person who is content with life, it takes some doing to . . . keep a good heart and not make plans for gradually getting clear of it all; and when, in addition to these things, one finds one's dearest friend quite estranged, one simply doesn't know where one is. I mean this as much for you as for myself. . . . Only I would like to implore of you—help me even in this matter, so that the relation which offends you may not degenerate, but remain as it is. Let me confide in you again—let me say one quiet, heartfelt word to you about it, and then I shall hope that all that was between us will be completely and happily restored.

What makes these letters unique in Goethe's life is the fact that they were inspired as much by worldly wisdom as by kindness, as much by gratitude as by diplomacy. They were written by a man who only in them—and even in them but intermittently—laid aside the mask he habitually wore, because he was remembering the time when no one saw his face as this woman had seen it, she whom he now sought to retain more for her sake than his own. Therefore he adopted a tone of gentle friendship to soften the effect of the defensive passages, and took no notice of the harshness which her letter must have contained.

Their love had died; but he as it were covered its grave with green grass, when in this letter he wrote only of duty and Fritz, of things that interested them both, but never referred to their past, nor directly to his own love for her. For an abandoned mistress there is nothing more painful than the consciousness that no one makes a claim to those hours which her lover now spends with a younger woman. But, being a diplomat, Goethe did not shrink from almost depreciating Christiane to her rival; and while he often reassured Christiane with the same words he had once written to Charlotte, he was at the same time writing of her to Charlotte as a "poor little thing." In the second letter, which he need not have written at all, there is an unmistakable return to the one-sided devotion which had been the mark of their friendship in its first great days. To confide in her had, he said, become a necessity to him; he does not ask her to requite his confidence with hers, and he gives her a final proof of how entirely he does "confide" in her, when he implores her help in this new passion, and longs to talk it over with her like a brother. How little he understood her pride, still less her jealousy! Whether she answered or not, we do not know. Seven years go by without a written word.

But after the short space of two years, she seems to have felt more kindly disposed towards him. She confessed to a woman-friend she was sorry for Goethe and could have wept about it all. About this time her husband died. But five years after the rupture, she took her revenge when she wrote the drama of *Dido*.

Goethe, on his side, closed the record of his longest love-affair with the sadly apathetic, purposely unimpassioned epigram:

Eine Liebe hatt' ich, sie war mir lieber als alles!
Aber ich hab' sie nicht mehr! Schweig und ertrag den Verlust![1]

It is like the clang of a heavy hall-door. The man who is leaving that house has no intention of wandering drearily through the streets—he is on his way to another, newly constructed abode. Those two lines were his farewell; they were followed by no song or elegy, no haunted hours of reverie. From the epigrammatist two lines were wrung. The poet had nothing to say.

The poet, indeed, had nothing to say throughout all this period. It was a strain rather than a delight to complete his collected edition on his return. His mind, more intent on truths than on imaginative creation, more scientifically than artistically inclined, turned from "consecutive compositions; the fragmentary style of erotic trifles better suits my present state." *Tasso* gave him most to work on. But in that instance too it

[1] "Once a lover was mine, she was of all the most cherished!
But I have lost her for aye! Bear thou in silence thy loss!"

was more a personal impulse that impelled him to the task than a desire to finish and reshape the piece. According to a later confession, he wanted to shake off some impressions and memories of Weimar which still clung oppressively to his mind.

Faust, which was to have been finished in Rome, appeared as a fragment—that is to say, scarcely differentiated from the original draft.

In the volume containing the lyrics, which he said was the *summa summarum* of a whole life, we see the earliest signs of the attempt, which afterwards became so marked, to cover up his tracks. He omits, softens down, and (on æsthetic principles) so fuses one experience with another that it is impossible to assign date and incident to any poem. This effort to objectify his work after the event is a very extraordinary contrast to his itch for self-confession; and when we see the man who called his life-work a prolonged autobiography carefully obscuring the details of that disclosure when they were concerned with others—which is to say, with women—we cannot refuse this further proof that Goethe's confessions were regardless of his own person, but full of consideration for others.

What he wrote at this time was influenced by the events of that agitated period—sometimes directly, sometimes symbolically. *Reineke Fuchs*, that profane Bible, he found it a relief to remodel after the shocks of the Revolution; and at the same time it was good practice with its several thousand hexameters, which he challenged Herder, Wieland, and Knebel to improve upon. The two comedies on the Revolution—*Gross-Cophta* and *Bürgergeneral*—are *pièces de circonstance* and nothing more. They are of no importance in the canon—they are of the stage pure and simple, the latter being boiled down from an opera. The third and most important play—the very modern-mannered *Aufgeregten*—is no more than a fragment.

To persevere with the drama in the grand style, after *Tasso*, he needed—and lacked—both actors and repose of mind. He knew that well, and shut his conceptions away like jewels, unsuitable to such dangerous times.

Thus throughout this whole period there was no great work, nor any new development in style except the twenty-four Elegies. In those he retrieved the fresh note of his youthful lyrics, though the form was entirely different, both psychologically and artistically speaking. And even they remained long in his desk.

For then, and through decades to come, Goethe was discouraged from attempting the grand style by the crying lack of an appreciative public. If he seemed petrified throughout these years, if he fled from the turmoils of the time to the Fortunate Isles of domesticity and scientific research, it was due to the change of taste in a public which he had consistently despised while he possessed its suffrages. Now that change struck home—not to his heart, but to his theory. Or was there not indeed something tragic in the fact that just when what he had learnt in Rome had caused him to deduce the value of the classic from the interest taken in art by an entire nation, his own nation should be beginning to turn from him to newer writers?

It was only for a brief while in his youth that he had felt it a happiness to be in touch with the best men of his time. Ever since Weimar he had abjured the national appeal, had written a few things for the few, so that the first edition of his collected works could scarcely have spelt success. Now, when he definitely came forward as a national poet, even the stirring *Egmont* was little talked of or acted, while *Iphigenie* and *Tasso,* then first published, left everyone cold. There was no attempt to stage them; all Germany was agog for the dramas of Schiller, who had publicly and adversely criticised *Egmont.* The revolutionary spirit of the age was averse from abstract beauty—subjective treatment, the intrusion of the dramatist's personality, was demanded, and was found in other poets. While Heinse's *Ardinghello* was the theme of universal praise, three of Goethe's works—the *Faust* fragment, *Tasso* and the volume of lyrics—were on their first appearance discussed almost exclusively in the letters of his literary contemporaries.

On the whole, he felt that the scepticism about German culture which had grown on him in Italy was confirmed in his own person. While his German publisher was dismayed, *Iphigenie* was at once translated into verse in England.

The average German is an honest, decent fellow, but of the originality . . . of a work of art he has not the smallest conception—which is to say, in a word, that he has no taste. Roughly speaking, it is comprehensible enough. Variety of scene and exaggerated treatment tickle the coarser minds in the audience, while the more cultivated are attracted by a certain vulgar sincerity. . . . A well-sustained middle-course, departure from which is attended by the risk of either sinking into the platitudinous, or soaring into the realm of absurdity.

Impossible to overlook the note of personal pique in that passage from a private letter of Goethe's.

Is it astonishing that his mind, which was already turning away from art, should have found in the incomprehension of his age another pretext for abandoning the Muses? The temper of his soul and the temper of the time, his isolation and his trend towards scientific truth—both private and public circumstances pointed him to research, to natural science. "I feel pretty sure that, as things are, I shall devote myself exclusively to it." Between forty and forty-five Goethe completed the two most important of his observations in this sort, and laid the foundations for the third.

In every particular instance Goethe's research-work followed the same mystical course as did his poetry and his experience. His eye saw the object, his genius envisaged the universal, his individual self made the connection. This path from perception by way of vision to the law was that which the lyric poet, the Minister, the scientist, consistently pursued; and whether it would take him minutes or years depended solely on the scope and intricacy of the matter in hand. As with Leonardo and Kepler, so with Goethe—casual experience was raised to vision, and vision widened to embrace the form; "for it is with these phenomena as with poems—I did not make them; they made me." Even the modes of endeavour which his manifold gifts called forth in Goethe were undifferentiated; it was the same spirit which, in its own highly individual way, projected itself on events no less than on phenomena. As arrogantly as Faust did Goethe turn to the symbol of the macrocosm, that he might feel himself to be God; as humbly as St. Francis did he submerge himself in his microcosm, that he might feel God in him.

That was why as artist and statesman no less than as scientist he never began by seeking the law—he merely felt that there was one. As a poet and man he gave examples, as an investigator he found prophetic outlooks. Goethe's achievements in physics, born of perception, fostered by intuitive generalisation, are no more than rough drafts for laws which he was prevented from elaborating either by want of time, or the resistance of his anti-philosophical sensuousness. But, as the draughtsman, he was always free to make use of his intuition for later investigation of the given problem. Here as elsewhere all his knowledge was derived from his personal apprehension of things, and even his logical fallacies could prove fruitful, because they were psychological verities.

"A perception of this kind," he now said of his vertebral theory of anatomy, "always has . . . one quality of the esoteric—that as a whole it can be expressed but not demonstrated. In detail it *is* demonstrable, but one can't completely round it off." And so he insisted, quoting an old saw, that we should never seek to take Nature by violence.

> No—I pursued her cautiously by observation and experiment, and was content when she was so good as now and again to confirm my view. When she declined to do that, she did not fail to show me some other way of perception. To inquire about the purpose—to ask "Why?"—is wholly unscientific; one gets a little further with "How?" For if I ask, "How does the ox come to have horns?" I am led to consider his organisation, and so to see at once why the lion has none, nor can have them.

Thus all his discoveries were, in this higher sense, empirical. He could not make minute investigations, nor could he specialise; and though distrust of a scientist-poet's exactitude might be excusable, he was found to be more careful than many a pure scientist, and was never accused of inaccuracy by any of his opponents. Rather it was he who uttered a warning against hasty conclusions. "Genius," he said, in one of the earliest of the papers against Newton,

> . . . is by its nature inclined to lay down the law to phenomena, to take them by storm. . . . Far more difficult for genius is the determination—often, alas, deferred too long—to give credit to phenomena for all they imply; and though it may succeed, by its productive

GOETHE AT THE AGE OF FORTY-FOUR

energy, in creating its own microcosm, it usually does violence to the macrocosm by preferring to make a coherent whole of a few experiences which are easily to be apprehended, rather than to combine several experiences in a spirit of humility, with the hope of discovering, at long last, the natural connection between them.

It was to this fresh, simple, unsystematic procedure—natural to a self-taught student—that he owed the perfect candour of his eye. He did not make his discoveries by sedulous exploration like Vasco da Gama, nor even indirectly like Columbus; Goethe was like Red Eric, a buccaneer on the high seas—and yet not wholly so, for Goethe's intuition said to him: "Here is a new continent." Indeed it seems as though this explorer-by-intuition was not intended to find the thing he definitely sought, for when he sought the primitive plant, for example, it was not to be found.

His was the eye which, on the promenade at Padua, observed the fan-shaped palms as it might have observed the human heart—as lovingly, as thoughtfully. It was the same eye which eighteen years before had seen anew the tower of Strassburg Cathedral and discovered the plan in the torso. When, so observing, he detected the modification between the leaves of the stem and those of the blossoms, and between these and the stamens, the secret of the leaf's anatomy was revealed to him—that which enables it constantly to take another essential form. And hence he called the leaf the fundamental type of plant-organism, and based a system on this law of metamorphosis.

And as a side-issue he followed up such experiments to their logical consequences:

> At the heart of this law lies the restriction to which every creature is subject—that it may not exceed its measure. Thus one part cannot encroach without causing another to deteriorate; nor one part wholly prevail without causing another wholly to perish.

These are first principles which were later to issue in his theory of dynamics.

His mind had long conceived the idea of a similar abstract type in the animal-kingdom—ever since he had discovered the intermaxillary bone in man. Fusion or reconstruction (he had then said to himself) causes increase or decrease in size, or else the atrophy of certain parts must have obliterated an original type, if we find that there remain even the rudiments of organs, no matter how unnecessary these may have become. The construction of the botanical kingdom from the metamorphosis of plants was to him in no way different from the transformation of the larva into the butterfly; there too a homogeneous origin resulted in differentiated forms—only in the plant the organism was the same, and in the butterfly it was different. Even in the higher animals this eurhythmic identity was evidenced by the vertebral column, though there the continuity seemed to elude the eye.

Thus far his meditations had led him years before—and now, on a visit to Venice, his servant one day picked up a skull in the Jewish cemetery on the Lido, and laughingly presented it to his master as the skull of a Jew. Goethe saw at once that it was a portion of a man's skull; and then, remembering the thrilling discovery, ten years ago, of the intermaxillary bone, his eye discerned what no one before him had discerned—that the skull too consists of vertebræ. And instantly he felt that "he had taken a great step towards comprehension of the structure of animals."

Every bone, he now told himself, is in itself a part or fragment of a vertebral nucleus—and thus he was the first to grasp a guiding principle of comparative anatomy. But this did not content him; he soon went further and concluded that:

> a universal type, progressing by metamorphosis, is characteristic of the whole organic creation, is observable in all its divisions at certain intermediate stages, and must therefore be at least postulated in man, who is the most highly developed organism, even though it takes so modest a place as to be actually imperceptible—

the Darwinian postulate, discerned seventy years before the younger Darwin.

So fruitful was Goethe's work, when its basis could be confined to the sense-perceptions. But just as he scorned all "invented" writing, and wrote poetry only when it came to him—just as he held no theories of government which did not naturally ensue from his own experience—so did his genius warn the scientist off the ground of speculative science. Only once, misled by the object, did he transgress against this law of his being. Unconsciously he then overstepped the frontiers of his own nature; and no sooner had he entered that alien realm in which the sense-perception can deceive, instead of guiding the observer clear-eyed to the goal, than he became involved in a confusion of thought from which he was unable to escape throughout the forty years which followed.

Goethe's theory of colour, his campaign against Newton, is one of the strongest proofs of his dæmonic nature. That enigmatic force which impelled him—in love, from desire to its satisfaction; in endeavour, from adoration to contempt of the active life; in poetry, from pure beauty to the cosmic orchestra—that force which through all his life conducted him from devotion to scepticism and back again to devotion, was now to invade the most untroubled sphere he knew, that of the light itself, his phenomenon of phenomena; and he was to wrestle, dæmonically misled, for an erroneous conception! While defending it against the analysis of the profane, he himself turned analyst; and it is as though the indignant god of light had retaliated on the devotee who presumed to think that his divinity could be dissected.

Newton taught that light was of varied kinds, differentiated by the colour-sense of the eye. This heterogeneous light yielded combinations of colours. White was the fusion of all the colours. Every colour was affected by an altered combination of the light, hence it must derive from the light; bodies merely caused it to be perceived. The prism caused the light to diverge at a certain angle.

This doctrine, which he had half-forgotten when he first began his investigations, Goethe repeatedly made physicists expound to him. He apprehended it rightly, but stuck to his point—which was that white light could never be a product of coloured light; and though all his experiments yielded the same results as Newton's did, his theory is impossible of acceptance, because all Goethe ever did was to insist on Newton's fallaciousness, without demonstrating exactly in what it consisted. Physicists of every school united in upholding Newton; Goethe stood derisively alone in the opposite camp.

He taught that all the colours were denser than white—had an element of shadow in them. But as the mere combination of light and darkness yielded grey, colours must be the product of some other alliance of light and shadow, and were perceived in the faintly nebulous atmosphere of blue and yellow—the sky and the sun. This nebulous medium gave the light that element of the opaque, of the material, which was necessary to the production of colour. Colour was more than light; a combination of light and shadow could alone elicit colour—or, as in his old age he once expressed it in verse:

> Einheit ewigen Lichts zu spalten,
> Müssen wir für Torheit halten,
> Wenn euch Irrtum schon genügt.
> Hell und Dunkel, Licht und Schatten,
> Weiss man klüglich sie zu gatten,
> Ist das Farbenreich gesiegt. [1]

Goethe was defending his worshipped phenomenon against the professors of physics—not only that light which they were intent on dissecting for him, but even the eye through which he had learned to worship that light! He was defending his God. Hence his long-lived error, hence the persistence of his passionate campaign.

Disappointment with Germany, avoidance of cold weather, opportunity and above all the pulsing of an expectant, lonely heart caused him to absent himself four times in the course of four years; but, driven by unrest as he was, unrest perpetually drove him home again. The Dowager-Duchess's presence in Venice was only a pretext for departure; he had no sooner reached Nürnberg than he was conscious that he felt no desire to go on, and once again his heart had foreseen what was to be. If in the earlier sojourn Venice had struck him as too lyrical, what he now complained of was the cold April, the hoggishness of the national life, the imposture and filth which prevailed in that

[1] "Light, a deathless Whole, to sever
We must hold unwisdom ever,
Fallacy too mild a word.
Radiance, dimness, wisely wed them,
Light and shade, adroitly shed them—
Of the colour-world you're lord."

wilderness of stone and water. He invoked boredom as the Mother of the Muses; the Italian tongue alone retained its former magic, and he complained of being master of only one language:

> Deutsch zu schreiben. Und so verderb' ich unglücklicher Dichter
> In dem schlechtesten Stoff leider nun Leben und Kunst.[1]

Thus completely can a master underrate his medium, when he happens to incline to another! And it was the same captiousness which now made him declare, with the exaggeration of overwrought nerves, that his love for Italy had received its death-blow.

The real cause of his disappointment was homesickness for Christiane. His first trip to Italy had been a flight from an aging mistress who seemed the symbol of a period in which *he* was aging—had been the hope of regaining tone and youthfulness in the South. His second was pervaded with longing for a young mistress at home, and he could only cast about for some transient compensation. On each occasion his mood created the land after its own image; and so now the two classic types of women, one in the South, the other in the North, disputed the ground:

> Schön ist das Land! doch ach, Faustinen find' ich nicht wieder,
> Das ist Italien nicht mehr, das ich mit Schmerzen verliess . . .
> Südwärts liegen der Schätze wie viel! Doch einer im Norden
> Zieht, ein grosser Magnet, unwiderstehlich zurück.[2]

And looking at the waves of colour in the sea at sunset, flaming and tossing round the ship, he thought of Aphrodite, from whose flames a son had issued for him and his beloved.

And yet, even now, his longing was shot through with resignation! His view of the Italians was arrogant and acrid; he maintained that they cared for nothing but eating, procreating, and nourishing their children; and cynically, sadly, he admonished himself:

[1] "German author—and so, ill-fated, as poet I squander
Life and art in the worst medium that language has known."

[2] "Fair is the land! but ah, Faustina here I retrieve not,
This is no more the Italia, left with an ache in my heart . . .
Beauties many I see in the South! But one in the Northland
Draws me, a magnet how strong, how irresistible, home!"

Merke dir, Reisender, das und tue zu Hause desgleichen!
Weiter bringt es kein Mensch, stell' er sich, wie er auch will.[1]

In such moods, now bored, now erotically languishing, he withdrew still more decisively than of yore from social life, frequented taverns and booths more constantly than at any other time, observing and portraying—in the suppressed *Epigrams*—prostitutes and hucksters. He had love-passages with little girl-acrobats and dancers, spoke of the poet as a conqueror of women, and in a public-house the tone was something new in him when he shouted, as if to purchase oblivion:

Aber auch mir—mir sinket das Haupt von Sorgen und Mühe . . .
Liebes Mädchen! ein Glas schäumenden Weines herbei.[2]

Suddenly the expected Princess made her appearance in Venice, and Goethe resumed the courtier's mask. Of the sojourn nothing survived for him—and us—but a sheaf of epigrams, the portrait of a rope-dancer, and the revelation from the ram's skull.

He ended his forty-third year in the French field, and even there he was at bottom half-hearted from first to last. "It's outrageous that I've never yet seen a review," he had written the year before to the Duke, in the character of pure observer; this time he said he wanted to find the fields sown with soldiers instead of plants and stones. Unenthusiastically, scarcely out of curiosity, more with a desire to play up to the Duke—in short, once again because he wanted to escape from the unrest of his lonely heart, did Goethe turn soldier.

We lead a restless sort of existence here, and yet it's thoroughly boring for the most part. . . . My life is very simple. I scarcely ever leave my tent of late; I revise *Reineke* and write down optical observations. . . . I see many people, with most of whom I have

[1] "Voyager, mark it, and see that thou doest likewise, returning!
More shall no man achieve, think of himself as he may."

[2] "And for myself—myself heavy-headed, weary, and anxious . . .
Bring to me, pretty maiden, a glass foaming over with wine!"

little in common. . . . I shall not rush into danger—one gets no thanks for it, and has nothing to show but the damage.

When the camp was in bad humour, he would recount the adventures of St. Louis, which were much more disagreeable, to the circle in the evenings; at night would read French improprieties to the Duke, or else write, like any adjutant, to his colleague at home: "Our dear Prince, who is well, cheerful, and active . . . sends you his kindest regards . . . There is no doubt that he values you as you deserve that he should." One seems to read between the lines that the Duke, sitting by, had been given a friendly hint: "Wouldn't it be well to send a gracious message to old Schnauss?" He spent half a night walking with a Prince behind the vineyards, and explaining his theory of colour till the peep of dawn.

He played the part of intelligent amateur, and took his baptism of fire. The effect was only to be conveyed by an image; he said it was like being in some torrid region, and so permeated by the heat that one felt as if fused in the element—as if one's blood were ignited. Goethe, as on the sailing-ship at Capri, looked death in the face with the composure of a man who does not regard it as final, since he believes in metempsychosis.

At the end of the eighteenth century, war was a problem in which Goethe could take but scant interest. "There lay the poor dead and wounded, and the sun was setting gorgeously behind Mainz." That is all. Even when they had to make a difficult retreat, he merely alluded to the anxiety, privations, and hardships which "we" had to bear. In such moments he came very near exchanging speculation for a definite creed; and in a somewhat ironical spirit promised himself that he would never again complain of boredom in the theatre at Weimar, where at any rate one was under a safe roof. Amid the confusion of the flight he, in the kitchen-cart, sat conning a Dictionary of Physics, because "he should not much mind being interrupted in that sort of reading"; but he was glad, for all his coolness, to get on horseback again. Once restored to home-comforts, he sang the most cheerful of the Psalms of David to the Lord who had redeemed him from the mire, and hoped to awake from his bad dream in the company of his mother and his friend.

There was one personality of the campaign, one individual fate which remotely moved him, and that was not because of the man's reckless daring. His feeling for Prince Louis Ferdinand was inspired not nearly so much by the Prince's romanticism as by his own urgent efforts to keep him out of the firing-line. But on the other hand, he was profoundly affected by the thought of the shepherds who had been robbed of their herds, and into whose horny hands were pressed, in compensation, worthless bank-notes dating from the days of the King deposed. The mettlesome hero, intent on risking his life, seemed to him even in practice merely foolhardy, and therefore to be restrained; but Goethe felt an affinity with the suffering shepherds and compared their destinies with those in classical tragedy.

Restricted to headquarters as he was, his general view of war was necessarily so superficial that he could not but despise it.

> First they are the fearless destroyers, then the compassionate healers; they have a collection of set phrases for inspiring hope in the most desperate situations. Hence a sort of hypocrisy, quite unique, and totally different from the parsonical and the courtly varieties. . . . This, in fact, is a regular puppet-play, wherein I act the (melancholy) Jaques in my own peculiar fashion.

How alien to his spirit was the war-machine, how reluctantly he obeyed the Duke's summons to follow him a second time into the field, is evident from the verses which he wrote, before he had even set out, to celebrate his return:

> Und wie wir auch durch ferne Lande ziehn,
> Da kommt es her, da kehrt es wieder hin—
> Wir wenden uns, wie auch die Welt entzücke,
> Der Enge zu, die uns allein beglücke.[1]

But only in the sense of wanting to extricate his person and his work from the turmoil of the time did Goethe desire "that small sphere." His mind was gripped, was even fascinated, by the age—it tested his universality to the utmost that history could.

[1] "And as through distant lands we wend our way,
One thought alone sustains us through the day—
However fair the world, our fancy turning
To that small sphere which holds our bliss, our yearning."

Here too it was not the day but the century which stirred his imagination; and this is merely confirmed by his withdrawing, in the first agitated years, from any contact with the general political situation, and seeking oblivion in the "small sphere" of affection, scientific research, and study in general. The campaign in which he had taken part had inclined him towards the Monarchists who wished to restore the legitimate rulers, and against the Revolution. Since, instead of reaching Paris (maps of which he had had bound into his field-books), he was involved in the rout of the Royalist army behind Valmy, it must be conceded that Goethe's practical experience of the Revolution was almost entirely that of defeat.

The dæmonic element in him could not but sympathise with the Revolution, while his genius, at this time intent on repose and somewhat rigorously conservative, could not but be against it—so that his instinctive abstract sympathy suggested a negative judgment, and ultimately led him to impartial contemplation.

He had two moments of insight into the ensanguined future. When, four years before the fall of the Bastille, the Necklace-Affair became known, he shuddered "as at the Gorgon's head." The prestige of the throne seemed to him to be undermined, he foresaw its annihilation, and the future rose before him like a spectre. So instantaneous, so overwhelming, was the impression made upon him that his friends afterwards told him they had thought him off his head that day. Everything that in his letters and works he had complained of during his ten years as Minister—the frivolity of princes, the arrogance of the nobility, the oppression of the poor—points to a democratic scepticism, and now his view was confirmed by international politics. The same Cagliostro whose crime he now saw as a horrifying symptom, he had suspected three years before; and writing to say so to Lavater, he had added to his doubts the very significant admission: "I have indications, not to say information, of a vast fraud, hovering obscurely. . . . Believe me, our moral and political world is undermined by secret passages, cellars and cess-pools."

Are not these words, which ostensibly express no more than fear of upheavals eight years before the Revolution, pregnant with unspoken condemnation of that society whose recklessness he had often enough tried to restrain, within the narrow compass of the little State in which he was Minister of Finance? Only the physician who has seen how frail is the organism will be quick to recognise the threatening symptom.

In the fourth year of the Revolution Goethe was a witness to the first defeat of a paid army by a voluntary national force. Stunned by an event which had seemed beyond the bounds of possibility, the Generals and officers were sitting round the camp-fires on the evening of the lost Day of Valmy, and apprehensively discussing the situation. Finally they turned to the civilian—after all, he was an author, a thinker, perhaps he would be able to say something encouraging. Then, among the uniforms, Goethe spoke out, and he said: "Here and now begins a new historical era: and you can all say you have been in it!"

Goethe's answer was equivalent to a deed; and as in a long life he was but seldom called upon for immediate action, that answer, thus and then enunciated, is unique in his career. A defeated man (or at any rate a man on the defeated side), the friend and Minister of a defeated ruler, by position, education, and prejudices a Royalist— and instead of an imprecation or some facile prophecy, an electric intuition! This was no cannonade, yet the irresistible flash of the idea had something in it of the cannonade. And it did flash upon the conquered men as might the crucifix appearing among clouds of smoke in place of a tattered standard; so that while he destroyed their self-confidence, he instilled into them the deeper trustfulness of those who are the instruments of destiny. And all in a few words, struck out at a moment's notice on the night of defeat!

Those are the two visions of the seer.

The observer, too, stood awed and penetrated—for Goethe did once actually *see* the Revolution. A year after Valmy his position was reversed; he was on the winning side. Mainz, in which the Jacobins had let themselves be invested, had fallen; and from a window of the re-conquered town Goethe watched the tragic exit of the French, who were permitted to march out to the strains of the *Marseillaise*. He felt it as a poet would:

That Revolutionary Te Deum always has something mournful and foreboding about it, no matter how arrogantly it is played; but this time they took it very slowly indeed, to suit the funereal pace of their horses. It was moving and terrible—a most poignant sight, as the horsemen, tall haggard men of a certain age, with faces that matched the music, rode past. Individually one might have compared each of them to Don Quixote—taken together, they were highly impressive.

And when, right before the Duke's tent, some infuriated citizens were preparing to lynch a departing Jacobin, Goethe stepped forward imperiously, saying they had no right to visit their sufferings on individuals. The Republicans had free egress; God and the authorities would judge them. And he pacified the mob.

But though in presence of the conquered he thus boldly took their side, because the question was one of sheer humanity, it was not so easy to see clear when hampered by his official position. When in Jena at this time there was a rising of students, because troops to the number of fifty had been drafted into the town to keep order, Goethe, in his capacity of Minister of Education, showed a very unusual violence of feeling. But furious though he was with every individual rebel, it was to him that everyone looked for the most conciliatory measures. He undertook to negotiate between the troops and the students; finally the troops were withdrawn. And he was so enthralled by the many "interesting scenes" that at moments he regretted being obliged to carry out his plans for a proposed journey.

So powerfully did the measureless, the lawless, fascinate the dæmon in Goethe, once he was obliged to look it in the face. But his imagination, too, was gripped by the vastness of this vast movement. In his *Aufgeregten* he makes the Magistrate envy a Countess, who has returned from Paris, her good fortune in having been a spectator of the mightiest performance that the world had ever beheld. "A witness of the blissful intoxication which fell upon a great nation in the moment of first feeling itself free and unshackled." To the Countess's sceptical rejoinder the Magistrate replies: "To blunder in a great cause is always more praiseworthy than to be right in a small one." It is as though we heard a distant echo of the Shakespeare speech at Strasburg, twenty years ago.

Ere long his political instinct warned him that the ferments abroad were spreading to Germany. It vexed him to see, in his friends' houses on the Rhine, the busts of Mirabeau and Lafayette among the Lares and Penates. These friends had been in Paris, had seen the two great men act and heard them speak, and they had been, "as Germans are unfortunately apt to be, stirred to imitation, and that at a time when anxiety about the left bank of the Rhine has been transformed into a genuine peril." He was angry to find his compatriots playing with ideas which would prepare a similar fate for Germany, to hear high-minded men propounding fantastic hopes, without any real knowledge of themselves or the situation. Many of his friends were for the Revolution—Herder, Knebel, Wieland, and others such as Kant and Fichte, Klopstock, Bürger, Stolberg; "all running about with bellows in their hands—when, as it seems to me, they had better be looking for cold-water jugs." When Fritz von Stein praised a Hamburg merchant-prince who had joined the Reds, Goethe said angrily that the *Marseillaise* would not sound well at the groaning dinner-table of a rich man!

As soon as he began to reflect like a prudent man, the trend of his judgment was all in favour of order, and against the upheaval. He had from of old believed in the genius, not in the mob; in the star, not in the supers—yet had striven to subordinate himself, when sharing in the government of the country. And now, in a mood of ironic reminiscence, he demanded the same from others:

> Alle Freiheitsapostel, sie waren mir immer zuwider:
> Willkür suchte doch nur jeder am Ende für sich.
> Willst du viele befrein, so wag es, vielen zu dienen,
> Wie gefährlich das sei, willst du es wissen? Versuch's![1]

Goethe knew that, as regarded his own monarch, he was a Monarchist. This second motive for his aloofness from the Revolution derived from a fundamental trait in him—that gratitude which was the simplest expression of his devotion.

[1] "Always obnoxious to me was every apostle of freedom:
Each was solely intent on doing himself as he willed.
Wouldst thou emancipate peoples, begin by attempting to serve them.
Wouldst thou learn what the risks, waiting that servitor? Try!"

Because the man upon whom (for all his critical independence of feeling) he must always look as his benefactor, was a Royalty, Goethe could support no anti-Royalist movement; and that was why he hoped the Revolution would be confined to France, where he could contemplate it coolly.

His heart had been always, and his plans had been at first, in favour of the lower classes; in critical moments he had never taken his stand with the rulers, with whom he was the sought rather than the seeker. But Goethe was always for evolution, and now he had to suffer the reaction against his democratic influence—to see the freedom of the Press, of thought, endangered, to see Fichte's and Hufeland's lectures in Jena frowned on by the neighbouring States, the Jena literary journal prohibited in Prussia. Force, it seemed to him, would never be efficacious towards the order which he desired.

For love of order—a third principle of his being—made him shrink from chaos and anarchy. "It is part of my nature, once for all. I had rather commit an injustice than suffer disorder." That this was no mere pedantry, resembling that of his father, the whole structure of his character goes to prove—indeed, the twenty-five years since in Leipzig he had seemed to be possessed with the idea of destroying himself and his genius, knew no more ardent purpose than that of combating the dæmon which urged him to irresponsible violence, clouding his judgment and betraying his highest aims. Only a man who felt that himself and his work were no less powerfully menaced by the perils of spiritual anarchy, could at times have displayed such vehement antagonism towards an international movement whose vastness could in other moments overwhelm his imagination.

Just then, Goethe was making an effort to master the events as a dramatist. In the two short plays already alluded to, as well as in the *Erzählungen deutscher Ausgewanderten* (*Tales of German Emigrants*), he attempted the satiric vein; in his *Märchen*, the symbolic; and later in the pastoral of *Hermann und Dorothea*, and the classic *Natürliche Tochter*, the idyllic and tragic. Now he was writing *Die Aufgeregten* (*The Terrorists*), and in that, by his own admission, he set forth his political confession of faith for the men of his time.

In this comedy, so deft as to be among the most valuable of Goethe's fragments, a doctor, a magistrate, and a bailiff instigate the peasants to end a lawsuit by violence. This lawsuit has been dragging on, between the lord of the manor and the Imperial Chamber, for years; and, inspired by Parisian models, these lesser revolutionaries defend their rights with bullets. Types of the aristocrat, the bourgeois, and the peasant are presented with the utmost impartiality; and there is delightful art in the way they are made to understand one another when brought into contact, and yet are never allowed to pass the bounds of pure comedy.

At the very end of his life, Goethe said he could still sign the Countess's views—they had been his own at the time.

> I was rewarded with all sorts of charming epithets which I had better not recapitulate. . . . Moreover, I was profoundly convinced that no great revolution has ever been the fault of the people, but of the Government. Revolutions are quite impossible while the Government is steadily just and steadily vigilant, so that it meets the people's desire for timely ameliorations, and does not oppose them until it is obliged to yield to pressure from below.

This practical realism is a summary of Goethe's political attitude during the Revolutionary epoch.

For realism was now his guiding principle, and never more markedly than in these years.

> Generally speaking [says Carl, one of the German Emigrants], it seems to me that every phenomenon as well as every fact is interesting only for its own sake. To explain it, or relate it to other events, is usually no more than an amusement of the mind, and we are taken in by it—as, for example, by scientists and historians. But an isolated action or event is interesting not because it is explicable or probable, but because it is true.

This paradoxical gibe, which so transparently masks the author of the speech, does indicate what was at the bottom of Goethe's mind. To his old friend Stolberg he declared, in resolute opposition to the other's fanatical propaganda, that he clung to the teaching of Lucretius and believed that life could suffice for all our pretensions. The yearnings which in his youth he had perhaps too fondly cherished, he now did his utmost to combat; yearning "was not fit for man, could not suffice him; and so his quest was for complete temporal satisfaction."

But just because the ebullient Faustean mood was rare with him, now that he sought a stoical composure, he seems to take his stand with Mephisto when, in one of the two new dialogues between them, he makes the latter reason cynically with Faust:

Mephisto.

Das will Euch nicht behagen.
Ihr habt das Recht, gesittet Pfui zu sagen.
Man darf das nicht vor keuschen Ohren nennen,
Was keusche Herzen nicht entbehren können.[1]

In the practical sphere, too, the middle-aged Goethe began to oppose the mysticism which had tinged his youth, and was to tinge his old age. He prevented the establishment of a Masonic lodge in Jena—indeed he induced a colleague there to lecture on the chaotic state of the secret societies, and make a simultaneous attack in print, so as to proclaim open hostility "between ourselves and the fools and knaves."

And following the law of Goethe's development, which always curved upwards in a spiral, the scepticism of the Leipzig student was now, after twenty-five years, resuscitated—only with loftier motives and on a higher plane. "The rest will be, and is welcome to be" (so he wrote from camp), "as it is written or not written in the stars." But he did not fail to see that he was in danger of becoming a fatalist, and it was thus that he summarised his destiny:

Götter, wie soll ich euch danken! Ihr habt mir alles gegeben,
Was der Mensch sich erfleht; nur in der Regel fast nichts.[2]

[1] *Mephisto.*

You'll not permit such jesting?
Your right to cry me shame is past contesting—
We should not name to ears of chaster brothers
What their chaste hearts insist on, like the others.

[2] "Gods, of my thanks am I debtor? Yea, ye have given me all things
Asked of men at your hands. Yet is it naught, of a truth."

With this strange two-edged thanksgiving he turned to his gods in the bitter-sweet weeks at Venice; and how unmystical his feeling then was he once indicated. It appeared, he said, that he was thought to take the most transcendental things in too earthly a sense; yet the gods of the Greeks were not enthroned in the seventh or tenth heaven, but on Olympus, and it was not from sun to sun, but more probably from mountain to mountain, that they took their one gigantic stride!

This very earthly faith, which was a quasi-scepticism, is nowhere more cynically set forth than in Mephisto's words, when Goethe—at the conclusion of the second new dialogue—seems to close the case for himself in these lines:

> Und hätt' er sich auch nicht dem Teufel übergeben,
> Er müsste doch zu Grunde gehn![1]

This glacial frame of mind leads to observation, compromise, sociability; but being entirely egotistic, is apt to make intercourse with others only a deeper loneliness. In this way Goethe's attitude towards sociability and seclusion took a new aspect. In the preceding decade he had more and more resolutely withdrawn from social life, that he might find himself; now he resorted to it again, that he might lose himself. The sense of being oppressed by numbers who were harmful to his productive energies or his moments of insight, had driven him to isolate himself; now he was driven back into society by a sense of sterile loneliness.

Disillusioned with the austere schooling to which, under Charlotte's goads, he had submitted at thirty—in the belief that it would lead to an harmonious organisation of his nature, and for that hope renouncing social life—he was now, at forty, taking a wider range. In Charlotte's day his thin pale face, his absent look, together with what was mirrored in his poetry, had betrayed so much to the world that he was driven to seclude himself; but now he had found a mask, a bearing, a manner which enabled him to move as it were incognito in society. He who for so long had stimulated those around him by the myste-

[1] "And even though he had not bargained with the Devil,
He must at last have come to grief!"

rious element which glowed within his breast, now constrained himself to frozen contemplation, unapproachable even by the critical sense. The "Here and Now" of the classic form of life became his ideal:

> I was leading a rather unconscious sort of life, from day to day as it were. . . . I developed an idiosyncrasy, which was that I never speculated about anyone who happened to be expected or anywhere I happened to be going, but let things make their own unanticipated impression upon me. . . . In much the same way I never cared what personal effect my presence or way of thinking might have upon other people, for I often found that I aroused quite unexpected liking or disliking, and sometimes both at once.

It was inevitable, then, that Goethe should begin to strike other people as a prig, an oddity. In the field, with his stiff bearing, serious expression, long hair, "streaming like the wool on a distaff," his effect was provincial, disconcerting, haughty. Strangers who brought letters of introduction to him at Weimar were dismayed by the absent-mindedness that would suddenly overtake their host, and astonished at the way he would unexpectedly leave the rooms of other people. Keen observers testify that he often made faces; and nobody could understand how it was that this master of language, so accustomed to society, often seemed at a loss for a word, and had to be helped out.

But an intelligent official, who made friends with him on a journey, perceived why it was that Goethe was never animated unless he was in a genuinely friendly atmosphere. He saw that Goethe was incapable of small-talk, and yet could not very well avoid it with strangers; while, once he was on terms, his ideas came thronging to his lips. Like an algebraist he reckoned in quantities, not numbers. At Münster, where the tone of society was devout, he felt a personal sympathy which made him give and enjoy the tolerance which best befits human intercourse; and to a Bishop, who was also a man of the world, he seemed at once friendly and aloof: "He is a very unhappy man, and must be perpetually dissatisfied with himself."

Of these very years, when he travelled so much and saw so many more people, Goethe himself said afterwards that his need for human intercourse had diminished, his decisive trend towards natural philosophy having made him more self-centred than ever:

I could find no master, and no fellow-students, and had to depend on myself for everything. I should have spent my time all alone in the solitude of the woods and gardens, in the obscurity of darkened rooms, if a happy domestic relation had not had its soothing and refreshing effect upon me during that strange period of my life.

His life, he said, was a mystery even to his closest friends; they could not imagine how any man could be so aloof as he was then, and had been for a long time.

For in these years his duality again became strongly apparent. It was now—in the *Emigrants*—that he first launched the idea of the two souls, which not until later, in the mouth of Faust, was to become the watchword for antithetical natures. Not until now had he found the philosophical authority for his first principle—from Kant's physics it leaped at him that attraction and repulsion were inseparable from the nature of matter, and from this he deduced "the essential duality of all substance."

This characteristic of his own nature he now stated afresh. Since the presentation of Tasso and Antonio, ten years earlier—since that attempt to take the measure of, and express, himself—he had shaped no other dialogue of self-communion. Now the old voices, which fifteen years ago had died away, broke out afresh in the antiphonies of Faust and Mephisto—nay, their two new dialogues were the first real expression of the two conflicting forces, for in the original *Faust* they spoke (save for two brief passages) only of the immediate predicament, that of Gretchen.

But the new scenes, written at forty, and irrelevant to the drama, display more arrestingly than any others the mighty to-and-fro of the pendulum which swung within the soul of Goethe. So subjective are these scenes, so entirely is any dramatic disguise stripped from them, that Faust—in the fragment—begins in the middle of a sentence, and Mephisto suddenly appears for no reason at all! These passages must be read as the hieroglyphic of his soul, and nothing more. The following instance will suffice:

Faust.

Ich fühl's, vergebens hab' ich alle Schätze
Des Menschengeists auf mich herbeigerafft.
Und wenn ich mich am Ende niedersetze,
Quillt innerlich doch keine neue Kraft.
Ich bin nicht um ein Haarbreit höher,
Bin dem Unendlichen nicht näher.

Mephisto.

Mein guter Herr, Ihr seht die Sachen,
Wie man die Sachen eben sieht;
Wir müssen das gescheiter machen,
Eh' uns des Lebens Freude flieht.
Was Henker! Freilich Händ' und Füsse
Und Kopf und Hintrer, die sind dein—
Doch alles, was ich frisch geniesse,
Ist das drum weniger mein?[1]

Here we are listening to the quintessential dialogue that persisted in Goethe's breast; between forty and forty-five it was incessantly renewed. It explains to all the vertiginous images which made the man a puzzle to his contemporaries, and to posterity.

This is the nadir of his battle for harmony. It is the climax of his self-analysis. And, beyond yea or nay, it is the deadlock.

It is as though the solitary were aching for a human voice.

[1] *Faust.*

The treasures of the mind that I have hoarded,
Now I possess them, seem an idle show;
I count them up at last, yet am accorded
Nothing of soul-revivifying glow.
Not by a hair's-breadth have I risen higher,
No nearer to the Infinite Desire.

Mephisto.

My dear good sir, the view you mention
Answers to that which all men hold.
Life needs more delicate attention,
Joys must be caught ere yet we're old.
Why, you have hands and feet, deuce take it!
And head and hind-parts, as I see—
Use them; your sport will never make it
Less of a sportive world for me.

CHAPTER IX

PROTEUS

"... Because my existence seems to be infinitely subdivided."

IN a large bleak well-lit room some hundred young men are standing in a row, heels together, heads and bodies very upright, for before them looms the stern and fateful figure of their aged ruler, the Duke of Württemberg. He is about to present the prizes to the students of his Military College. Behind and beside him hovers a semicircle of Court-officials, exchanging whispered remarks, and there are some guests as well—the Duke's young cousin of Weimar, with his friend, the author and Minister. The Duke has been praising the zeal and ability displayed by some of the candidates, and has just received a list from the Instructor. He reads out the names of the most distinguished students, who approach him in turn, and then, with a look which has more of admonition than approval about it, he presses a prize into the right hand of each. The recipients thank him mutely with the prescribed gesture, anxiously observant of his face, for he inspires them with awe.

There is one, and only one, who does not gaze into the master's face, who hears nothing, does not even see the winners of that reward which he would so much like to win himself. His eyes are riveted on the form of the visitor who stands a little in the background, sombrely attired. That silent man—as silently this other seeks to fathom him. So that's what a poet looks like, when he's famous and full of honours!

No more dazzling, no grander, than that? He is pale and thin, something like his Werther. . . . Now he has turned his wide, penetrating gaze on me, and now—if I could only hold it with my own, if I could only rush into his arms, and cry "*Et in Arcadia ego!*" But arrogant you are; you do not look into my soul as should a poet, you do not dream of what is pulsing through my veins. . . . Now you are bowing before the Duke, who has expressed a desire to speak with you; you're smiling and nodding; you are the servant of Princes, a mere courtier, after all. How I hate them all! And you too—you who have been false to your genius! Your pallor is that of ennui, your thinness that of dissipation. No, you are not a poet, any more. . . .

"Friedrich Schiller!" the Duke calls from his list. The youth awakes from his dream, steps forward, much embarrassed, plants the prescribed kiss on the hem of the master's coat, and returns to the ranks. He might be walking in his sleep.

A book! [he is thinking now]. You press a book into my right hand? O Duke, some day I mean to press a book upon your heart, that will turn it to stone! So this is your prize? And I am twenty years old. When I'm thirty, like that man there, I intend that a prize made of evergreen leaves shall be pressed upon my brow, and *he* shall see the nation give it me!

Eight years later, on a tranquil evening in August, Schiller is sitting with a glass of Rhine-wine before him in Goethe's *Gartenhaus*. He has left the Military College behind him, he has travelled and wandered, known poverty, known glory, but the vision of Goethe has persisted through it all—of Goethe standing there, so taciturn, and never for a moment dreaming that genius was being awarded a prize under his very eyes. Then he had come to Weimar, and the intellectuals had received him with open arms; but where was the man whom the visitor, with his admiration and his envy, his grudge and his reverence, his curiosity and his scepticism, at last might have put to the proof? Goethe was then domiciled at Rome; and only his house was to be seen, and only his *Gartenhaus* at that, for it was there that Goethe's friends had assembled on his birthday, inviting the new poet to be present. . . . So Schiller clinks glasses with Knebel to the proprietor's health, in the little house where Goethe had lived for six years; Schiller drinks Goethe's health, the absent Goethe's—and it is mid-summer.

A queer mixture—what he hears about the eccentric at

Weimar. Some are hostile and speak ill of him; a few are enthusiastic and speak well; and these few are undoubtedly the best people there. The Mistress of the Horse at the Court of Rudolstadt, her daughters, the Lengefelds (Schiller's most distinguished acquaintances)—don't they all speak admiringly of Goethe's genius? But their friend, that Frau von Stein . . . his reputation has already suffered from her acerbities. Many an official in Weimar purses up his lips when the visitor asks about Goethe. How long does he mean to stop away, what can he be doing? Anyhow, he gets his quarter's salary regularly from the Treasury. And once more Schiller feels the old resentment.

> What luck the fellow has, what an easy time of it, while the rest of us have such a struggle! Is he a bigger man? No; but he was born with a silver spoon in his mouth, and so he was better educated; he's lucky, that's all, and ten years older too!

And with tongue and pen he joins in the aspersions that he hears everywhere on Goethe.

When Goethe returns in the following June, Schiller's curiosity reaches its climax. "I am impatient to see him; few mortals have interested me so strongly"; and he bids his friends "say as many flattering things as possible." Soon Frau von Stein comes to visit the Lengefelds in the country; and from the lips of this lady, who must know, Schiller hears nothing but cold depreciatory remarks about the home-comer. "O my prophetic soul!" he thinks—but then he comes across a copy of *Iphigenie,* reads it again, and "it gave me a very delightful day, though I had to pay for my pleasure by the overwhelming conviction that I could never produce anything in the least like it."

But anyhow—won't he come to call upon me? And (how completely mistaken!) Schiller writes to his friend: "Goethe would have visited me if he had known how near I was to him, when he was passing through to Weimar. We were within an hour of each other." You will be within a few minutes of each other, Friedrich Schiller—and yet he will not look at you!

For only a few weeks later, on a brilliant Sunday in September, when people could still spend the day in the open air, they meet at a nobleman's country-house. The Herders are there, so is Frau von Stein.

"At last I can tell you something about Goethe," writes Schiller to his friend Körner.

My first look at him was rather destructive of all I had heard about his charm and personal beauty. He is of middle height, holds himself stiffly, and walks stiffly too. He looks reserved, but his eye is very expressive and animated, and one watches eagerly for its kindling glances. Though he looks stern enough, there is something very kind and sweet about his expression. . . . We were soon introduced, and he was very easy to get on with. Of course it was a big party, and everyone wanted to speak to him, so I couldn't be much alone with him or talk about anything but commonplaces. . . . I doubt that we shall ever become very intimate. Many of the things which still interest me, many of my hopes and wishes, are to him past experiences; he is . . . too far in front; we can never meet as fellow-travellers, so to speak. . . . His world is not my world; our outlooks seem to be essentially different. . . . Time will tell, however.

And that is all? A chat with Goethe about the Neapolitans and other Italian matters? A gay Sunday-party, in the company of ladies who are his friends or his enemies—and yet the stranger had proudly supposed that this was to be the historic day when Schiller and Goethe had looked one another in the face for the first time. How little has he seen through Goethe's mask—scarce more than that he wears one. He is mortified because Goethe did not draw him apart, or say one word about the link between them. But his self-confidence comes to his rescue, telling him not to be distressed, and he measures himself with the other, informs his friend, "We are too different ever to come together"—but hastens to add that "time will tell."

Time went on, and Schiller was still waiting. . . . When on that Sunday he had vainly hoped for a personal word from Goethe, his review of *Egmont* was in print—one might say, his attack on *Egmont*. Well that it was written but not yet published—so that the two men could exchange their first handshake without nervousness on one side and wounded vanity on the other. Soon enough Goethe was to read into that review the general atmosphere which surrounded his return. Schiller grudgingly saw in Goethe the darling of the gods, who conquered the world without fighting it; Goethe grudgingly saw in Schiller the usurper of the Muses' realm, who thought that he could conquer *them* without a struggle. His own twenty years wrestling with the chaotic in the service of form, his desperate search for the gold that lay in the dæmonic depths of him—this was what Goethe had to see arraigned, not only abroad but at home; for this young man was beginning to reinspire the Germans with the chaotic ideal. And he was to make friends with him? Even if he could manage not to hate him, his ideals would still be obnoxious.

But Schiller, for whom Goethe's ideals had always been inspiring if uncongenial, *was* beginning to hate him personally. From October onwards he spent the whole winter in the same little town with him, living round the corner, so to speak, consorting with his friends, frequently seeing Knebel and Moritz—but never a sign from Goethe, nothing but a polite deadlock, on the one or two occasions that they did meet. And Schiller was getting desperate. He had to listen by the hour to Moritz, reading eulogies on Goethe; and the more he pumped out about Goethe from this colleague of his enemy's, the more Schiller writhed. When Moritz returned to the stately abode where *he* was at home and where Schiller might not even set foot, and thence came back to Schiller, the latter was always hoping to hear that Goethe had "said something, the other day, about *Don Carlos*." Through all his antipathy pierced the desire to be judged as a poet by that poet—though it were to be condemned.

Goethe would neither give judgment nor even speak. All he wanted was to get Schiller out of the place. Already he seemed to see people cautiously pointing him to the new dramatist, and it dismayed him. On his return, he had found his friends changed; they were listless, evasive, and he did not intend to have a rival forced on him in that way. For Goethe, in whose work and projects Schiller felt an ardent if reluctant interest, took not the faintest interest in Schiller's art. To get him out of the town, he set up a new professorship in Jena for the poet. And he was in so frantic a hurry with this subtle scheme that he caused Schiller to be approached in December; and when Schiller agreed, Goethe obtained the Duke of Gotha's consent the very next day! Together with the official offer, he caused Schiller to be informed by

GOETHE AT THE AGE OF FIFTY

letter that he might make all his arrangements—it was as good as settled. Schiller was now obliged to go and thank him. "Meanwhile I paid a call on Goethe. He has taken any amount of trouble about this business, and seems to be very much interested in what he believes to be to my advantage."

A man of the world, with some knowledge of human nature—can Schiller have failed to perceive his rival's motive? Did he not see that it was with the Weimar Minister that he held converse, and that that Minister was careful not to set foot in the illimitable region which was for both their spiritual home? So fervent was his desire to win over the One and Only that in those days his penetrating insight was obscured.

And there was something else to obscure it, upon which Goethe had likewise reckoned, basing his attitude to Schiller on that very circumstance. After ten years of a distressful, uncertain, nomadic existence, Schiller now, at thirty, was anxious for official recognition—wanted a position, settled means, a house; wanted, in short, that repose from external anxieties which would further his intellectual aims. It is true that with the Lengefeld sisters, who were simultaneously the recipients of his confidences, he assumed a pathetic attitude of "heroic resignation," saying that the appointment had been "forced down his throat," that he would like to draw back, and praising "golden freedom." As a matter of fact, since he was not yet officially appointed, he *could* at any moment have drawn back—but he simply did not want to, for to his friend Körner he confessed that he was very glad indeed of the post. He wanted to cast anchor; and while trying to get out of his love-affair with the brilliant Frau von Kalb, he was looking out for a rich and well-born wife, for his heart was set on having money and standing at long last.

"That fellow, that Goethe is always in my way," he now cried frankly to his friend, and made no concealment of his grudging envy for a destiny which had made it so easy for "that fellow" to obtain such incomparable advantages. Indeed, before ever he went to Jena, he poured forth all the passionate mixture of love and hatred with which Goethe had filled him:

The idolisation of Goethe which Moritz keeps up—and which goes so far that his most mediocre productions are regarded as canonical, and every other kind of literary work is consigned to outer darkness—has somewhat restricted my intercourse with him. . . . To be often in Goethe's company would make me miserable. Even with his nearest friends he is never for a moment really spontaneous, he won't expand on any subject whatever; in fact, I believe him to be extraordinarily egotistical. He has the knack of fascinating people, and gaining their hearts by small as well as great attentions, but he always manages to keep apart from them. His kindness is well-known, but he must always be as a god, he never gives *himself*—and that seems to me a consequential . . . sort of attitude, designed in reality for the satisfaction of his self-love. People ought not to let a man of that kind domineer over them. It makes him quite detestable to me, though I love his intellect with all my heart and think highly of him. I look upon him as one might upon a pretentious prude, whom one must get with child so as to humiliate her socially. It is a most peculiar mixture of love and hatred that he has inspired in me—a feeling unlike any other, something like what Brutus and Cassius must have felt for Cæsar. I could destroy his intellect, and yet go on loving him. . . . His brain is now at its best, and his opinion of my work is, so far as I know, more hostile than favourable. And as I care most, at bottom, to hear the truth about myself, he of all men whom I know is the one who could best do me that service. So I intend to surround him with my spies, for I myself will never ask him a single question on the subject.

Never did Schiller so define his feeling towards Goethe as in this tempestuous letter, which indeed reveals little about Goethe, but much about Schiller—with his literary integrity, his artistic incorruptibility, his reverence for the great and the beautiful, and at the same time his ambition, his jealousy; and in the image of the pretentious prude, his passionate and virile craving to conquer the thing he loved. He never afterwards wrote for Goethe in so fiery a strain as here he writes against him; and this hostile temper obscured his perception of character. True, Schiller never at any time entirely revised this most mistaken view of what Goethe really was, but there are cordial words of tardy recognition for the unselfishness he did come to appreciate, despite Goethe's coldness of manner. At this particular moment Schiller saw no deeper into Goethe's soul than all the world did—and for a century afterwards, even most Germans.

In a year and a half Schiller was sitting—a married man and a professor, son-in-law of a Thuringian nobleman, honoured by students, savants, and writers—in his tasteful house at Jena. His wife had been known to Goethe from her childhood, Schiller himself frequently met him at the houses of common friends, so there is nothing to surprise us in Goethe's having gone (it is uncertain whether only once or on several occasions) to Schiller's house. The conversation, reports Schiller, soon turned on Kant.

> Goethe is quite incapable of taking a firm stand about anything. His view of philosophy is entirely subjective. . . . Generally speaking, his methods are too sensuous for me—too tactile. But his intellect is on the alert in every direction, striving to construct a synthesis for itself—and so I consider him a great man. In other respects he can be silly enough. He is growing old; and woman's love, against which he has so often blasphemed, seems to be getting its own back. I fear he is about to make a fool of himself, and suffer the usual fate of an elderly bachelor. His girl is a Mamsell Vulpius—she has a child by him. . . .

Schiller's position was steadily improving. Two years later —it was no longer to be avoided—Goethe produced *Don Carlos* at his Court-theatre, but the coolness between them persisted. For six long years Goethe never said or wrote one recorded word about Schiller! He afterwards declared:

> I refused every overture from persons who were intimate with us both. . . . His essay on *Anmuth und Würde* (*Charm and Dignity*) was equally little calculated to ingratiate him with me. . . . There were certain acrimonious passages which I could see were intended for me—they displayed my creed in a false light.

Schiller's position went on improving. He was full to the brim with promising schemes. Cotta had perceived a great political journalist, as well as a poet, in Schiller; and now, under his editorship, he founded a monthly literary journal to which Schiller's name, together with generous payment, attracted authors. The two brothers Humboldt, working at Jena in the flush of their youth, Fichte, and many others, were already at

Schiller's disposal when he bestirred himself to net the three big fish—Herder, Kant, and Goethe—in the name "of a group which sets unlimited value on your work."

When Goethe opened Schiller's letter, he knew that to hold back now would do him more harm than it would the new magazine. Prudence counselled him to mount this rostrum; in his reply he congratulated himself on his collaboration "with such fine fellows," and in the rough draft of his answer we see him gradually revising his expressions until they become really cordial.

A month after this letter the two poets met at the Society of Natural Science in Jena—real neutral ground. By chance (as we are pleased to call Providence) they left the hall together. Schiller deplored the mere dabbling in natural science to which a layman felt himself condemned.

Meanwhile they had reached Schiller's house.

> Our conversation [reported Goethe afterwards] tempted me in; I eagerly introduced the subject of the metamorphosis of plants, and showed him what a primitive plant was like. He listened to, and looked at, everything with great interest and remarkable quickness of apprehension, but when I had finished, he shook his head and remarked, "That is not an experience; it is an idea." I was taken aback and somewhat annoyed, for our breaking-point could not have been more sharply defined. My ancient grudge raised its head, but I controlled myself and replied: "I rather like the notion of having ideas without knowing it—and actually seeing them under my eyes!"
>
> Schiller, who was much shrewder and more tactful than I was, and moreover was more desirous of pleasing than of vexing me, on account of the magazine, retorted in the best Kantian manner; and as my stubbornly materialistic outlook gave occasion for lively argument, we had a pitched battle which ended in a deadlock—neither of us could say he had won. We both considered ourselves invincible. Remarks like the following made me quite unhappy: "How can we ever postulate an experience which shall be adequate to an idea? For the essential peculiarity of the latter is that no experience can be congruous with it."

When Goethe left the house and walked to his own quarters through the July evening, he said to himself: "Though Schiller regards as an idea what I describe as an experience, the two conceptions must have some quality in common." And went back to Weimar next morning.

One day, soon after their talk, he availed himself of the opportunity of sending back a proof for the magazine to write thus: "Remember me kindly, and be assured that I shall very greatly enjoy a frequent interchange of ideas with you."

Goethe was well aware of the value and significance which the recipient would just then attach to every one of those words—and it was in statesmanlike fashion that Schiller treated the inestimable utterance. As Goethe was away from home, he let four weeks elapse; then he wrote to him—and can we call it a letter? It was a philosophical treatise on the mind of Goethe, of the kind which is publicly promulgated on the death, or possibly on the birthday, of an aged celebrity, but had never before been privately presented to a man in the prime of life—and Schiller's only pretext for offering this unexpected monograph was a preliminary passage in which he said that Goethe's conversation had stimulated what he called "the whole mass of his ideas." Schiller wrote thus:

> . . . Your unerring intuition possesses, and possesses in much greater abundance, everything for which analysis laboriously searches, and it is only because you possess it as a whole that your own abundance is hidden from you. . . . Minds like yours, for this reason, seldom know how far they have penetrated, and how scant is their need to borrow from philosophy, which can but learn from them. . . . Long since, though from afar, I began to follow the operations of your intellect, and to observe with ever-renewed admiration the path you had marked out for yourself. You are searching for a first principle in Nature, but you are doing this in the most arduous of all ways. . . . From the simple organism you have climbed, step by step, to the more highly evolved, and now your effort is to construct genetically the most complex of all—the human being—from the materials implicit in all Nature. And by using Nature's methods to reconstruct him, you seek to penetrate the mystery of his technique. A great and truly heroic conception. . . . You can never have hoped that your life would suffice for the attainment of such an aim, but merely to set foot on such a path is grander than to reach the end of any other—and your choice is like that of Achilles in the Iliad between Phthia and immortality. . . .

This is how I see the course taken by your intellect, and whether I am right or wrong, yourself best knows. But what you can scarcely know (because genius is always the greatest of mysteries to itself) is the beautiful accordance of your philosophical instinct with the clearest deductions of speculative reason. . . . It is true that the intuitive intellect is solely concerned with the individual form, and the speculative as exclusively with the species. But if the intuitive intellect is that of a genius intent on discerning the law of necessity in the empirical world, its creations will always be individuals, but will display the characteristics of species; while if the speculative intellect is that of a genius and does not lose sight of the experience which it seeks to transcend, its creations will be of the nature of species, but will possess the element of personality and relate themselves to material substance.

But I perceive that I am in the act of writing a treatise instead of a letter . . . and should you fail to recognise your own aspect in this mirror, I beg you earnestly not therefore to reject it.

Follows an enquiry whether *Wilhelm Meister* may appear in the magazine.

My wife, together with my friends, send kind remembrances, and I remain most respectfully, Your obedient servant,

F. SCHILLER.

A philosopher wrote this letter—and a man of the world. The literary man is out of sight, and so a purely literary recognition of the object was irrelevant. Assuredly this was the first adequate summary of Goethe's development; never before had he had, and very seldom was he to have, the opportunity of reading such deep things about himself. But it was the path of the intellect, not the pilgrimage of the human being, that Schiller had there delineated; and for the space of eleven years, to the end of his life, he was never, despite closer contact, to attempt even a sketch of Goethe's character—astonishing in such a psychologist, and only to be explained by the purely intellectual attitude of Schiller towards this relation. (Neither poet ever attempted to portray the other in his literary work.)

But the diplomatic art with which, in this letter, Schiller disguised his real purpose was supremely effective. With what subtlety he treats Goethe as the purely instinctive genius who knows nothing about himself—and yet he was perfectly aware that Goethe knew everything about himself! How haughtily, at the same time, he excludes him from his own realm, that of philosophy! How boldly, and yet with what high reverence, he shows him that his stupendous aim is impossible of attainment! How gently he proffers himself, even though his mirror should present the image of what was not! For this letter was a big bid—with its reverence for the greater man, chivalrously acknowledged as such, but always with the far-reaching corollary that Schiller's reason is in sweet accord with Goethe's intuition, that Goethe is in fact an intuitive, and Schiller a speculative, genius —and that therefore none but Schiller is born to comprehend Goethe.

Goethe had once or twice written this type of letter to his Duke; and just as those epistles had ever, after all the wishes and rebukes, been voluntarily concluded with the formula of obedience, so now Schiller, on closing the door of the Holy of Holies, suddenly and frigidly remained most respectfully his obedient servant.

But in the same moment Goethe re-opened the door. For it was twenty years since . . . nay, never before had he had such a letter! He felt the grandiosity in Schiller's view of him—in what an historic, what an heroic light was he regarded! And in his gratitude he did what he hardly ever (and in these particular years never) undertook to do; for it was he, the ten years older man, who first used the word Friendship. He accepted this courtship as may a beautiful woman, who is aware of the distinction she confers, and refrains from too precipitate and wholehearted a response to the ardour of a suitor. It is the strangest of betrothal-letters:

> On my birthday—it is my forty-fifth—I could have had no more welcome present than your letter, in which with a friendly hand you recapitulate my existence, and by your sympathy stimulate me to more assiduous and enthusiastic application of my energies.

From that conversation he too dated an epoch; it seemed

> as if, after such an unexpected encounter, we were bound to go on in each other's company. I have always known how to value the genuine,

> and very rare, sincerity which is apparent in everything that you have written and done, and by this time I can claim to know something of you through your intellectual production, especially in recent years. . . . All that is of me and in me I shall gladly share with you. For as I have a very lively consciousness that my aim . . . far transcends the measure of our human capacities, I should like to lay it fully before you, and in this way not only be indebted to you, but also perhaps interest you. How great the privilege of your sympathy will be for me, you will not fail to see if, on nearer acquaintanceship, you perceive in me a certain perplexity and vacillation which, though I am very well aware of it, I cannot get over. . . . I hope soon to see a great deal of you, and then we shall talk over many things.

The novel, he said, had been delivered to a publisher. "Fare you well, most cordially, and remember me to your circle. Goethe."

He makes it quite clear that his partner in the proposed marriage of minds will be welcomed as a coadjutor in his realm, and need contribute no more than the said "genuine sincerity," which will be sufficiently valued. But of what Schiller himself actually is, Goethe seems to have no idea at all; for although Schiller's productions are before him and have become very famous, he is here cordially invited to unveil himself to his new friend. There is never a hint at equality.

Nevertheless, Schiller was conscious of victory; and he was right in so far as he had taken Goethe's confidence by storm. His interest (Schiller reflected) would be aroused by deeds. He got rid of his susceptibility, concentrated on the phrase about their going on in each other's company, and extended its application by saying that "we shall keep together for whatever may remain of the journey, and with the advantage that those who travel the latter part of a long road in one another's company always have most to say." In this way he established not only a lifelong friendship, but one which Goethe was to profit by to the end of his career.

Schiller now wrote ardently—much less philosophically than in the first letter of carefully restrained enthusiasm. He alluded to himself in a strain resembling that of a Posa, and while chivalrously affecting to take a back seat, stepped with dignity into his proper place:

To make much of little is what I need and desire; and when you know something more of my poverty in what is called acquired knowledge, you will perhaps find that in some respects I have not failed to do so. . . . *You* have a kingdom at your disposal—*I*, only a numerous progeny of concepts. . . . My mind really works best in the realm of symbols, and so I hover, like a sort of hybrid, between ideas and perceptions. . . . Commonly the poet in me takes the reins when I mean to philosophise, and the philosopher when I sit down to creative work. . . . But unfortunately, now that I am beginning to have some idea of my mental powers, and some knowledge of how to use them, my physical energies are threatened by disease. . . . But I shall do what I can, and when the building finally collapses, I shall at least have saved something from the flames—some right to survive. . . . I confidently lay these confessions before you, and I venture to hope that you will receive them in a spirit of affection.

A fine phrase—that of the poet taking the reins when he means to philosophise! Into what pulsating rhythms he fashions his confession—in this letter one seems to see the pen flying over the paper, while the first had been carefully composed and revised.

It was in a spirit of affection—as the younger man had requested—that Goethe answered these lines, at the same time inviting him to Weimar. Schiller, accepting the invitation, asked only for indulgence towards his delicate health. But as if re-assuming the old mask of pride, he made a point of telling Körner that "he could not well refuse" Goethe's persuasive invitation to stay with him, and that their intercourse would have far-reaching consequences for both; while to his wife he wrote that he heard on all sides "how very much Goethe looks forward to knowing me better." Much more coolly did Goethe inform his friend Meyer that Schiller had a very refreshing effect on his stagnant ideas; and even at the end of three months he was saying dispassionately: "For the present I am a good deal mixed-up with Schiller and the Humboldts, and it seems as though we might keep company for quite a while."

This fortnight's stay in Goethe's house took the aspect of an inventory of all the goods which each partner in the marriage of souls could contribute. A programme was drawn up—they were to correspond æsthetically, with a view to further revelations.

> We know now, my dearest fellow [wrote Goethe to Schiller on his departure], from our fortnight's conference, that in principle we are agreed, and that the range of our perceptions, thoughts, and activities sometimes coincides and sometimes approximates, which will be in many ways advantageous for us both.

And with this begins their correspondence, their collaboration in the magazine, and a new grouping of German writers.

When they contracted this alliance—which was to survive, with occasional slight vicissitudes, for nearly eleven years—the allies were aged respectively forty-five and thirty-five. But it was the younger man whom suffering had made pale and fragile; the elder collaborator was sunburnt and vigorous. Schiller was taller, with a spare, lanky figure; Goethe was broad of beam, and now looked more thickset than of yore—he was already beginning to grow stout. Schiller's liquid deep-set eyes looked out from an oval-shaped face; his pale brow was more remarkable for breadth than height, but there was something splendid in its rugged outlines; the colourless but sensuous lips might have belonged to a priest; the straight, short, prominent, hawk-like nose jutted out boldly, imperiously, from the face, and in its curves seemed concentrated all the sensibility of the head. Goethe's head was now tending to squareness; the arch of the brow, above the eye-sockets, was high rather than broad; the long nose, despite its slight obliquity, was almost classical in effect compared with Schiller's; the thin close lips were folded resolutely, but the eye seemed to irradiate the universe with its sombre brilliancy, and make the visible its own. Schiller's handwriting was like a large swift rushing wave, streaming in creative urgency over the paper; Goethe would form some letters with such care as to make them a work of art in their own convention.

Schiller, the youthful Councillor and courtier, paid great attention to dress. He would order the most expensive materials for his evening clothes, kept open house, had at thirty-eight set up his own carriage and horses (which Goethe had never done till the end of his forties), and in the first year of his marriage he and his wife had never gone as far as Leipzig without valet and maid. He shone in society, and in his Court uniform with epaulettes had actually, in the ante-room, been taken by Mme. de Staël for an officer of high rank. Goethe dressed very simply, had already given up the peruke and side-curls, scarcely ever went to Court and seldom into society, lived, though a Minister, like a private gentleman, wanted to seem forbidding, said very little indeed. Schiller, accustomed to learn from books rather than from people, a stranger to outdoor life, consumptive and always in dread of hæmorrhage, spent much of his time indoors, was in no way athletic, and would sit through the long summer-evenings in a stuffy room, smoking and taking snuff.

Sleepless on most nights, he could never be sure of his mornings; sometimes he did not eat anything before eight o'clock dinner, on his bad days had to stimulate his energies by alcohol, and did his best work when the barometer was low. Goethe depended on its being high, went early to bed and got up betimes, never wrote except in the mornings, would spend whole weeks in his little summer cottage, had resumed his rides and his skating, and between forty and fifty enjoyed his best health. The atmosphere which suited Schiller Goethe declared to be poisonous for *him*, and one day, when the smell of rotten apples rose to his nostrils from his friend's desk, he had to fling the window open lest he should faint.

Schiller, often distracted by his numerous undertakings, was for a time entirely debarred from literary work by his disease. Goethe disposed of his duties and business-affairs as fast as he could, so as to devote himself to study and creative composition. Want of method in the one made public life a burden to him; the other found routine a help. And yet Schiller needed to separate the dream and the business far more than Goethe did, because he made many more worldly plans, and then had carefully to divorce his art from them.

Schiller, at the moment of his collaboration with Goethe—and it is to this moment that our antithesis refers—was in danger of becoming a journalist. He was, in Goethe's words, shaping well as an editor. For his gifted, refined, politically atheistical intellect many proprietors were contending; and Schiller, who wanted power and money, might possibly, but for his disease and but for Goethe, have entered on that career. Friends of his youth had early seen in him a born diplomatist; Goethe said that he was as great at the tea-table as he would have been in the

Council of State. He was good at negotiations, subterfuges, intrigues; and everything of that kind in his dramas is better, and moreover much more relevant and more frequent, than in Goethe's. He was supremely clever at getting hold of the best brains for his magazine, as well as at advertisement; and he enjoyed both activities.

Goethe's gifts were the direct contraries of these.

As a contemplative being, I am a stubborn materialist, so that I am incapable of desiderating anything whatever from the objects I perceive, and the only distinction I can make between them is whether they interest me or not. On the other hand, when it comes to any kind of action I may say that I am a rabid idealist—I do not enquire into circumstances, but insist that they shall conform to my ideas.

Schiller's spirit of enterprise was not wholly the outcome of his money-making ambitions. The inward will-to-power was also responsible. Goethe, in his old age, seems to point to this.

Schiller [he said to Eckermann] was much more the aristocrat of our group than I was, and much more cautious about what he said. Yet he had the remarkable good fortune to be accounted a special friend of the people.

Schiller was haunted by the idea of contemporary and posthumous fame, when he sat down to write. What with critiques, attacks, competition, gossip, and party-feeling, his correspondence was immense; and although his only successes were as a dramatist, he was vexed by any journalistic failure—would talk of his blood boiling, and was very deeply wounded when his *Muses' Almanack* was torn to pieces between eulogy and censure. Goethe, who for twenty years had given up trying to please the Germans, answered amusedly in these sage words: "Unless we can be like the heedless sower in the Gospel, who casts his seed without caring what becomes of it, we ought to have nothing to do with the public."

In the sphere of passion, likewise, Schiller's masterfulness is the antithesis of Goethe's more feminine self-surrender. Schiller had scarcely broken with his mistress before he warned his new love against her, and when the latter became his bride, he sought to make her his obedient pupil. His relations with Frau von Kalb, with the separated wife, Caroline, and her sister Charlotte —respectively his sister-in-law and his wife—were all going on at the same time. As soon as he was married he invited Caroline to live with them; and when she married again he obtained a house and an official position in Weimar for the pair, because he himself lived there. But for all that his relations with his wife were happy—at any rate he called her "dear Mousie" in his letters. Schiller was sensual and domineering in love, Goethe gave himself up, heart and soul—therefore he loved only one woman in all his life, and in the more literal sense he never had two mistresses at a time. To this one woman, it is true, his words were such that when Schiller's widow read Goethe's letters to Frau von Stein, she was startled by their passion, and confessed that Schiller could never have loved like that—"he was really incapable of sheer passion."

The contrast between the literary work of Goethe and Schiller follows naturally from these antitheses. Schiller very cleverly defined it in his allusion to his own self-consciousness and Goethe's spontaneity, but that is only the first element in the problem. Goethe himself, in his old age, traced a connection between Schiller's talent and his arrogant bearing, but melting eyes. He said that Schiller attacked a big subject boldly, but was prone to fluctuate in his treatment as time went on. "He saw the thing from the outside, as it were, and only so. A tranquil inward evolution was not for him."

In those words, Schiller's greatness, his limitations, and the difference of his method from Goethe's are precisely defined. Schiller looked about for his material; Goethe came across his. Schiller selected; Goethe experienced. If the one was content with allegory, the other expanded everything into a symbol.

The more profoundly Goethe felt this to be his own method, the better could he fathom the contrary one of his friend, who always interested him in the way that a natural phenomenon might have done.

You are really, while you are actually at work, in darkness, and the light can scarcely be said to be in you; but when you begin to reflect, the inward light shines out and irradiates your environment, yourself, and others. With me both processes are fused, and not wholly to the advantage of my work.

The necessary consequence of this was that Schiller was attracted, by temperament and gifts, to the theatre, while Goethe was repelled by it. Schiller genuinely enriched the German stage with eight or nine pieces; Goethe, with his most important dramas, merely irritated his audiences; and while Goethe's plays are only now beginning slowly to be appreciated for their profoundly dramatic qualities, Schiller's, after the space of a century, have not yet lost any of their effectiveness. Tragedy follows tragedy, for humour scarcely finds a place. Schiller makes the very most of his dispassionately selected subject; he gives his *dramatis personæ* the highest possible expressiveness—indeed, he even tried to instil his frenzy of passion into Goethe's plays.

Both men, as creative artists fashioning types of humanity, treated parentage and nationality as secondary factors. How Goethe could forget father and mother in the service of his vocation has already been shown. Schiller was very fond of his mother, but lived always at a distance from his parents. We know what Goethe thought of nationalism, and to Schiller he wrote: "Patriotism, as well as personal heroism, has had its day, like clericalism and aristocracy." Schiller, whose material was nearly always of foreign origin, said—in almost identical words—in this thirtieth year of his life: "Patriotic enthusiasm is, generally speaking, important only for the nations which have had their day; it belongs to the morning of the world. . . . It is a poor, paltry ideal to write only for one nation." Or take this about his public, whom he could not complain of as far as outward enthusiasm went: "The Germans want sensations, and the more commonplace these are, the better they are liked."

Even from their most removed standpoints—those of thinker and observer—they sometimes beckoned to one another. Schiller was carried away by *Wilhelm Meister* (a work so entirely unlike him) because it contrasted so vividly with his own cold philosophy; "for all Nature is pure synthesis, and all philosophy antithesis. The poet is the only authentic human being, and the best philosopher a mere caricature compared with him." So he wrote—and it was precisely then that he again began to turn away from philosophy.

In his philosophical friend Goethe entirely failed to see a purely speculative nature. Indeed, he expressly attributed to him a peculiar mixture of observation and abstract thought; and Schiller himself, speaking of his method of work, once made the strange confession that a musical kind of mood would come upon him, for no particular reason, before he began to write.

But before all and above all, the two minds resembled each other in the purity of their earnest endeavour—nay, with extraordinary unanimity they both, independently of each other, hit upon the same metaphor for that endeavour. For Goethe—as he wrote at thirty in his diary—designed to build up his life like a pyramid; if that should prove to be beyond him, the mere attempt would answer for his earnestness. And, "Every one builds his own pyramid," wrote Schiller in almost identical words at the same age; "even if he cannot achieve the spire, he could assuredly have found nothing better to do."

At these points the curves of their natures approximate. But normally and in general they were poles apart; and to the end of their association Goethe's phrase, after their first talk, held good—neither was victor, neither felt himself to be defeated. For directly we cease to talk of the degree of genius possessed by each—directly we are concerned with their characters and how these are shown forth in the life and work of both, they must be ranked side by side as equally matched rivals and essentially different men.

Thus—Schiller's desire was to dominate, Goethe's to influence. Schiller never gave himself entirely to any human being, but always entirely to his work; Goethe always gave himself to those who loved him, and only sometimes entirely to his work. Schiller hammered at his composition with cold intensity; Goethe modelled it with a loving hand. For Schiller life came second to work—that was why he went about his enjoyment in so awkward a manner; for Goethe life was the radical element in work—that was why his existence flowered with such seeming spontaneity. Schiller always reflected when he felt; Goethe was always observant, even while reflecting. Schiller planted one tree after another; Goethe sowed his seed.

For Schiller could hate as deeply as he could love, and he is the rival of his own heroes, as Goethe is—with the difference that the heroes of Schiller are condemned as evil-principled by their creator, while Goethe's are complex human beings (just as the so-called hero is), "good and bad, like Nature." Only once did Schiller comprehensively delineate himself—as Wallenstein. He believed in the existence of Evil, and so it was only the Good in himself that he dramatised; Goethe, by harmonising the equally matched contending energies, sought to elucidate the mystery of his own soul. Schiller wrestled clamorously with the world; Goethe silently with his dæmon. Schiller struggled; Goethe grew.

But there is one thing which can cause the figure of Schiller suddenly to take on the softly glimmering patina of a noble bronze, while Goethe's always seems panting to extricate itself from the white marble block. This is, that Schiller was perpetually conscious of death; and if we did not already know it, we could divine from the sequence of his works that it would terminate in a premature and fiercely resisted death. When Goethe's friend Meyer once met Schiller on the promenade, he wrote that his face was like that of the crucified Christ in a picture—and this was many years before the end. An internal fever drove him onward at an ever more frenzied gallop; it is as though he were crouched, breathless, on a fiery steed, pursued by the black horseman, and glancing behind him every morning to see if his adversary had gained on him once more last night—and so it went on for years. Hence it was that in the last and most fruitful decade of his life, when all his circumstances were propitious, he was irresistibly and perpetually impelled to heap tragedy upon tragedy.

Gravely and helpfully, with sympathetic understanding, Goethe watched that spectacle. *He* was to see his eighth decade; illnesses with him were short, sharp, critical. He believed in life, he shunned tragedy, for death was not his foe—he had lived from the beginning in fond communion with death. For Goethe believed in metempsychosis.

It is thus that the silhouettes of Goethe and Schiller define themselves against the evening horizon of the eighteenth century, at the time when they concluded the pact which, from Goethe's forty-sixth to his fifty-seventh year, was to enrich his life with intellectual companionship. The natures and experiences of both men urged them, though from widely differing impulses, to this association. Schiller had every motive, human and divine, to persuade him; while Goethe, after ten years of intellectual isolation, eagerly caught at a mind which could comprehend his own.

What did Schiller, what did Goethe, gain from that alliance?

Schiller gained a friend.

Failing energies and super-sensitive nerves, lack of experience in ordinary ways of living, and an unpractical wife, caused him, with his exacting claims upon existence, to look round for help —and what better could he have found than in Goethe's kindness and knowledge of the world! Goethe rented a house in Weimar for him and furnished it, sold him his summer-cottage in Jena, chose carpets for him, asked in August how much wood he should order for the winter; he let Schiller live for several weeks in his *Gartenhaus,* procured quarters in the Palace for him and his wife, offered him money, got a position at the Court of Weimar for his brother-in-law.

Goethe's practical kindliness was inspired by a wholly unselfish heart—as usual, he fondly devoted himself to Schiller, once he had made his choice. "Our lives are so closely intertwined that whatever happens to you, I feel in my own person." When Schiller's father died, at a time when one of his children was seriously ill, Goethe "had not the heart to forsake him in his present state"; for as Schiller seldom went into society, he had few visitors.

And, giving his heart, he enfranchised Schiller's mind. Now, upon eight years empty of poetic work, followed nine in which Schiller wrote six great plays, all his ballads, and a quantity of lyrics—that is to say, his life-work. At first Goethe's productions were more fruitful for Schiller—even when, or even because, they were so foreign to his own method—than any that he wrote himself. *Wilhelm Meister* especially led him (as he confided to Körner) most blessedly away from speculation and towards the concrete. But eventually his conversations with Goethe, pursued through hours and weeks, together with their correspondence, re-awakened his productive energies, and his hope was to distil their quintessence into his succeeding works. None but this intercourse, he confessed, could have so extended his boundaries. If Goethe paid him too short a visit, Schiller would complain that he had not been able to outpour his heart. "I never leave you without having something implanted in me"; and to a woman-friend he spoke of the most inestimable of all men he had ever met, and the most blessed event of his life.

Above all, Goethe relieved him of any anxiety about the performance of his plays, and not only opened to him a rich stage on which he could see both his old and his new pieces, but also became Schiller's stage-manager and producer. And so the dramatist's most valuable means of instruction was unconditionally at Schiller's disposal for ten years—a stroke of good luck which had scarcely ever fallen to a German author. At the new theatre every fifth night was, at first, a Schiller-night—later, it was every third. *Wallenstein*, *Carlos*, *Maria Stuart* were there, and there alone, more frequently performed than even Kotzebue's popular plays.

The new house was to be opened with *Wallensteins Lager* (*Wallenstein's Camp*). For a year and more Goethe had been discussing the trilogy, scene by scene, with its author; now, as Schiller had written no prologue, Goethe wrote one for him, and other passages were introduced, altered, or rejected. Goethe, alone in Weimar, was solely responsible for the scripts, the music, and the costly dresses. Then Schiller arrived, and the rehearsals proceeded.

In this and subsequent dramas the great antithesis between the two men had a favourable influence (despite several stormy encounters) on dramatic art—for it led to productions in which Schiller's part was, as colleagues testify, to inspire the actors with a sympathetic comprehension of their rôles, and Goethe's to see that everything looked as it should.

Even on the first night of *Wallenstein*, Goethe was writing to the author about a cuirass, a cap, a scarlet cloak. At the same time, after long revision, he wrote an article in a leading journal to tell the Germans what they were to think of the drama. He also, in Schiller's name, offered the trilogy, before it was finished, to the Frankfurt theatre for sixty ducats. All this Goethe did for the author who was definitely putting him in the shade—for the leader of that younger generation which was upsetting all that he had taught Germany—for Friedrich Schiller, who had attacked him both privately and publicly.

And this period of happiness—as husband, official, author, and dramatist—brought about by Goethe's advice and assistance . . . what was its upshot? So far as the alliance was concerned, a "No" for Schiller. In his moments of insight he felt that he was the second, and always would be; and after reading *Wilhelm Meister* he expressed that feeling in exaggerated terms by saying that after such an æsthetic treat, he could not possibly go on with his own botching.

What did Goethe gain from Schiller?

Firstly, a more secure position, if likewise a contested one. The pages of *Die Horen*, Schiller's magazine, were for him, who had long lacked such an organ, a welcome outlet, an opportunity for bringing much to light which had hitherto been mouldering in his desk; and though he "knew the farce of German authorship inside out," he was seized with the desire to edit a magazine once more. "How long is it," he may have reflected, "since one read manuscripts, wrote reviews, made up numbers? Twenty years? Where are the companions of those days? Merck is dead, Schlosser a recluse, Lavater a monomaniac; only Herder is still near me, but rancour and discontent are making him old before his time."

New names appeared in these pages—Fichte, the Humboldts, the Schlegels; but Schiller surpassed them all in *élan* and initiative. But he seemed over-anxious for publicity, while Goethe demanded complete anonymity for his contributions, if in his position he were to collaborate "freely and gladly."

The *Horen*, one might say, used Goethe as a rallying-point. This made him feel younger, "and moreover it is to be remembered that we get a fine scope when we weld with one hand, and with the other take as full a stretch as Nature permits us."

The great thing that Goethe gained in Schiller was an intelligent listener. Such an one he had always wanted and seldom found; and when found, the other had never been creatively productive, and so had not been able to inspire *him* to productiveness. Frau von Stein was, in that sense, no use to Goethe as an audience—she was merely a receptive vessel, not a light-reflecting mirror. Herder, born to be Goethe's as no other was, had even when teaching him to a great extent destroyed his own great influence—and utterly destroyed it when he was called upon to listen. It was not until the years before the Italian sojourn that his intellectual friendship with Goethe was an untroubled, tranquil relation.

Now Goethe was finding two more besides Schiller. W. von Humboldt and Meyer were in these years assured by him of his deepest gratitude for their comprehension, just as Schiller was. Moritz he even overestimated, until Meyer came upon the scene. And yet Schiller remains the only man whom Goethe then acknowledged—with Homer and Shakespeare—as the typical artist. Who else, in long private letters, paid such homage to the whole body of a work, and showed such understanding of its details, as Schiller did with *Wilhelm Meister?* Even Jacobi had the impertinence, in a captious letter about the book, to refer to certain passages "which at the moment he had not time to look up"!

Schiller was ready to devote months to studying it, "and so, in a loftier sense of the word, deserve the name of your friend. . . . Farewell now, my dear, my honoured friend"—so the finest and longest of Schiller's letters concludes. Only after so much of jealousy had been atoned for was it possible for one writer thus to surrender himself to another. Alien as Goethe's dramas inevitably remained to Schiller—since to accept them would have been to condemn his own—he was stirred by the novels and Elegies, where art-forms hitherto unfamiliar to him were provocative of eager æsthetic discussions.

For it was this which made Goethe loud in his praise of intercourse with Schiller—that no one was so good at solving æsthetic problems; and if, after three years, he thanked Schiller demonstratively for having rejuvenated him and made him a poet again, he said the same thing in quieter, more measured words to their friend Meyer: "My intercourse and correspondence with

Schiller, now that I look back upon it, still seems to me of inestimable value."

Goethe's longing for really intelligent criticism was almost entirely satisfied by Schiller. He incessantly demanded a frank and decisive opinion about the various parts of the novel, for even in æsthetic friendships (he said) it was affection alone which saw all the excellence; and it took an incorruptible affection to see, nevertheless, what lapses there were; "and no words I could add would better express the unique position I am in with you, and you alone."

But, despite all this, Goethe had to do without any proof of true friendship. Wholly though *he* gave himself, Schiller was able to separate his heart—which was inherently less capable of personal affection—from his intellect. Never could Goethe have addressed such words to Schiller as, for instance, these to his devoted Swiss friend, Meyer, to whom he confessed (in the third year of his alliance with Schiller): "That we should have found one another is one of the happiest events in my life." Because Schiller's wife—beautiful and amiable in her way, but neither distinguished nor capable—shared, for love of Frau von Stein, in the latter's hatred of Christiane, Schiller was able to spend the happiest decade of Goethe's life in close proximity to him, without having a word to say about Goethe's wife! Resolute to make a social position for himself, this pagan poet of freedom adopted a disapproving attitude, like any Court-parasite, towards their "connection." Else how can we account for the fact that Christiane, whom he knew to be married to Goethe, is scarcely mentioned in the two volumes of Schiller's letters?

When Goethe sent him *Der Neue Pausias und Sein Blumenmädchen* (*The New Pausias and his Flower-Girl*), which was an allegory of Christiane, Schiller did make one allusion to her—but in what words? "I wish you a right good night after a pleasant evening, and may the lovely Muse who watches over you so vigilantly by day be pleased to consort with you in the same, though more material, beauty by night." So coarsely did Schiller touch upon Goethe's love. When Christiane gave birth to a child of Goethe's, Schiller congratulated him in three words without so much as mentioning the mother, and he was equally reserved when the child died immediately afterwards. Again, when in the eighth year of Goethe's friendship with Schiller Christiane once more gave birth to a child:

> I have just heard by chance that I have to congratulate you on a happy event in your household. I want to hear this confirmed by yourself. . . . Remember me very kindly to the little girl, and be assured of my warmest interest.

For weeks Schiller had stayed with Goethe, under Christiane's hospitable care, and after many years she had even been once in his house with Goethe and her boy. Goethe had, in Schiller's company, markedly alluded to his "married state"—but Schiller's coldness went so far that even during their daily intercourse in the small town of Weimar, Goethe did not venture to tell him of the expected or the accomplished event. Finally Schiller wrote that he "had" to congratulate and mentioned the "little girl." Goethe accepted the designation quite gratefully, though from Schiller it sounded derogatory enough, and answered that the little girl would be very much pleased with his message.

Once more the child slipped out of life, and once more Goethe, who for the first time in six years had again been made a father and had instantly lost his child, was obliged to keep silence with Schiller about an event which most profoundly grieved him.

"Things are not well with us, as you may perhaps have noticed in me at the opera yesterday"; and when Schiller at last made inquiries, Goethe thanked him: "The mother . . . sends her kindest regards and values your sympathy."

So little did Goethe receive in return for so much done by him for Schiller's wife and children! What worlds of feeling are held in check by the formal phrases—what strange thoughts must have passed through Goethe's mind, amid his domestic joys and sorrows, at the sight of his friend! How entirely Schiller misjudged Goethe's marriage is shown by his expressed regret that Goethe should have been led, by false conceptions of domestic happiness and dread of marriage, into this unfortunate connection, which "he was now too weak and soft-hearted to break off—but, after all, these failings were the defects of his noble qualities." And Schiller was, at this time, finding *his* bliss in domesticity with two sisters! Even æsthetically he would have none of Christiane, for to the fine character of Therese in *Wilhelm Meister*, for whom Goethe's wife was the model, his critical friend could promise but few admirers.

From everything which intimately concerned Goethe in this decade, not only from Christiane, Schiller held aloof. And it is typical that he, who signed himself "Yours ever" to a dozen people, at the best addressed Goethe as his "dear," and on a single occasion as his "loved," friend; while Goethe, infected by this coolness, never got farther than "most valued" friend. Schiller publicly broke with the Schlegels, who at this time were Goethe's admirers and often at his house. With Frau von Stein, despite her rupture with Goethe, he remained intimate. Even after her reconciliation with Goethe, she could actually entrust the manuscript of her pamphlet drama, *Dido,* in which Goethe was caricatured, to her friend for his criticism.

We are in the third year of the poets' alliance. It was at its zenith, letters were flying, visit succeeded visit—at such a time, one would think, Schiller would have felt obliged politely to decline reading this attack of his woman-friend upon his man-friend, so that he might not seem to take sides in the unmistakably set battle. At any rate, he might have handled it in ruthlessly æsthetic fashion, or at the very least have delicately hinted that the figure of her hero reminded one a little too much of the original in some respects.

Schiller wrote a rhapsody upon it! In a long ecstatic letter he declared that the piece had

interested him inexpressibly, in every respect. Besides the general sense it gives one of a fine, tranquil, mellow, intellectual atmosphere . . . it recommends itself to me, I might say especially recommends itself, by the faithfulness with which a tender, nobly feminine nature—with which indeed our friend's whole soul—is therein depicted. I have read few things, indeed I might almost say I have never read anything, which so clearly and simply, so truthfully and unaffectedly, revealed to me the spirit from which it flowed, and so it has moved me more than I can say. But besides it is so individual and authentic that one might reckon it among the confessions of a noble nature to itself and of itself, and then it is so poetic——

whereupon follows laudation of the style as such. He has heard from his wife, he continues, that the authoress is willing that her work should be copied. Should Goethe too receive a copy, "give me a handsome proof of your friendship, and you shall never regret having presented me personally with this charming poem."

Could an enemy of Goethe's have taken sides more unmistakably? Not only does this great critic declare himself to be in raptures with the style (which happens to be execrable), but he is even more so with the confession, with the threnody so mournfully chanted by "their friend's" soul over its own sorrows, and has never been so moved as by its tones! And in this drama Schiller had just read these words of Ogon, who was Goethe: "Exalted sensibilities are the outcome of a disordered digestion; nothing I have been saying to you [about ideals] applies to me." And his mistress answers him, in the play:

> Once I was deceived in you; but now I see only too plainly, in spite of your beautifully-dressed hair and well-made shoes, the little horns and hoofs and other attributes of the Forest-Dweller, and to him no vow is sacred.

By this sort of writing Schiller declared he was moved; a few days afterwards he wrote to the original of Ogon:

> This absence of yours from Jena seems to me longer than I can say. . . . And I have missed the most indispensable of all encouragements in my work. Do come, as soon as you can. . . . I shall but the more greedily and thirstily devour every word you say to me. . . . Kindest regards from us all to you.

We read, and silently marvel, asking ourselves: *Was* Schiller Goethe's friend?

What Goethe's heart was deprived of in this intercourse had its origin in Schiller's self-centred nature. What Goethe's intellect had to dispense with belongs rather to his own appointed lot of isolation. Neither Schiller's labours nor his personal inadequacy was the reason for his failing Goethe in the thing that mattered most—Goethe's own nature must bear the blame. Hence it was not the fault of Schiller, but of Goethe's uncharacteristic attempt at an intellectual alliance, if Goethe had unchangeably to stand alone in all the critical moments not only of his daily, but likewise of his intellectual, life. Goethe nowhere attributes any stimulating influence upon any of his works to Schiller, nor did he follow his advice on any essential point.

Their longest and most interesting interchange is concerned with *Wilhelm Meister*. This work, when the alliance began, was about half finished. Other parts were sketched-in and as a whole it was already arranged for, when Schiller's first letter asked for it for the *Horen*. But it was not concluded, and but for Schiller would perhaps have remained a splendid torso. Instead of that, Goethe was constrained to finish it; and Schiller's influence seems to have destroyed the vivacity and colour of these final portions. While they were ostensibly discussing epic composition (as Goethe afterwards confessed to his interlocutor), he was always thinking of the situations in his novel. The signs of this are only too apparent. With the fifth book began those debates between the two authors—and with the fifth book begin the debates in the novel, too! To give an instance: For the first time a chapter of Goethe's opens with such very unconvincing words as: "One evening the company were arguing as to whether the novel or the drama deserved the preference," whereupon follows a dialectical extract from the correspondence with Schiller.

Two works only seem to owe much to Schiller's influence—the stage version of *Götz,* in which the poetry is a good deal sacrificed to theatrical effectiveness, and that sterile fragmentary *Achilleïs,* which was the outcome of theories on material and form. For Goethe was then wandering in a thicket of theories, and he found in Schiller the impassioned æsthete whom he sometimes sought and sometimes merely suffered. It reached such a pitch that Goethe, whose entire work was a mirror for his personality, took pleasure in a mutual adoption of each other's manner for anonymous articles in the magazine; and accounted for this by the egregious argument that "they would both gradually shed their mannerisms, and improve their general style." But when, after five years, his patience gave out and he suddenly resolved to abjure all theories in favour of real work, Schiller stuck to his philosophical outlook, and more insistently than ever proclaimed theory to be the pre-eminent link in the chain.

Nowhere can we more plainly perceive the boundaries of Schiller's sympathy than in the illuminating dialogues of Goethe's old age, where he tries to extend those boundaries as far as possible. "What would have become of me without Schiller's promptings?" asks Goethe; and after such an exclamation one at least expects to hear the watchwords for the great works that followed. But Goethe answers himself thus:

> If the *Horen* had not fallen short of contributions, I should never have written the conversations of the German Emigrants, nor translated Cellini; I should not have composed any of the ballads and lyrics, as they stand in the *Muses' Almanack*, the Elegies would not —then, at least—have been published, nor would the *Xenien* (*Epigrams*) have gone buzzing about.

Yet (since as regards the Elegies, it was only a question of publishing a finished work) all these, with the exception of three or four ballads, might never have been written, and the value of Goethe's achievement would be in no way diminished. He himself, at other times, acknowledged the meagreness of a harvest which was the result of so much labour, and when he was old cried angrily: "The time I wasted with Schiller over the *Horen* and the *Muses' Almanacks!* . . . I can't recall those enterprises without feeling annoyed—they were utterly fruitless for us both!"

Sooner than this, he regretted the most notorious work of that decade, the only one in which Schiller collaborated—the *Xenien* (*Epigrams*).

Isolated, attacked, partly dethroned, Goethe was at that time in the very mood for parody; but even his enmity usually soars above personalities into the sphere of the universal, and he can slaughter half-a-dozen undesignated literati in a single quatrain:

> So will der Spitz aus unserm Stall
> Uns immerfort begleiten,
> Und seines Bellens lauter Schall
> Beweist nur, dass wir reiten.[1]

[1] "The Pomeranian dog we feed
Follows us, ever present;
No one would know we ride, indeed,
But for his bark incessant."

Personal polemics he had abjured for twenty years; in these days his dæmon was alive only in the depths of his being, and was to make itself heard in the new *Faust* dialogues. About this time he counselled Schelling, Hufeland, and the Schlegels to make up a literary quarrel, and rebuked Schelling for the polemical conclusion of an article.

So it was only as a "brain-wave" that he one day suggested to Schiller the insertion of critical letters to the editors of the magazine. But Schiller's canniness thought to perceive that Goethe wanted a "field of battle," and he did not follow up the idea of confronting authors with their public. Instead he arranged for something like a voluntary attack of the editors on their own means of subsistence; anyone who then wanted to defend himself would have to accept "our" conditions; they must act first and make their suggestion afterwards; "it will do us no harm to be considered 'wild men.'" Goethe gradually gave in. First of all, he found in Martial's Epigrams a model for the attack desired by Schiller, and threw off a dozen distichs. Again Schiller was electrified, arranged for their continuation, and published sixty-six distichs of his own.

Goethe wanted to attack cliques, schools, views; Schiller's contentious spirit drove him to annihilate individuals either under their own names or the most transparent of disguises—he talked of a declaration of war. He spurred on the dæmon in Goethe; and although it suited neither his temper nor his years, Goethe once more did what was required of him, and on his side now pleaded for a pedantic "continuity"—so that between them they composed about a thousand distichs, sometimes in collaboration, but finally published no more than five hundred or so in the *Almanack*, thus giving cause for offence to some eighty literary men.

Schiller's epigrams are keener, wittier, more venomous—they are the better ones, as his *Tierkreis* (*Zodiac*) alone would prove. He took public, critics, rivals more seriously, because he wanted to dominate. He let fly at the friend of Goethe's youth, Count Stolberg, and forced Goethe to acquiesce.

The sensation was immense and universal. Goethe was thought to have suborned Schiller, though Goethe's dearest foes could not understand how "that slinking malingerer had ever allowed himself to be persuaded into such a schoolboy prank." And when the victims retorted in more distichs, witty and malignant, it was Schiller's turn to foam at the mouth over such treatment of honoured names and declare that they must be passionately refuted. Goethe, on the contrary, had gleefully looked forward to the answers; and now, when Schiller lost his head, was ready to be more careful, rejected Schiller's retort as taking things too seriously, and planned a jesting answer, saying: "The fat's in the fire, and time is on our side."

Suddenly, when Goethe was preparing a satirical refutation of the attacks for the new number of the *Almanack*, Schiller called a halt. Worldly wisdom ruled again; his fury was overpast.

Schiller's negative influence on Goethe ends with this episode. How little he personally understood him, despite his profound appreciation of single works, is nowhere more clearly to be seen than in a letter to Meyer, where he tries to get the latter to persuade Goethe (who was then in Switzerland) not to revisit Italy and thus waste time and energy that should be devoted to work.

> When one man out of a thousand *does* succeed in making a beautiful, satisfying synthesis of himself, it is my opinion that he can do nothing better than express himself in every conceivable way; for no matter how far he may get, he will never improve upon that offering.

Schiller considered Goethe, at forty-seven, to be a finished product. There was no further evolution for him, and to express his completeness in ever-new forms was the only task left to him.

If such a psychologist as Schiller was blind to the lifelong conflict in his friend, how profound must have been Goethe's loneliness. If the most powerful contemporary intellect could so misapprehend him—who helped him, by sheer affection, to bear that utter isolation? His beloved helpmeet.

In this period, while Goethe's mind was enlivened by Schiller's interest, his heart was nourished by Christiane's devotion, her fresh youth, her cheerfulness and unassumingness, while at the same time her capable hands and vigilant care kept perfect order among his possessions and personal comforts. This decade, when he saw so much of Schiller, was also Christiane's prime; it was the meridian of their marriage, clouded only by the death of their children. For now she was flowering into what only the poet in Goethe could have foreseen when he found her—the self-reliant, active, happy-natured being, creating such an atmosphere as, long ago, his mother had created for the boy.

There was much in common between these two women, and on a visit of Christiane's to Frankfurt, they took the most cordial liking to one another. This points clearly to the hereditary element in Goethe's love for Christiane. Both women had sunny natures, warm hearts, and active bodies, with native intelligence and little education; they were courageous, devout, and virtuous —the Councillor's widow a little the vainer of the two, Christiane a little the simpler. But such natures do better as mistresses and wives than as mothers, when the mother has to feel her way between father and son in a saddened married life; and on the whole it was a more grateful task to be Goethe's wife and the mother of his son than to be Councillor Goethe's wife and Goethe's mother. Both were uncritical, and at bottom uncomprehending, of the human phenomenon so closely connected with them,—but when the mother bestirred herself for the son, her work was usually undone by her dual and difficult position, while the wife was not called upon to strive for the husband's advancement, nor to prepare a career for him. On the one occasion that she did intervene, her fearlessness pulled the wires successfully.

Nor were their destinies very different. From a narrow sphere of intercourse and thought, genius dragged both into the light; and in the long run neither proved wholly adequate. The elder woman's spontaneity lost much of its charm in the course of these ten years; a great deal that in her old age, posing as Goethe's mother, she said and wrote was more pretentious than dignified—only a son could have let it pass in silence. But when Christiane at last fell between the two stools of spontaneity and "behaviour," it must sometimes have been distressing for a husband. Frau Goethe out of six, and Christiane out of five, children had lost all but one at a tender age; and however different a value we may set on the two survivors, the sorrows and joys of two much-bereaved mothers are no different in quality. For Goethe's development his mother was negligible, since his education came from his father; his progress from sixteen onwards was entirely uninfluenced by her. But Christiane was the wife with whom Goethe, by his free choice, spent the three middle decades of his life. Late in that life he wrote this, in memory of her:

> Ich wünsche mir eine hübsche Frau,
> Die nicht alles nähme gar zu genau,
> Doch aber zugleich am besten verstände
> Wie ich mich selbst am besten befände.[1]

When Goethe entered the room, in Christiane's time, he was welcomed by a frank look from a young cheerful healthy face, which expressed contentment and intelligence, and there was only one question in the eyes: "What would you like—can I fetch you anything or do anything for you? Nothing in the world can interest me unless your brow is clear!"

Christiane was sweetly grateful. "I pray God," she wrote to him after fifteen years together, "that in return for your kindness He may be kind to you in every way . . . but you shall find me just as grateful through all eternity." When she consulted an old doctor about an ailment, she impressed upon him not to send his answer direct to her, because Goethe might open it and be uneasy. The children of Schiller's wife, who would not associate with her, Christiane willingly had in her house for weeks at a time. If an employé at the theatre was to be replaced, she would manage to get the position for a deserving person who really needed it; for an official in distress, with whom she had only the most remote acquaintance, she begged an advance from Goethe, saying, "You won't turn a deaf ear to your rabbit." Throughout her life, she provided for her brother and sister.

Never did Christiane try to conceal her origin—she was never

[1] "I only ask for a pretty wife,
Without too strict a view of life,
But some things she by heart must get—
The things whereon my heart is set."

anything but the girl of the people, whose face had been her fortune. When in later years she went over what Goethe's mother had left on her death with the niece "who had never seen her before," the latter declared in astonishment that "people were very unfair to her; she had been so generous and sweet about the division of goods, when if there had been anything mean about her, she would certainly have betrayed it."

She always pined for her lover when he was away; and when he was working in Jena it must sometimes have been with a mixture of amusement and annoyance that he read her touching attempts to lure him home again:

> Your room, and the whole house, are in good order, and await their master with the utmost impatience. Perhaps your work would go better here than it used to lately. You can dictate in bed here, just as you can at Jena, and I won't come to you in the mornings until you want me. . . . I can't be happy at home without my love. . . . Tomorrow I'm going to kill time at my ironing.

If she had no word from the absent one, she could not eat all day, and then everyone in the house complained of her tempers; even after thirteen years she counted the days and nights till he came back, and congratulated herself on its being "one less today." And when she was allowed to visit him at Jena, or go to fetch him home, she timidly asked beforehand whether she should alight at the Palace or the hotel. When he delayed altogether too long, she pretended that the child was pining for him, but he was not to let himself be put out by that, "for it was our fault, after all, that the poem wasn't finished." And Goethe would put down the appealing letter, to write:

> Das ist die wahre Liebe, die immer und immer sich selbst bleibt,
> Wenn man ihr alles gewährt, wenn man ihr alles versagt.[1]

But when it came to the point, she had the right sense of her position. Coming home from Frankfurt, she bought new clothes for her return, "so as to be a little smart," because people would

[1] "That is the true devotion, which knows not a shadow of turning,
Whether one grants or denies every fond wish of its heart."

know she had been at Frankfurt. And she always used *Sie* to him before other people. Goethe, on his side, knew how to silence any gossip that happened to come to his ears.

To the Leipzig Fair, whither he had preceded her, he told her to come in a good carriage, because all the world would be driving about in their best; and Schiller and others testify that Goethe would never suffer a word to be said against Christiane. But it was not until he was fifty that he began to appear in society with her, and then it was away from home. At Lauchstädt the students in the theatre applauded them both equally, but she said very little about it; and any compliments that were paid her she attributed to her charming frocks.

But Goethe's friends and foes in Weimar were unchangingly malicious. The two Humboldts, like Schiller, repeated all the latest tales about "little Christiane"; and when a tactless official asked her in the theatre if it was true that the Privy Councillor was desirous to marry, she had a sudden attack of bad spirits, complained that they were envious of her having the best box, and that she did not want to see anybody, "for I hate people more and more every day." But at her side there was a comforter who had gone far along the road towards misanthropy. "As regards people in general," answered Goethe, "show them every politeness in your power, without looking for thanks. That causes one many vexations in individual cases, but on the whole it makes for pleasant relations."

"Then I will go my own way," we seem to hear her clear sweet voice reply. "I'll be a good housekeeper, love my love, and make our boy the light of my eyes, and later on pay stiff visits to any extent."

How well they understood one another—the grey-haired man of the world with his genius, and the middle-class woman in her prime with her native intelligence! What simplicity there is in this written dialogue, so harmonious, so unpretentious! And at once her spirits revived; he could again call her his little child of nature, his angel in the house, and fondly smile when she spelt a word as it was pronounced in Thuringia—"*Einsegelibter*" instead of "*Einziggeliebter*"—or scraped out a blot on the paper, or invented comic euphemisms for the state of pregnancy, or came to grief with her grammar—as did Frau Goethe and Lotte

Schiller and the Duchess Amalia. He could smile, for he had never sought or wanted a cultured wife, and all his life he was the same—he who re-created the German language, and never quite mastered the art of punctuation.

> Welche Schrift ich zwei, ja drei Mal hintereinander,
> Lese? Das herzliche Blatt, das die Geliebte mir schreibt.[1]

Yes—what was she writing today, what had she thought of to amuse him? "It's very queer that the novel won't go; but perhaps it's going now—you mustn't lose heart too soon. With us there's been great spinning." How whimsical, how amusing, to contrast his work with her own! Was it unconsciously done?

Perhaps. But how well she understood the management of her difficult husband, Knebel's wife has told us. She, like Christiane, had long been the mistress and then the wife of an equally enigmatic being, and had known the Goethes well for twenty years.

> Christiane [she wrote after Christiane's death] had a great deal of native, clear intelligence, and a sunny temper. She knew how to encourage him, and exactly what tone would be good for him. Goethe could not have found a wife better suited to his temperament. . . . He often told us that when he was absorbed in some idea, and thoughts thronged into his mind so tumultuously that he really could not find his way among them all—he would go and explain the case quite simply to her, and would be astonished at the way in which with her quiet, native shrewdness, she would always find the right way out. He said he owed her a great deal in that respect.

He talked to Christiane about *Hermann und Dorothea,* before he began it, and afterwards wrote about its progress. She did not fail to pray that it should go well, but when he asked for a carriage-rug to be sent to Jena, she took it into her head that the work was going all wrong, and "so my prayer has been no use this time." She could give a vivid description of an unruly

[1] "Which the letter I twice, nay, oftener, three times running,
Read? The affectionate words written to me by my love."

student who had made a noise in the theatre, and when some official dogged her steps with pretended deference and vowed that she must order her garden-manure from him, since if she asked for his life he would give it her, she added the quaint comment: "But that makes me all the more afraid of him." At a visit to a palace she picked out Cranach's pictures as the best, and for half a night she could not tear herself away from reading Tieck's *Genoveva.*

True, it was only by renouncing any attempts at education that Goethe could have kept such simplicity unspoilt. At some naïve question put by her after twenty years of life together, Goethe at the dinner-table turned to a friend and said: "That is what delights me about her. She is always so utterly herself."

Had Christiane any passions?

She liked wine, as Goethe did. At first she drank less than he, then quite as much; but in her life of fifty years there is no credible witness to her ever having been more than merry. Once she regretted there being no Malaga in the house; on another occasion that she hadn't drunk a whole bottle the other day; and she had a white frock made "so that when you come back, we can have some nice little champagne-suppers." Frowned on by society, she made friends with actors and was to be seen at masked balls with young men, or laughing and singing in the mornings, dressed for riding. On these pretexts, contemporaries founded the legend that she drank to excess; and posterity has eagerly embroidered it.

But it was the theatre which attracted her most, as food for her feminine curiosity, and at the same time as neutral ground where nothing could happen to vex her. From her visits she would send reports to Director Goethe on the cast and the audience; but when she found fault with a new Ophelia, she added honestly that it was only because she was like a girl of whom Goethe had a high opinion. Sitting in her box, she liked to look pretty; and the better she succeeded in this, the more indulgent was her lover—he was indefatigable in contributing materials, shawls, and hats, and consulted his expert in art-needlework about the design for an embroidered gown.

A practised and daring horsewoman, she was very fond of riding, and at the end of her thirties learnt driving too; but above all she loved dancing—indeed, it was her only real passion. Her flirtations were always innocent, and what could better prove her innate sense of fitness than the well-attested sincerity of these words: "I could have lots of little affairs here, but I don't care to. When you are with me, I make eyes at lots of people, but when you aren't, it's no fun." But if it was a question of dancing, her partner could not be sufficiently handsome or graceful. Nothing elated her more than being engaged for all the dances straight off, and having worn out a pair of new shoes in one night with a fine dancer. In his early youth Goethe had sometimes done much the same, and when he was forty had danced with her fairly often; but now he was sedater and lazier, and even held a theory that every kind of dance bordered by its very nature on affectation. Strange irony of fate—that genius should invest itself with these dullnesses at the very time when his most unaffected of companions was reducing them to absurdity by her flying skirts and laughing eyes! Did he not laugh himself, perceiving it?

Raum und Zeit, ich empfind' es, sind blosse Formen des Anschauns,
Da das Eckchen mit dir, Liebchen, unendlich mir scheint.[1]

Nothing made their long companionship dearer to Goethe, or more effectually contradicts all the legends about her, than her constant activity; and if he always sought light-hearted and simple-natured women as a counterpoise to his own difficult and complex nature, it was because he was active himself that he also needed an active woman as companion. They both filled their days to the brim; and though the one ruled, as it were, a household of masterpieces, and the other made a masterpiece of housekeeping, that only helped to turn the harmony of their daily life into a perfect unison. So she could sum it up without *arrière-pensée:*

Your work is splendid, for what you have once done will last for ever, but with us poor drudges it's quite different. I had the kitchen-garden in such good order, all planted and everything. In one night

[1] "Space and Time, I am learning, are merely modes of appearance,
Since a corner with thee, darling, seems infinite now."

the snails had eaten nearly everything I had put down, and I shall have to do it all over again. . . . We can't have anything for nothing, and I won't allow it to vex me.

In that house there was neither self-indulgence nor sloth. They went to bed betimes, and by six o'clock in the morning he was sitting at his desk, while she was usually to be found at the potato-bed. Christiane could buy and sell horses, and knew that they must be in good condition before they were auctioned; she advised him in the purchase of more land for a vegetable-garden; and the things she sent her husband at Jena in the way of beer, wine, or meat, and the fruit he sent to Weimar, took up no less, but likewise no more, space in their letters than in his to Charlotte, long ago.

Christiane had to keep accounts, control their expenditure, answer enquiries; and if no one came to their Friday at-home, she would lament the beautiful wasted wood-fire. She sold home-grown asparagus too, and her own discarded clothes, made new skirts out of old materials, and when Goethe wrote to say that Cotta (the publisher) had sent some lovely brand-new louis-d'or, "which I shan't enjoy in the least until I count them into your hand. . . . Which would you rather have—a gold-piece for yourself to spend as you like, or something for the house?"—he must have smiled when he read her answer. It was a long story of two second-hand gauze frocks, one of which was to be had for two-and-a-half thalers, but she intended to buy one that cost two louis-d'or; "and if you don't like it, I can always sell it again with a lace edge and make money on it. But if *you* had been here, you would certainly have bought me a new one!"

That is Christiane—very economical and rather vain, capable and utterly devoted, with something of Therese in *Wilhelm Meister;* but able at a pinch to become Clärchen too, as she was one day to prove.

Viele der Veilchen zusammengeknüpft, das Sträusschen erscheinet
Erst als Blume; du bist, häusliches Mädchen, gemeint.[1]

[1] "Violets fastened together in clusters then and then only
Look like flowers—of thee, housewifely maiden, I think."

The brilliant Therese, it is true, had sadly to confess "that undoubtedly intellectual men look out for good housekeepers, though their hearts and their imaginations may crave for other qualities." Christiane had better fortune, for the qualities by which she had charmed the lonely man—her youthful heart and her capacity for love—remained the firm basis of their union throughout thirty years.

And so, though daily life might be prosaic, he was unchangingly her lover, and never tired, through decades, of showing her tender little attentions. Goethe was not now the obedient servant he had been to Lili and Charlotte, but still less did he want, like Schiller, to domineer. He gave public expression to his estimate of his wife when in his will he made his son his heir, but gave her a life-interest in his property.

After nine years, this: "I love you very dearly, and you only; you wouldn't believe how I miss you. Only now do I wish I was a richer man, so that I could always take you and the boy with me on my travels." Again, after thirteen: "Joyfully shall I . . . press you to my heart and tell you that every day I love you more and more." And after fifteen: "On the very next opportunity send me your last new danced-out pair of shoes that you write to me about, so that I may once more have something of yours to press against my heart." Written by Goethe at fifty-four, when he was the father of a boy of fourteen.

And yet, in that hard-fought existence, not even this gift from Tyche could be free—for this, too, he had to pay.

Four or five years after the beginning of their union, Christiane's sister and aunt moved into Goethe's house and stayed there to the end—her brother, too, lived there for a long time. Quiet people, the Vulpius family; but for all that a family, entailing obligations, with their own claims, their own friends, very unsuited to Goethe—strangers, who though they did not sponge upon him made all the more fuss about finding something to do. Here were three uninteresting middle-class down-and-outs, undesirable denizens of the stately mansion, belonging neither to Goethe's social nor his family life. True, it never came to quarrels or scenes; but still there was the unemployed brother to help, and in his interest Goethe wrote quantities of letters.

And there was a lover of Christiane's sister, a run-away young nobleman, for whose return the clergyman on the parental estate appealed to Goethe, and Goethe had to answer him, arrange and provide for it. Yet his native kindliness forbade him to drive out his mistress's family.

What was the result? Without knowing it or at all desiring it, they drove him out; and while he left the handsomest house in Weimar to a trio of lower-class bourgeois, with whom he was not really even connected, he set up a bachelor-establishment in Jena which consisted of two apartments in the Palace, scarcely capable of being warmed, and an occasional room in a lodging-house. So that Goethe, without being married, had to bear all the burdens of married life. Once he spent four, once nearly six, months out of the year at Jena.

It is true that at Weimar there was also the everlasting racket to which as Minister, Manager of the Theatre, and social personality he was subjected, and this too played its part in driving him away; even Schiller, when afterwards he lived in Weimar, had sometimes to take refuge in Jena for his literary work. There they could both be poets again, the one eager for success, the other for flights into the empyrean of the mind; and Goethe, sitting in Knebel's old study (long since deserted by the latter), said fondly that in no other place had he known so many productive hours. Soon he sent for a dozen of the choicest engravings from his collection: "so that I may have something to delight my eyes." In the evenings he would argue with Schiller, or in the circle of scientists and friends of which he once said that it was "like a fairytale."

Not that Christiane was forbidden an occasional visit, with or without the boy; and once or twice he went *sub rosâ* to Weimar, late in the evening, when he would have the back-door into the garden left open for him. Early next morning he would be off again to Jena—a three hours' journey each way. Does it not sound like the prank of a Crown Prince, stealing at night to his vigilantly guarded mistress? And it is an author of fifty, free to choose his place of abode, to arrange his affairs as he pleased, who slinks secretly in the dark through the back-door of his own big house to see the wife who had lived with him twelve years, for the space of a few hours.

And yet it was on this loved woman's account that his absences became more frequent and more prolonged!

> You know that at home I can't concentrate sufficiently to get through my arduous work. . . . There is a lot to do still, and I must be quite alone for it. . . . I beg you not to come here unexpectedly; I must stick to my usual routine and stay here till I've finished this one piece; then we shall be happy together again.

With such fatherly gentleness did he excuse himself to her.

He expressed himself more forcibly to Schiller:

> As I couldn't get away to Jena, my household has had to give way to *me*, for there's one thing certain—that without absolute quietude I can't produce anything whatever . . . and that not merely the voices, but the very presence in the house of people I love and value, entirely dries up my fount of poesy.

As the inmates of his house grew older and their claims more diversified, he sometimes had occasion to shake his head very gravely over the situation. He had lived irreproachably in the little State for twenty years, and now it was his to kowtow to subordinate officials for a passport for "Frau Vulpius and son." Once, when he had brought his family over to his mother in Frankfurt for three days, he found it more advisable to pack them back home at once.

On the whole, when his wife and son had paid him a visit in Jena, and he was left sitting quietly over his papers, at work again, Goethe must sometimes have asked himself: "Is it not strange that that brief beautiful encounter should have expanded into a destiny of which I had not then the remotest conception? Are we never permitted a lovely fleeting instinctive fancy, inconsequent as its origin in a summer morning? Primitive, classic as it was, is this relation now becoming ponderous? Ought we not to part friends, and each resume the liberty that was voluntarily sacrificed?"

The boy's education, too, suffered from the divided claims of society and authorship, for this was the critical period between six and eighteen. Goethe, who understood and loved children, who had been almost entirely responsible for Fritz von Stein's upbringing, who had done so much for Lotte Buff's brothers and sisters, and for Carl August's, Herder's, and Jacobi's children, was far from neglecting his own son, especially in his childhood; and the boy loved him in the early days, and delighted in being with him. He was allowed to take part in the Festival Procession at Ilmenau, dressed as a little miner, and was put to bed by his father in the evening. If he happened to be playing with a little girl in the Palace-yard at Jena, and Goethe, leaving his desk, caught sight of them from his window, he would let down little tit-bits at the end of a string for the children to catch, a game which greatly delighted them. Or he would make a pumpkin-head for the boy, like a devil with eyes of flame, or paint him a scene for his toy-theatre—and little August would sit, like his father before him, gazing at the shadow-play, and Doctor Faust would come on the scene, and the devil too—but the best fun, according to the boy, was when the cat suddenly upset the candle.

But it may have been that Goethe, at fifty, was too old, or too absorbed in his manifold activities. At any rate, the father and son were destined never to know that intimate and lasting affection which is the outcome of real mental contact in early years. For Goethe delayed too long his instruction of the boy.

The little we really know of August's childish years—for his letters were dictated by his teacher in imitation of Goethe's style, and that the father should have permitted this was a mistake, to begin with . . . that little gives the impression of a lively, plucky, practical-minded, rather rough sort of boy, who laughed at his mother when her cucumbers did not do so well as his, who teased his play-fellow, Schiller's son, because he was "afraid of everything," who bought himself "a great lot of siskins," but gave away a rare little bird because he did not want to be bothered finding food for it, who cruelly killed a mole, and liked to hear the pigs scream when they were being slaughtered. When one day he found a little silver trinket in the garden, he sold it for a penny. But he was quick at languages, had a good memory, and when his father read him Schiller's latest Turandot-riddle, he guessed it before Goethe did.

When he was growing up, Goethe would take him away with him in the summer; but the result was more to enliven the father than to educate the son, for the boy seems to have been incapable of really getting anything from Goethe. He preferred his mother's company, and of all the gossip one bit is undoubtedly true—that she always took him with her to the theatre, that Goethe never prevented it, and that so he grew up to be fonder of amusement than of any serious study.

Paternal feeling developed every civic virtue in him. He was conscious of this, and nothing could exceed the joy it gave him. . . . Oh, the strange exactions of society, which begins by perplexing and misleading us, and ends by demanding more of us than Nature herself. . . . Man is born for a limited sphere. He can comprehend its simple, immediate, unchanging aims. . . . Directly he sets foot in the great world, he knows not either what he desires or what he ought to do, and it matters little whether it is the mere pressure of events or their greatness and splendour which dismays him. "In America" [said Lothario], "I thought I should be able to get something done. . . . How differently I see things now and how dear, how precious, to me is the place I know best!"

"I remember the letter," replied Jarno, "which even then I received from over the sea. You wrote: 'I shall come home; and in my own house, under the trees of my own garden, among my own people, I shall say: *Here or nowhere is America!*'"

Here or nowhere, at the end of his *Lehrjahre,* Goethe hints at the reasons for his becoming a provincial at fifty. But besides—and we must lay stress on this—there is something of a desire to generalise an extremely individual case, as if to convince himself that he could not have done otherwise, that this was his appointed lot. "The aim of life is life itself," he wrote at this time to Meyer; and taken together with all that Goethe sought, attempted, began, abandoned, avoided, lauded, and disapproved, the aphorism denotes nothing more far-reaching than a sense of reality which, from a fiercely bubbling spring, had broadened into a river serenely submissive to its burdens of ships and barges, and flowing tranquilly onward through the spacious plain. In the powerful well-controlled stream of Goethe's middle-age, the cities of men were mirrored, with their towering spires and modest houses, and he conveyed their argosies from place to place. It was so that Goethe became a bourgeois.

As a youth, his burgher-blood had enjoined self-control in his most ecstatic moments. In his middle thirties it had kept him a thrall, between fits of despair, to state-obligations; about forty, it turned him into a resolutely sober-minded tourist. Now, in the fifties, we get the citizen, with wife and child, with a legion of accepted and self-imposed duties, definitely "settled down," remote from the great world and its events, but likewise from the intellectual centre of his country, and maliciously entitled by his enemies "the most cultivated man of the century." We get, in short, a power-house of intellect, which was capable of infinite extension.

And how different he was to look at! Eight years after Lips had delineated him, he refused to send that likeness to an admirer, for now (he said) it no longer really resembled him. Besides Bury (whose portrait is here reproduced), Jagemann, Meyer, Tieck, and the woman-artist Bardua painted him in these years—the man who now declared that dreamless slumber was the most refreshing; who never bared his throat; the portly thick-set Goethe, with fat-fingered hands, with fleshy cheeks and a double chin (which he was fond of pulling at) and bags under his eyes, with their look of weary penetration behind the glasses he had now more frequently to wear. Such he was at this time, living and working from within outwards along a line more marked by breadth than depth; everything that stamps the bourgeois now stamped him, and thus for ten years from this period.

He was the bourgeois who is happiest at home—though (as he said in verse) the nations might be raging in far-away Turkey; for almost in the words of his Leipzig citizen he remarked, when reading a travel-book about Morocco, that he thanked God he was in Lauchstädt. Humboldt's invitations to Paris could not tempt him away from quiet Weimar, where a visit from Mme. de Staël was epoch-making; he might sentimentalise about the cradle of the new epoch, envy Humboldt and Cotta for all they saw and enjoyed there—but the farthest he would go was over to Leipzig for the Fair, and there he gaped at London in the panorama! For the first time in his life he appreciated Frankfurt, and there is a touch of pursiness in the remark

> that the Frankfurt bankers, merchants, stockbrokers, shopkeepers, Jews, players, and managers were a thousand times more interesting to him, because at any rate they had some end in view, even though they might put a spoke in other people's wheels.

In his letters and diaries there is scarce an allusion to the European upheavals; and when the Rhine Confederation was established, he could actually note in his diary: "Quarrel between servants and cab-drivers on the bridge, which excited us more than the partition of the Holy Roman Empire."

He was the bourgeois, still more intent than of yore on the preservation of order. When Fichte protested against his rule in the name of liberty, he was infuriated—so much so that, though he thought most highly of his ideas, he acquiesced in the Professor's resignation for official rather than personal reasons.

At this time he was strongly addicted to note-books in which, when travelling, he collected the sort of information that today we find in Baedeker—regulations, price-lists, ceremonies, placards and proclamations, census-returns and statistics; and this practice he began in his native town, of all places, methodically documenting what his eyes and his intelligence had been familiar with for decades! At home, likewise, the catalogue-habit became more and more pronounced. If he wrote a new Elegy, he instantly began to "plan a new series of Elegies," and drew up this grotesque literary programme: "The second will probably deal with the craving to cross the Alps for the third time, and in that spirit I shall . . . continue."

He was the provincial good trencherman: the time had come for enjoying one's food in quiet! Since his early forties he had begun to drink a good deal—gradually arriving at one or two bottles of wine a day, and to that measure he mostly kept until the end of his life. In his fiftieth year he said that there was hardly anything he now enjoyed except meat and wine. Sometimes he would have as many as fifty bottles sent to Jena, besides dessert-wine. To a publisher from Bremen, who sent a case of fine wine as an inducement, Goethe delivered the second part of his *Zauberflöte* and left the price to him. The publisher sent another consignment of wine. In the diary, between entries about literary work and business, appears one about the first asparagus of the season, and in the second Epistle Goethe actually arrived at singing the praise of pickled cucumbers.

He was the well-paid prosperous bourgeois, more deeply concerned with figures than even when he had been President of the Council. Even now, at fifty, though his house had been presented to him, he possessed no other property, no certain income but his salary, which from thirty-six to sixty-six brought in sixteen hundred thalers a year. But now he had made up his mind to live at his ease; he refused himself no engraving, gem, apparatus, or book which he needed for his collections or studies, and he kept open house (though he cared little himself for anyone in particular), had friends to stay, and gave generous presents.

From this time forward Goethe stuck to Cotta, who was becoming very powerful (and from whom in four decades or thereabouts he obtained a hundred and fifty thousand thalers and nine thousand florins); but he did not refuse himself to other publishers. When Unger asked for material for a new volume of Goethe's writings, which was appearing with him, Goethe (who meanwhile had promised his next work to Cotta) said neither Yes nor No. For their contributions to the *Horen*, and later to the *Propyläen*, Schiller and Goethe received such payment as had hitherto been unheard-of in Germany—which is the only possible explanation of Goethe's having translated Cellini, or extracts from Mme. de Staël's books. For the four annual numbers of the *Propyläen*, of which he was only part-author, he stipulated for terms which exceeded his yearly salary as Minister; and when the enterprise failed, as it soon did, he at once advised the publisher to try again! It was only the great success of the *Zauberflöte* which induced him to write a second part, though Mozart was by that time dead; but the characters, dresses, and decorations could be made use of again in all the theatres of Germany, and Goethe demanded a hundred ducats from a Viennese composer for the text.

He intended *Hermann und Dorothea* for Vieweg's *Almanack*,

and though two-thirds of the work were written, the publisher was not allowed to see it—he had to make a blind offer for "an epic poem in two thousand hexameters."

Finally, at the end of this decade, Goethe re-sold his works for the first Cotta edition. There was very little new material—beyond a few lyrics, *Achilleïs*, and *Elpenor*, nothing except a third of *Faust*. Nevertheless, he asked and received, for the five-year rights of this edition, ten thousand thalers—a sum which only Voltaire had ever before attained to. There was some excuse for Schiller's writing, rather bitterly and tactlessly, to Cotta that Goethe set too high a price upon himself, and no publisher ever stuck to him. But Goethe wrote in high spirits: "It would seem that, since we literary men came short in the cosmic division of goods, we are accorded one important privilege—that of being paid for our follies."

Yet before he received this large sum, he had again been obliged to borrow—this time from his whilom servant, Philipp Seidel. He did not allow this circumstance to lead to any familiarity. When he repaid a portion of the twelve-hundred thaler loan, which had been advanced from savings made for the most part in Goethe's service, his tone was very definitely that of a master to whom the creditor had every reason to be grateful: "Herewith a jolly lot of double louis-d'or." This was the same Seidel to whom in former days he had, out of the riches of his intellect, made a present of a prose version of his *Iphigenie*, and to whose criticism he had gratefully lent an ear. Now, when Seidel handed out his contribution from the modest affluence which in Goethe's eyes was so contemptible, it was repaid with a gesture of cool indifference, as a mere nothing.

On selling the epic, Goethe had made his one mistake in household economy—he had bought (under Christiane's persuasion, it is true) a little property near Weimar, which he had not inspected before purchase. Now he occasionally spent a few summer-weeks there, laid out some winding walks in the park, and on one occasion Herr von Goethe—Minister, savant, eccentric, and literary man—was to be seen buying horses at the horse-fair. Then he quarrelled with the tenantry, and evicted one dishonest farmer only to find another who had peculiar ideas about arboriculture. Village-festivals, visits, a distillery, finally finished the work of creating a deficit for this great economist, who had once reformed the finances of two Duchies. And the good bourgeois was more upset by the mismanagement than by the monetary loss.

Yet it cannot have greatly surprised him, for from the first he had talked of this possession in a tone of somewhat shamefaced irony; and as if to symbolise his remoteness from that one aspect of his life, he had usually stopped with his neighbour, the vicar, instead of in his own country-cottage.

In former years, whenever a land-owning friend had sought to initiate him into the secrets of preparing the ground for crops, he had said that dilettantism in such serious matters was not for him, and now he at once farmed out his land. But he could not resist giving an occasional hint to the experts. Moreover, he liked his country-sojourns, "because I hand over the daily grind to someone else, and thus enjoy a sort of comfort and easy-going indifference to which I have long been a stranger."

This shows us plainly why Goethe was bound to come to grief in that little enterprise. Not that he lived romantically, like a poet, in the country, nor experimentally like a scientist, nor counting the cost like a President of the Council—he lived like a townsman on holiday. But to do that was to contradict his whole attitude towards life. However, this very fact may give us a clue to his motive, for Goethe in his maturity never took any step out of heedlessness or weakness. It would seem, then, that as he had long contemplated regular marriage, he wished to give Christiane a house of her own, as a way out from the difficult position created for them both by his residence in Weimar.

In the end she, with her practical good-sense, was glad to get rid of the property at no great sacrifice, after five years of doubtful enjoyment of it; and in his old age Goethe smilingly summed up the episode in the words: "It was everything—except any use to us." When he sold it, he characteristically made a synthesis of his feelings. It was of no service to him, "for I have renounced the earth in both the economic and æsthetic senses of the word."

A more than doubtful, or at any rate by no means characteristic, pronouncement, quite contradicted by this particular epoch in his life.

For Goethe in his fifties was no longer the thinker, candidly intent on the truth of things, and striving ever and only upward—and was not yet the poet, clear-eyed, winged for realms of freedom hitherto unknown, which he was soon to become. At this time he was more than ever in the toils of actualities and persons; and the wish which had ruled the immediately preceding years (and which was then a symptom of recovery in a heart benumbed by solitude)—that wish tc be companioned at any price had now subdued itself to the claims of daily life, had lost its intensity and vehemence, was more normal, more commonplace, more accommodating. But even now he had his days of misanthropy, and after a tiresome visit would consider the building of a higher hedge around his life, and keeping his writings sacred from the eyes of men.

> So I shall always travel incognito, prefer quiet clothes to smart ones, and in conversation with strangers or slight acquaintances choose trivial subjects or at any rate a trivial treatment of the subject, appear more frivolous than I really am, and thus, as one might say, stand between myself and my presentment of myself.

Here Goethe for once confesses to the reserves which his self-sacrificing but disillusioned spirit had been driven to practise and which later degenerated into a formality of manner that gave an intentionally false impression to his contemporaries and posterity. And at the same time he shows how a reluctantly adopted misanthropy works out in actual human intercourse. It was only by the aid of such unnatural reticence that Goethe, in his fifties and afterwards, was able to dispense with the iron mask worn in his forties—that so much slighter a disguise could now permit him to be more approachable, more agreeable, yet not less secretive.

> In this life, which we can get through the better the more indifferent we are, our chief aim should be to divert people's attention from ourselves and others, to keep our passions in check, and find our pleasure in things which do not depend on them.

It was on this unadventurous basis that Goethe resumed social intercourse as an author and savant, with more animation than when, as a statesman, he had fled his fellow-creatures. In Jena there were Professors who honoured and feared him; and to judge by the accounts that young men who were recommended to him gave of their first impressions, it would seem that every one of them stood in awe. At intellectual tea-parties he was to be seen standing stiffly under the chandeliers in a flood of light, surrounded by a semicircle of the erudite, who listened to him with open-mouthed curiosity.

The youthful Jean Paul, who told him some home-truths, nevertheless prevailed so far that Goethe warned Schiller against either over-praising or decrying him. To the young man himself, however, who was only too anxious to draw out Goethe on the subject of his works, he stood on the defensive; for one whole evening he, as it were, held him in check, and finally the boyish, inspired sceptic could find no point of attack, and was reduced to concluding his account with: "Also, he eats a great deal."

Mme. de Staël, who was then touring Germany, complete with note-book and interviews, Goethe at first tried to elude; but later, respecting her intellect and disliking her loquacity, he laid many a good-humoured trap for her, from which the clever lady always escaped. But when she informed him that she intended to print every word he said in France, he became more reticent and more cautious.

When, some time afterwards, Goethe was reading aloud some Scottish ballads at a tea-party in the house of the brilliant and wealthy Johanna Schopenhauer, and asked the ladies to repeat the refrain in chorus after him, a Professor's wife burst out laughing. Then she knew the lightning of his eye, the thunder of his voice: "Very well—I shan't read!" The horrified hostess intervened; universal obedience was guaranteed, and the ladies, keeping time with their chins, all recited the refrain in chorus—a scene so comic that only Goethe's authority could prevent them from giggling. Such was the end of one sociable endeavour when, a man of fifty, embarrassing and embarrassed, he sought friendly intercourse after an all too prolonged seclusion. Is it astonishing, then, that he preferred to sit down to his wine with the cheerful Christiane in her best frock, sure of warm-hearted affection?

For friends to whom his heart could really speak were almost wholly lacking. Schiller and Meyer, whom as kindred thinkers he usually brackets together, were not really, in that sense, a refreshment. Schiller was in bad health, and preferred to work in the evening, which was Goethe's favourite time for talk—moreover, his head was as full as ever of business-projects. But it was he who in these years could best give Goethe companionship. Meyer, who was a sort of permanent boarder in Goethe's house, was more a combination of teacher and graduate than a talker on equal terms. For him of all men Goethe felt the strongest affection; for among them all Meyer was the only one who had no designs on his intellect and influence, who was always receptive and always responsive, so that it was a true marriage of intellects, and endured to the end. When Meyer came back after a second visit to Italy, Goethe congratulated himself on their reunion, which would make up to them both for the separation, as if he were talking to a woman; and when his friend fell ill, he spoke of their love and their unique relation to one another.

And who else was there to devote himself? Was not everyone, at bottom, intent on getting something out of intercourse with Goethe? Was anyone ready to sacrifice his time, his heart, his energies? There was Knebel, but he must have felt that, as Goethe's audience, he was supplemented and surpassed by Schiller. Besides, he was now doing some original work, whereas hitherto he had been at most a translator, and by his productiveness he was putting some strain on his friend's sincerity.

More straightforward was the now increasingly intimate relation with Voigt, whom Goethe had at once distinguished from other young legal officials, and had gradually promoted to the title of Excellency and one of the principal Ministries in the Duchy. High-minded and energetic, shrewd and disinterested, here at last was the nature which believed in Goethe's heart and was unalterably grateful. Now indeed, after ten years of testing, he could feel that his highest hopes were gratified when he read: "I wish . . . I could have you always at my side. May I be able, one day, to requite you in some way. . . . For I cannot imagine what my existence would be like without you."

But those others, who had seen Goethe through his first decade in Weimar, sometimes affectionately, sometimes disapprovingly—what had become of *their* attachment? The destiny of genius—to disappoint its friends, because their love would have it keep to the one path marked out by them! The destiny of friends—to abandon the dæmonic being, instead of learning and unlearning from him! Almost all the friendships of his life were outlived by Goethe, but not more than one or two by reason of his longer span of years. Guiltless and guilty, as with women, his dæmon wrenched him from nearly all to whom he once had clung.

Charlotte's hatred had evaporated. She was approaching sixty, her hair was turning white; her son was soon to marry and make her a grandmother—so that the formal recognition which had been exchanged in a drawing-room not more than a year after their rupture, was with Schiller's help worked up into a reconciliation; and as in former years she had sent her boy to Goethe that he might be shaped on that pattern, so now Goethe, to the same end, sent little August to the ageing woman. For never had Goethe depreciated her powers, and he now desired that his son should breathe the rarefied atmosphere which was hers—little, indeed, though the boy could breathe in it at all. However, little August served to bridge the abyss; the adjacent households were brought into some sort of contact—and although Charlotte did not associate with Christiane, she put in a plea for the first asparagus, which the good-humoured Christiane, "as you weren't there, sent over by the chickabiddy." Christiane herself raved about Fritz von Stein as the finest dancer she had ever admired from the gallery at the Court-ball; and August told his father in a letter about a little picture that Frau von Stein had given him after dinner, "and she gave me eight pennies too."

". . . She gave me eight pennies too." Goethe read, smiled, and thought of many things. Soon the moment arrived when he could again do his hostile mistress a service—he intervened with the Duke for Fritz's transfer to the Prussian Army, and so the first note from Goethe's hand that she had unfolded for seven years began with counsel and help. But how did it end? "And suffer my poor boy to rejoice in your presence, and mould himself after your image. I cannot think without emotion of your wishing him so well."

" . . . My poor boy." Charlotte reads, and remembers how in that last letter, seven years ago, he had alluded to Christiane as "the poor girl." May she not feel rehabilitated, in the purest intellectual sense of the word, by Goethe's choice of such expressions? Only two years back, she had distilled her venom into the Dido-drama. But now. . . . One grows milder as one grows older; and she, who knows every accent of Goethe's voice, consoles her wounded pride with the humility of his tone in mentioning his housekeeper's child to her—and Charlotte sits down to the writing-table which Goethe had designed for her those twenty years ago, and seizes her pen, and sets upon her answering sheet of paper (after all the malignity in verse and prose) one human word, a word from the depths: "Surely you must feel it very natural that my heart should be irresistibly drawn to your child."

Now it is Goethe's turn to read—and smile; for only a few weeks earlier he had made a forsaken mistress say, at the end of his *Lehrjahre:* "We women have this peculiarity—that we can care very deeply for our lover's children, provided we do not know the mother, or else heartily detest her." And when shortly afterwards he passes her house with his seven-yeared son, and sees her sitting in the orangery, he turns in—and Goethe and Christiane's boy, one after the other, kiss Charlotte von Stein's delicate fingers. . . . Goethe keeps silence about this incident but Charlotte writes to a woman-friend, and is surprised and ashamed that she could so long have misjudged him. . .

Yet for all that—a year later she entrusted Schiller with her pamphlet upon Goethe!

He, however, invited her again to his house, usually with her niece or other ladies, sent fruit as of old, showed her his collection of coins, and occasionally even took something like the old tone with her: "May I beg of you to brighten this gloomy morning with your presence?"

Soon after the unsuccessful campaign against the Revolution, the Duke had come back as a Prussian General; and as he could not now do any strenuous military service he began to assert himself somewhat more as the sovereign, and there were a few slight collisions between him and his Minister of Education and Theatre-Director.

Goethe, who had left the Duke behind twenty years ago, now needed only the faintest indication of royal caprice to make him keep his distance—and so this second half of their respective careers, though closely connected by propinquity and public activities, was in no sense a really intimate relation. When we consider the ever-widening divergence between their characters and ways of life, we are at first inclined to wonder why, in spite of all, Goethe stayed in this sphere of intellectual authority and security, and why the Duke repudiated every attempt of Goethe's enemies to separate the pair.

But Goethe understood the Duke, and if the Duke had ceased to understand Goethe at all, he did hit upon a most pregnant phrase to describe the pedantic travel-letters: "It's amazing what a pompous chap he has become!" He seems to have lost all interest in Goethe's work, and approached him as Court-poet pure and simple when he wanted Voltaire's *Mahomet* translated for the Court-theatre.

Carl August showed no such interest in any of Goethe's later writings as he bestowed on this forced labour, which was entirely alien to the translator; he suggested some slight modifications, and dated a new epoch in the history of the German stage from the production!

But Carl August's growing interest in Nature-study sometimes brought him and Goethe nearer to one another; they prepared papers, procured specimens, together, and we cannot but admire the Duke's modesty in decking all his questions and proposals of visits with such phrases as: "With your permission I shall call upon you this evening in Jena—I am bringing something to drink. . . . I shall be immensely obliged by your kind acceptance." But only very seldom do we find "Dear old man," and only once "Keep me in your heart."

But never again was Goethe to be lured out of the citadel of formalities.

In connection with the building of a new palace of which Goethe was in official charge, the Duke's interference sometimes drove him to despair which, though clinging to the last remnants of courtly behaviour, could not resist a phrase or two of blighting irony:

Our monarch has an excellent eye for the suitable and the convenient . . . only he is rather apt to sacrifice beauty of form to those ends. . . . Your Serene Highness believes that my presence at the works may be useful, and, little though I am myself convinced of it, I can only respect that belief.

The days were long gone by when the two men had fraternally confided in each other about their pranks and projects, their ideals and follies!

Sometimes there was a renewal, but the old days seemed to hover timidly like ghosts which were forbidden to revisit the glimpses of the moon. In one such instance Goethe, for a second as it were, cast off his reserve. When the Duke sent him, under a transparent pseudonym, a few of his own verses, Goethe's answer took this malicious turn:

The impenetrably disguised poet . . . is really to be congratulated upon the very peaceful—one might almost say, empty—moments of inspiration granted him by the Muses, which indeed are a prime necessity for productions of this kind.

And then—once more it was Eros who really brought them together; that is, the Eros of men over forty. A few years after Goethe's union with Christiane, the Duke, weary of passing fancies, set up a dual establishment, and he too chose a Weimar archivist's daughter. Before long Goethe stood godfather to Caroline Jagemann's son, just as that son's father had stood godfather to Christiane's. Caroline was as well an actress at the Court-theatre, which was financed by the Duke and managed by Goethe—and thus three people found themselves in a position which might afford material for a dozen comedies. But life's developments were to turn it into a semi-tragedy. There was friction even now. Goethe begged to be relieved of the Court-theatre managership, having had enough of it four years ago, but the Duke, though neither warmly nor urgently, held him to his post. So that Goethe had to look after this Jagemann girl, who continually tried to injure him with their common friend; and the concatenation is sufficiently amazing when we find the ruler of the Duchy contending for his concubine's prestige—for Schiller would not receive her in his house, and so Carl August begged Goethe to persuade him, as it would improve her social position. His letter thus concludes: "I leave all this to your wise management. Farewell."

The third and most remarkable of the friends of Goethe's youth was also lost to him before he died. In reality, Goethe had lost Herder as soon as he had gained him—for the ardent devotion of the youthful poet had felt itself repulsed by the bigoted criticism which nevertheless he always wanted to hear. No other man was so sedulously and so sincerely courted by Goethe, but their relation was like an interestingly unhappy marriage—in the first ten years at Weimar it had its good moments, followed by coolness, and then again by good moments; for some time then the barometer stood at temperate; and finally they declared open enmity.

The "split" which occurred between them at the beginning of our present period—when the Herders, with threatening words, demanded of Goethe that he should obtain a wholly inequitable grant for their sons' education from the Duke—shows Goethe in a hitherto unprecedented position, and an entirely fresh light. This is his tone towards a woman-friend whom he is obliged to rebuke, though he does not intend to abandon her cause: "To speak with you," he writes to Caroline Herder, who was the one to approach him, "would hardly be advisable at this heated moment. . . . You have written what I ought never to have had to read—I could not but expect to hear what I prefer not to listen to." This monumental reproof is followed by thirteen practical points which are designed to make the situation clear to all concerned, and in which he dismisses both her appeal to the Court and her attack upon himself.

I give you free permission [he concludes] to hate me as you might hate any other stage-villain, but I beg you thoroughly to understand me, and not expect that I shall reform in the fifth act. . . . I pity you for having to seek the support of people whom you do not like and think so slightly of, whose existence can give you no pleasure, and to whose satisfaction you feel in no way bound to contribute. . . . Nevertheless, be sure that behind all the arguments you put forth in favour of your claims, I do not really mistake you. . . . I shall not read any reply you may make to this letter, and shall never again allude to what has taken place. . . . I know very well that no one is thanked for his utmost, when once the impossible has been demanded of him, but that shall not prevent me from doing what I can for you and yours.

After this dazzling sword-play, he obtained from the highly incensed Duke the grant so unjustifiably demanded by the Herders. But Herder resented the episode for years; and when he published a two-volume work on German literature, he vented all his jealousy, all his venomous depreciation, in the five words with which he abolished Goethe's art: "Unsympathetic, precise description of the visible." Those were Herder's last public words on Goethe.

But they could not let one another alone—this Herder and this Goethe. The spell was mutually magnetic, because they were such poles apart. Scarce three years after their rupture—and Goethe was again induced by friends to support another and still more questionable appeal for money for Herder's children. Again, after prolonged persuasion, he obtained the desired grant—basing his appeal upon Herder's intellectual eminence.

Now there was a possibility of reconciliation; the Herders occasionally came to Goethe's house, and once when his friend was dining with him Goethe put him at his right hand, though Schiller and Jean Paul were fellow-guests. At this very time Herder started a periodical in opposition to Goethe's *Propyläen*.

Immediately afterwards a fresh quarrel blazed up. Goethe wanted the chorus at the theatre to be reinforced at need by school-boys; Herder protested against a theatrical manager having his finger in the educational pie. Herder and Goethe, once purely intellectual antagonists, spurred only by their respective dæmons, ended by opposing one another as stage-manager and superintendent of schools, the helpless victims of their extraordinary destinies.

But once more Goethe bestirred himself in Herder's interest. The latter had, after getting the Duke of Weimar to provide for his son's education, got the King of Bavaria to ennoble himself, so as to ensure that son's future by making him heir to landed property; and Goethe persuaded the Duke to accord, without a patent of nobility, some gradual official recognition of Herder's title. "More when we meet" (so Goethe ended his last letter, that about the title)—"when I come to drink your health. Thine, Goethe."

It was the end of September, and Herder was ill, but no one dreamed that he had barely three months to live. Had *he* perhaps some prescience of it, and did he want to be intellectually reconciled with the greatest personality in his life, before that life came to an end?

It would seem so.

In November they were both stopping for a while in the palace at Jena. They visited one another, and one evening Herder began—after six years of silence on matters of the mind!—for the first time to praise Goethe's work.

Quietly and sincerely he opened the subject by giving the highest commendations to the new version of the *Natürliche Tochter* (*The Natural Daughter*), and Goethe felt "the most intense and exquisite pleasure." Something of the old concord, something like his youthful sense of friendship, came over him—and more untroubled than it had ever been before. But his friend had never been master of his own dæmon; and precisely as he finished his song of praise with its critical ground-bass—he suddenly, as by some irresistible compulsion, flashed his other aspect upon Goethe, and remarked: "For the rest, I prefer your *Natural Daughter* to your natural son!"

Goethe was struck to stone. He was fifty-four at this time, Herder was sixty; for thirty years and more this man had picked him to pieces, had bantered and derided him—and now, in that hour of renewed confidence, he epitomised their lifelong battle in a gibe. By Goethe's own account,

> this horrible false card had a really terrific effect upon me. I looked him in the face and said no word, and our many years of intercourse,

thus as it were symbolised, seemed to me hideous in the extreme On this we parted, and I never saw him again.

Here or nowhere we plainly perceive how deep was the affinity between the figure of Mephisto and the character of Herder. But we also perceive once more that Goethe too had some instinctive sympathy with Mephisto, for only one who was conscious of a modicum of such endowment could have been perpetually, as by a wizard spell, attracted to its possessor. Nowhere in all Goethe's symbolic career is the Mephisto-strain in Faust, the Faustean in Mephisto, more apparent than in the story of this dearest enmity and its conclusion.

When some weeks later Herder died in Weimar, Goethe did not come back from Jena, nor did he mention the event in his diary or his year-books. But when Mme. de Staël simultaneously arrived, and he wrote in a letter that he was glad of her visit, because a richly intellectual nature could make him forget the spectral visions of these winter-nights, it is evident that despite his silence he had been stricken to the heart—and Mephisto's tragically cynical spirit pervades his bitter allusion to the depressing time of year, "when I can very well understand how Henri III had the Duc de Guise assassinated, simply because it was miserable weather; and when I envy Herder for lying in his grave." That evening Goethe had spent with friends, where a beautiful girl had been surrounded by young men.

And yet once more—when twelve years had gone by, Goethe wrote for the only man to whom he owed anything that wonderful epilogue to *Dichtung und Wahrheit* wherein the mighty intellect of that enigmatic being is shown forth in a portrait which to this day the Germans revere.

Shortly before, he had heard unmoved of Lavater's death, and by Corona Schröter's end he seems to have been equally unmoved. Perhaps she had been present, a few months before her death, one evening when under Schiller's management some young actors were giving the first public performance of *Iphigenie.* Must they not both have recalled that other day when they themselves had played Orestes and Iphigenia, before a youthful, animated Court? Twenty-three years ago. . . . It was a spring-day then as now, but then it had all been pastime, a flash of genius—set down on paper only a few weeks back, and acted a few days after the last lines were written. And to-day they both sit stiffly in their boxes, and glance occasionally round the house. Old Knebel there with his young wife—do you remember? He was Pylades, alert and gay. And there, bull-necked, somewhat vacant, somewhat gloomy, sits the Duke in his Royal box—the Duke who had insisted on being Pylades next time, so that even in play he might do whatever his friend was doing. . . . Sometimes still older memories would hover about him, like players who have played their parts. Lili had asked him to interest himself for a friend, and her wish had been coldly obeyed. Lotte Kestner had wanted him to recommend her son as a doctor; from Wetzlar, where she was paying a sad visit, she had written—dwelling, woman-like, upon old times. "My best regards," Goethe had answered, "and think of me in those places where we have spent so many a pleasant hour." Commonplace enough, surely? But even that had then seemed to him too sentimental—and he had crossed the sentence out of his rough copy! However, when a month later he had had to write again to Wetzlar, he had permitted himself a warmer tone: "How I should like to be once more beside you, on the lovely Lahn," and then had brought the correspondence to an end.

His letters to his old mother had become balder and balder; and it was not until she had had his August to stay with her, and the fifteen-year-old boy was always talking about his granny, that Goethe, who had had to swallow so many an insult to wife and son in Weimar, became more affectionate and wrote: "We all send our fondest, best, and most grateful love." When for the last time he stopped with her in her new lodgings, he tried in vain "to do some work in that house"; and when he was departing—never again to see his mother—he said goodbye presagefully, "and not without emotion, for it was the first time, after so long, that we had got a little used to each other again." So aloof was the expression, even when Goethe wanted to remember his mother most kindly.

It was only under the light shed by poetry that his youth

could move the elderly man to any deep emotion. What an impressive retrospect is that dedication to *Faust,* so regarded—how haunting, how pregnant, do the stanzas sound, when we read them as the epitome of fifty years! There he sits, before the sallow dog's-eared sheets of the old Fragment, turning them over and wondering, while:

> Gleich einer alten, halb verklungnen Sage,
> Kommt erste Lieb' und Freundschaft mit herauf.
> Der Schmerz wird neu, es wiederholt die Klage
> Des Lebens labyrinthisch irren Lauf,
> Und nennt die Guten, die, um schöne Stunden
> Vom Glück getäuscht, vor mir hinweg verschwunden.
>
> Sie hören nicht die folgenden Gesänge,
> Die Seelen, denen ich die ersten sang.
> Zerstoben ist das freundliche Gedränge,
> Verklungen ach! der erste Widerklang.[1]

Is it surprising that the first verses with which, after decades, he resumed the work of his youth should be as an elegy on that youth, which till now he had been desirous only to discard, to forget? Moments wherein the realist gives up the game—seconds wherein he yields to the flowing tide of emotions.

For now he was entrenching himself more deeply than ever behind a tenfold palisade of activities, wintering as it were until the spring should come again in glory. And life and work went placidly on in the well-defended Castle Goethe, where everything had a certain amplitude—Platonic friendship and a bourgeois Eros, household and position, time and space. And

[1] "Like some old saga half-forgot they hover,
First-love and friendship, mine in other days.
Grief is new-born—its echoes I recover,
Filling Life's labyrinthine, broken ways:
By names of dear ones, torn from hours enchanted
Long long ago, remembrance now is haunted.

They do not hear the song that I am singing,
They, to whose souls I sang the first of all;
Scattered the kindly troop, no plaudits ringing
Now will, alas! that earliest praise recall."

similarly in this man, between the middle forties and fifties, the practical intelligence seems to have been in its most diversified phase—in every direction warmth and energy streamed from the great power-house, but only a few beams reached the sphere of infinity. It is Proteus who moves in ever-changing forms before our eyes, and it was now that he used the word Protean to define that amazing power of presentment which he demanded from himself in literary work. But even literature was then but one mode of presentment.

The tree of duties—that smaller, that indigenous tree which Goethe on his return from Italy had chosen to plant in the soil of his life's garden—will quickly take root in familiar ground, will spread in all directions, and is not always easily cut down. The Privy Council, which at twenty-six he had entered as the least of its members, now—twenty-five years afterwards—submitted to his Presidency as the senior in rank. But he was concentrating at one point only; he left most of the work and responsibility to Voigt, and in fact was Minister of Education sole and simple.

Nevertheless, though his days of unbounded energy were over, he kept such a firm hand on his office and conceived his duty in such a sense that not only the documents he signed, but correspondence begun and carried on by him alone, deal with such subjects as these among many others:

A gardener applies for exemption from military service; an innkeeper is desirous to set up a billiard-room; someone neglects to have saucers put under the flower-pots in the Botanic Garden; there is strife about the rating of master-builders, journeymen, and masons in the palace-works, or trouble about the menu for the luncheon to be given a foreign architect from the court-kitchens, and the estimates for beer, bread, and table-linen; or again about the shape and varnish for the shelves in a provisional arrangement of a library, or the cheapest mode of conveyance from the mason's of the stone to be used in a memorial. Besides all this, there are private instructions to the police on the conditions under which an excellent cook, dismissed for outbreaks of temper, is to be reinstated; or on the arrest of a servant who had gone off his head when in foreign parts.

And all of a sudden he perceives the extent and the excess of all these activities.

Symbolic! [he thinks, and echoes Schiller's groan.] As a matter of fact, we poets ought to be treated as Luther was by the Dukes of Saxony—forbidden the streets and shut up in a mountain-fortress. I wish someone would do it to me, and then my *Tell* would be finished by Michaelmas.

A few years after his return, Goethe's duties had been augmented by the management of the theatre, but in the early days he felt no real interest in it, nor it in him. It was not until Schiller took a hand that the work became a vital question.

Did this task suit Goethe?

Many of his characteristics, much of his training, were of the right sort for that sphere. His thoroughness protected him, and protected the theatre, from the dangers of a visionary director; he reformed the finances, appointed box-office keepers and limelight-men for tours in the provinces, set up a regular system of free passes, and was always courteous when personally importuned for stalls.

His philosophical outlook on the world saved the theatre from "tendenciousness"; he struck out every personal allusion in the pieces presented and refused those which were based upon anything of the sort. His universality would suffer no "one-part" performers, and he challenged the prevailing fashion by training all-round actors. If a performer were naturally impassioned, he would soon be cast for a phlegmatic character: "So that he may learn not to 'act himself,' and be able to assume a personality which is alien to him." He turned his knowledge of the world to good account in selecting his company by manner and appearance, and his connoisseurship inclined him to historical productions.

He commanded such respect that at rehearsals his word was law, and when an actor grumbled at having to take a small part as a gamekeeper, Goethe disarmed him by threatening to act the character himself. When at a performance of *Die Räuber* there was some disturbance among the audience, he quelled the tumult with a few stern words from his box.

Other characteristics were not so propitious. Goethe's systematic method of work was here confronted by the business which of all businesses is least amenable to system; and he was ever and always at the mercy of his period and his public. His unerring taste clashed with the Duke's desire to make the theatre pay, or at any rate not to lose by it, and so Goethe often had to produce bad plays which were considered likely to draw.

On the whole, he was unimaginative in his management, and that as it were of set purpose. He was a poet who had never been stage-struck, even in his youth, and as an amateur-actor his appearances had been more in the nature of social events than anything else. Now even the slight fancy for the footlights which had coloured the original version of *Wilhelm Meister* had been left far behind.

The one thing which might have been expected to attract him—the staging of his own dramatic works—he had long abjured. "I have written in opposition to the stage," he said of his plays. No wonder, then, that this essentially untheatrical human being and artist should have been, both before and behind the curtain, more of a level-headed mentor than an inspiring influence! And the most striking manifestation he could have given of what this activity meant to him was that Goethe the Dramatist, whose plays were so purely classic in form, so unadapted to the age, so "unactable" or at any rate so unacted, should have stood haughtily aloof from Goethe the Manager. In short, during twenty-six years of managership, the dramatist may be said to have proudly withdrawn his own best works from the manager's eye, rather than that the manager was prudent enough to decline them. Only thus is it explicable that so great a master of dialogue should, in his theatrical capacity, have learnt so little in the way of dramatic effect that at the zenith of his technical stage-career he wrote the most unactable of all his plays—*Die Natürliche Tochter*.

His duties were endless. Goethe himself engaged every actor, chose every play, rehearsed the whole repertory, wrote prologues, supplied translations, made alterations, controlled the box-office and the policing, personally produced many pieces, built a summer-theatre in Lauchstädt. In twenty-six years he arranged the programmes for more than four thousand performances. Two-thirds were of the spoken drama, one-third being devoted to opera, operetta, and a miscellaneous bill of fare. Four hundred and fifty plays, of which four hundred were novelties—fifteen in a year—each with an average of eight performances, were produced under his management; and these figures alone testify to a standard of organization which was very remarkable for the period.

In his character of impresario he had the plays read in his own house, where he would sit at the head of a long green table, tapping with a key when he wanted silence—and with his strong feeling for musical rhythm, he would often wave the conductor's wand. To a mind so swayed by the sense of universality, so intent on subduing the part to the whole, *ensemble* was inevitably the ideal—his aim was to construct a sort of aristocratic republic in the theatrical realm.

For his insight into the psychology of the actor was profound; and on those lines he dealt with his players, thus winning more of respect or affection than he ever had in his governmental work, where the reserve and precision which characterised him had had a chilling influence. He founded a school of dramatic art and drew up a code of first principles for its teaching—always, however, keeping a musical ideal before him; and so he conducted rehearsals as though they were operas, directing the pace, the crescendos, the *forte* passages. Every step, every gesture, no matter how trivial, was meticulously rehearsed.

Moreover it was his aim, at a time when the actor was still looked upon as more or less of a vagabond, to improve the social position of the stage. He invited the best performers to his house, and both in and out of Weimar his example obliged many persons of rank to do the same. Christiane was his best aide-decamp there. It was proposed to assign professionals a small box for their visits to the theatre, but he rejected it as an unworthy little pigeon-hole. When his colleague wanted to dismiss an actress because she had love-affairs with officers, he intervened, saying that her private life was not the management's business; but he himself kept free of all entanglements, and never had an intrigue with any of his company. He was the fairest of disciplinarians; when one member of the company boxed the ears of another, he devoted days to hearing the case before he punished the offender, and wrote seven letters about it. The question of whether another member had merely abused or actually struck a fellow-actress he thought worth five weeks of investigation, in which he himself took down most of the evidence!

Such respect for the actor was in strong contrast to the thoroughgoing contempt of the public for the profession. It was certainly Goethe's intention to teach the people a better way, but he did not propose to use persuasion—his idea was to show, not how much, but how little he cared for their opinion. He made use of armed force to this end of creating public respect for the stage. Hussars were stationed in the house to see that everyone kept off his hat before and after the performance, and they were equally energetic in restraining any hostile demonstrations, for he had nothing to learn about the public's incapacity for true criticism. "Once for all, the public needs to be bullied; and no matter how it kicks, it will submit in the long run." Thus he resolutely ignored both puffs and abuse of his players, for he knew only too well how capricious and ignorant is the judgment of the masses.

Thinking so slightly as he did of the public taste, is it surprising that Goethe suppressed his own plays, instead of bringing them forward? Even *Götz*, in its new stage-version, was only very rarely staged under his management; and likewise with *Stella*, which in Weimar was thought improper. For *Iphigenie*, *Tasso*, and *Faust* he had neither public nor players. The two last were never performed under Goethe's management; *Iphigenie* and *Egmont* were done a few times when Schiller took the reins. Only the slighter pieces, *Clavigo*, *Die Geschwister*, *Die Mitschuldigen*, *Der Bürgergeneral*, remained in the repertory. During the first few years Goethe staged none of his own plays; after some considerable time he did put on a few. At this time the other German theatres, too, fought shy of him; even the most popular of his pieces, *Götz*, was—despite the remodelling—acted only seven times in all during the last thirty years of Goethe's life!

Director of the Court theatre, and Minister of Education for the Duchies—and yet these also are but two aspects of this Protean being.

In that period Goethe's universality was at its perilous zenith.

As a stone falls faster the longer it takes to fall, so it would seem to be with life. Mine, for all its outward tranquillity, is swept along more violently every day. The many scraps of scientific, artistic, and practical knowledge which in my younger days I got together, now intermingle, obstruct one another, throng upon me to such an extent that I need all the sense of order I possess to keep my head at all. . . . And thus a futile, laborious existence interminably goes on, like the Arabian Nights—each fable growing out of that which has gone before.

It would be easy to give some idea of the fantastic yet impressive power of emission in his flashing intellect by pointing to his work on diseased ivory and his plan for the biography of a frozen tiger. But entries in his diaries will by their variety afford us a more interesting standpoint, since we may regard them as legends under the dissolving views of Goethe's life at the zenith of his worldly career.

In the morning got the fourth canto [of *Hermann und Dorothea*] right, and sent it to be copied. Read Froschmäusler on the various species of insects. In the afternoon with G., chemical experiments on insects. Continued galvanic experiments. The Duke in Jena all day. In the evening to Schiller. Influence of Reason and Nature on the actions of human beings. . . . In the early morning corrected my poem; then to the anatomy of frogs. Rest of the morning in Schiller's new garden, talking over its laying-out; went through the First and Second cantos again before this. . . . In the morning tabulated colours. Oyster-supper in the evening. Afterwards "Oberon's Golden Wedding." Ramadan and the Bayaderes. Letters to Humboldt and Vieweg. Ideas for an itinerary. In the evening at Schiller's—consulted him about it. Expedition to Weimar (see Letter-book). Indian Romances, conclusion. Looked through the Schlege essay. Thibaut [master-builder]. In the evening, Lord Bristol. Morning, Character of Lord Bristol. V, and St. came; talked over the proposed contract with the latter, and with the former, about an advisable place for the ice-grate. At Schiller's—various observations about characters. His *Diver* Romance. Talked about comedy. . . . In the evening at Loder's. A billiard-ball in a dog's stomach, one-third digested in twenty-four hours. . . . In the morning corrected final portion of Cellini. Letter to the Duke. Drafted a letter about new ice-grate. Theatre-business settled in afternoon. Various epochs of architecture in St. Peter's. In the evening at Schiller's—talked about naïve and sentimental writing, with reference to our own individualities.

He was fifty years old, and here is the account of how he spent a stay of six summer-weeks in his former garden-house:

(1) Collected my short poems; (2) Took this opportunity of studying rhythms; (3) Winckelmann's Letters reviewed; (4) Took this opportunity of studying his already published letters as well as his early writings; (5) Read Herder's *Fragments*, as bearing upon the literature of that period; (6) Made the acquaintance of the moon, with the aid of the telescope and selenotopography; (7) Began to read the *Athenäus;* (8) Hurried up the building at the Palace; (9) Judged the Prize-drawings; (10) A long letter arrived from Humboldt, and was revised for use in the *Propyläen;* (11) Was of some use at a few rehearsals of the Amateur Dramatic Society; (12) Paid a few visits to the Exhibition at the School of Art.

Goethe could only have made himself master of so many provinces of the mind by doing a little at a time of a great many things. In his youth, the only works he can really be said to have written at a sitting had been *Werther* and *Clavigo;* but now he definitely taught himself to exchange the *tempo furioso* of his method for the balanced pace of the mediæval artists. He now scarcely ever put all himself into one impassioned production; but would have in hand a quantity of different things in early stages, at which on one day or another he worked hard, and it was as though the alternation refreshed instead of confusing him. Goethe's day, throughout all this second half of his life, was more like a great organiser's than a researcher's, a Minister's, or a poet's.

His letters play a considerable part in these labours; they fill a thick volume yearly. The business-like temper of this decade is reflected in his cool matter-of-fact epistles to all and sundry; they were more polite than of yore, and all the more formal for that. Even to strangers he would frequently write an essay or short statement—the latter merely informative, the former for publication later on.

Everything was catalogued; he was determined to have chapter and verse for everything. Goethe had the creative kind of memory which from the remotest regions of thought and experience can call forth the right analogue at the critical moment; his was not of the reproductive type to which everything is immediately present. Satirical engravings from Paris were catalogued for the magazine, ideas and sequence of scenes for *Faust*, price-lists for the travel-diaries; for so

I can synthesize a great mass of material. . . . I have filled a few useful note-books already [he wrote from Switzerland] in all of which my information is . . . written down or pasted in. Up to this the most kaleidoscopic stuff imaginable. . . . It will help me to be circumstantial about ever so many things.

But not only about this extremely tedious guide-book stuff—about all Goethe's literary work in this decade it may be said that to be "circumstantial about ever so many things" he simply wrote about them; hence his manipulation is often, nowadays, less interesting than the fact that he undertook to manipulate such material at all. Magazines—that is to say Goethe's desire to extend himself and to make money—led him, under Schiller's misguidance and guidance, straight into multifarious realms of scribbling. "It will make a useful paper for the *Propyläen*"—on such grounds he would seek to justify an article which was entirely out of his line. Every journalistic detail, moreover, was earnestly discussed, usually by his own desire—such as the different colours of the magazine-covers, the cleansing of the copper-plates with turpentine, the setting-up and printing, done in Weimar, so that they might always be "thoroughly up-to-date."

The magazines bring us naturally to the prize competitions for German painters, which were held year after year; but were so entirely literary in conception that they have left nothing of any value behind them. *Pictura ancilla Poetarum.* If a passage from a classic writer was set for illustration, the details of the environment were so meticulously prescribed by Goethe (as President of the Committee) that no self-respecting landscape-painter cared to compete. The pictures would then be exhibited. It is still more grotesque to find the two great dramatic poets of Germany offering a prize for the best comedy of intrigue!

At this time, too, Goethe was reviewing for several papers.

Amidst all this task-work some masterpieces suddenly raise their heads. The review of Winckelmann is one of these; and in this Goethe, faced for the first time with the task of presenting a life in pure narrative form, selected his method with so sure an instinct that the little piece must be regarded as the pioneer of psychological biography, for never before had the chapter-headings of a Life stood thus: "Paganism. Friendship. Beauty. Strokes of Luck. Character. Society. Strangers. The World. Christ. Passing Over."

And just as his literary activities were less inventive than accumulative, so as a scientist he was less of a discoverer than an encyclopædist. "Optics are progressing, though just now I approach them more from the practical point of view."

So he was back at his cataloguing, his classifying, had paper-bags made for him, and did in fact finish the didactic and half the historical and polemical portions of his Theory of Colours. And again, all this re-modelling of material about which he had long since formed his own ideas, was more for the sake of "being circumstantial" to his own satisfaction in genetic matters than of contributing to that satisfaction in others.

Proteus could change into a poet in the twinkling of an eye—there was no pause in the shadow-play. And here we get an arresting light upon the baroque style of his mental architecture at this time: "The output of time and energy I have expended on these studies I can put to no better use than turning them to account for a poem"—and so he proposes to make magnetic attraction "the theme of a poem; one must try one's hand at a part, when the whole might prove to be beyond one." If for "poem" we substitute "dépôt" or "branch," we might be considering a prudent business-man who, if he has failed at one point, at any rate proposes not to come entirely to grief. Of his more important projects he spoke in a like matter-of-fact way;

of the most subtle things he would say that he was "working hard at them," and even of poems he would talk, before they were finished, in terms of the number of pages or hexameters. The success and selling-powers of works of art were more frequently alluded to than of old.

This provincial common-sensical state of mind inevitably kept him to epic poetry; and, writing almost nothing in dramatic form (and that little by no means actable), he maintained that epic poetry was ruled by reason, while in the drama blind Destiny held the reins! He became increasingly and perilously submissive to his material during this prosaic period.

Though in conception *Wilhelm Meister* belongs wholly to earlier years, some of the second part—the *Lehrjahre*—was not written at all until the beginning of the present phase. The work had dragged on too long, and finally it came to weigh on Goethe's mind; hence the latter half has lost something in ease and animation. He had come, tired-out, to the end of a long road; yet—very uncharacteristically—he declared that the completed book was his great work.

One thing is certain—that throughout this second half there is an undertone of weariness. The characters are inanimate, and still more so is the manner—sometimes it is tedious, sometimes cut and dried, sometimes grandiloquent. And everywhere the author, grown respectable and growing old, seems trying to account or apologise for the verve of his youthful beginning.

Hermann und Dorothea is—with the exception of *Die Natürliche Tochter*—the only one of Goethe's more important works which belongs to the Schiller decade; for *Wilhelm Meister* and *Faust* were but awaiting completion. This idyll, suggested by accounts of an incident in the Salzburg region, was conceived and written more rapidly than anything had been since *Werther*, and resembles it in brevity and finish. Two-thirds were written in nine days, and the conclusion, after a pause, took him no longer. Another point in common with *Werther* was its success—not, it is true, quite so sensational; and (as with *Götz*) that success was the outcome of a misunderstanding.

For Germany believed that it had been presented with the pattern German epic, and certainly the provincial homeliness which was an element of Goethe's mood at this time, the miniature-painter's touch, as it were—in short, everything that was Dutch in him came out in the eclogue. The names are tinged with this spirit, like the scenery and the domesticities, the social standing and the interests of the personages; in no other of his works is there such intimate and tender observation of simple, kindly, narrow lives. The German middle-class read the poem in this sense, and gratefully accepted it from the first moment of its publication.

It was well that the nation had no idea of what Goethe himself thought of the Germanness of his work.

In Hermann I have for once, as far as the material goes, given the Germans exactly what they want, and so they are overjoyed. I am wondering now if one could not write a drama on the same lines, which every theatre in the land would be obliged to produce, and which everyone would pronounce to be superlatively excellent, the author not necessarily being of the same opinion.

Is there not a note of disdain, of aloofness, of bitterness in that, as coming from the long-unrecognised poet in the moment of a national triumph? Shall we give a yet plainer indication? "If I were younger," he subsequently wrote to the translator of his work in Paris,

I should arrange to pay you a visit, and learn something of French customs and localities. Perhaps I should then succeed in writing a poem which, translated by your hand, might not be ineffective as a companion-piece to *Hermann und Dorothea.*

Goethe regarded *Hermann* as an experiment in form. The piece was the outcome of a desire to reproduce, in a purely classical dress, what Voss had done before him—but with a modern theme. Germans, however, can truly apprehend the vivid sensuous beauty of the figures in the story only through their counterfeits on canvas or in stone; for the rhythms of this poem could never come home to German hearts. Even Goethe's diction could not conjure with the German hexameter; and so his most popular poem, next to *Faust,* is unquotable, unrecitable, to this day.

Similarly, does anyone ever quote the Epigrams in Germany? But all the world knows the brief quatrains from Oberon's Wedding, which continue the satiric themes of the Epigrams; and if we would realise to the full the intractability of the hexameter, we should listen, immediately afterwards, to the miraculously gossamer verse in which, at the very same time, Goethe derided the "German Parnassus." Only the happy accident that the original draft of *Faust* had been composed in the short measures characteristic of German folk-rhyme has endowed the nation with a poem round which it can comfortably get its tongue.

Towards the end of this period, however, there are moments of a lighter, brighter manner, which remind us of Schiller's having called *Wilhelm Meister* "a magic-lantern."

> Sind es Kämpfe, die ich sehe?
> Sind es Spiele? Sind es Wunder?
> Fünf der allerliebsten Knaben
> Gegen fünf Geschwister streitend,
> Regelmässig, taktbeständig,
> Einer Zaubrin zu Gebote. . . .[1]

Did ever any of Goethe's poems begin with such sparkling gaiety, such fleet-footed grace, as does this *Magische Netz?* And some free translations (such as *O gib vom weichen Pfühle*) or those brief stanzas beginning "*Die Sterne, die begehrt man nicht,*" or the slightly ironic sentiment of a lyric like *Schäfers Klagelied,* or, again, the charming conceit at the end of the Cuckoo-song, "*mit Grazie in infinitum*"—these all herald a new note as of light-heartedness acquainted with grief, which makes itself felt towards the end of this period.

[1] "Battles, are they, there before me?
Are they revels? Mystic dances?
Five the youths, and none are fairer,
With five sisters fair contending,
Time they keep, as if to music
Some enchantress bids them follow. . . ."

Even in his ballads Goethe abjured the tragic, at a time when Schiller, next door, was inspired by none but themes of that calibre. Hence the action of *Die Natürliche Tochter*, too, is interrupted before it reaches tragic heights. Vainly did Goethe strive to do what Schiller, at the same period, was doing so easily—to simplify his *dramatis personæ* as in the classic dramas of fatality. Whenever he lacked the detail which his powers of intuition could transfigure into the typical—whenever Goethe had to deal from the start with the type pure and simple—he fell short both as poet and researcher. His work would then be frigid, would lack atmosphere—would be "a noble *ennui*," as Mme. de Stäel, said; and we feel cheated, so to speak, when Eugenie and even the Duke make their effect by a few magnificent but fortuitous exhibitions of character—thus proving themselves to be invented for the occasion—rather than as personages dedicated to the priesthood of ideas.

Faust and his Theory of Colours he described as importunate spectres, which must be dealt with and laid at long last; and indeed it was only by the sweat of his brow and the pressure of circumstance that the poet, as recalcitrant as ever he had been, succeeded in finishing the first part of *Faust*. He was now fifty, and he added about eight hundred lines to what had been written between twenty-two and twenty-five, and augmented but slightly towards the end of his thirties. The new material increased by a third the Fragment then published, and perhaps we can nowhere more plainly perceive the different attitudes of the youthful and the elderly Goethe than in the following words: "The old (and though serviceable, absolutely chaotic) manuscript has been copied, and I have arranged the parts separately, in sequence, numbered on a systematic scheme."

It was after a fashion so entirely undæmonic, so ample and so sanguine, that Goethe seems to have addressed himself to rekindling and polishing-off the once pulsating fragment.

And yet in solitary hours he would confront it with a kind of silent anguish, as though his youth, his whole life, were there mysteriously conjured up before his eyes.

Suddenly, without transition, as he turned some classic page, Goethe encountered Helen. And unhesitatingly—since she had her place in the old puppet-play of *Doctor Faust*—he brought

MASK OF GOETHE AT THE AGE OF FIFTY-EIGHT

her on the scene, writing three hundred lines for Helen, the Chorus, and Phorkyas, which are purely classic in form and sentiment. Begun thus arbitrarily, the fragment does not, for all its irrelevancy, interrupt the action of the drama; and Goethe wrote that "the beauty of my heroine's situation so enchants me that I shall be wretched if I find I have to burlesque it later on. Indeed, I feel no slight inclination to base a serious attempt at a tragedy on this beginning."

Goethe's conviction that the world of Southern classic art was a higher, more sublimated region of the spirit was so profound that when he reconsidered his scheme, and saw that he had arranged to include Helen in the original Faustean universe, he found the word "burlesque" upon his lips! He had not yet bridged the gap between the old and the new versions.

Immediately after he had sketched the Helen episode, he fell seriously ill; and no sooner had he recovered than he resumed the work of his youth at the critical point, and (in two months, at fifty-two) completed the First Part of *Faust*—that is to say, the conclusion of the first monologue and Easter-Day, the walk taken by Faust and Wagner, the second monologue, and the wager with Mephisto. Four years then elapsed, before he thought of publishing this First Part as it stands to-day—and then it was to be as a Fragment. The war prevented publication for three years more—it is as though some fatality pursued the work which Goethe had begun so long ago.

But then *Faust* stood still for twenty-four long years—from fifty-two to seventy-six—before he began to write the Second Part.

The works of this period would have done little to revive public interest in the half-forgotten poet, had not *Hermann und Dorothea*, figuring as a German epic, added fresh lustre to his name. When Goethe stepped out of his immediate narrow circle, he was confounded by the national incomprehension of him. At fifty, he was classed as thirteenth in the ranks of German lyric poets!

More depressing was the want of appreciation among his friends. Nearly all of them condemned *Wilhelm Meister* and the *Elegies;* he ought not, they said, to have introduced the *Schöne Seele* (Beautiful Soul) into the brothel that *Meister* was, nor whores into the pages of the *Horen*. Stolberg actually made a solemn holocaust of the book, and had the confessions of the Beautiful Soul separately bound for him. Two women, who had known him twenty years and ought to have understood him, had these things to say of *Meister:* "When he deals with lofty emotions," wrote Frau von Stein, "he always flings some dirt at them, as if to deprive human nature of any pretensions to the divine." "One never knows," wrote Caroline Herder, "whether he is in earnest or not. . . . His manner is quite too invidious." So seldom did he hear any discriminating praise that Schiller's searching criticisms or Humboldt's expositions of *Hermann and Alexis* were sufficient to encourage him.

The phalanx of new-made enemies also acted as a kind of incentive. With his Epigrams he had made the mistake of setting up a clique when he was growing old, and exposing himself to public attacks in a way which for him was imprudent. In their retorts the victims designated him as a ram, as Aries, as a wether of the flock, and jeered at his natural son.

Finally Kotzebue, smarting under some social rebuffs, set up a clique in Weimar against Goethe. A proposal for an ostentatious tribute to Schiller, at Goethe's expense, in the theatre there, was officially turned down by Goethe in his capacity of Minister —unwisely enough, for it enabled his opponents to accuse him of jealousy, though the whole intercourse of the two poets proved the contrary. A group of young writers who hailed *Wilhelm Meister* and Goethe as their ideals, were sure to be attacked by Goethe's enemies whenever he showed them any favour or produced their works.

This caused him, for the first time, to lay an autocratic hand upon the freedom of the Press: he simply would not suffer a word to be said against his management in Weimar. On the first night of a play of Schlegel's there were outbursts of derision. Goethe rose, came forward, and standing sternly at the front of his box, called out to the pit: "No laughter, if you please!" When, next day, an editor withheld half the criticism of the play from his inspection, Goethe took the extreme step of threatening him with the Duke's intervention—

for I will either be relieved of this task altogether, or protected against such infamies for the future. . . . I will suffer no more of this kind of thing in Weimar, while I hold my official position. I beg you to let me have your decision before four o'clock, for as soon as that hour strikes, my report shall be made to His Royal Highness.

The attacks were discontinued, but Goethe took a further step —he requested Wieland to close his magazine thenceforth to that antagonist!

Soon afterwards a marked demonstration in favour of Schiller was made in the theatre by some students, and had the most unpleasant consequences. The faculty in Jena was written to, the Professors were rebuked for the behaviour of their sons, there was a general explosion of feeling against Goethe's autocracy, several Professors left for other colleges, the famous literary journal was stopped, Kotzebue openly exulted, and the whole University of Jena was in danger of being boycotted!

Goethe's reaction to this uproar was a frantic effort to fill the vacant places and set things on their feet again, for he enjoyed most of the work he did at the Jena Academy. He devoted four months almost entirely to this business, personally invited every possible specialist to contribute to the new literary journal which at great pains he established in Jena to replace the other, now edited at Halle.

All this is important to our knowledge of Goethe only because the incident awakened one of his lesser passions, love of power— which, no matter how great the provocation, would never have been thus conspicuously displayed except in his provincial phase. Goethe, who never really desired either to dominate or to possess, was at this middle period of his life repeatedly a prey to selfishly autocratic impulses.

On the whole, during this decade, he took his official position more seriously than when it had made much greater demands on his time. Now, when he had long ceased to idealise public life in any respect, he seemed determined to play up to his little world's view of him both as Saxon Minister and German author. Goethe's attitude was quite as much the outcome of provincial self-consciousness as of genuine contempt. At this time he deliberately chose to give other artists a wrong idea of himself.

Jean Paul was awe-struck when he entered Goethe's house. Even the pictures and statues were enough to unnerve him, as he waited with Knebel.

At last the god made his appearance—cold, monosyllabic, uninterested. For instance, Knebel remarked that the French were entering Rome. "Hm!" was all the divinity said. He looks vigorous and full of fire; his eye is an abode of light. . . . But at last he woke up; it was not only the champagne but the conversation about art, the public, and so forth that did it—and behold! One was in the company of Goethe. He does not blossom out and pour forth as Herder does; his talk goes deep and is very quiet. His reading is like nothing so much as the roll of thunder, interspersed with the softest possible rustlings of rain—it is absolutely unique. At the end he read us, or rather acted us, a splendid unpublished poem where you could feel his heart flaming under the icy surface, so much so that he ended by pressing the hand of the enthusiastic Jean Paul. . . . By Heaven, we are going to like each other, after all.

Schopenhauer's mother gives a similar account of how Goethe was always rather taciturn and as it were embarrassed, when he first came in—until he knew who was there. He would be carefully dressed in black or dark blue, his hair curled and powdered. But when he thawed and began to tell a story, he acted every character who spoke in it. That is why there are so many different descriptions of Goethe; and when disparagement appears in them, we may safely attribute it to the incapacity of the person concerned to capture his interest. A daughter of Frau Brentano's says that he was cold and priggish and looked like a Frankfurt wine-merchant, but Mendelssohn's daughter, at the same period, raves about him in a high-flown tiresome fashion.

A young engraver on wood failed to obtain access to Goethe in Weimar and was taken to the rehearsal of a masque, disguised in a domino. They pointed out the poet, excitedly conversing with his colleague in the auditorium, and continually jerking at his golden silk domino. And standing close to Goethe, who was finding great fault with the affected posturing of one of the actors, the stranger—nervous but adventurous—joined in and upheld the excited manager, who eagerly poured his grievance into this sympathetic ear. He was right, said the artist, and did well to be angry; and at last Goethe broke into a laugh—"but all of a sudden, as if recalled to his dignity, asked me with a positively terrifying austerity: 'But with whom am I speaking? Who are you?'" Tremblingly the young man produced his letter of introduction from under the folds of his domino. Goethe recognised the name of an artist he admired, arranged to meet him again under a certain pillar, and when he came back, invited him very cordially to his house.

With youths of impressionable and ardent natures he was always at his ease, and was quite like a father to them, though he treated them on terms of perfect equality, calling them his friends. It was as though he wished to be rejuvenated by mixing with young people. He would scarcely let Fritz von Stein out of his sight, saying he missed him too much, "for in bygone days I understood you so thoroughly and was of so much use to you, and I need you even more now that you are so advanced and experienced while I am growing older and a little one-sided." Young Voss was allowed to visit him at any hour of the day; Goethe would read Sophocles with him in his dressing-gown, and gave a dinner-party for him when he took his Doctor's degree. They would take long walks together, discussing philosophical questions.

But none the less, Goethe's self-esteem was such that he regarded his theatrical management as an historical event, and some of the correspondence about it as matter for publication. Sometimes his attitude was positively regal. When some gossiping critical indiscretions about the Weimar theatre appeared in Cotta's *Allgemeine Zeitung*, Goethe (though it was barely a year since his big contract with the publisher) gave him a slap in the face:

If you set any value on our pleasant relations in the past, if you have any sense of the charm of our intercourse, put an end to this unworthy chattering, which cannot fail to destroy our mutual confidence in a very short space of time. No more! Goethe.

This self-esteem, increasingly conspicuous in his public demeanour and actions, was much reinforced by a stronger sense of intellectual certainty and philosophical grasp. At this period he discovered in Schelling—for the first and only time in his life—a thinker whose system included his own visionary, poetic range of thought. The amateur physicist and research-worker felt himself vindicated by this young student of natural philosophy.

In Schelling's system Goethe's contemplative intellect found none of the repellent atmosphere, suggestive of a Polar landscape in its arid desolation, of the Kantean scheme with its uncouth categories, its hailstone-shower of *a priori* conceptions. The new thinker's organ-point was the World-Soul—a spiritual conception of the universe; nor did he contemn imagination. Symbolism was at the heart of his æsthetic, and Goethe was a true Schellingite when he stated his formula thus: "What is the Universal? The individual case. What is the Particular? Millions of cases."

Goethe, whom Schiller's speculations had always intimidated, driving him back with a confused sense of antagonism into his own domain, now for the first time ventured to give some of his verses a title of purely philosophical import, and to promulgate his ideal of that blend of poetry, thought, and observation which had been good enough for Plato and his followers, but not for Goethe's contemporaries. "The World-Soul"—so he now entitled a lyric which was ostensibly one of good-fellowship, but embraced a complete outlook on the universe as seen by a man of fifty. In this poem Goethe's God-Nature was for the first time hymned in joyous alternation, as by a festive company at table. It is the mystical counterpart to the Pan-inspired *Ganymede* of the boy; and all that had surged within him through those thirty years of spiritual stress lies hidden here beneath the superficial aspect of a whimsical profession of faith. The light that never was on sea or land had dawned in Goethe's firmament.

A blend of materialism and magic—such was the form taken by religious faith in this man of fifty. When Schiller, steel-clad in cold philosophy, was discussing Wallenstein's belief in the influence of the stars, Goethe remarked that astrology was based

on an obscure sense of a vast cosmic whole. Experience tells us that the nearest planets have a decisive influence upon weather-conditions, vegetation, and so forth; and since man's upward evolution can only be gradual, it is impossible to say at what point that influence ceases to prevail. Thus man's prescience of his destiny inclines to take the further step of supposing that influence to embrace social conditions, such as fortune and ill-fortune. I should not even call it superstition —it lies so close to our nature, and is as acceptable and workable as any other belief.

The recusant, we perceive, is carefully feeling his way back to the native region of his soul. How apologetic is the materialist, how hard put to it the scientist, how reverential the biologist, when confronted by this image of the Divine, and feigning oblivion of the mystery which envelops it! And yet Goethe, when he uttered those intensely characteristic words—"man's prescience of his destiny"—set the whole question in the sphere of mystic thought. And now, too, his dream was of the "Lord of the earth, coming for the sixth time as one of like nature with ourselves, at one with us in joy and pain." This God, and this Bayadere, indeed might seem to dawn upon us from some intermediate world of faëry—approaching one another from their polar distances to find, to lose again, and amid the flame at last to know each other in a marriage of true souls!

Towards the end of this period there was a tendency no less marked to superstitious beliefs, much more so than in the past of some decades ago. Goethe would dream a number and take a lottery-ticket, would be secretive and deceptive about his plans. He who in bygone days had made fun of Caroline Herder's forebodings and dreams was now dismayed when, sending good wishes to Schiller, he wrote "*last* New Year's Day" instead of "this year's." He tore up the sheet, but on the fresh one had the greatest difficulty in avoiding the ominous word, and on that very day he told Frau von Stein of his premonition that either he or Schiller would go that year. Four months later, Schiller was dead.

The old wonder, the old worship, filled his soul as of yore—that underlying sense of the superhuman. Young Voss heard him, at fifty-five, speak ardently, with flashing eyes, of susceptibility to emotion, and rage against the *nil admirari* attitude—"as if any living soul could believe anything in the whole of God's world to be less than a marvel and a sacred revelation of the

Divine." In this vein he talked for an hour; then took his candle and went off without a Good-night.

It was the revival of his faith at the end of this period which tuned his mind to so confident a mood; and he needed it, for he was beginning to feel old.

At forty-seven he spoke of the end of his career, and soon afterwards of the disappointments belonging to the second half of life. "The new," he wrote at another time, "is, in our maturity, no longer a new thing, and the strange special case is of rare occurrence; one seems to be going downhill faster all the time." He commended Tieck's delight in youthful talent as an insurance for the future, which showed comprehension of the art of life; and when at the Court of Gotha they got up a surprise-party for his birthday, with a ceremonial cake on which the fifty-two candles threatened to set fire to one another, it was in a mood of elderly sadness that he recalled the birthdays of his childhood when, instead of these crowded symbols of the years, the candles all had plenty of room.

Work was the only refuge from such merciless reminders. Once, in mystical mood, he expressed it thus: "Well, however it be, I am forcibly swept round my zodiac, and every sign in it gives me something different to do." He was less exalted when, proudly confident, he said to Schiller: "We will await the favours genius may grant us in the autumn of life." It was his time for seeking rejuvenation and solace from the Muse whom he so touchingly invokes in the apologetic Prologue to *Hermann und Dorothea:*

> Denn du bist es allein, die noch mir die innere Jugend
> Frisch erneuest und sie mir bis zum Ende versprichst.
> Aber, verdopple nunmehr, o Göttin, die heilige Sorgfalt!
> Ach, die Scheitel umwallt reichlich die Locke nicht mehr:
> Da bedarf man der Kränze, sich selbst und Andre zu täuschen.[1]

[1] "For it is thou, thou alone, who freshly dost ever restore me
Youthful feeling, and say: 'So it shall be to the last.'
Ah, but redoubled must fall, O goddess, thy heavenly bounties!
See, no more do the locks richly encircle my brow:
Hence the laurels are needed, to cheat myself and the others."

This is Goethe's first explicit acknowledgment of a sense of growing old—this mood in which he promises himself a phase of unresting endeavour.

He sought other means, however, of solving the dilemma of grey hairs and a young heart:

> Das Leben ist des Lebens Pfand, es ruht
> Nur auf sich selbst und muss sich selbst verbürgen.[1]

In that passage from *Die Natürliche Tochter* sounds the old fearless materialism. He tackled the problem differently in his programme for *Faust*, as now sketched; and the first and second portions of that work might very well be taken as the programme for the first and second portions of Goethe's life. Looked at in juxtaposition, they are highly significant: "Personal enjoyment of life as seen from without, in the backwater of passion: First Part. Enjoyment of action, directed outwards, and conscious enjoyment, beauty: Second Part." Finally, the problem of growing old became one with the old problem of the dual nature, which in the lines spoken by Faust about the two souls is more conspicuously in his mind than ever, though even there in only one of its manifestations.

On the whole, Goethe's polarity seems in this homely phase to have been more manageable, more normal—more legitimate, so to speak. He now boldly extended the law of polarity to embrace magnetic, electric, and similar influences in Nature; and now, too, in his new manner, he drew up a "scheme" for the various forms of sensation which brooded and thrilled within his being—centripetal and centrifugal, the former passive and conceivably vacuous, the latter active and frequently called forth by immediate objects. Thus on one side of the scale he set reclusiveness, apathy, languor as vacuous sensations, a blend of physical requirements, timidity, lost innocence, vague symbolism, regret for or expectation of an unspecified beloved, a weakness peculiar to dreamy natures—and on the other, the centrifugal side, he classed aspiration, ambition, conscience, love of travelling, plant-

[1] "Our life is pawned to Life, its only pledge
Is of itself, itself the sole redemption."

ing for posterity, premonitions, appraisement of existence, shooting, fishing, building, road-making, representation.

Goethe's dual nature was the supreme inspiration for the new *Faust*-scenes, and Schiller went so far as to declare that the duplexity of human nature was the essential idea of the work—the unsuccessful effort to unify the divine and the physical elements in man; and with great perspicacity he continued: "The devil, because of his materialism, gains the verdict from the intellect; Faust, from the heart. But sometimes the parts seem to get mixed, and the devil turns into an advocate for divine reason as against Faust." Again, Goethe himself said in the afterwards rejected Envoi to *Faust:*

> Und hinterwärts mit allen guten Schatten
> Sei auch hinfort der böse Geist gebannt,
> Mit dem so gern sich Jugendträume gatten,
> Den ich so früh als Freund und Feind gekannt.[1]

Broadly speaking, in this period he was so absorbed in Mephisto (who, in reality, was never at all a disturbing influence in the original conception of *Faust*, but merely Faust's evenly-matched opponent) that in a conversation about the work with a young Professor of History—the longest conversation we have of Goethe's—he always took Mephisto's part against Faust.

But it was the inevitable logical result of all the defensive measures taken in this Protean decade that the dæmonic element in his nature should be somewhat obscured. We seldom read of any outbursts of wrath; nor do we often hear (with the exception of Faust's great curse) in verses, prose, or letters that clamouring of his soul, enamoured of the universal as it was, for air, for felicity. If he was attacked by fits of impatient revolt at futile labour, we see him somehow managing to get rid of them; for—in his own remarkable words to a friend—"It is better to relinquish once for all than to be for ever in a rage about yesterday, to-day, and to-morrow."

[1] "With every kindly spirit relegated,
That Evil One shall vanish from my sight,
With whom the dreams of youth too fondly mated,
Whom, friend and foe, I early read aright."

Slowly, and with cautious tread, he was at the end of this period climbing the green hill of serenity.

Since the outbursts of his youth with their savagely satirical tendency, Goethe's humorous writings had constantly revealed a stern, frowning habit of mind. Something of Northern heaviness which even the South could not conjure away, had pressed ever more weightily upon the spirit which, between his middle twenties and forties, had striven so earnestly to find repose in the common activities of humanity. The earlier manifestations of the new temper had a strain of crude jocosity which was somewhat provincial and old-fashioned; but probably this note was, after the tension of the last decade, the same sort of relief to Goethe that it is to posterity. For instance, he gave Schiller a comic description of all the gifts which his friends in Jena had made him in a recent week, ranging from an amputated foot to a crab-supper. Or he sent a messenger to wrest *Wallenstein* from the still hesitant author, saying that "he represented a detachment of hussars, with instructions to take possession of the Piccolomini, father and son, at any cost. . . . By order of the Melpomene Commission of Investigation into the Wallenstein Disturbances, graciously appointed by Messrs. Goethe and Kirms." Such moods inspired poems like his *Séance*, with its forced march of capital letters, or *Musen und Grazien in der Mark* (*The Muses and Graces in Prussia*), or *Der Neue Alkinous* (*The New Alcinous*) where the Jena School is parodied.

But it was only at first that Goethe's newly revived humour was so cumbrous; it soon became fleeter-footed—in the end it grew wings. Eros dwelt on the way to Serenity.

Even Eros, though, makes rather a rough clownish entrance at the beginning of this period. The uncouth stanzas of Mephisto and the Chorus were evidently introduced at this time into the Paralipomena to *Faust*, and it is likewise with the interlineations in the Walpurgisnacht.

In the third version of *Götz* some burning scenes with Adelheid, which belonged to the original conception, were restored; the *Neue Pausias*, and above all *Alexis und Dora*, are aflame with sensual exultation; and the two great ballads end in a blaze of erotic triumph.

Moreover, there are many more of those charming, felicitous

gracious social remarks which were almost unheard during the twenty years we have been considering. At a ball in Jena a young writer, at the height of the dancing, asked him if he was going to stay much longer, "Longer than I had thought I should—as long as it is so delightful. I have so many friends here, and one makes so many pleasant acquaintances, that I don't know when I shall depart; but I shall soon be returning to Jena for work." And when the young man applauded him for his interest in youth, Goethe answered: "When I see around me all this growing, all this budding, in other people's children and my own, as here to-night—that is life, is it not, life in its essence? What else could remind me that I am, and am what I am?"

We cannot fail to catch in such remarks those minor tones which some of us who come after him find more ravishing than many a famous passage in his works—and in phrases like these, casually uttered between two dances, we are listening to the first notes of the overture to a new Goethean manner.

Soon his song soared into the blue, and an April blitheness now informs a succession of brief lyrics—of a kind that he had not attempted for thirty years, but in his youth could never have fashioned with such skilful, tender hands:

Tage der Wonne,
Kommt ihr so bald?
Schenkt mir die Sonne,
Hügel und Wald?[1]

Or that glorious one, also written at fifty:

Was zieht mir das Herz so?
Was zieht mich hinaus?
Und windet und schraubt mich
Aus Zimmer und Haus?[2]

[1] "Early, O smiling
Day, you are come,
Sunlit, beguiling
Hill, forest, to roam."

[2] "What tugs at my heart so?
What tugs me, and fast

Or perhaps those graceful, airy *Weissagungen des Bakis* (*Prophecies of Bakis*), where a heavy-laden soul begins to make friends with the universe, in stanzas full of a radiant serenity. The "magic-lantern" effect which Schiller's penetrating eye had discerned in *Meister*, is here in full force.

And though these few unfamiliar poems, for all their beauty, are more like milestones on the path of this pilgrim-spirit than monuments of his genius, their music does lead us straight back to Goethe's spiritual home. For only of kindliness is serenity born; both are gifts of maturity, and flower late and warily in natures driven by mysterious urgencies.

When Humboldt lost one of his children, Goethe wondered whether to send him *Die Natürliche Tochter* would console him or open the wound afresh. To an actress, who sent her adolescent son to the Weimar theatre with some misgivings, Goethe wrote: "You will have patience with your bantling, if you should hear too often of some trifling imprudence. I always think of these babes, cast upon a world of strangers, as of birds allowed to fly about in a room."

For the building operations at the Palace he engaged the workmen without the intervention of the master-builders, for these latter always took a commission on the wages. He wrote to consult his colleagues on the Council as to whether the library-attendant might be permitted to ask for a Christmas-box from those who used the library, "for this might easily lead to a general system of importunity."

A letter about a servant's tip—is not this typical of the odd things we come upon in characterising these twelve years, which lie like a vast lake, circumscribed yet often apparently shoreless, along the frontiers of Goethe's old age?

But while all this Protean endeavour sought to elude the well-marked enclosure, Tyche, who had rather neglected Goethe during these ten years, made up for it to posterity by preserving a single page—more valuable for the history of that soul than a thousand others. It is a fragment from the beginning of this period, but was not discovered among his unpublished papers till a hundred

---

Entwining me, drags me
From indoors at last?"

years later—a note without preamble or superscription, written in the third person, probably so that the secretary to whom he dictated it might not know it related to himself, for Goethe gives us here a summary, one might almost say of his whole endeavour up to nearly fifty.

A tireless energy, a poetically-conceived passion for self-development both spiritual and material form the focus and the groundwork of his existence; once that fact is grasped, all else that may seem contradictory is explained. Since this passion knows no rest, he is forced, if he would not feed upon empty air, to turn his attention outward; and as he is not contemplative but merely practical, meet externalities on their own terms. Hence the many false shots at plastic art, for which talent—at active life, for which adaptability—at science, for which perseverance—are equally lacking; but since his attitude to all three is consistently inquiring, and he is himself irresistibly impelled to demand actuality in materials and contents, and unity and suitability in form, even these misdirected endeavours are not without fruit both spiritual and material. . . . In practical affairs he can be useful, when these are directed by a definite purpose; and finally, in one way or another, a permanent achievement is the reward, or at worst he finds he has done something worth doing as a side-issue. When hindered, he is not at all pliable; but he gives in or opposes with all his might, holding out or dismissing the subject, according as his conviction or his mood get the upper hand at a given moment.

He can bow to circumstance, to emergency, and the demands of necessity, art, and craftsmanship; but he cannot bring himself to look on calmly at work done by rule of thumb, yet pretending to proficiency. Ever since he grasped the fact that in science the measure of culture attained by the inquiring mind matters more than the actual phenomena with which we deal—ever since then he has but the more regularly pursued and delighted in what had formerly been an occasional uninspired endeavour; nor has he . . . entirely lost interest in the other two activities, but practises them now and then, only with more of perception and acceptance of the limitations which he knows to be his. And the more because the cultivation of any one mental faculty to the best of one's ability will prove beneficial to every other.

The special character of his poetic efforts is for others to define. Unfortunately his temperament has created many hindrances and difficulties for him in the handling of his material no less than of his form, and he has attained to some degree of perception only when the period of unabated energies has gone by. An idiosyncrasy which both as artist and man has always swayed him is a certain susceptibility and mobility which is at the mercy of direct impressions, and must either ignore immediate objects or make them a part of itself.

If this self-portrait confirms our delineation in all its particulars, it no less thrusts upon us, in its staggering dispassionateness, Goethe's perception that all perception comes too late.

But even so, these twelve years might seem to have been almost empty of developments, had they not been salutarily and profoundly disturbed by four great crises.

Only the first of these was voluntary—the plan of another trip to Italy. Yet can we call that obscure and potent urgency by the name of will, of purpose? Was it not rather a propulsion ever freshly renewed in Goethe's being since his return from the South? He thought of collaborating with Meyer in a great book about Italy. But in truth, though he was scarcely conscious of it, something far stronger impelled him. For the second time he was craving escape from the all too mundane, too importunate environment of his life; and again it was escape, too, from the woman—like Charlotte of yore, a symbol of his state. For the second time he was planning a kind of flight from Weimar. He had sent Meyer on before him. Years and days, military campaigns, were to intervene between the two; and it is typical of Goethe's then remoteness from mundane events that the name of a young General meant no more to him, when he first heard it, than a portent which might prove dangerous to a single work of art—he hoped that a picture despatched to him by Meyer "would escape the omnipresent and omnipotent Bonaparte's clutches."

Not yet did he dream of the heights to which that name was to lead his imagination. Still, as of yore, he regarded contemporary history from the mere standpoint of whether the war would keep him out of Rome or suffer him to get there. But though he consulted Meyer, who was ill and returning to his native Switzerland, on the best route they could take for Rome, he talked (now as then!) to the Duke and Christiane of a short visit to the Lake of Zurich.

The uncertainty got on his nerves. When the prospects seemed favourable, he was sociably inclined; when they were not, he resorted to working on *Faust*, so as to have "a path of retreat into the cloudland of symbolism and ideas." This labour was the best anodyne for his restlessness, during the one quiet month it lasted—he said that "the work promised to spread like a vast outgrowth of fungus, to the general astonishment and consternation. If my trip falls through, my only hope is in this piece of skylarking." So monstrously did Goethe exaggerate his craving for the sunny South that he could thus monstrously depreciate the most northern in atmosphere of all his works! In this state of vacillation, which in his maturity never arose from anything but a sense of loss of external liberty (and was therefore of very rare occurrence) he spent a whole summer, leaving *Faust* to its fate before long and getting through the days as best he could; "and I am vain enough to compare myself to Orpheus' lyre, which sounds but accidentally as it is borne upon the billows to the open sea."

At last there seemed to be nothing to prevent his starting. He engaged his lodging before he set out, made his son his heir, insisting upon even his old mother's renunciation of all her claims upon his property, burnt countless records of his life and loves, and then was sorry he had done it. Such, before he left his home—perhaps for ever—and contemplated the orderly volumes of his letters, was Goethe's hesitation between discretion and biography.

Now he settled down for weeks beside the Lake of Zurich, and ransacked the region with Meyer. A queer pair they must have seemed to many a God-forsaken Swiss hamlet, as they wandered about, poking their noses into everything, wool-gathering, botanising all over the place.

And then, for the last time in his life, he stood upon the Gothard Pass, and again he was stirred by the symbolism of this boundary between two countries, tongues, climates—two worlds, to both of which he belonged, and wished he could belong more whole-heartedly. And once more, for the third time, he turned his back upon the Pass. Here, twenty-two years ago, he had stood and looked back longingly to Lili. Here, eighteen years ago, he had stood and looked back longingly to that Duchy where he had hoped, with all the force of his being, to build himself a sure abiding-place. And eleven years ago he had hurried over another Pass, eastward, with the same South for goal—driven onward by the disillusionment and perplexity in which that Duchy, and the inextricable spell of one woman in it, seemed to have entangled him inextricably for evermore.

Now he was nearly fifty, more easy-going, inured to moderation in every pleasure of the senses. The war was not much of a nuisance, people could travel, others were not deterred—the war was no real reason for changing his mind. Why then did Goethe for the third time turn tail at the threshold of Italy?

He was a husband and father—and that called him back. He had fled of yore from Charlotte; now he hurried back to Christiane, not because his love for her was a deeper, but because it was a happier, thing. Woman-like, her instinct had warned her that she might lose him; yet assuredly it was not the mere dread of danger for him, but the healthy impulse to preserve the happiness she knew which made Christiane plead with such unwonted urgency: "I implore you by everything there is in the world, not to go on to Italy just now! You love me so well that you will never let me lose my prayers!" And she made the boy, too, appeal to his heart, and tried another method herself: "If you do go on to Italy or take any long journey, and won't let me come with you, Gustl and I will start off to follow in your tracks, for I would rather go through any sort of tribulations than be without you so long again!"

Such cries as these plucked at the greying Goethe's heart; and he answered:

So far as the danger is concerned, there was nothing to prevent my going on to Italy . . . but I could not bear to be so far away from you. If it proves impossible to take you, I will give up the idea of seeing Italy again. . . . I can . . . say that it is only for your sake and the boy's that I am returning. . . . Already I could wish to be at home with you, to bid you good-night and good-morning in the green alcove, and have you bring me my breakfast. . . . It's a bad business, this going away—something like being dead.

He knew what he was giving up, and yet he had to give it up. Of his vacillation between North and South the best witness is *Amyntas,* then and there composed.

No sooner back than his laments began again in full force! Profound were his sighs, as he looked through what Meyer had written. When he thought of the Niobe, he could have ordered his carriage for Florence; Humboldt in Rome was commissioned to kiss the Giustiniani Minerva's hands for him; and when Wolf, the Homeric expert, came so near as Halle, the place seemed to Goethe "a Southern country." He chose Greek plays of the Romantic period in preference to any others for the theatre, so that he might see the classic sculpture come to life, and in an essay at this time it was all summed up in: "The Southern race is the enkindled race."

The second crisis? In the middle of this period a severe illness brought him near to death for the first time since his twentieth year. Afterwards he called it "the great, ferocious illness." Like that earlier one, it too broke out alarmingly with scarcely any warning, was perilous in the extreme but short-lived, and left him ailing for years. And just as then our interest did not lie in the physiological causation of an ailment (which on both occasions pointed to some disorder of the blood, with fever, ague-fits, and heart-trouble) but in its psychical consequences—so now posterity seeks to discover the underlying moral cause of so acute, so abrupt a visitation. This time it was a stone in the kidneys, an affliction to which strong drinkers are frequently subject; and he wished he had the organs "of one of those healthy Russians who fell at Austerlitz." The preliminary symptoms were slight. He caught cold at the Palace, and collapsed in the ever-dreaded month of January; there were weeks of fever, a short period of horror in which his eyesight seemed to be going; the household was distraught, the Duke lent a helping hand—and in his delirium Christiane heard the sick poet quoting verses, probably from a *Höllenfahrt Christi* (*Christ's Descent into Hell*), which had been wrung from the boy of sixteen in the earlier ordeal.

Through it all his scientific impulse persisted. He daily dictated for his diary an account of his state on the day before.

On that following the crisis which nearly cost him his life: "Last night, too, was very restless. High delirium. In the morning at eight o'clock there were three hours of sleep, the spasms decreased in frequency and the swelling of the eye diminished." Of course the data were given him by his nurses; but that he should have asked for them and dictated them as dispassionately as though he were doctor instead of patient, is a fresh proof of Goethe's ability and resolve to keep cool in the throes of fever—a symptom of the polarity of his nature.

The first thing the convalescent asked for was music; and the first letters he was able to write have music in them, as it were—a solemn Largo from him who could breathe and see once more. He fingered the texture of his life anew, and found that "none of the threads seem to have broken; the mixture goes on as of old, and even production seems to be peeping round the corner."

Soon—behold!—production came out of its corner. That time-honoured poem of his youth, that fragment, once rejected as a torso, lifted a haughty head and stepped forth as though determined to inhale the renewed vitality and offer it up in gratitude for Death's overthrow. There seems to be some mysterious connection between *Faust* and the two illnesses which endangered Goethe's life at nineteen and at fifty-one. The former led the sceptic to make his first acquaintance with the mystic writings which were condensed into the beliefs and superstitions of Faust, as originally conceived; the latter led the materialist back to a coherent continuation of Faust's first self-communings, which had formerly broken off upon a dissonance. But for these two momentous physical interruptions the fragmentary poem would scarce have been either begun or completed.

His body, with its fifty years upon it, took longer than before to revive. Five years of recovered activity could but slowly restore the shattered constitution; and so the two succeeding times of crisis found Goethe still in precarious health. He was still ailing, though it was four years since his illness, when Schiller's last year on earth began. By Christiane's account he was "scarcely ever really well, and many were the occasions when one could not but think him on the point of death. . . . The attacks were usually of regular monthly occurrence and attended with the severest pain, to which he was obliged each time to succumb."

It was at this period that Schiller collapsed, never again to rise from his bed. Goethe had always hitherto been of the greatest help to him in these attacks, and his mere presence had seemed like a recall to life.

Now they were both sad, ailing, and grown older. Schiller declared he was completely undermined. There they both lay or sat in their well-heated houses, a few hundred yards between them, each accustomed to cheer the other in his hours of weakness —and all they could do was to exchange notes like prisoners. As time went on, Goethe got better, Schiller worse. Goethe did visit him, a week before the end. Schiller wanted to go to the play, but Goethe felt unwell, and said a last adieu to him at his hall-door. Soon afterwards he sent him some pages of his Theory of Colour: "And may you soon be quite yourself again!" Then both men had a relapse. Christiane was frightened about Goethe; Schiller, in the midst of a feverish renewed activity, fell seriously ill again.

It was the end. No one dared to tell the other invalid; Meyer could not bring himself to utter the words. "I see," said Goethe, "that Schiller must be very ill indeed." Christiane said he had been unconscious for some time; then she pretended to be asleep, so that Goethe might not work himself into a state of alarm. In the morning he asked: "Schiller was very ill yesterday, wasn't he?" His wife began to sob. "He is dead?" asked Goethe firmly. Then he wept. They did not tell the invalid a word about Schiller's inglorious funeral.

> I felt as if I had lost myself, and I *have* lost a friend [he wrote soon afterwards] whom to lose is the loss of half my being. I suppose I ought really to change my way of life altogether, but at my age that is out of the question. So I just live from day to day, and do the first thing that turns up.

Is there not a note in that of the sort of annoyance, of estrangement, with which a King might deplore the retirement of his most trusted Minister? In that very same month Voss was obliged to leave Weimar; and Goethe exhausted himself in passionate complaints and reproaches to Voss's son, saying that he had had to submit to the loss of Schiller, but Voss's departure "was not the fault of destiny; men had brought *that* about." The fine flower of his friendship with Schiller had faded; but that his familiar intercourse with Schiller or Voss should be broken up by death or departure was more than Goethe could endure in these particular years. He took weeks to recover from such personal grievances, inflicted on him by destiny or the will of another.

When he did begin to consider how they could best honour the dead genius, he was quite himself again. For soon after the brief dejection caused by Schiller's death, Goethe began, for the first time in many years, to recover health and vitality. That this was no accident, but a law of his being which made him always feel spiritually regenerated when a crisis was over, a comparison with future losses will prove.

Not more than three weeks after Schiller's death, Goethe had planned a great tribute to his friend in the shape of a choric threnody. But it came to nothing, as did his earlier plan of finishing *Demetrius*. The epilogue to the dramatic version of *Die Glocke* is the only epitaph to that wonderful alliance which we possess; and once more we feel, when reading those verses, that Schiller does not pervade Goethe's life as do Herder and Jacobi but moves through its third act like some impressive but transient figure in an episode. It is an ideal image of Schiller which Goethe gives us in the lines:

> Nun glühte seine Wange rot und röter,
> Von jener Jugend, die uns nie entfliegt,
> Von jenem Mut, den früher oder später
> Den Widerstand der stumpfen Welt besiegt! [1]

Just as after that brief subjective anger and real sorrow for Schiller, a heightened vitality was apparent in Goethe, so in the fourth of these crises—the upheaval in public affairs which threatened to break him down—he seemed on the contrary to be filled with all the ardour of his youth; for now the threads of his

[1] "Redder upon his cheek the rose shone glorious,
That rose of youth which poets keep for aye,
That courage, soon or late to be victorious,
Though the dull world withstand it many a day."

public and private life were strangely intermingled, and this is the cardinal point in the chronicle of that Protean period's final years.

Christiane, hitherto mistress, mother, and house-keeper, had in these recent semi-invalided years become Goethe's nurse as well; and as he lost courage and health and felt the support of her strong capable hand, the relation between these two (soon to have been united for twenty years) began slowly to take a different form. An ageing, ailing, increasingly solitary man at the end of his fifties was conscious of being upheld and stimulated by a brave cheerful woman at the beginning of her forties; and if hitherto he had paternally guided her steps as though she were his child, he now clung to her ripe youthfulness as that father in his grey hairs might have done.

For now he owed her such gratitude as she had formerly owed to him, and in gratitude—the emotion to which he was most susceptible—Goethe was second to none. Ever since the first years of their union he had treated Christiane as his wife; and now he felt himself her debtor until the world, too, should treat her so. So that the intention of marrying her which he now cherished was dictated by his feeling for her, not by any suggestion from without, and still less by Christiane's influence. Not a single word in any of their letters, spontaneous as a rustic song, no hint from any of their numerous enemies, gives the least handle to the conjecture that she (as would have been comprehensible enough after all their years together) made any attempt to persuade him into marriage.

But though Goethe's gratitude made him anxious to regularise their union, the tragic irony of Fate decreed that their life together lost in intimacy when the outward bond was more defined. Goethe married Christiane just when he was beginning to feel that he needed her presence less; and his inward dilemma had been earlier revealed, when he congratulated his friend Knebel on the regularisation of a similar bond: "In such cases it always comes to this—one has to choose between two sacrifices." But even then he did not make that choice.

In the summer after Schiller's death, Goethe, restored to health, wrote these earnest words to his mistress: "I thank you for all the love and devotion you have shown me recently; may you be rewarded for them in good measure, and I hope, while I live, to contribute to your happiness by every means in my power." It sounds frigid, but from Goethe it meant a promise; and on his birthday he had something warmer to say: "If it goes well with me I shall rejoice for your sake especially, since wherever I have known delight I have silently wished for you."

In the winter he was ill again for a while, and Christiane was in a state of utter despair, for her sister and aunt, then inmates, died in the house. Later, in the summer, she and Goethe quite regained their strength, but in different places and by different methods.

While Goethe in Carlsbad was re-entering social life and beginning to sketch and geologise, Christiane too had left home, but was alone for the first time in her life. Her kindred were dead; August, at seventeen, spent much of his time with his companions in the hill-country among the castles, Goethe was living in Bohemia—so Christiane betook herself to Lauchstädt, where she was received with open arms by the company at the theatre.

But there, remote from Weimar and on holiday, even aristocratic circles condescended to pay her some attention. She was now received in some sort as Goethe's wife; she rode and drove, was considered pretty and amusing, much might be conveyed through her to the powerful Minister, and therefore she was courted. It turned her head a little, to be invited to tea-parties and balls by the nobility. But now her accounts of it all left Goethe cold; he merely wrote that she was to make hay while the sun shone. "I was pretty sure that you would be spending more money, anyhow. And now farewell to you, with your luncheon-parties, dinners, dances, and theatres."

In September both were back in the house at Weimar.

Suddenly consternation and terror filled the neighbourhood. Napoleon's victorious army was advancing on Central Germany. Many people fled. Goethe did not stir, did not even remove his papers; it was as though he thought, like Danton, in misanthropic pride: "They will never dare!" He quietly went on with his theatrical work, putting on a play to the resentment of the company, for the house was almost empty. Goethe entered his box and gave the signal to begin. The paltry operetta was sung by very nervous voices; when it was over to-morrow's programme was announced.

To-morrow was October 14, 1806.

At Jena, on that day, a battle was fought which changed the course of history. Prussia was vanquished, and with Prussia the Duke of Weimar, who had again become a Prussian General. Sitting in his house, Goethe could hear the cannons. Fugitives came rushing into the town, the theatre was converted into a hospital; the French followed up their victory, and by that evening the entirely defenceless town of Weimar was in their hands. Nobody knew where the Duke had gone when the lost battle was over. The Dowager Duchess, her Court, and many officials had fled before that day. Only the reigning Duchess Louise, and Goethe, the Minister-in-charge, remained at their posts. His whole existence was at stake—he must have known it, for Napoleon's aim was to annihilate the Duke, and he could easily have seized the Minister instead of the fugitive ruler.

Goethe did as the emergency demanded. His son and secretary were the first people he sent to meet the French Hussars (now riding in by the Frauentor near by) with wine and beer; he himself went over to the Palace—with a young Hussar-officer. It is uncertain whether the young man then gave Goethe his name. He was Lili's son, now in the service of France.

Sixteen Alsatian troopers were quartered on Goethe—tired, good-humoured fellows, amenable to food and drink. At the same time some fugitives from the town collected in the back-premises, seeking refuge from the looting soldiery, as though their poet's and Minister's house were a place of sanctuary. Christiane was indefatigable in providing food, clothing, and shelter; forty beds were made up, and the table-linen was used as bed-linen.

Then in the dead of night was heard a violent hammering of butt-ends on the door, and two armed tirailleurs demanded entry. Those already installed refused it. The newcomers hammered still harder; Riemer, the secretary, at last opened the door, and gave them food and drink. They then asked for the master of the house. Goethe, who till now had kept out of sight in his own two rooms, appeared in his dressing-gown on the staircase, carrying a candle. He asked them if they had not had all that they could reasonably require. "His dignified imposing figure, and the intellect in his face, inspired them with respect," says Riemer. Then he withdrew.

But no sooner was he gone than the pair, intoxicated by fighting and drink, began to bluster more violently than ever, demanding beds; and finding there were none to be had, they rushed upstairs to Goethe's room and covered the defenceless man with their weapons. They might have wounded or killed Goethe —a couple of drunken tirailleurs on the night after the Battle of Jena.

But Christiane rushed up the back-staircase from the garden, bringing a man with her, and threw herself between them. With superhuman strength, born of the emergency, and aided by the man, she drove out the soldiers and bolted herself and Goethe into the room. The drunken men stumbled cursing down the broad Italian staircase of the silent house, flung themselves on the beds which stood in readiness for the Marshal and his staff, and when the Adjutant at last arrived at break of day, he drove them out with the flat of his sword.

Goethe, unarmed and defenceless, had been saved by his mistress—that fact has never been disputed. To the brave, loving Christiane Vulpius the world probably owes the last twenty-five years of Goethe's life, in which the *Diwan* and *Wahlverwandschaften* (*Elective Affinities*), *Pandora, Wahrheit und Dichtung* (*Fact and Fiction*), the second parts of *Wilhelm Meister* and *Faust*, were written.

Again Goethe had stood immovable in a short-lived crisis, wholly the victim of circumstances. Scarcely was it over—on the very next morning—than his soul seemed filled with a rapture of grateful emotion. The danger was past; on that following day the Marshals of the French Revolutionary Army took measures to ensure Goethe's safety; their safe-conduct designated him as "*un homme reconsidérable dans toutes les acceptions du mot.*" Denon, Director-General of the Paris Galleries, who accompanied Napoleon and had known Goethe in Venice, was now his guest, and had portraits painted both of him and Wieland.

Meanwhile Goethe was unwearying in reassurance of his friends. All his notes are quiet, manly, even cheerful. He was at his very best—Paris had come to Goethe, the Empire was as it were installed in his house; he felt it all to be a stimulating event.

But the diary was kept as meticulously as in the most halcyon periods; and nowhere is its pedantry, its wilful affectation of provincial detachment, more ludicrous in effect than in those days of the Battle of Jena. It is as though Goethe had held the white-hot hours in a great pair of pincers, and plunged them into a cold bath of biography, so as to render them innocuous:

October 14: Morning cannonade at Jena, followed by a battle near Kötschau. Rout of the Prussians. In the evening at 5 o'clock the cannon-balls smashed in the roofs. At half-past five the chasseurs entered the town. At 7 conflagration, looting, a fearful night. Our house saved by stability and good luck. *15th:* Marshal Lannes in billets. *16th:* Lannes gone. Immediately afterwards, Marshal Augereau. Extreme anxiety in the interval. . . . Dined with the Marshal. Several introductions. . . . *17th:* Marshal Augereau left. *18th:* Denon arrived. . . . With Denon to the Duchess. Received. Late in the evening, at Court. . . . *19th:* Wedding-day.

For just as in the past Goethe had been haunted for a year and a half by the Werther-mood—his love for Lotte, the suicide of Jerusalem—then suddenly in a flash to feel the whole experience crystallise within him and write *Werther* in the course of a few weeks . . . so now, after that night of mortal peril and rescue, he gathered into one great impulse all the wishes, all the obligations, all the inhibitions and claims which for many a long year had revolved round the question of his mistress's position—and, four days later, was married to her.

He wrote to the Court-Chaplain of Weimar:

These recent days and nights have confirmed me in a long-considered purpose—I intend that my young friend, who has done so much for me and has gone through these hours of trial by my side, shall be fully and formally recognised as my wife. . . . Please give the messenger, if he finds you, an immediate answer, and oblige. Goethe.

Was Romeo more insistent with the Friar? We know that Goethe had engraved within the wedding-ring the date of the day which had been so near to seeing the end of him and his Prince.

On the Sunday after the Battle of Jena, Goethe was married to Christiane in the vestry of the Court-chapel, in the nineteenth year of their life together; and the witnesses were their son of seventeen and his private tutor.

In that moment all the elements of Goethe's strange career seem to be shuffled together like a pack of cards—complete freedom from prejudice, swift resolve after prolonged consideration, trust and gratitude, sense of duty and self-respect prevailing over appearances and worldly advantage, world-history regarded merely from an extremely subjective standpoint—and to crown all, a Court-chapel and a private tutor. But as though nothing had happened, the relentless diary goes on:

"*19th:* Wedding-day. Denon came back from Erfurt. . . . *20th:* Showed Denon the medals. . . . Spent the day at Court. . . . In the evening at Mme. Schopenhauer's. Letter to Herr Cotta. . . ."

His attitude about his wife was uncompromising. He presented her to his intimates and business-friends with the words: "I introduce my wife to you with this testimony—that ever since she first entered my house, I have known nothing but happiness with her." And when a newspaper wrote that amid the thundering of the cannon of Jena Goethe had seen fit to marry his housekeeper, he merely sent Cotta a stiff intimation that he considered it unseemly; but in his rough draft we find these proudly indignant words:

> I am not of sufficient importance for my domestic affairs to be made the subject of a leading-article. But if there should be any suggestion of that kind, I am of opinion that my country owes it to me to take this step of mine in a serious spirit, for my life has been, and still is, lived in that spirit.

On that night of Jena, Goethe looked death in the face for the fifth time. In his youth he had felt that mystical methods had saved him; on the boat near Capri he had been the poet and the dreamer, submissive to destiny; under the hail of bullets he had felt his pulse like a scientist; on the day after the crisis of his illness he had noted "extreme danger" in his diary. On the night of Jena he had stood defenceless, as it were naked, before the drunken herald of victory, and let himself be rescued by a guardian angel of that sex which he served throughout a lifetime.

But ever and always to look death in the face—his own death or his friends'—was for him but to know renewed vitality. And now he made haste with his writings, sending enough belated manuscript for three volumes to Cotta; for "the dilatory days are over, the pleasant hours when hope tells a flattering tale of finishing one's attempts, and doing what one had only dreamed of doing."

A new tone, is it not? The malingerer, the bourgeois—over them both the ardent panting breath of hurrying life has swept; and it is as though Goethe were not referring only to his Fragments, but felt so powerful an impulse to new life and new endeavour that new masterpieces too must come of it.

The long ramble on the table-land was coming to an end. Goethe stood face to face with his grand climacteric.

PART III

TRAGIC VICTORY

"Only he who has been the most sensative can become the hardest and coldest of men, for he has to encase himself in triple steel . . . and often his coat of mail oppresses him."

CHAPTER X

EMPYREAN

"Ich weiss, dass mir nichts angehört
Als der Gedanke, der ungestört
Aus meiner Seele will fliessen,
Und jeder günstige Augenblick,
Den mich ein liebendes Geschick
Von Grund aus lässt geniessen."[1]

GREEN is the shade of the large hanging-lamp, and its light, falling on the table with its piles of books and drawings, leaves the talkers in semi-obscurity; but on the piano in the distance two wax candles sparkle, and cast a softly golden gleam upon a young girl. Who is it that she reminds one of to-day? Only of herself, of her childhood?

A delightful household, this of Frommann the erudite publisher in Jena. Here they are not for ever talking of French spies and magazine articles; here one can breathe a clearer loftier air. There is a volume of Petrarch on the table, though Frommann's great friend and adviser from Weimar is no lover of the sonnet. However, these have caught the sceptic's fancy; he examines the print, paper, and binding, turning over the leaves while his hostess pours out his tea.

Goethe, back in Jena a fortnight now, likes to spend his time here. The November evenings are getting longer and longer; the brief spell of daylight does not give him either light or air enough to make up for lost time—those few hours are too few, what with

[1] "I know that naught belongs to me
But thought, from out my spirit free
To take its flight unchidden,
And every moment sweet and fair
That fate shall fondly let me share
To full enjoyment bidden."

laboratory- and library-work and short walks with old Knebel in the morning and evening mists, for much pacing up-and-down of the little room in the Palace where he works and eats, and dictates articles, reports, letters. Comfortable eating and sleeping conditions, the charm of that affectionate spoiling to which he has been accustomed for twice ten years, the dignity of large reception-rooms, his many and various collections—all these are lacking in Jena, and yet . . . here alone is peace, is concentration; no theatre, no Court, above all, no family. If only the shortest day, that mortal enemy, were over—then one could breathe deep again and look forward to the distant spring. . . .

A soft prelude sounds from the piano. Instantly everyone stops talking, chairs are turned round—what is she going to sing? "*Der Erlkönig,*" thinks Goethe, after the first few notes, and the waves of melody envelop him in a cloud of reminiscences. Is it really twenty-five years since we were acting that comedy in Tiefurt, and Corona sang the song? Only twenty-five years—is it possible? It seems more like centuries since I was Petrarch to that lovely Laura. . . . How beautiful this girl has grown, prettier every year; a maiden in her flower, and only three or four years ago she was a short-skirted child with lanky arms. Or did she not then look as like a little grown-up girl as she now looks like a child? So spiritual, in the white gowns she always wears; and how wistfully the large dark eyes look out from the delicate pale face, appealing, expressive as the sweet low voice—but the rich luxuriance of the plaits that encircle her little head has its own tale to tell. Such lustrous black hair answers for passions which at eighteen she can know nothing of and perhaps the dainty nose will one day tilt more piquantly than now above the small faintly-tinted mouth which is opening to sing those old verses of mine? . . .

Her soul sheds no light as yet—it is like unburnished metal; but her beauty and youth suffice to stir the heart of Goethe, at fifty-nine, as it has not been stirred for twenty years. When Minna Herzlieb was only fifteen, her gentle charm had enthralled him; on her account he had spent many evenings in her foster-parents' house, a silent admirer of her childish grace.

To-night, seeing what Nature has done for her, seeing her flower as it were beneath his gaze, he knows her better; to-night,

GOETHE AT THE AGE OF SIXTY

too, Christiane is farther from his heart—moreover, in the meantime a new, a vital urgency has taken hold of him. Since those days of peril—peril in the field and peril at home; since the Schiller-period of theorising and argument, now little more than a wonderful memory, he has known physical regeneration. He has ceased to grow stout, his heart is pulsing for life, for poetry—and this girl, to-night, is as a symbol of new youth for Goethe's soul.

. . . Too late! A creature like this would look upon him as a father. Ah, why did he lead—and for so long—that empty life of theorising and wool-gathering? Other men *do* something, other men are for ever on the go; it is only our sort that sits dreaming, shaping images of beauty long gone by, possessed for how brief a space! O Epimetheus! O ever-fleeing moment!

And, saying good-night to the girl, to his hosts, he makes up his mind to avoid this house with its perilous attractions—and does henceforth absent himself, to the surprise of his friends. But he, back in his little room, cannot sleep that night. What had he better do? he asks himself over and over again, and feels shut out and old, condemned to refuse himself what he fain would venture. But in the morning—for the first time in many years, involuntarily, almost unconsciously, submissive to the Muse who will not have her prompting disobeyed . . . at last, as of old, Goethe begins a poem, and these are the first lines he sets upon the paper:

> Kindheit und Jugend, allzu glücklich preis' ich sie,
> Dass nach durchstürmter, durchgenossner Tageslust
> Behender Schlummer allgewaltig sie ergreift
> Und, jede Spur vertilgend kräft'ger Gegenwart,
> Vergangnes, Träume bildend, mischt Zukünftigem.[1]

And on the twelfth morning of his chosen remoteness from the beloved girl, he wrote nearly all we possess of *Pandora*, that most glorious of his fragments. The poet's dream of youth restored, beside the restrained and beautiful emotion of a man grown old; steadfast wisdom, hand-in-hand with passion; a smile at his own

[1] "Childhood and youth, for this I hold them blest indeed,
That after days of tumult, days of joy, outlived,
Swift slumber in its arms will take them, warm and close,
And, blotting out the present's all too potent spell,
In dreams will blend the past with days that are to come."

pain! With this work Goethe inaugurated ten years of pure music—it was the overture to a new mode of composition, a completely realised rendering of experience, after fifteen years of sterility. From the sublime background stand forth Prometheus and Epimetheus, the two brothers with their offspring; and, as ultimately in *Faust*—but more conspicuously, because the pair are so insistently contrasted—the poet here uses his passions and his inhibitions, the essential traits of his character, to construct his living, breathing figures.

Slowly from the darkness emerge the antagonistic brothers who have their abode in Goethe's breast, and who rule the two halves of the scene as they rule the two halves of his soul: Prometheus, the infinite energy—but slumbering near, the infinite imagination, Epimetheus rapt in dreams.

It is his duality, sounded upon a deep low chord in unison; and that first closing phrase can thrill us with its grave calm passion. The Dream and the Business—and resignation alone can harmonise them.

And then the girl in her white dress, with her dark eyes and hair, springs to quick life when instead of Pandora, her daughter Elpore, a vision in the father's dream, breathes in his ear:

. . . Die du verkennst und kennst, die Tochter ist's.
Epimetheus: So komm in meinem Arm!
Elpore: Bin nicht zu fassen.
Epimetheus: So küsse mich!
Elpore: Ich küsse deine Stirn
Mit leichter Lippe—Fort schon bin ich, fort.[1]

With what hesitant tenderness, here and still more in Elpore's epilogue, the poet's imagination dwells on Minna's fragile, supple form!

And then, something that had never happened before to Goethe came to pass. In the midst of his imaginative renunci-

[1] . . . "Thou knowst me not, and knowst—thy daughter I.
Epimetheus: Come then to my embrace!
Elpore: Thou couldst not grasp me.
Epimetheus: Then kiss me, child!
Elpore: A kiss upon thy brow,
So light, so fleeting—I am here no more."

ation, life knocked at the door; a Promethean virility of emotion awoke in the dreamer. It was on a morning in December that a man entered his room—a man with the face of a faun, frank and ambiguous, grotesque and romantic: the young Zacharias Werner whose plays, now being acted all over Germany, were making more of a sensation than any of Goethe's ever had. A false prophet, a deceiver of souls, himself deceived; and as Goethe found him "interesting and even lovable" because of his contradictions, he went with him next evening to his friend's house.

Werner, all nerves and vagaries, began to read passages from his own plays and poems, sonnets among them. The guests caught fire; they poetised too, till the room became the arena of a little tournament of song, under the hanging-lamp. Of course there had to be a goddess, and of course she was Minna Herzlieb. Werner, in a charade, composed a sonnet on her name.

Then, in a flash, Goethe felt the contest between admiring versifiers to be really a contest between admirers who happened to be versifying. His jealousy was twofold—and as he soon began spending his evenings in the girl's society between poesy, music, and magic-lantern shows, *Pandora* had rather a long rest. Youth and art were about him, setting his spirit free—Goethe was in love, and he was writing sonnets. His diary gives us the literary data, and shows together with the sonnets the synopsis of a love-story which lasted barely a fortnight, but left deep marks both before and behind it.

"Sonnet-fever," Goethe called this mood. Petrarch was the model, but Goethe's beloved was drawn into much more possessive arms:

> Doch wandt' ich mich hinweg, und liess sie gehen
> Und wickelte mich enger in die Falten,
> Als wollt' ich trutzend in mir selbst erwarmen—
> Und folgt' ihr doch. Sie stand. Da war's geschehen!
> In meiner Hülle konnt' ich mich nicht halten,
> Die warf ich weg—sie lag in meinen Armen." [1]

[1] "But then I turned aside, and let her go,
And pulled my cloak of white more closely round,
As if to warm my heart some other way—
Yet followed. She stood still. And it was so

Occasionally, in this garland of seventeen masterpieces (which to-day are scattered anyhow among the poems and called merely "Sonnets"), the paternal note is struck. She could have been his grandchild; that thought recurs amid all the passion.

But suddenly upon the older Goethe fell the fatality to which the younger had succumbed. That dæmon, the dreaded turmoil, upheaval, distraction of his Ego—*that* must be fled at any cost, whether it took the form of Mme. Branconi's beauty, or of a piece of work, or of a fragile girl who was half a child. On the seventeenth of December he was still with his friends, with his darling; Knebel alone knew that he would be gone on the morrow. It was a flight from Jena to-day, as thirty and forty years before it had been from Sesenheim and Leipzig, from Wetzlar and Frankfurt, and finally from Carlsbad, when he escaped to Italy. This man's life was built up on catastrophes brought about by Eros. The next day he packed his trunks and rushed away with no adieu. But now he knew better how to turn flight into victory. "Swift Parting" is the pencilled title on the manuscript of that poem, smouldering with hidden flame, which was later inserted among the collected lyrics under the colourless name of *Abschied.*

He went home, thinking, "Soon we shall be in Weimar, a Minister again, a husband and father again"—and in this mood he suddenly began to tell his travelling-companion, Riemer the secretary, all about his love for Lili! To Lili herself—so chillingly replied to a few years ago—he as suddenly, during those Jena love-days, wrote of his "infinite delight" at seeing "some lines from your dear hand, after all these years. I kiss them a thousand times in remembrance of the days which I count among the happiest of my life. Your ever affectionate Goethe." Lili's image always haunted him, whenever he felt youth pulsing in his veins.

But alas! *Pandora* became as remote from him as those early poems which had been snatched at rather than wooed. "Pandora is a darling (*herzliebes*) child," he wrote, gaily punning on Minna's name, to Knebel who had been partly confided in, and had heard the sonnets read aloud in Jena.

That hateful grew the mask; swift I unwound
And flung it from me—in my arms she lay."

But Eros had stirred in his sleep and was not soon to be lulled to rest again. Whenever Goethe succeeded (the dæmon exorcised) in linking Eros with his genius, that brighter companion of his path, everything in life and work seemed to take a happier turn. From that brief winter-love, which in true Goethean fashion was but the outbreak of an attraction felt for years, his genius evolved for him not only the drama and the sonnets, but a third work—a novel.

For in those productive December-days, which Goethe had been wont to call his hibernation, the electric experience suggested the idea of *Wahlverwandschaften* (*Elective Affinities*), first conceived as a short story. What had soared to a heaven of music in the transcendentalism of *Pandora*, in the rhapsodical fervour of the Sonnets, was in the novel devoted to an adoring portrait of Minna Herzlieb. True, no single episode in the book is faithful to the actual experience; but, as Goethe said, there is not one that *he* did not experience. When someone pestered him with questions about this story, he replied, in his character of stark materialist, that he had always written from experience, not out of the air—for "I have always held life to be more authentic than my invention"; and again in a later year-book we come upon a phrase which startles no less than it thrills us: "No one can fail to see in this novel the record of profoundly passionate suffering—a wound which winced from any healing touch, a heart for which its own recovery was something to be feared."

For Ottilie and Minna Herzlieb are one, as Werther's Lotte and Lotte Buff were one. The elusiveness, the maidenliness, the fleet sweet grace that fled yet glanced behind, the woman in the child, the child in the woman—the tremulous, instinctive warmth of Ottilie seems drawn from life, and all *was* drawn from Minna.

Charlotte too is in some respects modelled on that Charlotte whom Goethe wooed for ten long years, to possess yet unchangingly to serve, to be happy with at times and yet to suffer through. Both Charlottes are the formative influence in their circles—that wise, passionless influence of the older woman. The futile self-tormenting of this later Charlotte (and of the Princess in *Tasso* too) is wholly Charlotte von Stein's, when the woman in *Elective Affinities* says: "If we think of all the people we have seen and known, and own to ourselves how little they have been to us and we to them—we feel so sick at heart!" And the second Charlotte is again the first, when she finds the self-imposed rupture unendurable after all, and counsels Ottilie to distrust her own self-immolating heart, for "how swift, how sharp is our awakening, when we find that what we thought we could do without has never ceased to be the thing for which we really lived!" So, in Goethe's conception of her and his reminiscent sense of what she must have suffered in the past, might Frau von Stein have spoken of his return and her later reconciliation with him. But there is not a trace of their actual circumstances, nor of any posthumous apology for his long-ago invasion of the Stein household. How should there have been, when their former relation was a thing so extinct that a perfectly new one had been able to spring up between them!

The author himself does not resemble his hero, either in character or temper, as he did his Werther; for while *Werther* was a monologue, in the novel of his declining years Goethe is again, as always except in *Werther*, both hero and rival. It is true that there is little of him in the Captain, and a great deal in Edward. But the Captain's laconic hand holds the pen throughout—not that "most lovely hand" which he praises in Edward; and it is the Goethean hand which makes the Captain sketch plans, design avenues, make estimates, organise court-ceremonies, draw up rubrics—as it is with that hand, too, that finally he restrains his all too wildly pulsing heart, when he resolves that the woman and her friends shall keep their peace of mind. The author could stand before his glass and see it all—a *profil perdu* of the white-haired Goethe, for the Captain is older than his years.

And Edward younger. Here we have the adolescent Goethe's impetuous temper: "If she loves me, as I think she does, as I know she does, why does she not make up her mind, why does she not dare all, escape and fling herself into my arms? She ought to, I often think—and she could!" With one dispassionate phrase, indeed, Goethe as it were cast a protecting arm round Edward. "Edward," he wrote soon afterwards to a friend, "—he at least seems to me inestimable, because he loves with all his heart!"

And this, and nothing else, is the theme of the book—one wild-fire passion. Goethe had written nothing like it for limpidity since *Werther;* and so *Werther* is its nearest affinity, despite the world of difference in style.

The first real signal from the Muse of Goethe's rejuvenation is this—that in his sixtieth year he began and finished a work of such passionate intensity as he had not even conceived since his twenty-fifth. His over-long preoccupation with scientific research and experiment was avenged by the belated blaze which scorched him in the next ten years of his life. "Great passions are mortal illnesses. What might cure them makes them but more dangerous than before. . . . Passions are merely the enhancement of defects or qualities." Such is his commentary on his theme; and to-day we can understand neither the opinion of contemporaries, which held the book to be improper, nor that of posterity, which has explained it as an ethical defence of marriage. There had just been a great many divorces in Goethe's circle; and when he was interrogated on the subject, he gave an evasive answer.

There is no question that these words were meant to be taken seriously: "Marriage is the beginning of civilisation, and represents its highest development; it tames the wild beast in man"—but they are put into the mouth of a third party, the *raisonneur* of the book; he who utters them is neither hero nor rival. This Count, who comes butting into the quadrangle of the lonely castle from the great world without, is no lascivious stripling, no figure of caricature; he is a sage worldling, and his whole character, his whole past and present experience, go to prove that he is Goethe's mouthpiece, and not a mere *raisonneur*, when he suggests the idea of marriage on a five-yearly contract. Goethe explicitly says that Charlotte, reflecting on this pleasantry, feels it to have a profound moral significance, and merely regrets that Ottilie, in her extreme youth, should be present at such discussions.

The "election," born of the affinity and attraction between certain elements and certain human beings, is in neither instance a free electron, even though it may at first appear to be so. When passion works so imperiously in the lovers that in the arms of the unloved a child with the beloved's features is generated; when this magic law of attraction has its will with the younger pair; and when all this is prepared for by occult similarities in habits and names, dates and figures—we have the manifesto of Goethe the Materialist's revived credulity, the first signs of which were considered at the end of the preceding period.

There are certain things which Fate resolutely takes charge of. In vain do reason and virtue, duty and all things we hold sacred seek to obstruct her path; that which is right in her eyes, though not in ours, is bound to be, and so she has her way in the end, let us behave as we may!

That these are not Edward's words, but Charlotte's, the most dispassionate, the most clear-sighted of the four concerned, is a plain proof that it represents the outlook—nay, the teaching—of the whole book.

Was not this tragic sense of the inexorable utterly opposed to Goethe's distaste for tragic themes? Why shun tragedy for thirty long years, if the issue was to be a tragic novel?

We might well ask—and the whole nature of the man as it was at sixty would seem to be entirely different from that which had so lately begun to unfold in him—were not this book the first to be illuminated by that wide serenity which the end of his fifties slowly inaugurated in Goethe. It is indeed a different lightness of heart from that which gave such animation to the first part of *Wilhelm Meister*. Now it is the acquired serenity which at sixty—and in general throughout the decade from fifty-seven to sixty-six, our present theme—filled Goethe to the full. In that clearer air he soared on surer wings to ever more exalted heights; Goethe was at his zenith. This period is as well (except the years of adolescence at Strasburg and Frankfurt) the most productive which, as a poet, he enjoyed.

Goethe wrote the tragic *Elective Affinities* in the brightest weeks of summer, amid the gaieties of Carlsbad, six months after he had conceived it amid the secret agitation of those winter-evenings in Jena—finishing the first part almost as rapidly as *Werther*. And this was much more of a feat, for now he did not write in a locked room, but surrounded by women and royalties, in the whirl of adventures, driving-parties, conversations.

Here he soon found himself among women who were so happily scattered over different neighbouring spas that like a young man—though as a young man he had never done it—he could choose and alternate between them. Here, entering his sixtieth year, his mood for some months of summer was what it had never been before. For the only time in his life Goethe became the women's darling. They sent him roses, sent him their pictures, they adored and flirted with him, becoming a mistress or a tender dream.

With Minna Herzlieb, the briefly loved, the swiftly renounced, begins (for the first time in twenty years) a procession of beloved women, almost immediately after his marriage. It is as though Goethe's will-to-freedom permitted him to be constant only while he was not bound. For the space of eighteen years he had kept faith, by his own free will, with the mistress of his heart; in the first year of their regularised union he broke that faith.

Not with Bettina Brentano. This daughter of Maximiliane Laroche (with whom Goethe in his Werther-period had had a brief passionate affair, until her husband forbade him the house) came to Weimar at the time of his love for Minna Herzlieb. She was twenty-two years old; and though she chose to call herself a "child," the dates at any rate are somewhat against her. But she represents herself as being a child in appearance and feeling—and was in reality anything but naïve in every respect. With literary gifts, but not a writer; with an æsthetic cult for self-surrender, but never surrendering herself; artificial to the core, incapable of spontaneity, sensual without passion, pruriently lascivious, entirely self-centred, eternally acting up to her idea of herself, yet with nothing of the player's naïveté—Bettina is the crowning bloom in the hot-house of pseudo-Romanticism, the pattern for those countless provincial stragglers who for a century strove to be "in the movement."

She would have as little place in a Life of Goethe as she actually had in his existence, were it not that by her *Correspondence of Goethe with a Child* she distorted his image in Germany as his bitterest enemies scarce succeeded in distorting it. For it was she who set up a Goethe for the market-place, by investing that unfathomable nature with the one attribute of all others which it never possessed—sentimentality, sugariness, "hot air." It was not for some time that research proved a number of her "Goethe-letters" to be fabrications, and this discredited her on the topic for which the German nation most had cherished her—those accounts which she represented Goethe's mother as having given her of Goethe's youth, and which Goethe himself, with some hesitation, excluded from his reminiscences.

At first he good-humouredly submitted to her bombardment of declarations, letters, presents, no doubt thinking of the mother whom he once had loved, of the grandmother to whom he was attached, for during this erotic period he was inclined to be weak wherever women were concerned. But to become Goethe's beloved was what the "child" could not by any means accomplish. Very likely he saw through her from the first of her hysterical letters, for he soon wrote to Christiane, who could not bear her: "These few lines have done her more harm with me than all your and Wieland's backbiting." He called her "thou," because she implored him to; and would sometimes write: "My pretty child. . . . My little friend. . . . Thy letters remind me of the days when I was perhaps as foolish as thou art. . . . In reality one can give thee nothing, because thou wilt always get it for thyself, one way or another." When she returned to Weimar after her marriage with Achim von Arnim, Riemer gives her away to us in his account of how Goethe always changed the subject when she wanted to make love to him, pointing out the comet, for instance—"and she was baffled; the meteor with its long tail shooed off the persistent fly, the child who was a married woman (not so very young) and wanted to settle down on his knee."

At last Bettina insulted Goethe's wife in public, by the use of a coarse word. Goethe forbade her his house. But she, no longer permitted to write to him, busied herself with the sonnets to Minna (which had appeared in the interval), paraphrasing them in prose as Goethe-letters addressed to herself, so as to indicate that the Sonnets too were meant for her—even the charade upon Minna's surname. However, she was shrewd enough not to produce these documents till after Goethe's death. But he, in his very old age, when he was inclined to be indulgent to everyone, called Bettina "that troublesome gadfly."

Three or four other women occupied his thoughts during that amorous Carlsbad summer. Young and aristocratic, reserved and slender and naïve and fresh—Silvie von Ziegesar. Mature, dark and beautiful, impassioned, intellectual and experienced, the typical highly cultivated Jewess *pur sang*—Marianne von Eybenberg, born Meyer.

From this Marianne he shortly fled, leaving Carlsbad for the neighbouring Franzensbrunnen, there (as he wrote to his wife) to take the cure for gout. But with Silvie at his side he wrote to her rival, Marianne: "Why did you say, dear, that I ran away from you! In reality I was carried off and am now in custody. . . . Attraction and counter-attraction." He was quite well again, he said, and had discovered a volcanic peak which reminded him of Italy. Would she borrow some money from Riemer, "for I've run through my whole bundle of notes. And now a fond farewell for the present. . . . And write soon, dear—please, please! . . . Addio. Goethe."

Is this a white-haired, elderly man? Did his voice ever ring out so gaily in the adolescent years of perplexity? Did that heavy-laden heart ever before breathe so freely, in an air so clear? Not even in Italy!

But a few weeks later (apparently he had been bantered about her) he took a firmer tone with Marianne, and advised her "to think of him in silence, for it has come to my ears that people don't quite approve of your too flattering references to myself. So long as we ourselves know what we have in one another, it is quite enough." That is the tone of a man who has made his conquest.

Meanwhile Silvie, at Franzensbrunnen, was his star. "Daughter, mistress, darling—white and slim": so he addressed her in a long lyric written for her birthday. In the evenings he would go about alone with her, walking "in the bosket" or "behind the houses"; would read *Tasso* aloud to her, and when in a fortnight he departed, the diary notes: "With Silvie . . . for a walk. Bag packed. Beforehand! Leave-taking."

Marianne had scarcely left Carlsbad before he lost his heart to a Fräulein von Knabenau, lady-in-waiting to a Duchess who was fond of him, and beautiful like the rest. To her, as to the rest, he read aloud from his new stories and *Pandora*—and made these fair ones representatives of the parts written for the goddesses. On her departure the lady sent him a tender note in a rosy envelope. Had any women in the past done as much for the poet who did so much for women? "If you could know, dear lovely one, how delightful it is to be looked at by you (for your mirror can't tell you), you would be delighted yourself."

But one or two years later he cooled off. Marianne was too political for him; he ceased to visit the lady-in-waiting; Silvie alone, the youngest and freshest, still haunted his dreams.

Carlsbad offered him women and a great deal of gaiety. The three succeeding summer-holidays, each lasting for three or four months, saw Goethe, at sixty, for the first time immersed in that brilliant society. In his Weimar days he had shunned such circles, had hated the visits to other German Courts; in Italy he had lived like any nobody, consorting exclusively with artists; in the field he had been a silent observer. Now he was more frivolous and more inclined for the company of frivolous, fast-living, much-travelled women and men of cultivated tastes. Far from his wife and son, he lived like a fine gentleman who happened to be an author as well, with his secretary and valet; and as his work too went on wings, we can now for the first time say that—irradiated by his genius, untormented by his dæmon, loved and loving—Goethe was enjoying life.

He was quick to establish himself in Carlsbad after his usual methodical fashion, talking of his little *ménage* and determined not to seem, either to himself or others, a mere bird of passage. Hence he was always among the earliest arrivals, got up at five o'clock so as to be the first at the Pump-room and (for reasons of hygiene) in the baths; breakfasted at eight, dictated, took a walk, and spent all the afternoon in society. Feeling so well as he usually did in these days, he soon completely regained his vigour, and the cure did the rest.

Here he was not so economical as at home, for the Austrian currency, depreciated by a third, covered half his expenses. To his wife and son, and to the Princesses in Weimar into the bargain, he sent the prettiest of little presents, reflected that in the long winter at home one would want something to amuse one, and bought a tea-service, some porcelain, and some Bohemian glass. "My chief amusement is inventing everything I can think of to amuse *you*," he wrote Christiane. "For I must tell you in strict confidence that I have ordered you another fillet in old paste."

But despite all these attentions towards wife and son—how pleasant it was to be away from them!

When Christiane, from Weimar, complained of cold-shouldering, he put himself on the same level and gave tranquil advice: "Don't worry about it, and it will soon go out of your head. There are plenty of blackguards who make it their business to belittle my work, but I pay no attention, and just get on with it."

So she clung to him as her rock of refuge; and all the fun of their first years together was mingled with all the seriousness of the later developments when, between smiles and tears, she wrote him this touching appeal:

> And have that Bettina and that Frau von Eybenberg arrived in Carlsbad yet? They say here that Silvie and the Gotters are to be there too. So what will you do, between all your flirtations? Rather *too* many! But you won't forget your oldest one, will you? Think of me a little, too, sometimes. I mean to trust you absolutely, whatever people may say. For you are the only person, you know, who thinks of me at all!

Even if he had been free, such words could not but have deterred him from entering into any serious relation with a young girl—just as his marriage would not have deterred him from a separation, unless he had still cared for Christiane.

Since in these spas he sought the society of cultivated, fashionable people, he naturally consorted most with the nobility, who at that time were almost the only representatives of such a world in those watering-places. It is in this light that we should regard Goethe's increasing intercourse with people of rank, at the same time bearing in mind the heresies which for decades had kept him aloof from Court-life! Moreover, these noblemen were nearly all men who have made German history or at any rate were behind the scenes; and when we see Goethe, in his summer-sojourns, conversing with Stein, Blücher and Metternich, Lichnowsky, Liechtenstein, and Colleredo, living in constant intercourse with the ex-

King of Holland, Napoleon's brother (who had the room next to his at the hotel), and enjoying the company of Prince-Bishops and Dukes, Silesian and Polish Counts, Prussian Generals, English Peers, and *émigrés,* we must recognise that this was the way he could best hold dialogues with himself about contemporary history. For just as in Nature he could grasp none but the tangible fact, so in the "Here and Now" he had to use eyes and tongue before he could comprehend its leading figures.

There was for him a tenderer, deeper sense of this clearer air in the intercourse that for four weeks, at Teplitz, he enjoyed with the young, lovely, suffering Empress of Austria. Here he was face to face with the authentic Queen, adorned with every charm that Nature and intellect could shed; and as her life, overshadowed as it was by sorrow, gained upon his imagination, his feeling for her became tinged with something of the Tasso-sentiment which years and experience had unlearned. And this would perhaps have broken into flame had he not been able to divert it to the beautiful and intelligent Lady O'Donnell, her lady-in-waiting, and let himself go in that direction so far as befitted a courtly existence.

For the Empress, unconventional and intuitive, felt at once that he was the One and Only. Every day she begged him to read to her, secretly trying to penetrate to the arcana of poetic art; and one day she set him, with all her gracious deference, the task of making a play out of a lovers' quarrel. Goethe, the very next day, hit upon the idea of *Die Wette* (*The Wager*); on the following one he dictated the little comedy, which is far more psychological than comical, and was evidently modulated with masterly skill for a Royal audience. Perhaps he remembered that, forty years ago now, another such task had been set him, and that he had written *Clavigo* in the same spirit. Then it had been a middle-class girl, now it was an Empress, whom he obeyed; Goethe was now, as always, the one to do service. When the Empress herself achieved a little play, he actually condescended to memorise the principal part, and only the premature departure of the Court saved him from having to act it.

Goethe, in these weeks, was as lively as a young man, getting up amusements and observing with ironic complacency how his own Duke, who was sometimes of the company, looked on at his conquests. Several times he thought of going to Vienna, whither everyone was inviting him—indeed he confided to Christiane that the consequences of the Imperial intimacy were "incalculable." But after all he was rather glad of the Royalties' hasty departure, for the Imperial comedy had in the end got upon the nerves of the provincial in him, and "now, as you may suppose, it is time to have done. But as she delights in that kind of thing beyond anything and is so incredibly kind, tactful, and sympathetic, everyone does his very utmost for her."

But every thought of social ambition, everything that in hours of fatigue had influenced him for or against the Empress, vanished into nothingness when in his narrow winter-quarters at home her vision haunted him afresh. Then he complained to the beautiful lady-in-waiting that he had had to teach himself

> not to talk about our adored lady; for even the nicest people . . . don't fail to impress upon me that I am raving about her, when *I* think I am talking the plainest prose. . . . But if I am a man in a dream, I don't want to be awakened; and so I keep my distance from people who think they are looking at the truth when in reality they are only seeing the commonplace.

Even in these circles Goethe was not to be imposed upon by rank or titles. Of a certain Duke of Gotha he afterwards wrote, and wrote publicly, that "in a somewhat feeble fashion he had been good enough to be politely disagreeable."

But for all his sociability he stuck to his methodical ways, and only withdrew from the erudite Wolf, in Carlsbad, because the philologist was something of a busybody. He would spend half the day with an obscure economist from whom he could get information, and whom his diary, usually reticent about personal opinions, praises as an excellent fellow. He took six-hour walks with an old mineralogist; and had long talks, like those of thirty years ago, with Carlsbad specialists about buildings, schools, the murrain in Bohemia. He made researches into the origin of the limestone so much used in the region, calculated how the Pump-room management could afford stoppers for their bottles, made a note of a meeting at Eger with an old waiter from Erfurt, and of his driver's racy expressions on seeing a procession pass—just as he had, when a student, taken down the words used by the peasant-woman who brought eggs to his mother.

It was a refreshment after the Weimar air, which would occasionally blow over even to Jena; he said he was glad to be months "without hearing a word about German literature, and especially erudition and science, for I haven't looked at a newspaper or gone to a single theatre. It makes me feel as though I were living in an age of gold, in a paradise of innocence."

All the works belonging to that period and place are redolent of this sociable light-hearted mood, for he had never written much in the winter, and the gayer summer-weeks had nevertheless always been his best time for work. Narrative pieces were of course what now attracted him; he enjoyed playing with his characters in the lively mood which at that time possessed him; and nowhere was that easier than in the fable-like short stories, and some tales which later found a place in his *Wanderjahre*, such as *Die Neue Melusine, Die Gefährliche Wette* (*The Dangerous Wager*), *Der Mann von 50 Jahren, Das Nussbraune Mädchen.* Hence, too, the change of tone, when he told his friends thus frivolously of the arduous *Wanderjahre:* "Probably Wilhelm will come across some fine children, whom I am bringing up here and there *sub rosâ.* I particularly recommend the Nut-brown Girl, who is my pet just now. If you meet Pandora, be kind to that beloved child!"

For in the spas of Bohemia Goethe found at last that sophisticated public for whom, twenty years ago in Rome, he had resolved exclusively to write. His *Elective Affinities* he sent "really as a circular letter to my friends, so that they may give me a thought now and then in the various ends of the earth. If into the bargain the mob should read this little work, I shall not take it amiss."

Even his Theory of Colour, which on its publication at this time the specialists tried to annihilate by abuse or silence, became a craze in these circles; and Goethe, who had been adamantine in his defence of this work against the scientists, derived great amusement from the perplexity his two thick, erudite volumes caused his polite new friends.

How different is every utterance of Goethe's heart at this time—he who through decades had suffered from misanthropy and dejection, and only when certain he could not be heard, had dared to breathe one word from the depths of his being!

But the loveliest thing those days of liberty brought forth was the end of that *Pandora* which had been begun in so melancholy a November mood. Now, in the earliest weeks at Carlsbad, his miraculous phrasing drew the splendid forms out of the dark night of the spirit into the light which was their native sphere—and in the whole range of Goethe's works there is nothing of such radiant serenity as the final scenes of that fragment.

Now for the first time the Dionysian note rings out from Goethe's soul—not only in the personages, but in the rhythms and images as well. The gods, who in the *Prometheus* fragment written at twenty-five stood only for the enemies of man, here carry the whole action on their shoulders; and it is from their mouths—with all the dæmonic influences potent in the old *Prometheus* exorcised—that Goethe's resonant harmonies peal forth with such triumphant mastery.

A new voice is heard—a voice which in the early work spoke only as the prisoner at the bar, and in the beginning of *Pandora* was not audible at all. Eros, irresistibly driven onward by Helios, departs because she must; but, departing, flings this counsel backward to the Inexorable:

> Fahre wohl, du Menschenvater! Merke:
> Was zu wünschen ist, ihr unten fühlt es;
> Was zu geben sei, die wissen's droben.
> Gross beginnet ihr Titanen; aber leiten
> Zu dem ewig Guten, ewig Schönen
> Ist der Götter Werk! Die lasst gewähren![1]

Goethe so profoundly felt these concluding words to be a summary of his faith that with his dying hand he set them as an

[1] "Go thy way, Procreator! Mark me:
All desires ye know, on earth abiding;
All that shall be given, know the heaven-born.
Great, O Titans, your beginnings; but for guidance
To the eternal good, the eternal beauty,
Only gods suffice. Them suffer gladly!"

epilogue to the last volume of his collected works. Is this in truth the utterance of a vanquished Titan? If we have understood the early Prometheus-fragment—if we have understood Goethe's whole youth—in the light of an inborn dæmonic force held in check by creative genius, we shall read into these lines of his riper age no recantation, but the majestic heavenward gesture of a serene, strong-hearted man at the zenith of his career.

As one not conquered by the gods, yet sceptically clear-sighted for human values, the Goethe who could love speaks, as the old Prometheus, against his human personages, but only because in the youthful work he had trusted them too far; and he who there defiantly rejected Minerva's mediation does not bow his head to-day. But instead of Minerva's reasoned discourse—she who pleads for the gods as a mortal woman might—the voices of the gods themselves now ring in his ears, it is divine discourse to which he hearkens now, from them who are victorious without battle. Here or nowhere Goethe's poetry approaches the authentic Greek, the Mozartian, world of his adoration. Pandora herself was designed to be the fairest, purest, of incarnations. "Beauty, piety, tranquillity"—such she was to be in his synopsis for the continuation.

But then the poet laid the work aside, no doubt convinced that to pursue a work of art harmoniously for long was forbidden him, or at any rate too grudgingly conceded him, by his dæmon—and so where Pandora's voice should have sounded, Helen's takes up the tale. Goethe never did presume to make the gods he believed in his mouthpieces. Reverence and incertitude were equally opposed to that; and the music which in the last year of his life he heard and rendered back to us, was sung by mystic, not celestial, choirs. Only in *Pandora* did his genius thrust its brow against the cloudless vault of sunlit heaven.

And so—he himself did not understand his poem! Only as a mystery, he wrote, could it affect the reader, inspiring him with sympathy or repelling him, without his being able to say why. Three years afterwards—no more—he stood amazed at his own creations. But when it was suggested that he should complete the work, his answer was this dark saying—that whenever he tried to lift his most precious things they always fell from his hands;

so he soon ceased to look at those glowing embers, and then they went out.

Weimar and even Jena, whither he always had to return for the winter from these pleasant sojourns, would have depressed him even though the days had not been short and cold. He had taught himself, true master of the art of living, to keep the fires of his temperament alight through the long winter.

His first proof of that mastery was frequent separation, prolonged as far as might be, from his family with whom he was on the best of terms, though he could not live for any length of time too close at hand. By now he had familiarised Christiane with Jena, where she made friends; and they played a regular game of exchanging quarters, for when he left Jena for home with his secretary, she generally had to decamp from the house in Weimar with the companion whom he had engaged for the sake of appearances, and that she might have someone to amuse her. The end of it was that the companion and the secretary (Riemer) got married. This arrangement soon went on wheels; no one was injured, no one put out: "This makes it so that on Thursdays you will find the coast clear, have all your comforts, while we shall gain our few hours in Weimar—so everyone gets something out of it."

Certainly Christiane kept much of what he first had loved in her, even now at the end of her forties. A bust at Weimar shows her to have still been beautiful, something in the style of a Roman Empress; and a year after their tardy marriage, she and he still talked of "our bedroom" when at home. But she was growing fat; and as she was full-blooded and moreover danced too much and took a good deal of wine, she fell into bad health and had to take cures, in the very years when Goethe had grown slender again and felt so rejuvenated. It is a kind of symbol of their evolution—they were both young and slim when they first met, and then (in every sense of the word) expanded; but now their physical constitutions, temperaments, energies, habits, and desires led them on totally different paths. "I don't feel strong enough to stand joys and sorrows as I used to do"—so Christiane complained from time to time, while Goethe gained in vigour every day.

She remained as deferential, grateful, housewifely as ever; and as Privy Councillor's wife and Her Excellency she was indefatigable for humbler folk. She was glad that her visits to Court were so few and far between; indeed it was Goethe who now insisted on her going into society—and in that he made a mistake. He bade her pay calls on the Weimar ladies "even if only for a quarter-of-an-hour"; he had to insist on her looking up certain people when she was in Frankfurt, and this called forth the only command which we find in a correspondence of thirty years: "It is my wish. You know I never like to say 'my will.'"

For their circles differed more than they themselves did. If she did not care to associate with his friends, he was still less attracted by hers. And her craze for dancing, which he had looked upon indulgently when she was in her thirties, now began to be a little ridiculous by reason of her corpulence. When at forty-three she was again having dancing-lessons, and would take the three-hours' journey to Jena for the sake of a ball, always with students and officers, the town began to talk and say that the ladies of Goethe's household were like vultures haunting the Army. He gently warned her, but gave no commands. "Only don't let yourself be tempted by a ball which I am told they are going to have here on Thursday. I could not bear to encounter you in the Mühltal."

Though the increasing fastness and unhealthiness of Christiane's life made no difference in her affection and gratitude, there was less attention to his little fads—he had more frequently and more urgently to remind her of his carefully-numbered commissions, "so that they mayn't all come pouring in at once and create confusion, as unfortunately has been the case before now"; he had to entreat her "most pressingly" to forward his standing-orders of joints and wines to Jena; and now it was he who kept her in mind of the garden and remembered about planting and watering, for she had ceased to do much with her own hands. If she neglected to write to him in his solitude at Jena—for Minna Herzlieb was away, perhaps by some secret arrangement—he warned her, half in fun: "You should remember that flirtations are hanging fire, but may have to be resorted to if you are quite so neglectful. With this threat I make my very fond farewell."

And so, with long intervals of separation, their happy relations continued undisturbed, though not seldom there were sharp encounters. Two years after their marriage the Duchess, at a masquerade, at last permitted Goethe's wife to be introduced to her. An hour later, Christiane was seen with her party, "making a great noise in the supper-room, everyone half-seas over, champagne flowing, corks popping, ladies squeaking, and Goethe standing in a corner, silent and stern." Among a hundred malignant reports, so exaggerated as to be their own refutation, this one seems to bear the stamp of truth, for it comes from a woman-friend—and it shows Goethe in a position which one knows not whether to call merely painful, or tragic. In such moments he needed all his kindness to forgive his wife for being what she was; for, as he put it about this time in *Elective Affinities*, "the most enlightened of men has no better opportunity of displaying his equanimity" than in marriage.

Goethe's sense of estrangement from his son kept pace with the boy's growth, and here there was no former depth of feeling to supply what the present lacked. Of the boy he had sometimes had hopes; in the student he could not but perceive that talent of any kind was completely absent; and the one thing he prized in his son was at best pedantry, showing itself to the third generation in tidiness about letters and pocket-books.

Otherwise the lad at seventeen was a conceited youth, alternating between apathy and unruliness, to whom his father, in his first term at college, had to shout "Don't go mooning about the place," and whom he held to be a sponge upon his mother. For the rest August could hunt, wear ever-new waistcoats, insist upon having silk stockings, solicit his father for new pistols and an expensive sword, though he was not at any time an officer.

Cool and friendly are the letters to this son, quite impersonal, often uninteresting. Goethe never used, either in the text or the signature, the word Father. Any attempt at improving him was kindly made; he wasted his energy in explaining to August why he kept him on a small allowance, or would like him to devote a little more time to his letters, so that they might be legible.

Either the boy's pernicious tendencies were as yet undeveloped, or Goethe's paternal vigilance was insufficient to discern the dangers attendant on August's inadequacy. The one hope seemed to be—find him a safe position!

So Goethe wrote a begging-letter to the Duke, asking that his son should be officially appointed to an assessorship,

> for which both father and son herewith most humbly apply to Your Royal Highness. Neither will fail to testify, by assiduous attention to their duties, how deep is their sense of the inestimable value of Your Royal Highness's gracious interest and most flattering confidence.

Never before had Goethe taken so obsequious a tone with any man alive. To Princes and Emperors he had used the ceremonial phrases of compliment, but had always treated the essential matter with manly self-respect. It is painful to think of his now having to adopt, in a son's interest, so servile a manner—he, the prince of German authors, friend of this Duke and of his House, whom he had served for more than thirty years as Minister!

It is as though he could not transgress against his own decree of personal aloofness without injury to his dignity. He had never had the sense of inherited family-obligations. From one decade to another he had left his mother unvisited; and when she now died, in Goethe's sixtieth year (he having seen her for the last time in his forty-eighth) the event is just mentioned in two of his letters, and in his year-book briefly alluded to.

And it was likewise with his own son. August, the sole survivor of five children, had only for a few years of his boyhood been near to his father's heart. Goethe's work and temperament had caused him to keep as aloof from his parents and from his child as if they had been strangers.

Nevertheless he looked carefully after their interests, whenever that was in his power. When Cotta—as his contract permitted—wanted to produce a new pocket-edition, Goethe protested in one of those letters, as friendly as they were business-like, which had been his resource in the old days of stress with the Duke. His household (he said) were horrified at the idea, which in case of his death would be injurious to their interests. "I feel very much of a stranger to myself, when I use the word 'advantage.' . . . And yet I must think of these things, unless, after a laborious and frugal existence, I want to be in debt when I leave the stage."

After this highly coloured picture, he threatened not to go on with his biography unless he was paid two thousand thalers for every volume, and concluded with "Yours, in esteem and confidence." When finally it came to a new contract for a second edition of the works in twenty volumes, for which he demanded sixteen thousand thalers, he pointed out the usefulness of the biography in drawing attention to the new edition.

He consented to let the Mannheim theatre produce the remodelled *Götz* only on condition that the receipts of every third performance should be guaranteed as a "benefit" for the author. He expected neither pleasure nor profit from the drama: "I much prefer novel-writing, for everything that in the theatre is against the author is to his advantage in the novel."

His inheritance on his mother's death—a half share of what his father had left, amassed entirely by his grandfather, the Goethe who had been a ladies' tailor—amounted nominally to about fifty thousand marks, but the war had greatly depreciated its value. This was all that, beyond his wide education, Goethe inherited from his forebears, and it came to him in the sixtieth year of his life, when he no longer needed it.

As Christiane's energy and interest diminished, Goethe, finding that in this period of literary activity he had more free time, and being in a good-humoured frame of mind, himself did a good deal more about the place. There are many letters about a juniper-tree which had been broken in a storm; he brought all sorts of things home from his travels, including even a chest which contained a thousand corks, and wrote the following international-provincial note:

> The French Emperor has not yet got through. . . . Herewith I send a quantity of mignonette-seed, and a very little pansy-seed, because it is rare. So have the place under the stone . . . well weeded . . . and sow it at wide intervals with the pansies.

He twice lodged a semi-official representation about a skittle-ground in his neighbourhood; and the functionary who received it may, if he was a reader of *Faust*, have similingly remembered Wagner at the city-gate, when he read Goethe's ground of complaint: "It may seem to be no more than a slight concussion . . . but the noise is quite as tiresome as if it were louder."

Goethe stayed at home a good deal. He rarely went out to dinner, often to tea, but to the house that had of late been so frequently shut up, guests now came in throngs. At early noon and evening, during the winter, friends and new acquaintances would be received in Goethe's sitting-room, the most welcome being young Countesses or beautiful actresses; and so this most sociable period of his life resembled, in Goethe's old age, the youth of Wilhelm Meister—his intercourse was with the aristocracy and the stage. His old friends were dead, it is true, but it is also true that Goethe did not want old people about him—he wanted youth and pretty women. Knebel was the only survivor of the early days; Goethe and he had again drawn very near to one another after Schiller's death.

Charlotte von Stein, now approaching seventy, continued to receive frequent visits from Goethe, and letters which were full of significance for her, though almost impersonal and supposed to be read by the ladies of the Court as well. Charlotte declared that she disliked meeting Christiane; "but as he is very fond of the creature, I don't mind it now and again, if he likes." Twenty years after their rupture—her hatred was undying! But Goethe, on his side, confided to Christiane that he never could feel sure of Charlotte; and once, writing of a woman-friend that she was charming but that one always felt depressed after being with her, he added as if to make his meaning clear: "Just as it is at Ackerwand"—where Frau von Stein lived.

On the other hand, a new friend had during the last decade won Goethe's heart through their artistic sympathy. If Meyer, his practical expert on the plastic arts, had become his bosom-friend—taciturn, zealous, kindly—and was to remain so to the end, Zelter was from this time forward his trusted adviser in musical matters, likewise taciturn, zealous, and practical, and, likewise, so to remain. These two specialists, whom Goethe discovered—one at forty, the other at fifty—and drew into his circle, became (quite apart from their artistic functions) the friends and brothers of his heart.

To Zelter, who surpassed Meyer in temperamental gifts, Goethe was personally attracted by his North-German quickness and energy, his virile intelligence, independent career, and (as with Meyer) absolutely unselfish devotion to art. For in both men love of art was more marked than talent—Meyer being a great connoisseur and æsthete with little gift for painting, and Zelter an agreeable composer with remarkable musical insight and untiring energy in the performance of great works. Both men—like Schiller, about ten years younger than Goethe—were "thorough," genuine and unpretentious, practical and downright; they did not seek out Goethe, he discovered them. Their portraits speak for them. In Meyer's contemplative nature there was something of Goethe's Epimetheus; he compared the enterprising Zelter to his Prometheus. This pair, who came to him from the world without, but whom he resolutely drew into the closest intimacy, may be likened to the pair who dwelt in Goethe's inmost self, and so constantly appeared in his literary work. In that sense, these two last of his friends are, once more, symbols of his polarity.

From Zelter's first visit, he was Goethe's priest and devotee. "I thank God hourly with a humble heart that I have seen your face at last." And Goethe, too, instantly appreciated him: "There is something positively Promethean about the sort of man you are, something that I can only wonder at and revere. . . . All good to you, dear sun, and go on with your work of warming and enlightening us." When Zelter, later on, wrote to tell of his step-son's suicide, Goethe began his answer with a rush of spontaneous affection:

> Thy letter, my beloved friend . . . has grieved me to the heart, nay, crushed me, for it found me in a mood of very serious contemplation of existence. . . . Thou hast answered to Death's probing touch with a note of golden purity, refined in the crucible.

For forty years Goethe had never offered himself in brotherhood to any man. In this instance his heart cried out—the heart to which nothing in the world was so comprehensible as unsullied, steadfast character. This longest of Goethe's correspondences was at first of a purely practical nature; Zelter became as it were his ambassador in Berlin, and everything that in these years tended to promulgate the Goethean spirit there was the result of Zelter's propaganda.

Zelter showed Goethe the way in musical matters, but it was not he who first aroused his interest in them. Goethe had found and grappled to himself Herder, Charlotte, Schiller, Meyer, when they were necessary to him as exponents of the things he sought to make his own—and in the same way he now felt the need of musical knowledge and grasped at Zelter's aid. For this is, in a dual sense, Goethe's musical decade. Like mysticism, music had never been absent from his life; but in his middle period both had been obscured, for in that phase of sententious materialism his impetus had been towards active work and scientific research rather than towards the things of art and literature.

Now he was constructing a world for himself in this region of the mind, and it was to be both school and social centre. Following Zelter's example, he got up a little Choral Society, which for several winters assembled every Thursday evening in his house for practice, and on Sunday forenoons would perform before an invited company.

Moreover, he wrote a quantity of convivial songs for music, which Zelter set for his Berlin choir, and someone else would more or less improvise for the gatherings at Goethe's house. So through the rooms the *Ergo Bibamus* would peal, and the humanist took heart again—Goethe's resonant bass could even be heard among the singers.

At the same time he steeped himself in the study of counterpoint, and was combative about the theory of the origin of minor modes or the exclusive right of the diatonic to be called the normal scale. He even thought of writing a book upon acoustics, and drew up a detailed synopsis for it. And one morning in Carlsbad, Goethe—sixty-four, all alone and palpitating—seized on a sheet of music-paper and there set down an arrangement for four voices of the *In te Domine speravi*, afterwards comparing it with one he had got Zelter to make, so as "to be once for all convinced of my own delusion."

Even if we knew nothing of Goethe's love for music, his attitude towards Mozart would suffice to show how authentic was his taste. He had deeply studied Mozart at Weimar and constantly produced his operas; in his declining years he frequently ranked him with Raphael and Napoleon; and in two utterances of his middle period he put his finger on the point where Goethe and

Mozart part company—*Faust* could only have been set to music in the manner of *Don Giovanni*, but *Don Giovanni* "stands by itself, and when Mozart died, all hope of anything resembling it was at an end."

It might have been supposed that Goethe had nothing to do but sample the talents of young composers, from the quantity of packets which at this and subsequent periods were sent him by unknown musicians, whose veneration had an eye upon the advantage of a word of praise from Goethe. When, among the many, Schubert's *Lieder* arrived, it was an evil fate which made even the appealing letter of the unknown composer powerless to induce Goethe to open the packet. Of other masters, all were either dead or unborn—except one, the sole contemporary who was of equal stature with the older Goethe. With him he did make acquaintance, and him he recognised for what he was.

Fatality—in that it was not the younger Goethe! For when in the whole history of the arts would two great spirits have been more profoundly in sympathy than Goethe and Beethoven, had they but met in their tempestuous dæmonic periods! When the older Goethe dreamed of *Faust* with accompanying music in the style of *Don Giovanni*, it was of Beethoven as the nearest approach to Mozart that he longingly thought for the composer. When the original draft of *Faust* was being written, the young poet would have wanted the most undiluted, the most un-Mozartian Beethoven for his rhythms and visions. Beethoven was closely akin to the Goethe of the most German, the most Herculean of the poet's phases; and indeed Beethoven *had* been deeply stirred by *Egmont*, the work which casts so clear a retrospective light upon that period. But as it was, Beethoven at forty, with the stormy splendour of his work and his untamed personality, encountered a Goethe of sixty-two, who after decades of struggle had risen to the heaven of his *Pandora*, and was just at the beginning of his loftiest and serenest epoch.

Everything that Goethe's genius had wrested from his dæmon, after a lifetime of warfare, was arraigned when Beethoven's ravaged countenance, Beethoven's sombre accents, met his eyes and ears; and if that encounter had taken place in the heart of the vast labyrinth which was Goethe's middle-period, he would menacingly have bid the stranger:—"Go—nor invade my magic circle!" The chaos from which he had so painfully emerged, the Promethean battle which he had left behind him, Goethe saw revived for his imagination in Beethoven; his own youth, so pitilessly and so long reviled, arose from its grave. And because it was only now, a conqueror at the zenith of his career, to light and to serenity at last attained, that he met the other great dæmonic being, Goethe could comprehend him. Before this period, he would never have sat down beside Beethoven's piano; now he felt armed at all points against any and every tempter. During Goethe's most Mozartian phase he came in contact with Beethoven—hence his admiration, hence his imperfect sympathy.

It was in Teplitz during his daily intercourse with the Empress, surrounded by potentates and pretty women, as excited as a boy, as a poet, could be, yet weighing and calculating possibilities like an old man, like a worldling—it was there and then that he encountered Beethoven, and spent three or four afternoons and evenings in his company, visiting him, driving out with him, hearing him play.

We seem to see the two. In a small ill-furnished lodging-house apartment, Goethe—just come from the Empress, looking young and handsome, serener and richer now, intrepid and emancipated, lord of life, master of his dæmon—sits at a wretched piano alone with a man devastated, pallid, ill, and very hard of hearing; alone with Beethoven, whose fingers are rushing headlong over the keys. It is a summer-evening, and the candles are flickering. . . . When at last he goes, Goethe feels stirred to the depths: "He played magnificently. . . . I have never beheld so concentrated, so powerful, so intense an artist!" Never before or afterwards did Goethe use such words about a musician.

When, later, his own sphere was invaded by that strange elementary force, he was conscious of a certain aloofness. In Beethoven's settings of his lyrics he sometimes felt that he had been misrepresented, here by amplification, there by contraction, of his meaning; the rendering was seldom exactly true—but always he would declare: "Beethoven has done wonders with it."

Yet none the less Beethoven's temper and attitude were

inevitably alien to Goethe. "His talent has utterly amazed me"—so he wrote to Zelter—"but unfortunately his is a most savage personality. Certainly he is not entirely to be blamed if he finds the world a detestable place, but the effect is none the less disadvantageous both for himself and others." Beethoven's deafness (he said) was as regrettable as it was injurious to himself, for he was laconic anyhow, and the deafness made him doubly so. Beethoven saw it in the same light. "What patience the great man has had with me! What good he has done me!" But on the other hand, this: "The Court-atmosphere suits Goethe too well—better than it ought to suit such a poet." This accusation of worldliness, common to everyone about everyone else, may be regarded as merely symbolic of that difference in their spiritual evolution which could not but keep them apart.

Eleven years afterwards, Beethoven sent a subscription-list to the Courts and the rich patrons of art in Germany, for the publication of his great Mass; and with his petition to Goethe wrote these words, so moving in their reticence:

> I have written a great deal, it is true, but have gained almost nothing. But now I am no longer alone; for more than six years now I have been father to my late brother's son. . . . A few words from you would make me very happy.

When this letter from the ageing Beethoven reached Weimar, Goethe (who was then seventy-four) was so seriously ill that two doctors had given him up.

Fatality, this also—which to the deaf impoverished genius closed such a source of spiritual and temporal succour; for those were years in which Goethe's soul would assuredly have responded to him who so could render suffering and strife. A short time before, Beethoven, when someone suggested his writing music for *Faust*, had exclaimed, with arms raised to heaven: "That *would* be worth while—I could do something with that! But I have had three works in hand for some time now. . . . When they are done, I'll have a try at *Faust* at last!"

It was the same with Kleist. In a purely dynamic sense his period of *Sturm und Drang* had had an esoteric affinity with that of the young Goethe; but the strain of intense morbidity in Kleist was strongly opposed to the pantheistic outlook of Goethe's riper years. Goethe did not depreciate Kleist's talent; he merely disliked its tendency. His own endeavour was to render the antique in terms of modernity: in *Amphitryon* it seemed to him that the two worlds were, artistically speaking, poles apart. In the *Zerbrochene Krug* (*The Broken Jug*) he saw extraordinary beauties; but when *Penthesilea* appeared, Goethe must have felt that the whole of his antique world was menaced by Romanticism! Long afterwards he said:

That poet aroused in me, for all my genuine desire to enter into his mind, a frequent sense of horror and repulsion, as might a body which Nature had intended to be beautiful, but which was in the grip of an incurable disease.

Previously, however, he had managed so to shake off this after-growth of repulsion that he could examine it dispassionately, for:

Mit den edlen, lebendigen Neuen
Mag ich wetteifernd mich erfreuen.[1]

Goethe's arduous endeavour to enter into the minds of those who were his very antipodes went on for years; and if he was first attracted and then repelled by the Romantic School, that fact has no bearing upon his own development. Goethe was the great Unromantic all his life long, yet in the previous period he had gone some way with the Schlegels, with Tieck, and even with Jean Paul—and in the same spirit he now went some way with Zacharias Werner.

That "remarkable man" had originally fascinated Goethe by the sparks he could strike from the Jena circle; perhaps he felt some secret gratitude to him for having made his affection for Minna Herzlieb break into flower from the bud so long closed. But the element in Werner which derived both from heaven and hell, the faith which illuminated that faun-like face of his, was his

[1] "With proud new life, in young hearts beating,
I love to feel myself competing."

chief attraction for Goethe, recalling as it did, though at an infinite distance, Merck, the friend of his youth.

Goethe thought highly of Werner's gifts, and when he was taken to task for this, he wrote:

> Wie doch, betrügerischer Wicht,
> Verträgst du dich mit Allen!—
> Ich leugne die Talente nicht
> Wenn sie mir auch missfallen.[1]

But if pure poetry was in question, he would stand no nonsense; and when Werner one evening at Goethe's produced a sonnet in which the moon was compared to the Host, all Goethe's suppressed hostility suddenly broke its bonds—he flamed forth, he lost his temper, declaring that he hated that kind of perverted religiosity and would never countenance it. "You have spoilt my dinner for me—you have made me forget myself before these ladies!" Werner turned pale and said not a word; and Goethe soon left the room, in search of composure. Later, Werner wrote from Rome to say that Ottilie's self-sacrifice (in *Elective Affinities*) had made him feel inclined to turn Catholic. This time Goethe answered with good-humoured amusement, but there was a touch of *Götz's* mailed-fist when he added: "But don't, I beg of you, strew any allusions to the crown of thorns before my feet!"

In that scene at the dinner table Goethe quite literally turned his back upon the Romantic School. For the thing of all others that he, so rigorous with himself as he was, must have detested in the young Romantics was their fatal facility, their pride in being chaotic, their affected serenity so different from that of Mozart, who, just because he was unromantic, knew real serenity of soul. "There are plenty of people who know what they want to do, only they would like to stroll up to it, quite casually."

Those are not the words of a worshipper of strict form, from which indeed at that time Goethe tended to depart; they are an expression of the anger aroused by such self-conscious ranters in

[1] "But what a humbug you must be
To get on with so many!—
Because a talent mayn't please me,
I don't deny there's any!"

a strong spirit, whose aim it was to shape, though in obedience to them both, his life and art.

It was the pretentiousness of the Romantics that, after such a fight for life as his had been, he could not away with—their arrogance, and their self-seeking too. And they, who had begun by adoring him, fell upon him tooth and nail when he would no longer be called their champion.

They admit that we have influence; to insight they lay sole claim; and to use the former to the latter's advantage is their hidden purpose. Real belief in us is no part of their programme. I do not blame them, but neither do I choose to live in a fool's paradise, or to support uncongenial views against my own conviction.

Even in Friedrich Schlegel, whose intellect he never ceased to admire, the apostolic attitude annoyed him. Goethe thought his conversion an instructive example of how the highest endowments of reason and talent, if their possessor persistently plays the Veiled Prophet, will end in the hocus-pocus of the magician's cave.

Their next move was towards Brahminism—a good advertisement; and what at the outset of the rococo-period had been a slender flame now smouldered as on altars of sacrifice. And Goethe sardonically looked on, and grew but the more trenchant in his repudiation of their mysticism as his own welled ever more crystalline from the depths of his being! The old man rejuvenated might well have felt himself a pagan in presence of these Christians; yet, none the less, from the altar of Goethe's life the great sacrificial flame rose in august solemnity, and with scarce-concealed arrogance he declared, heroically prophetic, that a century would elapse before their grandchildren and great-grandchildren would find pleasure or profit in his works.

In so exalted a frame of mind, the importunate daily round could be more easily endured than in the years when a gigantic resolve to learn and to achieve had often run its head against the limitations of a Saxon Duchy. By this time he had lived so long in the neighbourhood of a Court that his attitude was like that of an enlightened scion of nobility, to whom that life is inevitable, in the nature of things—it can scarcely even be called resignation. In such a place he did not propose to do very much, but he had ceased to be resentful of it.

The Duke saw less and less of him. "It will be a great pleasure to me," wrote Goethe to the Duchess, "to pay my tribute in his Residency, though it be but for a few days, to that admirable ruler to whom, with equal confidence and affection, I have dedicated my existence." A singularly grandiloquent sort of compliment to the friend of his youth, now returning from the war! And much the same tone, though a trifle more cordial, marked Goethe's first use of the new title when at the Congress of Vienna he congratulated Carl August on having been promoted to the rank of Grand-Duke.

For the finishing-touch had been put to their estrangement by Carl August's supplementary spouse. She was that actress Jagemann whom we have glanced at; and with her increasing influence over the Duke, she was trying to undermine Goethe's already diminishing authority at the Theatre. She set herself to gain complete control over the repertory, the assignment of parts, the appointments to all offices.

Christiane's idea of separating the operatic and dramatic sides was adopted; and in one of the lengthy memorials which Goethe composed at this crisis, he embodied his views in this despotic formula: "Privy-Councillor von Goethe has sole and unlimited control over the artistic arrangements connected with dramatic performances"; and he made it very clear that "artistic arrangements" was to be construed in the widest possible sense. This he called his ultimatum, and would hear of no exceptions. The Duchess finally smoothed matters over, and Goethe made the mistake of sticking to his managerial position.

Of yore the various threads, so flexible at first, had indeed grown refractory to the pattern, but would still obey the weaver's hand in some degree. Now they were hopelessly entangled—and it is tragi-comical to observe how the straightforward, steadfast Carl August contended against Goethe, not about constitutional matters but those very theatrical affairs in which he had never aspired to any special knowledge; and how behind their broad backs two women, each an upstart mistress, skirmished with one another—till in the end a third, the dispassionate secluded Duchess, had to call a truce!

But Goethe, though vexed and wounded, managed not to lose sight of the ideal pursued throughout all the strange vicissitudes of his existence; and every one of his personal frustrations seems to have been dismissed from his mind when at this time he said in confidence to a friend: "The Duke is of that primal dæmonic breed whose inflexible natures have something of the quality of granite—they can neither bend nor be destroyed. He will always come unscathed out of every peril." In those manful measured words he seems to epitomise his whole relation to the Duke; and if we are as conscious as he was of all the restrictions and contentions upon which they shed so illuminating a gleam—a gleam which twenty years of the unknown future were to see still flickering as from a smoky torch . . . we are also conscious that here for the first time, so far as that relation goes, we see Goethe as it were in equilibrium between his youth and his old age.

For now, at sixty, he was mature and serene enough to look indulgently upon his youth. With ironic detachment he contemplated, from his heights, those distracted aberrations; and reflecting, found the lines which best epitomise them:

> Du hast an schönen Tagen,
> Dich manchmal abgequält?—
> Ich habe mich nie verrechnet,
> Aber oft verzählt![1]

As before, the entrance upon a new decade was surrounded by symbolism. On the threshold of his thirties he "had been conscious of strange emotions"; and so it was now on his sixtieth birthday, with its challenge to a retrospective survey. Very likely he recalled, that day, the serious-minded thirtieth anniversary, when he and the Court had paid tribute to the pleasure-loving Duke in verses and festivities; or the fortieth, with no one to cheer his loneliness but the young pagan mistress, already carrying under her heart the first of his sons; or the fiftieth, when the old

[1] "Wert many a day tormented,
Though heavenly-blue the sky?—
I never summed up wrongly,
But often paid too high!"

garden had seen Proteus follow with his telescope the moon as she went up to the sky. And on that morning, surely he must have passed in review the works of each decade, with last year's achievement bringing up the rear? First had come *Iphigenie,* then the Roman Elegies; next, from this æsthetic *quod-libet,* the Ballads rose to memory—and to-day *Elective Affinities* was nearly ready for the printers.

Surrounded by the things he loved, warmed by the affection of his friends, unperturbed by official duties, Court, and renown, he was sitting on that August morning in the garden at Jena between old Knebel and his pretty wife—when lo and behold! a carriage with Christiane inside, and Christiane had brought three young actresses along with her, thinking that, whatever else might be afoot, Goethe would be sure to enjoy feeling young on his sixtieth birthday.

Directly after this day, when the last touch had but just been put to the novel, Goethe—heretofore so chary of touching old documents, and never unless for an *auto-da-fé*—began to look up his old diaries and, as the cold weather began, to dig himself in like a hibernating animal among his Tales of a Grandfather. It was not long before the impulse to shape and form was stirred by the scope and novelty of this task; and in sweeping outlines—as when he had thought of writing the history of Duke Bernhard of Weimar—he now laid out the ground for his own biography.

But as he prepared himself to write the history of a human being, and contemplated the young man with whom he should have to begin, it came over him "how one may seem more worth while when one is shallow, crude, and undeveloped than when one encounters one's-self in one's abundance, elaboration, and accomplishment!" This is the first time that the older Goethe ever gave expression to a kind of envy for the dæmonic genius of his early days, as he looked down upon him from the altitudes of his serenity.

The portraiture is so intimate, so penetrating, so entirely free from any tinge of complacency, that the later sub-title, *Dichtung und Wahrheit,* is not to be construed as the mental reservation of an author paltering with the truth. By *Dichtung* he undoubtedly meant no more than the "re-modelling" indispensable to a survey of such distant years. The actual facts (not only about the period but about Goethe himself) are at first touched with a gingerly hand; but gradually they assume more prominence, so much so that the book must be regarded, in its most interesting chapters, as a source-work of the first importance.

Whenever he was hampered by regard for persons still surviving, Goethe preferred silence to tactful evasions. Though the world was agog for revelations about the *Werther* episode, he chose to ignore his Wetzlar novel rather than give pain to Lotte Kestner, now widowed and living in Hanover; and in his generalised portrait of her, the one intimate allusion he permitted himself was this enchanting turn of phrase: "Lotte—for I think she would like me to call her so. . . ."

Friederike was able to read her story just before she died. But when Lili's moment came, he found that no consideration for her could persuade him either to ignore or to throw a veil over that most sovereign of his passions—and at this stage he suddenly interrupted the narrative, to resume it at a point after the death of Lili many years later. His mother, for whose delineation he had been supplied with material by Bettina, he preferred (when it came to transcribing these notes) to leave unsentimentalised; hence we have only one or two allusions which would have been a great disappointment to her, had she ever read them.

He found it easier to deal with the friends of his youth. Most of them—Behrisch, Salzmann, Lenz, Merck, Lavater, Herder—were dead; Jacobi is most fondly portrayed; and Klinger at this time received a cordial letter from Goethe: "Life is just like the Sibylline Books—the nearer to its close, the more precious. Farewell; and remember me, as in the beginning and the middle, so to the end!"

What grateful tributes he could pay to his old friends, ignoring any estrangements there might have been, is shown by the votive-tablets to Lavater and Herder, here as it were propped against the mighty tree that was his life.

But what sort of picture does he draw of himself? His diary at the moment of beginning the book has these deep sayings, an open sesame to the student of that spirit:

Ironical view of life in the higher sense, by means of which biography assumes a superiority over life. Superstitious outlook, whereby again one stands back from life. By the former method the intellect and the reason—by the latter the sensibilities and the imagination—are indulged. . . . Physiology lies at the heart of it all. Physiological, and pathological too, as for example in the passages relating to organic Nature. . . . This to be carefully distinguished from any definitely morbific state of mind. . . . Anyone writing a self-confession runs great risk of falling into melancholy, for one is owning up to the morbific, the peccant, side of one's nature, and is never at liberty to confess to one's virtues.

That seems to be a revelation of something far transcending a biographical method. Was not the form taken by Goethe's whole life the outcome of an objective survey and a superstitiously-conceived endeavour, and did not the individual thereby sublimate his experience, yet find himself perpetually drawn back to it by imagination and sensibility? In this programme for the delineation of a life we have, besides, the programme for that life itself.

At the same time, it is all a well-considered manipulation. Such writings should not be too serious (so he admonished himself); one should give them a certain special kind of wings—for with this book Goethe desired, for the first time in his life, to gain popularity. While

all my earlier works were written for myself because I wanted to write them, so that in that way I could afford to wait a dozen years or more for many of them to gain acceptance . . . with this work I want . . . to please my fellow-countrymen, but especially my friends.

No work of Goethe's, with the exceptions of *Werther* and *Hermann*, won such instant popularity as *Dichtung und Wahrheit.* The book laid the foundation for the renown of his old age; and, as he had foreseen, aroused interest in many of his earlier achievements, which were regarded as fragmentary renderings of this whole. All the world was eagerly awaiting a continuation.

But if anyone is curious about what the author kept in the background of his ironic *dĕcor*, let him turn to the sketches for this work; and there he will find himself staring at these tremendous words:

My life one long adventure. Not the adventure of striving to bring to perfection what Nature had implanted in me. Endeavour to acquire that which she had *not*. Tendencies as often right as wrong. Thence perpetual torment bereft of any genuine enjoyment.

So did Goethe, even in his serenest phase, hold commune with himself, surveying that vast Titanic wayfaring of whose aberrations his biographical confession says in so many words that it does not represent more than "the thousandth part."

In like manner, the third masterpiece completed and published by Goethe in this epoch of four masterpieces—the *Theory of Colour*—is in its best portions an outcome of the same spiritual temper. What at forty he had begun in a manner purposely dry-as-dust, he now at sixty actually thought of turning into a novel! And now, too, he took to satirising his colour-antagonists in rhyme; and it was in this humorous vein that he first epitomised the affinity between himself and his Theory, the reason why he was so devoted to it. The polarity of light—that was it; and he found a far-reaching symbol to express it:

Armer Tobis, tappst am Stabe
Siebenfarbiger Dröseleien,
Kannst dich jener Himmelsgabe
Reinen Lichtes nicht erfreuen;
Nicht erlustigen dich im Schatten,
Wo mit urgebotner Liebe
Licht und Finsterniss sich gatten,
Zu verherrlichen die Trübe.[1]

Then the colours are marshalled as in a grand march-past, each with its own emblem; and it is then too that the exultant reverence he felt for Nature takes chiselled form in these splendid words: "The eye owes its very existence to light. From inert

[1] "Still to fumble colours seven,
Hapless Tobit, art thou bidden,
Light, pure light, that gift of Heaven,
From thine eye for ever hidden?
Mayst thou never bend, elated,
O'er the nuptial couch primeval,
Where the light and darkness, mated,
Glorify the gloom coeval?"

animal ancillary organs light evokes an organ which shall become light; and so the eye learns to give light for light, emitting an internal ray to encounter that from without."

And now, obedient to the scheme of his psychical evolution, Goethe the scientist turned from materialism to symbolism. It is marvellous—the synchronisation, the ubiquitous unfolding, in that nature whose growth was so akin to Nature's own, of the blossom upon every branch in his old age. If it was one and the same Goethe who in his life and his work, in Nature-study and art-criticism, had moved by the light of reason throughout twenty years, so now it was one and the same Goethe who, living and writing, criticising and investigating, grappled the universe to himself, to contemplate it with trustful vision, irradiate it with symbolic truth, adore it with tender irony. Goethe's research had fused with Goethe's faith.

More and more symbolic grew his ideas about Nature—more and more do such passages in his letters and conversations recall Leonardo's day-books. His was the recondite suggestion that animals and plants, which in their ultimate phases would be scarce distinguishable from one another, might conceivably be evolved from the primal state—plants by concealment from light, animals by extreme exposure to it. He closed an argument with chemists with the observation that for the lower organisms a terminology typical of the higher would become the usage; and "it will go so far that for the more advanced intellects mechanical and atomic demonstrations will be entirely supplanted, all phenomena appearing as dynamic and chemical; and in this way the divine principle in Nature will become more and more clearly evidenced."

All this led to the most astonishing changes of front. He who had always looked askance at astronomy and mathematics as too abstract for him, holding aloof from stars and numbers in a heresy of superterrestrial conviction, now lauded astronomy as the one science which proceeded from accepted data to certain and illimitable conclusions. "Divided by continents and oceans, astronomers, most gregarious of recluses, have all the elements of their science in common, and so they can build as on the solid rock." His principal quarrel with Newton had been for the inconclusiveness of his experiments, as contrasted with the radiant clarity of Goethe's own Promethean vision. But now to Schopenhauer, Kant's young follower, with whom Goethe was arguing his colour-theory, he exclaimed in words of flame: "What? You affirm that light exists but by virtue of your perception? Never! You would not be there at all, if light did not perceive you!"

And now it was that such lines as these could say the last word for him:

> Was wär ein Gott, der nur von aussen stiesse,
> Im Kreis das All am Finger laufen liesse!
> Ihm ziemt's, die Welt im Innern zu bewegen,
> Natur in sich, sich in Natur zu hegen,
> So dass, was in ihm lebt und webt und ist,
> Nie seine Kraft, nie seinen Geist vermisst.[1]

Henceforth his intellect is as a mighty river in full spate. One almost shrinks from any detailed treatment of the features in a portrait of such majestic unity. Goethe's faith, as it was at sixty, had been foreshadowed in his scientific work, and was inevitably constructed out of identical elements.

> For an old pagan like me, it is a very strange experience to see the Cross erected upon my own territory [the reference is to Werner] . . . and yet it is not entirely repugnant to me. . . . It ought by this time to be just what I should like—to live and die the last of the pagans. . . . For myself, so variously constituted as I am, I can never be satisfied with only one way of thinking; as a writer and artist I am polytheistic, while as a scientist I am pantheistic, and both with equal conviction. If, as a moral being, I wanted a personal God, that God would assuredly be forthcoming.

There we have the formula for the creed of Goethe's earlier old age, and for its evolution.

[1] "A God who in external force consisteth,
One who the All around his finger twisteth!
Nay— he is blent with every cosmic motion,
Nature and he so fused in deep devotion
That all which lives and moves and is in him,
His energy, his mind, fill to the brim."

It was only in opposition to the pretensions of Christian belief that he professed so primitive a paganism. In his moments of deepest insight Goethe was now drawing near to the mystical temper of the antique faiths, in consonance with the more and more mystical bent of his scientific research. The metamorphosis of plants and a belief in the Eternal Return are only two forms of the same spiritual perception; and one day, in a dialectical correspondence with an intimate, he wrote down this most amazing scheme, as his "general confession of faith":

(a) Nature contains all that the Ego contains.
(y) and something more.
(b) The Ego contains all that there is in Nature.
(z) and something more.
b can perceive *a;* but *y* can only be surmised through *z.*

With such a sense of what Nature stands for, is it surprising that he now turned again to the study of the mystics and alchemists, the Kabbala, and Pico della Mirandola, re-established a Masonic Lodge which had been closed for twenty-five years, and even drew an occasional horoscope?

He said at this time that man was irresistibly impelled to take refuge in the unconscious, for in that he was rooted; at another time he called his own works "Vestiges from a former existence"; on a third occasion these ironic words fell from his lips: "I often seem to myself like a magic oyster, washed over by mysterious waves of ocean."

Emotions such as these proceeded from and contributed to a wonderful serenity of mind. The conflicting voices in his soul were better harmonised—but neither was yet silenced.

In these years, he found endless new ways of expressing the polarity in the universe and in himself:

There are two worlds. When one of them is angry the other does not ask why. . . . For a God and for a dumb animal dispassionateness is the supreme condition; hatred and love, victory or death, dominion or subjection—these are only for men. . . . As if overstrain, illness, were not likewise conditions of Nature! So-called health can only consist in an equilibrium of contending forces.

Goethe had now, after a lifetime of spiritual conflicts, attained to a kind of glad security. His dæmon was quiescent, in these years, as never before or afterwards it had been or was to be; and the love which he extended to the world and man was a universal, all-embracing love. It was the Eros of a Goethe grown old—and thus a manifestation different in kind from that of the earlier period. One mark was a patience with all and sundry, which had hitherto been foreign to him; and it was now that the philosopher could say: "All the world over there are plenty of poor devils, each more or less panic-stricken. Others, who have known what it is to be like them, look on at their antics in a spirit of forbearance." And again: "Hatred is like an illness—like the *Miserere*, turned the wrong way round."

This was an Eros which armed him with a steel so true that none could pierce his breast. The transition between his moods of grave serenity and sportive ease was as subtle as ever. One day he would declare that even joyous music could induce melancholy; the next he would enjoy hearing his acquaintances caricatured upon the piano. His heart held the balance true. "It is no effort to me to be indulgent, for my harshness and severity are only factitious—only bluff." One might quote as many as two dozen aphorisms which give expression to this temper:

> Lass nur die Sorge sein,
> Das gibt sich alles schon;
> Und fällt der Himmel ein,
> Kommt doch eine Lerche davon.[1]

All burdens weighed light upon him now. Problems were wrestling-bouts, contentions games of skill. Goethe's most strenuous hours were bright with a clear radiance hitherto unknown. And we listen, open-eyed, to utterances wherein he seems eager to shed a retrospective stream of gaiety even upon the times gone by:

[1] "Abide the hour, for all
Is but a passing thing;
And should the heavens fall,
A lark will earthward wing."

I want to get as much fun as possible out of everything I do. . . In my youth I did that, unconsciously; and now I propose to do it, consciously, for the rest of my life. Useful? I leave that to you! *You* can use me, if you like; but I can't consent to do anything "on sale or return." . . . I don't hand myself over as a tool, and all professionalism means being a tool—or if you prefer a more flattering word, an organ.

Had such insight as this taken less than a generation to visit him, how much he might have spared himself! And yet it was because nothing was spared him that such spiritual conquest could be his in his old age. For how organic, in its slow gestation, was the change in Goethe! Only in that light can we comprehend how the sombre misanthropic seeker after truth could now sing thus:

> Gibt's ein Gespräch, wenn wir uns nicht belügen,
> Mehr oder weniger versteckt?
> So ein Ragout von Wahrheit und von Lügen,
> Das ist die Köcherei, die mir am besten schmeckt.[1]

In truth, it was the Goethe of sixty and sixty-five—and that Goethe alone—who could get anywhere near such a degree of harmony, the utmost ever permitted to his antithetical nature. The dæmon was at his feet for once, if only slumbering—that dæmon which had always hitherto disturbed the joys of equilibrium.

All this is to be read in Goethe's face—so much younger-looking, so much handsomer. On a spring day in his sixtieth year the poet, Count Baudissin, saw him for the first time, and says:

I swear that I have never seen a handsomer man of sixty. Brow, nose, and eyes are those of the Olympian Jupiter, and the eyes absolutely unpaintable and incomparable. At first I could do no more than feast my own upon the beautiful features and the magnificent olive complexion; but afterwards, when he began to tell stories and gesticulate, those two black suns seemed to be twice the size, and they

[1] "Is there a language, sometimes apprehended,
A chiaroscuro—or is this but dream?
Such a ragout, of truth and untruth blended,
Were the concoction I should best esteem."

gleamed and sparkled so divinely that I can't imagine how anyone can face their lightning when he is angry. . . . He has got rid of his former corpulence, and his figure is now faultless in its symmetry. . . . In conversation his gestures are full of fire, and exquisitely graceful. . . . He speaks low, but with a voice of splendid quality, and neither too fast nor too slow. And the way he enters a room, the way he stands and walks! He is one of the born Kings of the world.

From the mask at fifty-eight, the voice would come upon a darker key. Here the discords in the head, re-echoing those in the soul, are not refined away into beauty. The features are still immobile, as in a plaster cast; the asymmetry in the two sides of the face is conspicuous. But the lofty brow bears marks of anguish, graven by the tool of destiny; the great eyes have widened thus in their unresting watch for the true faith, the dignity in that strong virile nose is his own work. The lips droop at the corners; and though they can smile, the smile is no Olympian gift—it is the conquest of a mortal man.

Such had Goethe become, in body and soul—to such a degree of harmony had he pressed on, when two events befell him, which are the mountain-peaks in this second half of his life.

At this time he encountered Napoleon and Hafiz.

As powerful as the influence of sex upon kindred natures, mutually drawing them together in a relation which has something both of hate and love, is that of genius upon genius. The craving to behold himself as in a glass will ever urge the genius towards his compeer—only, like any other creature, eventually to find the way back to his native solitude; for self-love, vigilance, distrust keep him continually, warily, poised as it were on one foot for flight. To seek and fear his kind, then, is for the dæmonic being, solitary as the genius is, a natural process. Goethe, in whom both types were included, had spent more than forty years in a vain quest—and yet, with his venerative instinct, felt but the more intimately drawn towards his great contemporaries.

It was chiefly the work of destiny, but also the result of his chosen remoteness from artistic life, that the few by whom he could have measured himself had eluded him. He had missed meeting Lessing and Winckelmann in Leipzig; Voltaire had left Switzerland when Goethe visited it; Klopstock he remembered as a dignified man of the world with whom he had spent a few hours; Herder had always done everything he could to spoil his own effect; Goethe had seen through Wieland at a glance. With Schiller the case was so complicated that friendship had been difficult to bring to birth at all; and their gifts being as little akin as their natures, theirs was an artistic alliance rather than a mutual flame of genius. He never met the great German thinkers, for Kant never left his eastern town, to which Goethe was as little attracted as to Kant himself; Schelling and Hegel were, among other things, too young to set a standard for Goethe. And Mozart, whom as a boy he had listened to on the piano, came too soon for him, as Beethoven came too late.

Men of action would have made a deeper impression on this man of action; especially because, as a writer, he always longed to behold the kind of man whose prototype in history and legend he sought to portray. Frederick the Great was an old man when Goethe came to Potsdam. But even through the absurdities of his courtiers Goethe had been able to divine the spirit of "old Fritz," though by mysterious dispensation he was absent at the time of Goethe's visit. Romantic natures in men of action were always unattractive to the Goethe of the middle and later periods, and so Louis Ferdinand had left no lasting impression upon his observant eye. But there was one thing which might have challenged his attention, and possibly have taken him by storm—the atmosphere of Paris in those years of the 'nineties; and above all Mirabeau, whose mind was adored by Goethe's friends—and his busts as well. But inner conflicts, such as we have indicated in an earlier chapter, had kept Goethe out of Paris; and even if he had visited the city, there would have been certain inhibitions to overcome—inhibitions of which he, as a Conservative and a teacher, was always conscious with an orator so alien in spirit from himself.

But when General Bonaparte came upon the scene Goethe was instantly captivated—though his temper forbade him any great admiration of warlike deeds, and even in Cæsar and Frederick he esteemed the monarch rather than the General.

But as the years revealed Bonaparte's enterprise in all its vastness—as a host of anecdotes, inspired both by love and hatred, showed forth the antique valour, the downright forthright grip, the ineffable range and latitude—in short, the mighty dæmon in the little man who at thirty-five, a lawyer's son and a lieutenant, stood in possession of the Kingdoms of the earth . . . then Goethe forgot the anarchical beginnings of that towering flight, forgot as if they had never been the weeks of the campaign in which he had suffered with his countrymen for the restoration of the Bourbons; and could forgive this latter-day hero the Revolution, nay, could feel it to be retrospectively justified by genius such as this. From the Day of Austerlitz he called him "my Emperor."

Goethe, who had never striven for authority, loved authority and hated anarchy. Nothing more clearly demonstrates how sublimely he conceived of the hero's part in history, how wholeheartedly he could relinquish the traditional order in favour of the heaven-sent genius, than this enthusiasm for the greatest "self-made man," besides himself, to whom the age had given birth. It was the impossible which came to pass when this Saxon Minister, this member of a vanquished nation, this poet, felt that in France, in the conqueror, in the great man of action, the electric spark in him had met its answering spark—that he had found, as in a brother, here at last the elements which were his own twin elements, the Genius and the Dæmon.

> We forswear the prodigious as long as we can, and maintain a wilful blindness to the elements of which it is composed. But when one listens to an unsophisticated description of this Emperor and his environment, one cannot but perceive that there never has been, and probably never will be, anything like it. . . . His legend reminds one of nothing so much as the Revelation of St. John. Everyone feels that there is a quality in it which he cannot define.

When on one occasion the talk turned upon genius and morality, Goethe declared that such figures transcended the moral law, and were like natural phenomena such as water and fire; for a God could only be measured by the stature of a God.

"Napoleon combines the most contradictory characteristics

—his love of the miraculous really belongs to the poet; his delight in overcoming difficulties to the mathematician."

There we have Napoleon's character in outline, and from that outline Goethe's eye could logically deduce his downfall; for what could ever have overthrown him save the inordinate preponderance of his imaginative over his mathematical faculties, as typified in that Alexander-like Eastern campaign, the first to be based on erroneous calculations?

But this is yet another indication of their spiritual affinity—for what else could have so complicated, so destroyed the blissful harmony of Goethe's existence as did that very play of inborn energies, taking shape in ever-renewed attempts at the consummation of a life of action, forcibly discriminated from that of the imagination? Napoleon, pointed by destiny to the deed, was doomed to fall if ever he should trust his dream; Goethe, pointed by genius to the embodiment of his dreams, must wait for victory till he should sacrifice the deed to the poet's dream. Precisely at the dividing-line between these two courses—Goethe at the zenith of his attainment, Napoleon immediately before his tragic error—the two men met for a brief hour, mutually to gaze in one another's starry countenance.

Goethe, when this hour came, was in his sixtieth, Napoleon in his fortieth, year. Five years earlier, Napoleon would have been disappointed to behold a fat Goethe—Goethe to behold a fat Napoleon. For both it was the propitious moment.

When, since Socrates had sat with Alcibiades at the Symposium, since Seneca had given counsel to his Emperor, had one speck of space, one little room, enclosed two human beings of such self-acquired authority? Was this really possible, so recently as in the days of our grandparents—that two men should, in the course of a few decades, have made themselves legendary figures, have shaped spiritual dynasties—that two sons of the bourgeoisie, born as it were invisibly among a thousand more in the street of a town like any other town, should in that space of time have raised their mothers to such rank that one reigned as Empress-Mother at the Tuileries, and the other could enter a drawing-room on the majestic words: "*Je suis la mère de Goethe*"!

When at the end of September, 1808, Napoleon came to Erfurt before the Spanish campaign, he was at the zenith of his fame. Four kings and thirty-four reigning princes were there assembled to do honour to the parvenu.

Those days found him inwardly in a state of extreme tension; he felt that he was at the apex of his powers, yet some dæmonic presentiment seemed already to warn him of the end. How else can we explain the uneasiness which just then assailed him concerning the alliance with Russia? "If Alexander is as friendly to me as you suppose," he said to Talleyrand, who has recorded the interview in his Memoirs, "why is he taking so long to sign the Alliance?" He walked up and down the room excitedly: "Do you know why nobody will join in with my luck, why everybody hesitates? Because I have no children, and they all think it will come to an end with me! It is unfortunate for the world—and we must alter it some day."

With the Tsar, who travelled by way of Weimar, Carl August too came to Erfurt, bringing an immense retinue. Goethe alone held aloof. Everything, it would seem, ought to have attracted him to Erfurt in the mundane phase through which he then was passing. Did he fear reality, with its grand disillusionment? Did he wish to be personally summoned? When after a few days he *was* summoned, but only by his own ruler, he hesitated long; and it was only Christiane's sure instinct which could persuade him to take the short journey.

He came into such a medley of diplomats, soldiers, and courtiers of every nation as he had never beheld till then. On his second evening he made the Minister Maret's acquaintance at a tea-party. Next day, Maret told the Emperor that Goethe was in the town. Instantly he was summoned to an audience.

I am summoned to the Emperor's private room. At the same moment Daru is announced, and at once admitted. I hesitate on that account. But am again summoned. I enter. The Emperor is seated at breakfast before a large round table; at his right, somewhat removed from the table, stands Talleyrand, Daru a little nearer on his left. . . . The Emperor beckons me closer. I remain standing at a respectful distance. He looks at me attentively, and says: "*Vous êtes un homme!*"

SILHOUETTE OF GOETHE AT THE AGE OF SIXTY-TWO

I bow profoundly.
"How old are you?"
"Sixty years old."
"You are well preserved. You are, I know, the chief dramatic poet of Germany."

Goethe demurs, and alludes to Schiller and Lessing. All Napoleon knows of Schiller is his *Thirty Years' War*, which is not to the Emperor's taste. Goethe defends Schiller. Napoleon changes the subject, and asks if "the academicians" in Weimar get on well together. Goethe points to Wieland as the most renowned. Napoleon requests that he be asked to Erfurt.

Then Daru takes up the tale. He sings Goethe's praises, as he has heard them sung in Berlin, alludes to his translations from the French, particularly Voltaire's *Mahomet.*

I will at once inquire [says the Emperor] whether we can have the play acted here. You ought to hear it in the French, but it is not a good piece; and very convincingly shows how unfitting it is to make a world-conqueror reveal himself in so unfavourable a light.

Then he touches upon *Werther*, which he has read seven times and had even taken with him to Egypt. He makes various comments (which Goethe afterwards described as very just) and then His Imperial Majesty says:

"*Je n'aime pas la fin de votre roman.*"

"*Je ne croyais pas que Votre Majesté aimât que les romans aient une fin.*"

Upon this, the Emperor puts forward his objection to Werther's ambition having been used to bring about the *dénouement:* "That is not natural, and weakens the reader's impression of the overwhelming influence which love had had upon Werther. Why did you do it?"

Goethe laughs—as he affirmed in two of his letters (or as his more considered narrative, written much later, has it: "I smiled"); and answers that though certainly no one has ever before taxed him with that error, he thinks the Emperor perfectly right, and must confess that there *is* something not quite authentic about that passage. But is there not some excuse for the artist if he resorts to artifice for producing certain effects which could not be achieved by simple natural means?

The Emperor seemed to take that for an answer; he recurred to the drama and made several very interesting remarks which showed that he scrutinises the tragic theatre much as a judge's keen eye does the evidence in a criminal case, and has been much exercised by the absence of spontaneity and authenticity in the French theatre. In the same way, he disapproves of the drama of fatality, and said that it belongs to the dark ages:

"What is fatality to us of to-day? Policy is Destiny for us."

Then he turned again to Daru, and continued their discussion of war-contributions. Goethe withdrew into an embrasure, and looking round the room, recognised Berthier and Savary. Soon big, long-haired Marshal Soult came in with a report upon Poland.

Then "the Emperor stood up, marched straight at me, and cut me off, by a sort of military manœuvre, from the rest of the row I was standing in. Turning his back on them all and addressing me in a low voice, he asked me if I was married, had any children," and so on. Then he inquired if Goethe was enjoying himself in Erfurt.

"Very much, and I hope these days are going to be of service to our little land."

"Are your people contented?"

"I hope and believe they are."

"Monsieur Göt, you ought to stay here the whole time, so as to describe the effect of this great spectacle upon your mind."

"I should need the pen of a classical author for that . . ."

"Your Duke has invited me to Weimar. He was rather badly-behaved for a while, but he has got over that."

"If he was badly-behaved, Sire, he was pretty well punished for it—but perhaps I ought not to offer an opinion upon these matters. At all events, none of us can refuse him our admiration."

For the third time the Emperor recurred to the tragic drama.

It should be a school for Kings and peoples. That is the highest service a dramatist can render. You ought to write a play on the death of Cæsar, as it should be written—a finer thing than Voltaire's. *Ce travail pourrait devenir la principale tâche de votre vie. Dans cette tragédie il faudrait montrer au monde, comme César aurait pu faire le bonheur de l'humanité, si on lui avait laissé le temps d'exécuter ses vastes plans. Venez à Paris! Je l'exige de vous!*[1] .

Then he invited Goethe to the theatre that evening, when he would find several ruling monarchs among the audience.

"Do you know the Prince-Primate? Well, you will see him to-night, slumbering on the King of Württemberg's shoulder. Have you met the Russian Emperor? You ought to dedicate something about Erfurt to him!"

"I have never done anything like that without regretting it."

"Our great writers thought differently, under Louis XIV."

"Doubtless, Sire; but we cannot be certain that they never regretted it."

Goethe always answered

quite naturally. The Emperor seemed to like it, and translated it into his own phraseology, but rather differently from what I could have permitted myself to say. . . . He seldom listens quite passively; either he nods thoughtfully or says "*Oui*" or "*C'est bien*" . . . and would usually add, "*Qu'en dit Monsieur Göt?*"

And then I seized an opportunity to ask the Chamberlain by a gesture if I might take leave, on which he nodded, and I immediately did so.

This audience, granted to one another by Goethe and Napoleon, lasted more than an hour.

In that hour the two minds recognised each other. Napoleon expressed this after his laconic fashion in the three words with which he received Goethe, and which probably were not "*Vous êtes un homme*," but (as Riemer reports them) "*Voilà un homme!*"; and in another way by silently accepting Goethe's championship of the Duke. But above all—how could he have paid a higher compliment to a German dramatist than by requesting him to take a theme of Voltaire's and do better with it, instead of lauding the French school as something from which the

[1] "Such a work might become the principal task of your life. In that tragedy, you should show the world that Cæsar might have made the happiness of humanity, if he had been given time to carry out his vast plans. Come to Paris! I insist upon your coming!"

vanquished *ignorami* might learn their business! Indeed he frankly decried the French theatre as false and artificial—and here we may remind ourselves that after all it was not a Frenchman who spoke, and that it was easier for Goethe to get on with this half-Italian. Finally the Emperor invited a German to Paris, there to write for his Imperial Theatre; and as Napoleon must have known what an insult this would have been to the poets of his nation, we cannot but ask ourselves: "What was at the bottom of it all?"

The theatrical programme for the Erfurt sojourn gives us our answer. When Napoleon insisted upon the significance of the tragic drama, he meant every word he said. He had made a thorough study of it; as a young man he had written for the stage. Amid all the business of state, he had carefully chosen the pieces to be acted during these few days, and they were designed to give food for reflection to his royal guests. For "policy is Destiny for us." When Talleyrand had contrived, with a great deal of trouble, to get Goethe a good seat—the whole of the front row being reserved for crowned heads, and the second for Crown-Princes—Goethe could listen to many a vicarious expression of His Imperial Majesty's mind. On the first evening, in *Mithridate*, Napoleon's hatred for England found voice "by command"; on the second, in Racine's *Iphigénie*, Talma, by the same Imperial behest, delivered the lines in which the self-made man is glorified. But when finally, in *Mahomet*, one of the prophet's devotees exclaimed:

> Qui l'a fait roi? Qui l'a couronné? La victoire!

Goethe could see all eyes turn to the Imperial box, and when Omar went on to proclaim:

> Au nom du conquérant et du triomphateur
> Il veut joindre le nom du pacificateur,

Napoleon, from his place, indicated by a gesture that that was his intention also.

At such moments Goethe must have felt what a tribute had been paid him by the conqueror of the world when Napoleon asked *him* to proclaim the greatness of Cæsar, and hence Napoleon's own. Never—since his youthful days—had Goethe, now sixty, been stirred by any definitely national enthusiasm; and now he was called upon to forget his nationality and give expression to an enthusiasm which had for years possessed him. The Roman note was struck in Goethe's soul—it was as though Cæsar and the antique world had taken shape before his eyes.

And, thus ranked above Voltaire, must he not have seen himself as the avenger of the German school to which his youthful writings had belonged—the school which Frederick the Great had contemned, when he summoned Voltaire to Potsdam? Did it not appear as a grand belated vindication of the German *Sturm und Drang*, when the master of the world selected just this Goethe, out of all other poets, to summon to Versailles? Goethe might well have felt the laurels of the rhapsodists, of Homer, on his brow when Fortune chose this amplest, this serenest epoch of his life to favour him in such a sort. As the poet pure and simple—as what he had now at last perceived himself to be—he was challenged to stand forth by the Lord of Europe, to whom he had never paid tribute by so much as a single word.

Indeed, he had entered the Emperor's private room as one armed for defence; and though in all his movements—as he walked, stood, bowed—he had held himself as befitted a man of the world, his general tone towards the Emperor had been less complaisant than the Emperor's towards him.

For Goethe and for Weimar the after-effects of those days were far-reaching. "Napoleon is our patron saint," wrote Voigt, the Minister of State. Weimar was exempted from active service, Jena was indemnified, Wieland excelled himself in courtly paradox, calling Napoleon the mildest, most unassuming man in the world. Goethe was enraptured with Talma; and the Imperial delegate, appointed to the surveillance of Prussian espionage in Weimar, translated *Faust* into French.

But why did not Goethe go to Paris?

The idea long occupied his mind; he made repeated inquiries about the expenses and necessary arrangements. Yet he never once went even to Vienna—he no longer felt any need to go there. To see Italy with his own eyes had been his heart's desire, because the Southern element in his soul demanded its long-delayed sustenance. But what did he want with Paris? At thirty-seven he had irresistibly fled "over the hills and far away"; but at sixty he smiled—and stayed at home.

What we might call Goethe's unhappy love for Germany was never put to a severer test than in the years when he saw his fellow-countrymen—of whom he would fain have been prouder—thrall to the hero's hand, yet at the same time "bucked-up" as never before. Goethe's affectionate scepticism about the Germans is explicable when we consider his temperament and his experience. After a short-lived phase of fanaticism, fostered by youthful revolt against French domination in the frontier-provinces—after an infatuation, lasting for years, for German Gothic, German landscape, German chivalry, Goethe at twenty-five had found and encouraged in himself a somewhat crude and confused, but gradually more purposeful (and at thirty challengingly emphatic) dislike for the climate and scenery, the history, policy, and temper of his native land. This he developed into a reasoned and systematic antagonism, which every fibre of his being helped to intensify.

When, in his adolescence, he had ardently surveyed the boundless universe from behind the mask of Faust; when three times he had stood upon the Gothard Pass to look down longingly on Italy; when in the Trentino, just below the Pass, he had felt as if new-born, or amid the world-convulsions had lamented that he was not a son of England, free from the first drawing of his breath; when, a South-German, he made lifelong moan over Thuringia's ruder winters; when he envied Voltaire and Rousseau, Tasso and Ariosto, because their voices were the voices of their land; when as his own Wilhelm Meister he took refuge with the strolling players from provincial heavy-handedness; when he immersed himself in classic art, to paint more radiant gods, more radiant men beneath a bluer sky; when Schiller, in that first letter, showed him what endless circumlocutions might have been spared him had he been of Italian birth . . . always it was the old, the Faustean, cry, embodying itself in Goethe's craving for beauty and warmth, for air and liberty. It was the German, the Hohenstaufen, spirit, winging from Mainz to Palermo, the Isle of the Blest. It is—it ever is—the dark, the cloud-encompassed dæmon of the North, glad thrall to him of the radiant South.

And yet, throughout his eighty years, he hardly ever left that German land, and came back sooner than he need have come from his one great Southern pilgrimage—just as the German Emperors were perpetually drawn from Palermo to the Rhine. And yet, again, his mind had from decade to decade steeped itself afresh in study of the magician-doctor whose shadow had loomed upon the pathway taken by his adolescent feet, and never left him till he stood before the Gate of Transformation. A Northern poet, whose delight was in Southern themes—and whose masterpiece could scarce have been more Northern in conception!

It was because he loved it and would fain have been afar from it, because he could cast his German skin and yet could never long be absent from his land, that Goethe rebuked Germany more severely and more affectionately than ever a German had done before him. But the marked neglect shown by his fellow-countrymen, of which he could not but be conscious, necessarily embittered his attitude. He was filled with an anger which, humanly speaking, was more than justified—if, in a metaphysical light, unreasonable—when he beheld the sudden right-about turn of his compatriots, who had for two brief moments sung the praises of two superficial adolescent works. How could he have divined, at that time, that the people had shown a sure instinct in abandoning the poet who was tentatively abandoning them! And how could they, in their turn, have then divined that he was the elect who should lift them, and the tongue in which he wrote, to loftier planes of life and art?

No one can say whether Germany was first to turn its back on Goethe, or he on it. For Goethe's growing resistance to the Northern side of himself inevitably tended to make Northern themes distasteful to him, and thus brought about the isolation and oblivion which could not fail to wound his spirit. One thing is certain—that Germany, simpler, cruder, more prosaic (as the great public must always be), loved its poet little from his thirtieth to his sixtieth year; while its poet, subtler, deeper, and kinder, none the less loved Germany throughout, though to his sovereign eye her soul lay bare.

Banal, at any time, to inquire of creed or patriotism—frivolous, and worse than frivolous, when concerned with a spirit so eminently German as to create a new language for his nation. Of this, in his last years, he would say, with the greatest modesty, that at best he might be said to have surpassed Luther in subtlety, now and then!

What, then, could the French mean to Goethe! Their Emperor (in whom, besides, he felt the Southern strain) was in his view a timeless, raceless portent—the object of a purely personal adoration as creative energy incarnate.

And when it came to the subjection of Germany, Goethe was not only possessed by a vague instinct that the issue would be salutary, but was intellectually convinced that Germany deserved her fate.

At Jena German power went to the devil because the Germans had no initiative . . . Germany is naught, but the individual German is much—although they like to believe the opposite. The Germans will have to be, like the Jews, uprooted and dispersed the world over, before all the good which is in them and which would work towards the well-being of all nations, can be brought out. . . . "Many men, many minds"— that may be called the motto of our nation. . . . They have a bad habit of undoing their best work by inordinate demands, though mediocrity is their native sphere. . . . I am so sick of the imbecility at present displayed in every department that even in their distress the Germans strike me as ludicrous, for their despair arises simply from the fact that an end has been put to their bungling methods. . . . These fools of Germans keep up an outcry against egotism—would to God that long ago there *had* been some frank solicitude for their own and their families' interests! Things would look very different if it had been . . . . Though the Germans are not materialistic in tendency, it is none the less difficult to move them to an ideal end.

Countless similar judgments are to be found in Goethe's confidential letters and conversations during the most distressful years, and nothing could be less like the voice of a poet. Rather might we think to be listening to that of a relegated statesman. He who thus speaks is a statesman in voluntary retirement; and through the larger indignation we can catch the echoes of the vast disillusionment he had suffered, thirty years before, during his own endeavour in a small German enclave. But later too, when the country had raised its head again, Goethe—untroubled by the apparent change of view—epitomised his fondly critical perception of the German people in one of his most penetrating deliverances, when he refused to be instrumental in founding a German Literary Association.

> I am afraid that now as of yore they will misjudge, undervalue, hinder, retard, persecute, and injure one another. . . . This habit is the less likely to be shed because it derives from a superiority . . . which is, that perhaps no other nation is wont to have so many eminent men contemporaneously living within its borders. But now observe this. Each individual among these remarkable men finds it as much as he can do to develop himself to the full; hence it ensues that since the German takes nothing for granted and is given (though without at all resembling a butterfly) to perpetual transmutations, he goes through such a series of metamorphoses, not to say stages of evolution, as the most faithful of historians is unable to keep track of. . . . Everyone who is conscious of his own individuality begins from the very beginning, all over again—and who is without his right to such self-consciousness? . . . Well, then, as this heterogeneity must in the immediate future steadily increase, while . . . on the other hand the great mass of those whose soldierly activities effected the salutary change have an unquestionable right to *their* opinions, simply because they have got something done—the conflict cannot fail to grow fiercer and fiercer, and the Germans be more than ever split up into very small parties, if indeed they do not fall into complete anarchy.

The Jeremiads over "Germany destroyed" drove him to utter despair, for deeply though he sympathised with the private sorrows caused by the war, and anxious as he was to console the sufferers, it was irksome to be obliged to conceal his impatience, "when people whine about an entity which was doomed to destruction, whose birth no living man had seen, nor ever cared twopence about."

His vision grew more and more catholic. He was emphatic in repudiating the mass-sentiment of hatred for the enemy. The only vital question for him was Civilisation or Barbarianism; and he owed much to French civilisation.

In Goethe's words, war is a disease in which the forces useful for recovery and health are dissipated in the service of something alien and abnormal. He was soon to learn, too, from the narrative of a cavalry-officer, that the soldier "speaks more rationally and temperately of the whole thing than the entire pack of do-nothing Philistine onlookers"; and he exclaimed to those who stuck it out at home:

> Nicht grössern Vorteil wüsst' ich zu nennen,
> Als des Feindes Verdienst erkennen.[1]

For everything tended to make that spirit, strenuously seeking to outsoar the temporal and the national, inimical to race-enmity; everything inevitably made him the friend of international friendships.

> Our life [he said immediately after Jena] does not point us to isolation and separation from other nations, but rather to the utmost possible degree of intercourse. Our civic existence is not like that of the ancient world. On the one hand, we are much more emancipated, more unconventionalised, and less one-sided in our views than they of antiquity; and on the other the State makes no such claims as would oblige us jealously to maintain, on its behalf and for its purposes, an exclusive patrician class. The whole trend of our civilisation, the Christian religion itself, points us to inter-communication, the communal life, submission, and all the social virtues which make us yielding and complaisant, even at the sacrifice of all the emotions and susceptibilities—nay, the rights—which belong to a barbarian state of society.

It was now Goethe's steadfast purpose to give practical proof of this super-national outlook in a nationalist work of art. He was pressed to publish a kind of Golden Treasury of folk-songs, which should revive the German spirit. Much tempted by the idea, he wrote a long glowing preface of inestimable value, which to this day lies neglected; for as in that period of hallucination, so now—posterity has been incapable of comprehending how the first of German poets could have proposed, in a time of national

[1] "No greater gain for the human spirit
Than a sense of our foeman's merit."

distress, to introduce foreign strains into a German anthology, on the ground that "it was high time to draw attention, and children's attention especially, to the merits of other nations." For the Germans (he continued) had little native inspiration; individuals had aimed high, "but what has been achieved is far less than we care to admit to ourselves or others." On the other hand, they had nearly always proved themselves to be good translators, and in this way all paths to civilisation could be made to converge.

In advance of the age as it was, this work might have been Goethe's national achievement during the period of German subjection. It was too nobly conceived to be then carried out.

The year of German liberation dawned. Prussia revolted; Young Germany sang songs, and sabres were rattled.

Goethe, staying in Dresden, heard the voice of German aspiration, of national self-confidence. Theodor Körner, sword at his side, welcomed the poet with military swagger; his father stood near, and beside the two was Ernst Moritz Arndt. Goethe heard and saw these ardent spirits; cordially did he shake hands with the two poets of freedom, but he said: "Stop short at rattling your chains—the man is too big for you! You will not be able to break them!"

His compatriots stood gazing open-mouthed at one another when Goethe was gone—but the spell of his personality was so powerful that Arndt himself publicly applauded him, in that same year, for his quiet persistent endeavours.

During the three days of the Battle of Leipzig, Goethe received the French Ambassador, examined excavated skulls, studied English history under Elizabeth, read *Gil Blas*, revised the proofs of his biography, wrote the epilogue to a foreign drama, in the hope of making a better ending for a mediocre play entitled *Graf Essex*. There is no doubt that this *Essex* really inspired Goethe to an epilogue on Napoleon's day of doom; for during the course of those four October days in which Napoleon's destiny fulfilled itself almost under Goethe's eyes, he—Goethe, whose duty it was, as German poet and Minister, to rejoice in victory—assumed the mask of the Queen of England that he might cause these words to be spoken upon the boards of a Saxon theatre:

Wer Mut sich fühlt in königlicher Brust,
Er zaudert keineswegs, betritt mit Lust
Des Stufenthrones untergrabne Bahn,
Kennt die Gefahr und steigt getrost hinan.
Des goldnen Reifes ungeheure Last,
Er wägt sie nicht; entschlossen wie gefasst
Drückt er sie fröhlich auf das kühne Haupt
Und trägt sie leicht, als wie von Grün umlaubt.
So tatest du. Was noch so weit entfernt,
Hast du dir anzueignen still gelernt,
Und was auch Wildes dir den Weg verrannt,
Du hast's gesehn, betrachtet und erkannt . . .
Der Mensch erfahrt, er sie auch, wer er mag,
Ein letztes Glück, und einen letzten Tag.[1]

All the sympathies of the genius were with the Emperor in flight. If hitherto Goethe had despaired of a German victory, now he was dubious of the victor's staying-power.

But August his son, unsoldierly as he was, had joined the colours merely because every other young man was doing so—to find that the Duke, as a Russian General, was about to lead a German corps across the Rhine; and Goethe did put forth all his authority to keep that son at home. He approached the Duke in a respectful document, with the request that his son might be exempted from military service, "in the interests of reconstruction"; and so exaggerated this pretext as to declare that he would be deprived of his son's "indispensable aid," adding: "It would make my position unendurable—indeed, I might even say it would put an end to my existence." Here Goethe appears

[1] "The man with mettle in his kingly breast
Ne'er hesitates to take with fearless zest
The perilous mined pathway to a throne,
Sees well the risk, but pushes coolly on.
The weight of that gold fruit, though vast it be
He reckons not—calm, resolute is he,
And on his dauntless brow will press it down
To bear it lightly as a laurel-crown.
And thus you did. Howe'er remote the prize
You made it yours through silent, long surmise;
Though round your way wild beasts were gathered thick
You saw them, tracked them, knew their every trick . . .
Man knows, let man be mighty as he may,
His last good-fortune, and his last great day."

as the aged father who is not prepared to sacrifice his only son, because no pulse in his heart beats to the ideal patriotic tune.

The following passage in the *Literaturzeitung* I wish you to take to heart, and say nothing about it. Our men and women must on no account be led to imagine that Germanism is identified with Christianity and chivalry; for the former was extraneous to Germanism . . . and the latter, likewise a foreign product, is in many ways contradictory of the fundamental idea of German national freedom.

Such was Goethe's state of mind, as confided to his son, in the January which saw Blücher cross the Rhine. His public attitude he soon had the opportunity of setting forth in a ceremonial piece of writing; for when Paris had fallen and Napoleon had made his first abdication, there came to Goethe from the Berlin Court a request to write a pageant for the King's re-entry. *Des Epimenides Erwachen* (*The Awakening of Epimenides*), written in a few hurried weeks, is far from being a Court-pageant —it is a real poem. In this piece, half-allegory, half-satire, Goethe in his most light-hearted period, and with great expenditure on music, scenery, and stage-devices, takes the most affectionate of rises out of him who commissioned it, His Majesty, and the German people.

The vanquished foe was the inspiration for every "passionate speech." One is reminded of lines from the second *Faust* when the Dæmon of War (Napoleon) exclaims:

Kein Widerspruch! Kein Widerstreben!
Ich kenne keine Schwierigkeit,
Und wenn umher die Länder beben,
Dann ist erst meine Wonnezeit.
Ein Reich mag nach dem andern stürzen,
Ich steh' allein und wirke frei;
Und will sich wo ein schneller Knoten schürzen,
Um desto schneller hau' ich ihn entzwei. . . .
Ein Schauder überlauft die Erde,
Ich ruf' ihr zu ein neues Werde.[1]

[1] "Oppose me not! No protestation!
What difficulty baffles me?
When round me trembles every nation,
I know the thrill of ecstasy.

At the end the poet makes a clean breast of his feelings about this war, this foe, this peace. As Epimenides, Goethe is shown in the Prologue as one under the guidance of his tutelary spirits, sleeping on a couch; as Epimenides, he awakes when the action is over. Was he not, in those seven years between Jena and Leipzig, dreaming and taking soundings, withdrawn, insistently aloof from the age in remote countries and centuries—had he not pilgrimaged even to the primitive rock of China?

Doch während meines Schlafes hat ein Gott
Die Erd' erschüttert, dass Ruinen hier
Sich auf einander türmen . . .[1]

—and Epimenides-Goethe shrinks in terror, thinking he is lost in a world unknown. But ere long he recovers, and is himself again; and now he proclaims himself the people's loyal priest. But then Goethe confesses with a smile, which we may be sure no actor could have smiled to his satisfaction:

Wie selig euer Freund gewesen,
Der diese Nacht des Jammers überschlief,
Ich konnt's an den Ruinen lesen,
Ihr Götter, ich empfind' es tief!—
Doch schäm' ich mich der Ruhestunden;
Mit euch zu leiden, war Gewinn:
Denn für den Schmerz, den ihr empfunden,
Seid ihr auch grösser, als ich bin.[2]

Let crumbling realms on realms be scattered,
I stand alone, supreme in power;
Are bonds drawn closer, swift they're shattered,
I cut them loose in one short hour. . . .
The earth is all one shuddering fear,
I bid her rise, a new-born sphere!"

[1] "But while I slept, a god came down to earth
And shattered it, till ruin piled on ruin
Here I behold around me . . . "

[2] "How blest your friend, who calmly slumbered
Throughout that night of woe and fate,
I read in ruins all unnumbered—
O gods! I know my happier state!
Yet restful hours must shame my spirit;

With that smile he at last consigns the problem to the archives; nor does he find it hard to turn away, for his soul is already afar in time and place.

Long before he saw Italy, Goethe had begun to use Italian themes. When at last he did behold the country, it seemed no more than the continuation of a dream, and he felt no surprise at anything he saw with his waking eyes—landscape and vegetation, people, cities, and works of art all served but to confirm his pre-vision. Twenty-five years later, at sixty, Goethe had emotionally and intellectually—nay, even stylistically—pilgrimaged in spirit to the East; but not as a thirsting devotee, impregnated with its magic through books and pictures, as of yore with Italy. This time it was more like a sleep-walker, unwitting of his path. With such ease as could only, in a consciousness so highly-cultivated, betoken a second youth, he displayed, quite without set purpose and with the utmost beauty, a perfect mastery of an Eastern poet's methods—and this between his sixtieth and sixty-fifth years.

It was the serenity in his soul which would not be denied expression in song; and once again, it was only song which could enhance that serenity. In the East all this lay ready to his hand—in those regions of the East which, pregnant with the ancient wisdom yet not dulled to Brahmin quietism, know the fullness of life through the more positive and liberal creed of Mahomet. Proverbial wisdom has its native home there, for wisdom there is both old enough and young enough to express itself in aphorisms; and song too lives among a people, worn in battle, who rejoice in the firmly drawn boundaries of their existence. There the weapons hang above the silken rugs; and the Divan of the Chieftains and the Divan of the Viziers and the Divan of the Pundits assemble among their many-coloured yielding cushions, yet never lose the energy of body and of mind which acts as a centrifugal force. Ripeness—that is the mark of Arabia, after her centuries of battle and victory; and ripeness was the mark of

---

More had I gained, to bear with ye
That anguish—yours is higher merit,
Greater are ye than I can be."

Goethe at the zenith of a life of struggle. He must have felt the breath of those lands within him before ever he opened one of their books.

Wisdom and love, the Persian singer's themes, filled the rejuvenated poet's spirit, ere he knew Persia. A swarm of aphorisms summarised, in these years, his fond yet critical conceptions of God, modality, the universe; and the little songs that here and there break forth again are akin to aphorisms. Far in the dim inane of an earlier period the hexameter panted laboriously to its predestined end.

Goethe's rhythms now soared on airier pinions. His humour goes hand-in-hand with his eroticism, stumbling about the foothills, wandering through the valleys, clambering up the mountains, circling through space. The richest lyrical years that Goethe knew—far richer than those of his adolescence—dawned in music and rejuvenescence.

> Zwischen Weizen und Korn,
> Zwischen Hecken und Dorn,
> Zwischen Bäumen und Gras,
> Wo geht's Liebchen? Sag mir das. . . . [1]

And even more like a diffident young lover is the message sent with some flowers to a pretty girl:

> Der Strauss, den ich gepflücket,
> Grüsse dich vieltausendmal,
> Ich hab' mich oft gebücket,
> Ach wohl eintausendmal,
> Und ihn ans Herz gedrücket
> Wohl hunderttausendmal! [2]

[1] "'Twixt the rye and the corn,
'Twixt the hedge and the thorn,
'Twixt the trees and the grass,
Whither away, my dainty lass?"

[2] "A many times a thousand
These flowers for you I've blessed,
And stooped—say, times one thousand
To pluck the very best,
And times a hundred thousand
All to my heart have pressed."

So closely was he drawn in spirit to the threshold of the East, yet knew it not.

Then there appeared in Vienna the first translation of Arabian poetry.

Goethe was not a stranger in this realm, either. As a youth he had planned a drama about Mahomet, had paraphrased the Song of Solomon, had studied the Old Testament thoroughly and repeatedly, had thought of versifying the Vedas. A few years before this he had studied the Thousand and One Nights; and yesterday, as it were, some Chinese poems. So he was well-equipped for the Arabian adventure.

Yet what would all his knowledge have been to him if the foreign land had not despatched to his borders, as to a veritable Prince punctilious for etiquette, a tribute-bringing herald who bowed before Goethe as though seeing himself reincarnate! His name was Hafiz.

But throughout this eastward pilgrimage his eye was fixed upon the peak of Olympus, glittering afar; and as he turned to the Land of Morning he made sure that that height, once the cynosure of a lifetime, stood impregnable behind him, towering upon the borders of both kingdoms. Goethe never exchanged the Greek form for the Arabian; he merely absented himself, smilingly, like a blissful traveller sojourning for a space in some land of dream.

For at sixty-five, at this height of inspiration, not even the inveterate observer, not even Goethe, had any need to see with eyes what he already carried in his heart. That is why this journey, taken in no travelling-carriage, was the only one which brought him no sort of disappointment. He had spent two years in Italy, studious, strenuous, collecting and watching, laboriously shaping, writing not at all. Now, older by nearly a generation, he strayed for the space of two years over Persia, over Arabia, giving as much as he took, collecting as much as he bestowed—and singing, always singing, with such wayward ease, such fire, as never of yore in his ebullient youth, as never afterwards in his contemplative old age.

And wantonly, without title, without purpose, without a thought of any more to come (how differently from those recent years when a single idea for an Elegy had been the instant occasion for a plan embracing a new series of Elegies), like a man intoxicate, like a boy, Goethe one day, after studying Hafiz and Firdusi for a few Thuringian summer-weeks, dashed down these lines on his paper, half in the old life, half in the new:

> Auch in Locken hab' ich mich
> Gar zu gern verfangen,
> Und so, Hafis, wär's wie dir
> Deinem Freund ergangen . . .
> Wer sich aber wohl besann,
> Lässt sich so nicht zwingen:
> Schwere Ketten fürchtet man,
> Rennt in leichte Schlingen.[1]

And he called the whole *A Warning*, and laid it aside. But already *The Talismans* had submissively shed their Eastern form for a masterly Western rendering:

> Lasst mich nur auf meinem Sattel gelten,
> Bleibt in euren Hütten, euren Zelten!
> Und ich reite froh in alle Ferne,
> Über meiner Mütze nur die Sterne![2]

And next day, and for many another day, there came coveys of little aphorisms, of tender songs; and he wrote them down quite clearly, with scarce a correction—as he had been wont to do in his youth with the waking dreams of his white nights; only now it was always in the broad sunshine of summer-days that he recorded them.

[1] "Curls about the heart that twine
I have not resisted,
So my fate like thine had been,
Hafiz, sadly twisted . . .
But we longer-headed ones
Prove in this thy betters—
He in silken reins who runs,
Shies at heavy fetters."

[2] "Saddle me my horse, and learn my mettle!
Ye that will in huts and camps may settle,
I will ride away, exultant singing,
O'er my caftan stars of heaven swinging!"

This was a youth new-born, who now as forty years ago obeyed the esoteric law of his being in that he watched his desire come gladly hastening towards him—and smilingly awaited its arrival, singing a leisurely sweet song the while to the fair Unknown.

. . . But it was full summer by this time, and people were talking about Wiesbaden. The Main, the Rhine—for twenty years, almost, he had not seen them! Not long since, he had refused to revisit the altered places which were going to be part of his biography. Now he suffered himself to be persuaded—in the name of Hafiz, he would fain see the old made new:

Gutes zu empfangen, zu erweisen,
Alter, geh auf Reisen!
Meine Freunde . . .
Haben nicht an mir gelitten,
Ich hab' ihnen nichts abzubitten;
Als Person komm' ich neu.
Wir haben kein Konto miteinander,
Sind wie im Paradies selbander.[1]

Scarcely was Goethe seated in the carriage ere the waking, lucid dream began. The country was gay with the hues of a Thuringian summer, yet this traveller was asking himself:

Sind es Zelte des Wesires,
Die er lieben Frauen baute?
Sind es Teppiche des Festes,
Weil er sich der Liebsten traute? . . .
Ja, es sind die bunten Mohne,
Die um Erfurt sich erstrecken
Und dem Kriegesgott zum Hohne
Felder streifweis freundlich decken. . . .[2]

[1] "Give and take—old man, if that's your pleasure,
Travel yield's full measure!
My companions . . .
Have not found my ways too trying,
No indulgence I've been buying;
Unknown am I to all.
We keep no reckonings with one another,
Each, as in Paradise, our brother."

[2] "Are they tents the Vizier builded
For his women fairest, dearest?

By the evening—behold seven poems, and to Hafiz he owed them all! "When did I experience these things?" thought the biographical side of him. And if we follow his pedantic mood and restrict ourselves to comparing the number of his lyrics, we find that those inspired by Strasburg fill only eight pages (and not many have been lost), that the four years of his deepest passionate experience fill sixty, and that then, throughout his entire middle period, counting every little aphorism, there are three hundred pages for thirty years. But now he writes half as much again in two years—and even if we must stop there, we have already, for twenty-five years of Goethe's old age, twice as many poems as for the twenty-five of his youth.

And he was the lover of humanity in these, and some little songs against hatred might almost be called love-songs. Someone happened to gaze wonderingly at Goethe in his carriage—a beggar ventured to approach his table at an inn . . . little sayings, light as the breath of a sleeping child, flowered from every encounter, and all are instinct with kindliness. Then—so soon!—he gathered them all together into a German Divan, and it was instantly given a name: *Östlicher Diwan vom westlichen Verfasser* (*Eastern Divan by a Western Writer*).

Even the old diary strikes a younger note; and where of yore it hoarsely remarked: "Letter to the Chamber-Assessor von Goethe," or "His Excellency Voigt here," or "Colours of the fourteenth century classified," or "Forty-fourth bath"—it now sang very softly, and with only the slightest of stutters: "Magnificent day. . . . Another magnificent day. . . . First stork first reaping. . . . Think of going to Rüdesheim. Glorious to be so near the Rhine. Clear sunrise. . . . Never tired of gazing."

The whole world of men, hitherto apt to avoid him as a unsociable or haughty being, now saw how brilliant and kind his eyes could be; and on the promenade at Wiesbaden the very

---

Are they silken festal carpets,
And his best-beloved nearest? . . .
Nay—but scarlet poppies burning
Laugh the war-god to derision,
All the fields of Erfurt turning
To a fair forgetful vision. . . ."

school-girls ventured to request a complimentary message for their teacher, which he instantly wrote for them.

Never were Goethe and the world in such unison as during this summer—he wished the whole world well, as it wished him. Nay, the unprecedented came to pass—the *Frankfurt General Post-Office Gazette* took notice, for the first time in its existence, of its fellow-citizen's presence in their midst, and in the quaintest of phrases announced the arrival of Goethe, "the greatest and oldest surviving hero of our literature."

For most astonishing things were happening to Goethe's fame in these years, as if the fame too were sharing in the re-juvenescence. Of a truth, his name had never since the *Werther* days been so continually on the people's lips as at this very period of political emancipation—of which Goethe took so ex-tremely critical a view. It was as though the nation, in its renewed self-consciousness, felt the need of an intellectual leader, and could turn only to one of the old guard if it were to know real confidence. The word "hero" in that singular tribute was with-out precedent in Germany. *Werther* lay forty years behind him, and was out of fashion; no German could keep a line of *Hermann und Dorothea* in memory; *Götz* was forgotten, the poetic dramas incomprehensible; *Faust* was unactable and known only to the intellectuals; *Wilhelm Meister* was "very queer" and *Wahlver-wandschaften* "immoral"—forbidden to young people.

But *Dichtung und Wahrheit* won all hearts. Reflective and idyllic, it struck the Germans as German to the core; and the nation—which had insisted on regarding the literary Minister at Weimar as an adventurer—now looked with amazement on one corner of the vast battle-field, one fragment of a life so deep, intensely felt, and full that it had kept the poet true to his high calling. And there was something to move the "great heart of the people" in the modesty with which he dwelt only on his errors. Besides all this, a series of lyrics in lighter mood had gradually made their way into popular favour. So, because they happened to need him just then, the people took Goethe back to their hearts at this precise moment of national exaltation, when his own spirit was sojourning in Arabia—and there was some indwelling justification for what seemed a misconception. For whether it was the cause or the effect of this mood—this Rhine-

and-Wine mood of the spirit—one thing is certain: Goethe now began to immerse himself afresh in German art.

A young man named Boisserée had taken the first bold step. Arriving at Weimar from Heidelberg the winter before, with good introductions, he had spread out drawings and plans of Cologne Minster upon Goethe's table, and shown him how German they were. Goethe had hummed and hawed, growled and grumbled "like a bear with a sore head," had had a week's battle with himself before he could confess to being convinced—but (as great natures are) was only the more attracted to the young man who had beheld him in his weakness. He had promised to go and see Boisserée.

Now the young collector (who has preserved the most invaluable conversations for us, and reported them with dispassionate and arresting convincingness) induced him to come from Wiesbaden to see his pictures; and so Goethe for the first time beheld a fine German collection—he who throughout sixty years had really studied nothing of the kind beyond a few Dürers and Cranachs. Now he was confronted by Roger van der Weyden's *Tod der Maria.* He gazed for some time; then he said, as though he were speaking of Bach: "The truthfulness in that smites one in the eye!" But when he had studied and admired them all, he drew this conclusion: "The finest things I have got out of it" (he was speaking of travel) "are some bas-reliefs from the Cella of the Parthenon (in plaster), the Pallas Velletri, the infinitely beautiful torso of a Venus, and perhaps the head of a Venetian horse"—and soon afterwards he wished he could sleep in a gallery of sculpture, so as daily to awake among the Greek gods.

One day there came to Wiesbaden an old Frankfurt friend. This was Councillor von Willemer, a tall, vigorous, graceful man in the middle fifties, clever, worldly, and satirical—twice a widower before he was forty, and the father of several children. He had long retired from affairs.

This man had, many years before, discovered a girl who had originally come from Linz with her poverty-stricken mother in a company which was nothing more or less than a troop of gipsies; and was then as a soubrette-dancer, fifteen years old, displaying her gracile childish limbs to the ravished old bankers and young poets of Frankfurt. He was a connoisseur in women's charms, and he had made up his mind to take charge of this girl, buying her outright from her mother.

And when she grew into a great beauty, and her foster-sisters were married, and Willemer himself was getting older—what could be more natural than for her benefactor to court her, win her, and omit to marry her? Both were happy in their union; gradually he ceased to be regarded as her father; he took her with him on his travels, and in summer they lived outside the town in an old tree-girt country-house as happy as the day was long.

Now Marianne, just thirty, at the zenith of her charms, graceful and full-breasted, thoughtful and sensuous, imaginative, brilliant, and provocative—like the most charming of Austrian women—stood at her lover's side and held out her hand to Goethe.

Eagerly did he accept Willemer's invitation to his "tannery" near Frankfurt; and at sixty-five Goethe found, for the first time in decades, a house in which he really enjoyed being a guest for a few weeks.

He was seldom to be seen in the mornings. He drank his wine, in the forenoons, out of his own silver goblet; he dressed for dinner, and would often drive into town; but later, in his white flannel coat, he would be in sociable mood. He would find some work to do among the flowers with a handsome pocket-knife, and in the September evenings would tell stories and recite, read and talk; they would play and sing Mozart's arias, would drink and laugh upon the terrace that looked out on the Main; and many of the early drinking-songs in the *Divan*, written but yesterday, would be read aloud by the poet over his wine. Sometimes (Boisserée writes) tears would come into his eyes as he read.

But what were Marianne's feelings while she sang Goethe's songs to the piano, the windows standing open upon garden and river? Hafiz now added to the earlier love-songs, addressed to nobody in particular, one or two new ones in which there was already perceptible something transcending the long-ago witchery of Christiane:

Über meines Liebchens Äugeln
Stehn verwundert alle Leute;

Ich, der Wissende, dagegen
Weiss recht gut, was das bedeute. . . .[1]

Could Willemer have told them too? He knew women, and had early divined the danger threatening him from this grey-haired rival; for nine days after Goethe's appearance, Willemer had made Marianne, who had been his so many years, into his lawful spouse! The haste with which the master of the house made certain of his mistress is surely Goethe's swiftest and least welcome success with a woman!

Nothing was farther from his thoughts than to disturb their bliss, for he really valued his friend, and in this mood of airy fantasy could still put up a good fight against falling in love with a real live woman. Was he not Hafiz of Shiraz? Was it necessary to possess Marianne before he could sing Zuleika? He easily steered clear, and after these vaguely sentimental weeks of dalliance went home with a heart at ease.

In Jena and Weimar Goethe contrived to get pleasantly through the winter, and for the first time in many years he saw the New Year in at a public ball. It was full of promise for him. He steeped himself in his Arabian dreams, forgetting temporalities. What on earth did they mean by their Congress at Vienna? Was it the real world that they supposed themselves to be parcelling out?

I am ready to toil to my last breath, if only I don't have to attend any diplomatic dinners in Vienna, where everyone spends his time eructating over the latest piece of villainy. . . . One soon becomes unable to distinguish between dream and real life. That is, if the word of the enigma were not love and fidelity.

With Zuleika, however, he played hot and cold; and if there were some love-songs in this winter, they seem to have been

[1] "When my darling glances sideways,
Whom she looks at no one guesses;
I, all-wise, alone can tell them
Who receives those mute caresses."

uninvolved with glances of any kind, quite in the air, of Eastern inspiration wholly.

At last the sun came out again. True, the world was in an uproar; for from Elba a certain person had suddenly descended on Paris, and the gaieties of the Congress ended in confusion. Goethe smiled, for even the Old Guard could not close Persia to him. Frankfurt, indeed, was not far from the French frontier—for there can now be no doubt that he returned to the tannery that summer. But he seems to have entirely lost interest in the Emperor, who had so long been his idol.

Goethe came into contact with Baron von Stein, and learnt to know and value him better, now that he had a more open mind upon German questions. By this time Waterloo had been fought—his hero was a prisoner, after all. Goethe praised Stein's confident faith, to which he owed a clearer sense of the next world; and when he drove alone to Cologne, there to study on the spot young Boisserée's plans for finishing the Minster, he turned and found that Stein, who had happened to come too, was standing behind him in the building. Arndt was with Stein, and he relates how they suddenly caught sight of Goethe under the striving pillars, gazing at one of the Cathedral pictures. Two years had gone by since Goethe's chilling words to the young soldier and poet; the present moment confirmed Arndt and refuted Goethe, yet the younger man stood silently apart. And when someone in Stein's party showed signs of wanting to say something controversial, Stein laid a finger on his own lips and said: "Hush, boys—no politics, please! He would not like it. It is true that we can't be enthusiastic about him in that respect, but after all—he is too great. . . ."

It was a pure amazement for Goethe to find himself at this time greeted with "fanatical enthusiasm" wherever he went on the Rhine. He had not been accustomed to it in any corner of the world—in Weimar he was too well-known, in Prussia too little, to have experienced personal tributes.

Undoubtedly his complete openness of heart was the key to all other hearts. Never had his charity been so warm, so wide. Only a couple of years ago, he had grumbled when his amanuensis fell ill in Carlsbad; now he nursed his sick valet, pitied him more than himself, and smiled to think that with such a figure and at such an age he could still pull on his own stockings. He invited antediluvian friends of his youth to wine-parties—among them that Riese to whom he had written such extraordinary letters from Leipzig.

He grew restless as the summer-heat increased—and about the middle of August he unexpectedly drove up to the door of the tannery. He stayed six weeks. Again the country-house life went on to the blithest of tunes—harmony seemed to reign supreme. But Hafiz and Zuleika were drawn towards one another by invisible forces, daily growing more and more irresistible. Goethe's songs became very much more highly coloured, and right into Marianne's eyes he looked while singing like a latter-day Romeo:

> Deinem Blick mich zu bequemen,
> Deinem Munde, deiner Brust,
> Deine Stimme zu vernehmen,
> War die letzt' und erste Lust. . . .
> Eh' es Allah nicht gefällt,
> Uns auf Neue zu vereinen
> Gibt mir Sonne, Mond, und Welt
> Nur Gelegenheit zum Weinen. . . .[1]

He still tried, however, to elude the spell; in the beginning of September he went to Frankfurt town for a week. Now they were parted, now they could be more explicit than when in the same house, now to write and send verses was in the natural order of things. And there, at the inn, he took a half-sheet of green paper, and wrote upon it, in characters that seem to gallop across the sheet:

> [1] "In your eyes to gaze adoring,
> Watch your lips, your bosom, move,
> Hear your voice in music soaring,
> Once was all I asked of love. . . .
> Now, while Allah still delays
> Our rebirth to fairer morrow,
> Sun, moon, world, are all my days
> Seen through tears of yearning sorrow."

Nicht Gelegenheit macht Diebe,
Sie ist selbst der grösste Dieb;
Denn sie stahl den Rest der Liebe
Die mir noch im Herzen blieb. . . .[1]

Would she answer? Had she not made some pretty little verses before now?

Next day arrived a small envelope—and Goethe, who had laid a thousand verses at ladies' feet, was now for the first time answered in verse by a beloved woman. But what had come to her? It could not take the master's keen eye two minutes to perceive that love, in a single night, had turned a graceful poetaster into a true poetess, for her answer was this:

Hochbeglückt in deiner Liebe,
Schelt' ich nicht Gelegenheit;
Ward sie auch an dir zum Diebe,
Wie mich solch ein Raub erfreut!
Und wozu denn auch berauben?
Gib dich mir aus freier Wahl!
Gar zu gerne möcht' ich glauben—
Ja, ich bin's, die dich bestahl. . . .[2]

When they met again, both were on fire. In the house of the Frankfurt patrician, surrounded by the provincial proprieties of the nineteenth century, the Eastern play-acting blazed into passion; and under the social forms he could conceal his emotions from the husband and her environment when in the evenings, singing their songs in the garden-room, he decked her out with a turban of white muslin, secretly crowning Zuleika.

[1] "Thieves made by Occasion—never!
She's herself the thief, I say:
Stole from this poor heart for ever
What was left of love away."

[2] "With your love a raptured being,
I will ne'er Occasion chide;
Shameful thief for you, but seeing
All she gives me, my fond pride!
Nay—why talk of theft so sadly?
Give yourself, nor think of grief!
I could fancy, all too gladly—
Yes, I was myself the thief!"

Then he resolved to break away. Was Wetzlar to repeat itself once more? Again he felt himself, the guilty guiltless, to have invaded an untroubled relationship between two people whom he loved. He saw the Goethe-Fate stand threateningly before him. Already it was time—still it was time—to go. The month was September, the moon was at the full. The last evening is described by Boisserée (who in the character of his disciple spent a few days in the country with him) as cheerful and rich in amusing incidents. But when Marianne sang *Gott und die Bayadere,* Goethe was nervous, fearing it might be too much for her—it was almost her own story. Next she sang some of Mozart's arias, and finally a song from *Don Giovanni.* Goethe applauded and even declared she was his little Don Juan. Then he decked her with shawl and turban, and read aloud his new songs to Zuleika.

But for this same last day Goethe's diary contains, among social records, these revealing, unmistakable words: "Discovery. . . . Ostensible departure." In this twilight mood, between anxiety and gaiety, listening with panting hearts, usually dragged back to the social scene, but always tranced in their Orient dream . . . in this mood they parted, for Goethe went with his young disciple to Heidelberg—but the others promised to visit him there in a week's time. Was it a sudden thought of the lovers, who had respected their friend's roof, to meet in another place under cover of a journey? Did she perhaps make it a condition, before she would let him go? Only one thing is certain—that in these days of their parting such passion broke out in both of them as Goethe had not known since Lili's time.

Marianne's impatience took wings; she persuaded her husband to hasten their departure for Heidelberg; and when Willemer appeared, at an astonishingly early hour, at Boisserée's table, Goethe leaped up, rushed into his room, and all he could say in his confusion was: "We can't go on eating, while the ladies are waiting in the hotel!" So Marianne and Willemer's daughter were fetched in all haste, and then Goethe came back.

They had three days to themselves in that Heidelberg autumn weather. She timidly slipped a sheet of paper into his hand—something she had written on the journey; and Goethe read:

Was bedeutet die Bewegung?
Bringt der Ost mir frohe Kunde?
Seiner Schwingen frische Regung
Kühlt des Herzens tiefe Wunde . . .
Und mich soll sein leises Flüstern
Von dem Freunde lieblich grüssen,
Eh' noch diese Hügel düstern,
Sitz' ich still zu seinen Füssen. . . . [1]

The poet gazed in wonder at the sheet of paper; and when later on he incorporated this (and four other lyrics of Marianne's) in his *Divan*, he altered it for the worse in three places, and for the better in only one. He stood amazed at her reckless abandonment to a love which had grown so silently, now to break out with ardour such as this. All things seemed possible, all things desirable, in these three days, to the old man grown young; and when he drew her name in Arabic characters on the sand, when he wrote some verses comparing the ripe chestnuts on the Palace-terrace to his love, when he made the twin-leaves of the gingko-tree symbolise the mystic Two-in-One of lovers' dalliance . . . all suddenly his passion broke through the eastern Web of Maya, and he sobbed out these lines:

Ist es möglich? Stern der Sterne,
Drück' ich wieder dich ans Herz!
Ach, was ist die Nacht der Ferne
Für ein Abgrund, für ein Schmerz! [2]

But then the fire sank a little. From the red-gold blaze of a first embrace there sprang, opalescent, fables about the origin

[1] "What shall be the consummation?
Frolic Eastern wind, art bearing
Happy hours? Thy fresh elation
Cools the heart that knows despairing. . . .
Whisper softly, whisper gladly,
Saying: 'So shalt thou be greeted;
Ere those hills have darkened sadly,
Silent at his feet be seated!' "

[2] "Can it be? Thou star supernal,
Once again upon my heart!
O abyss of night eternal,
O the pain when lovers part!"

of the Cosmos—born of Goethe's innate loneliness and the tragic, insoluble enigma of man's existence. And yet again, unexpectedly, the song flared up to full intensity:

> So, mit morgenroten Flügeln,
> Riss es mich an deinen Mund,
> Und die Nacht mit tausend Siegeln
> Kräftigt sternenhell den Bund. . . .[1]

Fifty years ago, well-nigh—and he had sung:

> Die Nacht schuf tausend Ungeheuer,
> Doch frisch und fröhlich war mein Mut:
> In meinen Adern welches Feuer,
> In meinen Herzen welche Glut!"[2]

The aubade of the Strasburg student, as he mounted his horse after the love-battle won in Friederike's arms! Never since that day had Goethe thus depicted passion in its blaze of triumph. So, since his genius was ever his loyal companion, we must conclude that throughout the decades even that vital spark had scarce shot to such heights as in the Sesenheim days and these. It is as though, after Titanic wanderings of the spirit, he had returned to the zones where youth leaps exultant in the heart—zones in which of late he had begun again to dally.

The Dæmon had burst his bonds once more. The set game, the circumspect conquest of his spirit, of his years, seemed likely to be lost; Hafiz with his enfranchisement and Zuleika with her radiant smiling were sternly arraigned—and then, as of old, the dispassionate decree of reason sounded in Goethe's pulsing heart. He must flee.

Forty years ago—and he had stood at a selfsame parting of the ways, when he left Lotte and Kestner alone together. But to-day the struggle was fiercer. Then Lotte's No had defined the

[1] "So the rose-red wings of morning
Swept me on to lips of thine,
And, her myriad stars suborning,
Night the bond shall seal and sign."

[2] "Weird monstrous forms were born of night,
But I could play the hero's part:
What fire within my veins alight!
What pulsing passion in my heart!"

situation for him; now it seems incredible that Marianne, with her theatre-blood, a bourgeoise only by an extraordinary turn of fortune, dazzled by his glory, stirred by his devotion, should have refused to follow him whither he would. But he did not feel young enough for the folly of carrying her off; and besides, now to forsake Christiane seemed to him, eighteen years after *Amyntas*, utterly unthinkable. Tree and ivy—that was how he thought of it. Everything seems to say that it was Goethe who once more resolved on relinquishment, and as an old man accepted the destiny which had four times convulsed his youth, and made him into a poet.

He tore himself away after three days, letting her return with her husband to their beautiful home, whither he promised to come for a while on his return. Marianne wrote, on the day they parted, her other little masterpiece to the West Wind: "*Ach, um deine feuchten Schwingen, West, wie sehr ich dich beneide. . . .*" [1] But Goethe, during those days, wrote these lines on a stray sheet of paper:

> Locken, haltet mich gefangen
> In dem Kreise des Gesichts!
> Euch geliebten, braunen Schlangen
> Zu erwidern hab' ich nichts.
> Nur dies Herz, es ist von Dauer,
> Schwillt in jugendlichstem Flor;
> Unter Schnee und Nebelschauer
> Rast ein Ätna dir hervor.
> Du beschämst wie Morgenröte
> Jener Gipfel ernste Wand,
> Und noch einmal fühlet Hatem
> Frühlingshauch und Sommerbrand.
> Schenke her! Noch eine Flasche!
> Diesen Becher bring' ich ihr!
> Findet sie ein Häufchen Asche,
> Sagt sie: Der verbrannte mir! [2]

[1] "Ah, of thy rain-burdened pinions, West Wind, is my spirit envious."

[2] "Love-locks, keep me prisoned ever,
Captive of the face ye frame!
Dear brown snakes, from me shall never
Sound a word of grief or blame.

Godlike was the gesture with which he crushed down the leaping flame within. His dæmon had grown strangely compliant —a thrall, not a master. How he had stormed, of yore, in innumerable pages to Käthchen, Lotte, Lili! It had taken Goethe a lifetime to find this Archimedean lever.

The carriage bore his beloved away—he felt: "It is for ever"; and he must have believed that she would be the last woman in his life. There he stood in Heidelberg where his genius had led him; and only by a word did he show that once more the hard-fought combat had been won—by dropping just a single rhyme in the above-quoted verses, thus mutely bidding his reader substitute for "Hatem's" name the name of Goethe—called for by the rhyme, and suffusing the Eastern original as by international anticipation of history.

The collapse came very suddenly. In a few days Goethe resolved to leave Heidelberg; he said, "I am making my will!" His young companions tried to persuade him to stay—but he was afraid he might fall ill, he could not sleep, and finally he gave Boisserée some of his poems to read, saying, "I must get out of this place." In the diary: "Sad, troublous farewell."

He had held out for ten days after the parting, seeming to live in a state of inward ardour, haunted by a strange medley of past and present memories, some long gone by, some recent—Lili, Carl August, Minna Herzlieb. But on the day of that sudden impulse to make his will, when he rushed away from Heidelberg, and—for the sixth time in his life—fled from a woman beloved, he wrote two letters which make it clear that on that day he resolved to conquer himself and lose not a moment before relinquishing, once and for all, the whole relation. To the woman

---

April to this heart is bidden,
Green the meadow, green the lea;
Under snow and fog-drift hidden,
Blazes Etna, all for thee.
Like the rosy morning, certes,
Thou dost shame the gloomy hill;
May and June—they both are Hatem's
Once again at thy sweet will.
Fill the glass with diamond-flashes!
For this goblet goes to thee!
If she finds a heap of ashes,
She will say: 'He burnt for me!'"

herself he dared not announce his resolution to avoid the tannery; but to Willemer's daughter he wrote:

Only think—up to yesterday I had hopes of seeing you any day, and now I'm hauled by the hair through Würzburg home. . . . Forgive these splutters and blots—they represent my state of mind. Adieu to the other two. May they always be united as they are now! And I too. G.

Almost literally, what he had written at twenty-three to Kestner and Lotte. To-day he was sixty-six.

But with a wonderful manly restraint he wrote at the same time to Willemer:

I've had a hundred imaginings of when, how, and where I should see you again for the first time. . . . But now it's all up! And I'm hurrying through Würzburg homewards, consoled only by the thought that, submissively and quietly, I am taking the appointed path, and so may think with unremorseful yearning of those whom I leave behind. But even that is more than befits my state, for there is a rift which cannot be ignored, which I would be loth to widen, but would fain put an end to. Cordial thanks for all your kindness and affection. But these thanks, to be fitting, must bring some sadness with them. You, who understand the heart, will know how to convey all I mean. So these words will serve for you both—who are so enviably happy in your union.

On the day he returned to Weimar he sent Marianne, as agreed between them, a letter in Arabic cipher; and, turning to the same ciphers and numbers in her own copy of the Arabian poems, she read the rune:

Die Einsamkeit ist schön,
Sobald die Freundin meine Freundin ist.
Aus meinem Kopfe geht
Die Sehnsucht deines Aufenthaltes nicht,
Weil dort das irre Herz
Des armen Fremdlings wie zu Hause ist.[1]

[1] "To be alone is well,
So long as my belovéd still is mine.
For ever in my head

To Willemer he dedicated an Arabic work as from "his grateful guest, Hatem." His native town and the tannery, his friend and Marianne, Goethe never saw again.

It was the middle of October when Christiane fondly welcomed him back to the big house. The cold weather had set in already; the large stove had to represent the sun. He slowly settled down into the accustomed life of active contemplation.

Tranquilly he collected his new poems. . . . Where did that happen, now? On the Neckar? On the Euphrates? Uncommonly pretty pieces there are among them, especially those about her. . . . He must have a talk with Riemer about the arrangement.

The yearning to be with thee doth abide,
For there my heart can rest,
Poor alien heart, at home a little while."

CHAPTER XI

RESIGNATION

"Give a thought to the hermit who, cloistered in his cell, yet hears the ceaseless roaring of the sea."

AMONG the tops of the olden pine-trees a bay-window glitters from the highest storey of the inn overlooking the river, outside the town of Jena. It is the beginning of February, but the season is mild; and here, on the south side, an old man (who even in his youth had needed more warmth than do his fellow-countrymen) can scent the Spring as he suns himself in the feeble radiance. What is he doing up here in the snug little room at which he had often looked enviously as he passed, then had engaged by the day, and finally had come to sleep in? Is he dreaming, writing poetry?

He is working. But every now and then he lets his eyes rove to the hills and the surrounding country, and drinks in the lesser beauty that symbolises the greater. "Among these pine-tops I live as in the Land of Goshen, cheerful and serene, while over Nineveh-Jena broods the black cloud of politics." Through the arches of the bridge at his feet he can see the raftsmen skilfully making their way down the river.

One man is enough to do the work. . . . The logs go lolloping along behind; some are stranded, God knows where, others whirled round in the current. . . . To-morrow the water may rise high, float them all, and bear them many miles to their destination, the hearth-place. You see that there is no necessity for me to waste my time on the daily papers, when the most perfect of symbols are spread before me for the looking at. . . . The old man amid the pine-tops, rocked like a raven in his eyrie.

There he defines the essential temper of his spirit for the next few years—serene relinquishment, ironic contemplation, cosmic wisdom within a narrow circle; and that temper of the spirit is the sole explanation of his curious fancy for this remote abiding-place.

And now, when he does take to verse at all, it is more in the way of arranging than of composing. The Muses have once more deserted him, and during this period—from his sixty-seventh to his seventy-fifth year—will but rarely and remotely attend upon his utterances. Seldom do we catch an echo of that richest of all his phases, so recently passed away.

How far it seems! Is it really only two years and a winter since in Heidelberg, convulsed by desire and passion, warned by experience, he had for the first time wrested of his own accord—entirely of his own accord—a tragic victory over his dæmon?

Since then he had carefully collected the gifts of his genius, arranging them in sections, adding scholarly notes—for Goethe was in truth not merely Hafiz the Singer, but Hafiz the Scribe as well. True, he had not acquired the difficult tongue of Arabia, but its beautiful script was his; for hours he would copy those mysterious arabesques, once he even began a letter to the reigning Duchess with an oriental invocation, and his *Notes to the Divan* are not mere explanations, but the crowning proofs that, if rather by irruption than a formal siege, he had made himself master of a civilisation.

And now the veteran Goethe could, like the experienced statesman he was, heedfully partition the provinces of his well-nigh boundless realm among contending powers, and keep them united by no other bond than his own sense of synthesis. This was his only means of guarding himself against the imperious assaults of public upon private life. The system he imposed upon his spirit is perhaps nowhere more evident than in this decade, so scantly poetic and yet for that very reason the more laborious—and ended at last by the dæmon's once more upsetting the entire Art of Life.

Christiane is dead. He who in his pine-top eyrie thinks and dictates, arranges and classifies, is alone and a widower. Though during the decade just gone by he had been more and more frequently driven away from his well-ordered household, because it had always been full of strangers, he now—when it was resounding to new voices, new movements—missed the only being who had always drawn him back to home. Christiane's last year of life had been, despite many brave rallies, a period of suffering; and since that year was for Goethe one of his richest and brightest and most expansive, the spiritual gulf between them had inevitably widened in the long run. That it never, even then, became estrangement—that Goethe never felt any secret resentment against his wife for having had to part from Marianne—is yet another proof of the fineness in both their characters, and of a concord which neither rank nor social conditions, gossip nor jealousy, free-love nor marriage, fame nor intellect . . . in short, which only death could rend asunder.

On the day she died he had looked from the window of his room, and seen the June sunlight contending with the cloud-rack. He had found a sheet of paper, and written:

> Du versuchst, o Sonne, vergebens
> Durch die düstren Wolken zu scheinen!
> Der ganze Gewinn meines Lebens
> Ist, ihren Verlust zu beweinen.[1]

And on another day—we know not when—he put into his dear woman's mouth this touchingly modest epilogue, in which everything that had sometimes been a source of uneasiness to him is transmuted by grateful recognition:

> Ein rascher Sinn, der keinen Zweifel hegt,
> Stets denkt und tut und niemals überlegt;
> Ein treues Herz, das, wie empfängt, so gibt,
> Geniesst und mitteilt, lebt, indem es liebt;
> Froh glänzend Auge, Wange frisch und rot,
> Nie schön gepriesen, hübsch bis in den Tod.
> Da blickt ich ihn noch manchmal freundlich an
> Und habe leidend viel für ihn getan.

[1] "O thou sun, how vainly art striving
To illumine cloud-rack of sorrows!
And mine the sole gain of surviving—
Her loss to lament through the morrows."

Indes mein armes Herz im Stillen brach,
Da sagt' ich mir: Bald folgst du ihnen nach!
Ich trug des Hauses nun zu schwere Last,
Um seinetwillen nur ein Erdengast.[1]

That House had long been deprived of the solicitude lavished upon it by Christiane in her youthful days. What had kept the pair united—and fruitfully so—through all the conflicts of their life was her skill in smoothing things down at the theatre. But with failing health she lost interest in this as in other things; and when shortly before her death Goethe's favourite pupil let himself be enticed away to Berlin by a new Director, the Goethe-party was crippled. Goethe had repeatedly declared that Christiane was his one remaining link with the stage-world; and so, on her death, he would have done well to abandon all connection with the Weimar house, which he had long ceased to love, while its master had long ceased to love his presence there. But instead of resigning, Goethe made a fresh start, resumed entire control of the dramatic side, and proposed to arrest the gradual dry-rot and regenerate the Weimar stage. His principal aim, no doubt, was to prepare a field of action for his idle son, from childhood all too familiar with that sphere. Six months after Christiane's death—at the New Year—he appointed August to the Board of Directors, and both by words and deeds made it plain that he intended to inaugurate a new era for the Theatre. The earliest weeks were rife with instructions, reports, and innovations; for more than ten years Goethe had not been so often in the House, nor held so many committees of inspection, nor taken a hand in so many productions.

[1] "A reckless disposition, foe to doubts,
That acts on impulse, and reflection scouts;
A loyal heart that, as it takes, will give,
Enjoy and share, and best in loving live.
Bright-giancing eyes, a cheek whose roses blend,
No beauty, yet attractive to the end. . . .
How fondly would my gaze upon him rest!
I suffered much for him, and did my best.
When this poor heart seemed like to break for pain,
I said: 'Thou soon shalt see thy dead again';
The burden of the House,* too vast, I bore,
And willed to live for him a few years more."

* "The House" refers to the Weimar Court Theatre.—*Translator's Note.*

Did he fail to perceive how this zeal incensed his opponents? Had he forgotten that that Jagemann who now controlled the operatic side was his Duke's supplementary wife into the bargain? It is as though some external force were driving him, as though he were (as in his youth) to be bludgeoned by Destiny into fuller knowledge of himself and the world!

So it went on for ten long weeks—went on till March,

Then there came into Goethe's life, which so many human beings had helped to shape, the first dumb animal that was to affect it. A strolling-player inquired if he might not exhibit his famous trained poodle in Weimar too. Goethe refused—not on the dog's, but on the theatre's, account.

He had, indeed, repeatedly inveighed in print about the barking of dogs, and had never had any of his own since his student days; but he disliked them as little as he did any other product of Nature. Cats he even liked to have about the house, and he once compared them to fallen Princesses of the leonine race. With a tame adder displayed to him by a clergyman, he had tried to make friends. The Duke was always surrounded by dogs, and when August brought home a huge English mastiff, Goethe willingly suffered it to remain. The older he grew, the more kindly disposed he was to animals; he never, it is true, was much interested in their souls; it was more compassion that he felt for them.

But on his stage he would not suffer animals to appear—and that is no matter for surprise. However, this actor found his way to the Duke. Carl August wanted to see the dog, and bade the manager ask Goethe to reconsider his decision. Goethe refused for the second time—now on the disingenuous pretext that animals were not even allowed in the auditorium. The Duke read Goethe's minute.

For forty years he had never allowed Goethe to tyrannise over him—because Goethe had been shrewd enough never to take the law into his own hands. After that one grand effort of the first decade he had given up the contest once for all; and throughout thirty years had devoted himself solely to the cause of education, in which he had to some extent a free hand.

But the Theatre had been from the very first a bone of contention about which friction, more or less unpleasant, had periodically recurred. When Goethe lost interest in it after Schiller's death, the favourites of the Favourite had seen to it that hers became all the more engrossing. This affair of the poodle brought matters to a head. Goethe had just reasserted himself—to give in now would have been to let his opponents triumph over him. But that was precisely what the Duke, too, was feeling. The deep grudge which these two men, despite their friendship, had in reality cherished for a generation, now for the first time—but also for the last—stepped into the light of publicity from out the little circle of their intimates. Attracted by a sympathy which had been naïve in its precipitate expression, each had in a few years recognised how different he was from the other; and when they awoke to this glaring discrepancy and considered men and things in general by its light, each realised with a mixture of fascination and horror how inextricable were the bonds that held them together. For Goethe and Carl August lived side by side for fifty years as in a marriage begun in love, continued in good-will, to culminate at last in estrangement. Throughout whole decades each went his own way, entirely regardless of the other, to be happily reconciled in their old age through habit and environment, activities and friends. The Duke had never seriously considered the final dismissal of Goethe, and every motive, both practical and ideal, urged Goethe to remain.

But that after forty years of friendship this which now came to pass should have been possible, is a fresh proof of the irreconcilability of their natures. The one was formative and practical, the other wanton and destructive.

Child's-play for the Duke to ring the curtain up upon the dog, despite Goethe's double veto! But this was not merely an instance of the commonplace autocrat, who ordains in his wrath what he could not accomplish by fair means. It was much more. It was a grand advertisement of his authority over his friend, the consciousness of which had often made him unpleasantly overbearing. The inferior dæmonic being defying the superior one—in that light Goethe's refusal must have struck the Duke; and he thought to have defeated Goethe when he ordered the dog to take the stage. We see that no poodle, but an eidolon, was in question. The Duke commanded the performance.

On the evening he heard this, Goethe's dæmon leaped to life once more. Should he make the Duke a scene, tell him home-

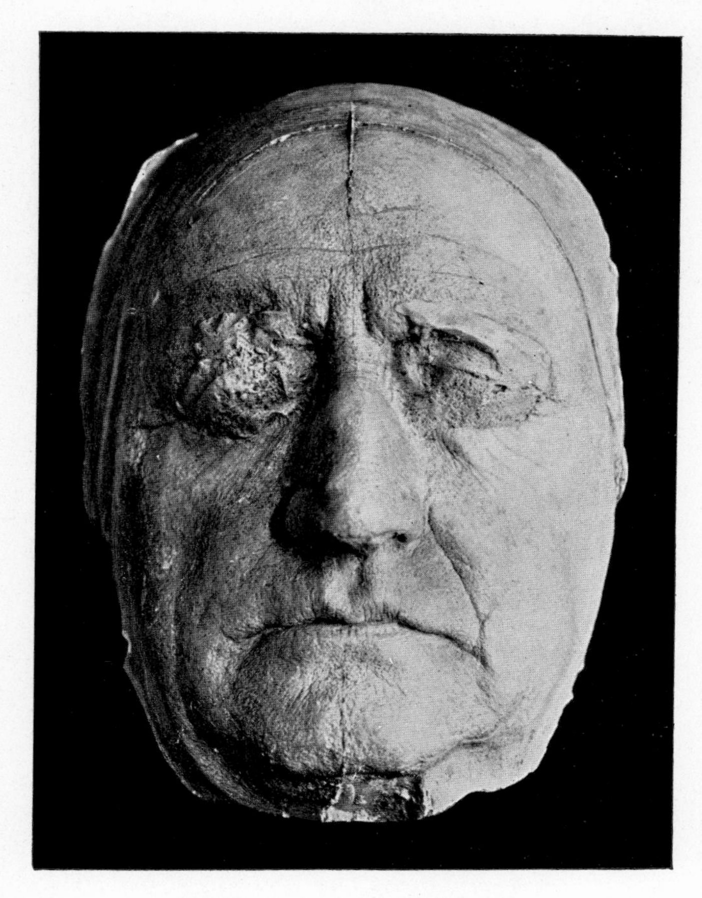

GOETHE AT THE AGE OF SIXTY-SIX

Photograph from a mask

truths kept back for forty years—and then leave Weimar? Should he silently acquiesce and allow the performance? How often had Goethe stood confronted by such pros and cons before a woman, on the critical day when he had either to link her fate with his or leave her altogether! Overcome by the possibilities of either decision, he had always solved the problem in one way—flight. To-day, too, this seemed to him the only course; and despite the precision with which in his old age he was wont to make his arrangements, he now took only a few hours to resolve on flight to Jena—packing, though, more extensively than ever before, and taking sufficient manuscripts, drawings, and apparatus for an uninterrupted stay from March to August!

When next day the stage-manager made his appearance, Goethe was gone. Simultaneously the Duke received a message from him—he begged to be allowed to absent himself from the dog's performance. The sensational news was soon all over the little Capital. Frau von Stein and Frau von Schiller were anxious to mediate through Knebel—Goethe returned an evasive reply. At Jena he remained, by no means in seclusion, writing tranquilly—indeed, by visits and committees, he there emphasised his position as Minister of Education.

The Duke, however, incensed by the exit of his distinguished friend and antagonist, was not content with regaling the town and the nobility by the sight of the dog on the Court stage—a poodle who, like that other poodle, seemed to have a devil in him. The Duke would have felt himself to be a beaten man if he had calmly acquiesced in Goethe's flight. So he took the extreme course: on the day after the dog's appearance he decreed Goethe's dismissal from the Directorship, saying that some recent expressions of opinion had convinced him that Goethe would wish his services to be dispensed with. As he simultaneously notified the Board of Directors of his decision, it was irrevocable.

But Goethe, in one of his cleverest letters—which feigned devotion, but was really full of oblique malice—proclaimed the Duke's defeat before the Areopagus of the intellect.

Your Royal Highness, as has so often ere now been your gracious pleasure, meets—indeed anticipates—my wishes. I have been hoping I might now be permitted to entertain them. . . . Will you, then, accept my respectful gratitude for all the favours I have enjoyed in the course of business; and I trust I may be graciously allowed, in the future, to exercise some influence upon that department in which I may lay claim to a certain amount of knowledge and practical experience.

His son (he went on) also wished to retire, since "in my present position I can only be concerned with affairs which require ripeness of judgment and calm deliberation." His presence in Jena was useful; "and therefore I venture to ask for an extension of leave. . . . Your Royal Highness's most obedient servant, W. von Goethe."

The Duke got no pleasure out of his victory—for after all, he loved his mighty antagonist! Two weeks later he betook himself to Jena. It seems that he paid Goethe a surprise visit at Knebel's family dinner-table—he is even said to have embraced him. That he took any steps to reinstate him in the position from which he had just kicked him out is very far from being proved, and moreover would have been quite out of character. Goethe resigned, and held his peace. Why—once more the question assails us—why did he remain in the town, and in office? Practical considerations can have had no more to do with it now than they had had thirty years before, when he returned from the South to find himself superseded in affairs, and cold-shouldered by his circle. Renowned, highly-salaried, and as an author still more highly paid—a widower, and the father of but one son, he was now in every sense free to turn his steps homeward, or anywhere else he pleased on the inhabited globe. And he must, besides, have guessed what indignation all Germany would feel when it became known that Goethe had been dismissed from office on account of a poodle. Germany would have taken his part, if he had left Weimar. Why did he stay?

Because he saw that in this sphere he could find scope for his energy; because in this uninspired phase some impetus to practical work was vital for him, at the age of sixty-eight; because, in spite of all, he could be sure of the Duke's real amity; because he could perceive every single one of the articulations in this stupid senile quarrel as clearly as those in a skeleton—because he had learnt wisdom, and because, by remaining, he conquered. Goethe was not at all like the Persian poet whose story he was now telling in the *Notes to the Divan*—that Firdusi who, after toiling thirty years, received too scanty a reward from his sovereign, and left the Court to die a man embittered.

By remaining and holding his peace, Goethe greatly increased his silent influence. Several actors left the Court stage as a protest, came to see him in Weimar, and confidentially imparted to him what admiration was felt for his

gigantic display of energy and his Brahminical power of patient endurance—indispensable, throughout well-nigh thirty years, for making something out of nothing. And that something was—however it might recently have dwindled—so fair a thing that I felt great reluctance to abandon it, and was sick at heart to cry: "*Rentre dans le néant dont je t'ai fait sortir!*" Haide's statement of particulars, though prudent and sensible enough, gave me a glimpse of the slough of despond into which before long they would all be plunged. We had at least kept the wine in the stage of fermentation, but now it was turning sour with a vengeance, and everyone knows the pace that goes at.

What a mixture of derision and pride, of grief, soreness, and malicious satisfaction! The wounded heart could torment itself like a boy's—the mature spirit could resign itself like an old man's.

Could resign itself, in every sphere. That voluntary relinquishment by which he put an end to rejuvenescence, poetry, and love, was now followed by the two relinquishments imposed on him by Destiny. The fond brown eyes of his dear companion were shut—the eyes which had never looked anything but fondness to the end; and the manly loyalty in those of his master and friend had in the end been clouded over. The hand which had a thousand times been given with the fraternal *Du* (so long now unresponded to), in assurance of his old-time faith, could now without a qualm sign the rescript which banished the same friend —an old man—from the House of his creation.

A year and a half—no more—since the farewell evening with Marianne, followed by the June day of Christiane's death, when Goethe himself lay ill in bed. Schadow, at this time, took a mask of the face. And indeed, to play with words, the mask was finally torn from the face of this man of sorrows by one individual's utterance: "*Voilà un homme qui a eu de grands chagrins.*" A diplomat had said this of Goethe, and Goethe translated it: "Which means, a man who has made no easy job of life."

The look of resignation was never absent from Goethe's face, though it was susceptible of much variety—now exorcised by contemplation, now kept under by activity. But since the time, nearly fifty years ago, when that look had been the mark of the Wertherish Goethe, it had never (not even in the loneliness of his fortieth year) been the distinguishing trait of his countenance. Now it pervades the relentless fidelity of the mask in Schadow's bust, and the profile portrait by Jagemann.

Stoicism, compounded of manifold spiritual elements, rules the different phases of Goethe's seventies. When something caused him to re-read *Werther*, he said he could not understand

> how a man to whom the world had appeared so absurd in his youth could possibly have contrived to stick it out forty years longer. The enigma is partly explained by the fact that everyone has something of his very own in him, which he thinks to make good with by letting it have its way. This queer notion makes fools of us, day after day, and so we grow old without knowing how or why. If I look at the thing closely, I can see that nothing but the talent I happen to possess has sustained me through circumstances which did not suit me, and in which I became involved through miscalculation, accident, and entangling affections.

Such revealing soliloquies, which scarcely anyone but Zelter was allowed to overhear, and which posterity almost blushes to assist at, lose nothing but rather gain in sadness by the irony which makes the old man's mode of expression so different from the bitternesses of his youth. In his youth it was hopeful despair; in his age it was despairing mockery. And that is the undertone in the later-born songs of the *Divan*, sonorous as the ground-swell of some imperishable Largo:

> Lasst mich weinen! umschränkt von Nacht
> In unendlicher Wüste.
> Kamele ruhn, die Treiber desgleichen,
> Rechnend still wacht der Armenier;

Ich aber, neben ihm, berechne die Meilen,
Die mich von Zuleika trennen, wiederhole
Die wegeverlangenden, ärgerlichen Krümmungen.
Lasst mich weinen. . . .[1]

But what kept the balance of his resignation true was the manful confidence in the other scale—the confidence that waited upon the veteran's melancholy, the same feeling that had made him, as a youth, suddenly fling aside every thought of death, "and I made up my mind to live." This is the way he speaks of the talent entrusted to him by God:

Ich brauch' es zur Rechten und Linken,
Weiss nicht, was daraus kommt.
Wenn's nicht mehr frommt,
Wird er schon winken.[2]

And it was then, too, that in a dialogue before the gates of Paradise, he looked the reluctantly inquisitorial houri in the face and cried, a poet unafraid:

Nicht so vieles Federlesen!
Lass mich immer nur herein:
Denn ich bin ein Mensch gewesen,
Und das heisst ein Kämpfer sein.
Schärfe deine kräft'gen Blicke!
Hier durchschaue diese Brust,
Sieh der Lebenswunden Tücke,
Sieh der Liebeswunden Lust![3]

[1] "Let me weep, by the night engulfed,
In the infinite desert!
The camels rest, their drivers beside them,
Counting, mute, stands the Armenian;
While I, not far away, am reckoning the distance
That parts me from thee, Zuleika—reckoning, counting
The endlessly lengthening, harassing labyrinths.
Let me weep, then. . . ."

[2] "To right and to left I bestow it,
What comes of it, can't say.
When past our day,
He'll let us know it."

[3] "Not so ceremonious, pray you!
Let me pass the gate at last:

German as is the splendid sonority of these lines, worthy to adorn the scutcheon of the Muses, it is nevertheless something more than the form which makes this Western, this Protestant, confession of faith an Oriental poem. Whenever he could, during these years, Goethe held fast to the spirit of the East. In it he perceived all the elements befitting the poetry of an old man:

Unquestioning acquiescence in the unfathomable will of God; a serene vision of the pulsating flux, the incessant convolutions and involutions, circle-wise, spiral-wise, of the terrestrial rhythm; love, affections, hovering between two worlds; all matter purged of its dross, symbolically evaporating. What more can Grand-Daddy want?

With the last five words he at one stroke sets this confession of faith (addressed to Zelter only) in the light of another relinquishment—putting a comprehensive minus-sign before all forms of dogma.

During this period Goethe's nervous susceptibility became more and more marked—for while the strong-hearted cheerfulness of the immediately preceding years had faded away from him, the most sensitive part of his nature was exposed to the batterings of the world and Destiny. The subtlest of his observers had to describe as "unusual" an evening on which Goethe was "cheerful, reasonable, sympathetic, instructive—no pique, no irony; nothing violent or repellent."

Very far removed from the harmony which it had taken him sixty years to acquire at all, in this retrograde phase Goethe had to redouble those hygienic methods which even as a youth he had practised. Zelter was on his way to visit him, when his daughter died; Goethe was asked to break the news to his friend. He, who regarded all unprofitable agitations as superfluous, because to him the inexorable was the only school for the spirit, said nothing

---

I have been a man—what say you?
Does not that mean battles past?
Yours are eyes of piercing vision;
Look into this breast and see!
Life-wounds—those were spite, derision;
Love-wounds—those were ecstasy."

to Zelter and sent the letter containing the news to his room on their first evening, adding some lines from himself of heartfelt sympathy and consolation. Afterwards, to a third person, he described the whole incident as "vexatious."

His trustiest weapon against Destiny was now as forty years ago—occupation. In occupation the veteran took refuge, as had the man bidding farewell to youth—yet not as he! When we consider from without the ceaseless activity of the life which this man of seventy pursued year in, year out, we are reminded of the strenuous period of practical work to which he had condemned himself at twenty-seven.

But spiritually considered, the two phases are radically different. During the most fruitful portion of a man's existence Goethe had of his own choice well-nigh completely abstained from production, that he might gain practical experience; now he filled one of the most unfruitful with occupations, merely that he might survive.

Again, as ever until that brief halcyon-time of serenity, we find him inventing countless emblems, phrases, and metaphors for his dual nature. The sage among the pine-tops was only one of the shapes it now assumed; in other moods the familiar dæmon would burst the bonds of resignation, as never before but in his youthful days. Once more he was plunged into the strife of warring impulses, once more victory seemed out of the question. On the day that the mortal combat of his soul should be decided once for all—on that day Goethe would die!

Of such a savage Goethe is the tale of a summer-night which he spent with the contentious philologist Wolf, and Meyer. The ever-argumentative Wolf he then "brutally" sat upon. "Fortunately or unfortunately I had drunk so many more glasses of Burgundy than was good for me that I could not control myself. Meyer sat by, composed as usual, and I don't think he liked it." But such violence, he adds (and it is more like self-reproach than censure) will come home to Wolf, as it did to Herder. "Examine yourself, then, to see if you are made of similar stuff—*I* do, every day."

If there was any noise in the house, such as a quarrel or a mishap, Goethe used immediately to call out: "Quiet! Quiet! for Heaven's sake!" But the fact that he sometimes called out like this when the noise was over shows that he had to bid himself be quiet; and it was a man of seventy who dashed off these electric lines:

Was hast du denn? Unruhig bist du nicht,
Und auch nicht ruhig, machst mir ein Gesicht,
Als schwanktest du, magnetischen Schlaf zu ahnen.—
Der Alte schlummert wie das Kind,
Und wie wir eben Menschen sind,
Wir schlafen sämtlich auf Vulkanen.[1]

Now, as in the past, Goethe perpetually speaks of the systole and disastole which formed part of his dual nature; and in one of the little biographical sketches—splendid *torsi*, so long left to moulder neglected in one dust-covered volume of the series of sixty—he finds the happiest of expressions for the old problem: "The reason within us would be a great power if it only knew with what it had to contend. Our nature is always taking fresh forms, and every one of them is an unexpected enemy for that good-humoured equable reason of ours."

Two external events tended to encourage Goethe's renewed zeal for work. Weimar, at the Congress of Vienna, was raised to the rank of a Grand Duchy, and almost doubled in extent; then Voigt, who was Goethe's nearest colleague in the administration, died; and Goethe's duties were vastly increased. As from this time forward the improved revenue at last enabled him to work out former schemes, his energy could indeed spread its wings.

The Public Library, collections of coins, drawings, antiquities, the School of Art in Weimar—and in Jena seven scientific laboratories and the Botanical Gardens, the School of Medicine, the Observatory, the Chemical Institute and Library, were henceforth

[1] "What ails thee then? Thou art not restless now,
Yet cannot rest. I see around thy brow
For sleep magnetic timid craving flutter.—
The old man sleeps as children sleep,
And mortals all, our couch we keep
Where far below volcanoes mutter.

controlled by him alone. As soon as he took the helm the Observatory was renovated, a veterinary college was established, all institutes were enlarged, archæological work was set going again, the Botanic Museum was founded, the Library re-orientated, under the greatest architectural difficulties. As the taking-over of the old revenues by the new State necessitated the removal of the most important Treasury-officials, Goethe had himself to wind up all the old accounts, and open new ones; and indeed he could have found, as matters stood, no better expert, for had he not been Finance Minister in the past?

He had shed every illusion; and, never having been dazzled by personal power, could look with perfect indifference upon the much-aggrandized Duchy. When the new States first assembled to do homage in the great hall of the new palace, which he himself had helped to build, Goethe stood beside the throne of his monarch, now promoted to be His Royal Highness. Goethe was nearest to the Duke's right hand, his ageing back constrained to the courtier's erectness, the orders bestowed by Napoleon and the Tsar glittering upon his gold-laced Court uniform. He looked into the circle of nobles and citizens, now for the first time representing their country; and in all that Palace-Chamber there was no one so unmoved as he.

He gave his friends an unemotional account of the ceremony—indeed, when there was talk of an intellectual association, such as Wilhelm Grimm suggested to him, he confessed that he had "from of old wandered about these indigenous regions without ever feeling them to be his abiding-place." How literally, in the intellectual sense, he used the phrase, could not be more clearly demonstrated than by his having omitted these drafted words from the letter, fearing that they might reveal too much to the outer world!

It is true that there were practical reasons for this sense of complete aloofness. Goethe disapproved of the new Constitution given to the land, in accordance with promises made at the Vienna Congress, by Carl August—and by him almost alone among German rulers. He transformed the old Privy Council into a Ministry of State; in the diets he gave citizens and peasants such a share in the government as corresponded with modern ideas.

Goethe was opposed to any kind of majority-voting. With

real humility he had, especially in his middle period, appealed to his friends to follow him into the arcana of his art; from Herder, Schiller, Knebel, Wieland he had taken advice on the form of a stanza; even now he would ask the most intimate of his pupils for their verdict, which he sometimes made use of; and he never ceased, in his grey hairs, to feel himself a beginner in the sphere where he had been from the first a master. But when practical questions on which he had thoroughly reflected were fumbled with and interminably discussed by a dozen different colleagues, it was only by great self-control that he could bear it at all, and many a groan or curse was confided to private documents.

And now was he, for whom politics had always represented an art, to shake in his shoes before a shopkeeper from Apolda or a cabbage-grower from Kochberg, lest such an one might refuse to vote him the desired amount for Greek casts on the Education Estimates!

> The mass of men has from all time been united only by prejudices and stirred only by passions; even the loftiest aims are in this way perpetually obstructed or indefinitely postponed; but [he was careful to add] no matter for that—the best will get done, if not at once, in the long run; if not by direct means, as an ultimate consequence.

Here Goethe is revealed as looking both ways, exactly as he had done twenty-five years ago during the Revolution. As a practical statesman, as an expert and adept, he desired oligarchic rule; indeed, had Goethe been born to a crown he would never have yielded a tittle of his authority, but would have reigned precisely as Frederick did, perhaps as Joseph did—serving of his own free will where he could have commanded. That had been his method at the Theatre, where alone he was supreme. But as a thinker and a seer, he saw on the horizon the "cloud no bigger than a man's hand"—the cloud that meant Democracy. In his own life he had contrived to strike the balance between liberty and subjection. This was now his aim in the public sphere; and anything in the pages to come which may seem contradictory or illogical, is—once more—nothing but the outcome of his dual nature, which inevitably alternated between cleaving and leaving, prizing and despising, creating and contemplating. So that the veteran's frame of mind is, again, only to be explained by the essential elements in his nature, which held fast to the established fact in the belief that the ideal would emerge from it.

In his public life this looking-both-ways is strongly evidenced by two instances which affected his own realm of letters. Together with the new Constitution, Carl August had given his land the freedom of the Press, while everywhere else in Saxony autocracy and the Censorship prevailed. So of course the little land of liberty attracted critical brains, to augment the many others which already made the Poet's City, and the University, richer in them than in poets and specialists. Five new journals, springing up in the small city of Jena, attacked the new Constitution as being regarded by foreign lands in the light of a dangerous experiment, and by their own as a caricature of liberty. The Duke foamed at the mouth—he had meant so well! He proposed to dismiss the Professor who edited the most acrimonious of these sheets—for a few months after the accorded privilege, he could not without stultifying himself suppress the newspaper.

Goethe advised the exact reverse—to suppress the paper and leave the editor alone. After all that he had suffered, throughout forty years, from the stupidity and tactlessness of the Press, he could not but despise it—while the scientist, in his view, was sacrosanct, was not even to suffer rebuke! "It is pluckier," he said, "to let one's leg be cut off than to die of frost-bite." And he scribbled these lines:

> O Freiheit süss der Presse!
> Nun sind wir endlich froh:
> Sie pocht von Messe zu Messe
> *In dulci jubilo!*
> Kommt, lasst uns alles drucken
> Und walten für und für;
> Nur sollte keiner mucken,
> Der nicht so denkt wie wir.[1]

[1] "O land that now rejoices,
In Freedom of the Press!
Hark to the thousand voices
That chant our happiness!
Come on—we'll all be printed,
And rule the roost, you'll see.
No word be ever hinted
By him who won't agree."

Such was the angry derision with which he greeted the freedom of the Press.

Youth at the Universities, disappointed by what, instead of the promised emancipation, had ensued from affiliation with Germany after the fight for freedom, had now conceived a positive hatred for Austrian and Russian hegemony—and this was precisely what Goethe had foreseen, and what had prevented him from joining in the jubilations over the new era. When all the world was singing:

> Gott Dank, dass uns so wohl geschah:
> Der Tyrann sitzt auf St. Helena![1]

Goethe's rejoinder was:

> Doch liess sich nur der Eine bannen—
> Wir haben jetzo hundert Tyrannen.[2]

When the Jena students invited their brethren from all Germany for the 31st October, 1817, to celebrate Luther's tercentenary at Luther's Wartburg, Goethe uttered a word of warning—and was of course accused of upholding the party of Reaction. But the Duke sanctioned the arrangement whereby his Professors led five hundred German students from Jena to Luther's stronghold, there to celebrate Emancipation. Some of these young men, at the end of the day, combined to build a bonfire and burn, amid inflammatory speeches, the most embittered writings of the Reaction. Rumour fanned the flame—the little auto-da-fé became a vast conflagration, Weimar and its administration fell under suspicion as a centre of revolutionary thought; Hardenberg arrived with the Austrian Ambassador on a special mission; the rulers of France and Russia were shaking their fists in the background, terrified for their thrones if German intellect should revolt. The affair, in short, was magnified into a crisis of State.

And Goethe upheld the youngsters! The bonfire at the Wartburg kindled his old heart; and as his enemy Kotzebue's

[1] "Thanks be to God—we sing Hurrah!
The tyrant's dumped on St. Helena."

[2] "Yet only One is gone to his place—
A hundred tyrants now we face."

political writings had at last met their fitting fate among the rest, he had a double draught of satisfaction. Fearing the consequences, he had advised against the ceremony; now, when youth was arraigned, he took part with their idealism. "They're so attractive, these young people—with all their faults, which will be got the better of quite soon enough. If only the seniors weren't so asinine! For it's they who really spoil the fun." So he wrote confidentially to his son. In his public capacity he played the responsible Minister, and was sternly silent when one of the ringleaders in the Wartburg incident ventured to approach him. But the student was no sooner gone than Goethe declared that he had had the greatest difficulty in preventing himself from taking the culprit in his arms and saying: "Dear boy—don't be so silly!" Then he went on to imagine fondly how the young eyes would have flashed at him; but instead he had had to administer a sedative to "the dear hotheads for their own good."

Does it not read like a scene from one of Schiller's plays—the philosopher, the fond father, and forced to act the cold worldling's part in the service of reason!

> On the principle of upholding the established order, and preventing revolution, I am in entire agreement [with the Monarchists]; but not as to the means to that end—by which I mean that they put their trust in stupidity and obscurantism; I, in reason and enlightenment.

In this cleft stick between natural and political prejudices, owning allegiance to neither party and looked askance at by both, he sought solace—resigned in that as in all else—in a comparative study of the spirit of the age.

While his mere routine-work, in this period, waxed daily, he allowed the Court likewise to take up a good deal of his time. It was easier than before to get on with the circle there represented—friends and enemies were dead or grown old; memory, embellishing the past, spread a gracious patina over the relations of those concerned in it. The third generation was growing up, and Goethe's intercourse with Carl August's grandchildren was so patriarchal that he good-humouredly declared that they regarded him as one of the ancient fixtures of the house.

He was always inventing graceful little attentions with which to cheer the Duchess's embittered old age. All through the winter the Duke and she came once a week to his house, there to view interesting novelties or antiquities. Goethe became as a museum to be frequented in the days of growing old, when people want to replace, to forget, so much.

In public his courtly attitude grew more and more punctilious; it was as though he revenged himself by senile stiffness for a servility which no one demanded of him.

Upon this occasion I had the unexpected pleasure of my house and garden being honoured by the presence of Their Imperial Highnesses, the Arch-Duke Nicolaus and the Archduchess Alexandra, accompanied by our own most gracious Royal Highnesses. Her Imperial Highness the Archduchess was so gracious as to allow me to inscribe some lines of poetry in her tastefully- and splendidly-bound album.

Indeed, he even played the Court poet again; and anything he accomplished in this, his seventieth year, was superior—in the opinion of his friends and of posterity—to what he had formerly done in the Court masques. The Empress-Mother of Russia, as the guest of her relatives, was given an exhibition of what Weimar could do in the way of poetry; and to this end the old gentleman led a retired life for quite a long while that winter. And when Goethe slaved for six weeks and said "Bravo!" to himself at the end of them, something brilliant was to be looked for. This festival-piece was nothing less than an Epilogue upon Weimar's Golden Age, at the conclusion of which Goethe himself wore the cothurnus as Phorcias, commenting on his own lines.

Weimar's river, the Ilm, was the supposed narrator of all that it had seen in those decades. Allegorical figures entered, singing the praises of Herder; Wieland's characters advanced to the rhythm of Wieland's measures; from Schiller's plays the dramatis personæ, familiar to all present, appeared in turn and when the Ilm, gladdened by the general applause, should have proceeded to the laudation of the only one among the Weimar poets who still survived to write these verses, the doubly involved author extricated himself from his dilemma with the utmost tact. Then came the turn of Mahomet and Götz, Adelheid and Iphigenie—

nay, of Mephisto and Faust themselves, who had never yet trod the stage in actuality; and with what a courtly bearing did Mephisto, before this little Court, propound the devastating veracities with which in later years he was to regale a great Imperial one!

And when on that festal evening those figures passed before their poet's eyes—his own and those of his departed friends—and he, sitting between his sovereigns, looked down upon the crowded house and saw the son of Schiller in Götz's mask, and his own son, August, in that of Mephisto—how like his own ghost he must have felt!

That was his adieu to the Court which it had certainly not been given him to turn into a Court of Ferrara; but "we have preserved the antique honour of Weimar; though I, God willing, have bid an eternal farewell to all such vanities."

Even in his own home Goethe had to practise resignation. Christiane's death had robbed him of his companion without delivering him from the racket which had so often driven him away from her; and now that in his age he needed even more care, and would have liked a still stricter routine in his household, he had again to face his old lot—always to give, seldom to receive.

A year after Christiane's death, he had got his son married; and if it was his father who induced August to settle down and found a bride for him, the bride, too, was thinking more of the father than of the son she took for husband. August was now at the end of his twenties, promoted to be *Kammerrat* and, under the new dispensation, associated with his father's official duties. He had grown handsome—there was even a look of Goethe about his eyes. The weak, round chin and cheeks derived from his mother; but in height he outstripped both parents, and through the exercises taught him by his father had acquired the true Greek symmetry. But there was a fierce unruly element in his composition which neither work nor affection availed to mitigate—and in fact he was given little of either. But he still seemed susceptible of improvement; and it was to remove him from a way of life which was always erratic, sometimes coarsely dissipated, and often intensely miserable, that Goethe found a wife for him, and began—so we are told—by making the mistake of separating him from a mistress, instead of waiting till his own volatility should do the work.

Ottilie von Pogwisch, of the North-German, impoverished nobility, was slender and pale, delicate, intelligent, and gifted, tormented by an unquenchable thirst for love and romance—which, however, she was not so reckless as to seek outside the shelter of a Court. When she became a member of Goethe's inner circle and comfortably shared his spacious house with him, she was not so much in quest of the young man's love or the old man's intellect, as of the great house and the great renown, which would give her desirous soul an outlet and confer upon her prosperity and a name. Though at first she was but partly conscious of this, a few years proved that it was her real purpose. To Goethe, whose last fifteen years she tended, the occasionally charming but often ailing and moody young lady meant little more in the beginning than a "daughterling," such as of yore he had been wont to choose for himself in a more normal and less egotistic fashion.

Discipleship—which was what he now chiefly desired in young people—he did not find in August and Ottilie; they were scarcely even listeners. Ottilie preferred to collect first editions of Goethe's works, to receive the Court in his house, and to represent the Goethe-dynasty at Berlin before the Hohenzollerns.

But even these things pleased her only when she happened to be in the humour for them. She was given to crazy infatuations which made her utterly scorn the social joys which yet she could not do without, and neglect household, father, husband, and children in favour of some handsome exquisite of the Court, especially if he happened to be an Englishman. Everything with which Weimar had reproached the defenceless Christiane, Ottilie revelled in for years under the shelter of the law.

Yet how little she did for her father, of those things which Christiane had so long done for her husband!

It was a semi-resignation here too, for Goethe. August's married life soon became a source of anxiety, and was often punctuated by quarrels. In a few years it showed as definitely unhappy; and as all this went on in Goethe's house, and only too often in his presence, the young pair did little to cheer him, and he was soon feeling lonelier than before. And as the young wife filled the house with her relatives, had her sister to stay for months at a time and her mother too on frequent visits, as Court interests, love-affairs, and dress (with a literary atmosphere superimposed) took precedence of all other topics, Goethe now did as he had done twenty years ago when Christiane introduced her relatives—scarcely more alien to him—into the stately mansion. He betook himself to Jena, there to dwell for months, on two occasions for as much as half a year. As of yore, his abode there consisted of two exiguous rooms (for the pine-top eyrie had been only one spring's refuge); and this, because the house where he could collect his mind and his treasures, happened to be just what the young people wanted as a focus for *their* activities.

But Goethe made no claims. The closer his association with the life of a fellow-creature, the more impossible it was for him to make it serve his own interests. In his old age he expected absolutely nothing from his fellow-men; and the completeness of his disillusion made him but the more serene. To his powerful vision their antic figures were transparent, and it was with the scientist's absorption that he observed an interior mechanism which was all too human in its functioning.

On several occasions he was unable to show hospitality to foreign notabilities, because supplies had failed to come from Weimar; and his only reproach was a casual remark in a letter that his servant "had to make out as best he could, and send the hat round perpetually." Even when he was the giver, the thankless young pair would take no trouble for him. Sending Ottilie a melon from Jena, he requested her

> *urgently*, to send back the seeds and if possible those of the former one too—for gardeners set an excessively high value on the good kinds. So as to impress upon you the desirability of taking this small amount of trouble, which moreover may be of advantage to yourself next year, I beg to announce that a quarter of a hundredweight of manuscript-music has arrived, which will be dispatched on receipt of the desired seeds.

So that all he had to thank Ottilie for was a couple of grandsons.

These years made Goethe a nominal grandfather several times over, for from all Germany came requests that he would be godfather to children whose parents had once had some slight connection with him; and whenever he was asked if a boy might be christened Wolfgang he would beg that his name might be William—for that was Shakespeare's name. It was now his turn to become a real grandfather.

Meanwhile I am occupied with the education of my grandson, which I deliberately conduct on the principle of giving him his own way in everything—hoping by this means to have him on his pins before his parents return. . . . With true grandfatherly infatuation. . . . I regard him as the most charming little creature in the world, and in sober fact I do feel that this great empty house and grounds are full, now he is here.

And when, as the boys grew older, they would rush all over the house with their little girl-friends, he would send them down sugar-plums (which with inextinguishable faith in his childhood's memories he always procured from Frankfurt) to play lotto with, and perhaps keep quiet for a while.

Since his children spent the money he earned as though it were water, he had to worry over expenses as in his old days; and Goethe, who had scarcely saved a penny, was obliged at seventy to calculate that he had better stay in Jena for the moment, for August was on Court-duty, and Ottilie "dined out so often that there were fewer household expenses at Weimar."

True, in his old age he was more meticulous than ever about most things. With his grey hairs he grew more and more like his father in that way.

Das mach' ich mir denn zum reichen Gewinn,
Dass ich getrost ein Pedante bin.[1]

The perpetual re-arrangement of his papers became a passion with him. He appointed sums to his various assistants for the publication of his posthumous works; and once when he returned from his summer holiday at a watering-place he was much gratified to find that they had prepared a portfolio for him, in which everything that came from his hand was carefully arranged in good order.

[1] "I haven't a doubt but it's better for me
A pedant unabashed to be."

On a return visit to Carlsbad, walking along the principal streets, he was delighted to discover that he knew all the street-signs by heart. When someone, driving with him, warned him that the carriage might upset on the bad road, Goethe said laughing that Napoleon could have had no better coachman than his; but when he happened to have with him a piece of black spar with which an admirer had presented him, he was worried all the time lest this should get any harm by the jolting.

In money-matters Goethe had grown so discreet that he, who dictated every single thing he wrote, often settled his accounts with his publisher with his own hand. From Frankfurt, for which he had no sort of sentimental feeling, he removed his inherited capital on the ground that he did not wish to contribute towards the rates, and for the same reason renounced his citizenship!

When the Duchy was re-organised he had no scruple in urging his claim to an increased salary, and this frankly on the score of his renown. The Duke granted him three thousand thalers a year—at that time an unusually high salary.

Goethe needed the money for his collections, his comforts, above all for his children—but also for the open house it pleased him to keep with them. During one winter there were guests in that house nearly every evening, while on every Thursday there was a large party; and he seems to have partly depicted his social ideal in the life of that uncle who, in the *Wanderjahre*, likes to be hospitable and inhospitable as the fancy takes him, dines from a travelling-kitchen which follows him everywhere, and waxes eloquent about the new arrangement in hotels of dining at separate little tables.

For Goethe liked society best when he was certain of being able to get away as soon as he wanted to. At their formal parties he now made a practice of appearing only when all the guests had assembled, and had been received by his son and daughter. On such occasions he was inclined to be stiffly ceremonious, wore all his orders and stars, was very much His Excellency—this to protect himself from being button-holed by the sort of guest he did not care about. He usually stood with his hands behind his back, and himself described this attitude as one which betokened certainty of one's rank, did not preclude a nearer approach, and properly belonged only to Princes. When he received friends in the middle of the day he did not at once shake hands with them—and, even when they were leaving, only if he had enjoyed the visit.

But any man whose work and achievements he admired, Goethe would astonish by the warmth of his reception. If a young physicist, with whom he had exchanged letters on their special subject, came to the house in Weimar, he would take him into his own room on the first visit; and, while they stood sketching and measuring, would break the loaf brought him by his servant in two pieces, so that he and his visitor might share it without ceremony.

To judge by many accounts, it was with an embarrassing mixture of fear and veneration that everyone for the first time ascended the broad staircase; and as Helen's beauty is best conveyed to us by Homer's description of its effect upon the Trojan veterans, so we can get our best idea of Goethe's personality from the impression it made upon visitors. Either they were afraid of him beforehand and became natural and confidential under his gaze, or else they had promised themselves to tell him home-truths and fell silent before those great eyes. In either event, fear played its part with everyone.

Even the uncertainty of how he would behave, which had to be reckoned with, derived from the very roots of his being.

I have an idiosyncrasy, [he wrote at seventy,] which has been both fortunate and unfortunate for me, in that it has led me to give more or less than was desired, but very seldom just *what* was desired. For my old friends it has been a source of mingled pain and pleasure.

The death of his old colleague in office, Voigt—one of his few surviving old friends—was a great loss for him. In a feverish, almost illegible hand Voigt wrote, on the day before he died, these words to his old friend:

. . . wanted to write you this last word while I could. Harrowing thought—the last word to Goethe! Ah, dear Goethe, but we shall live together in spirit . . . till I see that word written high above the stars. Perhaps to-morrow in the script of Heaven! Your Voigt.

It did not occur to Goethe that he might go to see his friend, who lived only two streets away from him. He answered on paper:

> Forgive me, most revered of my friends, for having left your treasured lines unanswered for twenty-four hours. Noble, to remember your old friend and bid him farewell in such a sacred moment—inestimably precious for him. But I cannot let you go! When our nearest and dearest prepare for a journey, which sooner or later will bring them back to us somehow, we try to dissuade them; and surely when it is the most solemn of all departures, we are called upon to be recalcitrant. So allow me to hope for the best. . . . Now and ever your most faithfully attached . . . J. W. Goethe.

Ghastly—this cold, stilted tone towards the dying man who had breathed such a tender yearning farewell to his friend! Goethe, who had never seen a fellow-creature die, and had scarcely ever visited a graveyard, now as before avoided the spectacle—and, as though he had never reflected upon that mysterious change, addressed his friend on his dying-day (and probably too late) with a semblance of cheer and affection. His letter has all the metallic hardness in which that tenderest of hearts was driven to disguise itself. Every word in this letter is studied; not one adjective could be changed for the better, and even the signature is unique in its mingling of formality with intimacy—for usually he signed his surname alone, unless ceremony demanded the particle of nobility.

Truly, at such moments, it seems to be made of glass—the heart of Goethe, crystalline, transparent, hard; and yet at other moments, even in his most advanced years, to be a heart pulsing with warm humanity. "It is certain" (he had said when he was no more than sixty) "that only he who has been the most sensitive can become the hardest and coldest of men, for he has to encase himself in triple steel . . . and often his coat-of-mail oppresses him."

His relation with Frau von Stein was strangely sublimated now. Her son, whom he addressed as "My dear friend and son" and Herder's son too—were now "fine young men," as Goethe said; though neither in them nor in Schiller's and Wieland's posterity was there any sign of remarkable talent. Charlotte had once more proved how different her nature was from Goethe's when she wrote to her son about *Dichtung und Wahrheit:* "I could not let the public into my secrets as he does." But she, who after Christiane's death was admitted to something like her old intimacy with Goethe (as though Charlotte, who was about twenty years older, had ultimately got the better of Christiane by surviving), did at last find the right phrase to characterise him: "I might call you the One who Gives."

Yet what Goethe now felt for her transcended by far their mutual memories. The woman whom he had loved at thirty and fled from at fifty, he now—at seventy—ranked with his idol Shakespeare, and expressed it in these words:

> Einer Einzigen angehören
> Einen Einzigen verehren,
> Wie vereint es Herz und Sinn!
> Lida! Glück der nächsten Nähe,
> William! Stern der höchsten Höhe,
> Euch verdank' ich, was ich bin.
> Tag' und Jahre sind verschwunden,
> Und doch ruht auf jenen Stunden
> Meines Wertes Vollgewinn.[1]

His fidelity to Knebel, Meyer, Zelter, was inviolable; his anxiety intense, whenever any of them happened to be ill. For some time his circle had been enlarged by a musician and a philosopher—the former a boy to be delighted in, the latter a youth to be argued with and admired. When Goethe was sad and lonely, sitting in the wintry gloom among his many disillusions, the twelve-year-old Felix Mendelssohn, whom Zelter had discovered, would come rushing up the broad staircase of the Weimar house; and he was never tired of listening to the handsome boy's improvisations on the piano—he would caress and spoil him, calling

[1] "Only one for heart's emotion,
Only one for mind's devotion—
Heart and mind communing so!
Lida! thou the bliss beside me,
William! thou the star to guide me,
All I am to ye I owe.
Days and years must fly, must perish,
Yet those deathless hours I cherish,
Best and rarest life shall know."

him his David who could exorcise his bad dreams when he was feeling ill.

Schopenhauer was instantly appreciated by Goethe, although his misanthropically self-conscious nature irritated the older man. Long before Schopenhauer produced his principal work—when he was little more than a boy—Goethe declared that he had a remarkable brain. Later he called him a man misunderstood by most people, but undoubtedly very difficult to know, and he initiated him into chromatics. But when Schopenhauer went farther than he did in his fine *Versuch über das Sehen und die Farben* (*Essay on the Perception of Colour*) Goethe wrote these testy lines:

> Trüge gern noch länger des Lebens Bürden,
> Wenn Schüler nur nicht gleich Lehrer würden.[1]

From a single sheet of paper we get a wonderful indication of the mutual comprehension between those two minds, for Schopenhauer's whole personality, the dangers threatening him both as a man and a philosopher, are hinted at in the lines written by Goethe in his album:

> Willst du dich deines Wertes freuen,
> So musst der Welt du Wert verleihen.[2]

And Schopenhauer recognised the truth there was in this, and—despite all his misanthropy—so passionately revered the personality of Goethe that he tore out every other page in his album, but kept that one till he died.

Zuleika's image gleamed afar. Of no other woman did Goethe keep so long such tender, thrilling memories. It was no more than he deserved—for had he not relinquished her that he might not spoil the happiness of his two friends? Now he could write to both; and gifts and remembrances came and went, in pleasant, untroubled, often whimsical fashion.

Marianne and Goethe never saw one another again, and so they could love to the end. As a youth he had always, when he

[1] "This life and its load I could gladlier shoulder,
If pupils would wait to teach till they're older."

[2] "To get from your gifts the sum of pleasure,
You must judge the world by a kindlier measure."

lost his sweetheart, lost her whole household with her, having loved them as one—but now he could keep both with a clear conscience. A box in which she had sent him fruit from her garden was returned with a medallion of his head and these touching verses:

Eine Schachtel Mirabellen
Kam von Süden, zog nach Norden.
Als die Frucht gespeist geworden,
Eilt sich wieder einzustellen
Das Gehäus, woher es kommen.
Bringet keine süssen Früchte,
Bringt vielmehr ein ernst Gesichte,
Das im Weiten und im Fernen
Nimmer will Entbehrung lernen.[1]

Do we not feel through the graceful, tender melody a renewal of sadness—a smiling-down of the heavy-laden heart, as in the days of his *Divan?*

Fifty years ago, he had sent his picture to Lotte Buff with these lines.

's ist ungefähr das garst'ge Gesicht,
Aber meine Liebe siehst du nicht.[2]

A poet's life had drawn a great sweeping line between these two inscriptions; yet the morose adolescent of Goethe's Werther-days, with his many meretricious flourishes and the sophisticated sprightliness of his rococo-rhymes, seems an older man than the writer of that midget masterpiece, with its German touch of real earnest.

[1] "Mirabelles, a box of beauties
From the South came northward fleeting.
When we all had finished eating,
Said the box: 'And now your duties
Are to pack and send me homeward.'
No sweet fruits it now will bring you,
But a grim old face will sing you:
'Far, though far away for ever—
I can do without you never.'"

[2] "A fairly good likeness of ugly me—
Ah, but my love you cannot see."

About this time Goethe made a private note: "When a man, as is the way with lovers, has opened his heart and kept nothing to himself, he has given a present which he cannot take back; and it would be impossible to injure or leave defenceless a once-loved being." Here he gives us an outline-sketch of the Goethean Eros—first, wholly feminine . . . in surrender and bestowal; then, wholly masculine in protection and helpfulness. And it was so that Goethe loved throughout his life, wooing and serving, honouring and protecting—never claiming, never contending, never the master.

The literary work of this period was all uninspired—continued, left unfinished, or concluded as it were by chance. He wrote a great deal, but—if we disregard isolated lyrics—nothing which can compare with any one of the four principal works in the preceding phase.

Didacticism was the note of all his verse at this time—the rhymed proverb flowered high in these anomalous years, and the epigrammatic form made it easy for him to take up a critical attitude towards the world and the age, their men and the work to which they gave birth.

One evening he was sitting alone with Ottilie, and telling her "a little tale of the sort I often invent. She wanted to read it, and I had to confess that it only existed in my imagination." But as he dictated it to her, it grew into a short story; and when he put it together with those so rapidly composed twelve years ago in the happy weeks at Carlsbad lo and behold! there resulted, in the most natural way in the world, the scheme for the first *Wanderjahre*—published by the author of seventy-two after he had brought Wilhelm Mesiter's *Lehrjahre* to a conclusion. He might have given those *Lehrjahre* the sub-title of "The Years of Desire"; and he now did give these *Wanderjahre* the profoundly expressive description of "Years of Resignation."

There is no comparison between the depth of wisdom in this volume and that of the *Lehrjahre;* but the way the episodes were strung together was too casual for it to equal the former work in construction. Besides, the idiosyncrasies of his older years enter even into the merest technicalities of this work—the circumstantial way in which letters and manuscripts are produced and exchanged by the characters corresponds to the pedantic tabulations, the cut-and-dried diaries, of the ageing Goethe.

Even the pieces which he frankly described as episodes "from my life"—the first half of the *Italienische Reise* and the *Campagne in Frankreich*—often lack the ease, and always the breadth, which had made the earlier portion of his biography so brilliant. This does not result from the period therein depicted, but from the period at which the work was done. The rejuvenated man of sixty had not lost his power of describing his youth; the stoical septuagenarian had to fasten on the Italian and Field-service documents if he was to recover anything at all of the earlier effect.

The impression we derive from the "Day- and Year-Books" in which he annotates the records of the last thirty years, is that of a positively frost-bound senility. Precious self-revealings and maxims are obscured by masses of nebulous tediousness, almost all his spiritual experiences are ignored, his works are barely alluded to; while on the other hand every Prince and Duke who happened to cross Goethe's path in this year or that is meticulously mentioned. Of Christiane's death, or Herder's, or of the time when the Duke dismissed him from the Theatre, there is not a word to be found. But the Duchess's broken arm is bewailed.

Nowhere is the "polar landscape," which to many Germans even then stood for an image of the veteran Goethe's inmost self, more manifest than in these official annals, which yet have almost nothing to say about the soul of the old man. While his mental realm was extending beyond all compass (though the spiritual powers were inadequate to supply centrifugal energy) Goethe despatched to his outermost frontiers mail-clad legions who—dumb, marble-cold—should watch lest any unauthorised foot profane the sacred soil.

And yet, all unafraid, self-confident, he could sum up his youth and his old age—sum up the whole mysterious problem of his being in these light-hearted lines:

Wüsste kaum genau zu sagen,
Ob ich es noch selber bin.
Will man mich im Ganzen fragen,
Sag' ich: Ja, so ist mein Sinn.

Ist ein Sinn, der uns zuweilen
Bald geängstet, bald ergetzt,
Und in so viel tausend Zeilen
Wieder sich ins Gleiche setzt.[1]

At this time Goethe made the oddest attempts at sentimentalising his youth for his private eye, though he was giving such a frigid account of it to the public. For a philologist he wrote a bowdlerised commentary on the "abstruse" poem *Harzreise im Winter*. Yet at the same time he was recalling those so-called "mad days" with great pleasure, at his dinner-table.

But every illusion was pricked like a bubble when one thing happened—when any of these sublimated figures of his youth ventured to appear as its own ghost in Weimar. More than forty years after the final adieu in Wetzlar, the widowed *Hofrätin* Kestner, with a tall daughter from Hanover, arrived at Weimar —*una pœnitentium*, once known as Lotte. Goethe set up an attack of gout, excused himself, sent them tickets for his box, put off this (to him) extremely unwelcome meeting as long as he could. Ultimately Lotte made "the acquaintance of a stranger— an old man whom I should never have known to be Goethe; and even so, he made anything but an agreeable impression on me." And yet, at bottom, there was nothing worse between these two old people than a book which had carried her name round the civilised globe.

When the creative impulse slumbered in Goethe, the critical always awoke. At this time he established, in the journal *Kunst und Alterthum*, a sort of Veterans' Home for æsthetic opinions; for the six volumes published by him in the last sixteen years of his life are for the most part of his own authorship. Upon contemporary literature in almost every European country, upon

[1] "Never did I know distinctly
What 'myself' might mean for me.
On the whole? I say succinctly:
'This is what my mind must be'—
For there is a mind that thinking
Tortures now, and now delights;
This, a thousand verses linking,
Somehow sets itself to rights."

plastic art in almost every age, upon coins and gems, upon songs, speeches, biographies, upon natural rights and policies, he there pontificated—ostensibly, as a rule, reviewing new works of art, but always so prone to take a general view that in the event these volumes comprise the veteran Goethe's complete æsthetic.

With renewed enthusiasm and longing the old man's saddened contemplation fastened on antiquity; and nothing in this decade excited him to such a pitch as the rumours of the Parthenon Frieze—the suspense, and then the pictures of it, as brought to London by Lord Elgin.

And when the sketches of the recently discovered frieze of Phigaleia reached him in his pine-top eyrie, Goethe wrote: "It is abysmal in its profundity and power—one feels two thousand years younger and better the moment one looks at it."

Ease and blitheness in art—these alone he desired, exacted. During this difficult self-sacrificing era of the spirit, it was by these that he judged all achievement; and Mozart's and Raphael's names fell constantly from the old man's lips.

It is not until now that his letters and conversations can be reckoned among his important works—from their number and interest, but chiefly as the ground-plan for a critical judgment which (in most instances with a view to later publication) was now used to elaborate his maxims and essays. Goethe, in his old age, dictated something like three hundred letters every year, of which more than a quarter treat of outstanding events, persons, or tendencies. Many he would read to his friends before despatching them. In his business letters, especially those to the Duke, he used a system of continuously numbered sections; but as private matters frequently broke in, there would crop up, say in *No. 1*, an opinion on a new book of memoirs; and then: "*No. 2:* A passion-flower stands on my desk . . . I take great delight in it, though it distracts my thoughts. *No. 3:* And I take the liberty of enclosing a message from Frege" (the banking-house).

For the signature to his intimate letters the septuagenarian adopted a couple of formulas which are all the more touching when they are irrelevant to the actual contents. "And so ever and for ever yours"—that was his chosen conclusion to his friends, and it always has the effect of sending a lifelong farewell. But the other phrase, with which in his youth he had always, and even in his middle age sometimes, conjured his friends, was scarcely ever used—it does occur to Knebel, but even to him only once or twice: "Love me." The stoic said that no more to anyone. Now that he could love more universally, he did not need to beg for any individual's love.

The veteran Goethe expanded most in conversation. . . . As everyone hears what he carries in his heart, any isolated account may easily distort the image of Goethe; and what friends profess to have heard him say must be reckoned by psychological weights and measures. It is only the sum of all his conversations which can give us the image of him—especially that which the six most renowned interlocutors have drawn for us.

Of these, the Councillor of Legation, Falk, seems the most suspect because of his remarkable intelligence, which is prone to mingle Goethe's ideas with his own. Boisserée and the Swiss Soret are faithful and perceptive, but their opportunities were few. Eckermann is usually true to fact because so unimaginative, but his long-winded answers are tiresome. His renown really derives from the steadiness of their intercourse, and the confirmation afterwards given by Goethe to a part—not all!—of his accounts. But nearly all of his narratives depart from the living word, and are couched in a pseudo-classic style which spoils the effect; while the third section, published by Eckermann sixteen years after Goethe's death, and really taken over from Soret's French notes, is stylised beyond recognition, and not seldom demonstrably erroneous.

Of his occasional visitors the only ones who have given really illuminating accounts of conversations with Goethe are Riemer, a highly-cultivated psychologist, and Müller, an equally cultivated man of the world. They alone, in their Memoirs, give us a comprehensive portrait of the old Goethe. Doubtless Meyer and Zelter were the friends who got the most personal confidences by word of mouth, because Goethe knew that they would for ever hold their peace.

At this period Goethe was *Præceptor Germaniæ*. He had lived to be an historical figure; and having taken his whole experiences in an historical sense, he was not too modest to make arrangements for posterity.

"Take your time over the study of my posthumous works,"

he wrote to Schubarth, his commentator. "This I advise, not because the works are by me, but because in them you have a complex of emotions, thoughts, experiences, and results which all bear upon one another."

A young poet could often charm the veteran by an expression —a stanza—a look—a gesture. He sometimes commended the verses of modest, well-bred young people whose efforts have passed into complete oblivion; but when Heinrich Heine, in his student-days, came and confided to Goethe that he was writing a *Faust*, it must be confessed that Goethe dismissed him with the remark: "Have you no other business in Weimar?" He detested writing to programme, in every sense.

Generally speaking, he shunned more carefully even than before the vast, chaotic type of talent, preferring graceful Goethe-Epigoni—not because they imitated him, but because they were more unlike himself in his youth than the former were. And yet, all of a sudden, he would say something of this sort: "Higher aspirations are by their very nature more admirable, even when unfulfilled, than lower ones perfectly carried out."

To foreign poets Goethe was much more indulgent—he would even permit them to be Romantics. But in Germany at that time the Romantic school was becoming more and more dangerously allied with Catholicism and the Reaction, while abroad it was otherwise, and so did not trouble him. He called attention in several articles to Serbian songs and Russian poems; he praised and translated Manzoni; Greek students sent him their modern heroic ballads, and while he was advertising these for them, they were translating his *Iphigenie* into Neo-Greek.

Foreign renown, which was only now really beginning, was the weapon he most coveted against his adversaries. From essays upon his work, from translations and books about him, appearing in Paris and London, he would make extracts with his own hand, "to show my friends that it is not (as some would fain persuade the nation) the indiscriminating applause of the mere mob." And indeed this foreign fame did seem to make his position stronger in Germany. True, certain of his works still failed to make their effect. The *Divan* was held to be untimely and obscure; and Goethe was continually, as of old, annoyed by the appreciation of early works at the expense of new ones. And if anything of his did happen to be acted, it was usually by amateurs. When Prince Radziwill, in the little Monbijou Palace at Berlin, experimented with some scenes from Goethe's *Faust*, the Earth-Spirit wore a mask representing—Goethe!

Nevertheless Goethe, whose fame had revived of recent years, was gradually becoming the National Sage. "Strange, but quite natural, that human beings should ponder on our last days as if they were Sibylline books, though they looked with such insulting composure on the fireworks of the earlier volumes." It was not until now that Goethe's personality captured the imagination of his fellow-countrymen. The queerest questions came to him from afar; strangers would consult him about their marriages, their business-affairs, so that he could smilingly call himself a father-confessor. Princes and pundits, travellers and dilettanti, sent him stones and coins; there came amethysts from Kamchatka (and it was like being transplanted again to the regions of the *Divan*); while some antique church-plate was actually presented to the pagan by a collector.

In Frankfurt they took heart of grace, and (after Goethe had been suffered to renounce his rights as a citizen, instead of being presented with the freedom of the city) made up their minds to erect a memorial to the septuagenarian. He was personally consulted by the committee; but it was not until an artist so renowned as Rauch came to model him for a statue that he changed his attitude, declaring that he had done with false modesty, and was ready to co-operate as if someone else were concerned. He began by remarking that the site chosen for the memorial was too remote and too damp, and suggested instead the vestibule of the Library, where other men might be placed beside him. Finally he even wrote an article: "Considerations on a memorial to be erected to the Poet Goethe in his native town"; and this article is yet another symbol—the strangest alloy of pedantry and naïveté.

More the Sage than the Poet, more the busy man than the creative artist—so Goethe appeared at the beginning of his seventies; and he was again devoting the best part of his energies to natural science, from which the poetic phase of the preceding period had caused him almost entirely to abstain. Nowhere does the old man's eager elasticity take so splendid and so youthful a stride as in this era; for now begins the last of his metamorphoses, the gradual rending of the veil behind which he had lived his inward life, and accumulated all his creative forces. Individuality was now merged in the Universal.

The grand pitched battle between poet and thinker which had convulsed his writings, his thought, his existence for decades—that symbol, as it were, of his dual nature—was now at last to be fought to a finish, and Goethe was conscious that the decisive moment was approaching.

My whole attention [he wrote at seventy-three] is now fixed upon the question of how far special and individual tendencies divorce the perceptions of the observer from the logical processes of the thinker—and especially those which operate in the same sphere, and attract and repel one another as living beings do.

Once more he was projecting that inner conflict from out his breast into the universe, that so he might more clearly apprehend it.

Like Leonardo, Goethe in his old age never abandoned his reverent investigation of the particular for contemplation of the universal. Like Leonardo, he plodded on patiently at the details, faithful to the lowly endeavour of an entire lifetime, for whether it was a stone or a colour, a plant or a cloud:

Und es ist das Ewig Eine,
Das sich vielfach offenbart:
Klein das Grosse, gross das Kleine,
Alles nach der eignen Art;
Immer wechselnd, fest sich haltend,
Nah und fern, und fern und nah,
So gestaltend, umgestaltend—
Zum Erstaunen bin ich da.[1]

[1] "One, the deathless, manifested
In the Many—this I see;
Small is great, great small, attested
Each by its own entity.
Ever-changing, never ranging,
Near and far, and far and near,
Forming now, and now transforming—
I to gaze in awe am here."

GOETHE AT THE AGE OF SIXTY-EIGHT

This was a sage who never wearied of testing his underlying pantheistic emotion by ever-renewed observation; but now he was not urged by materialistic scepticism—rather by a sort of confident curiosity, very much as a lover, without doubting her, will test his beloved that he may be the more fondly convinced of his mastery. Nurtured by his father on world-history, challenged by talent and energy to a life time of many-sidedness, Goethe was now beginning—he whose influence as veteran, teacher, educationist, was so far-flung—to preach one-sidedness.

Many-sidedness really does no more than prepare the element in which one-sidedness, having sufficient margin, can effectually operate. . . . To confine one's self to one craft—that is the best way. For a limited brain, a craft is at worst a craft; for a better one, it is an art; and the best of all, in doing one thing, does everything—or, to be less paradoxical, in the one thing done well it sees a symbol of everything that is well done.

He himself, who was renouncing so much both in life and poetry, entered on new realms of thought with fearless confidence, and did not abate his investigations into the old ones. A journal of his own, "in the service of science as a whole, especially morphology," which he ran alongside *Kunst und Alterthum,* was henceforth the channel for Goethe's scientific writings on physics, botany, zoology, geology, mineralogy, meteorology.

A new discovery in chromatics, which led to definite results, he first announced to his son in words recalling those wherewith he flung the new-found intermaxillary bone in Herder's face. Thirty years lay between, but from the tone one would not imagine them to be more than ten at most:

. . . that the moral dispensation of the universe . . . has graciously suffered me, as I once hoped but scarcely expected, to solve the enigma of entoptic colors which has so long occupied me, and for the last ten weeks has utterly distraught and befooled me, but has been at last got the better of . . . It was not like holding an eel by the tail but a dragon by the throat—and I throttled him so unrelentingly that he had to give in.

When a disciple of Hegel's founded a special chair for Goethe's Theory of Colour in his Berlin Academy, he told several friends of it—much uplifted, and hoping "after thirty years of non-recognition, to win a decisive and dangerous game at last, supported by young eager intelligences."

New geological studies confirmed or refuted the old. He had once thought of bringing chromatics into a novel; and now, in his *Wanderjahre*, he created a geologist-hero. Montan's emotions are those of Goethe—and so much so that to-day it is not Goethe himself but Montan whom we think to see, when Goethe suddenly made his carriage stop, bent over an ordinary stone in the road, and (by his companion's account) stood gazing and tapping, and saying softly to himself: "Well, and how do *you* come here?"

Following the example of an Englishman, he now took up the new science of meteorology; and was not deterred by the prospect of beginning in a small way what could only prove fruitful in a large one. From one day to another he made himself a "Cloud-Calendar," classified cloud-forms, arranged that the warders of towers all over the country should keep a look-out for meteors, published tabular forms for officials and amateurs, and was incessant both in private and public appeals for observation of the skies.

With Goethe's symbolic apprehension of the visible world, it is not surprising that now, towards the end, scientific research, poetry, and faith should have imperceptibly merged in one another; and that—even by posterity, considering him—they are to be divided only by the most heedful of hands. How true it is that poetry is the connecting-link between science and faith, Goethe showed unmistakably when, from this time forward, he took to publishing his profoundest poems in the morphological magazine—so that the maturest productions of the septuagenarian had to be sought for between the covers of his scientific journal.

> Im Namen dessen, der sich selbst erschuf,
> Von Ewigkeit in schaffenden Beruf . . .
> So weit das Ohr, so weit das Auge reicht,
> Du findest nur Bekanntes, der ihn gleicht,
> Und deines Geistes höchster Feuerflug
> Hat schon am Gleichniss, hat am Bild genug.[1]

[1] "Now in his Name, who did himself create,
And evermore doth form, doth generate. . . .

Side by side with the manful composure of such a mood existed all the more feminine instincts. Imagination and faith survived to fight the old battle with the scientist's tenacity; and though Goethe fulminated against the telescopes that bring us too close to the arcana of Nature, he could laugh to scorn those who parroted Haller.

> "Ins Innre der Natur"
> —O, du Philister!
> "Dringt kein erschaffner Geist!"—
> Mich und Geschwister
> Mögt ihr an solches Wort
> Nur nicht erinnern!
> Wir denken: Ort für Ort
> Sind wir im Innern. . . .
> Natur hat weder Kern noch Schale,
> Alles ist sie mit einem Male.[1]

And under the stern superscription "Ultimatum" he soon afterwards reiterated almost word for word the last two lines.

When we touch upon the conflict between sensuous perception and dream, we have penetrated to the core of Goethe's religion. Never is it more difficult of apprehension than in this penultimate period, wherein a complex of spiritual tendencies, impulses, and counter-impulses threatened to make even his political attitude uncertain. Here as there we shall find our way only by an undeviating gaze into the heart of his being.

> Far as the ear, the eye, can hear or see,
> Only the Known will make him known to thee;
> Thine ardent spirit, though it scale the sky,
> Symbol and image still must satisfy."

[1] "'To Nature's inmost core'
—O Philistine!—
'No mortal mind may pierce!'—
For me and mine
That phrase you fondly air
Is not so telling!
We hold: Or here or there
In her we're dwelling. . . .
Not husk is Nature, no! nor kernel;
She is the All-in-One Eternal."

Kindliness is not religion—it is a trait of character; and indeed Goethe at his kindliest is Goethe at his most controversial, in the doctrinal sense. If gratitude and worship, sisters to kindliness, always filled Goethe's heart in an unbroken continuity, it is equally true that he was much more actively benevolent at some periods than he was at others. Work had never made him hard, if misanthropy had made him cautious; and now stoicism, unsullied by any hatreds, removed all inhibitions of that kind. No one knows how much Goethe, for all his pedantry and aloofness, did for others. Vehemently opposed though he was to the larger issue of universal suffrage, his servants and subordinates were personally devoted to him; and if as an official he figured as an enemy of the people, in private life he was a spiritual healer and counsellor, the advocate and helper of the oppressed and of his friends. A hundred letters now supply a connected narrative of what then was known only to individual persons.

In that sense the veteran Goethe was a Christian; but in that sense, so was the young Goethe. And yet he was a Pagan, and remained one to the end. For everything which might be adduced as a symptom of change of heart in his advanced age, turns out to be no more than a social or æsthetic, an historical or academic, recognition.

Both Churches now made tentative approaches to the old heretic, for it was felt that such a soul was worth saving. Goethe first learnt to appreciate Catholic teaching at the age of seventy. Closer intercourse with Austrian aristocrats, issuing from the hands of the Jesuits as accomplished men of the world, and with Bohemian prelates, the Headmasters of admirable schools, gave Goethe—who had seen little of Catholicism in Germany, and in Italy only its decadence—a clearer idea and a more logical comprehension of that mighty influence; and when in Carlsbad he was induced to hear some missionary sermons, he confessed that he could find "not a trace of monkishness or sacerdotalism."

Yet even when looking at the pictures of Martin Schön, whom he loved, he exclaimed regretfully:

If only the rascal had stuck to the Magi instead of going in for that detestable Passion! . . . Eleven hundred virgins—at any rate that's an element in which an artist can let himself go, and be as happy in the odour of sanctity as any gay dog of them all!

When he recommended, as a subject for painting, the Lord walking on the sea with Peter sinking beside Him, he in the same breath suggested Thisbe, eavesdropping at the hole in the wall!

"No doubt," he wrote in ecstasy about a Danæ by a contemporary of Veronese, "a thing like that seems foolishness to our experts, who so revel in Holy Families." He was against the idea of summoning Schelling to Jena (though he always spoke admiringly of his teaching and character) simply because Schelling had embraced the Catholic faith, and Goethe did not desire "to see that old obsolete stuff re-introduced in a new mystical-pantheistic abstrusely philosophical, though (tell it not in Gath!) by no means despicable form."

A single incident, contradicted by a hundred others, seems at this time to indicate a more amicable attitude. When Chancellor von Müller was reading aloud to Goethe, then seventy-two, a passage upon the contrast between revealed and natural religion, Goethe vehemently exclaimed:

Damned rhetorical flourishes, that's what they are—putting a false gloss on everything. What has made the Christian religion prevail over all others, how has it become mistress of the Universe—and deservedly so—if not because it has incorporated the truths of natural religion in its teaching? And then what becomes of your "contrast"? The frontiers are conterminous, I tell you!"

He found that certain secular tenets of the Protestants were congenial, and his praise of the Reformation as a liberating force is a plain proof that he was very far from conversion in any form—for as a born Protestant, and an artist and mystic into the bargain, he could, after fifty years of paganism, have chosen no other creed than Catholicism. When the tercentenary of the Wittenberg Thesis was approaching, Goethe spoke up for Luther, and said that the two Testaments stood respectively for Law and Gospel—for Necessity and Freedom. This he thought of making the theme of an oratorio—and no one can read his synopsis without a fervent regret that it never came to the birth. He intended to begin with the thunder of Sinai, with "Thou shalt!"—and end with the Resurrection of Christ, with "Thou wilt!"

Nothing came of it;

for, between ourselves, the only interesting thing in the whole business is the character of Luther, and it is also the only thing that really impresses the big public. All the rest is the same sort of wish-wash that descends upon us every day of the year. . . . And so you will come to see that the greatness and glory of our forefathers is to be found, in all its pristine beauty, when they speak for themselves; for what God says in the Koran is true: "We have sent no nation a prophet who does not speak directly to the people!" Thus, the Germans were no nation until the coming of Luther.

Among the voices which whispered to Goethe, thinking to save that soul while yet there was time, one spoke in accents which he had not heard for nearly fifty years. Augusta, Countess Stolberg had certainly—though she had never seen him—not forgotten Goethe. She was an earnest member of the Moravian Brotherhood; and she devoted nine days to the composition of the beautiful letter she wrote him.

He seems to have answered immediately; and nowhere in the whole range of his confessions (and scarcely from any other human spirit) shall we find such noble acquiescence as in this letter from Goethe at seventy-three, to a woman once worshipped from afar, a saintly nature elected to uplift him. Dignity and humility, complete spiritual immunity, lent him these gentle chastened accents of assent and dissent, with their silver music:

. . . All my life long I have been sincere with myself and others, and through all my striving here below have ever looked above—as you and yours have looked. Let us then work together while yet it is day. . . . And so we need take no thought for the morrow! In our Father's House are many mansions, and he who has given us so fair an abiding-place here will assuredly care for us in the Beyond. It may be that what we failed in here we shall accomplish there—to know one another face-to-face and love one another still more truly. Remember me in tranquil trust and faith.

With these exquisite words Goethe closed the door and withdrew into his own kingdom; and the sexagenarian poet who had said he was a polytheistic artist and a pantheistic scientist, shows at seventy as a scientist oblivious of his Muse, a Pantheist through and through, as those didactic poems, heralding his Nature-studies, testify.

Yet Goethe now drew the line more stringently than he had done of late; and no doubt fully conscious of the supremacy to which the best German minds were beginning to look up, he refused to be identified with any sect or secret society.

When my eyes shut and my brain loses control, it is extremely refreshing to fall into natural slumber. When I reflect that I was a friend of Lavater's, who attached religious value to this miracle of Nature, it often seems to me very strange that I was not led away, but behaved exactly like a man walking beside a river without the least desire to bathe in it. That shows that it must have been natural for me, else it would not have lasted into my old age. . . . (But if) the inexpressible ever did contrive to get expressed, we should not take it so literally as all that. And so the poet, if he wants to be modest, must recognise that his state is neither more nor less than a waking sleep; and indeed I do not deny that a very great many things have come to my knowledge when I was in a dream-like condition.

Is not the boundary-line perceptible—so fine, yet so decisive? This believer shrinks from all dogma; this scientist, whose mysticism embraces the All because its source is the All, will be seduced by none into betraying his nature by acceptance of the formulæ of transcendentalism. At no price will Goethe, in his old age, surrender his eye and his reason, which have revealed to him the universe. Goethe gave his fellow-creatures all that his vision gave him—but they were not suffered to urge upon him as a principle what he possessed as a divination.

True, he could still be superstitious as in the preceding decade, when he traced a decided connection between the news of Napoleon's escape from Elba and a Napoleon-ring which on that very day, after a prolonged search, was restored to him. Nevertheless, the words spoken in trance by an Indian conjurer (whose tricks had delighted him) he tested afterwards with an Orientalist sceptical as a criminal judge. For it was to himself as well as others that he uttered the pregnant warning:

Suche nicht verborgne Weihe!
Unterm Schleier lass das Starre!
Willst du leben, guter Narre,
Sieh nur hinter dich ins Freie![1]

No mistaking there the line he means to draw against the "fools that rush in"—for what had been revealed to him, Goethe the Poet revealed to none but them who had wisdom.

As poet, indeed, he did now create the most mystic of all his characters; and suffered her, in her supremacy to meet his wandering Wilhelm—for Makarie is an astrologer; and

it would seem that to Makarie the correspondencies of our solar system were from the beginning so clear as really to seem part of her being—first in repose, then gradually evolving, and finally revealed with such vividity as she could not mistake. At first these visions were a source of distress to her, then she began to take pleasure in them, and the fascination grew with every year.

When the "magic manuscript of a family of alchemists" had to be sold to relieve their poverty, Goethe procured it at a high price for the Library, and wrote under the report for his colleagues—who might have derided or blamed him—the singular words: "Consideration! And sympathy!" Of Giordano Bruno, the Orphic mystics and their commentaries, he made a prolonged study at this time.

And so on a day in October, all the elements—scientific research and prescient perception, emotional and intellectual adventures joined forces for a poem. In its strophes genius is ever present, together with all the aspirations, experiences, misgivings, engendered in the twilight of a mystical yet discerning and vigilant faith. They were written in a cold glow of spiritual exaltation; and (as Goethe afterwards acknowledged) embody

perhaps the most abstruse conceptions of modern philosophy. I am inclined to believe that poetic art is possibly the only instrument

[1] "Break not into holy places!
Shroud the corpse, and leave it lying!
Worthy fool, wouldst live? No prying—
Vast enough the rearward spaces."

which can at all suffice to express such mysteries; they would have an absurd effect in prose, because they can only be conveyed by contradictions which the reason is not prepared to accept. Unfortunately, with things of this kind, the will avails little for consummation—they are gifts and graces of the moment which come unbidden, casually as it were, after long gestation.

Aboriginal incantations, spoken over the destinies of mortals: so he called these runes, which were collectively entitled *Orphic Mysteries*, and calmly printed as introit to a new morphological essay—strophes which are at once a profounder and a clearer paraphrase of the veteran Goethe's faith than any other confession as that rhapsody on Nature had been for his middle period.

When Goethe wrote them down he can scarce, for all his prescience, have been conscious that a few years were to bring him yet another gift and yet another ordeal, which should once more embroil the five primeval forces of his Orphic poem. In his seventy-fourth year Goethe was brought into contact with a young man, and a girl, who perplexed him, attracted him, and were swiftly swept away from him.

While the man of seventy, busy and uncomplaining, was working, experimenting, writing in his restricted sphere of Weimar and Jena, the thirty-yeared Lord Byron was pursuing his headlong career. For the first time in many years old Europe was regaled by the spectacle of an artist who made his life more famous than his work, although the work was no less a product of genius than the life was. That wild-fire existence consumed itself in one quick flare of dæmonic energy, sensuality, and melancholy; and was a literal, if grossly exaggerated, embodiment of the lines in which Goethe—at the very time of Byron's birth—had unbosomed himself during the Roman dream, through the lips of Faust:

> So tauml' ich von Begierde zu Genuss,
> Und im Genuss verschmacht' ich nach Begierde.[1]

[1] "So am I tossed between desire and bliss,
And, having bliss, am with desire consumed."

Surpassing genius destroyed itself in Byron, because it sought adequate material in vain—for even his poetry was no more than a cry. "Napoleon robbed me of the first place." So Byron, whose star rose with Napoleon's, complained; and arrogant as it may seem, there is a profound truth in the saying. A Peer of England, beautiful, gallant, highly-cultivated; but, as the result of an unhappy marriage, ostracised, driven from his native land, an outlaw from the society to which he belonged by right of birth, which he regarded as the best in the world, which devoured his verse and held him up to contumely—such was the Byron who for well-nigh a decade tossed about Southern Europe, the lover of one of the loveliest and proudest of Italian women, the friend of the most distinguished intellects, the first artists of his time; world-renowned for the passion and gloom of the poems which were always so much the same; for ever craving the fiery deed, the gallant action, all energy and all indolence—the perfect type of the uncontrolled dæmonic being, who puts no rein upon himself, and least of all the rein of his genius. In sober truth, this is the formula for Byron's life—the dæmon, destroying genius.

At every point the life of Goethe was the antithesis of this. His dæmon overcome by genius, his whole existence a battle with himself; the world shut out by walls of such artful construction; a clutch at every form of activity for the saving of his soul; deliberate concentration on a narrow sphere; the inward self the focus of all endeavour—and thus, the soaring sweeping flight of eighty years of life slowly bearing him, in his supreme fortitude, to the peak which seems to touch the stars. No competitor had been able to disconcert Goethe; for they who took a different line from his were less than he, or else came quickly to the ground.

Not until he was nearly seventy, then, did Goethe meet his match in a poet. How his heart must have burnt within him as he saw Byron rush uncontrollably on to spheres in which he himself had never been at home, to phases which he had always shunned—and yet saw, too, a poet's life enact itself in the grand style which, whatever Goethe might tell himself, had its own way of defeating the world. It is the ebb-tide gaze of the old man in his resignation at the young man in his wilfulness; it is some abysmal resentment, never even to himself confessed; it is the reflective envy of a tragic victor for the more dazzling Defeated—this and these it is which explain Goethe's enthusiasm for Byron.

From the first the personality fascinated him more than the poetry. It was only gradually that he got used to Byron's poetry, "which at first repelled me by its hypochondriacal passion and violent self-hatred; and, though I wished for closer contact with his great personality, threatened to make his Muse entirely alien to me." What was it that made this impression on Goethe, who was very chary of attributing "a great personality" to his contemporaries, and—take it for all in all—really confessed it in none but Napoleon? He never saw or spoke to Byron, so that the supreme fascination passed him by; Byron had never *done* anything to speak of, and his writings began by irritating rather than convincing Goethe.

It was nothing but the unmistakable genius speaking from Byron which attracted him; the apocalyptic frenzy of the man, depicted in a hundred anecdotes, the pace, the furore, the passion, the *Weltschmerz*—of yore, in the young Goethe, no less fierce, no less convulsive. The dimensions of this career, the journeyings, the love-affairs, everything by which the English poet, with neither army nor throne, had worn himself out—these were the influences; for if he contrasted their youthful periods, Goethe fell short of Byron only in the limitations of his home-life, in the dullness of his career as a Frankfurt advocate, in the mereness of society as represented by a banker's house at Offenbach, in the lesser proportions of the Parliament House at Weimar, and of the marriage he made there, and of the local paper he conducted there.

In cosmic emotion (as the retrospective Goethe was well aware) this young foreign poet was by no means superior to himself in his youth; but with his title, his means, his women, horses, travels—with the whole anarchic glamour of his poetic career, he cast a spell over Goethe. For the career, with its amoral, its challenging note, was Napoleonic; and Napoleon's tyrannous course, like Byron's, overwhelmed all Goethe's fundamental principles of law and order. Here as there it was—over and above the success—the mighty personality, of which Goethe throughout a lifetime had felt the absence in his contemporaries, and which he knew to be chiefly of inward growth in himself. A like poetic genius, born as a German bourgeois, would have left the veteran Goethe cold. But the complete, undeniable unity of Byron's life and poetry made him able to admire both Byronic manifestations, because his own endeavour had been to see life and poetry as mutually stimulating forces.

Yet at the same time Goethe's vision could discern, in the heart of Byron, all the blindnesses, the exaggerations and untruths, the self-conscious sentimentality. He called his a talent born to torment itself, saying that his "mannerisms," both in life and poetry made it well-nigh impossible to judge him aright. "He has often enough confessed what it is that torments him . . . and scarcely one human being has any sympathy with the unbearable pain over which he broods so incessantly, and which he is for ever flinging in the face of the world." Even about Byron's *Manfred,* which was a deliberate variation on *Faust,* Goethe (amid the general admiration) went so far as to say in his review, "that the lurid glow of an infinite, grandiose despair becomes fatiguing at long last." Indeed he even said, so late as this, that in six months he would perhaps declare against Byron!

Instead, his expert critical judgment suddenly veered round to passionate enthusiasm; and as Byron's later works can scarcely be considered notably superior to his earlier ones, it must have been his conduct which brought this about. As his fantastic manner of life became more and more talked of, Goethe found it easier to understand and admire the poems it inspired—particularly as Byron now approached him with a dedication. Never had such a step affected Goethe's judgment—and scarcely even the manner of his acknowledgment. But now he was most marvellously uplifted by the young Lord's veneration. In a published essay he had already told the romantic anecdote about the murder of a Turkish mistress of Byron's, and attributed his persecution-mania to that incident; and generally speaking he had adopted—in defiance of his wonted scepticism—the tone of the legend woven through all Europe round that frenzied career. "What a wounded heart must be that of the poet," exclaimed Goethe, referring in this essay to the history of a Spartan king "who chooses this story out of all antiquity, to identify himself with so tragic a fate!" Then he spoke of "that singular career, that singular poetry, in all their eccentricity, made the more arresting because their parallel will not be found in any bygone century, and hence we have no material of any kind by which to measure them." Finally he makes use of such superlatives as had never before appeared in any criticism from Goethe's hand; and in reviewing *Cain* and *Don Juan* writes of a "work of boundless genius," of "a revelation not before communicated to man," of "a poet without his equal"; and declares that he "would not have Byron other than he is."

In private he spoke more robustly, saying that *Don Juan* was wilder and more grandiose than any of the former works, but wearisome by reason of the perpetual repetitions. If Byron had been a painter, he added—and we perceive that he appreciated this poet's knowledge of society—his pictures would have fetched their weight in gold.

So that when Byron wanted to dedicate his *Sardanapalus* to Goethe, and caused this to be conveyed to him, and when the dedication somehow failed to come off Goethe—to whom Byron's written words had by some curious chance been lent, had them lithographed, and sent copies to his friends. When the succeeding work (*Werner*) really was dedicated to him, he declared that he felt it almost beyond his power to acknowledge it adequately!

Then Byron himself afforded a better reason than heretofore for admiration of his personal life. He sailed for Greece, equipped with insufficient funds and few followers, but with any amount of romantic feeling and craving for action, there to support the Greeks in their revolt against the Turks. Byron was nearly thirty-six; Goethe was twice that age. He beheld a young chivalrous nobleman, who loved to trace his descent from Thor, the god of thunder, preparing himself to fight for Hellenic freedom—beheld a poet endangering his life out of passion for an ideal; he felt that the action was in the grand style, and that his own life had never known such a moment. And from that day Goethe, who had lately heard of his Emperor's death, was in possession of a new hero. Did he not know that it was more out of fatigue and satiety, out of a craving for the sensational, out of a premonition that the Fifth Act of his life lay here—in a word, that it was wholly as an adventurer that the poet decided on this plan, with the idea of which he had toyed two years before, suggesting it to a friend as an excuse for an interesting journey. Even if Goethe could have divined all this, he would not have let himself divine it.

Then there came from Genoa, where Byron was waiting to embark, a charming note in which he introduced the bearer, who was a friend of his, to Goethe. And the old poet's every pulse thrilled for the young hero; he hastened to send him a message before he sailed, and (while ostensibly wishing him Godspeed) tenderly summed up his whole fate, his whole nature, and all his genius and folly, in a few lines—closing with this profoundest of a poet's well-learnt lessons, directed straight at Byron's quivering heart:

> Wohl sei ihm doch, wenn er sich selbst empfindet!
> Er wage selbst sich hochbeglückt zu nennen,
> Wenn Musenkraft die Schmerzen überwindet,
> Und wie ich ihn erkannt, mög' er sich kennen![1]

At the last moment Goethe's lines reached Byron. Would he answer in verse or in more precious prose? A formal note hastily scribbled, speaking only of himself and his setting-out, thanked Goethe for "your verses sent me by my friend"; and there was only one sentence which gave a glimpse of his perplexed, excited state. Goethe's words (he said) he would take for a good omen, and hoped on his return to visit him.

But Goethe, stirred by the thought that a poet had no time for writing because he was on the eve of sailing for Hellas, was moved by the letter, declared himself to be vastly honoured by Byron's having found time "to answer with a whole page of writing, which the recipient has preserved among his most precious papers, as the proudest testimony to the connection existing between us." Byron sailed; and for something like a year very little was heard of him.

In a letter referring to Byron Goethe spoke of old age saying that it asked for documentary evidence, which for younger people was too much of a tax. This partly explains the puzzle. It was not his years alone which made Goethe's attitude what it was, but they had something to do with it. But above all, it may have

[1] "Though of himself be all his contemplation,
Blessings attend him! He whose Muse can quell
His earthly pain has godlike compensation—
I know him; be it his to know as well!"

been a premonition that this figure of Byron might turn out to be material for poetry. How could the equanimity of old age have been subject to such overmastering excitement, unless it were engendered by some creative purpose? We shall soon see.

That agitated letter of Byron's which Goethe, as though presciently, treasured as a *Moriturus*, reached him on a summer-day in Marienbad, when he himself was stirred to the depths. He had fallen in love, and she whom he loved was nineteen years old. He himself was seventy-four.

This was the third year that Goethe had stayed, as a paying guest, with the family of a Frau von Levetzow to whom he had made love in Carlsbad fifteen years before, and whom he had compared to Pandora. Her daughters were now grown up; in his first summer with them Ulrike, the eldest had been seventeen; and he had played and laughed with her, and given her a few lessons. When he had presented her with the new volume of *Wilhelm Meister*, and she had asked him about the earlier ones, he had sat himself down beside her in the garden and told her the story of Wilhelm's *Lehrjahre*, for she was not then permitted to read that book.

It was in the second summer that he fell in love with her. "I am in a bad way," he had exclaimed a few weeks before in Weimar, "for I am not in love, and no one is in love with me, either." This was the first word of the kind that had fallen from Goethe's lips since his parting with Zuleika some years ago; and it speaks more of vague yearning than of a definite access of impassioned sensation. So it would seem that Ulrike caught his eye more because she happened to come at the psychological moment, than because his vision of her induced that moment. For of all the women whom Goethe admired, Ulrike seems to have had the smallest degree of personality—she seems to have signified no more than the general atmosphere of youth, its dancing, laughing charm, as it were in a type, an allegory; and as she was the last to make that old heart blossom like the rose, she might almost stand for a symbol of sublimation, generalisation, in Goethe—the old man desires a maiden; and the maiden happened to be this girl, for Goethe.

Not that she was not charming, with her brown curls (in which she resembled Marianne and Christiane) and her deep blue eyes;

but she was merely to herself his "daughterling," a title she was proud of because a kind father had conferred it on her—and moreover a very famous man, whose works indeed one was not allowed to read, but which would seem all the more splendid when one could. But there is no sign that by the magic spell of love Ulrike, who was half a child, succeeded in getting a glimpse of this old man's Olympus, as some young men had before now not failed to do.

Goethe saw it all. Poetically, he never sought to present her as a creature of flesh and blood—she was no more than the melody running through his verses. In the *Äolsharfen* (*Aeolian Harps*) he said his farewell, the phrases rippling softly over the ache in his heart; and when in this ethereal dialogue his voice takes up the tune, it is to Goethe's sense of the pain love means for all of us that we are listening.

Er:

Ich dacht', ich habe keinen Schmerz;
Und doch' war mir so bang ums Herz,
Mir war's gebunden vor der Stirn
Und hohl im innersten Gehirn—
Bis endlich Trän' auf Träne flietzt,
Verhaltnes Lebewohl ergietzt.
Ihr Lebewohl war heitre Ruh—
Sie weint wohl jetzund auch wie du.[1]

But he was careful not to send her such verses, after having given her only a few laconic aphorisms; and when he wrote to her six months afterwards from Weimar, it was in this decorous style:

Your sweet letter, my dear, has given me the greatest pleasure. . . . Though her fond Papa is always thinking of his loyal, lovely daughter,

[1] "*He:*

I thought that I had done with pain;
And yet my heart knew fear again,
My brow was as with iron bound,
No thought within my brain I found—
And then the tears flowed free and fast,
And I could say Farewell at last.
And her Farewell was calm, was gay—
Perchance she weeps like thee to-day."

your welcome image has never been so vividly present to him as of late. And now I know why! Those were the very days and hours in which you were thinking of me in a dearer sense than usual, and feeling that you wanted to say so from far away. . . .

Then he sends messages to her kind mother, whom he had been given to thinking of as a star in days gone by; "and so, my dearest, I claim your daughterly remembrance again, and very soon. Your truly attached, J. W. von Goethe."

Can we not divine the trouble in the heart of this paternal lover? That phrase, which of yore had always been his in a thrilled moment: "That's it—*now I know why.*" And the subtle compliment to her youth, her "kind mother" so definitely relegated to the blind-alley of the past—yet always, and so insistently the dear old Dad and his daughterling!

When he was writing such lines, with their delicate harmonics, he did not know that Death was standing at his shoulder—soon to step forth into the light.

For suddenly, in February, Goethe was attacked by severe illness, with rising temperature and eye-trouble. He was delirious, had to spend eight days and nights in his armchair; two doctors gave him up for lost, though he fought bravely. "Practise your arts by all means, but you won't succeed in saving me! . . . Death is all round me, in every corner of the room . . . I am lost."

On the tenth day he flew into a rage, because the doctors forbade him the Kreuzbrunnen water in which he put his faith. Angrily he cried: "If I am to die, let me die in my own way!" He insisted on having the Kreuzbrunnen, next day he was better —was soon complaining because someone had not kept his diary going for him, and after a few days talked of his illness as a thing of the past. None of the accounts says a word about wisdom and resignation, readiness to go and weariness of life; every one of them tells of the will-to-live, of vigour, crossness—this side of things.

For it was simply because Goethe willed to live, not because he drank the Kreuzbrunnen, that he got over this mortal attack. He was determined to have a second rejuvenescence.

And so in June he for the third time visited his Marienbad

friends, declaring that new blood was running in his veins and that he had not felt so well for years. But his nerves were on edge; for in these summer-weeks he was tormented by his infatuation—and by this time the girl's eyes must have been opened. They were seldom alone together. Her sisters were usually on the scene; the group was supposed to be studying crystals, and he would bring them chocolates, look on at their dancing, and often be with them till midnight. And when in August there was a temporary separation—for the family were going to Carlsbad, whither Goethe was shortly to follow them—he so far forgot caution in his cautious Diary as to illuminate the situation with these laconic words: "Met the sisters. Great fun, escorting the carriage. . . . A moment on the terrace, and in the room. Ante-room lit up. . . . Thoughts of the past. Considered my next step. . . . Quiet night. Refreshing dreams."

That "next step" which he was considering was—marriage.

And once more the Goethe-Destiny fulfilled itself. Two generations between him and Ulrike! But the atmosphere in which he was just then living was erotic. Carl August (who was also of the party), the Duke of Leuchtenberg, and some Viennese nobles, had more or less appropriated various lovely women; and Society and beauty, all around him, were turning Goethe's head. He consulted his doctor on the question of marriage; and as the doctor did not advise against it, Goethe got more and more restless.

Fantastic dreams of eleventh-hour happiness fevered his brain; but at the same time he had to consider his son and daughter-in-law, his repute and his dignity. At the close of a long life of inward growth, with few sensational incidents, how could he venture on anything so paradoxical, so abnormal? Now, as *Præceptor Germaniæ, now* in his grey hairs bring home a bride of nineteen for the Weimar scoffers, the youth of Germany, to gape at—he, Goethe, cynosure of the world!

But what was the good of this fame, of that strenuous life of endeavour, if a soul which had for sixty years withstood the world might not now, at last, step forth in all its freedom and defiance with a public challenge to the world? Had not the Peer-Poet arrogated such liberty to himself, and by his tameless appetites that knew no bounds captivated Europe but the more surely?

Yes: Byron, to whom Goethe that very spring had paid tribute for his inexhaustible self-expression, and who was now, as the finishing-stroke, on the eve of that high-flown expedition to Hellas, under the critical or fervid gaze of foes or friends—a glance at that contrast must in those impassioned days have lent irresistible impetus to Goethe's decision.

For it was precisely then that, enclosed in a letter from Ottilie, he received that hurried note from Byron, just sailing from Leghorn; and Goethe, who happened to be writing to his daughter-in-law and making a quasi-confession of his dalliance in phrases of ambiguous mock-earnest, went on to say:

> At this moment comes . . . Byron's letter. What different strings I shall have to touch, in my answer to it! The fairy-tale I am in the middle of here will be finished in a few days. . . . Enough, for the present. Anything else I may have to say shall be kept till we can talk, perhaps for one of our midnight sittings. . . . But read between the lines a great deal that will only be seen in its true light when this is over—and you will understand the bitter-sweetness of the cup which I am now draining to the dregs. How solemnly impressive Lord Byron's farewell words must have seemed to me in moments such as these, you will readily guess: it was like being told the most vital news at a masquerade. . . . Such a consummation could be the outcome only of a dæmonic youth intent on enjoyment and the common human aims; and now, to its own amazement, called upon to accomplish more than it can ever have willed or dreamed. Forgive me! But the constant mutual companionship of such excellent, reasonable, intellectual people as we are has at times (to my despair) somewhat tended to stagnation—we have felt the need of a third or fourth person to complete the circle. . . . May all come to pass as I think and hope it will. . . . In the fondest sense, Your loving father, G.

A letter that might have come out of *Elective Affinities*—all background as it were, full of appeal and persuasion, caution and coaxing, with its exaggerated adoration of youth, its recognition of the "years that bring the philosophic mind"—and yet! Here is the boy again; the boy who will not be denied his love, the lonely longing boy . . . in this letter to Ottilie, signed for the first time with the name of Father!

And yet again—as he saw everybody's gowns and hats disappearing into everybody's trunks, and in anticipation felt the loneliness of the deserted Terrace, behold another woman comes upon the scene, and on the instant he loses his heart to her! This one was in her early thirties, like Marianne before her; an artist like Marianne, but very much more beautiful—indeed, with Lili and Corona, who belonged to nearly half a century ago, she was the most beautiful woman whom Goethe ever loved. Slender, mobile, profoundly imaginative and yet absolutely spontaneous: so she was afterwards described by a connoisseur, and he adds that the upward look of her eyes had something about it both of witchery and childishness.

She was a Polish woman, Maria Szymanowska, and Goethe soon found himself taking a walk with her in the rain. But she was married and the mother of children, besides having brothers and sisters to provide for; her only mode of self-expression appears to have been music of exquisite quality and romantic interpretation; and so she represented—what with her art, her nature, and her lot in life—the sort of divinity whom a man does not actively desire, not even Goethe in his amorous state. His Byronic mood grew upon him as he yielded to the swelling tide of erotic emotion; for besides the Polish pianist there were her charming sister and a German diva, so that Goethe, with Ulrike far away and only her glove to console him (like Faust with Gretchen's scarf), flung himself, a Werther redivivus, into a sea of music and tears.

The impression he gives at this time is of gentle low-pitched sentimentality, easily stirred to lachrymose emotion, and somewhat uncertain of its direction. He could never have enough of the lovely Pole's piano. "If music be the food of love, play on!" And when after a few days she departed, the immediate effect was an impetuous cataract of verses, beginning:

> Die Leidenschaft bringt Leiden! Wer beschwichtigt,
> Beklommnes Herz, dich, das soviel verloren?
> Wo sind die Stunden, überschnell verflüchtigt?
> Vergebens war das Schönste dir erkoren!
> Trüb ist der Geist, verworren das Beginnen;
> Die hehre Welt, wie schwindet sie den Sinnen![1]

[1] "With passion cometh pain. Who shall appease thee,
Care-burdened heart, such loss upon thee falling?

A new note runs through the poet's lyricism now—the Byron note; for here, and soon again, all these overwhelming encounters mix and are as one in the soul of Goethe, grown so old. It was because he was ready for such a mood that Byron was dear to him; and it was because Byron was dear to him that this mood took possession of him so strongly.

On the evening before his birthday, in Carlsbad (where he soon joined the Levetzows) he saw the girls at a ball; and looked on until "a Polish lady asked me to dance the final polonaise with her. So I went round with her, and in the changing of partners most of the pretty young things came into my hands." So Goethe danced, the chosen girl clasped to his breast, in the seventy-fourth year of his life. September and separation were coming nearer—he would soon have to make up his mind.

And Goethe confided in the Duke, who had so often in the past called upon *him* to be father-confessor, and go-between too. It may have been with satisfaction and a little malicious pleasure that Carl August, whose amorous youth had brought upon him many a mute reproof from Goethe, undertook the commission now entrusted to him, and gave his opinion on it. With all ceremony the Grand Duke of Saxe-Weimar and Eisenach approached Frau von Levetzow with a request for her eldest daughter's hand on behalf of his chief Minister of State, Privy-Councillor von Goethe; and as the proposal was not at first accepted, we ask ourselves whether it was mother or daughter who was against it.

If her mother had consented—so Ulrike maintained in her old age—*she* would have agreed. This seems the more probable because—as Goethe's verses and Zelter's notes testify—she had received, by this time, not the senile advances of an old man out of an *opera bouffe*, but the impassioned kisses of a youthful lover!

At any rate, there is no doubt that her mother begged for time to decide. On this uncertain footing Goethe had to take leave of

---

Where are the hours, too swift, that once could
ease thee?
Vain to know beauty, past beyond recalling!
Sad is my soul, perplexed the short sweet story,
Scarce can my sense retrieve that world of glory."

them. And then, as soon as he had left the girl behind, his passion broke all bounds; and one day driving homewards, he wrote the most powerful of all the poems of his old age—that Marienbad Elegy which he always loved as a parent loves a late-come child, and which was, like other of these poems, written under the spell of Byron. He felt like Tasso now, and chose some lines from his own *Tasso* as the motto for these twenty-three strophes.

When for half-a-century—when since *Werther*—had Goethe suffered such accents to break from his soul? Where else does the battling, insatiable dæmon give such vent to his frustrated wrath? Ineffable—the tempest in that heart, for ever aching to snatch the moment, for ever robbed of its "Here and Now," of its bliss. It ebbs and flows here like the sea, yet never finds-the-shallows where the ninth wave may lull itself to acquiescent peace. The day of travel which created this poem may be regarded as exceptional, as the crisis of a mood almost unique with Goethe and its issue contrasted with the myriad utterances of ripe balanced wisdom which stand in opposition to it. Yet, even so, it was on such a day that the floodgates were opened, and his spirit could soar into the light, the air, soothing itself with the plangent, reiterated lament—for when all is said it was always Eros who laid bare the essential Goethe. But that it was a man of seventy-four who now as in the Lili-days sobbed out—if in a more exacting form—the unslaked thirst for happiness, for youth, for the woman possessed, for that equilibrium of the spirit which Hafiz had, like him, known instantly when with Zuleika all his being seemed to drain itself away . . . this does drive on us the lesson that even superhuman self-control, in the last issue, is but self-control—a flimsy rope that will break in the critical moment. After wayfarings such as no human being but he could well have permitted himself, he seems to have returned to his source, to have forgotten all the harmonies of Arabia, all the symmetries of Greece—he seems, as a psychical entity, never to have changed from adolescence to old age.

The last thing he wanted was to write a letter to the girl that day, and so he forced himself to compose a rhymed note:

> Am heitzen Quell verbringst du deine Tage,
> Das regt mich auf zu innerm Zwist:

Denn wie ich dich so ganz im Herzen trage,
Begreif' ich nicht, wie du wo anders bist.[1]

In that graceful form he allowed his passion to take shape on paper—a rococo-trifle, with the great elegy pouring from his soul like a long-reverberating echo, but kept hidden away in his portfolio.

Meanwhile, from the two spas rumour had penetrated to Weimar—"Goethe is going to get married." On his return to the Weimar house, a scene ensued; the bitterest ordeal Goethe had to endure from his fellow-creatures in eighty years of life.

When in his youth three girls had thrown him over, there had been certain ties, certain circumstances, to account for it and make it comprehensible, if not consoling, to Goethe. When on his return from Italy, with a heart full of love, he found friends and mistress estranged and worshipping new gods who were his enemies, he could reflect that the change in him was as much to blame as they were. When his fatherland forgot him and youth sought to depreciate him, he felt the transiency of such literary fashions, and salted the bitter bread with mockery. When the Duke, after fifty years, dimissed him from the theatre which he had made into the leading German house, after all it was only inherited authority resuming its ancient privilege.

But now his only son, who owed him everything—existence, rank, repute—set his face against the father of seventy-four, furious at his daring to assert himself in his own house, and (we may safely conjecture) suspecting him of intent to divide that son's inheritance with a stranger. "The brutal, heartless disposition of his son," (so the Chancellor, who is our best witness, writes of this period) "and Ulrike's," (this was Ottilie's sister) "harsh one-sidedness and shallow naïveté were certainly not conducive to smoothing over such a crisis." And Charlotte Schiller's testimony is much the same—she says that it is true that Ottilie was ill and took no part in the discussions; but that her sister, who was quite at home in Goethe's house, egged on the

[1] "You dwell where springs gush hot; and I to find you
Must rend myself in twain, for since I bear
A heart within, and in that heart enwind you,
How can I think that you are otherwhere?"

son, who moreover was drinking hard and threatened his father with removing to Berlin.

And among these people stood—for a while almost beside himself—the aged Goethe, pleading, persuading; a man not born for domination and by no means desirous of it; solicitous only to divert the gossip by clear pronouncements against rash marriage-projects. But none the less he procured from a dealer some of the sort of medals that are supposed to be mascots, together with a larger one which prognosticated marriage-ties! We may be sure that no one knew this but the man who ordered them. To the Chancellor Goethe told only half the truth: "The De Staël once said a very true word to me: 'Il vous faut de la séduction!' Yes, I came home in good spirits, having been happy for three months. . . . Now I must dig myself in for the winter and carry on as best I can. . . . It's preposterous that Julie" (von Egloffstein) "isn't here this winter. Not that she has any idea how she attracts me, as little as she has of how I love her! To you I may say this, though on that point we are rivals. . . . But believe me, the old Merlin in his badger's-holt fills many a quiet hour with absent ones like these!"

Then he praised a country-life where one can do as one likes, saying he was the sort of gardener who never realises how lovely his flowers are until someone asks him for a bunch. And all of a sudden, he began to rave about the lovely Pole—evanescent as a zephyr, ethereal, immaterial, her voice so troubling to the nerves that one always wanted her to go back to the piano; and he fetched a specimen of her handwriting to show her character. Then, in his most moving tones, he read the Chancellor some of his verses to her.

Soon afterwards he took a fancy to be "at home" every day. The house was to be prepared for guests every evening—they would read and talk or make music, just as they felt inclined; and he himself would come and go at pleasure. "A sort of everlasting tea-party, like the lamps that everlastingly burn in certain chapels." Then suddenly he told the Chancellor something of the strain in the household, blamed Ottilie too, and doled out morsels of his love-story.

"There's a little affair going on which will give me a good deal of trouble yet, but I shall come out of it all right. Iffland could make a pretty thing out of it—an old uncle, head-over-ears in love with his youthful niece."

He would show his guests the landscapes he had painted only ten years ago, regret that he had quite lost his hand at the art, laugh at the dangling bonnet-ribbons worn by girls at that time, rave about the nobleman-poet: "No one but Byron will I hear of as my equal!" He commended the Persians, who had only seven renowned poets, and yet "among the rejected there were some small fry who were better than he was." If anyone got sleepy, he would fume at having wasted his literary history of Persia on young people and storm out of the room "with mock violence."

But after three days the Chancellor, arriving for the "everlasting tea-party," found that Goethe had forgotten all about the plan; and a week later he came upon him in a dejected mood: "Of immense, unsatisfied striving, a certain inward desperation."

Into these heart-sick quivering days, Goethe always the one to give in, always trying to find something he might console himself with—gentle affection, friendly faces, kindness, indulgence . . . into this vast solitude of soul there shone, that autumn, the mild radiance of the Szymanowska. All of a sudden she arrived with her sister—dressed in brown with white lace, and roses in her bonnet. For some days she visted Goethe regularly, playing to him in the afternoons and evenings; he invited people to hear her and moved about excitedly, claiming applause; then he arranged a concert, and when someone asked him if she played as well as Hummel, he answered: "You must remember she is a lovely woman into the bargain!"

At dinner in Goethe's house, after the concert, someone proposed a toast in remembrance of her. "I won't have any 'remembrance' of that sort!" cried Goethe passionately. "Anything great and beautiful and impressive that comes our way, can't be re-remembered from outside in; it must become part of our being from the instant we experience it. . . . There is no past, that we need look back upon regretfully. . . . Real regret can never be anything but productive, making a new and better thing out of the old. Haven't we all known that, in these few days? That sweet, noble creature . . . lives in us, with us, henceforth; and though she should try her very best to get away from me, I have her for evermore."

The next day, when she had arranged to leave Weimar, Goethe tried to be quite cheerful about it; but the Chancellor saw that the parting was causing him the profoundest sorrow—he wandered restlessly to and fro, and back again incessantly. It utterly upset him to see the lovely Pole in black. When she had left the house, he vehemently implored the Chancellor to bring her back—then, with tears in his eyes, he silently embraced her and her sister, and followed them with his gaze through the open door of the room. "I have much for which to thank that charming woman," he said afterwards. "Her friendship and her talent were the first things that gave me back to myself." So deeply was he conscious of the interplay of attractions, the universal element in his craving for love; and one doubts whether Ulrike herself, if she had come instead of the Polish pianist in those autumn days, could have made him any happier.

Scarcely were the visitors gone than Goethe fell ill again, almost as seriously at the end of this year as at the beginning. There was no one to nurse him; Ottilie was away, his son ill-tempered and sullen, and the secondary Ulrike never to be seen—until Zelter paid a surprise-visit, and was horrified to find his friend so neglected. Though he felt that Goethe needed a more intimate companion, he swore to remain until his friend was better, and so he did. "What did I find? A man who looked as if love, love with all the torment of young passion, were seething in his veins!"

Goethe told him the history of his heart in long talks together, and loved to hear Zelter's sonorous voice reading his great Elegy over and over again—the Elegy that he had copied in his best hand, and kept in the Carlsbad drinking-cup. He had it always beside him, like a bottle of medicine! And so the two old men sat alone together in the sick-room, and read the love-poem to one another.

But when the year drew to its close, and Goethe was ready with his new wall-calendar, all the protagonists could not keep the girl's image from once more becoming so vivid to him that he wrote to her mother these arresting, sensuously-inspired words:—

". . . If a slender, darling child bends down and picks up a little stone in memory of me, it will be a new treasure to add to the hundred attitudes in which she is present to my eyes."

Then he made several allusions to the happy second marriage of an old Court Councillor with many children, which had caused a brief sensation—and was careful to add that the young wife got on remarkably well with her step-children. "As I write, I am looking at the new wall-calendar for 1824, where the twelve months look as white as snow, no doubt, but also absolutely uninteresting. Vainly do I try to guess which days will be rosy for me and which dismal; the whole table is a blank, with wishes and hopes fluttering about it. May mine and yours encounter! May nothing—*nothing* prevent their fulfilment and their happy issue! In hopeful, expectant longing. . . ."

But though he hoped and expected, he had already begun to relinquish. There were the pressure from his family, the threatening tones of his furious son, the vacillation of the girl and her mother—for we have no proof whatever that this New-Year letter was answered by a final refusal. But above all, there was the ebbing of that last great spring-tide in his heart—for Goethe, wooing Ulrike, had been wooing womanhood, youth, vitality. The twilight in his soul, the soul that still hoped on while it relinquished, darkens the poem which, in the following March (for the Jubilee-edition of the novel, published fifty years ago) he addressed to Werther:

> . . . Zum Bleiben ich, zum Scheiden du erkoren,
> Gingst du voran—und hast nicht viel verloren. . . .
> Da kämpft sogleich verworrene Bestrebung
> Bald mit uns selbst und bald mit der Umgebung. . . .
> Ein glänzend Aussres deckt ein trüber Blick,
> Da steht es nah—und man verkennt das Glück.
>
> Nun glauben wir's zu kennen! Mit Gewalt
> Ergreift uns Liebreiz weiblicher Gestalt. . . .
> Doch erst zu früh und dann zu spät gewarnt,
> Fühlt er den Flug gehemmt, fühlt sich umgarnt.
> Das Wiedersehn ist froh, das Scheiden schwer,
> Das Wieder-Wiedersehn beglückt noch mehr,
> Und Jahre sind im Augenblick ersetzt;
> Doch tückisch harrt das Lebewohl zuletzt.

Du lächelst, Freund gefühlvoll, wie sich ziemt:
Ein grässlich Scheiden machte dich berühmt;
Wir feierten dein kläglich Missgeschick,
Du liessest uns zu Wohl und Weh zurück.
Dann zog uns wieder ungewisse Bahn
Der Leidenschaften labyrinthisch an. . . .

Verstrickt in solche Qualen, halb verschuldet,
Geb' ihm ein Gott, zu sagen, was er duldet.[1]

So profoundly had Goethe relapsed into pessimism—resigned, indeed, as at the beginning of this period, but with a heart no longer thrilling to the chords of truth and faith, stirred now by gusts of melancholy only. And as though Destiny were resolute to set her seal upon this mood, so that even the last lingering gaze at youth should henceforth be obscured—at the very time when those lines to Werther were written, Byron died in Greece; and by that death became, once for all, the legendary figure which the old man had loved to think him while he was alive. Every omen seemed to say that the course of Goethe's life had taken its final downward trend.

If then, after those half-envying lines to Werther, Goethe had

[1] "Elected, I for staying, you for going,
You went before—and little lost, so doing. . . .
Here in the clash of battle we, confounded,
Turn on ourselves, who are by foes surrounded. . . .
Of shining aspect, masking looks of woe,
A form draws near—and joy we think to know.

Oh, surely now we know it! Such the power
Of love, of woman's charm, in love's great hour. . . .
Yet warned too soon, too late, howe'er it hap,
He feels his wings are caught, he feels the trap.
To meet again is bliss, to part is pain,
Yet best of all, once more to meet again,
And years are turned to moments, such the spell;
Nay, at the last we know the thing 'Farewell.'

You smile, my friend—the sad, sweet smile well-known!
Cruel your death, but mighty your renown;
We followed, weeping, in your funeral-train,
Then left you—free for life, for joy, for pain;
Our wandering feet once more too surely set
On labyrinthine paths to wild regret! . . .

Snared by such torments, half his own creation,
Give him a God, to teach him acceptation!"

died in the seventy-fourth year of his age, he would have lost the great battle. It could not be—there had to come the ultimate ascension, when his soul should walk in light. But the man who wrote those lines was called upon to renounce the last faint possibility of simple happiness. When shortly afterwards the Levetzows wrote, asking if he would not be with them in the summer, he refused; and never saw them again.

CHAPTER XII

PHŒNIX

"Immer höher muss ich steigen,
Immer weiter muss ich schaun!" [1]

THROUGH the green shutters of the little window the earliest ray of light peers into a narrow room, to touch the old man's eyes to life. He wakes from a brief dreamless doze, and no sooner has he collected himself than he considers what is to be done to-day. Then he gets out of bed, puts on his white flannel dressing-gown, opens window and shutters. It is chilly, though the month is June, for it is only just four o'clock. As he draws back his head, his eye catches the reflection of his face in the pane. That face is his life-work.

The mouth is an old man's mouth—framed by two deep lines that speak of suffering and patience, and run from the bony chin to the powerful nose. It is sunken, for behind the thin close lips some teeth are missing; and as the skin of the cheeks and throat is furrowed all over with a network of wrinkles, under which the cheek-bones stand out arrestingly, there seems all the more splendour in the dark lustre of the sovereign eyes, and again in the brow whose lofty arch so majestically meets the halo of short silvery hair. For eighty long years those eyes have been the intermediaries between that brain and the world. In the shapes of moving clouds and the positions of passive stones, in the veinings of leaves and the jaws of prehistoric beasts, in the refraction of light and the glance of an enamoured maiden, they have sought untiringly to descry the image of God. They have sent forth messengers from the interior of that royally vaulted forehead to classify the visible, and re-establish the form first taken

[1] "Ever mounting higher, higher,
Ever farther I must gaze!"

by it. For a mysterious affinity, perceptible from the first has endowed the inmost soul of this man with some prescience, some clairvoyance; and it is simply because everything he has seen and learnt was a confirmation of pre-consciousness that to him so swift, so complete a synthesis has been possible.

Now he shivers slightly, and goes into the adjoining room, straight to the large stove—out of habit, as if it were still heated. With short shuffling steps he gets along. As bare of ornament as the bedroom (in which, besides the bed and washstand, there is nothing but a big, seldom-used armchair) is this work-room, lit by two windows. The table in the centre is cleared of everything but an inkpot and some pens—his trusty lifelong servitors, patiently awaiting him; the wooden chairs around it look uncompromisingly stiff and hard. Yonder on the desk is a row of plainly-bound books; from the door a diagram of acoustics issues a challenge to arithmetical ignorance; a few scientific appliances stand against the wall; no picture breaks the space, no easy-chair or sofa invites to repose—everything speaks of work and concentration.

Near the big stove a plain standing-desk holds some sheets of white paper in a parchment folder. Goethe goes to this desk, opens the folder, reads yesterday's work, writes on. He is now at the "Klassische Walpurgisnacht"; he makes several notes, to be expanded later, and then adds something to the poem in his clear script. Two hours go by in this dialogue between the solitary old man and his creations. Sometimes he walks up and down, looks out into the dewy garden—the earliest sounds from without rise to his ears, a bird-note, the beat of hoofs; and when he closes the folder again, he has written not more than a single page.

Now the household begins to stir. Friedrich the servant comes in, wishes His Excellency good-morning, and brings him a tempting breakfast. Newspapers have arrived from Berlin, Paris, Milan; the old man lays them aside unopened, for it is the letters that interest him. What is there? Another young man asking for an opinion on his poems; a request from a newspaper for a contribution, at his own price; a woman-painter, wanting to do his portrait; a letter of thanks for the *Neue Melusine* out of the *Wanderjahre*. Ah, but here is Zelter's vigorous handwriting—what news has *he* got, fond indefatigable fellow?

And while Goethe is reading, and smiling over art and Court-gossip from Berlin, and how the Professors have been arguing about the latest number of *Kunst und Alterthum*, a boy bursts into the room. This is little Wolfgang; and he gives his grandfather a brief bear's-hug, then pulls out the writing-table drawer which he has appropriated, so as to be sure of having a few toys upstairs when he wants them; and as he arranges his dominoes the old man looks on with secret satisfaction to see the fourth generation as tidy, as careful of its possessions, as his own father used to be in Frankfurt. Then the boy coaxes a handful of cherries out of his grandfather, who keeps a hoard for such occasions—and off with him again, and soon he is heard merrily laughing with the Secretary, Herr John, who enters unannounced.

Meanwhile the old gentleman has been dressing with Friedrich's help; and when he comes in and says good-morning to his secretary, he is wrapped in a long brown coat, under which high boots are visible.

While Friedrich is clearing away, John has taken one of the stiff chairs at the table and spread out his writing paper. Goethe sits opposite, resting his arms on a cushion; and in his still sonorous bass, which he can modulate to the most delicate intonations, begins to dictate in verse what he has just drafted. Soon he stands up, and strides to and fro in the little room, his hands behind his back; and without a pause he first dictates yesterday's diary, then an order for *foie gras*, then an article about the French translation of Goethe's Works, with quotations from the Parisian reviews, and then a few words about Neo-Greek heroic ballads.

In the middle of all this a stranger's name is brought to Goethe. He is introduced in no wise, save by the far-away address on his card. Goethe thinks it over while the servant waits, twists the card in his hands, reflecting on the certain waste of time, the possible gain of information . . . then he says, "Show him up," goes down a few stairs to the front part of the house, and enters a large, bright, rather too low-ceilinged room, while through the communicating doors of two others a young man comes timidly towards him.

The veteran, now bolt upright for the first time to-day, stands (his hands immovably behind his back) in the middle of the room, letting the stranger come all the way to him. While the young man stammers out a few embarrassed phrases, the old man

GOETHE AT THE AGE OF SEVENTY-SEVEN

gives him no help; but makes use of the moment to wrest the visitor's secrets, or as much of them as he can, out of his features, glances, figure, bearing, apparel, and choice of words, with concentration on which might hang the fate of a poem. Seconds like these are highly productive for Goethe.

Then with a stiff bow he indicates a chair, and takes one himself; and when the guest, terrified by his host's speechlessness and the steely arrows from his eyes, ventures on a compliment, there issues from that hitherto inarticulate throat a deep-toned "Hm!"—but it sounds so formidable that the guest is struck dumb. And then Goethe, without transition, begins a catechism upon conditions in the distant city, the foreign land; and as the other, warming to his task, brings up all sorts of interesting topics, the old gentleman hitches his chair nearer and questions pour from his lips—till the visitor, feeling more at ease, begins to plume himself on being able to give Goethe information. He is agreeably surprised when his host, getting up, lays a hand on his shoulder and invites him to luncheon at two o'clock, "for there are several other things he wants to hear from him."

Two minutes later Goethe is back in his work-room, and when he has walked up and down once or twice he goes on dictating his article, without having read over what had gone before.

When, in the course of two hours, he appears at the luncheon-table, Ottilie comes up to him. He kisses her on the forehead, does not forget to ask after her headache, pulls his grandson's curls, shakes hands with his son. This last begins to tell the latest gossip of the town in a loud blustering voice—the old man silently endures it, Ottilie tries to stop it, whereupon August scowls at her. Goethe sees it all and holds his tongue. "How is your sister Ulrike?" She shrugs her shoulders. The foreigner arrives, is introduced; Goethe continues their talk from the point where they had broken off in the morning. Fortunately the youth has a smattering of geology, and has provided himself with a few stones for the great man. When he brings them out, and Goethe sees that they are rare specimens, the stranger has completed his conquest; lo and behold! his host is pouring out his wine for him—but when he breaks off to answer August's irrelevant questions, he is gently called to order by the old man.

All this time Goethe is eating very largely of an abundant,

savoury menu. He carves a substantial fowl with his own hand, and empties a bottle of red wine which stands at his place (as at everybody's), but does not except by example urge anyone to drink. Then he confides to Ottilie that some artichokes have arrived, and everybody who behaves nicely shall have one. The basket is brought in. It came from Marianne in Frankfurt this morning—and as Goethe begins to separate the leaves of the prickly fruit, he falls silent for a while, absorbed in the construction of the plant. "Now he'll say something about his *Metamorphosis,*" thinks the stranger; but Goethe lays the artichoke aside without a word.

When luncheon is over he asks for a certain portfolio, and on Humboldt's geological maps he shows the guest where and how the stones that he has brought from home are distributed. Meanwhile Dr. Eckermann has arrived, and the family has disappeared. About four o'clock the guest is given the friendliest of farewells; and as he has previously persuaded Ottilie to make the usual request for him, he is handed, on leaving, a small sheet of paper on which a couple of lines in Goethe's handwriting are lithographed—in this instance, as in many others, made still more precious by his signature.

The carriage is now ready; and since none of the household seems desirous of accompanying the old man, Eckermann is requisitioned to-day, as on many another day. He sits on Goethe's left, heart and ears entirely at disposal; and as they drive along to the Belvedere (the old man wearing a blue cloth cap, and spreading a pale grey cloak over his knees) Goethe begins to talk about old times, about the Duke and Herder—idealising everything a little, for the June sunshine cheers one up, and besides one knows that this very evening every word one says will be written down by this faithful disciple—so it's better to mind one's p's and q's and say nothing so profound that Eckermann won't be able to grasp it, and nothing, either, that one does not wish posterity to know.

When they come home, Goethe goes through the house to the back-garden, putting on a little shade to protect his sensitive eyes (that are often ailing) from the light. That archery that Eckermann was talking about? And he sends for the tall Bashkiri—bow—a present that has hitherto been rather a white elephant. The young disciple and writer draws it skilfully, and shows the old man how to do the trick—and then the octogenarian for the first time in his life, takes a bow in his hand. He stands there, facing the setting sun—he draws, and shoots into the air, but the old arm can only propel the arrow a few feet towards the sky. Does the veteran envy the young archer's muscles? He turns to his border of mallows, and consoles himself with their colours.

Meyer—the laconic Meyer—now appears in the garden, and Goethe sits down with him in the mellow sunlight, and asks about the entries for the new painting-competition. Then they sit silently side by side—two old men who do not need to keep up conversation with each other.

At six o'clock Goethe resumes dictation in his study—a long letter about meteorology, full of new ideas, masterly in construction. Then arrives Riemer, now a Court-Councillor. How time does fly—can it really be Wednesday? He has brought back a volume of correspondence with Zelter, revised by him with infinite pains; and they go on to talk about deletions, modifications. Suddenly Goethe has an idea concerning a point at issue with Cotta, and makes notes for a letter to Boisserée, his agent in South Germany, who has the matter in his hands. Then similar notes for a letter to Zelter, his Berlin intermediary, who is negotiating with Rauch about a medal.

Sudden uproar in the corridor, boys' voices clamouring, and the grandsons rush in to say good-night, chaffing, begging for little favours. Immediately afterwards the Chancellor is announced. He brings in a breath of the world of affairs—they scoff and praise and disparage, and soon find themselves involved in an argument. Riemer, less sophisticated, less loquacious, but no less misanthropic and nearly as shrewd as the Chancellor, often upholds him against Goethe. So the three work one another up, and grow combative. Goethe speaks his mind—at first about the past, its personages, affairs, and actions, and the things he says are mordant, acrid; then he goes on to talk at large about his youth, his errors, waxing warm against his adversaries, against the thing called Fame.

When Müller has gone, Goethe (now in his dressing-gown again) begs Riemer to see about carrying out his suggestions;

and as the sitting has now lasted a long time and the servant has brought lights, he orders supper to be laid for his guest on the study-table. He himself seldom eats so late, but will drink a couple of glasses with him. Every ten minutes he uses the snuffers, for he allows no one else to tend the candles.

Then left alone, Goethe begins to read, late though it is, some of Niebuhr's lately-published *History of Rome*. Suddenly he starts—what noise is that? He listens a moment. Upstairs in August's quarters the son, come home intoxicated, is making Ottilie a scene. Goethe stands up, throws open the window, looks for Orion, calculates when Mars and Venus will be in propinquity again—then rings the bell. Friedrich helps him to undress. But he is very far from being tired yet. He takes a sheet of paper and writes:

Nachts, wann gute Geister schweifen,
Schlaf dir von der Stirne streifen,
Mondenlicht und Sternenflimmern
Dich mitewigen All umschimmern,
Scheinst du dir entkörpert schon,
Wagest dich vor Gottesthron.[1]

It is night. He goes into his room, lies down in bed, puts out the light and thinks of the lines with which, at the first ray of dawn, Thales shall continue the Walpurgisnacht.

Something like this was the routine of Goethe's day in the last eight years of his life. The old man worked in the two little rooms, received his visitors and talked in the handsome front rooms, went neither to Court nor parties nor the theatre, scarcely ever (and then for brief stays) left Weimar, and left Thuringia not at all. Sometimes he ventured on a little driving-excursion, in the course of which he would sit on a heap of stones by the highroad, carefully extract from its leather-case a little

[1] "When, of nights, good spirits creeping
Slumber from thy brow are sweeping,
When the moon and stars resplendent
Tell thee of the All transcendent,
Thou, in flesh immured no more,
To the throne of God dost soar."

gold folding-cup, and filling it with wine, lift it still more carefully to his lips.

And this narrowest of spheres, in which Goethe was to terminate his course—was it irradiated by tender affections? Did he achieve at last what he had striven for from the first, and for a while in middle-life had known in some degree?

The household which then he had got into such perfect order was now a melancholy failure. In broken health and spirits, idle, unoccupied, his only son inhabited the upper storey with a wife who was alien and hostile to him, who sought to forget her discontents in love-affairs and social excitements, wasting her talents, drifting, aimless, incapable of ordering or managing her house and servants—and between this pair two boys (and later on a girl) were growing up, almost entirely without education, example, or purpose. The daily life of Goethe at seventy-five was as cheerless as his life at twenty, in his parents' house, had been; but he, who once had so longed for marriage and children, normal happiness and tranquillity, now voluntarily (when he could) kept his family at a distance, ironically stoical; and when the children—usually unescorted—left home, the grandfather secretly congratulated himself.

Though Ottilie's extravagance made her precise old father-in-law extremely uneasy, she was so utterly incapable of managing a household that Goethe himself had to look after the smallest details, and in the end was obliged to instal a young nephew of Christiane's as a sort of steward, so as to get some relief from such cares!

If little cheerful Christiane had housed her relatives in the back-rooms, Ottilie, for hers, took such complete possession of the whole house that for Goethe's most intimate friend, for Zelter himself, no room could be found in a mansion which contained thirty—and he had to put up at the neighbouring hotel.

Sometimes the old man complained bitterly to the Chancellor of the disorder in the household, and confided such matters as Müller was careful to keep out of even his diaries. Frequently the master of the house had to do what he had often done before when his family was too much for him—take flight though it should be no farther than to the summer-villa nearby.

Though he still envied Byron his wide wild life—a life which Goethe could never at any time have led—Carlyle's, on the other hand, struck him as ideal. To study and write in the remote Scottish Highlands—he declared that such a married life, such a rustic existence, represented something "sincerer, more concentrated" than his own.

But how far he really was in spirit from these two, though in reminiscent mood the comparison could sometimes fret him! He now seemed resolute to cope no more with his environment, conscious that he needed all his remaining vigour for creative purposes. It is as though Destiny made amends to him at the last moment by teaching him to throw off the bonds of natural affection; for if the children gave him little, he did not give them much more.

Two boys, the only grandsons of this man who believed in heredity and had engendered five children—surely they must have had something of Goethe in them? No one disciplined them, and he was merely indulgent. The little belated daughter on whom was to fall the Goethean doom of early death, he admired for her beauty; and over her doubtful paternity (to be read between the lines in Ottilie's letters) the old man smiled, remarking with subtle irony to his intimates that the child reminded one of "foreign friends as well as of home-ones."

Walter played the piano, paid visits, was idle and frivolous; in little Wolfgang's eyes the grandfather did think to see a poet, and *he* was orderly enough, but

> it would never have done for him to be born a Peer of England—he would have behaved very badly indeed; however, I think a middle-class upbringing will suit him well enough. . . . I admit he has a very pretty way of forcing me to play some game or other with him before he goes to bed.

And of climbing on his knee too, and if reprimanded by a guest, of exclaiming that he was doing no harm—when he was asleep, Grandpapa could rest. Grandpapa would smile and let himself be pulled about, summing up his attitude for the guest in the sublimely ironic remark: "You see, love is always inclined to be a little disrespectful." When the house-tutor complained that he could not get the boys out of bed in the morning, the old man contended himself with saying: "Tell them their grandfather wishes it." The tutor comes to him again in a day or two. "Did you tell them?" "Yes, but it was no good, Your Excellency." "Hm," says Goethe—and there an end.

This dialogue took place during the last years of his life. Before then, he had had the severest of blows to face—the complete demoralisation of his only son.

For Goethe was really to blame for August's ruin. May he not sometimes have thought (as in Faust's exclamation over the sleeping shepherd-boy, Paris, kissed by Helen): "*Furchtbare Gunst dem Knaben!*" [1] But all he said in confidence was: "It is my son's misfortune that he has never recognised the Categorical Imperative." He might have said: "That his father never held that Imperative up to him." For though he had ordered August to be brought-up with the utmost simplicity, very circumspectly and by Goethe's most carefully-selected subordinate, remote from the luminary whose blaze might have scorched him, the boy had in fact spent his childhood between women, the Court, and the theatre; then had made a loveless marriage, been prevented from developing himself by travel, been kept at his father's side as a sort of adjutant to serve and work for him. Such a life as this was the sure destruction of just those elements in August which were most akin to Goethe; and if he was now—in his thirties—an utter wreck, it was the almost inevitable result of his parentage, tendencies, and training.

"I had rather they said, 'Goethe's son is a dolt,' than be able to say of me, 'He wants to play Goethe junior!'" This and other confessions, made by August in his last years to his friend Holtei, go far to explain his fate. It was not because his mother and father were hard drinkers—though no one ever saw either of them drunk—but because the son sought oblivion of himself in wine that he gave rein to an inherited tendency, and became a drunkard.

Take him for all in all, Goethe's son stands revealed as a thoroughly dæmonic being; and psychologically considered, he is what Goethe might have been if that gigantic force of will had not acted as a powerful corrective throughout eight decades.

[1] "Dire for the boy, that favour!"

For Goethe's genius was only one of the means—not the sole means—of salvation from the perils of being born with a devil in him!

If August was dissolute, if in his cups he was violent and blasphemous, none the less his room was full of papers, pictures, coins, geological specimens—all interesting to him and arranged with true Goethean pedantry. In society he was polished, courtly, elegant; and even in his rages there was often something heroic about him. At times, indeed, he reminded people (entirely against his will) of his father's ceremonious stiffness—Goethe's fetch, as it were.

When strangers spoke to him of his father he would abruptly change the subject, tell indecent Berlin stories, play the barbarian. He never spoke of Goethe's poetry—indeed he seemed to prefer Schiller. His favourite mode of escape from his heart-sickness was the telling of ribald anecdotes; but in the maddest of his letters or in convivial conversations, there would suddenly break out a desperate cry that revealed the *tædium vitæ* beneath.

He could not but hate his father. Why did Goethe prevent him from seeing the world?

Goethe, who had let his wishes be brought to naught by his son, held August as in a vice, dæmonically resolute, when the son wanted to go his own way—so disastrous was the mingled hatred and love between them. Goethe flinched before his furious offspring, when the happiness of his old age was at stake; the son wilted under the father's piercing eye, instead of indignantly asserting himself.

> Not one of you knows anything about me! You all take me for a good-for-nothing brainless fellow—but inside me here . . . the abysses! If you were to throw a stone into me, you'd have to listen a long time before you heard it fall!

One of the younger Goethe's sayings—that savage cry with its fine metaphor, so poignantly expressive. Goethe only once or twice complained to others of August's selfishness—otherwise his heart was a closed book. But there was nothing he did not know; and when (himself eighty-one) he at last suffered August to go to Italy, he gave him up for lost.

So there he sat in his narrow room—an old, old man; and though he could give others beaker after beaker of living water, sparkling to the light, not one of them could do the same for him. Riemer and Eckermann, the clever Doctor Vogel, the subtle Genevese Soret, laconic old Meyer, best of all, the Chancellor—these were the most interesting of his friends; and almost daily they received inestimable treasures—later, it is true, to some extent shared by posterity, but at the time by no one living. "Cribbed, cabined, and confined" the veteran must indeed have felt, when he thought of the animated circles in which the old Voltaire, the Titian of remoter ages, had been privileged to renew their youth! On one Whit-Sunday he was sitting in his shirt-sleeves, drinking with Riemer and Müller, when the Countess Egloffstein was announced. He sent a message, begging her to come in the evening instead; "not when I am with friends in whose company I am either pensive or above myself!"

He wasted hundreds of irretrievable hours on Eckermann, who with all his good-will could never be anything but the Wagner of *Faust*, and once absented himself for months because he had been offended. And when he did come back, he was at best little more than tactful and discreet, which made him to the end a useful intercessor in family-affairs. Moreover, his official work of registration and correction was arduous, and in addition to all this it was he who held the Chair for Englishmen who wished to study German Literature. Goethe certainly had Eckermann completely under his thumb. His had been the Mephistophelian rôle of persuading him to settle down in Weimar immediately after his first visit; for Goethe had seen at once what a valuable official Eckermann would prove, and so had held out inducements, though without offering any security of tenure.

Of Riemer, whom Goethe had made an official and teacher, their thirty years of intercourse made it natural for him to see a great deal; but the Chancellor was not so easy to get hold of. Goethe and he consulted together over any State-business that still remained in the former's hands—for after forty years of service the Duke had in effect pensioned off his old friend, without formally depriving him of position and authority.

Yet Goethe's heart was never really given to these men who so incessantly battened on his intellect. Knebel, Meyer, Zelter—they alone were and remained his last real friends.

In his seventy-ninth year Goethe sat for the last time at Knebel's familiar table in Jena. Knebel, now eighty-three, had silently tottered across the room to meet and embrace him; but now they did not enter eagerly upon some intellectual argument—they merely sat rejoicing in one another's company. Perhaps they thought of that twilight-hour in which, fifty years ago, the literary-minded officer from Weimar had first appeared in the poet's attic-room at Frankfurt.

Or was Knebel's head full of very different memories? He had wanted to be a poet; but Goethe had prized him only as a translator, and had let this be generally known. For years they had tacitly kept apart, without any sort of breach; during the middle-period Knebel had sometimes stood by Herder, who had been Goethe's opponent. It was as though in the temple of their mutual attachment there lay one stone against which each must be careful not to stumble—on Knebel's side one might define it as sublimated jealousy; and Goethe occasionally resented the fact that Knebel had never been his devotee.

For the last ten years they had very seldom met, though they were only a couple of hours' drive from one another. Goethe wrote to Knebel sometimes—now and then with a sudden access of startling ceremoniousness: "Dearest Sir and friend," signing himself with his full name and title! Upon which would follow a little poem, headed with a phrase unique in Goethe's correspondence: "To the dear companion of my life, Von Knebel." It was some indefinable attraction, suffused with memories, which in his best hours Goethe felt for Knebel; and when at the banquet held to celebrate his Jubilee year of office, Goethe (himself absent) entrusted the giving of thanks to August, and everyone was hanging on the words to which the son, in the father's name, would empty his glass, there was a stir of surprise and emotion when the toast was drunk to "my oldest surviving friend" Knebel—and while the two old men sat in their warm rooms at Weimar and Jena, the formal banqueting-hall was applauding to the echo that sensational coda to a friendship which had demanded some self-abnegation from both concerned.

And it is true that, on a general survey, Knebel was perhaps the one who for the longest time looked deepest into Goethe's soul.

When Meyer (who after his wife's death lived alone) fell ill, Goethe sent his secretary, whom usually he could not do without for a day, to help in looking after him. "The two old men," writes this secretary, "had by now grown as it were into one . . . . Often they would sit together for hours without speaking a word, content to be in one another's company"; and Goethe declared emphatically: "I don't want to survive that man's death!" or else he would say sadly: "Am I to be condemned to see him go?"

The most fruitful relation, however, was certainly that with Zelter; his letters were always a refreshment to Goethe. To Zelter went Goethe's most intimate confessions—and perpetually; to him alone he spoke so openly that sometimes he half-repented it, "for when one doesn't even like to say what one's thinking, how on earth can one bring one's self to write it?"—and off the letter would go at once, lest he should be tempted to keep it back! Zelter's serene temperament, his inexhaustible interest and energy for the things of art, was precisely the atmosphere that Goethe needed.

Even the Duke and Duchess were over seventy now. Carl August, who after a long, dull middle-age had regained all his youthful eagerness of mind, stood to Goethe in the same sort of relation as one of a married pair estranged for many years, and now happily reconciled in a mutual self-surrender. They had long ceased to quarrel about military matters, about policy and administration; for Goethe was in effect out of office, and Carl August was inclined to let things slide. The chief bond between them was natural science, in which the Duke grew more interested as he grew older; and the Goethe who had sought, in their young days, to amuse him with letters about flirtations and starry nights, later about recruits and high-roads, and later still about Professors and Theatre-directors—now wrote to him about the temperature of the earth, steamships, or the origin of the wood-louse.

But about his literary work he said as little now as he had in the past, for it was a regret to him "that as concerns poetry this high-minded Prince has never thrown off the influence of French materialism." Such was—a year before the Duke's death—the

German Poet's epilogue upon the intellectual equipment of his Prince and Pupil.

Nevertheless, they had renewed their mutual attachment. On the day of Carl August's Jubilee Goethe—then seventy-six—hid himself behind the Duke's bed-hangings at six o'clock in the morning, so as to be the first to congratulate him; and when the occasion was celebrated in the evening at Goethe's house, and the Duke shook hands with him on coming in, Goethe was heard to say very softly, with deep emotion: "Together to our last breath. . . ." But the Duke, quicker to recover himself, looked laughingly into his eyes and said like any poet: "Ah, eighteen—and Ilmenau—!"

The more little attentions the constantly rejuvenated Court showed to Goethe, the more stiffly punctilious he became. Even there his duties were all at an end. At the very most the Master of the Horse might ask the old Court-poet to name a new-born foal—or the Master of the Household very politely inquire if His Excellency could remember whether, fifty-four years ago, certain robes had or had not been provided for a Councillor of Legation? Whenever a handsome carpet was spread out upon the threshold of Goethe's house, Weimar knew that the Princesses were paying him a visit. If one of these ladies congratulated the old man on his birthday, he would answer in the language peculiar to courtiers: "The most gracious handwriting . . . so as it were dazzled me, that till now I have been able to find no adequate expression for the gratitude I owe"; and when there was an addition to the Princely family Goethe declared that the news had "transported him to the highest pinnacle of earthly happiness"!

Can Goethe, who had never truckled to any Royalty, have ended by becoming a time-server?

No—it was because all the elements of his personality were in solution that these forms and ceremonies grew upon him, as many another trait in this last portrait of his soul will demonstrate. Royalty: in the last analysis it meant for him legitimacy, meant law and order, and hence was to be swallowed whole —as for instance when he once said to Schiller, vexed by some desire of Carl August's: "I am bound to respect it." The more unflinchingly, as the long years went on, he worked his way upward from the unit to the type and from the type to the symbol, the more he was inclined to accept legalised authority as a law of Nature. But as Goethe's style, like every other old man's, tended to become a tissue of formalities, it would now and then break out into such grotesque servilities as those cited above; yet in truth they signified no more than his symbolic sense of kingship, his punctiliousness, and the fixed determination of a master-spirit—living, under the pressure of genius, an inward life of the utmost intensity—to come to a dispassionate understanding with the powers of this world, rather than hotly to contend with them as in his earlier years.

In the same way, those so-called "dumb audiences" in the course of which Goethe scarcely spoke at all, were really no more than the outcome of tediousness or tactlessness on the part of his visitors, whom he saw to be attracted merely by curiosity, with its inevitable result of futile conversation-making. On these occasions he would deal out such platitudes as: "How do you like Weimar? There's a good deal of intellectual life in the place, don't you think? We've done our best in that line, at any rate."

But anyone who had something to contribute would be surprised by the epic hospitality of his reception. With both hands extended Goethe would welcome young men who had written a good book or painted a fine picture. Scholars and artists, when they pleased him, were invited to luncheon every day of their stay in Weimar. On the second occasion, he would beg these birds of passage to go on from the precise point they had reached the day before. Young men had to submit to sitting down while he, standing, handed them sketch after sketch to look at.

For such guests there were all sorts of amenities—he would call upon the whole table to admire a good remark; but if the guest told an anecdote for the general ear, everyone waited to see whether Goethe testified his approval. If he toasted the painter Cornelius, everyone followed his example; even old Meyer, for whom no good thing came out of that Nazareth, had to toe the line—for this was a question of art-politics.

Moreover, Goethe would send his own tame portrait-painter to the hotel that he might sketch these interesting guests for his collection. Finally the "Goethe-Order" would be conferred. There were three classes of this: a Goethe-medal in copper—by

Bovy or Rauch—which in the last ten years he lavished so generously that he would send his various agents several copies for free distribution to the deserving. The same head in silver was given only to a few intimates; three, at the most, received the gold medal. When Goethe felt disinclined to hear Tieck read *Clavigo* aloud, Ottilie handed to Tieck's daughter some scarf-pins with Goethe's likeness on them, by way of compensation. On the evening of Carl August's Jubilee Goethe threw his house open in true regal fashion—everyone who liked could come in for wine and cake.

Sometimes he gave a formal evening tea-party. When all the guests had assembled and been welcomed by Ottilie and August, Goethe would appear in evening-dress, wearing his Star, with his hair beautifully done (he still had it singed every second day), holding himself bolt upright by sheer will-power, and would speak to each individual guest as a king does. Then the various groups would converse in low voices, intimates looking forward to the moment when the strain should be relaxed by his departure.

This extraordinary stiffness of demeanour in the old man who only yesterday would have been chatting over his wine or in the garden—this apparent affectation, the legend of which could for a century distort our conception of Goethe in his old age, was in truth no more than the outcome of embarrassment. The man who had most insight into Goethe's nature—that is, the Chancellor—told interesting visitors, whom he saw to be disappointed, of this psychological trait in the veteran; and everything else we know of Goethe's demeanour points to the same conclusion. Had it not been for this, he could have done himself justice as the brilliant, humorous man of the world that he was; yet it was men of that calibre who most noticed how frequently, on ceremonious occasions, he would be difficult and out of humour. The stiffness for which the Leipzig student—nay, even the schoolboy—had been derided, was now a mannerism serving to conceal the infirmities of old age. Scepticism had developed into misanthropy—and this, together with everlasting preoccupation of mind (for he was as chary of his time as of his highest favours) united to bewilder visitors, and posterity into the bargain.

Yet when a young painter, on taking leave, kissed Goethe's

hand, the old man laid both hands upon his head as if to bless him for his journey.

Grillparzer had three days to judge by. Disappointed, on the first, to find his ideal as strait-laced as a Spanish King, he would have preferred not to go near him on the next. But to his utter amazement, on the second occasion the old gentleman led him to the table with his own hand. Grillparzer was moved to tears, which Goethe was tactful enough to prevent anyone else from noticing. At table the guest kept crumbling his bread, and for a long time never noticed that Goethe, beside him, was gathering every crumb into a little heap with one finger. On the third day the garden was the place of audience; Goethe was walking up and down in his dressing-gown and the little peaked cap. "Infinitely touching," said the young poet. "He looked something between a King and one's father."

One day two Russian noblemen, brothers, arrived at Goethe's house—men of the world, a rare type of guest in that circle; and in the description given by one of them (who was an accomplished horseman, a traveller, a libertine, a patron of art, and there an end of him), we see this singular community under a fresh light. To him the intellectual arrogance of that narrow self-centred society seemed absurdly pretentious; and when at a large reception these aristocratic Russians found themselves looked upon as a species of queer foreign birds, and rather tactlessly interrogated about serfdom, while Goethe sat by in silence and seemed to revel in their embarrassment—this gentleman suddenly turned the tables and very loudly launched at him some far-reaching questions about his writings, their origin and intention, the company sitting round in silent consternation. Instead of Goethe, a professor undertook to answer; and when the Russian, irritated, begged him to speak French and the Professor retorted that what he was saying could only be comprehensible in German, the Russian revenged himself by the cutting remark that he believed, like Byron, that Goethe was nowhere so misunderstood as in Germany. Goethe changed the thorny subject by asking if supper was ready. Stiff and laconic with the Russian, he nevertheless shot a couple of stolen glances at him, which did not seem to be angry ones.

The next morning the Count was surprised at being invited to take a drive with the poet. "Yesterday," said Goethe, in the carriage, "you let fall some valuable remarks which made me anxious to know you better, for I am like Voltaire in this—that I desire nothing so ardently as the praise of those who refuse me their applause." Then he opened his mind about the worthlessness of fame, the pure love of humanity which had inspired all his works, saying that Byron had understood him better than the Germans did, only unfortunately he had never heard anything very directly about Byron's opinion of him. The Russian, who saw what Goethe wanted, had in fact seen a good deal of Byron in Venice—and that in his character of libertine and gambler.

So he had many a titbit for Goethe, and these were thoroughly appreciated; but he took care not to impart all Byron's comments. For Byron—so this Russian informs us—had often spoken of Goethe's hypocrisy with a great deal of humour but very little reverence, and had once said of him that he was an old fox who never came out of his den, and from there took a very high tone indeed. He had called *Werther* and *Elective Affinities* such skits upon marriage as Mephisto himself could not have bettered, both novels ending on so strongly ironical a note. Instead of these sallies, the Russian retailed only Byron's genuine admiration for Goethe's achievement as a whole. But Goethe very eagerly explained to the astonished Russian that most of that achievement was in the Second *Faust*—wherefore the Germans would one day declare it to be the most tedious of all his works.

This anecdote is a tragi-comic revelation of the narrowness of Goethe's social life at the end of his career—for what could be more grotesque than the anxiety of a very old man to win the confidence of an aristocratic cosmopolitan *roué*, who had nothing to contribute but a few remarks of Byron's about Goethe, dropped between women and wine at the Carnival of Venice? To say nothing of the cautious way the young cavalier avoided telling anything that might wound the old gentleman! Since the Herder and Schiller days, Goethe had perhaps never listened with such eagerness to a verdict upon himself as on that morning-drive with a nobody of a Crimean Court whom he barely knew—for when he spoke of Voltaire's jealous craving, he was not thinking of the Count, but of Byron.

What could fame signify to him now! In his youth it had not dazzled him; in his middle-age its default had sometimes embittered him; when he began to grow old he had included it, as a hard-won treasure, in the catalogue of his possessions; now it was a factor with which to reckon when something had to be achieved.

For now the old man was world-renowned, as he had not been since he was twenty-five; and truly it was a hard-won treasure, and centuries would not behold it fade! The youth of France made pilgrimages to Weimar, bringing translations and tributes; Carlyle begged for a testimonial from the German Goethe, to support his candidacy for a chair in a Scottish University; from England came a letter addressed "To his Highness, Prince Goethe"; and the young Berlioz, dedicating his *Damnation de Faust* to him, erased the word Monsieur in his letter, to improve it into "Monseigneur"! Geologists named a stone after Goethe; one German King sent him the cast of an antique he had procured, another that of a recently excavated Jupiter, and a third the old grandfather's-clock which had once struck the hours in his ancestral home.

But amid all this homage, he was not to be led away by the seductions of Fame—many decades had taught him too much about her fickleness!

In reality, they were never satisfied with me. . . . When I had laboured day and night at some piece of work, the world demanded, over and above, that I should prostrate myself in gratitude because it found the thing tolerable. When they applauded me, I was not to be so vain as to take it for a tribute; no, they expected some modest phrase of self-depreciation. But as I was strong-minded enough to show exactly what I felt, they called me arrogant, and to this day they call me so! . . . And of my lyrics, which survives? One or another may be sung now and again by a pretty girl at her piano, but for the real public they're as dead as mutton. . . . I'll tell you a secret—my things could never be popular . . . they are only for the few who desire and look out for that kind of thing, and are doing something like it themselves.

When the engraver Schwerdgeburth, in Goethe's last months, expressed a desire to make a drawing of him, he said he did not wish to be done again. But while he was giving his reasons for this refusal, the artist was devouring him with his eyes. He rushed home, drew him from memory, brought Ottilie the sketch; she showed it to her father-in-law—and, conquered by its excellence, the old man offered to sit as often as the artist liked. Even in his last days he eagerly inquired how the engraving was getting on. Thus, it appears, did Goethe wish posterity to see him. But when the Frankfurt Memorial, about which he had had some correspondence, fell through, he jotted down this haughtily ironic epigram:

> Zu Goethe's Denkmal was zahlst du jetzt?
> Fragt dieser, jener, und der.
> Hätt' ich mir nicht selbst ein Denkmal gesetzt,
> Das Denkmal, wo käm' es denn her?[1]

To complete this Memorial of his own, to round off his work, to protect it, became Goethe's last passion; and so far as that task involved him in worldly affairs, it shows the man of seventy-five as equal to the most exacting demands of business.

For now, and not till now, he grasped his works as a whole. He had begun by regarding them as "Vestigia," and had half-unwittingly, and then only piecemeal, collected these mementoes of his long pilgrimage; but now, when at this last his personality was in solution, when fellow-creatures and affections, the past and the present, all swam before his gaze as symbols of the whole, remotely distant—now there came to pass what had come to pass with other artists in youth or at any rate in middle age. Goethe began to forget his life, from whose ever-climbing crest those works had fallen to him as fruits may fall—and he discovered that though the trunk was withering away the fruits would endure, for they were apples from the Garden of the Hesperides.

With amazing energy, with a nervous eagerness, impatience,

[1] "What price the Goethe Memorial now?
Says he, and the same says she.
If I had not erected my own somehow,
Where *would* the Memorial be?"

and enthusiasm which seemed to say that this was the one chance left for salvage of the grand total, he set about making a final collection of his works, after a method never before attempted by anyone. He gathered round him a group of five men, including Riemer and Eckermann, and gave each a share in the critical and grammatical revision of all the text for sixty volumes, of which twenty were not to appear till after his death. He included all his magazine-writings, was indefatigable in arranging and re-arranging; and kept this up, as of yore his Ministerial labours, no matter what new work he was engaged in—for four whole years!

And what was the good of it, in the end? Could not the German commentators have done nearly as much, leaving Goethe to reserve his own time and energies for fresh productions? Was it not only an excessively subtle form of his characteristic pedantry?

No; it was more. It was a dæmonic determination to bring order, with his own hands, into the infinite endeavour, the straggling abundance; and so from a hundred separate works to shape, when all was done, a new, a single masterpiece—the life-work of Goethe.

But above all he wanted, by this achievement, to leave his house in order after the grand manner. Behind him stood his son, driving the old man on to "cut up well" when his eyes should be closed in death.

And so Goethe began by mustering up everyone he knew in the way of powerful personages—Kings and Dukes, Ambassadors, Ministers, and noblemen, to the end that Germany and its great ones should grant him a fifty-years' copyright, thus protecting his work for well-nigh two generations.

But once he was in possession of this magic key, still greater pressure was put upon him by his family to get the great business finished once for all.

Endless disagreeable negotiations—in the course of which Goethe himself dictated proposals "on my father's behalf" to be signed by August, thus submitting to the urgency of his heirs—led to friction with Cotta. In these incidents Goethe appears as the aggressive author, half-persuasive, half-menacing, while the publisher smoothes him down by tactful prevarications.

When it was all settled Goethe declared he had got very much the better of the publisher, and wrote two highly excited letters, one immediately after the other, with his own hand to Boisserée, who had acted as agent. He said that he looked upon him as Hercules coming to the help of Prometheus, and concluded with the heartfelt cry: "If you knew what I have gone through this year, you would not think such comparisons exaggerated!" Another hint at the pressure put upon him by the unsympathetic heirs who from their ambush lashed the aged poet mercilessly on.

A kindred passion informed the veteran's anticipation of the completed great edition. There was a similar monomania in his retrospect on his own life. He now regarded it as little more than the instrument of those works; and so he was for the most part critical in his view of the course it had taken—often bitter, many times enraged. His survey was vehement and unjust, in these days, even of what his life in the great world had brought him; he grudged his misdirected efforts and his wasted time:

> My only pleasure was my poetic meditation and creation. But how sadly that was disturbed, restricted, and hindered by my public position! If I had held more aloof from official and business-affairs and claims, and been able to live more alone, I should have been a happier man, and have done far more as a writer. But it was written that the wise words spoken to me soon after my *Götz* and my *Werther* should be proved true: "If a man has once done anything for love of humanity, humanity takes good care that he shan't do it again."

When he considered the colossal achievement of Lope de Vega, he regretted not having stuck more to his own craft. If he had remained in his summer-villa, he would have prosecuted his Nature-study with ever-increasing insight. If Schiller had not lured him on to æsthetic experiments he would have had more in the way of actual achievement to show. And were not his earlier works, written from sheer intuition, when he *knew* nothing, sufficient proof that a man does not need knowledge of the world before he can represent it?

It was thus that Goethe, reflecting, lamented his wasted youth; and he went on to lay stress on the contrast between the body of an adolescent, which is an ally to his energies, and that of an old man, which is their adversary. True, he had lived strictly by the best régime that science then knew how to prescribe—changing his food and drink from time to time so as not to be dependent on any, avoiding highly-spiced dishes, solicitous about sleep and wine, as being productive of energy; and his health had been consistently good except for inflammations which close work and shortsightedness repeatedly caused in his retina. How well he could take his wine is shown by his prowess at an Archery-Banquet given one autumn, when he—at seventy-eight—could drink the younger men under the table. But from his eightieth year onwards he was more absteminous in this respect, and contented himself with a glass of madeira and a bottle of light Würzburger a day.

Yet there were moods in which retrospection on his endeavour and frustrations went deeper, piercing to the core of his being. On a few autograph sheets—fragments on no particular theme and in no sequence—he (probably not until this period) communed with himself in this dispassionate, stern strain:

I have never known a more presumptuous human being than myself. . . . I never could believe that anything was to be striven for—I always thought I already possessed it. If a crown had been set upon my head, I should have taken it as a matter of course. And yet I was, in every fibre, a man like other men. But because I was always trying to put through something I had been fascinated by, which was beyond my powers, and to merit something which had been granted me, and was beyond my deserts—I do discriminate between myself and the man who is really no more than a visionary. First it was my follies which made me objectionable to other people, and then my serious aims. So do what I would, I was alone.

I was conscious of noble, lofty aims, but could never grasp the conditions under which I had to work. I was well aware of my deficiences, and of my redundancies too; and so I was always trying to develop myself both outwardly and inwardly. And yet I remained as I was. I pursued my every aim earnestly, with all my strength and all my loyalty; and I did often succeed in wholly overcoming adverse circumstances, but often too was broken by them, because I could not learn to concede and evade. And so my life went by in doing and enjoying, suffering and resisting, amidst the love, satisfaction, hatred, dissatisfaction of others. Let him who has known a like destiny, look in this mirror.

They are like a Largo on the organ in his Temple of Life—these sonorous phrases in which he seems to speak for Destiny, calling upon him to review his course. In them Goethe surveys with "cold commemorative eyes" the strivings and the frustrations imposed upon him by his nature—but that "And yet," which sounds in the heart of each fragment, suffuses the dark stormy atmosphere of those self-revelations with the warm sense of tears in human things.

These gentler moods would also bring some colour into the old man's retrospect, in that they induced remembrance of the women in his life. It is true that he gives but an impersonal sort of summary; and we find it difficult to believe that it is a man untiring in his devotion to women who says, at last:

> Women are silver dishes, in which we lay our apples of gold. My idea of women has not been divorced from actualities; but it was born in me or else came to exist in me, God knows how. So my female characters have all been indulgently conceived; they are better than those one encounters in real life.

This glacial comment was doubtless inspired by annoyance at the eternal curiosity about the original models for his personages.

Soon after their parting he wrote a few friendly letters to Ulrike's mother, clearing up all misunderstandings, and always inquiring for the whole family. When he met Minna Herzlieb again, twenty years after their farewell to each other, he said it was a strange sensation, and spoke of her charming, pretty manners; and now he gave the last of the sonnets to the world—that charade upon her name. Whether he ever heard of Lotte Kestner's death, we do not know.

When Frau von Stein, now in her eighty-fourth year, congratulated him for the last time on his birthday, he answered with some vague lines of verse, and concluded:

> The enclosed poem, my dearest, ought really to end: "But to find affection and love enduring for so many a long year in the lives of such close neighbours is the very best and highest blessing that can be granted to mortals." And so for evermore! Goethe.

Strange, that for the woman with whom his intercourse had been longest he could find nothing better than such stilted prose to express the sublimation of experience, now so familiar to his own spirit!

Marianne alone was still a living memory—because he never saw her again. To the end she remained for him the incarnation of pure blitheness of spirit, and of a passion for which art had been the only medium. He wrote to her often, and with his own hand: "Open your dear heart to me again, turn your sweet eyes to me" . . . so he would say, when she was too long silent.

Even his dead friends he seldom now called to mind. There is hardly a word of Lavater, an occasional allusion to Merck and Jacobi; but Herder, with whom he had never been able to strike just the right note, is most frequently mentioned. And when Eckermann (who knew *Dichtung und Wahrheit* by heart) speaks with Goethe of these men, and also of the women of Goethe's younger days, exactly as though they were historical characters, there is something eerie in the thought that the old man sitting by the big stove and answering his questions is one and the same person as the man in the book.

Schiller gave him a great deal to work upon. Their friendship is immortalised in what might be called an extensive dossier; and so, Crown-witness as it were for Goethe's middle-period, Schiller is continually in the box. When Goethe was revising this dossier, he felt that Schiller's letters were more pregnant than his own, and he contrasts them as though he had never before laid eyes on the correspondence. But to Zelter he had something to say in strictest privacy:

> Yet in truth there is something really instructive in the situation—two men, equally ardent in the pursuit of their aims, throw precious time away because they are both over-intellectualised, and moreover excited and perturbed by outside matters; so that in the end we have nothing that can be called a truly valuable outcome of their powers, tendencies, and points of view.

Thus we see that he had come to regard the work of this decade—which has been thought so important—as purely experimental.

Meanwhile it had been decided that Schiller's remains must be removed from their unworthy surroundings. Goethe was prominent in this exhumation; the moment came when Schiller's skull was brought to him for identification. And in the grinning object Goethe not only discerned the genius of the man—he had the courage to put the skull into a poem! The poet's soul took fire from the scientist's vision, and leaped into a glorious blaze of inspiration:

> . . . Wie mich geheimnisvoll die Form entzückte!
> Die gottgedachte Spur, die sich erhalten!
> Ein Blick, der mich an jenes Meer entrückte,
> Das flutend strömt gesteigerte Gestalten.
> Geheim Gefätz! Orakelsprüche spendend!
> Wie bin ich wert, dich in der Hand zu halten,
> Dich höchsten Schatz aus Moder fromm entwendend
> Und in die freie Luft, zu freiem Sinnen,
> Zum Sonnenlicht andächtig hin mich wendend?
> Was kann der Mensch im Leben mehr gewinnen,
> Als datz sich Gott-Natur ihm offenbare:
> Wie sie das Feste lätzt zu Geist verrinnen,
> Wie sie das Geisterzeugte fest bewahre.[1]

What other scientist has ever been privileged to behold thus transfigured the relics of a human existence? What artist, to put the experience into such lambent words with the cold skull between his hands? What friend, thus fearlessly to ignore his memories, his tenderness, and—where survivors are wont to weep and shudder—be conscious only of the "incessant soul" in Nature? Nowhere else does the warm stream of Goethe's ultimate sense of the Cosmos so interpenetrate the ice of his impersonal intellect.

And while he was writing those glowing lines he was assisting the anatomists to assemble Schiller's bones; he was ordering

[1] "That form—I gazed in awe and fascination!
Upon it still the stamp of thought supreme!
A sight that rapt me hence in contemplation
Of radiant hosts that people shores of dream. . . .
Chalice occult, thine oracles outpouring,
Set in this hand unworthy thou dost seem
To bid me turn, the grave like thee ignoring,
And, opening all my sense to open Heaven,
Feel the broad sunlight bathe my brow adoring!
What holier boon has life to mortals given
Than thus God-Nature's mysteries to range—
See how pure mind the stubborn bone can leaven,
See how the mind-engendered mocks at change!"

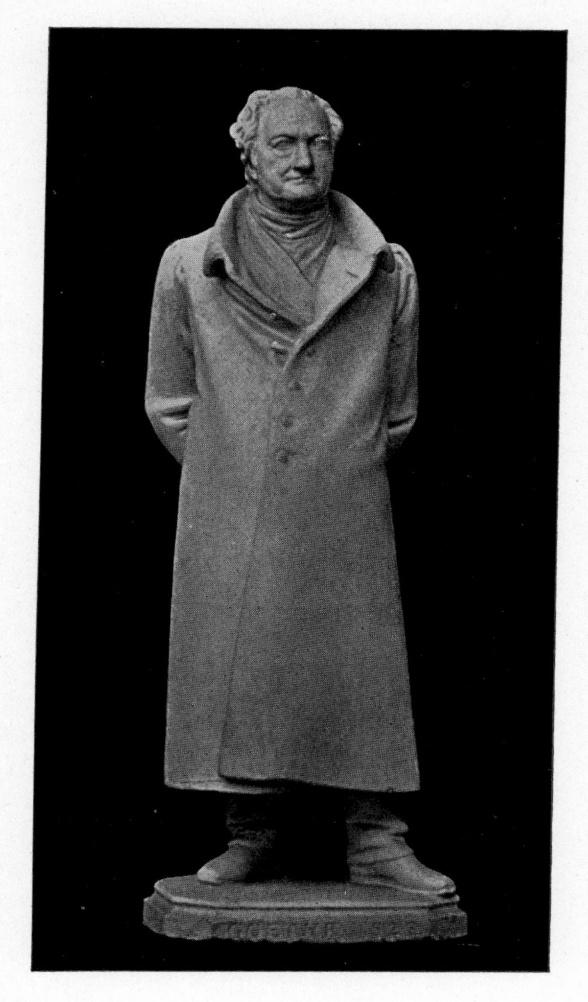

STATUETTE OF GOETHE AT THE AGE OF SEVENTY-NINE

designs for a little chapel, near the Royal Vault, in which he was to be laid at Schiller's side—yet, occupied with these things, he could close a letter telling a friend about them all with: "Work, while yet it is day!"

Still more instinct with emotion was Goethe's last Italian retrospect. He seemed determined to make those two years historic as the zenith of his life: "Yes, I may say that only in Rome did I feel what it really means to be a man. I never again touched such heights of exalted, enraptured sensibility. Compared with what I felt in Rome, I was never truly happy again." Was he conscious that it was not only Rome—that it was freedom, above all, which had made him so peculiarly happy there?

At eighty he had young acacia-trees planted with branches so grafted as to hang downwards, because they reminded him of orange-trees; and the division of his affections between the North and the South seems typified in his sending the gardener in Jena some grains for planting, taken by him from ears of Sicilian corn those forty years ago.

The old man's outlook on the times to come was quite in keeping with his review of those gone by—looking back, he was critical of details; looking forward, of things in general. Everything that opened a wider field for action was irresistibly attractive to his tireless spirit; everything that brought the nations nearer to one another, charmed his super-national feeling. Steamships and the acceleration of mails were stimulating to his imagination; in the *Wanderjahre* he foresees a successful experiment in telegraphy accomplishing the great end of wiring the course of time both by day and night all over the world—for he insisted on Time being held in the utmost respect as the highest gift of God to men. He sent most of his "wanderers" to America, as a final resort; for he admired the new outlook—in those days unsophisticated too—of her young men.

So far he could welcome the nineteenth century, which he saw shedding the spirit of Romanticism for that of productive energy. But though he was thus prescient of the international and socialistic ideas of our twentieth century, Goethe did not fail to indicate the dangers implicit in over-population, financial expansion, speed, machines, and the Mechanical Age in general. He was fond of calling it the "velocipedic" age, said he would not care to be young in "such an utterly artificial century," held riches and rapidity of communication to be corrupters of the youth of the period, and thought they tended to encourage mediocrity.

I cannot help thinking that the greatest evil of our times, impatient of slow growth as they are, is that one moment is swallowed up in the next, one day squandered for the sake of the next, and that people thus live from hand to mouth and take no time to dwell upon anything whatever. Why, we can get a newspaper at every hour of the day! . . . And hence every single thing that anyone does, attempts, writes —nay, every single thing he even hopes to do—is dragged into the light of publicity. No one may be glad or sorry, but all the rest must batten on it; and so the vortex spreads from house to house, from city to city, from realm to realm, and in the end from continent to continent, with incredible velocity.

He certainly may be called a seer in that passage; and writing to Zelter in a similar strain he concluded with the proudly prophetic words: "Let us preserve, so far as we may, the principles to which we were born; then we, with perhaps a few others, shall be the last representatives of an epoch whose like will not soon be seen again."

The enormous amount of work done by Goethe in the last eight years of his life was almost entirely that of a writer, and a writer was what he finally felt himself—as in the past—to be. The revision of finished works, the completion of those begun, represent only a portion of his labours. His official position and his fame no longer pressed so hard upon him, and anything he was called upon to do in those respects could be done by letter. It is in this period that his letters rank with his conversations as part of the Goethe-canon: there are from three to four hundred for every year.

He pursued a similar method to that with his visitors. Only those who had something to contribute were answered quickly. He found it more arduous work than in the past; and liked his letters to be dispatched directly he had dictated them, for when he read the fair copy next day he was often dissatisfied—and then he would put off his answer for weeks. Frequently he would stop at the end of a page—in the middle of a sentence, or even of a word; and conclude with a promise to continue, which he would do, after weeks had gone by, with the very same word. And so it once came to pass that Goethe implored one friend to get another to forgive him—he having found the latter's last letter of twenty-three years ago still unanswered, when he was arranging his papers!

For he could not teach himself a curt businesslike style of answering. On important letters, often filling several pages of print, he would call in Riemer to advise him; for Goethe never really mastered either punctuation or correct spelling, and whenever he wrote with his own hand, the orthography is that of the rococo-period.

He became addicted to ceremonious ways of signing himself—we find an instance of *hochachtungsvoll ergebenst* (Your most respectful and obedient servant); and even to those he knew best he nearly always signed his full name. But for his few friends there would usually be some special little flight of fancy at the end; not now "Love me," but such vaguer phrases as "And thus to the end of time," or "For ever and ever." On very rare occasions he would conclude with a boyish appeal: "Indulgence! Sympathy! Good-will!"

These letters range over every province of the mind; and if we combine them with his short studies and essays on artistic and scientific matters (which now filled fresh volumes), Goethe will seem to us, in the end, like a composer who spends blissful evening-hours at his piano, playing variations on the themes of his works.

While he was reading Scott, Manzoni, Victor Hugo in the originals; while he was writing Studies in the Minor Modes, and sealing them up like a boy until Zelter sent *his* for comparison; while he was reading, on an average, one octavo volume a day—he was also writing on Serbian folk-poetry, inquiring for the passage in Vitruvius where he decries fresco-painting, arguing about Mondragone's head of Antinous, about the difference between the haloes in the wall-paintings of Pompeii and of the Catacombs, answering questions upon the kind of stone used in the building of an antique Roman fortress in Bohemia, and finding, after a Jamaican visitor had been with him, that his information about that island was "pleasantly refreshed." Simultaneously he would be writing about water-caltrops, mango-seeds, Batavian vegetation; about Mexican mines, Heligoland granite and stearine-acids, about soot from plants, cuckoo-spit, and the entrails of the kangaroo.

His purely literary work took three principal forms in this final period—the lyrics, the *Wanderjahre*, and the Second *Faust* are the last monuments of the octogenarian poet.

Ripe wisdom falls naturally into a sententious form—and so some hundreds of *Zahme Xenien* (*Tame Epigrams*) are one of the principal legacies of his last decade. He liked the method, and used it for syllogisms upon God, upon reason and the universe, art and politics, his adversaries, contemporary productions, and the spirit of the age. With these may be classed some other hundreds of short apophthegms addressed to individuals.

It was only very rarely that a lyric poem shed its tranquil planetary radiance upon these intellectual fireworks. Only once (at any rate until he was eighty) does such a star shine forth, as though miraculously—equal to the supreme creations of his muse; and ultimately the outmoded "Luna" makes her re-appearance, as though the hoary poet were fondly recalling his juvenile effort:

Dämmrung senkte sich von oben. . . .[1]

On the other hand, the two final volumes of *Wilhelm Meisters Wanderjahre* display all the eccentricities of old age. The pro-foundest prophecies upon social and academic matters, a golden rain of wisdom in the form of aphorisms, are here mixed up with passages which are either too prolix or too confused to capture the attention.

If we read, together with this novel, the exquisite short stories of the same period (whose subjects had, thirty years earlier, been fortunate enough to elude the hexameter) it is clear that failing creative energy was not the essential reason for this deterioration in the *Wanderjahre*. It was rather that Goethe regarded that work as the great larder of his old age, and crammed

[1] "Twilight mists from heaven were falling. . . ."

things into it which properly belonged to newspaper-articles or letters.

And then, all of a sudden, the whole thing blazes up into so splendid a final chapter that we ask ourselves if this is not poetry in the disguise of prose! But not at all—for a pregnant parenthesis makes us feel as though saluted by a stiff-necked Indomitable: "*To be continued.*"

Goethe's dread was of having to add a similar parenthesis to *Faust*. True, *Meister* had been with him almost as long as *Faust* had, and no less urgently; but he felt that the former was a pastime, the latter a parable of life; and so he devoted his last, his sublimest powers to the poem, first conceived nearly sixty years ago.

> In goldnen Frühlings—Sonnen—Stunden
> Lag ich gebunden
> An dies Gesicht.
> In holder Dunkelheit der Sinnen
> Konnt' ich wohl diesen Traum beginnen—
> Vollenden nicht.[1]

The more he felt that here alone could he display all his genius, the more passionately did he desire to rescue *Faust* from its fragmentary state. It was impossible that he should regard the first part as anything but a fragment—and yet it is as though he dreaded the sight of the manuscript, as though his genius were awaiting some external impulse which should stir that valley of dry bones.

Just then, Byron died.

Goethe, already fired by the poet's Greek campaign, was now kindled afresh. To him that figure of Byron was simply incommensurable, and—between his critical faculty and his infatuation—he involved himself in a labyrinth of contradictions. Of no men did he talk so constantly in his old age, nor did he reflect so much on any (Schiller excepted), as Napoleon and Byron. He

[1] "When April's golden voices called me,
This face enthralled me
Long, long ago.
Englamoured then by youth and passion,
The dream I could begin to fashion,
But finish—no!"

never unravelled the enigma of either, and indeed said little of their actions and works, but much of their personalities and careers. Before Byron's death he had divined the real motive—desperation—for that Grecian adventure which at first he had regarded as pure heroism; he even came to describe it as a means of recreation, since a genius could not but be exhausted after such works; and when he heard of the death he was not overwhelmed, and said it had come at the right moment for Byron and poetry.

But, dead or alive, Byron haunted him perpetually. He had too well discerned in that phenomenon the alternative possibilities of a poet's life, barred to him by his chosen destiny. A few months sufficed to make him again see Byron as a radiant unblemished being, a "latter-day Lycurgus or Solon"—had he but survived; and he ended a poem on his death with the passionate words:

> Lasst ihn der Historia,
> Bandigt ener Sehnen,
> Ew'g bleibt ihm Gloria,
> Bleiben uns die Tränen.[1]

Not long afterwards he deplored the lawlessness which had ruined Byron. He had then been reading some English articles upon the Greek War and Byron's death.

About this time, a year after the tragedy of Missolonghi, he spent an entire February evening in talking of the scapegrace poet. This time he cast all the blame upon Bryon's rank, told anecdote upon anecdote, and was "inexhaustible" on the topic.

And in that same February Goethe, in the seventy-sixth year of his life, untied the string he had fastened round the *Faust* manuscript when he was fifty-two. Helen, sketched nearly thirty years ago in a few hundred lines, now came to life in a flash—through the remembrance of Byron; and when Goethe thus recalled his spirits from the vasty deep, the whole work, at one stroke, awoke from its trance-like sleep.

[1] "Leave him to Story!
Crave not more years—
His be the glory,
Ours be the tears."

A visitor tells us that Goethe spoke of Byron as a father may speak of a son. And into a son he now made him—Byron became Euphorion, Faust's son by Helen. That was the highest honour Goethe could bestow—and the only means by which he could lay Byron's ghost.

Indubitably it is to him, as the Boy-Charioteer, that Goethe speaks (in the First Act) as Plutus-Faust. No poet but might envy Byron that recalling!

> Wenn's nötig ist, dass ich dir Zeugnis leiste,
> So sag' ich gern: Bist Geist von meinem Geiste.
> Du handelst stets nach meinem Sinn,
> Bist reicher, als ich selber bin. . . .
> Ein wahres Wort verkünd' ich allen:
> Mein lieber Sohn, an dir hab' ich Gefallen.[1]

On one other man only did Goethe ever in his life confer the title of son. That was the farmer, Batty, from whom he had learnt husbandry at thirty. But the Boy-Byron is made to answer Goethe thus:

> So acht' ich mich als werten Abgesandten,
> So lieb' ich dich als nächsten Anverwandten.
> Wo du verweilst, ist Fülle. Wo ich bin,
> Fühlt jeder sich im herrlichsten Gewinn. . . .
> Bin der Poet, der sich vollendet,
> Wenn er sein eigenst Gut verschwendet.[2]

The Second *Faust*—as Goethe remarked—ranges from the burning of Troy to the taking of Missolonghi; and yet, though he could jestingly say: "It would be too amazing if I really

[1] "If I must needs bear witness, from my heart
I gladly say: Soul of my soul thou art.
Ever for me thy actions shine,
And thou hast riches more than mine. . . .
For all I make this proclamation:
Dear son, thou hast my approbation."

[2] "Thy proud ambassador myself is now,
So loving thee as nearest kin wert thou.
Thou dwellest in thy fullness. I on men
Lavish a splendour erst beyond their ken. . . .
The poet I, who best himself fulfils
When recklessly his holiest wine he spills."

brought it off!" he could not get rid of the uncomfortable feeling that it *was* beyond his power to finish it. When he began to work at it again, he first wrote the long-drafted conclusion, and then the *Helena*, hitherto a mere interlude. At the last moment he suppressed an introductory passage in which he had thought of preparing for her appearance and making the transitions smoother. Instead, he suffered the Interlude to stand by itself as a surprise, in the first edition of his Works.

The success achieved by the Interlude so stimulated this poet of seventy-eight, who certainly had not been spoiled by over-appreciation, that he now entered upon long digressions both prospective and retrospective. But he was saddened by the inevitable discovery that, at nearly eighty, he no longer had the same creative abundance as at fifty and during the *Divan* period. Now:

> I can work only in the morning-hours, when I feel refreshed by sleep and have not yet been put off by the little everyday worries. And even so, how much do I accomplish! At the very best one written page; as a rule no more than one could write on the palm of one's hand; and often, in an unproductive mood, even less than that.

No matter which we take for comparison, this Second *Faust* is the most effective stage-play that Goethe had written since the dramas of his youth. He knew this and was glad of it, and often said the conclusion was operatic. So that, æsthetically speaking, it is an important legacy as representing Goethe's lifelong wrestle, half-affectionate, half-hostile, with the dramatic form—a wrestle in which he never wholly conquered.

For he was by no means first the dramatic, then the epic, and finally the lyric, poet. The *Divan* and the second *Faust* are far more indicative of the great curve which makes him seem, at last, to hover lovingly over his early works. After having scorned the stage for decades and resolutely ignored his own dramatic efforts, he declared in his eightieth year that he would have liked to dictate a comic and a tragic piece, each in a week, if there had only been a few decent actors left in Weimar. "For a closet-play is no use at all. The poet must know what instruments he has to work with, and he must write his parts with full knowledge of the people who are going to play them." But that was precisely what Goethe never did; and even of the one apparent exception—*Iphigenie*—it cannot be said for certain how far the character was an anticipation, or a portrait, of the lovely Corona.

A tragic turn of mind, which at this last became evident in various ways, is clearly to be perceived in the realm of his art. In *Tasso* and *Iphigenie* (he said at this time) he had been able to colour the idealistic material with the sensual emotions of youth; but now he preferred material which (like the motley world of the Second *Faust*) was itself in some sort sensual; and he often regretted not having written, in his twenties, half-a-dozen pieces like *Clavigo*. For it was not until late in life—and too late for his happiness!—that Goethe perceived how the richness of his youth might have abounded in its own sense, might have enhanced his life with its own exuberance; and how seriousness and melancholy, passivity, all that his dæmon signified, had cheated even the poet in him of the moment which was now irretrievable. He would in these days often speak of that tardy recognition of the right tactics which comes upon a man when the campaign is over.

It was only now at the end that Goethe again professed the creed of spontaneous, as it were hallucinatory, creation, from which at one time he had declared he must escape to lucid possession of himself, to clarity and consciously pursued development—"if he were to survive"! After his long struggle for classic serenity (even when the Muse was prompting), after his perpetual theorising about poetry and his frequent obedience to his theories, he now finished by applauding that which was the outcome of a vague poetic impulse, of a beautiful accident as it were; he scouted all inquiries about the "idea" in *Faust*, in *Tasso*, and cared only for the sensuous appeal that they might have.

Indeed, when in its final phase we set ourselves to solve the great enigma of his soul, it is anything but harmony that we perceive in the picture so nearly finished. Neither love nor serenity, neither contemplativeness nor wise indulgence, characterise the Goethe of this decade. He is equally removed from Zeus and from Apollo—a defiant youth, a restless man, a stoical veteran confronts us now, whose aim is a purely literary one, though to him it shows as universal. It is only by the greatest perspicacity that we shall be able to discern the organic connection between the warring forces.

Vigour is predominant. *Faust* had slumbered in him for twenty years; and when he waked him from his haunted dreams in the beginning of the Second Part, the first word spoken by the sleeper refreshed was: "*Des Lebens Pulse schlagen frisch lebendig!*"[1] The cry might be taken as a parable of Goethe's final period.

He flung himself like a boy into the business of completing his works, for at his advanced age he felt that death was drawing nearer every day. To this final outburst of energy it is not alone the result which testifies, but the splendid words of proud humility which he uttered in confidence to his most intimate friends:

> Every morning challenges us to do what in us lies, and await possibilities. . . . Since God and his Nature have given me so many years for my possession, I know not what better I should do with them than express my grateful recognition by working like a young man. I want to show myself worthy of the blessings I have received, and I spend my days and nights in thinking and doing all I may to that end. "Days and nights" is no mere phrase, for many and many of the sleepless nights that a man of my age must spend are dedicated—not to aphorisms and general ideas, but to planning very carefully what I intend to do on the morrow. . . . And so I perhaps do more, and think to more purpose, in my doled-out days than others who can look forward to a longer future, who have the right to believe in and reckon on the day after to-morrow, and days and days after that.

And the old man was so adamantine in endeavour that he once accused himself of the "two greatest errors"—procrastination and hurry; and it was now that the whole question of how to keep research and daily life from encroaching on one another was decisively summed-up in the fine saying: "The highest art, both in study and social life, consists in turning your problem into a postulate—that's the way to get through." Did ever anyone more forcibly state the case for work as the core of life than the veteran poet in that monumental utterance?

[1] "The vital pulses beat with life renewed!"

It was just such a manful steady gaze, objective and unregretful, that Goethe in his ripest years could bend upon Eros.

> Und ringsum ist alles vom Feuer entronnen;
> So herrsche denn Eros, der alles begonnen![1]

In that mighty Chorus of the Sirens the great line of cleavage is drawn through the Second *Faust*, and the clarion note of his life peals out once more.

Everything now—even Eros—was pressed into the one service of "heightening his faculties," an expression which frequently recurs in these concluding years. He always now shows Eros as healthy, sensual, normal; designates marriage, which must be preserved in the interest of social order, as "essentially abnormal"; and when admiring a Dannæ gives vent to some sarcasms on the people who go into raptures over every Holy Family they see. And now, at last, he upbraids himself for his final re-modelling of *Götz*—meaning that he felt the loss of Adelheid's passion, which had made the original *Götz* so electric. He makes Faust on Peneus delight in the "fair young limbs of women"; in his last *Epigrams* the language is so frank that it can only be represented in print by asterisks; and one day he held this trenchant dialogue with himself:

> Wie bist du so ausgeartet?
> Sonst warst du am Abend so herrlich und hehr!—
> Wenn man kein Schätzchen erwartet,
> Gibt's keine Nacht mehr.[2]

Penetrated by the sense of this, he entirely abandoned any attempt at depicting love; and it is pathetic to find that master of love-scenes avoiding one at the end of the *Wanderjahre* for fear that "here youthful vigour might be found to fail me."

Since everything turned on his work, Goethe now in the service of his energies erected the hygienic practices, begun

[1] "And round us the blaze leaps, devouring and tall;
Then hail to thee, Eros, beginner of all!"

[2] "You've sadly degenerated;
Time was when at evening you glowed like the light!—
When no sweetheart is ever awaited,
How empty is night!"

sixty years ago, into a very stringent system. Anything that made for productiveness was cultivated; anything that frustrated it, given up. On books: "The little book will find it difficult to outwit the sentries at my frontiers." Or on his fellow-creatures: "One must not see old friends again. . . . Anyone to whom his inward development is a matter of importance should avoid this, for the dissonance can only perturb him, and the picture of the earlier relationship will be obscured." Or on his own works: "Why should I try" (it was thus that he rejected the impulse to finish *Die Natürliche Tochter*) "to recall to memory the uncanny things which lurk in that quarter?"

He refused to see or discuss anything unpleasant. When the old Theatre was burnt down, he would not let anyone come near him, for useless lamentations would have been intolerable; and he set to work at once on plans for the new building! When Ottilie was thrown from her horse and carried into the house, he never went to see her until her disfigured face had healed. When someone began to describe the condition of a man well known to him, who had broken both legs, he exclaimed: "Don't spoil my idea of him! I can see him now, full of energy and activity!" When an old actor died, Goethe sent for his son, came into the room, and said: "I have lost a faithful old friend, and you an excellent father. Enough!"—and pressing his hand, he vanished. When Zelter, whose stepson had killed himself in the past, now lost a son, Goethe looked at even this from an objective point of view: "A similar misfortune brought us very near to one another. . . . The present one leaves us as we are, and even that is a great deal."

Goethe's ultimate political attitude was the outcome of energy and the dissolution of personality. His conservative spirit became more and more manifest, more and more inclusive, towards the end—a confession of faith not only in social order but above all in authority. Now, far from the madding crowd, his outlook on these questions was as generalised as on other things—he saw them in the light of necessity. So it had been ordered—and he, who had revered the Emperor in the advocate's son because the man had known how to make himself accepted of the people, ended by revering every manifestation of power, whether conferred by God, ancestral right, or personality.

When Wellington's dictatorship was the theme of censure, the octogenarian Goethe defended the man who, be he what he might, had conquered Napoleon and India; and he made his position clear in these words: "Who has the highest power is right. We must bend our heads to him."

He felt that contemporary events now justified him by upholding his instinctive sympathy—classic in its ignoring of the moral standpoint—for men and deeds whose only vindication was success. "We don't ask what right we have to govern" (this extremely broad generalisation comes from the *Wanderjahre*) "—we govern. We don't trouble to ask whether the nation has a right to depose us—we merely take care that it has no temptation to do so." But in none of such sayings does he designate or mean the Divine Right only.

> I rank myself higher than the commonplace well-intentioned politician; and I say straight out that no King keeps faith—he cannot keep it, being constantly obliged to yield to the pressure of circumstances. On us poor Philistines duty lays the opposite obligation—not on the great ones of the earth!

That is Goethe's legacy to *Realpolitik*, vehemently delivered two months before he died.

And yet there was no one, at that time, whose vision of twentieth-century conditions was so piercing as his. His last political aspirations were for a League of Nations for foreign affairs, and socialised co-operation for internal ones.

He held that Free Trade in ideas and sentiments would be no less stimulating to the realm and the general welfare than to commerce; but that hitherto there had been none of the fixed laws and principles which were so useful, even in private life, for smoothing down innumerable contentions and fusing the communal existence into a more or less harmonious unity. Here he pointed out prophetically—and actually in the very words which are to-day on everybody's lips—the way to a League of Nations; and after having, in addition, designated national hatreds as typical of a very low degree of development, he had himself in mind when he spoke of a plane "on which all this kind of thing vanishes into thin air, on which one as it were looks down upon the nations, and feels the weal or woe of a neighbouring people as intimately as if it were the lot of one's own." To sum up, at the end of the *Wanderjahre* his ideal state is animated by the principle of a League of Nations—nay, the community itself is so described by its members.

Likewise with his last social conceptions—they are a whole century in advance of his time. Complete tolerance for all forms of religion and the service of God rules in Wilhelm Meister's Utopia. As regards property, Goethe points the way to Communism; but leaves us strangely in the dark about what definite measures he proposed to that end.

> If the whole community regards proprietorial rights as sacred, still more does the proprietor. Custom, youthful impressions, reverence for his forebears, aversion from his neighbour, and a hundred other things make the proprietor stubbornly opposed to any change in conditions. The more time-honoured such conditions are . . . the more difficult it becomes to accomplish in any wide sense that which, while despoiling the individual in some degree, would be of advantage to the community, and would moreover by reaction and co-operation prove unexpectedly so to the individual as well.

But it was to a song to be sung in his Utopia—a song which held the leader up to admiration—that Goethe entrusted his view of the widely differing forms of communal activity:

Du verteilest Kraft und Bürde
Und erwägst es ganz genau,
Gibst dem Alten Ruh' und Würde,
Jünglingen Geschäft und Frau.
Wechselseitiges Vertrauen
Wird ein reinlich Häuschen bauen,
Schlietzen Hof und Gartenzaun,
Auch der Nachbarschaft vertraun.

Wo an wohlgebahnten Stratzen
Man in neuer Schenke weilt,
Wo dem Fremdling reicher Matzen
Ackerfeld ist zugeteilt,
Siedeln wir uns mit den andern.
Eilet, eilet, einzuwandern
In das feste Vaterland!
Heil dir, Führer! Heil dir, Band![1]

[1] "To the back you fit the burden,
Giving each your careful thought—

With this confession of his social faith Goethe's energy died down—until the finishing of *Faust*. That energy, in former decades baffled by alternating moods of resignation, depression, and cynicism, was in his advanced old age no longer exposed to cross-currents such as these. But—in accordance with the law of Goethean polarity—all his other characteristics had meanwhile been reduced to a state of passive acquiescence.

Scepticism and imagination, irony and sense of beauty, now renewed their conflict. Never in all his dramas and novels, and only in a very few poems, had Goethe sung the beauty of a woman's body; nowhere had that beauty determined the fate of his heroines or of his own affections—possibly because absolute beauty had never been the object of his desire. But now, in his eighth decade, Helen makes her appearance—by no means as a classic symbol only, but in all her supremacy as the loveliest of women; and in that character she irradiates the central portion of the second *Faust*. No other Goethean hero ever spoke as Faust speaks to Helen at first sight.

This second *Faust* developed into the most fantastic of his creations. There are moments when one could think that the veteran who declared that his mind had never been clearer than when this work was written, had on the contrary been completely carried away by his phantom-forms; and that he might as in a parable have adjured himself in the words of his Mephisto to the jealous and indignant Faust, during the Court-entertainment: "*Machst du's doch selbst, das Fratzengeisterspiel!*"[1] Where in

---

Rest and honour, old man's guerdon,
Young man's, wife and work well-wrought.
Garden-hedge no segregation,
Mutual co-operation
Helping modest homes to build;
Neighbours all a friendly guild.

Well-laid streets, where men at leisure
Drink their glass in hostels new,
Where the fields in ample measure
Yield the stranger pasture too:
Such the realm that lieth yonder—
Thither, thither let us wander!
March we to the Fatherland!
Hail, O Leader! Hail, O Band!"

[1] "'Twas thou thyself who set these ghosts grimacing!"

the whole range of Goethe's collected works (the additions to *Pandora* alone excepted) are to be found such fairylands as bewilder us in the second *Walpurgisnacht*—such tossing seas with their griffins and sphinxes, their sirens, nymphs, and phorkyads? Where else has he been so inexhaustible in wizardry?

And yet this classic Phantom-Festival is nothing but one long succession of silvery ironies upon science and research, upon God, Art, and the Universe!

In the *Zahme Xenien* his irony is more acrimonious. Taken altogether, they represent a great outburst of wrath against opponents, dunces, hypocrites, Philistines. He saves his face when he advises a touch of irony in every positive statement—otherwise we should be bewildered and angered at each re-reading. At large receptions he liked to withdraw into a window-recess with an intimate, and deliver himself of malicious remarks on any guests whom he did not know.

This soon led to a still more lamentable frame of mind—that of a universal scepticism. Of youth and life he remarked that we never learn strategy until the campaign is over; and in his eightieth year he traced the course of man's development from the sensual child and the idealistic lover to the premature sceptic—"the rest of life is of no consequence; we let it take its course, and end up with quietism, as do the Indian philosophers."

One step further, and the veteran shows as a complete Mephisto. On the death of Zelter's son he wrote:

> A long life means surviving many things—so runs the melancholy refrain of our dawdling comic-opera sort of an existence. It's for ever sounding in our ears, vexing us, and yet making us resolve to work more assiduously than ever. To me the circle of those most nearly affecting me appears as a sibylline scroll of which one leaf after another gets consumed by the devouring flame of life, and vanishes like dust in the air . . .

Not otherwise had imagination and scepticism dwelt together in the Leipzig student; and just as of those conflicting forces neither had prevailed over the other, so now in the old man the combination of self-consciousness and humility which had marked his youth was as conspicuous as ever. In the Utopia of the *Wanderjahre* he makes reverence an essential element in education.

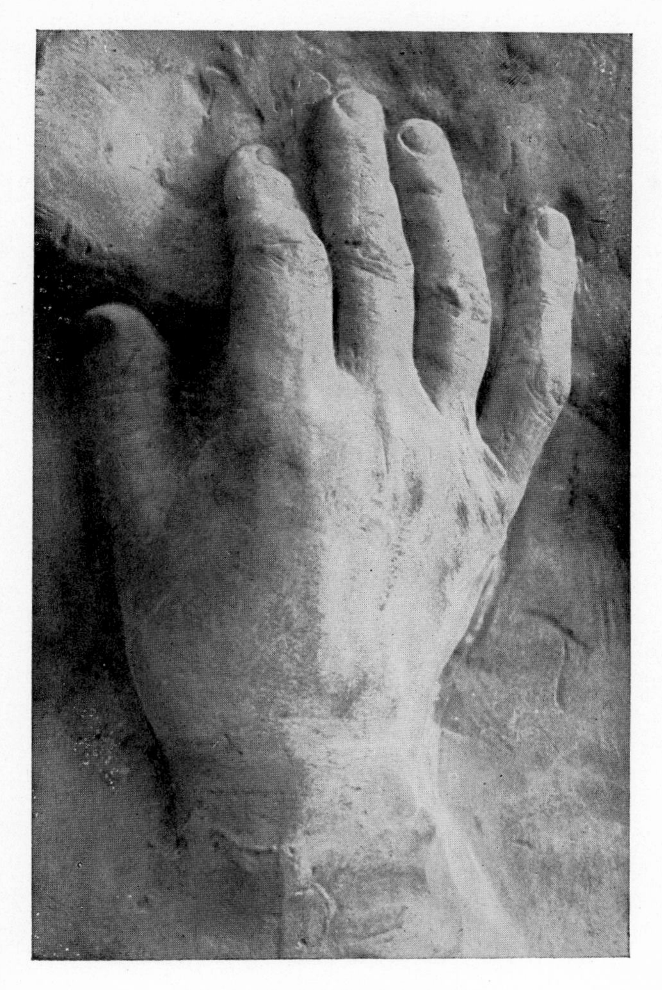

GOETHE'S HAND IN OLD AGE

And certainly he was aware of his own significance, especially now when he could feel and display his work as a totality. He was quick to acknowledge Tieck's merits;

but when they insist on comparing him with me, they make a mistake. I may be frank about this, for such as I am, I did not make myself. It is just as though I were to compare myself with Shakespeare, who did not make himself either, and who is undoubtedly a being of a higher order, to whom I look up, and who claims my veneration. . . . Anyone who has really learnt to understand my works and my character is bound to acknowledge that he has thereby attained to a certain freedom of the spirit.

Such were the final words of the man who very nearly *had* "made himself."

Still more vehemently, at this last, did he resent the restrictions and withdrawals whereby in his youth he had learnt to control his passions. The same impetuosity which marked his final bout of energy made Goethe's ageless heart pulse to anger and impatience, defiance and dæmonic pride. In the Chorus of the Passions, Eros alone was mute.

Like a champion the veteran now stood, erect and wrathful, before his works:

Wie mancher Misswillige schnuffelt und wittert
Um das von der Muse verliehne Gedicht.
Sie haben Lessing das Ende verbittert—
Mir sollen sie's nicht![1]

The Chancellor, who would fain have seen him chastened and rational, had frequently to see him rude and contradictious, violent and impossible.

His nervous irritability grew more and more marked. No one was suffered to interrupt him. If anyone used a phrase like "no other than," Goethe would snap his head off. And as to him who came in with spectacles on his nose, or was slow in taking the chair offered him, the old man could not contain

[1] "They sniff and they snort with their ill-natured noses
Round song that the Muses have poured in their ear.
They embittered poor Lessing, in earth who reposes;
But me—never fear!"

himself. He so dreaded the shortest day that he had to help himself over the critical date by incessant reading—but by the 17th of December he was already aglow with the thought that in a few days the sun would be coming closer. To the end he was a slave to the state of the barometer. Illness he feared as the worst of earthly evils.

He fell into rages more frequently than of old; and if at table he had been long and loud in abuse of anything, he would actually finish up with: "So I've been bad-tempered again! That's a good thing—it stimulates me!" True, only intimates saw him like this. When Cotta procrastinated over the publication of his works, the aged Goethe wrote a furious letter to his agent Boisserée, blew him sky-high, and told others of it afterwards. This dispassionate friend and disciple took notes of an evening at Goethe's: "Then invectives began again on Paris, German and French party-spirit, royal caprices, corruption of taste, idiocies, priest-ridden France and heresy-hunts in 'enlightened' Germany, and so forth."

Even his tidiness began to fall away from him, for at the end (as in his youth) he would seize upon torn bits of packing-paper or theatre-tickets, and use them for writing notes, verses, even ideas for the Second *Faust*.

A demagogue, whom he could not bear, inspired him to these words:

> Well, at any rate he stirs people up! That's the point, whether it's by hate or love. One must always be on the lookout for stimulation, so as to combat depression. . . . Yes, anyone who wants my society must sometimes put up with my bearish moods, as he would with the foible or hobby of another. Old Meyer is clever, very clever, but he won't come out of his shell, he won't contradict me—I can't stand it. Not a doubt but in his heart he's ten times more captious than I am, and simply thinks he would snuff me out if he began. If only he would storm and thunder at me—that would be fine fun!

Is this Byron at thirty, insatiable for excitement? It is Goethe at eighty, and it is again this old, old Goethe who like the youth he once was exclaims in a sudden access of black rage and despair:

Könnt' ich vor mir selber fliehn!
Das Mass ist voll.
Ach! warum streb' ich immer dahin,
Wohin ich nicht soll?[1]

Such lines afflict us. We feel as though there had been no assuagement—as though a pilgrimage without its parallel had done nothing to soothe that fierce spirit. But suddenly the old man's impetuous vehemence will melt into such wonderful strains as this:

Immer wieder in die Weite,
Über Länder, an das Meer,
Phantasien, in der Breite
Schwebt am Ufer hin und her!
Neu ist immer die Erfahrung:
Immer ist dem Herzen bang,
Schmerzen sind der Jugend Nahrung,
Tränen seliger Lobgesang.[2]

It is true that those passionate voices, contradicting one another in a duet of Goethe's composition, were now less insistent than of yore. In the second *Faust* his æsthetic aim was harmony; and anything that has the old effect of duality seems to have burst forth against his will, or else is treated as symbolic. Goethe's great dialogue with his own heart, which he had scored for the voices of Faust and Mephisto, is only twice resumed in the second part.

And it was long before he could make up his mind to send Faust straight to Heaven. In one of the old drafts we even

[1] "Could I from myself but flee!
My day is past!
Ah, wherefore struggle incessantly
To fail at the last?"

[2] "Ever farther through creation,
Over countries, to the sea,
Take thy flight, Imagination,
Here and there to hover free!
New is our experience ever;
Ever in the heart are fears—
Sorrows foster youth's endeavour,
Songs of praise are in our tears."

find: "Epilogue in Chaos on the way to Hell!" So baffling were Goethe's native reactions to his desire for unity.

The champion whose youth had been perpetually renewed (and hence perpetually exposed to fresh perils) by aggression, wrath, and dæmonic pride, was finally confronted by misanthropy, equanimity, isolation—and these too bade his ageless passions strive towards stoicism.

Sometimes the traits are indistinguishable. After all, is not misanthropy a genuine passion, and at the same time a renunciation? In such moods he perpetually arraigned the world, the public, and the age:

Das geht so fröhlich
Ins Allgemeine;
Ist leicht und selig,
Als wär's auch reine.
Sie wissen gar nichts
Von stillen Riffen;
Und wie sie schiffen,
Die lieben Heitern,
Sie werden wie gar nichts
Zusammen scheitern.[1]

And it was actually Goethe, entering on his eightieth year, who declared it to be the wish of his heart "to have been born on a South-Sea island as a so-called savage, for then he could have enjoyed existence in its purest essence, without any artificial flavourings!"

I know very well [he said at eighty-one] that I am a thorn in the side of many people—they would all like to be rid of me; and as they can't attack my talent now, they fix upon my character. One day I am arrogant, the next egotistic, the next a prey to envy. . . . If you

[1] "They venture lightly
On seas uncharted,
So gay, so sprightly,
No leak yet started,
And ne'er a notion
Of rocky places
That show no traces—
Good luck attend them!
But I've a notion
Some reef will end them."

want to know what I have suffered, read my *Xenien*. . . . A German author—a German martyr!

And so all his humane pleasure in imparting instruction was a thing of the past. Even as a poet, Goethe had in the end completely given up the idea of influencing his time; nor was he interested in what the future might make of his work. "As a matter of fact, I always studied Nature and Art in a purely egotistic spirit—that is, for my own edification. And I write about them merely for my own further development. What other people make of them is a matter of indifference to me."

Inevitably came the days when the old man—not from senility, as many visitors believed, but from a sense of isolation—let every conversation drop, and would merely make some such remark as "My good people, you're beyond help," or "You young folk must see to that," or "Well, that is really very fine"—or else he would do no more than grunt out his "Hm-hm!" But all the while, this was the sort of thing he was thinking:

Die stille Freude wollt ihr stören?
Lasst mich bei meinem Becher Wein!
Mit andern kann man sich belehren,
Begeistert wird man nur allein.[1]

He was unhappy until the door had shut for the last time, and work could begin again in the form of self-communion:

Da ich viel allein verbleibe,
Pflege weniges zu sagen.
Da ich aber gerne schreibe,
Mögen's meine Leser tragen.
Sollte heissen: gern diktiere;
Und das ist doch auch ein Sprechen,
Wo ich keine Zeit verliere:
Niemand wird mich unterbrechen.[2]

[1] "My wordless peace ye fain would shatter?
Leave me to wine, and go your ways!
With others one may learn some matter;
Inspired? That's for lonely days!"

[2] "Since I often now am lonely,
Speech upon my lips is rare;
Good for composition only—
Readers, this ye'll have to bear.

And yet in his misanthropic seclusion he taught himself the lesson of complete acquiescence; and then he ceased to be contradictious, and felt (as he says) that he and his contemporaries were in their way historic figures, so that he must not quarrel with anyone whatever. Thus he kept his best things for himself, in order—as he makes his Montan express it—that his equilibrium might not be disturbed by arguing about his dearest convictions. He said in his own person at the end that we should display only so much of our profoundest certainties as is necessary for retaining some advantage over others; and that even this would shed a mild radiance, like that of a hidden sun, over the things we did.

So in those hours of utter loneliness he was able to epitomise the history of his renunciation in pregnant epilogues; and his friends were told in confidence of the secret motives and instincts —now and immediately before now—sustaining him in his mortal combat, between genius and dæmon, for development and acquiescence.

> It never was my way to fight against institutions—that always seemed to me presumptuous; and it is possible that I entered Court-life at too early an age. . . . I never did more than touch it with the tips of my fingers. . . . My political colour was always subdued, say a pretty blue; I should have come to utter grief if I had taken it into my head to try for a glaring red. . . . I have always been regarded as a man specially favoured by Fortune. . . . But at bottom it has all been labour and sorrow, and I might go so far as to say that in my seventy-five years I have not known four weeks of genuine ease of mind. It was like the stone of Sisyphus, always having to be rolled uphill again.

Seldom did the old man reveal the joints in his armour more frankly than in these conversations, which at the same time rather confirm than refute the charge of egoism. But we must avoid the primitive error of regarding him as a man who in any sense designed to make his life a work of art. His own statement does a great deal to throw new light on his whole endeavour, in that

---

Rather should I say 'Dictation';
That, though speech it is, I know,
Wastes no time in explanation,
No one interrupts my flow."

it so very dispassionately sets forth what had animated him throughout his lifelong struggle.

In the second *Faust* renunciation finds its most definite expression. Here, though the treatment is more vigorous, more luminous, and therefore more effective than in the tumultuous whirl of the First Part, renunciation is at the heart of all. The adolescent Goethe had aspired to godhead when in his attic-room he made his Magician, his other self, cry into the rising fumes:

> Soll ich dir, Flammenbildung, weichen?
> Ich bin's, bin Faust, bin deinesgleichen![1]

But now the old man's heart was rent by no such jealous emulation. Yonder, where the mountain hid the morning-sun from the eyes that would fain look up into its glory—there, there only was the light that could dazzle his vision and thence he looked down on the cataract, and when the rainbow shimmered in it—

> Der spiegelt ab das menschliche Bestreben.
> Ihm sinne nach, und du begreifst genauer:
> Am farbigen Abglanz haben wir das Leben.[2]

So profound was Goethe's acquiescence.

For always he reminded himself, when *Faust* was resumed at varying points and he found that the central motive of the Second Part was still to be defined, that he had made a certain note in his Diary which ran: "Remorse for the earlier days, so overshadowed by sadness. Hardihood, self-possession—these alone can redress our liability to disaster." That is the same spirit which prompted him to reverence for constituted authority, in whatever form, and made him devote his last energies to the rounding-off of his work. But it is also the same which inspired his lifelong wrestle with the Here and Now; and assuredly, when

[1] "Flinch before thee, thou flame-born incarnation?
I am myself, am Faust, of like creation!"

[2] "See mirrored here man's conflict, man's persistence:
Think upon this—thou'lt comprehend more clearly:
That iridescent gleam is our existence."

in his middle-period he wrote the scene of the wager with Mephisto, it was that spirit which enabled him, as his Faust, to scorn the fair fleeting moment.

And now, at the end of his days, Goethe was to be filled with regret, as his Faust was with vexation of spirit. Now he would fain have retrieved that vanished Present, that he might take more pleasure in it.

But so rigorously was that spirit denied enjoyment of the Ideal Now that he could never even imagine its joys until he betook himself to the Inanimate. He recommended the keeping of a diary because it was instructive for the future, as shedding light upon inadequacies and errors. "We learn to appreciate the momentary, when we immediately make it historic." So completely was Goethe, even in his ripest years, debarred from possession of the instant's joys.

Is it surprising, then, that he perpetually postponed the issue of Faust's wager, attacking everything else rather than that solution—of which indeed he was not himself quite certain? He keeps his audience in suspense up to Faust's very last moments; so doubtful was Goethe, in the last year of his life, about the dénouement of *Faust!*

Among the many contradictions of his final phase one thing alone emerges clearly—his faith. To his ninth decade Goethe remained what he had been in his third—religious but not a Christian, upright but not a moralist, open to the Invisible but not contemptuous of the Visible, a believer in Eternity but not in Judgment.

The Christian teaching was to the end entirely alien to him, though the vehemence of his earlier attacks upon it had now been softened into irony. Except for an extremely apocryphal passage, which Eckermann—fifteen years after Goethe's death—theatrically includes among his last words, he only once expressed any recognition of it; but how? "Who in these days is a Christian, as Christ would have him be? Myself alone, perhaps, though you all think me a pagan!" This utterance occurred in a conversation about marriage and divorce; and the occasion, together with the key in which it was spoken, testify to no more than the old man's anger at the perversion of a teaching which he had always held in high estimation for its social value—just as in his old age he described Christ as a most interesting but enigmatic character.

The utterances which belie that isolated testimony are not to be overlooked. Not even to his secret diary did the Chancellor venture to confide what Goethe said in the way of invective about a new canon-law; he merely notes: "Acrid sallies upon the mysteries of the Christian religion, especially on the Immaculate Conception of Mary whose mother Anna herself is supposed to have immaculately conceived." Standing before a crucifix, Goethe observed that everyone who looks at it feels better, because he sees before him someone who has had more to bear; and of the latest religious poetry he said derisively that it was "slip-slop for invalids."

The Bible he declared to be a purely historical book. In the Utopia of his *Wanderjahre* three creeds are held in equal honour —the pagan, the philosophic, and the Christian, which as a trinity evolved true religion. Upon a man who held such ideas, the theologians of Jena could certainly not have conferred, at their Jubilee, the Doctorate Honoris Causâ, as was done in the other faculties; and so they had to confine themselves to a diplomatic message of congratulation. And they did not as yet know anything about his very far from "tame" *Xenien*, for it was posterity which first read Goethe's terse quatrain:

> Wer Wissenschaft und Kunst besitzt,
> Hat auch Religion.
> Wer jene beiden nicht besitzt,
> Der habe Religion![1]

The conclusion of *Faust* has led to the fallacy that Goethe turned religious in old age. In reality Faust, like Goethe himself, shows no sign of a conscience or of a longing for pardon. Nor is there any trace of a proposed sublimation—such as, for instance, in Dante's Rose of Heaven; indeed, the end of *Faust* was undecided right up to the last pages. Only a few years earlier Mephisto was to have been pardoned by God himself, his wager

[1] "He who has science and has art,
Religion too has he.
Who has not science, has not art,
Let him religious be!"

half-won; "and if Faust is to bear part of the blame, the old Gentleman's clemency will but enhance the cheeriness of the conclusion!"

But Goethe himself expressly said that everything in the conclusion which might seem to uphold the Catholic faith was merely a matter of treatment. On one occasion he even described it as a Bacchanal, and seemed anxious to account for it by saying earnestly that he had found the conclusion very difficult to render; and that,

> treating of such super-sensual, such almost inconceivable things, I might easily have lost myself in the void if I had not restrained my poetic flights by the use of clearly-defined personages and conceptions borrowed from Christianity and the Church.

Nor did Goethe's ultimate ideas about ethics conform to gospel-principles. His ethic was "pure humanity." After a life spent in the untiring service of the spirit and of Nature, a life of infinite self-conquest, all ethical conceptions must of necessity have struck him as insipid—and so he ignored them.

At the end of his days he was not afraid to stand by the axioms which others, when they feel the approach of death, are prone (in view of possibilities) to guard themselves by at any rate glossing-over. And when someone happened to speak of the conscience, this dauntless veteran exclaimed: "And are we really obliged to have a conscience? Who demands it of us?"

In the same way as he had admired the strong man in politics, he now at this last bestowed his deepest reverence on the two contemporaries who had been the great amoralists of their epoch—Napoleon and Byron. Napoleon alone he recognised as his superior; Byron alone as his equal. He often spoke of a great man of action as greater than a poet. Eckermann questioned whether Byron's works were of any real value for the human mind; and Goethe answered: "The daring, dash, and grandiosity of Byron—was that not formative? We must be careful not to attribute value only to the accepted Good and Beautiful! Everything that is great is formative, so soon as we apprehend it." He went so far as to declare that the First Roman Republic, entirely free from crime as it was, must have been to a certain extent tedious and tame, and that no self-respecting man could wish to have lived in it.

This great amoralist's unbosomings were at the end as racy as those of his youth had been. Do they imply that he had shed the all-reconciling kindliness which had animated the younger man? Was this heart, which strove to soar above our earthly spheres, to merge itself in the All so frozen that at last it had no feeling for mere fellow-creatures?

August had an accident on his travels—and Goethe wrote to him with his own hand, fearing that his amanuensis might reveal the bad news to Ottilie. Rauch wrote to tell him of a family-misfortune, without saying what it was. In the hour of receiving the tidings, Goethe answered in a long, a wonderful letter, saying what he did in such events to restore himself. To a poverty-stricken, unknown young man, who asked him for his works because he could not buy them, Goethe sent the necessary sum of money. He wrote a whole series of letters in recommendation of one of his disciples, told him exactly how to frame his official reports, what it was necessary to say and what to keep silence about in the service. He wrote detailed recommendations of the library-attendants, so that Orders might be conferred on them on festival occasions.

When the Court-gardener procured some acacias for him, Goethe sent a message to say that he would always remember him when he watched them growing. He sent a Governmental Secretary some grafts from his fruit-garden. To the widow of one of his gardeners, who gave him a blue hortensia on his birthday, he sent the plant back after it had stopped flowering, saying that he entrusted it to her care and begging that he might have it again on his next birthday, if he lived to see it, "as a sign of your affectionate remembrance." In the country, where there was not much to do, he let his servant take lessons in barbering and do a little gardening, so that he might be more useful to any future employer.

Neither Christianity nor ethics gives the clue to Goethe's faith. But science does—and especially now, when in that too he had left the particular behind, and attained a universality which in earlier days had seemed little more than a visionary aim. Not that his meteorological and botanical observations had been given up; but they all formed part of a great synthetic vision, for "the supreme thing would be to comprehend that everything actual is in itself theoretical. . . . We must not try to get behind phenomena—they themselves are the lesson."

This is the keyword to Goethe's final perception of the full identity of observation and vision, of insight and research, towards which he had been progressing for decades.

He more and more abjured any pretension to knowledge of objective truth. The physicist, he said, had nothing to do but adapt himself to phenomena—from that not only the human being, but the subjective truth, resulted. And while here too he returned to the intuitions and visions of his youth, he felt that all his relinquishments had raised him to a higher plane; and discriminated between the thoughtless ignoramus and himself in words whose proud humility is reminiscent of Plato:

Man's loftiest experience is that of awe; and if the phenomenon as such can awe him, let him be satisfied. He will get no higher, and should not seek to go behind the experience. . . . If ultimately I am content to stop at the pure phenomenon, that merely resolves itself into another acquiescence. But there remains a wide distinction—whether I acquiesce in the limitations of humanity, or at heart in a hypothetical inadequacy of my own restricted individuality.

On the whole, his transcendental creed inclined at the end to resemble that of his middle-years, but to depart from that of his youth and early old age. "In Nature there is a Knowable and an Unknowable; we must distinguish between them, reflect upon them, and have respect for both."

He took a magnificent stride from scientific knowledge to the Unknowable, and was inevitably a foe to all symbolists, of whose growing influence he was now made aware.

I am a "plasticist" [he said, pointing to the head of the Juno Ludovisi]. I have tried to make my mind clear about the world and Nature. And now come these fellows and kick up their dust, showing me things at a distance one moment, and in oppressive proximity the next, like *ombres chinoises*—Devil take them

In the same way he hated all sectarianism, and advised against making incomprehensible things the subject of daily thought and speculation. "Let him who believes in survival be happy and hold his tongue, but there is nothing for him to plume himself upon. . . . Absorption in ideas of immortality is for those in high positions, and especially for ladies who have nothing to do."

In such robust fashion the veteran even now showed his anger or scorn for pretensions of every kind. He did try to save something for science; and revealed all his tenacity in the confession that there might certainly be things that were hidden from research, but one could not desist from the attempt to come to close quarters until one was forced to acknowledge defeat.

Speaking quite generally, he confided to Zelter, in words which command our reverence: "I have the good-fortune, in my old age, to find thoughts arising in me which to pursue . . . it would be well worth while to live life over again."

But he was always and ever the devotee of the thing in evolution. "Evolution is a finer thing than completion." And again: "The Godhead is active in evolution and metempsychosis, not so in completion and torpor." Or in Faust's mystic words:

> Doch im Erstarren such' ich nicht mein Heil,
> Das Schaudern ist der Menschheit bestes Teil.
> Wie auch die Welt ihm das Gefühl verteure,
> Ergriffen fühlt er tief das Ungeheure.[1]

All the master-forces in the oldest Goethe—energy, acquiescence, faith—urged him to prove metempsychosis; and in his eightieth year he found these words, Promethean in their ageless vitality: "My conviction of our survival results from my view of energy—for if I work unrestingly to the end of my days, Nature is bound to assign me another form of existence, since this one can no longer contain my spirit." And with pagan simplicity he developed his idea to Zelter:

Let us work on until one or other of us is summoned back to the ether by the Cosmic Spirit! And may the Eternal One not deny us new

[1] "Yet will I not in torpor seek salvation,
For man through awe doth reach his consummation.
Though for that sense the world exact its price,
The Vast will grip his soul as in a vice."

activities, akin to those in which we have proved ourselves! If to these he should paternally add memory and an after-taste of the Right and Good that here below we have willed and achieved, we shall assuredly be but the better prepared to take our place as cogs in the cosmic mechanism.

The freedom of thought, the irrepressible vitality, which speaks in these sense-images of a supersensual world, entitle us to say of the oldest Goethe that by his vision of metempsychosis he vanquished death—now, though his days were nearly told, regaining a youth which, when it had been actually his, was sometimes overwhelmed by the suggestions of that mystery of change.

Halte dich nur im Stillen rein
Und lass es um dich wettern!
Je mehr du fühlst, ein Mensch zu sein,
Desto ähnlicher bist du den Göttern.[1]

There we have Goethe's ultimate faith: acquiescence that transcended death, life's battle well-fought establishing a claim—not before any judge, but as an appeal to the Reason inherent in Nature, who will not suffer such an exemplar to vanish from her ken. Steadily—nay, almost cheerfully—he envisaged the bourne from which he had nothing to fear and everything to hope. Yet not as a "Beyond"—rather, as a more strenuous Here, an interpretation of things past, a fulfilment of things purposed; for "no organic being entirely corresponds to the Idea therein implicit—the Supreme Idea is always unrevealed. . . . That is my God!"

Destiny was twice more to put his acquiescence to the proof.

In Goethe's seventy-ninth year the Duke died, on his return from a trip to Berlin. His last days, which were spent with Alexander von Humboldt, showed that his tameless nature had reached its breaking-point. He died, very characteristically without being really ill; it was simply that new energies failed

[1] "Do thou but hold thy peace and wait,
Though round thee storms be blowing!
And, conscious thus of mortal fate,
More Godlike wilt be growing."

him in his fierce assault on life. He passed away between sleeping and waking, buoyant but worn-out.

It was as though his friend's loss had given Goethe a new lease of life. His son brought him the tidings on an afternoon in June. He at once busied himself with a hundred unimportant matters, because his "painful state of mind" permitted of no continuous work; refusing to see anyone, but likewise to give any assistance in the aftermath of official business. He did not pay his respects to the widow at her country-seat, nor did he even write to her.

When the day of the funeral drew near he fled the place, "to escape those dismal functions whereby, as is only right and fitting, the crowd is symbolically shown what it has just lost"; and took up his abode in a pleasant little country-house which the new ruler had offered him.

Scarcely had he set foot in this Dornburg, which stands above the city of Jena—scarcely, after long years of town-life, had he felt the soil under his feet, seen vegetation and gardens around him, and the broad expanse of Heaven above—than his mind and body seemed purged to youth and freshness; and these two summer months, at the end of which he concluded his seventy-ninth year, were epoch-making for him. He was soon calling it his "as it were dæmonically-directed sojourn."

He would not suffer his grief to cloud the halcyon summer of those weeks—the Duke was hardly ever mentioned.

In Dornburg the old man was alone again for the first—and last—time. Though rejoiced to be away from his family and the town, he was by no means strictly reclusive. He was accessible to children, friends, guests; sent for wine and oil, books and maps, prisms and lenses, and had his secretary and his valet with him.

But when, before daybreak, he stood at his high-perched window and saw Venus retreat before the sun—when in the long summer-evenings, between mallows and roses, wind and sun, he strode up and down the little mountain-path . . . he would be penetrated by the sense of something symbolic, something that stood for his old age as a whole; and the sublime serenity of that silence born of the hills—he could not but feel it to be the expression of his final loneliness.

Es spricht sich aus der stumme Schmerz,
Der Äther klärt sich, blau und bläuer—
Da schwebt sie ja, die goldne Leier,
Komm, alte Freundin, komm ans Herz! [1]

And after those four throbbing lines it was given him to write four of his most exquisite Nature-poems—the last; for what followed was no more than aphorism or flash of thought.

To Zuleika, after all those fifteen years, his loveliest verses were written; the half-forgotten names fell from his lips once more, and as if in a last pang such formless rhythms as these might seem to hover sighingly round the crystalline rhymes and measures of the far-away *Divan:*

Nicht mehr auf Seidenblatt
Schreib' ich symmetrische Reime,
Nicht mehr fass' ich sie
In goldene Ranken. . . . [2]

To the rhythms of his youth, pulsating with emotion, the old man now went back. But gazing at the full moon, which had once enthralled him as the symbol of Zuleika, all the vigour in him poured itself into the gracious form that had inspired his happiest lyrics, and he wrote the invocation which ends thus:—

So hinan denn! hell und heller,
Reiner Bahn, in voller Pracht!
Schlägt mein Herz auch schmerzlich schneller,
Überselig ist die Nacht. [3]

[1] "Speaks now at last the speechless pain,
To bluer blue the ether clears—
And lo! the golden lyre appears:
Come to this heart, old friend, again!"

[2] "No more on silken page
I write symmetrical verses,
No more framing them
In golden tendrils. . . ."

[3] "Onward, upward! Still more purely
Shines thy path of cloudless light!
Heart that, throbbing, aches too surely,
Pulse to this transcendent night!"

BUST OF GOETHE AT THE AGE OF EIGHTY

And like a boy he sent the poem to Marianne, as a sign that he had been thinking of her; but, characteristically stoical, asked *both* if they had thought of him when looking at the same full moon.

And since for him individuality had ceased to be important, our picture too must make the transition and seek to show how Goethe's character, already delineated in some detail for the whole of his last decade, did now—in these closing years—attain to a yet higher sublimation of itself, so long as external circumstances were not of an agitating kind. We speak of the years between eighty and eighty-two.

His continuous good-health enhanced his energies. In his eighty-second year he had a sort of head-rest attached to his old wooden writing-chair; the grandfather-chair he never used.

Everything was subordinate to work and the saving of time. He now entirely abjured the reading of newspapers, received only a few visitors, refused to answer any attacks that were made upon him and was so sedulous about his health that he refused to inspect the Schiller-Album of Schiller's friend Caroline, because it was not good for him to look back on things of the distant past.

He regarded everything in an historical light—things which had happened long ago in foreign lands were no farther and no nearer to him than those which had happened yesterday in his own house. He did not even want to look at his own works again, once they were finished with.

Energy, vitality—these must be stimulated!

Came the death of the old Duchess Luise, whom Goethe had personally venerated for half-a-century—but he was sitting at wine with his friends; and while they talked louder so that he might not hear the passing-bell, he was telling them of new scenes for the second Walpurgisnacht, "for which he was daily bringing off the most astonishing things." Then he talked about people who had lived to be very old, and about Ninon de Lenclos. His tendency now was to insist upon an extension of the normal span of life. He said it was a pity that the Duke should have had to go "so prematurely"—at seventy-three.

Have I reached the age of eighty, to go on doing the same things every day? I try much more than others to think daily of something new, so that I mayn't become tedious. We must be always changing, always rejuvenating, ourselves—else we grow mouldy'

He had never talked so much of the dæmonic element in him as he did after his eighthieth birthday—because now the dæmonic mood was inhibited by lack of excitements, scope, and even volition. It was an octogenarian who launched this thunderbolt: "If I were to let myself go, I am capable of annihilating myself and my environment!"

Of his dæmon he said:

That element in me was not divine, for it showed in unreason; not human, for it had no understanding; not devilish, for it was beneficent; not angelic, for it could take pleasure in the pain of others. . . . It was like chance, because it was inconsequent; it had something of prescience, because it pointed to connections. . . . It seemed to deal arbitrarily with the necessary elements of our existence. . . . It seemed as if nothing but the impossible could satisfy it. . . . I tried to rescue myself from this terrible being, by my usual method of sheltering behind an image.

When Mendelssohn, who again was called upon to enliven him in Weimar, insisted upon his hearing some Beethoven, and Goethe from his corner listened to the first movement of the C Minor Symphony—he, who had always refused to recognise a world fashioned by hostile hands, cried out: "That's grandiose! That's very great! Quite mad! One could think the house was tumbling about one's ears!"—and he often spoke again of the tremendous effect it had had upon him.

The forces which made for stoicism likewise took a new lease of life. Irony, instead of being modified, became more blasting—the higher Goethe, as Faust, raised the pyramid of his life, the more sedulously did the Mephisto in him seek to undermine it. Of existence he spoke as "a fool's life"; to Zelter he once signed himself "Reineke Fuchs"; one evening he egged Mendelssohn on to deride women with him; and at noon on a certain day he talked the wildest nonsense about America to a couple of Russians, who did not dare to open their lips. Through an entire evening with Müller and Riemer he was the complete cynic, and said he wished he was an English Bishop with thirty-thousand a year.

Three months before Goethe's death, the Chancellor declared that irony was his favourite method of expression!

His final loneliness became sheer desolation. Goethe, who had always hymned the "Here and Now" and striven to grasp it—he, who like Faust attributed all the tragedy in his life to his having failed to seize the moment—Goethe arrived at last at this grotesque consolation: "There is something narrowing, restrictive, often painful, about the thing that is there. The thing that is not there, on the contrary, leaves us free, puts us at our ease, refers us to ourselves alone!"

Such were the bewildering consolations he had to clutch at in his old age, when his spirit had grown impatient of this mode of existence. The young Goethe had revolved in a circle which had well-nigh driven him crazy; and the old man still revolved in it, but now with smiling stoicism.

And was there nothing in his environment which could give him pleasure? Yes, there was something. A little bust of Napoleon in opalescent glass, "which alone is worth a journey round the world. It stands facing the rising sun. At the first beam it seems to sing with the glittering glory of all—*all* the colours, such as no jewel in the world can come near." Napoleon in opalescent glass, lit up by the morning-sun; the miracle of colour in the head of the conqueror; his Theory of Colour as it were vindicated by the Emperor—that was Goethe's last daily restorative.

In his faith, too, he got closer still to the phenomenon pure and simple.

But I [he cried] I worship him who has endowed the Cosmos with such creative energy that if a mere millionth part of it took life unto itself, the world would so pullulate with living creatures that no war, no pestilence, no deluge, no burning, could stem the tide. That is my God.

So chaotic was his sense of the Cosmos. But he gave no name to that sense—until at the last he heard of a communion to which he expressed a desire to belong.

A year before his death—to the very day—he wrote that he had lately heard of the sect of the Hypsistarians, who, "wedged between pagans, Jews, and Christians," had declared their intention to reverence the best they knew, and inasmuch as that must necessarily stand in close relation to the Godhead, to worship it.

And it was as if, from some Dark Age, a joyous gleam had flashed upon me, for I felt that all my life I had been aspiring to qualify for an Hypsistarian. But that is no small endeavour; for how is one to become aware of the best there is?

There is Goethe's ultimate creed, clothed on with dogma. That creed was soon to be tested for the last time.

August had got away at last. At forty he had succeeded in persuading his father to let him go; and it was only because Goethe no longer hoped to save him by his vigilance that he yielded.

Rome was the objective, Eckermann the companion. Like one seeking liberation and development after an over-burdened decade, Goethe had fled southward a few years before August's birth; like one desirous of ending tumultuously a lifetime of failure, August his son now fled—the one from activity and superfluity, the other from emptiness and passive despair. All that is implied in the contrast must have been a source of silent anguish to Goethe, when he let his son go free.

There was an unhealthy sort of exaltation in August's last letters from Rome—indeed, he wrote to his father twelve days before he died:

It is the first time in forty years that I have had a sense of independence and that among foreign people. . . . They have tried to lure me on—gaming, girls, women—these three last I had forsworn. So I shall return with clean hands, though in some ways I may have squandered more money than others have. . . .

This letter, from a man who was drinking himself to death, is full of subterfuges and reservations, and was written with an eye to the rarefied atmosphere of the bureaucratic Goethe-household—and the old man knew it was.

Then, at the end of October, August von Goethe died—the last of five children born to Goethe. When his body was dissected, the liver was found to be five times the normal size—the so-called "drunkard's-liver." There were no tears for him.

When Goethe's friends began to falter out the tidings, he cut them short, and only said like some ancient stoic: "I am aware that I engendered a mortal son."

But now there came a sudden pause in the slow work at *Faust*.

Perhaps Goethe—after the first shock—was relieved at the news. His son had long been too utterly lost to him. But the more implacably he had taught himself to see all things as parables, the more deeply must he have felt that son's death as a lesson in human destiny, and his childless old age as the revenge of that dæmon who had ever meddled with the destiny which was his own.

> Look for trials even unto the end! [he wrote to Zelter]. They have not failed you, my dear friend, or me either. . . . At such times nothing but a strong sense of duty can keep us going. I have no other anxiety than to preserve my physical equilibrium—everything else goes of itself. The body *must*, the spirit *wills;* and he who sees clearly marked out for him the path his will is bound to take, has no great use for reflection. . . . And so, over the graves—forward!

From the time of writing this letter, Goethe's life was heroic.

Again his personal grief seemed to stimulate his energies, again loss and sorrow bore him upward, again a new work forced its way upon the stage, just as the curtain seemed about to fall upon the drama of one man's life. For ten years the synopsis for the last volume of *Dichtung und Wahrheit* had been awaiting the working-out. Now, in a fortnight, he dictated nearly the whole volume! There are passages which make it the most impassioned portion of the whole book.

There he stood—alone, with no son, no one to love him—turning over the leaves of ancient diaries, and dictating such a sentence as this for his narrative: "Laughter and revelry lasted till midnight." He apologises to the reader for the lack of youthful vigour; yet lavishes wild gestures and excited words, speaks of his love for Lili, fifty-five years gone-by, as a foretaste of hell—and on every page of this work of his old age breaks out the forcibly repressed sorrow of yesterday, fused with the mighty sorrow that of yore had rent his very soul for the girl who had meant to him the world's woman.

And yet the remembrance of her loveliness excited him to hymn it again and again; again—after half-a-century—he wondered if they could not have married *quand même;* and he for whom love was over now confessed to an intimate:

> She was, in very truth, the first woman whom I loved deeply and truly; and I may say she was also the last, for all the little fancies I have cherished in the course of my life were slight and superficial compared with that first one. I was never so near to my true happiness as at that time. The obstacles were not really insurmountable—and yet I lost her! . . . I am not saying too much when I maintain that my coming to Weimar, and my presence in it now, were the direct consequences of that.

It was his re-awakened sense of the beautiful creature whom he had so often called a divine enchantress, which lured him into these exaggerated statements—apparently so oblivious of the moderation ruling his whole life. And indeed when he had brought the narrative to an end, his doubly overwrought being suffered a collapse—there was hæmorrhage from the lung. He was bled, and once again he recovered. With such marvellous precision did Goethe's body, after his eightieth birthday, respond to the agitations of his soul! After a few days the veteran was himself again—and again, as thirty, as sixty years ago, the crisis enhanced his vigour. "Still the individual hangs together, and is in possession of his senses. Good luck to him!" Yes—as one saved by special providence he resolved to earn the new gift of days, so as to make them truly his own.

At first, indeed, he had to resume the part of paterfamilias, for Ottilie was useless. Goethe had to reorganise everything, and alter his will—wherein he sought to restrain Ottilie from a second marriage by moral and pecuniary arguments. He had now no direct heir, and this so altered his views about his possessions that he even thought of selling his collections to the State. Again bequests and volumes of correspondence were divided among his fellow-workers. Before now he had said earnestly to a Bohemian friend that he would very much like to bequeath him "his affairs in Bohemia."

As this took up several weeks, the references to August himself were usually in this strain: "Since it was her husband's choice to live retired from the world in the aforesaid capital. . . ." The tone of the household improved after his death; Ottilie became fonder of the old man, there was no more quarrelling—but still disorder reigned unless Goethe saw to everything himself. For weeks the diary is almost daily concerned with household-matters. "Vulpius dismissed the cook with a just indemnity. . . . This off my shoulders, I could attend to more important affairs." Two days later: "Household-matters going on better. The supreme affair attacked—bravely and well."

The "supreme affair" was the finishing of *Faust*.

It was February. Goethe was in his eighty-second year, The most important parts of the work of his life were still to be added—the issue of the wager, Faust's victory or defeat; part of the Fourth Act was unwritten and about half of the Fifth. "And so, over the graves—forward!" Goethe cried to himself for the last time. He had set his house in order, had protected his works; everything was done except the making of the final decision, postponed for years, but lacking which his great work would be left a fragment. It makes one think of an aged monarch, hesitating over his last signature.

And then his creative energy blazed up for the last time. For thirty years he had known nothing like it, as he confessed to his doctor—who shook his head, knowing the aftermath in that nature of critical periods such as this. Goethe made up his mind to finish his work before his birthday—the birthday which was to be his last. Like Manto he felt: "I love the man who craves the Impossible!"

Thenceforward he called the finishing of *Faust* "the supreme affair"—and so in the last year of his life he set himself to an heroic self-abnegation, like Faust in the last year of his. For that neither had ever had, throughout a life-time, "a supreme affair" was all too surely the outcome of both Goethe's and Faust's essential natures. Now—when the door was about to shut—the first, the only one was snatched at, as though it might really offer a solution of the insoluble problem.

It was strange how, at this last, Goethe's ideas about Faust were bound up with the name of Napoleon. He grieved that there was no Napoleonic progeny—a son, he said, would not only have done heroic deeds, but would long years ago have joined with him in the great project of connecting the Rhine and the Danube by a canal. In Goethe's eightieth year a friend had awakened his interest in the new harbour at Bremen, the embankment of the fruitful Fenland region, and the Weser estuary; and Eckermann had found the old man surrounded by maps and plans for embankments, quays, and harbours. At the same period he had been excited about the Panama Canal, of which Humboldt had told him. He would have liked to see the three canals—the Rhine, the Panama, and the Suez—before he died; indeed "it would be well worth while to hold out for fifty years more, for the sake of those three great things."

This was worked into the conclusion of *Faust*. But even now he had no sort of fixed plan in his head. So late as the May of this last year of his life a draft for the Fourth Act says no more than: "Faust envies the dwellers by the sea, who resolve to stem the tides. He wishes to associate himself with them." He did not go any further with this idea until his last weeks of work.

And Goethe, very old, walking up and down and thinking, in these summer-mornings dictated his Last Act: "Faust, very old, walking up and down and thinking." At eighty-two he conceived his centenarian Faust. Himself must surely have inspired that heading—he must have felt how like he looked to his hoary hero, in whom he had been mirrored sixty years ago.

And, thus thinking, he winged his last stupendous flight:

> Noch hab' ich mich ins Freie nicht gekämpft . . .
> Stünd' ich, Natur, vor dir ein Mann allein,
> Da wär's der Mühe wert, ein Mensch zu sein. . . .[1]

[1] "I have not yet won through to liberty . . .
Confronting thee to stand alone, a man,
O Nature! that were worth our mortal span. . . ."

Then Care comes to him; she asks if he has not known her. And Goethe gives this answer, as from one born of Prometheus:

> Ich bin nur durch die Welt gerannt . . .
> Ich habe nur begehrt und nur vollbracht
> Und abermals gewünscht und so mit Macht
> Mein Leben durchgestürmt; erst gross und mächtig,
> Nun aber geht es weise, geht bedächtig.
> Der Erdenkreis ist mir genug bekannt—
> Nach drüben ist die Aussicht uns verrannt. . . .
> Dem Tüchtigen ist diese Welt nicht stumm.
> Was braucht er in die Ewigkeit zu schweifen!
> Was er erkennt, lässt sich ergreifen.
> . . . Im Weiterschreiten find' er Qual und Glück,
> Er! unbefriedigt jeden Augenblick![1]

Here and nowhere else we have the last word of Faust, of the "very old" Goethe. By the deepest law of his being must Faust, must Goethe, cause the Devil to lose the great wager of Supreme Contentment. Even in this penultimate moment sounds the defiant cry of Faust's and Goethe's unrest. Perpetually urged by his senses to let the Devil win, yet by virtue of his soul the victor when all seems lost, Faust can still, at this point, claim to have won; Goethe is still his dæmon's conscious thrall, yet master of his steadfast acquiescence; and when Care—as though she were the Devil's procuress—seeks to undermine that stoical courage, it is the veteran Goethe who shouts, in the character of Faust:—

> Unselige Gespenster! So behandelt ihr
> Das menschliche Geschlecht zu tausend Malen;

[1] "Over the world I have but scoured . . .
I have but wished, and seen my wish come true,
And wished again; and so, existence through,
Have stormed; at first an elemental being,
But now I'm something sager, more far-seeing.
The universe—of that my fill I know—
Beyond, our mortal vision may not go . . .
The world will speak to him who has the pluck.
Then wherefore through Eternity go trailing?
The tangible is here for man's unveiling . . .
Man must march on, his pain or bliss to buy—
He! whom the moment ne'er can satisfy."

Gleichgültige Tage selbst verwandelt ihr
In garstigen Wirrwarr netzumstrickter Qualen.[1]

She breathes in his ear that he is blind—and so, as though he were Destiny herself, in this last hour Goethe ceases to stand for his hero. Blindness was the heaviest trial that Goethe, the Light-Worshipper, could lay upon his Other Self. Yet Faust does not flinch. Extolling the inward eye, he turns to his work; and though Mephisto—still with no reason to hope he has won—has his grave dug before his blinded eyes, Faust, like Goethe, presses on in his last moments to achievement. He proposes to drain a marsh, to do battle with the elements, to look into the "bright eyes of danger"—every man's restorative.

And the old seer makes his blinded hero at last discern an ultimate purpose, through his inward vision of new contests on this scale. Once more he gives voice to his deepest faith, and it seems a variant of those Bible-words in the Authorised Version: *In the end was the Act.* So it is that Faust can cry, presciently:

Im Vorgefühl von solchem hohen Glück
Geniess' ich jetzt den höchsten Augenblick.[2]

Is this the solution? Has he not just told the spectre to her face that it is only by marching on that the man who has pluck can appease his ever-unsatisfied heart with momentary joys? It is no more than an evasion—this issue that Goethe found from the problem which had robbed his own life of happiness. To consummation, the thing for ever denied him, he ultimately looks forward: the figment of a future state, the fantasy—"My genius must save me!" so that for one brief instant he may delude himself into being master of his dæmon. It is an arbitrary identification of Faust, dying upon a dream, with a poet who

[1] "Accursed spectres! Yours it is to tell
The human race of ills it never knows;
Even on pulseless days ye cast your spell,
Your filthy network of imagined woes."

[2] "In foretaste of such bliss supreme, I know
That moment, the supremest, here below!"

rejects the piercing insight of his dæmonic human heart, that he may enjoy what is never to be his.

In all equity—so the lawyers say—Faust had lost his wager with the Devil; and had Goethe entered upon such an one, he—whose heart even to the last laboured under the Mephistophelian incubus—would for sure have morally lost it too. Because he "wanted to have done with it," he snatched at a solution for the insoluble, a solution invented *ad hoc* at the last moment, merely that he might attain to a consummation. And Faust, like Goethe, wanted to have done with it; and since he, like Goethe, suddenly took to believing in "a supreme affair," he lost all sovereignty over the devil, lost the salvation of his soul for an eidolon, for the belief in "a ditch."[1]

And yet he regained it—not as a victor, but through grace. In very truth the end of Faust was as that recent draft had foreseen: he did bear half the blame, but "the clemency of the Old Gentleman" took immediate effect, and the legal loser soared into the skies.

Thus, as it lies before us, the solution affects us as the brilliant artifice of a man who has set himself a problem, and will have harmony at any price. It is only when we look back upon Goethe's whole life, in its rhythmic alternation between action and acquiescence, that the end of *Faust* is irradiated by the sunlight of the Supreme Justice; and that to Goethe, the Wanderer, the word of grace is uttered from that sphere as erst to Gretchen: "Nay—is saved."

. . . But the work was finished, if not consummated: "The supreme affair brought to an end. . . . All that had been fair-copied bound up."

For the final pages had been ready for some years. Goethe had never let them out of his hands. He had fastened up the manuscript, and sealed it with his Morning-Star seal.

But he could not stop work just yet! Was it not only the end of July, so that he had reached his goal a few weeks too soon? He still had time. Instantly he began on all sorts of supplements to the finished works; but though his usual activities were gradu-

[1] This refers to Mephisto's gibe, when Faust speaks of the draining of the marsh, of the "ditch." "*Man spricht . . . von keinem Graben, doch vom Grab.*" ("They spoke not of a ditch, but of a grave.")

ally resumed, this final summer-campaign had drained his last energies. He felt it, and regarded any future days that might be his as an indulgence, for "it is really of no consequence now what I do, or whether I do anything."

With his household he lived in peace at last. Ottilie was older, quieter, readier for the duties that lay nearest. The old man was tactful with her; he let her tell him about her balls, minutely discussed some forthcoming charades, was still the one to look after the kitchen and the household.

The children too were easier to do with. Alma was beautiful and self-willed; Walter was composing arias, because he was in love with a singer; Wolf "writes tragedies and comedies, collects theatre-tickets, reads incessantly." Patiently the old man taught the boys to seal letters, keep drawers tidy, did not hinder them from going far too often to the theatre like their father before them, even allowed himself to be persuaded to listen to their rendering of one of Kotzebue's plays. When they drove out with him, they vied with each other in theatrical projects, and he would sit in the carriage, smiling and observing how "exactly like real poets they were, for when one was lost in enthusiasm the other was yawning, and when it was *his* turn the other one began whistling." But on one of their birthdays he "was deep in Nature-study, and could manage only to be good-humoured."

He still occasionally sent beetles and butterflies to collectors, in exchange for rare stones. And there was also some official work, for in his last months there was a very weighty correspondence with the Secretary of the Mineralogical Society in Jena about the paragraphing of diplomas, in which Goethe complained that the word "President" came too near the end of the page. There were continual advances of money, recommendations, patronage for artists. But the life seems to have gone out of it all, and a letter at this time concludes: "Peace and joy to all men of good-will especially the near and dear! And so henceforth!"

For his last birthday he withdrew to Ilmenau with his grandchildren, "so as to salute the ghosts of the past in a steady and settled frame of mind, with posterity around me"; and while in Weimar his bust was being unveiled amid ceremonial speech-making, exactly as though he were already a dead man, he himself was gazing at the tall lindens that he had planted with his own hands, here where he "had experienced as much of bliss as of trial, only to be reconciled in any lot by boundless activities—and where at least much was done which still has its own quiet influence." The grandsons, of course, wanted to see the colliers, wood-cutters, glass-burners. So he climbed, on foot, the heights where the belvedere stood. And where was that window-recess? He found it, and found too the words he had written more than fifty years ago on the wall:

Über allen Gipfeln ist Ruh.[1]

He stood silent for a while; then he went down to the valley.

Science in every department was in a state of commotion. Still he had outbursts of derision and rage because they were trying to squash his Theory of Colour, and his joy was great when a scientist at Prague arranged his studies in historical order. Again he made a vain attempt at accounting for the rainbow. In a long letter he advised a student to make some new chromatic experiments with the aid of a ball of cobbler's-wax.

Fossil animals and vestiges of plants, elephant's teeth which had been found in a Thuringian gravel-pit—these and many other things littered his table, "and would inevitably drive one mad if one plunged into the subtler modes of meditation on the æons." He was going on with his osteological studies, his ideas about plant-organisms. The conflict between Geoffroy St. Hilaire and Cuvier afforded him further proof of his metamorphic principles, and he wrote upon it once again. He was re-reading the whole of Plutarch with Ottilie, evening after evening—and at the same time was perusing, with amazement, the descriptions of the first English railway.

And when, a few weeks before the end, the talk turned upon his influence, he thus summed himself up:

What, if we wish to be honest, did I possess that was really my own, beyond capacity and inclination to see and hear . . . and render with some skill? I owe my achievements . . . to thousands of things and

[1] "Over all the hills is repose."

persons outside myself, which constituted my material. Fools and sages, clear-brained men and narrow-minded men, children and young people, to say nothing of ripe seniors—they all came to me, all told me how things struck them . . . and all I had to do was to catch hold of it, and reap what others had sown for me. . . . The main thing is to have a great desire, and skill and perseverance to accomplish it. . . . Mirabeau was quite right to make as much use as he could of other people and their capabilities. . . . My work is that of a composite being, and happens to be signed Goethe.

So, for ever unsatisfied with the momentary, he looked back upon his work and life; and one day he ventured once more to break the sacred seal he had set upon *Faust*, that he might add to the great scene, "which, so as to have done with it, I treated all too cursorily."

It was the middle of January. He glanced over the pages, on several days read long passages to Ottilie, touched it up in one place. But ere long he sealed the manuscript again—almost unchanged.

On a mild day in February he drove out to his old garden. There, four weeks before the end, he spent some hours alone.

Old Meyer still came and went and sat silently with him; and after Zelter's last visit Goethe noted: "Interesting talk about the past, present, and future." Both friends survived him only a short time—the one was to die seven weeks, the other seven months, after Goethe.

Only one woman's name still echoed through his heart. Six weeks before his death Goethe took Marianne's letters and sent them to her in a sealed packet: "Certain sheets of paper which point me back to the fairest days of my life . . . to guard them against all contingencies"—but she was to promise to leave them unopened till "an hour as yet uncertain." But the tender message did not satisfy him; once more a vision of Zuleika stirred his rhythmical sense to life, and he wrote:

Vor die Augen meiner Lieben,
Zu den Fingern, die's geschrieben—
Einst mit heissestem Verlangen
So erwartet wie empfangen—
Zu der Brust, der sie entquellen,

Diese Blätter wandern sollen,
Immer liebevoll bereit,
Zeugen allerschönster Zeit.[1]

That was Goethe's last love-token to woman.

Now it was March. He was hoping for the Spring, which he was never to see again. In the last three weeks of his life, Goethe unconsciously touched once more upon all the strings which had most affected his life and his work—all the regions of the mind, the subject-motives, the materials. What follows needs no commentary:—

He spoke of the inadequacy of speech, for "often we do not know whether we are seeing, observing, thinking, remembering, imagining, or believing." He fulminated against patriotic poetry, for the poet resembled the eagle, "which soars over countries, taking a bird's-eye view of them, and caring nothing whether the hare he swoops upon is running through Prussia or Saxony." He derided the sentimentalists who accounted for Lady Macbeth's deeds by love for her husband, and thought it "terrible, the way the century played up to and defended its weaknesses." He wrote to the astronomers in Jena, saying that they might now be preparing to give "a worthy reception" to the great comet which would appear in two years. He called the earth's motion round the sun the most sublime discovery of the human mind, more important than the whole Bible put together. He described a rare fossil as an interesting transition from the fern to the cactus. In the middle of March he wrote to W. von Humboldt, suddenly, almost without preamble:

The ancients held that animals learn from their natural enemies. I go further, and say that so do men, though *they* have the privilege of passing on the instruction to their organs. . . . The sooner man realises that there is a craft, an art, which can assist him in the syste-

[1] "Once with beating heart awaited,
Heart with reading never sated,
Now these letters home are going
To the other heart o'er-flowing;
Soon my loved one's eyes shall light them,
Soon the hand that then did write them,
Once again shall touch the page,
Telling of the golden age."

matic enhancement of his innate capacities, the happier he will be. . . . Suppose a man with musical talent, scoring an important composition—the conscious and the unconscious will stand in a relation similar to that of note-book and entry. . . . The human organs, by means of practice, training, reflection, success or failure, furtherance or resistance—and then again reflection—learn to make the necessary connections unconsciously, the acquired and the innate working hand-in-hand, so that a unison results which is the world's wonder. . . . It is over sixty years since my adolescent mind conceived *Faust* from beginning to end, and clearly. . . . But of course I was confronted with the great difficulty that purpose and strength of character had to achieve what really should have been done by the light of Nature, working in me of her own free will. But it would be a poor thing if, after so long, so active, and so reflective a life, it had proved impossible. . . .

The world is ruled by bewildered theories of bewildering operations; and nothing is to me more important than, so far as is possible, to turn to the best account what is in me and persists in me, and keep a firm hand upon my idiosyncrasies. . . .

Forgive this belated answer! In spite of my seclusion, the hours are rare in which I can find time to dwell upon and realise these mysteries of life.

Weimar. March 17, 1832.
J. W. VON GOETHE.

That is Goethe's last important letter. The last books he read were Balzac and Plutarch.

At this time a young man presented his album, and Goethe wrote his last verses in it—these admonitory, indeed misanthropic, lines:

Ein jeder kehre vor seinen Tür,
Und rein ist jedes Stadtquartier.
Ein jeder übe sein' Lektion,
So wird es gut im Rate stohn.[1]

The recipient of this was Bettina's son.

The visitors' door closed behind this youth. On the 15th

[1] "If each to his own business kept,
Clean were the town of scandal swept;
If all would practise what they preach,
Then were it well with all and each."

of March the old man caught cold, out driving. In three days he was so much better that he could get up; he looked over his engravings, and a new cholera-medal inspired him with ribald remarks as to the best design for such a thing. In this vivacious mood he did not fail to tell his doctor of hospitals and functionaries, invalids and poor folk needing assistance—all of whose names the doctor recognised. The next day he put his last signature to a subscription for a young woman-artist—forty-eight hours before his death, with a trembling hand.

For on this twentieth of March he suddenly collapsed.

Terrible nervous restlessness [reports his doctor] made the old man like a hunted creature—one moment in his bed, the next in his armchair. The pain, which was settling more and more definitely in the chest, wrung moans and loud cries from the tortured sufferer. His features were distorted, his face ashen, his eyes were sunken deep in the livid sockets, colourless, filmed over—he looked as though in the last throes of dissolution.

The doctor hastens to assuage his anguish. At last the invalid falls asleep in his chair. The next day, and the morning after, he seems a little better. On this last morning he asks for a French work on the July Revolution; it lies open before him, but he can do no more than turn the pages. He eats and drinks a little.

"Are you sure you haven't filled my glass too full?"

Then he calls for his amanuensis, and with his help and a servant's he rises and stands near his chair.

"What day of the month is this?"

"The twenty-second, Your Excellency."

"Then spring has begun. Maybe that will help us to get well."

It is past nine o'clock. He sits down again in the chair beside his bed; and now, when the mortal battle of one morning, the mortal battle of eight decades, is over—now at last he falls into a light slumber with continual dreams, for he talks in his sleep more than once. His friends catch the words: "Look—that beautiful woman's head with dark curls—splendid colouring—on a dark background——"

Then he says: "Please open the shutters, so that more light may come in. . . ."

And then: "Friedrich, give me that portfolio there, with the drawings. . . . No, not the book—the portfolio." And when they can find none: "Well, it must have been the ghost of it."

About ten o'clock he asks for a little more wine. After that he ceases to speak. But once more he looks round for Ottilie, and these are Goethe's last words: "Come, my daughterling, and give me your little hand—"

But the mind is still active, for in his semi-slumber he begins to write with the middle finger of his right hand in the air, until the hand sinks slowly down. They think they can distinguish the beginning of a "W".

Then he lay back in his chair and passed away, at the hour of his birth, towards noonday.

INDEX